Of the People

Concise Edition
Of the People

A HISTORY of the UNITED STATES

VOLUME 2: SINCE 1865
Second Edition

James Oakes
City University of New York Graduate Center

Michael McGerr
Indiana University-Bloomington

Jan Ellen Lewis
Rutgers University, Newark

Nick Cullather
Indiana University-Bloomington

Jeanne Boydston
University of Wisconsin-Madison

Mark Summers
University of Kentucky-Lexington

Camilla Townsend
Rutgers University, New Brunswick

New York   Oxford
OXFORD UNIVERSITY PRESS

Oxford University Press is a department of the University of Oxford. It furthers the University's
objective of excellence in research, scholarship, and education by publishing worldwide.

Oxford   New York
Auckland   Cape Town   Dar es Salaam   Hong Kong   Karachi
Kuala Lumpur   Madrid   Melbourne   Mexico City   Nairobi
New Delhi   Shanghai   Taipei   Toronto

With offices in
Argentina   Austria   Brazil   Chile   Czech Republic   France   Greece
Guatemala   Hungary   Italy   Japan   Poland   Portugal   Singapore
South Korea   Switzerland   Thailand   Turkey   Ukraine   Vietnam

Copyright © 2013, 2011 by Oxford University Press.

Published by Oxford University Press.
198 Madison Avenue, New York, NY 10016
www.oup.com

Oxford is a registered trademark of Oxford University Press.

ISBN: 978-0-19-992475-2

Printing number: 9 8 7 6 5 4 3 2 1

Printed in the United States of America
on acid-free paper

Jeanne Boydston
1944–2008
Historian, Teacher, Friend

Brief Contents

Contents

CHAPTER 19 The Politics of Industrial America, 1870–1892   566

CHAPTER 20 Industry and Empire, 1890–1900   592

CHAPTER 23 The Modern Nation, 1919–1928   **686**

CHAPTER **24 A Great Depression and a New Deal,
           1929–1940   716**

CHAPTER **28 "The Table of Democracy," 1960–1968   844**

CHAPTER **30** The Triumph of Conservatism,
1980–1991   **910**

Appendixes

Maps

Features

Preface

We are grateful that the first edition of *Of the People* has been welcomed by instructors and students as a useful instructional aid. Enhanced with even greater emphasis on American democracy and diversity, the second edition includes innovative learning tools that help students draw connections among topics and think critically. In preparing the second edition, our primary goal has been to maintain the text's overarching focus on the evolution of American democracy, people, and power; its strong portrayal of political and social history; and its clear, compelling narrative voice. To that end, we have broadened the representation of Native Americans, African Americans, and other minority groups to better show the full diversity of the American people. Recognizing the increasingly visual orientation of our students and society, we have included new diagrams to help students see the connections among events in each chapter. And we have strengthened the text's critical-thinking pedagogy because the study of history entails careful analysis, not mere memorization of names and dates. In response to feedback from instructors, we have also added a chapter outline and list of key terms to frame each chapter's text.

History continues, and the writing of history is never finished. The newest members of our author team, Camilla Townsend and Mark Summers, have substantially revised and expanded our coverage of Native American societies and the Gilded Age, respectively. For the second edition, we have updated the following elements based on the most recent scholarship:

>> **Chapters 1 through 3** have updated and expanded coverage of pre-Columbian America, including a fuller description of Native Americans and precontact civilizations of Latin America as well as native societies through the seventeenth century.

>> **Chapters 8 through 10** include updated scholarship on the new republic as well as integrated content on slavery in the Americas and additional content on Native Americans.

>> **Chapters 11 and 12 (previously 11 and 10),** on slavery and reform movements in the early nineteenth century, have been reordered and substantially revised to present a clearer picture of events that would ultimately erupt into violence. Coverage of the abolition movement appears in the chapter on slavery, which now immediately precedes the causes of the Civil War.

>> **Chapters 17 through 19** include updated scholarship on the Gilded Age, with more details about technological innovations of the period.

>> **Chapter 28** has a new title, "The Table of Democracy, 1960–1968." This emphasizes a stronger focus on issues of power and democracy also seen in Chapters 23 and 27.

>> **Chapter 31** now includes an account of the Obama administration through 2012, the death of Osama bin Laden, and the nation's continuing response to challenging economic circumstances. The Tea Party and Occupy movements receive coverage as well.

At Gettysburg, Pennsylvania, on November 19, 1863, President Abraham Lincoln dedicated a memorial to the more than 3,000 Union soldiers who had died turning back a Confederate invasion in the first days of July. There were at least a few ways that the president could have justified the sad loss of life in the third year of a brutal war dividing North and South. He could have said it was necessary to destroy the Confederacy's cherished institution of slavery, to punish southerners for seceding from the United States, or to preserve the nation intact. Instead, at this crucial moment in American history, Lincoln gave a short, stunning speech about democracy. The president did not use the word, but he offered its essence. To honor the dead of Gettysburg, he called on northerners to ensure "that government of the people, by the people, for the people, shall not perish from the earth."

With these words, Lincoln put democracy at the center of the Civil War and at the center of American history. The authors of this book share his belief in the centrality of democracy; his words, "of the people," give our book its title and its main theme. We see American history as a story "of the people," of their struggles to shape their lives and their land.

Our choice of theme does not mean we believe that America has always been a democracy. Clearly, it has not. As Lincoln gave the Gettysburg Address, most African Americans still lived in slavery. American women, north and south, lacked rights that many men enjoyed; for all their disagreements, white southerners and northerners viewed Native Americans as enemies. Neither do we believe that there is only a single definition of democracy, either in the narrow sense of a particular form of government or in the larger one of a society whose members participate equally in its creation. Although Lincoln defined the northern cause as a struggle for democracy, southerners believed it was anything but democratic to force them to remain in the Union at gunpoint. As bloody draft riots in New York City in July 1863 made clear, many northern men thought it was anything but democratic to force them to fight in Lincoln's armies. Such disagreements have been typical of American history. For more than 500 years, people have struggled over whose vision of life in the New World would prevail.

It is precisely such struggles that offer the best angle of vision for seeing and understanding the most important developments in the nation's history. In particular, the democratic theme concentrates attention on the most fundamental concerns of history: people and power.

Lincoln's words serve as a reminder of the basic truth that history is about people. Across the 31 chapters of this book, we write extensively about complex events, such as the five-year savagery of the Civil War, and long-term transformations, such as the slow, halting evolution of democratic political institutions. But we write in the awareness that these developments are only abstractions unless they are grounded in the lives of people. The test of a historical narrative, the authors believe, is whether its characters are fully rounded, believable human beings.

The choice of Lincoln's words also reflects our belief that history is about power. To ask whether America was democratic at some point in the past is to ask whether all people had equal power to make their lives and their nation. Such questions of power necessarily take us to political processes, to the ways in which people work separately and collectively to enforce their will. We define politics quite broadly in this book. With the feminists of the 1960s, we believe that "the personal is the political," that power relations shape people's lives in private as well as in public. *Of the People* looks for democracy in the living room as well as the legislature, and in the bedroom as well as the business office.

Focusing on democracy, on people and power, we have necessarily written as wide-ranging a history as possible. In the features and in the main text, *Of the People* conveys both the unity and the great diversity of the American people across time and place. We chronicle the racial and ethnic groups who have shaped America, differences of religious and regional identity, the changing nature of social classes, and the different ways that gender identities have been constructed over the centuries.

While treating different groups in their distinctiveness, we have integrated them into the broader narrative as much as possible. A true history "of the people" not only acknowledges their individuality and diversity but also shows their interrelationships and their roles in the larger narrative. More integrated coverage of Native Americans and African Americans appears throughout the second edition.

Of the People also offers comprehensive coverage of the different spheres of human life—cultural as well as governmental, social as well as economic, environmental as well as military. This commitment to comprehensiveness is a reflection of our belief that all aspects of human existence are the stuff of history. It is also an expression of the fundamental theme of the book: the focus on democracy leads naturally to the study of people's struggles for power in every dimension of their lives. Moreover, the democratic approach emphasizes the interconnections between the different aspects of Americans' lives; we cannot understand politics and government without tracing their connection to economics, religion, culture, art, sexuality, and so on.

The economic connection is especially important. *Of the People* devotes much attention to economic life, to the ways in which Americans have worked and saved and spent. Economic power, the authors believe, is basic to democracy. Americans' power to shape their lives and their country has been greatly affected by whether they were farmers or hunters, plantation owners or slaves, wage workers or capitalists, domestic servants or bureaucrats. The authors do not see economics as an impersonal, all-conquering force: instead, we try to show how the values and actions of ordinary people, as well as the laws and regulations of government, have made economic life.

We have also tried especially to place America in global context. The history of America, or any nation, cannot be adequately explained without understanding its relationship to transnational events and global developments. That is true for the first chapter of the book, which shows how America began to emerge from the collision of Native Americans, West Africans, and Europeans in the fifteenth and sixteenth centuries. It is just as true for the last chapter of the book, which demonstrates how globalization and the war on terror transformed the United States at the turn of the twenty-first century. In the chapters in between these two, the authors detail how the world has changed America and how America has changed the world. Reflecting the concerns of the rest of the book, we focus particularly on the movement of people, the evolution of power, and the attempt to spread democracy abroad. Chapter 20 shows how Singer, a pioneering American multinational company, began to export an economic vision of a consumer democracy along with its sewing machines in the nineteenth and early twentieth centuries.

While Singer wanted to sell sewing machines, Abraham Lincoln wanted to sell a war. But both believed their audience would see democracy as quintessentially American. Whether they were right is the burden of this book.

About the Concise Edition

We are very happy to present *Of the People* in this concise edition, designed especially for instructors who need to teach the survey in a short term, wish to assign readings in addition to the textbook, or prefer a more economical option for their students without sacrificing the primary advantages of the full edition. To meet this goal, we have included 75 percent fewer margin quotations and 60 percent fewer images than in the comprehensive edition.

New to the Second Edition
>> New visual reviews with connections.

Chapters now end with a diagram that lays out the important topics (based on headings and subheadings) and presents a brief summary of each as well as the ways they interrelate. Visual learners and all students will benefit from seeing the relationships among the topics illustrated.

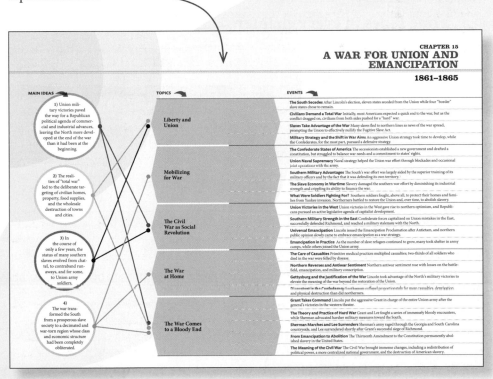

>> Enhanced critical-thinking pedagogy.

All chapters now end with both Review Questions, which test students' memory and understanding of chapter content, and Critical-Thinking Questions, which ask students to analyze and interpret chapter content.

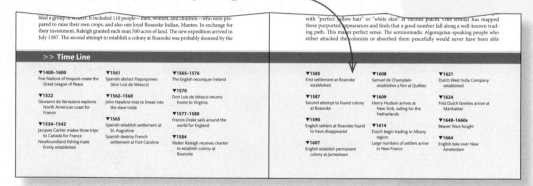

Review Questions

Conclusion   259

1. What were the key elements of Hamilton's fiscal and economic policies?
2. Why did political parties emerge during Washington's administration? How did the two parties differ, and why was the conflict between them so intense?
3. What was the Whiskey Rebellion? How did it reflect larger tensions in the early republic?

Critical-Thinking Questions

1. Why were foreign and domestic affairs so intertwined in the 1790s?
2. How fragile do you think the new nation was? What were the reasons for that fragility?
3. Could slavery have been eliminated in the 1790s?

>> Time Lines in every chapter.

bled a group or settlers. It included 110 people—men, women, and children—who were prepared to raise their own crops, and also one loyal Roanoke Indian, Manteo. In exchange for their investment, Raleigh granted each man 500 acres of land. The new expedition arrived in July 1587. The second attempt to establish a colony at Roanoke was probably doomed by the

with "perfect yellow hair" or "white skin" at various places. One scholar has mapped these purported appearances and finds that a good number fall along a well-known trading path. This makes perfect sense. The seminomadic Algonquian-speaking people who either attacked the colonists or absorbed them peacefully would never have been able

>> Time Line

▼1400–1600 Five Nations of Iroquois create the Great League of Peace	▼1561 Spanish abduct Paquiquineo (don Luis de Velasco)	▼1565–1576 The English reconquer Ireland	▼1585 First settlement at Roanoke established	▼1608 Samuel de Champlain establishes a fort at Québec	▼1621 Dutch West India Company established
▼1522 Giovanni da Verrazano explores North American coast for France	▼1562–1568 John Hawkins tries to break into the slave trade	▼1570 Don Luis de Velasco returns home to Virginia	▼1587 Second attempt to found colony at Roanoke	▼1609 Henry Hudson arrives at New York, sailing for the Netherlands	▼1624 First Dutch families arrive at Manhattan
▼1534–1542 Jacques Cartier makes three trips to Canada for France Newfoundland fishing trade firmly established	▼1565 Spanish establish settlement at St. Augustine Spanish destroy French settlement at Fort Caroline	▼1577–1580 Francis Drake sails around the world for England ▼1584 Walter Raleigh receives charter to establish colony at Roanoke	▼1590 English settlers at Roanoke found to have disappeared ▼1607 English establish permanent colony at Jamestown	▼1614 Dutch begin trading in Albany region Large numbers of settlers arrive in New France	▼1648–1660s Beaver Wars fought ▼1664 English take over New Amsterdam

>> Who, What.

This list of chapter-ending key terms helps students recall the important people and events of that chapter.

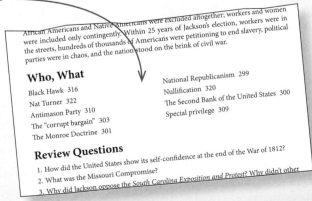

African Americans and Native Americans were excluded altogether; workers and women were included only contingently. Within 25 years of Jackson's election, workers were in the streets, hundreds of thousands of Americans were petitioning to end slavery, political parties were in chaos, and the nation stood on the brink of civil war.

Who, What

Black Hawk 316
Nat Turner 322
Antimason Party 310
The "corrupt bargain" 303
The Monroe Doctrine 301

National Republicanism 299
Nullification 320
The Second Bank of the United States 300
Special privilege 309

Review Questions

1. How did the United States show its self-confidence at the end of the War of 1812?
2. What was the Missouri Compromise?
3. Why did Jackson oppose the *South Carolina Exposition and Protest*? Why didn't other

>> New additions to "American Portrait," "American Landscape," and "America and the World" features.

These popular boxed features from the first edition have been updated with 10 new "American Portraits," 4 new "American Landscapes," and 5 new "America and the World" features.

Hallmark Features

>> Each chapter opens with an **"American Portrait"** feature, a story of someone whose life in one way or another embodies the basic theme of the pages to follow.

>> Each chapter presents an **"American Landscape"** feature, a particular place in time where issues of power appeared in especially sharp relief.

>> To underscore the fundamental importance of global relationships, each chapter includes a feature on **"America and the World."**

>> Focus questions at chapter openings.

CHAPTER

8

Contested Republic
1789–1800

AMERICAN PORTRAIT

>> Ona Judge Finds Her Freedom

Ona Judge was only 16 when George and Martha Washington brought her to Philadelphia in 1790. She was Martha Washington's slave, the daughter of Betty, an African American seamstress, and Andrew Judge, a white indentured servant who worked as a tailor at Mt. Vernon. According to the law of slavery, because her mother was enslaved, so too was Ona. When Ona was 10, she was brought to live in Mt. Vernon itself, as a playmate for Martha Washington's granddaughter. She was trained as a seamstress and body servant, and in Philadelphia, at the president's house, she worked as a waiter.

When Washington's term was ending, the slaves were told that they would all soon return to Virginia. Martha Washington planned to give Ona Judge to another granddaughter as a wedding present. Judge decided to liberate herself. "Whilst they were packing up to go to Virginia," she later explained, "I was packing to go, I didn't know where; for I knew that if I went back to Virginia, I should never get my liberty. I had friends among the colored people of Philadelphia, had my things carried there beforehand, and left Washington's house while they were eating dinner."

Judge's friends in the free black community hid her until they could find a way to smuggle her out of the city. The Fugitive Slave Act that Washington had signed in 1793 had made it a crime to help a slave escape bondage. Judge snuck out of Philadelphia aboard a boat bound for Portsmouth, New Hampshire, where, however, it was her bad luck to run into the daughter of the Washingtons' good friend, Senator John Langdon. "Oney?" she called out. "Where in the world have you come from?" The young woman could not understand why anyone would run away "from such an excellent place." "Yes–I know," Judge replied. "But I wanted to be free, misses; wanted to learn to read and write."

Told his slave was in Portsmouth–where slavery was still legal, although unpopular– Washington asked a government official to send Judge back, and to keep it quiet. Neither

continued

229

COMMON THREADS

>> What were the continuing disagreements about the power of a central government?

>> What were the conflicting values and ideas of citizenship?

>> How did the new nation negotiate with the European powers?

>> What was the status of slavery in the early republic?

OUTLINE

AMERICAN PORTRAIT: Ona Judge Finds Her Freedom

The Struggle to Form a Government
Creating a National Government
The States and the Bill of Rights
Debating the Economy

A Society in Transition
A People on the Move
AMERICAN LANDSCAPE: Philadelphia
The First Emancipation Movements
Conflicting Visions of Republican Society
The Culture of the Republic

Securing the Nation
Borders and Boundaries
Controlling the Borderlands
The Whiskey Rebellion
Other Revolutions
AMERICA AND THE WORLD: Citizenship in an Age of Revolution
Between France and England
To the Brink of War
The Administration of John Adams
Tensions at Home

Conclusion

England Attempts an Empire 51

AMERICA AND THE WORLD

>> Indians on the Thames

When we think about the cultural encounter between the Old World and the New, we tend to imagine European men coming ashore in a wilderness and meeting Native American people. Often, however, the encounter consisted of Indians docking at European cities for the first time. Over the course of the first century after contact, the colonizers brought hundreds of Native Americans back to Europe with them. Some of these Native Americans went on to take leading roles in the unfolding dramas.

The phenomenon began with Columbus and the Spaniards, but English colonizers also regularly kidnapped Indians. In 1530, an English captain explored the coast of Brazil (not yet firmly under Portuguese control) and reported that "one of the savage kings of the country was contented to take ship with him and to be transported into England." The indigenous man was brought to the court of Henry VIII. "The King and all the Nobilitie did not a little marvaile," The English spent a year

Raleigh's home for two years until the expedition sailed.

Sometimes indigenous people coming to London from the Spanish world did not disclose their Indian origins. Martin Cortés, Malinche's son by the conqueror, was given to Philip II as a page when he was a young man, and in 1554, his marriage to Queen Mary to London for his marriage to Queen Mary. He lived at court, where no one would have guessed that his mother had grown up in an indigenous chieftainship on the coast of Mexico.

At the start of the seventeenth century, when the English became more active in colonization, interest in Native Americans spiked. In 1603 Bartholomew Gosnold seized some Indians from the Rappahannock River and had them perform daring feats on canoes on the Thames for riveted audiences. (They died of the plague shortly after, and their people were still asking why about them when John Smith arrived in their country.) In The Tempest, Shakespeare

---

892 Chapter 29: Living with Less

AMERICAN LANDSCAPE

>> City Hall Plaza, Boston

On Monday morning, September 9, 1974, 8,000 to 10,000 whites gathered in the barren red brick plaza flanked by two drab, hulking structures of concrete and glass—Boston City Hall and the John F. Kennedy Federal Building. It was a stark setting for a rally that dramatized equally stark divisions of race, class, and politics in 1970s America.

The crowd, mostly working- and lower-middle-class white women, had come from Boston neighborhoods to protest the court-ordered busing due to start with the new school year in three days. As many as 1,500 protesters had come from South Boston, the predominantly Irish American center of opposition to the busing plan.

Crowd members were angry that their children would be bused to black-majority schools in Roxbury while black pupils would come into white-majority neighborhoods. Like the civil rights activists of the 1960s, these whites felt strongly that their own rights had been denied. The sponsor of the rally was the group Restore Our Alienated Rights—ROAR. "With Liberty and Justice for ALL?" one banner asked pointedly. Some protestors, evoking the Boston Tea Party of the Revolutionary era, threw teabags into the plaza's fountain and called for the "Second American Revolution." "We're not ready to quit," insisted the moderator, Rita Graul of South Boston.

The protestors, most of them Democrats, were also angry at their own party

their own. Senator Ted Kennedy, who, despite his Irish American heritage and longtime family ties to Boston, supported civil rights and busing. There were "Impeach Kennedy" signs in the crowd. One of the speakers wore a chicken mask representing "the white chicken, Sen. Kennedy."

To everyone's surprise, the "white chicken" suddenly turned up on the platform. But the protestors would not let Kennedy speak. One of the organizers pulled the plug on his microphone; Some crowd members turned their backs on him. "Give us our rights back," the protestors demanded. "God Bless America," they sang. "You're a disgrace to the Irish," some people yelled. "Why don't you put your one-legged son on a bus for Roxbury," one crowd member called. "Yeah, let your daughter get bused there so she can get raped." A crowd member even shouted, "Why don't you let them shoot you like they shot your two brothers."

"Why won't they listen?" Kennedy asked. One of the organizers, Thomas O'Connell, answered that "maybe now he knew what it was like to be deprived of his rights—the way we've been deprived of our rights." Stone-faced, Kennedy left the platform and headed toward his office in the building named for his brothers. Security held back angry protesters, who heckled him, turned thumbs down, and threw eggs and tomatoes. As he entered the building, crowd members banged on the big plate glass windows until one of them shattered.

Supplements

For Students

Oxford University Press is proud to offer a complete and authoritative supplements package for students—including print and new media resources designed for chapter review, for primary source reading, for essay writing, for test preparation, and for further research.

Student Companion Website at **www.oup.com/us/ofthepeople**

The open-access Online Study Center designed for *Of the People: A History of the United States* (comprehensive and concise editions) helps students to review what they have learned from the textbook as well as explore other resources online. Note-taking guides help students focus their attention in class, while interactive practice quizzes allow them to assess their knowledge of a topic before a test.

- **Online Study Guide,** including
  - Note-taking outlines
  - Multiple-choice and identification quizzes, (two quizzes per chapter, thirty question quizzes—*different* from those found in the Instructor's Manual/Testbank)
- **Primary Source Companion and Research Guide,** a brief online Research Primer, with a library of annotated links to primary and secondary sources in US history.
- **Interactive Flashcards,** using key terms and people listed at the end of each chapter, help students remember who's who and what's what.

Writing History: A Guide for Students, Third Edition, by William Kelleher Storey, Associate Professor at Millsaps College.

Bringing together practical methods from both history and composition, *Writing History* provides a wealth of tips and advice to help students research and write essays for history classes. The book covers all aspects of writing about history, including **finding topics and researching** them, **interpreting source materials, drawing inferences from sources, and constructing arguments.** It concludes with three chapters that discuss writing effective sentences, using precise wording, and revising. Using numerous examples from the works of cultural, political, and social historians, *Writing History* serves as an ideal supplement to history courses that require students to conduct research. The third edition includes expanded sections on peer editing and topic selection, as well as new sections on searching and using the Internet. *Writing History* can be packaged for free with Oakes's *Of the People: A History of the United States.* Contact your Oxford University Press sales representative for more information.

The Information-Literate Historian: A Guide to Research for History Students by Jenny Presnell, Information Services Library and History, American Studies, and Women's Studies Bibliographer, Miami University of Ohio.

This is the only book specifically designed to teach today's history student how to most successfully select and use sources—primary, secondary, and electronic—to carry out and present their research. Written by a college librarian, *The Information-Literate Historian* is an indispensable reference for historians, students, and other readers doing history research. *The Information-Literate Historian* can be packaged for free with Oakes's *Of the People: A History of the United States, Second Edition* (concise edition). Contact your Oxford University Press sales representative for more information.

Primary Source Documents

Our Documents: 100 Milestone Documents from the National Archives brings documents to life, including facsimiles side by side with transcripts for students to explore, explanations, and a foreword provided by Michael Beschloss. This primary source book can be **packaged for free** with Oakes's *Of the People: A History of the United States, Second Edition* (concise edition). Among the documents it contains are the Declaration of Independence; the US Constitution; the Bill of Rights; the Louisiana Purchase Treaty; the Missouri Compromise; the Dred Scott decision; the Emancipation Proclamation; the Gettysburg Address; the Fourteenth Amendment to the US Constitution; Thomas Edison's lightbulb patent; the Sherman Anti-Trust Act; the Executive Order for the Japanese Relocation During Wartime; the Manhattan Project notebook; a press release announcing US recognition of Israel; President John F. Kennedy's inaugural address; as well as many more.

Other primary source books that can be packaged with Oakes's *Of the People: A History of the United States, Second Edition* (concise edition) include Chafe's ***History of Our Time*** and Bloom's ***Takin' It to the Streets,*** as well as ***The Boisterous Sea of Liberty: A Documentary History of America from Discovery through the Civil War;*** and ***Documenting American Violence: A Sourcebook.***

For Professors

For decades American history professors have turned to Oxford University Press as the leading source for high-quality readings and reference materials. Now, when you adopt Oakes's *Of the People: A History of the United States, Second Edition* (concise edition), the Press will partner with you and make available its best supplemental materials and resources for your classroom. Listed here are several series of high interest, but you will want to talk with your sales representative to learn more about what can be made available, and about what would suit your course best.

Instructor's Manual and Testbank. This useful guide contains helpful teaching tools for experienced and first-time teachers alike. It can be made available to adopters on request and is also available electronically on the Instructor's Resource CD. This extensive manual and testbank contains:

- **Sample Syllabi**
- **Chapter Outlines**
- **In-Class Discussion Questions**
- **Lecture Ideas**
- **Oxford's Further Reading List**
- **Quizzes** (two per chapter, one per half of the chapter, content divided somewhat evenly down the middle of the chapter: 30 multiple-choice questions each)
- **Tests** (two per chapter, each covering the entire chapter contents: each offering 10 identification/matching questions, 10 multiple-choice, 5 short-answer, 2 essay)

Instructor's Resource CD. This handy CD-ROM contains everything you need in an electronic format—the Instructor's Manual (PDF), PowerPoint Slides (fully customizable),

Image Library with PDF versions of *all* maps from the textbook, and a Computerized Testbank, which was made specifically for the concise edition.

A complete **Course Management cartridge** is also available to qualified adopters. Instructor's resources are also available for download directly to your computer through a secure connection via the instructor's side of the companion website. Contact your Oxford University Press sales representative for more information.

Other Oxford Titles of Interest for the US History Classroom

Oxford University Press publishes a vast array of titles in American history. Listed below is just a small selection of books that pair particularly well with Oakes's *Of the People: A History of the United States, Second Edition* (concise edition). Any of the books in these series can be packaged with Oakes at a significant discount to students. Please contact your Oxford University Press sales representative for specific pricing information, or for additional packaging suggestions. Please visit www.oup.com/us for a full listing of Oxford titles.

NEW NARRATIVES IN AMERICAN HISTORY

At Oxford University Press, we believe that good history begins with a good story. Each volume in this series features a compelling tale that draws on a sustained narrative to illuminate a greater historical theme or controversy. Then, in a thoughtful afterword, the authors place their narratives within larger historical contexts, discuss their sources and narrative strategies, and describe their personal involvement with the work. Intensely personal and highly relevant, these succinct texts are innovative teaching tools that provide a springboard for incisive class discussion as they immerse students in a particular historical moment.

> *Escaping Salem: The Other Witch Hunt of 1692,* by Richard Godbeer
> *Sleuthing the Alamo: Davy Crockett's Last Stand and Other Mysteries of the Texas Revolution,* by James E. Crisp
> *In Search of the Promised Land: A Slave Family in the Old South,* by John Hope Franklin and Loren Schweninger
> *The Making of a Confederate: Walter Lenoir's Civil War,* by William L. Barney
> *"They Say": Ida B. Wells and the Reconstruction of Race,* by James West Davidson
> *Wild Men: Ishi and Kroeber in the Wilderness of Modern America,* by Douglas Cazaux Sackman
> *The Gentle Subversive: Rachel Carson,* Silent Spring, *and the Rise of the Environmental Movement,* by Mark Hamilton Lytle
> *"To Everything There is a Season": Pete Seeger and the Power of Song,* by Allan Winkler

CRITICAL HISTORICAL ENCOUNTERS

The objective of this series is to produce original books that focus on a major "critical encounter" in the American experience. "Critical," as used in the series concept, refers to a formative, vital, formidable occurrence or action with a major impact in defining the contours of American life. "Encounter" suggests a confrontation or clash, sometimes but not always contentious in character, possessing profound historical meaning and consequence. Each book in the series will present a fresh viewpoint or perspective that will serve to deepen and enrich knowledge about the book's subject.

> *The Battle of Ole Miss: Civil Rights v. States' Rights,* by Frank Lambert
> *The Making of a Patriot: Ben Franklin at the Cockpit,* by Sheila Skemp
> *For Ourselves and Our Posterity: The Preamble to the Federal Constitution in American History,* by Peter Charles Hoffer

PAGES FROM HISTORY

Textbooks may interpret and recall history, but these books **are** history. Each title, compiled and edited by a prominent historian, is a collection of primary sources relating to a particular topic of historical significance. Documentary evidence includes news articles, government documents, memoirs, letters, diaries, fiction, photographs, advertisements, posters, and political cartoons. Headnotes, extended captions, sidebars, and introductory essays provide the essential context that frames the documents. All the books are amply illustrated and each includes a documentary picture essay, chronology, further reading, source notes, and index.

> *Encounters in the New World* (Jill Lepore)
> *Colonial America* (Edward G. Gray)
> *The American Revolution* (Stephen C. Bullock)
> *The Bill of Rights* (John J. Patrick)
> *The Struggle Against Slavery* (David Waldstreicher)
> *The Civil War* (Rachel Filene Seidman)
> *The Gilded Age* (Janette Thomas Greenwood)
> *The Industrial Revolution* (Laura Levine Frader)
> *Imperialism* (Bonnie G. Smith)
> *World War I* (Frans Coetzee and Marilyn Shevin-Coetzee)
> *The Depression and the New Deal* (Robert McElvaine)
> *World War II* (James H. Madison)
> *The Cold War* (Allan M. Winkler)
> *The Vietnam War* (Marilyn B. Young)

PIVOTAL MOMENTS IN AMERICAN HISTORY

Oxford's Pivotal Moments in American History series explores the turning points that forever changed the course of American history. Each book is written by an expert on the subject and provides a fascinating narrative on a significant instance that stands out in our nation's past. For anyone interested in discovering which important junctures in US history shaped our thoughts, actions, and ideals, these books are the definitive resources.

> *The Scratch of a Pen: 1763 and the Transformation of North America* (Colin Calloway)
> *As If an Enemy's Country: The British Occupation of Boston and the Origins of the Revolution* (Richard Archer)
> *Washington's Crossing* (David Hackett Fischer)

James Madison and the Struggle for the Bill of Rights (Richard Labunski)

Adams vs. Jefferson: The Tumultuous Election of 1800 (John Ferling)

The Birth of Modern Politics: Andrew Jackson, John Quincy Adams, and the Election of 1828 (Lynn Parsons)

Storm over Texas: The Annexation Controversy and the Road to Civil War (Joel H. Silbey)

Crossroads of Freedom: Antietam (James M. McPherson)

The Last Indian War: The Nez Perce Story (Elliot West)

Seneca Falls and the Origins of the Women's Rights Movement (Sally McMillen)

Rainbow's End: The Crash of 1929 (Maury Klein)

Brown v. Board of Education *and the Civil Rights Movement* (Michael J. Klarman)

The Bay of Pigs (Howard Jones)

Freedom Riders: 1961 and the Struggle for Racial Justice (Raymond Arsenault)

VIEWPOINTS ON AMERICAN CULTURE

Oxford's Viewpoints on American Culture series offers timely reflections for twenty-first century readers. The series targets topics where debates have flourished and brings together the voices of established and emerging writers to share their own points of view in compact and compelling format.

Votes for Women: The Struggle for Suffrage Revisited (Jean H. Baker)

Long Time Gone: Sixties America Then and Now (Alexander Bloom)

Living in the Eighties (Edited by Gil Troy and Vincent J. Cannato)

Race on Trial: Law and Justice in American History (Annette Gordon-Reed)

Sifters: Native American Women's Lives (Theda Perdue)

Latina Legacies: Identity, Biography, and Community (Vicki L. Ruiz)

OXFORD WORLD'S CLASSICS

For over 100 years Oxford World's Classics has made available a broad spectrum of literature from around the globe. With well over 600 titles available and a continuously growing list, this is the finest and most comprehensive classics series in print. Any volume in the series can be **packaged for free** with Oakes's *Of the People: A History of the United States, Second Edition* (concise edition). Relevant titles include Benjamin Franklin's *Autobiography and Other Writings*, J. Hector St. John de Crèvecœur's *Letters from an American Farmer*, Booker T. Washington's *Up from Slavery*, and many others. **For a complete listing of Oxford World's Classics, please visit www.oup.com/us/owc.**

Acknowledgments

The authors are grateful to our families, friends, and colleagues who encouraged us during the planning and writing of this book.

Nick Cullather: To Isabel and Joey for (occasionally) allowing me to work, and to Melanie for the 16 best years.

Jan Lewis: I want to express special thanks to Andy Achenbaum, James Grimmelmann, Warren F. Kimball, Ken Lockridge, and Peter Onuf, who either read portions of the manuscript or discussed it with me. And I am grateful to Barry Bienstock for his enormous library, his vast knowledge, and his endless patience.

The authors would like once again to thank Bruce Nichols for helping launch this book years ago. We are grateful to the editors and staff at Oxford University Press, especially our acquisitions editor, Brian Wheel, and our development editors, Angela Kao, Frederick Speers, and Anne Kemper. Brian's commitment made this text possible; Fred's vision helped us shape the book's direction; and Anne guided the development of the second edition. Thanks also to our talented production team, Barbara Mathieu, senior production editor, and Michele Laseau, art director, who helped to fulfill the book's vision. And special thanks go to Linda Sykes, who managed the photo research; to Teresa Nemeth, our copyeditor; and to Mike Powers and Martha Bostwick, cartographers, and Deane Plaister, editor, at Maps.com, who created the maps; and to the many other people behind the scenes at Oxford for helping this complex project happen.

The authors and editors would also like to thank the following people, whose time and insights have contributed to the first and second editions.

Supplement Authors

Laura Graves
South Plains College
Instructor's Manual

Jim Jeffries
Clemson University
PowerPoint slides

Andrew McMichael
Western Kentucky University
Student Companion Website

Archie McDonald
Stephen F. Austin State University
Test Bank

Expert Reviewers of the Concise Second Edition

Hedrick Alixopulos
Santa Rosa Junior College

Matthew Isham
Pennsylvania State University

Guy Alain Aronoff
Humboldt State University History Department

Ross A. Kennedy
Illinois State University

Melissa Estes Blair
Warren Wilson College

Eve Kornfeld
San Diego State University

Amanda Bruce
Nassau Community College

Peggy Lambert
Lone Star College–Kingwood

Jonathan Chu
University of Massachusetts–Boston

Shelly L. Lemons
St. Louis Community College

Paul G. E. Clemens
Rutgers University

Carolyn Herbst Lewis
Louisiana State University

Martha Anne Fielder
Cedar Valley College

Catherine M. Lewis
Kennesaw State University

Tim Hacsi
University of Massachusetts–Boston

Daniel K. Lewis
California State Polytechnic University

Scott P. Marler
University of Memphis

Laura McCall
Metropolitan State College of Denver

Stephen P. McGrath
Central Connecticut State University

Vincent P. Mikkelsen
Florida State University

Julie Nicoletta
University of Washington–Tacoma

Caitlin Stewart
Eastern Connecticut State University

Thomas Summerhill
Michigan State University

David Tegeder
Santa Fe College

Eric H. Walther
University of Houston

William E. Weeks
University of San Diego

Kenneth B. White
Modesto Junior College

Julie Winch
University of Massachusetts–Boston

Mary Montgomery Wolf
University of Georgia

Kyle F. Zelner
University of Southern Mississippi

Expert Reviewers of the Concise First Edition

Hedrick Alixopulos
Santa Rosa Junior College

Guy Alain Aronoff
Humboldt State University History Department

Melissa Estes Blair
Warren Wilson College

Amanda Bruce
Nassau Community College

Jonathan Chu
University of Massachusetts–Boston

Paul G. E. Clemens
Rutgers University

Martha Anne Fielder
Cedar Valley College

Tim Hacsi
University of Massachusetts–Boston

Matthew Isham
Pennsylvania State University

Ross A. Kennedy
Illinois State University

Eve Kornfeld
San Diego State University

Peggy Lambert
Lone Star College–Kingwood

Shelly L. Lemons
St. Louis Community College

Carolyn Herbst Lewis
Louisiana State University

Catherine M. Lewis
Kennesaw State University

Daniel K. Lewis
California State Polytechnic University

Scott P. Marler
University of Memphis

Laura McCall
Metropolitan State College of Denver

Stephen P. McGrath
Central Connecticut State University

Vincent P. Mikkelsen
Florida State University

Julie Nicoletta
University of Washington–Tacoma

Caitlin Stewart
Eastern Connecticut State University

Thomas Summerhill
Michigan State University

David Tegeder
Santa Fe College

Eric H. Walther
University of Houston

William E. Weeks
University of San Diego

Kenneth B. White
Modesto Junior College

Julie Winch
University of Massachusetts–Boston

Mary Montgomery Wolf
University of Georgia

Kyle F. Zelner
University of Southern Mississippi

Expert Reviewers of the First Edition

Thomas L. Altherr
Metropolitan State College of Denver

Luis Alvarez
University of California–San Diego

Adam Arenson
University of Texas–El Paso

Melissa Estes Blair
University of Georgia

Lawrence Bowdish
Ohio State University

Susan Roth Breitzer
Fayetteville State University

Margaret Lynn Brown
Brevard College

W. Fitzhugh Brundage
University of North Carolina–Chapel Hill

Gregory Bush
University of Miami

Brian Casserly
University of Washington

Ann Chirhart
Indiana State University

Bradley R. Clampitt
East Central University

William W. Cobb Jr.
Utah Valley University

Cheryll Ann Cody
Houston Community College

Sondra Cosgrove
College of Southern Nevada

Thomas H. Cox
Sam Houston State University

Carl Creasman
Valencia Community College

Christine Daniels
Michigan State University

Brian J. Daugherity
Virginia Commonwealth University

Mark Elliott
University of North Carolina–Greensboro

Katherine Carté Enge
Texas A&M University

Michael Faubion
University of Texas–Pan American

John Fea
Messiah College

Anne L. Foster
Indiana State University

Matthew Garrett
Arizona State University

Tim Garvin
California State University–Long Beach

Lloyd Ray Gunn
University of Utah

Suzanne Cooper Guasco
Queens University of Charlotte

Richard Hall
Columbus State University

Marsha Hamilton
University of South Alabama

Mark Hanna
University of California–San Diego

Joseph M. Hawes
University of Memphis

Melissa Hovsepian
University of Houston–Downtown

Jorge Iber
Texas Tech University

David K. Johnson
University of South Florida

Lloyd Johnson
Campbell University

Catherine O'Donnell Kaplan
Arizona State University

Rebecca M. Kluchin
California State University–Sacramento

Michael Kramer
Northwestern University

Louis M. Kyriakoudes
University of Southern Mississippi

Jason S. Lantzer
Butler University

Shelly Lemons
St. Louis Community College

Charlie Levine
Mesa Community College

Denise Lynn
University of Southern Indiana

Lillian Marrujo-Duck
City College of San Francisco

Michael McCoy
Orange County Community College

Noeleen McIlvenna
Wright State University

Elizabeth Brand Monroe
Indiana University–Purdue University
Indianapolis

Kevin C. Motl
Ouachita Baptist University

Todd Moye
University of North Texas

Charlotte Negrete
Mt. San Antonio College

Julie Nicoletta
University of Washington–Tacoma

David M. Parker
California State University–Northridge

Jason Parker
Texas A&M University

Burton W. Peretti
Western Connecticut State University

Jim Piecuch
Kennesaw State University

John Putman
San Diego State University

R. J. Rockefeller
Loyola College of Maryland

Herbert Sloan
Barnard College, Columbia University

Vincent L. Toscano
Nova Southeastern University

William E. Weeks
San Diego State University

Timothy L. Wood
Southwest Baptist University

Jason Young
SUNY–Buffalo

About the Authors

James Oakes has published several books and numerous articles on slavery and anti-slavery in the nineteenth century, including *The Radical and the Republican: Frederick Douglass, Abraham Lincoln, and the Triumph of Antislavery Politics* (2007), winner of the Lincoln Prize in 2008. Professor Oakes is Distinguished Professor of History and Graduate School Humanities Professor at the City University of New York Graduate Center. In 2008 he was a fellow at the Cullman Center at the New York Public Library. His new book is *Freedom National: The Destruction of Slavery in the United States* (February 2013).

Michael McGerr is the Paul V. McNutt Professor of History in the College of Arts and Sciences at Indiana University–Bloomington. He is the author of *The Decline of Popular Politics: The American North, 1865–1928* (1986) and *A Fierce Discontent: The Rise and Fall of the Progressive Movement, 1870–1920* (2003), both from Oxford University Press. He is writing *"The Public Be Damned": The Vanderbilts and the Unmaking of the Ruling Class*. The recipient of a fellowship from the National Endowment for the Humanities, Professor McGerr has won numerous teaching awards at Indiana, where his courses include the US Survey; War in Modern American History; Rock, Hip Hop, and Revolution; The Sixties; and American Pleasure. He has previously taught at Yale University and the Massachusetts Institute of Technology. He received his BA, MA, and PhD from Yale.

Jan Ellen Lewis is Professor of History and Acting Dean of the Faculty of Arts and Sciences, Rutgers University, Newark. She also teaches in the history PhD program at Rutgers–New Brunswick and was a visiting professor of history at Princeton. A specialist in colonial and early national history, she is the author of *The Pursuit of Happiness: Family and Values in Jefferson's Virginia* (1983) as well as numerous articles and reviews. She has coedited *An Emotional History of the United States* (1998), *Sally Hemings and Thomas Jefferson: History, Memory, and Civic Culture* (1999), and *The Revolution of 1800: Democracy, Race, and the New Republic* (2002). She has served on the editorial board of the American Historical Review and as chair of the New Jersey Historical Commission. She is a member of the Society of American Historians and the American Antiquarian Society. She received her AB from Bryn Mawr College and MAs and PhD from the University of Michigan.

Nick Cullather is a historian of US foreign relations at Indiana University–Bloomington. He is author of three books on nation building: *The Hungry World* (2010), a story of foreign aid, development, and science; *Illusions of Influence* (1994), on US-Philippines relations; and *Secret History* (1999 and 2006), a history of the CIA's overthrow of the Guatemalan government in 1954. He received his PhD from the University of Virginia.

Jeanne Boydston was Robinson-Edwards Professor of American History at the University of Wisconsin–Madison. A specialist in the histories of gender and labor, she was the author of *Home and Work: Housework, Wages, and the Ideology of Labor in the Early American Republic* (1990); coauthor of *The Limits of Sisterhood: The Beecher Sisters on Women's Rights and Woman's Sphere* (1988), and coeditor of *Root of Bitterness: Documents in the Social History of American Women*, second edition (1996). Her most recent article is "Gender as a Category of Historical Analysis," *Gender History* (2008). She taught courses in women's and gender history, the histories of the early republic and the antebellum United States, and global and comparative history, and she was the recipient of numerous awards for teaching and mentoring. Her BA and MA were from the University of Tennessee, and her PhD was from Yale University.

Mark Summers is the Thomas D. Clark Professor of History at the University of Kentucky–Lexington. In addition to various articles, he has written *Railroads, Reconstruction, and the Gospel of Prosperity* (1984), *The Plundering Generation* (1988), *The Era of Good Stealings* (1993), *The Press Gang* (1994), *The Gilded Age; or, The Hazard of New Functions* (1997), *Rum, Romanism and Rebellion* (2000), *Party Games* (2004), and *A Dangerous Stir* (2009). At present, he has just completed a book about a Tammany politician, *Big Tim and the Tiger*. He is now writing a survey of Reconstruction and a book about 1868. He teaches the American history survey (both halves), the Gilded Age, the Progressive Era, the Age of Jackson, Civil War and Reconstruction, the British Empire (both halves), the Old West (both halves), a history of political cartooning, and various graduate courses. He earned his BA from Yale and his PhD from the University of California–Berkeley.

Camilla Townsend is Professor of History at Rutgers University–New Brunswick. She is the author of four books, among them *Malintzin's Choices: An Indian Woman in the Conquest of Mexico* (2006) and *Pocahontas and the Powhatan Dilemma* (2004), and is the editor of *American Indian History: A Documentary Reader* (2010). The recipient of fellowships from the National Endowment for the Humanities and the John Simon Guggenheim Memorial Foundation, she has also won awards at Rutgers and at Colgate, where she used to teach. Her courses cover the colonial history of the Americas, as well as Native American history, early and modern. She received her BA from Bryn Mawr and her PhD from Rutgers.

Of the People

COMMON THREADS

>> In what ways did emancipation and wartime Reconstruction overlap?

>> When did Reconstruction begin?

>> Did Reconstruction change the South? If so, how? If not, why not?

>> What brought Reconstruction to an end?

Reconstructing a Nation

1865–1877

>> John Dennett Visits a Freedmen's Bureau Court

John Richard Dennett arrived in Liberty, Virginia, on August 17, 1865, on a tour of the South reporting for the magazine *The Nation*. The editors wanted accurate weekly accounts of conditions in the recently defeated Confederate states, and Dennett was the kind of man they could trust: a Harvard graduate, a firm believer in the sanctity of the Union, and a member of the class of elite Yankees who thought of themselves as the "best men" the country had to offer.

At Liberty, Dennett was accompanied by a Freedmen's Bureau agent. The Freedmen's Bureau was a branch of the US Army established by Congress to assist the freed people. Dennett and the agent went to the courthouse because one of the Freedmen's Bureau's functions was to adjudicate disputes between the freed people and southern whites.

The first case was that of an old white farmer who complained that two blacks who worked on his farm were "roamin' about and refusin' to work." He wanted the agent to help find the men and bring them back. Both men had wives and children living on his farm and eating his corn, the old man complained. "Have you been paying any wages?" the Freedmen's Bureau agent asked. "Well, they get what the other niggers get," the farmer answered. "I a'n't payin' great wages this year." There was not much the agent could do, but one of his soldiers volunteered to go and tell the blacks that "they ought to be at home supporting their wives and children."

A well-to-do planter came in to see if he could fire the blacks who had been working on his plantation since the beginning of the year. The planter complained the workers were unmanageable now that he could no longer punish them. The sergeant warned the planter not to beat his workers as if they were still slaves. In that case, the planter responded, "Will the Government take them off our hands?" The agent suspected that the planter was looking for a way to discharge his laborers at the end of the growing season but

continued

479

before they had been paid. "If they've worked on your crops all the year so far," the agent told the planter, "I guess they've got a claim on you to keep them a while longer."

Next came a "good-looking mulatto man" representing a number of African Americans worried that they would be forced to sign five-year contracts with their employers. "No, it a'n't true," the agent said. They also wanted to know if they could rent or buy land to work for themselves. "Yes, rent or buy," the agent said. But with no horses, mules, or ploughs, the former slaves wanted to know "if the Government would help us out after we get the land." The agent had no help to offer, except for a note from the bureau authorizing them to rent or buy their own farms.

The last case involved a field hand who came to complain that his master was beating him with a stick. The agent told the field hand to go back to work. "Don't be sassy, don't be lazy when you've got work to do; and I guess he won't trouble you." The field hand left but came back a minute later and asked for a letter to his master "enjoining him to keep the peace, as he feared the man would shoot him, he having on two or three occasions threatened to do so."

Most of the cases Dennett witnessed centered on labor relations, which often spilled over into other matters, including the family lives of the freed people, their civil rights, and their ability to buy land. The freed people preferred to work their own land but lacked the resources to rent or buy farms. Black workers and white owners who negotiated wage contracts had trouble figuring out each other's rights and responsibilities. The former masters wanted to retain as much of their old authority as possible. Freed men wanted as much autonomy as possible, whereas freed women were forced to seek the patriarchal protection of their husbands.

The Freedmen's Bureau was in the middle of these conflicts. Most agents tried to ensure that freed people were paid for their labor and were not brutalized as they had been as slaves. Southern whites resented this intrusion, and their resentment reached sympathetic politicians in Washington, DC. The Freedmen's Bureau became a lightning rod for the political conflicts of the Reconstruction period.

Conditions in the South raised several questions for lawmakers in Washington. How far should the federal government go to protect the economic well-being and civil rights of the freed people? What should the federal government require of southern states to be readmitted to the Union? Politicians disagreed violently on these questions. At one extreme was Andrew Johnson, who, as president, believed in small government and a speedy readmission of the southern states and looked on the Freedmen's Bureau with suspicion. At the other extreme were radical Republicans, who believed that the federal government should redistribute confiscated land to the former slaves, guarantee their civil rights, and give African American men the vote. They viewed the Freedmen's Bureau as too small and weak to be effective. In between were moderate Republicans who at first tried to work with the president. But as reports of violence and the abusive treatment of the freed people reached Washington, Republicans shifted toward the radical position.

It went back and forth this way: policy makers in Washington responded to events in the South, and events in the South were shaped in turn by policies from Washington. What John Dennett saw in Liberty, Virginia, was a good example of this. The Freedmen's Bureau agent listened to the requests of former masters and slaves, his responses shaped by the policies established in Washington. But those policies were, in turn, shaped by reports on conditions in the South sent back by Freedmen's Bureau agents like him and by journalists like John Dennett. From this interaction the politics of Reconstruction, and with it a "New South," slowly emerged.

Wartime Reconstruction

For several years, emancipation overlapped with Reconstruction. Emancipation began early in the war and was not completed until the very end of 1865. Experiments with Reconstruction therefore began during the war, long before emancipation was complete. Indeed, what is known as "presidential Reconstruction" was also the crucial phase in the completion of emancipation. Congress and the president often had very different ideas about how to reconstruct the defeated Confederacy, but on one thing they agreed from the very beginning. Until the Thirteenth Amendment was ratified in December of 1865, state emancipation was the most legally secure means of abolishing slavery. Congress and the president therefore agreed that before any southern state could be readmitted to the Union, it had to emancipate its own slaves.

After that, however, came other contentious questions. What system of free labor would replace slavery? What civil and political rights should the freed people receive? During the war Congress and the Lincoln administration responded piecemeal to developments in regions of the South under Union control. A variety of approaches to Reconstruction emerged.

Experiments with Free Labor in the Lower Mississippi Valley

In November 1861, several of the Sea Islands off South Carolina were occupied by Union troops. The slaveholders fled the advancing Union army, leaving behind between 5,000 and 10,000 slaves. In December President Lincoln declared that under the terms of the First Confiscation Act they had been "liberated." So began the first notable "rehearsal for Reconstruction." Within months the abandoned plantations of the Sea Islands were being reorganized. Eventually black families were given small plots of their own to cultivate, and in return for their labor they would receive a "share" of the year's crop. When the masters returned after the war to reclaim their lands, the labor system evolved into what would become known as "sharecropping."

Southern Louisiana also came under Union control early in the war. The sugar and cotton plantations around New Orleans provided another major experiment in the transition from slave to free labor. Unlike in the Sea Islands, however, Louisiana's planters did not abandon their plantations, and tens of thousands of slaves were involved. Union commanders faced a dilemma. The plantation workers were no longer slaves, but their masters were still in place, so the plantations could not be broken up. And sugar plantations could not be effectively organized into small sharecropping units. The unusual labor system that emerged played an important role in the politics of Reconstruction.

Union general Nathaniel Banks, hoping to stem the flow of black refugees to Union lines and prevent the shocking numbers of deaths among blacks in the contraband camps, issued stringent regulations designed to put the freed people back to work quickly. The Banks Plan required freed people to sign yearlong contracts to work on their former plantations, often for their former owners. Workers would be paid either 5 percent of the proceeds of the crop or three dollars per month. The former masters would provide food and shelter, and African American workers were forbidden to leave the plantations without permission. So harsh were these regulations that to many critics Banks had simply replaced one form of slavery with another. But as harsh as it was, the Banks Plan was not slavery, and most of the freed people returned to work fully aware of the difference. The Banks Plan was implemented throughout the lower Mississippi Valley, especially after the fall of Vicksburg in 1863.

The Banks Plan touched off a political controversy. Established planters had the most to gain from the plan, which preserved much of the prewar labor system. Louisiana Unionists, who had remained loyal to Washington, formed a Free State Association to press for more substantial changes. Lincoln publicly supported the Free State movement and issued a Proclamation of Amnesty and Reconstruction to undermine the Confederacy by cultivating the support of southern Unionists. The Proclamation contained, in outline, the first plan for reconstructing the South.

The most important thing Lincoln's plan did was to require Louisiana to abolish slavery as the price for readmission to the Union. The precedent for such a precondition had been established earlier the same year for West Virginia. Lincoln quickly applied that precedent to the seceded states, beginning with Florida and Louisiana. But the attempt to establish a loyal government in Florida foundered, so Louisiana became the first great experiment in wartime Reconstruction.

Lincoln's Ten Percent Plan Versus the Wade-Davis Bill

Beyond requiring the abolition of slavery, Lincoln's Ten Percent Plan promised full pardons and the restoration of civil rights to all those who swore loyalty to the Union, excluding only a few high-ranking Confederate military and political leaders. When the number of loyal whites in a former Confederate state reached 10 percent of the 1860 voting population, they could organize a new state constitution and government. Abiding by these conditions, Free State whites met in Louisiana in 1864 and produced a new state constitution. It abolished slavery, but it also denied blacks the right to vote.

By the spring of 1864 such denials were no longer acceptable to radical Republicans. Unionists in Louisiana developed strong ties to leading radicals in Congress, such as Thaddeus Stevens of Pennsylvania and Charles Sumner of Massachusetts. Most radicals favored federal guarantees of the civil rights of former slaves, including the right to vote, and were prepared to use the full force of the federal government to enforce congressional policy in the South. Although the radicals never formed a majority in Congress, they gradually won over the moderates to many of their positions. When Congress took control of Reconstruction after the elections in 1866, the process became known as "radical Reconstruction."

The radicals were particularly strong in New Orleans, thanks to the city's large and articulate community of free blacks. In the spring of 1864 they sent a delegation to Washington to meet with President Lincoln and press the case for voting rights. The next day, Lincoln wrote to the acting governor of Louisiana suggesting a limited suffrage for the most intelligent blacks and for those who had served in the Union army. The suggestion was ignored. Free blacks in New Orleans and former slaves then demanded civil and political rights and the abolition of the Banks labor regulations. Radicals complained that Lincoln's Ten Percent Plan was too kind to former Confederates and that the Banks Plan was too harsh on former slaves.

Swayed by events in Louisiana, congressional radicals rejected Lincoln's plan. In July 1864, Congressmen Benjamin F. Wade and Henry Winter Davis proposed a different Reconstruction plan. Under the Wade-Davis Bill, Reconstruction could not begin until a majority, rather than merely 10 percent, of a state's white men swore an oath of allegiance to the Union. In addition, the Wade-Davis Bill guaranteed full legal and civil rights to African Americans, but not the right to vote. Lincoln pocket-vetoed the bill because it required Louisiana to emancipate its slaves as a condition for readmission to the Union. Lincoln believed that only he, as commander in chief, could emancipate slaves as a necessity of war. He included an emancipation provision in his own plan for Louisiana Reconstruction.

The Louisiana experience made several things clear. The radical Republicans were determined to press for more civil and political rights for blacks than moderates initially supported; however, the moderates showed a willingness to move in a radical direction. Equally important, any Reconstruction policy would have to consider the wishes of southern blacks.

The Freed People's Dream of Owning Land

Freedom meant many things to the former slaves. It meant that they could move about their neighborhoods without passes, that they did not have to step aside to let whites pass them on the street. Following emancipation, southern blacks withdrew from white churches and established their own congregations, and during Reconstruction the church emerged as a central institution in the southern black community. Freedom also meant literacy. Even before the war ended, northern teachers poured into the South to set up schools. When the fighting stopped, the US Army helped recruit and organize thousands more northern women as teachers. As a result, hundreds of thousands of southern blacks became literate within a few years.

More important, former slaves went out of their way to have their marriages secured by the law. In 1865 marriage became an urgent necessity for many recently freed slaves, particularly women. Under slavery, black women were valued in part for their labor and in part for their ability to reproduce more slaves. With emancipation, black women and their offspring were no longer valuable as property, and some planters, hoping to avoid the expense of caring for them, began expelling women and children from their plantations in late 1865. Desperate women quickly realized that their best hope for survival was the patriarchal protection of their husbands. Once married, their husbands would demand sharecropping contracts that allowed their families to live with them on the plantations. For the first time in their lives, black women across the South became what the law called "domestic dependents." Emancipation moved black women—no longer human property—out of slavery and into patriarchy.

Charlotte Forten Born to a prominent African American family in Philadelphia, Charlotte Forten was one of many northern women who went to the South to become a teacher of the freed slaves. Forten helped found the Penn School on St. Helena's Island in South Carolina.

The freed people also wanted land, without which they saw no choice but to work for their old masters. As the war ended, many African Americans had reason to believe that the government would help them become landowners. In early 1865, Union general William Tecumseh Sherman discovered how important land was to the freed people on the Sea Islands off the Carolinas. "The way we can best take care of ourselves is to have land," they declared, "and turn it out and till it by our own labor." Persuaded by their arguments, Sherman issued Special Field Order No. 15 granting captured land to the freed people. By June, 400,000 acres had been distributed to 40,000 former slaves.

Congress seemed to be moving in a similar direction. In March 1865, the Republicans established the Bureau of Refugees, Freedmen and Abandoned Lands, commonly known as the Freedmen's Bureau. The bureau became involved in the politics of land redistribution and controlled the disposition of 850,000 acres of confiscated and abandoned Confederate lands. In July 1865, General Oliver Otis Howard, the head of the bureau, directed his agents to rent the land to the freed people in 40-acre plots that they could eventually purchase. Many agents believed that to reeducate them in the values of thrift and hard work, the freed people should be encouraged to save money and buy land for themselves. From the bureau's perspective, redistributing land was like giving it away to people who had not paid for it.

The former slaves, however, felt they had more than earned a right to the land. "The labor of these people had for two hundred years cleared away the forests and produced crops that brought millions of dollars annually," H. C. Bruce explained. "It does seem to me that a Christian Nation would, at least, have given them one year's support, 40 acres of land and a mule each." Even Abraham Lincoln seemed to agree. But in April 1865 Lincoln was dead, and Andrew Johnson became president of the United States.

Presidential Reconstruction, 1865–1867

When Andrew Johnson took office in April 1865, it was still unclear whether Congress or the president would control Reconstruction policy and whether that policy would be lenient or harsh. As with so many Democrats, Johnson's sympathy for the common man did not extend to African Americans. Yet as wartime governor of Tennessee Johnson had struggled tirelessly to get slavery abolished in the state, and in his first year as President he demanded that the former slave states abolish slavery as a condition for readmission to the Union. Nevertheless, Johnson grew increasingly determined to reconstruct the South in his own way and blind to the interests of the freed people. In 1866 he drifted away from the Republicans who controlled Congress, becoming bitter and resentful in the process.

The Political Economy of Contract Labor

In the mid-nineteenth century, Congress was normally out of session from March until December. Taking office in April 1865, Johnson hoped to use the recess to complete the Reconstruction process and present it to lawmakers in December. At the end of May the president offered amnesty and the restoration of property to white southerners who swore an oath of loyalty to the Union, excluding only high-ranking Confederate military and political leaders and very rich planters. He named provisional governors to the seceded states and told them to organize constitutional conventions. To be readmitted to the Union, the seceded states were first required to abolish slavery, preferably by ratifying the Thirteenth Amendment. Johnson also required the states to nullify their secession ordinances and repudiate their Confederate war debts. These terms were far more lenient than those Lincoln and the congressional Republicans had contemplated. They did nothing to protect the civil rights of the former slaves.

Johnson's leniency encouraged defiance among white southerners. Secessionists had been barred from participating in the states' constitutional conventions, but they participated openly in the first elections held late in the year after Johnson issued thousands of pardons. Leading Confederates thus assumed public office in the southern states. As required, the former Confederate states began abolishing slavery, and in the fall of 1865 the last great wave of emancipation spread across the South. Right up to the end of the war most slaveholders hoped to retain their slaves, even if they were forced to rejoin the Union. When the last holdouts—and there were many thousands of them—were finally forced to accept emancipation, they were furious and resentful. As the new state governments were coming into existence, a wave of violence spread across the South.

Blacks who had been freed earlier were not immune to the reaction. Back in power, white southerners demanded the restoration of all properties confiscated or abandoned during the war. In September 1865 Johnson ordered the Freedmen's Bureau to return all confiscated and abandoned lands to their former owners, and in late 1865 former slaves were being forcibly evicted from the 40-acre plots they had been given by the Union army or the Freedmen's Bureau.

Alongside their emancipation ordinances, the Johnsonian state governments enacted a series of "Black Codes" that severely restricted the civil rights of freed people. In many states the Black Codes *were* the emancipation statutes. Vagrancy laws, for example, allowed police to arrest and fine virtually any black man. If he could not pay the fine, the "vagrant" was put to work on a farm, often the one operated by his former master. Even more disturbing to the

Freedman's Labor Contract Many freed blacks were forced into labor contracts like this one in the early years of Reconstruction. Harsh working conditions and reports of white landowners refusing to pay agreed-upon wages prompted many to argue that contract labor was little different from slavery.

former slaves were apprenticeship clauses that allowed white officials to remove children from their parents' homes and put them to work as "apprentices" on nearby farms.

Presidential Reconstruction left the freed people with no choice but to sign labor contracts with white landlords that restricted their personal, as well as their working, lives. In one case, a South Carolina planter contractually obliged his black workers to "go by his direction the same as in slavery time." Contracts required blacks to work for wages as low as one-tenth of the crop, and cotton prices were falling. It is no wonder that contract labor seemed little different from slavery.

Resistance to Presidential Reconstruction

In September 1865, blacks in Virginia issued a public appeal for assistance. They declared that they lacked the means to make and enforce legal contracts, because the Black Codes denied African Americans the right to testify in court in any case involving a white person. Many planters blocked the development of a free labor market by agreeing among themselves to hire only their former slaves and by fixing wages at a low level. Finally, there were many cases of black workers who had obeyed the terms of their contracts being "met by a contemptuous refusal of the stipulated compensation."

Across the South, whites reported a growing number of freed people unwilling to accept the humiliating conditions of the contract labor system. Some blacks refused to perform specific tasks, whereas others were accused of being "disrespectful" to their employers or to whites in general. Most important, thousands of freedmen declined to sign contracts at the end of the year.

As white backlash and black defiance spread, reports of violence flooded into Washington. A former slave named Henry Adams claimed that "over two thousand colored people" were murdered around Shreveport, Louisiana, in 1865. Near Pine Bluff, Arkansas, in 1866, a black community was burned to the ground by whites. Blacks were assaulted for not speaking to whites with the proper tone of submission, for disputing the terms of labor contracts, or for failing to meet the standards white employers expected. Through relentless intimidation, whites prevented blacks from buying their own land or attending political meetings to press for civil rights.

Northerners read these reports as evidence that whites were resisting emancipation and that "rebel" sentiment was reviving in the South. When Congress returned in December 1865, moderate Republicans were already suspicious of presidential Reconstruction. Radicals argued that the contract system made a mockery of their party's commitment to free labor, and insisted that the only way to protect the interests of the freed people was to grant them the right to vote.

Congress Clashes with the President

Increasingly distressed by events in the South, Republican moderates in Congress were radicalized. They accepted the need for a more active government in the South and endorsed voting rights for black men. President Johnson, meanwhile, became obsessed with fears of "negro rule" in the South. When he insisted on readmitting southern states clearly controlled by unrepentant Confederates, Congress refused. Instead, the Republicans formed a Joint Committee on Reconstruction to propose the terms for readmission, reflecting Congress's determination to follow its own course.

In February 1866, Congress voted to extend the life of the Freedmen's Bureau and empowered the bureau to set up its own courts, which would supersede local jurisdictions wherever civil authorities were not functioning properly. The bureau's record during its first year had been mixed. In the area of labor relations, the bureau often sided with the landowners and against the interests of the freed people. But it also emancipated thousands of slaves, provided immediate relief to thousands of individual freed people, and assisted in the creation of schools. The bureau's effectiveness varied with the commitments of its agents. Some agents sided instinctively with the former masters. The more idealistic agents often acted under difficult circumstances to protect the freed people from racist violence, unfair employers, and biased officials. Thousands of freedmen and freedwomen looked to the bureau as their only hope for justice; for the same reason, thousands of southern whites resented the bureau, and they let Andrew Johnson know it.

To the amazement of moderate Republicans, Johnson vetoed the bill to extend the life of the Freedmen's Bureau, claiming that the legislation would increase the power of the central government at the expense of the states. He invoked the Jacksonian ideal of the free market, insisting that the "laws that regulate supply and demand" were the best way to resolve the labor problem in the South. Republicans fell just short of the two-thirds vote needed to override the veto. Johnson reacted by attacking the Republicans in Congress and questioning the legitimacy of the Joint Committee on Reconstruction.

Origins of the Fourteenth Amendment

In March 1866 Congress passed a landmark Civil Rights Act. It overturned the Dred Scott decision by granting United States citizenship to Americans regardless of race. This marked the first time that the federal government intervened in the states to guarantee due pro-

The Freedmen's Bureau Led by President Andrew Johnson, attacks on the Freedmen's Bureau became more and more openly racist in late 1865 and 1866. This Democratic Party broadside was circulated during the 1866 election.

AMERICAN LANDSCAPE

>> **Race Riots in Memphis and New Orleans**

A few weeks after Congress passed the Civil Rights Act, white mobs in Memphis rioted for three days. In the year since the war had ended, the city's black population had multiplied four times over as former slaves fled the countryside for better opportunities in the city. But whites in Memphis grew increasingly hostile to the presence of so many blacks. "Would to God they were back in Africa, or some other seaport town," the Memphis *Argus* complained, "anywhere but here." Under President Andrew Johnson's terms for a newly reconstructed government, the old Memphis elite had been displaced by Irish politicians at least as hostile to freed people as the old guard. Conflict between whites and blacks broke out on the streets of Memphis.

In this atmosphere of heightened racial tension, one incident sparked a riot. On May 1, 1866, after two hack drivers—one black, one white—had a traffic accident, police arrested the black man. A group of black veterans tried to prevent the arrest. A white crowd gathered and began rioting in the streets. Over the next three days, white mobs burned hundreds of homes, destroyed churches, and attacked black schools. Five black women were raped, and nearly fifty people, all but two of them black, were killed.

Three months later, white mobs in New Orleans rioted as well. Once again, both the state and city governments were falling into the hands of former Confederates. But the New Orleans massacre had a more explicitly political dimension. Its well-established community of free blacks had, by the middle of 1866, grown disillusioned with the direc-

tion Reconstruction was taking in Louisiana and New Orleans. A group of radicals sought to bring the state's 1864 constitutional convention back into session. They proposed giving blacks the vote, stripping "rebels" of the franchise, and establishing an entirely new state government. The convention was scheduled to meet on July 30.

But as the delegates met, white mobs set out to stop them. Led by police and firemen, many of them Confederate veterans, whites first attacked a parade of about 200 blacks marching to the Mechanics' Institute to support the delegates. At the convention hall, the mobs began shooting and killing the delegates trying to escape through the windows, even after they raised the white flag of surrender. When the mob finally dispersed, 34 blacks and 3 white supporters had been killed, and another 100 had been injured.

The Memphis and New Orleans massacres quickly became political issues in the North, thanks in large part to Johnson's reaction. In late August the president undertook an unprecedented campaign tour designed to stir up voters' hostility to Congress, but his trip backfired. He blasted congressional Republicans, blaming them for the riots, and suggested that radical congressman Thaddeus Stevens should be hanged. Republicans charged in turn that Johnson's own policies had revived the rebellious sentiments that led to the massacres.

The elections of 1866 became a referendum on competing visions of what American democracy should mean. For President Johnson, "democracy" meant government by *continued*

AMERICAN LANDSCAPE *continued*

local majorities, which often meant white supremacy. For African Americans and a growing number of Republicans in Congress, genuine democracy demanded a firm foundation of equal civil and political rights. The results were "overwhelmingly against the President,"

the *New York Times* noted, "clearly, unmistakably, decisively in favor of Congress and its policy." The Republicans gained a veto-proof hold on Congress, and Republican moderates were further radicalized. Congressional Reconstruction was about to begin.

cess and basic civil rights. But Johnson vetoed the Civil Rights Act of 1866. Alongside the usual Jacksonian rhetoric about limited government, Johnson justified his veto on racist grounds. He doubted that blacks "possess the requisite qualifications to entitle them to all the privileges and immunities of citizens of the United States."

Johnson's actions and rhetoric forced moderate Republicans to confront him. The Republican Congress overrode Johnson's veto of the Civil Rights Act and passed another Freedmen's Bureau Bill. Again Johnson vetoed it, but this time Congress overrode his veto.

To ensure the civil rights of the freed people, the Joint Committee on Reconstruction proposed a Fourteenth Amendment to the Constitution. The most powerful and controversial of all the Constitution's amendments, it guaranteed citizenship to all males born in the United States, regardless of color (see Table 16–1). Although the amendment did not guarantee blacks the right to vote, it based representation in Congress on a state's voting population. This punished southern states by reducing their representation if they did not allow blacks to vote.

By mid-1866, Congress had refused to recognize the state governments established under Johnson's plan, and it had authorized the Freedmen's Bureau to create a military justice system to override the local courts, thereby guaranteeing the former slaves basic rights of due process. Finally, it made ratification of the Fourteenth Amendment by the former Confederate states a requirement for readmission to the Union. Congress and the president were now at war, and Andrew Johnson went on a rampage.

Congressional Reconstruction

Johnson's outrageous behavior during the 1866 campaign, capped by a Republican sweep of the elections, ended presidential Reconstruction. Congressional Reconstruction would be far different. It was an extraordinary series of events, second only to emancipation in its impact on the history of the United States.

Origins of the Black Vote

The Congress that convened in December 1866 was far more radical than the previous one, evidenced clearly by the emerging consensus among moderate Republicans that southern blacks should be allowed to vote. Radical Republicans and black leaders had been calling for such a policy for two years, but moderate Republicans initially resisted

Table 16-1 Reconstruction Amendments, 1865–1870

Amendment	Main Provisions	Congressional Passage (2/3 majority in each house required)	Ratification Process (3/4 of all states including ex-Confederate states required)
13	Slavery prohibited in United States	January 1865	December 1865 (27 states, including 8 southern states)
14	1. National citizenship for all men and women born in the U.S.	June 1866	Rejected by 12 southern and border states, February 1867
	2. State representation in Congress reduced proportionally to number of voters disfranchised		Radicals make readmission of southern states hinge on ratification
	3. Former high-ranking Confederates denied right to hold office		Ratified July 1868
	4. Confederate debt repudiated		
15	Denial of franchise because of race, color, or past servitude explicitly prohibited	February 1869	Ratification required for readmission of Virginia, Texas, Mississippi, Georgia. Ratified March 1870.

the idea. At most, moderates contemplated granting the vote to veterans and to educated blacks who had been free before the war. Not until early 1867 did the majority of Republicans conclude that the only way to avoid a lengthy military occupation of the South was to put political power into the hands of all male freedmen.

Andrew Johnson finally pushed the moderate Republicans over the line. Ignoring the results of the 1866 elections, Johnson urged the southern states to reject the Fourteenth Amendment. Frustrated Republicans finally repudiated presidential Reconstruction. On March 2, 1867, Congress assumed control of the process by passing the First Reconstruction Act. It reduced the southern states to the status of territories and divided the South into five military districts directly controlled by the army (see Map 16–1). Before the southern states could be readmitted to the Union, they had to draw up new "republican" constitutions, ratify the Fourteenth Amendment, and allow black men to vote. The Second Reconstruction Act, passed soon after, established the procedures to enforce black suffrage by placing the military in charge of voter registration. Johnson vetoed both acts, but in both cases Congress immediately overrode him. This was congressional Reconstruction at its most radical, and for this reason it is often referred to as "radical Reconstruction."

Radical Reconstruction in the South

Beginning in 1867 the constitutions of the southern states were rewritten, thousands of African Americans began to vote, and hundreds of them assumed public office. Within six months, 735,000 blacks and 635,000 whites had registered to vote across the South. Blacks

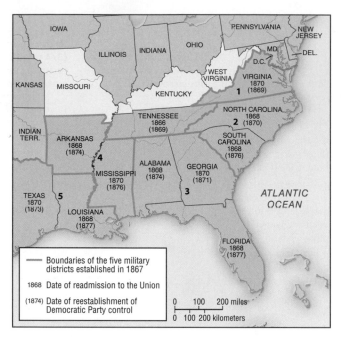

Map 16–1   Reconstruction and Redemption By 1870 Congress had readmitted every southern state to the Union. In most cases the Republican Party retained control of the "reconstructed" state governments for only a few years.

formed electoral majorities in South Carolina, Florida, Mississippi, Alabama, and Louisiana. In the fall these new voters elected delegates to conventions that drew up progressive state constitutions that guaranteed suffrage for all men, mandated public education systems, and established progressive tax structures.

The governments elected under congressional authority were based on an unstable political coalition. Northern whites were prominent in the southern Republican Party. Stereotyped as greedy carpetbaggers, they included Union veterans who stayed in the South, idealistic reformers, well-meaning capitalists, and opportunists on the make. More important to the Republican coalition were southern whites, or scalawags. Some of them lived in up-country regions that resisted secession and the Confederacy. Others had been Whigs before the war and were now hoping to regain some former influence. But new black voters were the backbone of the Republican Party in the South. They were a varied lot. Elite black artisans and professionals did not always share the interests of poor black farmers and farm laborers, but most African Americans were united by a shared interest in securing civil rights.

Although in the long run class and race divisions weakened the party, in the late 1860s and early 1870s the southern Republicans launched an impressive experiment in interracial democracy in the South. Racist legend paints these years as a dark period of "negro rule" and military domination, but military rule rarely lasted more than a year or two, and only in South Carolina did blacks ever control the legislature. Blacks who held office were largely members of the prewar free African American elite of teachers, min-

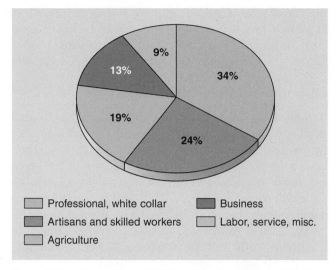

Figure 16–1 Occupations of African American Officeholders During Reconstruction Although former slaves were underrepresented among black officeholders, the Reconstruction governments were among the most broadly representative legislatures in US history.

isters, and small businessmen rather than sharecroppers or farm workers. These Reconstruction legislatures were more representative of their constituents than most legislatures in nineteenth-century America.

Achievements and Failures of Radical Government

Once in office, southern Republicans had to cultivate a white constituency and at the same time serve the interests of the blacks who elected them. To strengthen this biracial coalition, Republican politicians emphasized government support for economic development. Republican legislatures granted tax abatements for corporations and spent vast sums to encourage the construction of railroads. They preached a "gospel of prosperity" that promised to benefit ordinary white southerners.

In the long run, the gospel of prosperity did not hold the Republican coalition together. Outside investors were unwilling to risk their capital on a politically unstable region. By the early 1870s, black politicians questioned the diversion of scarce revenues to railroads and tax breaks for corporations. Instead, they demanded public services, especially universal education. But more government services meant higher property taxes at a time of severe hardship. White small farmers had been devastated by the Civil War. Unaccustomed to paying high taxes, and believing strongly in limited government, they grew increasingly receptive to Democratic appeals for restoration of "white man's government." Thus southern Republicans were unable to unite the diverse interests of their constituents.

Despite powerful opposition at home and lukewarm support from Washington, DC, radical governments in the South boasted several important achievements. They funded the construction of hospitals, insane asylums, prisons, and roads. They introduced homestead exemptions that protected the property of poor farmers. Republican legislatures established public school systems that were a major improvement over their antebellum counterparts. The literacy rate among southern blacks rose steadily. Nevertheless, public schools for southern blacks remained inadequately funded and sharply segregated.

The Political Economy of Sharecropping

Congressional Reconstruction made it easier for the former slaves to negotiate the terms of their labor contracts. Republican state legislatures abolished the Black Codes and passed "lien" laws that gave black workers more control over the crops they grew. Workers with grievances had a better chance of securing justice, as southern Republicans became sheriffs, justices of the peace, and county clerks and as southern courts allowed blacks to serve as witnesses and sit on juries.

The strongest card in the hands of the freed people was a shortage of agricultural workers in the South. After emancipation, thousands of blacks sought opportunities in towns and cities or in the North. And even though most blacks remained in the South as farmers, they reduced their working hours in several ways. Black women still worked the fields, but they spent more time nursing their infants and caring for their children. And the children went to school when they were able. The resulting labor shortage forced white landlords to renegotiate their labor arrangements with the freed people.

The contract labor system that had developed during the war and under presidential Reconstruction was replaced with a variety of regional arrangements. On the Louisiana sugar plantations, the freed people became wage laborers. But in tobacco and cotton regions, where most freed people lived, a new system of labor called sharecropping developed. Under this system, an agricultural worker and his family typically agreed to work for one year on a particular plot of land, with the landowner providing the tools, seed, and work animals. At the end of the year the crop was split, perhaps one-third going to the sharecropper and two-thirds to the owner.

Sharecropping shaped the economy of the postwar South by transforming the production and marketing of cash crops. Landowners broke up their plantations into family-sized plots, worked by sharecroppers in family units with no direct supervision. Each sharecropping family established its own relationship with local merchants to sell crops and buy supplies. Merchants became crucial to the southern credit system, because most southern banks could not meet the banking standards established by Congress during the Civil War. Storekeepers, usually the only people who could extend credit to sharecroppers, provided sharecroppers with food, fertilizer, animal feed, and other provisions during the year until the crop was harvested.

These developments had important consequences for white small farmers. More merchants fanned out into up-country areas inhabited mostly by ordinary whites, areas now served by railroads sponsored by the Reconstruction legislatures. With merchants offering credit and railroads offering transportation, small farmers started to produce cash crops. Thus Reconstruction accelerated the process by which southern yeomen abandoned self-sufficient farming in favor of cash crops.

Sharecropping spread quickly among black farmers in the cotton South. By 1880, 80 percent of cotton farms had fewer than 50 acres, and the majority of those farms were operated by sharecroppers (see Maps 16–2 and 16–3). Sharecropping had several advantages

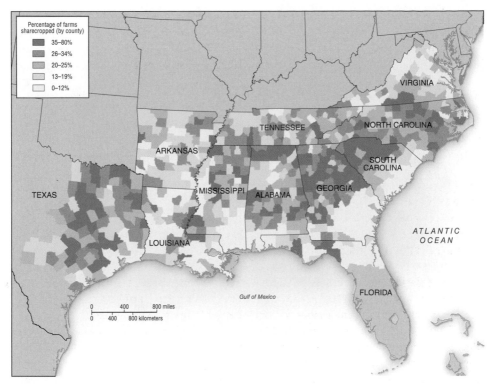

Map 16–2   Sharecropping By 1880 the sharecropping system had spread across the South. It was most common in the inland areas, where cotton and tobacco plantations were widespread before the Civil War.

for landlords. It reduced their risk when cotton prices were low and encouraged workers to increase production without costly supervision. Further, if sharecroppers changed jobs before the crop was harvested, they lost a whole year's pay. But there were also advantages for the workers. For freed people with no hope of owning their own farms, sharecropping at least rewarded their hard work. The bigger the crop, the more they earned. It gave them more independence than contract labor.

Sharecropping also allowed the freed people to work in families rather than in gangs. Freedom alone had rearranged the powers of men, women, and children within the families of former slaves. Parents gained new control over their children. They could send sons and daughters to school, or put them to work. Successful parents could give their children an important head start in life. Similarly, African American husbands gained new powers.

The marriage laws of the mid-nineteenth century that defined the husband as the head of the household were irrelevant to slaves, because their marriages had no legal standing. With emancipation, these patriarchal assumptions of American family law shaped the lives of freed men and women. Once married, women often found that their property belonged to their husbands. The sharecropping system further assumed that as head of the household the husband made the economic decisions for the entire family. Men signed most labor contracts, and most contracts assumed that the husband would take his family to work with him.

Map 16–3   Effect of Sharecropping in the South: The Barrow Plantation in Oglethorpe County, Georgia Sharecropping cut large estates into small landholdings worked by sharecroppers and tenants, changing the landscape of the South.

Sharecropping shaped the social system of the postwar South. It influenced the balance of power between men and women. It established the balance of power between landowners and sharecroppers. It tied the southern economy to agriculture, in particular to cotton production, impeding the region's overall economic development. Yet amid these changes, the Republican Party was retreating from its commitment to the freed people.

The Retreat from Republican Radicalism

By the late 1860s, fractures in the Republican coalition were weakening the party's commitment to radical Reconstruction. By 1868, the Republicans were presenting themselves as the party of moderation. The success of this appeal brought the last major achievements of Reconstruction.

The Impeachment and Trial of Andrew Johnson

Throughout 1866 and much of 1867, President Johnson waged a relentless campaign against Congress and the radicals. Inevitably, this conflict led to a struggle over control of the military in the South. The First Reconstruction Act placed the entire South under direct military power. The Freedmen's Bureau was a branch of the US Army. Judicial authority was vested in the provost marshals. The military also oversaw voter registration. But as the commander in chief of the military, Johnson removed dozens of Freedmen's Bureau officials who enforced the Civil Rights Act of 1866. He replaced Republican provost marshals with men hostile to Congress and contemptuous of the former slaves. In short, Johnson went out of his way to undermine the will of Congress.

Radicals called for Johnson's impeachment, but moderates and conservatives resisted. Instead, Congress hoped to restrain the president by refining the Reconstruction Acts and by using the Tenure of Office Act of March 2, 1867. This act prohibited the president from removing officials whose appointments required congressional approval, such as Secretary of War Edwin M. Stanton, who was sympathetic to the Republicans. A related statute required that all presidential orders to the military pass through General Ulysses S. Grant. Republicans hoped that this would prevent the president from removing military officials who enforced the Reconstruction Acts.

Congress's actions only provoked the president. In his veto messages and public pronouncements Johnson indulged in blatant racist pandering. He played on fears of "amalgamation," "miscegenation," and racial "degeneration." He expressed fear for the safety of white women, when the evidence suggested that black women were most in danger. In the off-year elections of 1867, northern Democrats played the race card successfully. Democratic victories erased many of the Republican gains of 1866 and inspired the president to defy congressional restraints. As a deliberate provocation, Johnson asked Secretary of War Stanton to resign on August 5, 1867. Stanton refused, and the president appointed General Grant as interim secretary of war. Stanton would not budge, so in February 1868 Johnson fired him. For this the House of Representatives voted to impeach the president and put him on trial in the Senate.

For all the animosity that Johnson had aroused by his obnoxious behavior, the senators trying him took their job seriously. Many were concerned that the Tenure of Office Act, which Johnson was accused of violating, was in fact unconstitutional. Others wondered whether his technical breach of the law was serious enough to warrant his removal from office. These and other doubts, along with Johnson's promise of good behavior in the future, led the Senate to acquit the president by a single vote.

Republicans Become the Party of Moderation

While Andrew Johnson was on trial in the Senate, voters in Michigan voted overwhelmingly to reject a new state constitution that granted blacks the right to vote. Coming on the heels of Democratic victories in 1867, the Michigan results were read by Republicans as a rejection of radical Reconstruction.

During the 1868 elections, Republicans repudiated the radicals' demand for nationwide black suffrage, arguing that the black vote was a uniquely southern solution to a uniquely southern problem. The northern states should be free to decide this issue for themselves. Congress readmitted six southern states to the Union, demonstrating that Republican policies had restored law and order to the South. By nominating General Ulysses Grant as their presidential candidate, the Republicans confirmed their retreat from radicalism. "Let Us Have Peace" was Grant's campaign slogan.

By contrast, the Democrats nominated Horatio Seymour, who ran a vicious campaign of race-baiting. The Democratic platform denounced the Reconstruction Acts and promised to restore white rule to the South. Seymour suggested that a Democratic president might nullify the governments organized under congressional Reconstruction.

AMERICA AND THE WORLD

>> **Reconstructing America's Foreign Policy**

Before the Civil War, Republicans associated expansionism with slave power and the Democratic Party. But with the triumph of nationalism, the Republicans equated overseas expansion with the spread of liberty. In 1867 Secretary of State William Seward negotiated the purchase of Alaska from Russia. The acquisition ignited expansionist dreams of eventual US control of all of North America, including Canada and Mexico, and "all the West Indian Islands."

The administration was equally adroit in its negotiations with Great Britain over the settlement of the so-called Alabama claims. In 1872 the English accepted responsibility for having helped equip the Confederate navy during the Civil War and agreed to pay over $15 million for damage to American shipping by the *Alabama* and other southern warships built in England.

In 1870, a diverse coalition came together to support the annexation of the island nation of Santo Domingo, now the Dominican Republic. The Grant administration strongly supported the treaty, and Republicans who had once objected to any scheme associated with slavery now endorsed annexation. It would, they claimed, allow "our neighbors to join with us in the blessings of our free institutions." Thus the abolition of slavery in the United States was said to have purified the motives for American expansion. Even Frederick Douglass endorsed the annexation of Santo Domingo as a way to help the island's inhabitants rise out of their grinding poverty. But Grant's aggressive foreign policy was not uncontested. Grant tried to bulldoze the treaty through Congress but was thwarted by Senator Charles Sumner of Massachusetts, the powerful chairman of the Foreign Relations Committee. Sumner took a principled stance against imperial ventures in general, but he was particularly concerned with protecting the independence of the black republic of Haiti, which shared the island with Santo Domingo. A handful of Republicans, including Carl Schurz and Oliver P. Morton, also opposed the treaty, but most of the party sided with Grant. Yet Sumner succeeded in having the treaty rejected, by a 28–28 tie vote, thanks to the opposition of Senate Democrats. They opposed annexation for racist reasons: they objected to incorporating into the United States an island populated by dark-skinned peoples of an inferior race. The prewar alignments on expansionism were reversed by the Civil War. Republicans spearheaded American imperialism, and Democrats largely opposed it.

Whereas the Republicans promised order and stability, the Democrats seemed to promise continued disruption. Northern fears were confirmed by the election violence that swept the South, incited by southern Democrats to keep black voters from the polls.

The Ku Klux Klan, which systematically intimidated potential black voters, was one of several secretive organizations dedicated to the violent overthrow of radical Reconstruction and the restoration of white supremacy. They included the Knights of the White Camelia, the Red Shirts, and the Night Riders. In addition to harassing and attacking African Americans, these organizations worked in the main to restore the political power of the Democratic Party in the South. They intimidated white Republicans, burned homes of black families, and lynched African Americans who showed signs of political activism. In 1868 the Ku Klux Klan served as the paramilitary arm of the southern Democratic Party.

As a means of restoring white supremacy, the Klan's strategy of violence backfired. During a wave of disgust that swept across the North, the Republicans regained control of the White House, along with 25 of the 33 state legislatures, and quickly seized the opportunity to preserve the achievements of Reconstruction.

The Republicans reinforced their moderate image by attempting to restore law and order in the South. Congressional hearings produced vivid evidence of the Klan's violent efforts to suppress the black vote. Congress responded with a series of Enforcement Acts designed to "enforce" the recently enacted Fifteenth Amendment (see "The Fifteenth Amendment and Nationwide African American Suffrage," following). After some hesitation, the Grant administration used the new laws to prosecute the Klan and diminish political violence throughout the South. As a result, the 1872 presidential elections were relatively free of disruption.

Reconstructing the North

Although Reconstruction was aimed primarily at the South, the North was affected as well, especially by the struggle over the black vote. The transformation of the North was an important chapter in the history of Reconstruction.

The Fifteenth Amendment and Nationwide African American Suffrage

Before the Civil War, blacks in the North were segregated in theaters, restaurants, cemeteries, hotels, streetcars, ferries, and schools. Most northern blacks could not vote, either because they were expressly denied the privilege or because of discriminatory property requirements that blacks alone were required to meet. The Civil War galvanized the northern black community to fight racial discrimination, with some success. In 1863 California removed the ban on black testimony in criminal courts. Two years later Illinois did the same. During the war, many northern cities abolished streetcar segregation. But faced with black voting, northern whites retained their racial prejudices. In 1865 voters in three northern states (Connecticut, Wisconsin, and Minnesota) rejected constitutional amendments to enfranchise African American men. In 1867, even as Congress was imposing the black vote on the South, black suffrage was defeated in Ohio, Minnesota, and Kansas.

The shocking electoral violence of 1868 persuaded many northerners that, given the chance, southern whites would quickly strip blacks of the right to vote. In Iowa and Minnesota, voters finally approved black suffrage. In 1869 Republicans passed the Fifteenth Amendment to the Constitution, which prohibited the use of "race, color, or previous condition of servitude" to disqualify voters anywhere in the United States. By outlawing voter discrimination on the basis of race, the Fifteenth Amendment protected the most radical achievement of congressional Reconstruction.

The Fifteenth Amendment brought Reconstruction to the North by overturning state laws that discriminated against black voters. In addition, Congress required ratification of the amendment in those southern states still to be readmitted to the Union. Virginia, Mississippi, and Texas did so and rejoined the Union. On March 30, 1870, the Fifteenth Amendment became part of the Constitution. For the first time, racial criteria for voting were banned everywhere in the United States, North as well as South.

Women and Suffrage

The issue of black voting divided northern radicals, especially feminists and abolitionists, who had long been allies in the struggle for emancipation. Signs of trouble appeared as early as May 1863 at the convention of the Woman's National Loyal League in New York City. The League had been organized to assist in defeating the slave South. One of the convention's resolutions declared that "there never can be a true peace in this Republic until the civil and political rights of all citizens of African descent and all women are practically established." For some delegates, this went too far. They argued that it was inappropriate to inject the issue of women's rights into the struggle to restore the Union.

By the end of the war, radical pressure for black suffrage in addition to emancipation caused a rancorous debate among reformers. Abolitionists argued that, although they supported women's suffrage, the critical issue was the protection of the freed people of the South. This, abolitionist Wendell Phillips argued, was "the Negro's Hour." Some women's rights activists felt betrayed. For 20 years they had pressed their claims for the right to vote. They were loyal allies of the Republicans and were now abandoned by them. It would be better, Elizabeth Cady Stanton argued, to press for "a vote based on intelligence and education for black and white, man and woman." Because voting rights based on "intelligence and education" would have excluded virtually all the freed slaves, as well as the working-class Irish, Germans, and Chinese, Stanton's remarks revealed a strain of elitism that further alienated abolitionists.

Not all feminists agreed with Stanton, and as racist violence erupted in the South, abolitionists argued that black suffrage was more urgent than women's suffrage. "I have always championed women's right to vote," argued Frederick Douglass, "but it will be seen that the present claim for the negro is one of the most urgent necessity."

Stanton was unmoved by such arguments. Supporters of women's suffrage opposed the Fifteenth Amendment on the ground that it subjected elite, educated women to the rule of base and illiterate males, especially immigrants and blacks. Abolitionists favored universal suffrage, not the "educated" suffrage that Stanton was calling for. The breach between reformers weakened the coalition of radicals pushing to maintain a vigorous Reconstruction policy in the South.

The Rise and Fall of the National Labor Union

Inspired by the radicalism of the Civil War and Reconstruction, industrial workers across the North organized dozens of craft unions, Eight-Hour Leagues, and workingmen's associations, all designed to protect northern workers who were overworked and underpaid.

They called strikes, initiated consumer boycotts, and formed consumer cooperatives. In 1867 and 1868, workers in New York and Massachusetts campaigned to enact laws restricting the workday to eight hours. Soon, workers began electing their own candidates to state legislatures.

Founded in 1866, the National Labor Union (NLU) was the first significant postwar effort to organize all "working people" into a national union. William Sylvis, an iron molder, founded the NLU and became its president in 1868. He denied any "harmony of interests" between workers and capitalists. On the contrary, every wage earner was at war with every capitalist, whose "profits" robbed working people of the fruits of their labor.

Under Sylvis's direction the NLU advocated a wide range of political reforms, not just bread-and-butter issues. Sylvis believed that through organization American workers could take the "first step toward competence and independence." He argued for a doubling of the average worker's wages. He supported voting rights for blacks and women. Nevertheless, after a miserable showing in the elections of 1872, the NLU fell apart. By then, Reconstruction in the South was also ending.

The End of Reconstruction

National events had as much to do with the end of Reconstruction as did events in the South. Reacting to a nationwide outbreak of political corruption in the late 1860s and 1870s, influential northern liberals, supporters of Reconstruction, abandoned the Republican Party in disgust in 1872. The end of Reconstruction finally came after electoral violence corrupted the 1876 elections. Republican politicians in Washington, DC, responded with a sordid political bargain that came to symbolize the end of an era.

Corruption as a National Problem

Postwar America witnessed an extraordinary display of public dishonesty. Democrats were as prone to thievery as Republicans. Northern swindlers looted the public treasuries. In the South, both black and white legislators took bribes. Corruption, it seemed, was endemic to postwar American politics.

If corruption was everywhere in the late 1860s and 1870s, it was largely because there were more opportunities for it than ever before. The Civil War and Reconstruction had swollen government budgets. Never before was government so active in collecting taxes and disbursing vast sums for the public good. Under the circumstances, many government officials traded bribes for votes, embezzled public funds, or used insider knowledge to defraud taxpayers.

The federal government set the tone. In the most notorious case, the directors of the Union Pacific Railroad set up a dummy corporation called the Credit Mobilier, awarded it phony contracts, and protected it from inquiry by bribing influential congressmen. The Grant administration was eventually smeared with scandal as well. Although personally honest, the president surrounded himself with rich nobodies and army buddies rather than respected statesmen. Grant's own private secretary was exposed as a member of the "Whiskey Ring," a cabal of distillers and revenue agents who cheated the government out of millions of tax dollars every year.

William Marcy Tweed The boss of New York's notoriously corrupt "Tweed Ring" was parodied by the great cartoonist Thomas Nast. Nast's portrayal of the bloated public official became an enduring symbol of governmental corruption.

State and city governments in the North were no less corrupt. Wealthy businessmen curried favor with politicians whose votes would determine where a railroad would be built and which land would be allocated for rights of way. State officials accepted gifts, received salaries, and sat on the boards of corporations directly affected by their votes. Municipalities awarded lucrative contracts to build schools, parks, libraries, water and sewer systems, and mass-transportation networks, creating temptations for corruption. The Tweed Ring alone bilked New York City out of tens of millions of dollars. By these standards, the corruption of the southern Reconstruction legislatures was relatively small.

But corruption in the South had particular significance for Reconstruction. Southern Republicans of modest means depended heavily on the money they earned as public officials. They were responsible for the collection of unusually high taxes and for economic development projects. For many, the lure of corruption proved overwhelming. The Republican governor of Louisiana grew rich while in office by "exacting tribute" from railroads seeking state favors. Corruption on a vast scale implied petty corruption as well: some legislators sold their votes for as little as $200.

Opponents of Reconstruction often used attacks on corruption to undermine Republican policies. Their strategy helped galvanize opposition, destroying Republican hopes of attracting white voters. Finally, corruption in the South stirred a backlash against active government nationwide, weakening northern support for Reconstruction. The intellectual substance of this backlash was provided by influential liberal Republicans, many of whom had strongly supported radical Reconstruction.

Liberal Republicans Revolt

The label "liberal Republicans" covered a small but influential group of intellectuals, politicians, publishers, and businessmen from the northern elite who were disgusted by post-war corruption and discouraged by the failure of radical Reconstruction to bring peace to the South.

Liberal philosophy was deeply suspicious of democracy. Liberals argued that any government beholden to the interests of the ignorant masses was doomed to corruption. They believed that public servants should be chosen on the basis of intelligence, as measured by civil service examinations, rather than by patronage appointments through corrupt party machines. To liberals, party politics was the enemy of good government.

Liberals grew increasingly alienated from the Republican Party and from President Grant. Above all, they resented the fact that the Republican Party had changed as its idealistic commitment to free labor waned and its radical vanguard disappeared. To emerging Republican leaders, getting and holding office had become an end in itself.

As Republicans lost their identity as moral crusaders, liberal reformers proposed a new vision of their own. In 1872 they supported Horace Greeley as the Democratic presidential candidate. The liberal plank in the Democratic platform committed the party to universal equality before the law, the integrity of the Union, and support for the Thirteenth, Fourteenth, and Fifteenth Amendments. At the same time, liberals demanded "the immediate and absolute removal of all disabilities" imposed on the South, as well as a "universal amnesty" for ex-Confederates. Finally, the liberals declared their belief that "local self-government" would "guard the rights of all citizens more securely than any centralized power." In effect, the liberals were demanding the end of federal efforts to protect the former slaves.

In the long run, the liberal view would prevail, but not with the voters of 1872. The liberals' biggest liability was their presidential candidate. Horace Greeley's reputation and Republican background were too much, and Democrats refused to vote for him. Grant was easily reelected, but Republicans saw the returns as evidence that Reconstruction was becoming a political liability.

The 1874 elections confirmed the lesson. Democrats made sweeping gains across the North, and an ideological stalemate developed. For a generation, neither party would clearly dominate American politics. The Republicans would take no more risks in support of Reconstruction.

During his second term, Grant did little to protect black voters from violence in the South. Not even the Civil Rights Act of 1875 undid the impression of waning Republican zeal. Ostensibly designed to prohibit racial discrimination in public places, the act lacked enforcement provisions. The bill's most important clause, prohibiting segregated schools, was eliminated from the final version. Southern states ignored even this watered-down statute, and in 1883 the Supreme Court declared the last major piece of Reconstruction lawmaking unconstitutional.

A Depression and a Deal "Redeem" the South

Angered by corruption and high taxes, white voters in the South answered the Democratic Party's appeal for restoration of white supremacy. As the number of white Republicans fell, the number of black Republicans holding office in the South increased, even as the Grant administration backed away from civil rights. But the persistence of black officeholders only reinforced the Democrats' determination to "redeem" their states from Republican rule. Democrats had taken control of Virginia in 1869, North Carolina in 1870, Georgia in 1871, and Texas in 1873. Then panic struck.

In September 1873, America's premier financial institution, Jay Cooke & Company, went bankrupt after overextending itself on investments in the Northern Pacific Railroad. Within weeks, hundreds of banks and thousands of businesses went bankrupt. The country sank into a depression that lasted five years. Unemployment rose to 14 percent as corporations slashed wages. To protect their incomes, railroad workers tried to organize a nationwide union and attempted to strike several times. The strikes failed.

As the nation turned its attention to labor unrest and economic depression, the Republican Party's commitment to Reconstruction all but disappeared. Democrats regained control of the governments of Alabama and Arkansas in 1874. In the few southern states where black Republicans clung to political power, white "redeemers" used violence to overthrow the last remnants of Reconstruction.

Mississippi established the model in 1875, and it became known as "the Mississippi Plan." Confident that Washington would no longer interfere in the South, Democrats launched an all-out campaign to regain control of the state government. Crude appeals to white supremacy reduced the dwindling number of scalawags. To defeat black Republicans, White Leagues used violence and intimidation to keep blacks from the polls. Republicans were beaten, forced to flee, and in several cases murdered. Washington ignored African American pleas for protection. In the end, enough blacks were kept from the polls and enough scalawags voted their racial prejudices to put the Democrats in power. Mississippi was "redeemed."

The tactics used in Mississippi were repeated elsewhere the following year, with dramatic consequences for the presidential election of 1876. Amidst a serious economic depression, and with an electorate tired of Reconstruction, the Democrats stood a good chance of winning the presidency. The Democratic candidate, Samuel J. Tilden, won 250,000 more votes than the Republican, Rutherford B. Hayes (see Map 16–4).

>> Time Line

▼1863
Lincoln's Proclamation of Amnesty and Reconstruction

▼1864
Wade-Davis Bill

▼1865
General Sherman's Special Field Order No. 15
Freedmen's Bureau established
Lincoln's second inauguration
Lincoln assassinated; Andrew Johnson becomes president

General Howard's Circular 13
President Johnson orders the Freedmen's Bureau to return confiscated lands to former owners
Joint Committee on Reconstruction established by Congress

▼1866
Congress renews Freedmen's Bureau; Johnson vetoes renewal bill
Civil Rights Act vetoed by Johnson

Congress overrides presidential veto of Civil Rights Act
Congress passes Fourteenth Amendment
Congress passes another Freedmen's Bureau Bill over Johnson's veto
Republicans sweep midterm elections

▼1867
First and Second Reconstruction Acts
Tenure of Office Act

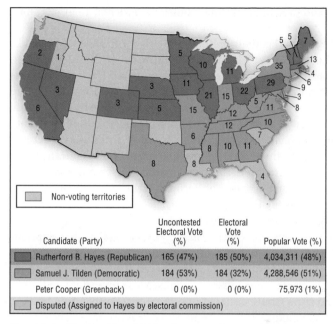

Candidate (Party)	Uncontested Electoral Vote (%)	Electoral Vote (%)	Popular Vote (%)
Rutherford B. Hayes (Republican)	165 (47%)	185 (50%)	4,034,311 (48%)
Samuel J. Tilden (Democratic)	184 (53%)	184 (32%)	4,288,546 (51%)
Peter Cooper (Greenback)	0 (0%)	0 (0%)	75,973 (1%)
Disputed (Assigned to Hayes by electoral commission)			

Map 16–4   The Presidential Election, 1876 In 1876 the Democratic presidential candidate, Samuel Tilden, won the popular vote but was denied the presidency because the Republicans who controlled Congress chose to interpret voting irregularities in Louisiana, South Carolina, Oregon, and Florida in a way that gave their candidate, Rutherford B. Hayes, all of the disputed electoral votes.

▼1868
Johnson fires Secretary of War Stanton
House of Representatives impeaches Johnson
Senate trial of Johnson begins
Acquittal of Johnson
Fourteenth Amendment ratified
Ulysses S. Grant wins presidential election

▼1869
Congress passes Fifteenth Amendment

▼1870
Fifteenth Amendment ratified

▼1872
"Liberal Republicans" leave their party
Grant reelected

▼1873
Financial "panic" sets off depression

▼1875
"Mississippi Plan" succeeds
Civil Rights Act of 1875 enacted

▼1876
Disputed presidential election

▼1877
Electoral commission awards presidency to Rutherford B. Hayes

But electoral fraud in South Carolina, Louisiana, Florida, and Oregon threw the results into doubt.

If all of the electoral votes from those states went to Hayes, he would win, but if even a single electoral vote went to Tilden, he would win, the first Democrat to win the presidency in 20 years. The outcome was determined by an electoral commission with a Republican majority, which awarded every disputed electoral vote to the Republican Hayes, casting doubt on the legitimacy of his presidency. What he did shortly after taking office suggested that he had won thanks to a "compromise" with the Democrats to end Reconstruction in the South. There is no proof that such a deal was ever actually made. Nevertheless, Hayes ordered the federal troops guarding the Republican statehouses in South Carolina and Louisiana to leave. This order marked the formal end of military occupation of the South and the symbolic end of Reconstruction. By late 1877, every southern state had been redeemed by the Democrats.

The following year the Supreme Court began to issue rulings that further undid the achievements of Reconstruction. In *Hall v. DeCuir* (1878), the Supreme Court invalidated a Louisiana law prohibiting racial segregation on public transportation. In 1882, the justices declared unconstitutional a federal law protecting southern African Americans against racially motivated murders and assaults. More important, in the Civil Rights Cases of 1883, the Supreme Court declared that the Fourteenth Amendment did not pertain to discriminatory practices by private persons. The Supreme Court thus completed the retreat from Reconstruction.

Conclusion

Inspired by an idealized vision of a society based on equal rights and free labor, Republicans expected emancipation to transform the South. Freed from the shackles of the slave power, the region would soon become a shining example of democracy and prosperity. If the results were less than Republicans expected, the achievements of Reconstruction were still impressive. Across the South, African American men and women carved out a space in which their families could live more freely than before. Black men by the tens of thousands elected to office some of the most democratic state legislatures of the nineteenth century. Thousands more black workers repudiated an objectionable contract-labor system in favor of a new compromise known as sharecropping. Furthermore, Reconstruction added three important amendments to the Constitution that transformed civil rights and electoral laws throughout the nation.

Nevertheless, the Republicans quickly washed their hands of Reconstruction. They left southern blacks unprotected in a hostile world. Sharecropping offered blacks little hope of real economic independence. Democratic redeemers excluded blacks from the substance of power. Tired of Reconstruction, Americans turned their attention to the new problems of urban, industrial America.

Who, What

Review Questions

1. What made congressional Reconstruction "radical"?

2. How did conditions for the readmission of states into the Union change over time?

3. How did Reconstruction change the South?

4. How did Reconstruction change the North?

5. What were the major factors that brought Reconstruction to an end?

Critical-Thinking Questions

1. Compare and contrast wartime Reconstruction, presidential Reconstruction, and congressional (radical) Reconstruction. What were the key differences between the three phases?

2. How critical was the failure of land redistribution for blacks? Was sharecropping an acceptable substitute for achieving economic freedom? Why or why not?

3. In what ways did the tactics of white supremacists in this period end up hurting their own cause?

For further review materials and resource information, please visit www.oup.com/us/ofthepeople

1) Blatantly discriminatory policies such as forced labor contracts and the "Black Codes" led to the radicalization of Republican congressmen and the end of presidential Reconstruction.

2) Freed slaves never received federal land grants, but many ended up as sharecroppers and helped shape the new social and economic systems of the post-war South.

3) Tensions between the executive and legislative branches of the federal government led to the first impeachment of a president in the nation's history.

4) Over the course of Reconstruction, the Republican Party transitioned from a radical platform of racial and social equality to a slow abandonment of those aims in the face of economic depression, labor unrest, and changes in public opinion.

5) Widespread electoral violence toward blacks by southern white supremacists persuaded northern whites to set aside their long-standing resistance to black suffrage and support the Fifteenth Amendment.

Wartime Reconstruction

Presidential Reconstruction, 1865–1867

Congressional Reconstruction

The Retreat from Republican Radicalism

Reconstructing the North

The End of Reconstruction

RECONSTRUCTING A NATION

1865–1877

EVENTS

Experiments with Free Labor in the Lower Mississippi Valley The plantations of the Sea Islands and southern Louisiana served as the earliest "rehearsals" for Reconstruction and sparked political controversy.

Lincoln's Ten Percent Plan Versus the Wade-Davis Bill Lincoln and congressional radicals debated the conditions under which Confederate states would be allowed to return to the Union.

The Freed People's Dream of Owning Land Former slaves carved out new communities and institutions, reunited with family members, and pursued land ownership.

The Political Economy of Contract Labor Free southern blacks were forced to sign labor contracts and adhere to new laws that severely restricted their civil rights.

Resistance to Presidential Reconstruction Blacks resisted the contract labor system and faced violent reprisals from southern whites.

Congress Clashes with the President Republican moderates in Congress grew more radical and challenged President Johnson's Reconstruction agenda.

Origins of the Fourteenth Amendment Congress passed the Civil Rights Act over Johnson's veto and proposed a constitutional amendment granting citizenship to all males born in the United States, regardless of color.

Origins of the Black Vote A more radicalized Congress passed two Reconstruction Acts and secured black suffrage in most of the South, again over Johnson's veto.

Radical Reconstruction in the South Southern Republicans launched an experiment in interracial democracy in the South.

Achievements and Failures of Radical Government Southern Republicans were unable to unite the diverse interests of their constituents but still boasted several important achievements.

The Political Economy of Sharecropping The rapid emergence of sharecropping reshaped the social, economic, and physical landscape of the postwar South.

The Impeachment and Trial of Andrew Johnson Tensions between Congress and the president resulted in impeachment and a trial in which Johnson was acquitted.

Republicans Become the Party of Moderation Facing opposition, Republicans transitioned into a more moderate position and nominated Ulysses S. Grant as their presidential candidate.

The Fifteenth Amendment and Nationwide African American Suffrage The Fifteenth Amendment brought Reconstruction to the North by overturning state laws that discriminated against black male voters.

Women and Suffrage Black suffrage left some women's rights activists feeling betrayed, and created tensions among radicals.

The Rise and Fall of the National Labor Union Postwar workers formed a national union, but it quickly fell apart after a miserable showing in the elections of 1872.

Corruption as a National Problem Corruption at the local, state, and federal levels—although widespread in both parties—allowed opponents of Reconstruction to undermine Republican policies.

Liberal Republicans Revolt A small but influential group of Republicans pushed for an end to federal protection of former slaves.

A Depression and a Deal "Redeem" the South Labor unrest, economic depression, and the end of military occupation severely diminished Republican commitment to Reconstruction and helped Democrats regain control of every southern state.

CHAPTER

17

The Triumph of Industrial Capitalism
1850-1890

>> Rosa Cassettari

In 1884 Rosa Cassettari left an Italian village near Milan and joined the stream of migrants from all across Europe bound for America. Others went full of dreams. "The country where everyone would find work! Where wages were so high that no one had to go hungry! Where all men were free and equal and where even the poor could own land!" But Rosa left behind her son to rejoin her brutal, abusive husband, Santino, an iron miner in Missouri. Unable to read or write, she expected the worst, and rightly. "All us poor people had to go down through a hole to the bottom of the ship," she remembered. Crowded in darkness, sleeping on wooden shelves, feeding from tin plates, Rosa felt no relief to see land. Cheated in New York and forced to make her way to Missouri with nothing to eat, she arrived in a shabby cluster of tents and shanties, where she added to Santino's wages by cooking for a dozen miners. With no doctors or midwives available, Rosa gave birth to a premature child alone on the floor of her cabin. The last straw came when Santino used his savings to open a house of prostitution. Rosa fled for her life, and friends helped her move to Chicago. Was this the Promised Land?

Rosa thought so. She worked hard all her life, knew hunger in bad times, and just got by in good ones. But she always found friends to help her and religious faith to comfort her. In time she found work at Chicago Commons, a settlement house founded to help immigrants get by in a strange, often bewildering city. She discovered a strength and courage she had never known at home. When she went back to Italy to bring over her son, villagers gaped. She was wearing a hat and new shoes and "they thought I was something wonderful." When she told them that poor people in America ate meat every day, they could not believe it. And she lived to see her children doing better than she had—not rich, but not in want.

Rosa was one of millions of people uprooting themselves worldwide in the late nineteenth century. They moved from the countryside to the city or from town to town. They

continued

shifted from less developed regions to places where industrialization was well under way. The magnet for most of the movement was a core of industrial capitalist societies, and the United States was just one destination among many.

Common laborers moved from place to place because jobs were unsteady, or they moved when work was finished. Hired hands plodded the roads in autumn following the harvest, spent winters working in Washington's lumber camps, and toiled by summer along the Erie Canal. African American sharecroppers in the South moved at year's end, eventually into cotton-growing districts, into towns and cities, or out of the South. White tenant farmers found new homes and better living conditions in company-owned coal- and textile-mill towns. Native Americans, their domains already in flux for centuries, now lost most of their lands to white settlement and were herded onto reservations. And all across America the children of farmers traded the charm and endless labor of rural life for the bright-lit, squalid metropolises of the East.

They went seeking work, and that meant working for somebody else, on terms that the employer set. It meant working with new, complicated machines, with foul air, dirty rivers, or ravaged land. Working people had been freed from the things that once tied them to the land, such as feudal dues and slavery. But wage labor often compelled men and women to shift from country to country, and finally from continent to continent. To watch Rosa Cassettari as she traveled from Italy to Chicago is to witness one small part of a process set in motion by global needs and once-unimaginable aspirations.

The Political Economy of Global Capitalism

The economic history of the late nineteenth century was sandwiched between two great financial panics in 1873 and 1893. Both were followed by prolonged periods of high joblessness and labor strife. Between the two panics, prices dropped. Farmers with crops selling for less felt the crushing weight of money borrowed when prices were high. Manufacturers cut costs by increasing production, by replacing skilled labor with technology, and by drawing on the international labor market for a cheaper workforce. Still, amid bouts of hard times, the American economy transformed dramatically and, for consumers and many workers, for the better.

The "Great Depression" of the Late Nineteenth Century

On July 16, 1877, workers for the Baltimore and Ohio Railroad struck at Martinsburg, West Virginia, over one wage cut too many. Within days the strike spread to the Pennsylvania Railroad, the New York Central, the Great Western, and the Texas Pacific. Governors ordered the strikers to disperse. They asked for federal troops and got them. Soldiers fired on protestors in Pittsburgh, and for a while confrontations between workers and armed forces fanned the flames of insurrection. "Other workingmen followed the example of the railroad employees," explained Henry Demarest Lloyd, a prominent social critic. "At Zanesville, Ohio, fifty manufactories stopped work. Baltimore ceased to export petroleum.

The rolling mills, foundries, and refineries of Cleveland were closed. . . . Merchants could not sell, manufacturers could not work, banks could not lend. The country went to the verge of a panic." The strike was broken, though a hundred lives were lost by that time. Alarmed state authorities went on an armory-building binge and recruited a National Guard to keep order or break strikes in the future. Between 1875 and 1910, state troops were called out nearly five hundred times.

The railroad strike of 1877 was fueled by an economic depression that began with the Panic of 1873 (see Chapter 16) and spread throughout the developed world. Immigrant arrivals in New York—200,000 every year between 1865 and 1873—fell to less than 65,000 in 1877. Although employment (and immigration) recovered in the 1880s, prices and wages continued to fall. Then in 1893 another panic struck. Major railroads went bankrupt, including four of the five transcontinentals. Over 500 banks and 15,000 businesses shut down.

The world was shrinking. In 1866 Cyrus Field's telegraph cable was laid under the Atlantic Ocean. Now Americans could read Europe's latest news the next morning. They could cluster at the depot to hear the latest box score, sent by telegraph even as the game went on. Railroads carried Pillsbury's flour from Minneapolis mills to Massachusetts; refrigerated cars carried Chicago's "dressed beef" carcasses to California; and the catalog brought the goods of a nation to every farm on the high plains so efficiently that consumers swore "by God, the Ten Commandments, and Sears Roebuck." Thanks to the steamship, midwestern wheat fed customers in Russia, and boards cut from the forests of the Cascades turned into flooring for plantations in Malaya. In Pittsburgh's steel mills, Slavic languages and Hungarian were as common as German and Russian in Lower East Side New York's needle trades. Capitalism, not just transportation, had mingled peoples together.

An industrializing and liberalizing Europe had cut families free from their traditional ties to the land. Many migrated to better themselves: some within Europe, some to South America or Canada, and many to America. In many Irish families, sending sons and daughters abroad meant money packets sent home to allow the rest to stay behind. Italians and eastern Europeans, known as "birds of passage," often came west only to earn money and return. But their cheap labor and that of millions who came to stay built the railroads and forged the steel. They slaughtered sheep and cattle in Chicago's stockyard district, "Packingtown," for Philip Armour and Gustavus Swift. Others worked as domestic servants, served behind store sales counters, or ran the sewing machines that met a national demand for ready-made clothing.

America Moves to the City

Between 1850 and 1900 the map of the United States was redrawn thanks to the appearance of dozens of new cities. In 1850 the largest city in the United States was New York, with a population of just over half a million. By 1900 New York, Philadelphia, and Chicago each had more than a million residents.

The industrial city was different from its predecessors. By the middle of the nineteenth century the modern "downtown" was born, a place where people shopped and worked but did not necessarily live. Residential neighborhoods separated city dwellers from the downtown districts and separated the classes from one another. Streetcars and

AMERICA AND THE WORLD

>> **The Global Migration of Labor**

Nineteenth-century migrants tended to leave areas already in the grip of social and economic change. Rosa Cassettari, for example, had worked in a silk-weaving factory in Italy. At first, the largest numbers emigrated from the most developed nations, such as Great Britain and Germany. Later in the century, as industrial or agricultural revolution spread, growing numbers of immigrants came from Scandinavia, Russia, Italy, and Hungary (see Map 17-1). As capitalism developed in these areas, small farmers were forced to produce for a highly competitive international market. The resulting upheaval sent millions of rural folk into the worldwide migratory stream.

Improvements in transportation and communication made migration easier. In 1856, more than 95 percent of immigrants came to America aboard sailing vessels. By the end of the century, more than 95 percent came in steamships. The Atlantic crossing took one to three months under sail, but only 10 days by steam. Beginning in the 1880s, fierce competition among steamship lines lowered the cost of a transatlantic ticket. But the great migrations were also related to political turmoil. In China, for example, the Taiping Rebellion of 1848 was accompanied by an economic disaster that rivaled the Irish potato famine of the same decade and sent some 300,000 Chinese to America's Pacific Coast between 1850 and 1882. They dug the mines, panned for gold, and laid track on the transcontinental railroad. A similar mix of forces impelled European immigration. The revival of employment in the 1880s spurred a revival of movement.

After 1890, immigration from northern and western Europe fell off sharply, as capitalist development made labor scarce in those areas. But by then agrarian crisis and political disruption had set off a wave of emigration from eastern and southern Europe. In southern Italy, citrus fruits from Florida and California arrived on the market, and protective tariffs thwarted the sale of Italian wines abroad. Straitened Italian farmers started coming to the United States.

Jewish immigration was propelled by different impulses. In the Russian empire, anti-Jewish riots erupted in 1881–1882, 1891, and 1905–1906, during which countless Jews were massacred. Anti-Semitic laws forced Russian Jews to live within the so-called Pale of Settlement along Russia's western and southern borders, and the May Laws of 1882 severely restricted Russian Jews' religious and economic life. In the 1880s, Russian Jews began moving to America in significant numbers.

Most immigrants came to America looking for work. Many planned to make money and then return home, as thousands of Italians and Slovaks did. (Some, discovering to their surprise that they had become more American than they expected, came back to stay.) Some came with education and skills, most with little more than their ability to work. They usually found their jobs through families, friends, and fellow immigrants. Letters from America told of high wages and steady employment. Communities of immigrant workers provided the support that newcomers like Rosa Cassettari needed. Some immigrants settled directly on farms, but the overwhelming mass lived in cities.

Map 17–1   Patterns of Global Migration, 1840–1900 Emigration was a global process by the late 19th century. But more immigrants went to the United States than to every other nation combined. *Source:* London Times Atlas.

commuter railroads brought middle-class clerks and professionals from their homes to their jobs and back, but the fares were beyond the means of the working class. The rich built their mansions uptown, but workers had to stay within walking distance of their jobs (see Figure 17–1).

Cities became more crowded, unsanitary, and unsafe. Yellow fever and cholera epidemics were frequent. Fires periodically wiped out entire neighborhoods. In October 1871 much of Chicago went up in flames. Immigrant slums sprang up in most major cities of America, as well as in mill towns and mining camps. In 1890 Jacob Riis published *How the Other Half Lives*, exposing conditions in downtown New York, the breeding grounds of vice, crime, and despair. He described a dark three-room apartment that six people shared. The two bedrooms were tiny, the beds nothing more than boxes filled with "foul straw." Such conditions were a common feature of urban poverty in the late nineteenth century.

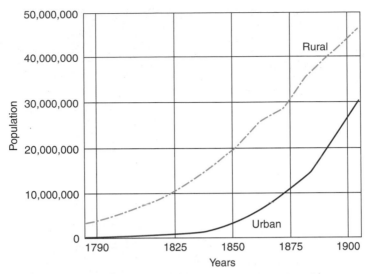

Figure 17–1   Proportion of Population Living in Cities, 1790–1900 While a growing proportion of Americans lived in cities, city dwellers would only outnumber rural Americans in the 20th century.

Yet during these same years urban reformers and technology made city life less dangerous and more comfortable. Professional fire and police departments made cities safer and less violent. Boards of health and quarantine laws brought epidemics under control. By the century's end, city dwellers could count on clean drinking water, efficient transportation, great museums, public libraries, parks, and a variety of entertainment unimaginable in the countryside.

By 1900, travelers walking down New York City's Bowery at midnight could feel safer, basking in the blaze of electric lights. Thomas Alva Edison's invention of the incandescent light bulb in 1879 was only one invention among many to dispel that darkness. He and other inventors created the dynamo to generate electricity, as well as alternating current to transmit power more efficiently. City dwellers would be the first to light their homes with electricity, the first to install telephones, and those most likely to receive mail every day, Sundays included. They would also be the ones most likely to eat fruits and vegetables out of season. Thanks to mass production, Gilded Age manufacturers would introduce canned foods into American diets. For those with money to spare, nothing could compare with the new, gigantic department stores, able to sell an endless variety of goods at the lowest prices because they dealt in such tremendous volume. Cities were the first places to have food chain-stores like Grand Union and A & P. Where else but Philadelphia would have Wanamaker's, with three acres of selling area and 129 counters, stretching two-thirds of a mile? Where else but New York would have a Heinz food sign six stories high, requiring 1,200 light bulbs? Cities showed off industrial capitalism's riches at their best, as well as its victims at their worst.

Nobody represented both sides of capitalism as well as a young Scots immigrant who came with his parents to Pittsburgh and started out in a textile mill for $1.20 a week. Fifty years later, Andrew Carnegie sold his steel mills to J. Pierpont Morgan for $480 million.

Wanamaker's Grand Depot Department Store, 1876 "Big business" in the late 19th century not only mass-produced goods but also sold them in large quantities at low prices. John Wanamaker's Philadelphia department store was among the most famous of these large, new retailers and funded Wanamaker's political activity against corrupt city officials.

The Rise of Big Business

Before the Civil War the only enterprises in the United States that could be called "big businesses" were the railroads (Map 17–2). Indeed, railroads became the model for a new kind of business—big business—that emerged during the 1880s. Big businesses had massive bureaucracies managed by professionals rather than owners and were financed through a national banking system centered on Wall Street. They marketed their goods and services across the world and generated wealth in staggering concentrations, giving rise to a class of men whose names—Carnegie, Rockefeller, Morgan, and Vanderbilt—became synonymous with American capitalism.

The Rise of Andrew Carnegie

Andrew Carnegie was an immigrant, whereas most businessmen were native born. His childhood in Scotland was marked by poverty, whereas most of America's leading men of business were raised in comfort. Certainly, few working families in the late nineteenth century could hope to match Carnegie's spectacular climb. Nevertheless, Andrew Carnegie was the perfect reflection of the rise of big business. In the course of his career, Carnegie mastered the telegraph, railroad, petroleum, iron, and steel industries and introduced modern management techniques and strict accounting procedures to American manufacturing. Other great industrialists and financiers made their mark in the last half of the nineteenth century. However, none had lives that took on the mythic proportions of that of the Scottish lad who came to America at the age of 12 and ended up the world's richest man.

Not content with his job at a textile mill, Carnegie enrolled in a night course to study accounting, and a year later he got a job as a messenger boy in a telegraph office. So astute and hardworking was Andrew that by 1851 he was promoted to telegraph operator. There he displayed a rare talent for leadership. He recruited bright, hardworking men and organized them with such stunning efficiency that Tom Scott, a superintendent for the Pennsylvania Railroad, took notice. In 1853, he offered Carnegie a job as his secretary and personal telegrapher.

Carnegie stayed with the Pennsylvania for 12 years during a time when rail construction soared. Petroleum refiners shipped their kerosene by rail. Mining corporations needed railroads to ship their coal and iron. His position at the Pennsylvania Railroad gave Carnegie an unrivaled familiarity with the workings of big business.

By the mid-1850s, the largest factory in the country, the Pepperell Mills in Biddeford, Maine, employed 800 workers, whereas the Pennsylvania Railroad had more than 4,000 employees. If an engineer arrived late, or if a fireman came to work drunk, trains were wrecked, lives were lost, and business failed. The railroads thus borrowed the disciplinary methods and bureaucratic structure of the military to ensure that the trains ran safely and on time.

J. Edgar Thomson, the Pennsylvania's president, was a pioneer of a different sort. He established an elaborate bookkeeping system providing detailed knowledge of every aspect of the Pennsylvania's operations. Based on that data, the company could reward managers who improved the company's profits and eliminate those who failed.

Carnegie succeeded. After Scott was promoted to vice president in 1859, Carnegie took his place as superintendent of the western division, where he helped make the Pennsylvania a model of efficiency. By 1865, with 30,000 employees and lines stretching east to New York City and west to Chicago, it was the largest private company in the world. It was also necessarily one of the most financially intricate. Railroads dwarfed all previous business enterprises in the amount of investment capital they required and in the complexity of their financial arrangements. A major line might require over a hundred separate kinds of account books. Railroads were the first corporations to issue stocks through sophisti-

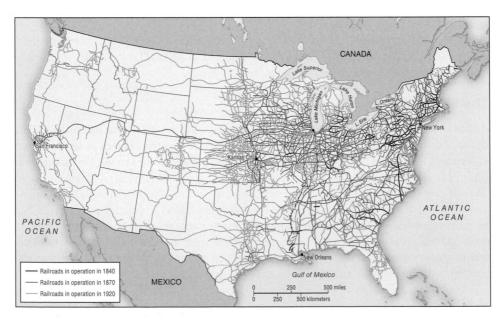

Map 17–2 The Growth of Railroads, 1850–1890 Railroads were America's first "big business." They set the model for running huge industrial corporations, and the growth of railroads fostered the iron and steel industries.

cated trading mechanisms that attracted investors from around the world. To organize the market in such vast numbers of securities, the modern investment house was developed.

Carnegie Dominates the Steel Industry

By 1872 Carnegie was 37 years old. He had proven himself both a master of the railroad industry and a brilliant manager. His Keystone Bridge Company built the first steel arch bridge over the Mississippi. Acquiring a controlling interest in the Union Iron Company, Carnegie had originally wanted to speed the flow of materials to the Keystone by making the two firms coordinate their operations. To pinpoint the most wasteful places in the production process, he adapted the Pennsylvania's managerial techniques and accounting practices. He also integrated operations: unlike other firms, his would not just melt iron ore into pig iron, but make bars of it, and turn those bars into beams and plates. Eliminating middlemen meant savings, and savings let him sell for less. As Carnegie put it, "Watch the costs and the profits will take care of themselves." But Carnegie was not content to dabble in iron. Steel was the future.

Railroads' needs drove steelmaking. Under the loads of larger, heavier trains, iron rails simply could not hold up for long. Though prohibitively expensive at first, steel rails lasted twenty years where iron ones needed replacement at five. Steel also proved better for making locomotives, boilers, and railroad cars. In the 1860s two developments cleared the path for the transition from iron to steel. First, Henry Bessemer's patented process for turning iron into steel became available to American manufacturers. Second, iron ore began flowing freely from deposits in northern Michigan. Andrew Carnegie was uniquely

The Eads Bridge The steel arches of the Eads Bridge across the Mississippi River at St. Louis were both an engineering marvel and a triumph of Andrew Carnegie's managerial skills.

placed to take advantage of these developments. With access to investment capital and Thomson for his partner, Carnegie opened his steel plant in 1873. Despite a worldwide depression, it turned a profit immediately.

Big Business Consolidates

In the late nineteenth century, every great industry conjured up the name of a magnate: Carnegie in steel, Gustavus Swift or Philip Armour in meatpacking, John D. Rockefeller in oil refining, Collis P. Huntington in railroads, and J. P. Morgan in financing (see Map 17–3). Actually, no single individual or family could own most big businesses because they took too much capital (financial resources). They were run by professionally trained managers. The highest profits went to companies with the most efficient bureaucracies. Because the businesses were so big and their equipment so expensive, they had to operate continuously. In an economic slowdown, an average factory could close its doors for a while, but big businesses could not.

With railroads and telegraph lines opening up national markets and new technology allowing mass production at lower costs, industries faced unprecedented competition. They met this challenge of competition and the need for a regular source of supply by adopting *vertical integration*. This was the attempt to control as many aspects of a business as possible, from the production of raw materials to the sale of the finished product. Carnegie did not just manufacture steel; he owned the iron mines and handled the marketing of finished steel. He also grasped two profit-making strategies that other firms, from breweries to makers of canned

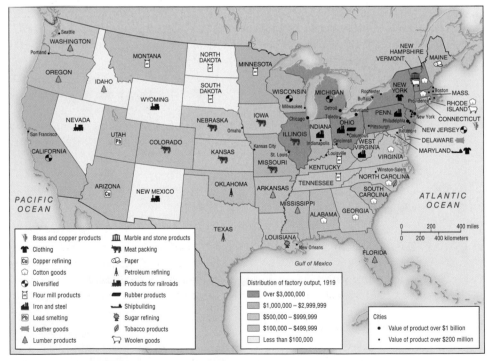

Map 17–3   Major American Industries, ca. 1890 An industrial map of late 19th-century America shows regions increasingly defined not by what they grew but by what they made.

goods, had learned: economies of scale and continuous flow. Bigger furnaces could produce steel more cheaply. Running them twenty-four hours a day, seven days a week, made every minute count. And with the help of the Jones Mixer, a container keeping pig iron molten, the biggest component in steel would be ready for immediate use. Rails poured into molds did not even wait in the plant to cool. Flatcars carried them outside, while others lined up to be filled. By such means over 15 years, Carnegie cut steel prices in half. Without these innovations, the gridwork of steel railroad lines would never have been—nor that new, lighter superstructure of girders that allowed the first skyscrapers to tower above Chicago and New York. John D. Rockefeller tried the other solution to cutthroat competition, *horizontal consolidation*: control of one step in the industrial process. Rockefeller had founded Standard Oil in 1867 in Cleveland, Ohio. Like Carnegie, Rockefeller hired the best managers and financiers to build and run the most efficient modern refineries and cut his dependence on railroad transport by investing in pipelines to carry the oil. However, he was also more willing than Carnegie to wipe out his competitors by any means available. Rockefeller squeezed from the railroads preferential shipping rates and rebates, the return of part of the standard price charged to other refiners—a critical advantage in a savagely competitive business. In 1872 Rockefeller began imposing on the regional industry the same control that he had already achieved in Ohio. As president of the National Refiners' Association he formed cartels, alliances with the major operators in other states. But the cartels were too weak to eliminate independent refiners.

Rockefeller found his solution in merging all the major companies under Standard Oil leadership. In 1882 the Standard Oil combine was formalized as a "trust," an elaborate legal device by which different producers came together under the umbrella of a single company that could police competition internally. In 1889 the New Jersey legislature passed a law letting corporations based in that state form "holding companies" that controlled companies in other states. Thus the trust gave way to the holding company, with Standard Oil of New Jersey its most prominent example. Within a decade, holding companies dominated some of America's largest industries.

Rockefeller and Standard Oil became a notorious example of how big business had changed the American economy, and, in the eyes of some, for the worse. Rockefeller's many charities never buried his reputation as a "robber baron," a term thrown at the titans of industry, transport, and finance. Exceptional in an age when most firms remained small and most industries stayed competitive (railroads mercilessly so), these "captains of industry" were admired and feared in equal measure.

A New Social Order

Americans took pride in having no such rigid class system as in Europe. Anyone could rise, and, as Rosa Cassettari noticed, the poor need not doff their caps before the rich. But class divisions ran deep, all the same. One could see that clearly, just by comparing Carnegie's Scottish castle with Painters' Row, where his unskilled workers lived in unventilated wooden houses without running water and with privies for all perched up the hill.

Lifestyles of the Very Rich

Between 1850 and 1890 the proportion of the nation's wealth owned by the 4,000 richest families nearly tripled. At the top of the social pyramid clustered some 200 families worth more than $20 million each. Concentrated in the Northeast, New York especially, these families flaunted their opulence. Spread more evenly across America were the several thousand millionaires made rich by cattle ranching, agricultural equipment, mining, commerce, and real estate. Most of America's millionaires traced their ancestry to Great Britain. Usually they were Protestant, mostly Episcopalians, Presbyterians, or Congregationalists. By the standards of their day they were unusually well educated and, more often than not, voted Republican. (Southerners remained firmly Democratic.)

The upper classes lived in mammoth houses. Some addresses became celebrated for their wealth: Fifth Avenue in Manhattan, Nob Hill in San Francisco, and Boston's Back Bay. Wealthy suburbs (Brooklyn Heights, Philadelphia's Main Line, and Brookline, Massachusetts) became privileged retreats. The richest families also built country estates that rivaled the stately homes of England and the chateaus of France, such as the palace-sized "cottages" along the Newport, Rhode Island, shoreline. The leading figures in New York's high society competed to stage the most lavish balls and dinner parties, in one case with hundred-dollar bills as party favors. It was left to the new middle class to display the traditional virtues of thrift and self-denial.

The Consolidation of the New Middle Class

In 1889 the *Century Dictionary* introduced the phrase "middle class" in the United States. The new term reflected a fresh awareness that American society had distinct gradations.

Professionals were the backbone of the new middle class of the nineteenth century. All professions organized themselves into associations—some 200 between 1870 and 1890 alone—that set educational and ethical standards for admission and practice. Corporations had to make their management professional. Business schools arose, teaching the science of accounting and the art of management. By 1920, 1,700 schools trained nurses, nearly all of them women. (At the same time, doctors' associations used their power over licensing to get rid of midwives; Rosa Cassettari was not the only one to do without.) Educators even gave a professional veneer to housekeeping by inventing "home economics" courses. States had a vested interest in professionalism, too. By 1900 most required association-drafted bar exams for lawyers and medical exams for doctors.

> The most valuable class in any community is the middle class, the men of moderate means, living at the rate of a thousand dollars a year or thereabouts.
>
> WALT WHITMAN, 1858

Behind the new professional managers marched an expanding white-collar army of cashiers, clerks, and government employees, mostly men. Their annual incomes far outpaced independent craftsmen and factory workers. They also had a better chance to rise. A beginning clerk might make only $100 a year, but within five years his salary could approach $1,000. At a time when a skilled Philadelphia factory hand made under $600, over 80 percent of the male clerks in the Treasury Department earned twice that.

Improved roads and mass-transit systems allowed middle-class families to escape the city's clamor and crowdedness, though suburbs, like city neighborhoods, were made for every income. The invention of oil-based house paints in the 1870s allowed owners to give the outside any color they pleased. Thanks to the mass-produced "Excelsior" mower and romantic associations with the Old South, the normal middle-class residence had a front porch and a lawn; but the crabgrass got blamed on eastern European immigrants, who supposedly brought it with them.

Only the most successful craftsmen matched the incomes and suburban lifestyles of white-collar clerks. Butchers might earn more than $1,600 annually, for example, but shoemakers averaged little more than $500. But while a shoemaker earned little more than a skilled factory worker, if he owned his own shop, he enjoyed an independence that middle-class Americans cherished. A cigar maker working on high-priced "seed and Havanas" had skills that gave him far more say in his work than the unskilled employees making two-cent "stogies" with a cigar mold. Pride and power, not just pay, defined job satisfaction. In carpentry and in the coal mines, specialized skills made workers hard to replace. But around them, labor-saving machinery was increasing a far more dependent industrial working class made up of people like Rosa Cassettari.

The Industrial Working Class Comes of Age

"When I first went to learn the trade," John Morrison told a congressional committee in 1883, "a machinist considered himself more than the average workingman; in fact he did not like to be called a workingman. He liked to be called a mechanic." Morrison identified one of the great changes in nineteenth-century America. "Today," Morrison lamented, the mechanic "is simply a laborer." Technological innovations replaced artisans with semiskilled or unskilled factory laborers. For traditional mechanics, this felt like downward mobility.

Because most factory workers and common laborers were migrants (or children of migrants) from small towns, farms, or abroad, few experienced factory work as a degradation of their traditional skills, as Morrison did. They had a chance to move upward from unskilled to skilled positions. Shop foremen might become storekeepers. Working-class families took comfort that their children had a still better chance of moving into the middle class. But industrial labor was a harsh existence for all factory operatives, who toiled long hours in difficult conditions performing repetitive tasks with little job security. Most luckless and hardest pressed were the common laborers, earning their keep by physical exertion. Their numbers grew throughout the century until by 1900 unskilled labor made up a third of the industrial workforce.

In 1900 women accounted for nearly one of every five Americans gainfully employed, mostly in unskilled or semiskilled labor. In northern middle-class homes, young Irish women worked as domestics, jobs held in the South by African American women. Jewish women sewed garments for as little as three dollars for a six-day week, Italians worked on lace and paper flowers in their tenements. A smaller proportion of women held white-collar jobs, as teachers, nurses, or low-paid clerical workers and salesclerks behind department store counters.

The same hierarchy that favored men in the white-collar and professional labor force existed in the factories and sweatshops. In the clothing industry, for example, units dominated by male workers were higher up the chain of command than those dominated by women. Indeed, as the textile industry became a big business, the proportion of women working in textile mills steadily declined. The reverse trend affected white-collar workers. As department stores expanded in the 1870s and 1880s, they hired low-paid women, often Irish immigrants, with none of the prospects for promotion men still had. White-collar work did not confer middle-class status upon women as it did upon men in the late nineteenth century.

Few working-class wives and mothers took jobs outside the home, but many took in boarders or did laundry. The poorer working-class families survived by sending their children to work. The rich sent their daughters to finishing schools and their sons to boarding schools; middle-class parents sent their children to public schools; anything beyond grade school ranked as a luxury among those less well off than that. Ten-year-olds could be found tending the cotton spindles or picking shale off the conveyor belts coming up from the coal mines. They ran barefoot through New York's streets hawking newspapers and lugged red-hot, newly cast bottles from the furnaces in glass factories. Only in Horatio Alger novels did "Mark the Match-Boy" strike it rich.

Division of labor allowed more goods to be made for much lower labor costs per unit. The introduction of the sewing machine in the 1850s, for example, gave rise to sweatshops where work was subdivided into simple, repetitive tasks. One group produced collars for men's shirts, another produced sleeves, and another stitched the parts together. Division of labor saved employers on training, and in industries where turnover was high, it kept the machinery running. Factory work was at best insecure, subject to swings in the business cycle. But unskilled workers also lacked the leverage to improve their own conditions. If Carnegie's workers, blinded or crippled on the job, got nothing more than the privilege of begging at the mill gates—if lung diseases were as common in textile factories as the

Packingtown The Industrial Revolution replaced small, local slaughterhouses with mass-production facilities like Philip Armour's in Chicago. Division of labor allowed the hiring of less-skilled workers to be assigned to specific tasks in separate departments. This artist caught the systematic quality, but not the actual squalor and unhealthfulness of "Packingtown" as it really was.

"mill-child's cough" and gangrene of the jaw among boys making matches—workers had no options beyond leaving and being fired.

Workmen's compensation was rare, retirement pensions unknown. Helplessness and the pool of surplus labor made organizing unions a challenge among the unskilled. Men laying railroad track or digging subway tunnels were always moving on, with common labor often seasonal and factory turnover high. In some meatpacking houses, it came close to 100 percent annually. A strike depleted workers' savings quickly. Exceptionally mobile and easily replaceable, immigrants increasingly came from places unfamiliar with the idea of organized labor and from cultures where religion defined identity more than class. Employers knew that by using them or, better still, black Americans as strikebreakers, they could turn race against race, native against foreigner. "Scabs," as those taking strikers' places were called, faced insult and threat. Some were beaten, others killed. Some firms built private armies to enforce control, but they could usually count on the police and state militia to help them win a strike.

Sharecropping Becomes Wage Labor

As the southern economy recovered from the devastation of the Civil War, many observers predicted a bright future for the region. Optimists saw a wealth of opportunities from untapped natural and human resources, a South freed from the inefficient slave labor system and ripe for investment.

Americans were building railroads at an exuberant clip, but southerners built them faster—on northern money. By 1890 steel mills lit the night skies of Birmingham, Alabama. Textile mills dotted the Piedmont Plateau (along the eastern foothills of the Appalachian Mountains from Virginia to Georgia). Southerners were migrating from the countryside to the towns, expanding cotton production into new areas, like the rich Mississippi delta soil. Yet ordinary southerners, especially African Americans, did not share in the New South's prosperity.

After the war most blacks toiled on land they did not own (see Chapter 16). In place of the master-slave relationship emerged a new labor relationship between landlords and sharecroppers. Merchants arose to supply the credit that kept this system alive. The most important question was who owned the cotton crop at the end of the year: the sharecropper who raised it, the landlord who owned the farm, or the merchant who lent the supplies to bring the crop in.

Legal resolution in favor of the landlord came by the middle of the 1880s. The courts defined a sharecropper as a wage laborer. The landlord owned the crop and paid his workers a share of it as a wage. Landlords also won a stronger claim on the crop than the merchant creditors. Under the circumstances, merchants were reluctant to advance money to sharecroppers. Many left plantation districts and moved up-country, doing business with white yeomen farmers. Trapped in a cycle of debt, white farmers in the 1880s began losing their land and falling into tenancy. Meanwhile, in the "black belt" (where most African Americans lived and most of the cotton was produced), successful landlords became merchants while successful merchants purchased land and hired sharecroppers of their own. By the mid-1880s, black sharecroppers worked as wage laborers for the landlord-merchant class across much of the South.

Sharecropping differed in two critical ways from the wage work of industrial America. First, sharecropping was family labor, depending on a husband and father who signed the contract and delivered the labor of his wife and children to the landlord. Second, because sharecropping contracts were yearlong, the labor market was restricted to a few weeks at the end of each year. If croppers left before the end of the year, they risked losing everything.

The political economy of sharecropping impoverished the South by binding the region to a single crop—cotton—that steadily depleted the soil even as prices fell. Yet most southern blacks found few alternatives. In time a few black farmers purchased their own land, but their farms were generally tiny and the soil poor. The skilled black artisans who had worked on plantations before the Civil War moved to southern cities, where they took unskilled, low-paying jobs. Northern factories were segregated, as were the steel mills of Birmingham, Alabama, and the Piedmont textile mills. Black women worked as domestic servants to supplement their husbands' meager incomes. Wage labor transformed southern blacks' lives, but it did not bring prosperity.

Hoping to escape poverty and discrimination, some former slaves moved west. One group, the Exodusters, moved to the Kansas prairie during the mid-1870s. By 1880 more than 6,000 blacks had joined them, searching for cheap land for independent farms. Like white farmers, the Exodusters fought with cattlemen. Blacks who settled in cow towns such as Dodge City and Topeka found the same discrimination they had known in the South. Still, some of the Exodusters did buy land and build farms.

Clearing the West for Capitalism

Passed during the Civil War, the Homestead Act was meant to people the West with independent small farmers. Millions came in the 40 years that followed and continued to take out titles until 1934. Their movement has become the stuff of legend.

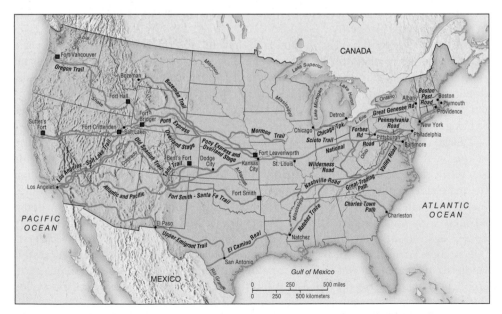

Map 17–4   The Overland Trail No transcontinental railroad existed until 1869. Even thereafter, most settlers moved west on a series of well-developed overland trails.

But these hardy individuals did not settle an empty prairie. Native people held it already. And far from escaping the world of industrial capitalism, the settlers brought it with them. By the time the director of the US Census declared the frontier "closed" in 1890, the political economy of the American West was diverse and ethnically and economically complex.

The Overland Trail

In popular images the West was a haven for rugged men who struck out on their own, but most migrants went in family groups, and the families were mostly middle class. Few poor people could afford the journey and still hope to buy land and set up a farm.

The journey across the Overland Trail (see Map 17–4) had become safer over the years. The US government built forts to supply migrants and protect the trail from (rare) Indian attacks. Mormon settlers in Utah had built Salt Lake City into a major stopping point and the heart of a thriving economy. On May 10, 1869, two railroads, the Central Pacific, building from California, and the Union Pacific, building from the Missouri River, joined at Promontory Point, Utah. This first transcontinental railroad line effectively replaced the five-month

Chinese Laborers Building Railroad This 1877 picture of a Southern Pacific Railroad trestle shows the crude construction methods used to build the first line across the Sierra Nevada.

journey of covered wagons with a trip of a little less than a week. Four more transcontinentals would reach the Pacific over the next generation. Out from them radiated branch lines and side spurs, to tie the West into eastern markets. Where the companies set down depots, towns sprang up, unlike in the East, where the towns came first and the railroads afterwards. Irresponsibly and sometimes crookedly financed, subsidized by all levels of government, their construction almost guaranteeing an eventual wreck (actual and financial), railroads became the symbol for the age. They represented to many Americans the enterprising spirit, the intrepid nature, and the arrogance of industrial capitalism. They turned Minnesota's Red River valley into a sea of wheat and dominated California's government. They also gave the army an unprecedented mobility that it would very much need. By the time the railroad presidents drove the golden spike at Promontory Point, the government had become occupied by the growing problem of Native American–white relations in the West.

The Origins of Indian Reservations

In 1851 more than 10,000 Native Americans from across the Great Plains converged on Fort Laramie in Wyoming Territory. All the major Indian peoples were represented: Sioux, Cheyenne, Arapaho, Crow, and many others. They came to meet with government officials who hoped to develop a lasting means of avoiding Indian-white conflict. Since the discovery of gold a few years earlier, white migrants had been crossing through Indian territory on their way to California, most of them already prejudiced against the Indians. US officials wanted to prevent outbreaks of violence between whites and Indians as well as between Indian nations. They proposed creating a separate territory for each Indian tribe, with government subsidies to entice the Indians to stay within their territories. This was the beginning of the reservation system, and for the rest of the century the US government struggled to force the Indians to accept it.

The government had good reason to advocate for reservations. At their worst, both whites and Indians behaved ferociously. Civilians in one territory raised $5,000 for Indian scalps, promising $25 for any "with ears on." At Sand Creek, Colorado, militia slaughtered and scalped over one hundred friendly Indians, two-thirds of them women and children. Fingers were cut off for the rings, body parts for souvenirs. In the northern Rockies, warriors led by the Northern Plains Indian leader Red Cloud lured forces from Fort Phil Kearny, killed them all, and stripped and mutilated the bodies. But Red Cloud could also say truthfully, "When the white man comes in my country, he leaves a trail of blood behind him." The reservation system was corrupt and badly handled. Agents for the Bureau of Indian Affairs cheated Indians and the government alike, sometimes reaping huge profits. But the reservations failed mostly because not all Indians agreed to stay within their designated territories, leading to armed confrontations and reprisals. "The more we can kill this year, the less will have to be killed the next war," General William Tecumseh Sherman declared.

Instead of extermination, the government opted for a more comprehensive reservation policy. Two treaties divided the Great Plains into two vast Indian territories. The Medicine Lodge Treaty, signed in Kansas in 1867, organized thousands of Indians across the southern plains. In return for government supplies, most of the southern plains peoples agreed to restrict themselves to the reservation. The Northern Plains Indians did not agree so readily. Inspired by Red Cloud, some insisted that the United States abandon forts along the Bozeman Trail. When the government agreed, Red Cloud signed the Fort

Laramie Treaty in 1868. (It was one of the last. Starting in 1871, the government stopped treating the tribes as separate nations. They were subject peoples, nothing more.)

Red Cloud abided by the treaties for the rest of his life. They failed all the same. Not all the tribes approved of the treaties, and on the southern plains, raiding parties gave the army all the excuse it needed for payback. On Thanksgiving Day, 1868, the Seventh Cavalry, led by Lieutenant-Colonel George Armstrong Custer, massacred Cheyennes at Washita Creek, Oklahoma. Among the fallen was Black Kettle, who had survived the Sand Creek massacre in Colorado and whose influence had brought other tribes to make peace at Medicine Lodge. President Grant's "Peace Policy" had replaced selfish politicians with high-minded ministers as its go-betweens to the tribes and emphasized negotiation and assimilation over war and expulsion. However, there was no peace out West; not for the Comanche, Navajo, Modoc, or Lakota Sioux. And those last, in one general's opinion, were the greatest light cavalry that the world had ever seen.

The Lakota had a chance to prove their skill in battle. In South Dakota the discovery of gold in the Black Hills in 1874 brought thousands of whites onto Indian territory. When the Lakota refused to cede their lands to the miners, the government sent in the army, led by the charismatic, headstrong Lieutenant-Colonel Custer. In June 1876, Custer made two critical mistakes. He divided his forces and failed to keep them in communication with each other. Custer and hundreds of his men were slaughtered at Little Bighorn, Montana, by 2,000 Indian warriors led by Crazy Horse.

"Custer's Last Stand" was the stuff of legends, but the real story came afterward. The Lakota could win battles, but not the war. Significantly, Crow warriors died with Custer. As in most other struggles, Native Americans served as scouts, adjuncts, and allies of the United States. There was never a united Indian resistance, because, as far as Native Americans were concerned, there were no such things as Indians. There were Blackfoot, Nez Percé, Arapahoe, and Comanche. They could be broken and beaten one by one, or turned against one another—and they were. The longer a war went on, the more tribes gave up or switched sides. The army had learned to adapt to a different kind of fighting. It hit the enemy in winter, when its forces were pinned down as they had been at Washita Creek. It destroyed not only Indian soldiers, but also villages and crops to starve them into submission. In the Southwest, it used Apaches to hunt down other Apaches and adopted mule trains in place of slow, cumbersome supply wagons.

The Destruction of Indian Subsistence

At the same time as the discovery of gold in the Black Hills, the demand for hides brought a different kind of gold rush to the plains: the mass slaughter of buffalo herds. Profit and sport drove the hunt, but cattlemen had no objection to opening up the range for their own stock. The army saw a bonus in anything wiping out subsistence for Indians off the reservation. "Kill every buffalo you can," a colonel urged one hunter. "Every buffalo dead is an Indian gone." Railroads joined in, sponsoring mass kills from slow-moving trains on the prairies. Some 13 million bison in 1850 dwindled by 1880 to a few hundred. The only buffalo a westerner was likely to see by 1920 was the one on the back of the nickel.

In the Northwest in 1877 the Nez Percés, fleeing from Union troops, began a dramatic trek across the mountains in an attempt to reach Canada. The Nez Percés eluded the troops and nearly made it over the Canadian border. However, hunger and the elements forced Chief Joseph and his exhausted people to agree to go to their reservations.

Indian Village Routed, Geronimo Fleeing from Camp Oil on canvas by Frederic Remington, 1896.

Pursued and deprived of allies one by one, Chief Sitting Bull and his last few warriors gave up in 1881. By then, most Indian wars were like jail breakouts: small, sporadic, and ugly. The ugliest came at Wounded Knee, South Dakota, in 1890. Fearing that a religious revival movement would stir up rebellion, soldiers gunned down over 200 Native American men, women, and children. Sitting Bull did not live to see it. He had been shot resisting arrest days before.

Sharing none of the settlers' fear of and less of their contempt for Indians, reformers hoped that reservations would function not just as holding pens, but as schools and civilizers. Lincoln's Commissioner of Indian Affairs, William P. Dole, believed that "Indians are capable of attaining a high degree of civilization." Like other reformers, Dole equated civilization with a belief in individual property rather than communal holdings, Christian values rather than native religions, and the discipline of the regular hours that farmers and workers, rather than hunters, observed. Accordingly, reformers set out, as one of them put it, to destroy the Indian and save the person. They introduced government schools on reservations to teach the virtues of private property, individual achievement, and social mobility.

The reformers' influence peaked in 1887 when Congress passed the Dawes Severalty Act, the most important Indian legislation of the century. Reservation land was broken up into separate plots and distributed among individual families. The goal was to force Indians to live like white farmers. But the lands allotted were generally so poor, and the plots so small, that their owners quickly sold them. Large tracts were kept in trust by the government and gradually sold off, purportedly to pay for uplifting and assimilating the Indians. By the early twentieth century only a few, sharply diminished reservations remained outside the desert Southwest. Native American cultures endured, but many Native Americans did not. Poverty, overcrowding, and epidemic disease brought their population to its lowest point. With the Indians subdued, the West lay open for economic development.

The Economic Transformation of the West

Hundreds of civilians died in Indian attacks during the late nineteenth century. More than 5,000 died building the railroads. Lawless violence and wild speculation were part of the western experience, as were struggling families, temperance reformers, and hardworking immigrants. By 1900 the West provided Americans with the meat and bread for their dinner tables, the wood that built their homes, and the gold and silver that backed up their currency. The West was being drawn into the political economy of global capitalism.

Cattlemen: From Drovers to Ranchers

The cowboy is the mythic figure of the American West: a rugged loner who scorned society for the freedom of the trail. In fact, cowboys were usually single men. They worked hard and played harder, spending their earnings on a shave, a new suit of clothes, and a few good nights in town. Civil War veterans, former slaves, displaced Indians, and Mexicans all became cowboys. Their pay was low, their work dangerous and unsteady, and their chances of reaching real independence were slim.

Longhorn cattle were as much a part of western legend as the cowboys who drove them. With the westward spread of the railroads, Texas ranchers began driving huge herds of Texas longhorns up the Chisholm Trail north onto the Great Plains. They brought the herds to railroad towns from which the cattle could be shipped, such as Abilene, Wichita, or Dodge City, Kansas. Cattlemen sold half of their stock to eastern markets and the other half in the West, some to the government for feeding soldiers and reservation Indians.

But the Texas longhorn had several drawbacks. Tough and rangy, it was more muscle than meat. It carried a tick that devastated many of the other grazing animals, and it also took a long time to fatten up. Investors began to breed hybrid cattle that were less hardy but with more beef and of higher quality. By the early 1880s, investors were pouring capital into mammoth cattle-herding companies. The Great Plains became seriously overstocked. The depleted grazing lands left the cattle weak from malnutrition, and in the late 1880s several devastating winters wiped out whole herds. It was said that a person could walk across Kansas and never touch ground, just stepping from carcass to carcass.

Open-range herding became so environmentally destructive that it was no longer economically feasible. Long drives became increasingly difficult as farmers fenced in the plains, but they also became less necessary because railroads could pick up cattle just about everywhere. By the 1890s huge cattle companies were giving way to smaller ranches that raised hybrid cattle. Cowboys became ranch hands with regular wages, like miners and factory workers.

In the mid-1880s, more than 7 million head of cattle roamed the Great Plains. As their numbers declined, sheep replaced them. Although sheep proved even more ecologically destructive than cattle, by 1900 sheepherding had largely taken the place of the cattle industry in Wyoming and Montana and was spreading to Nevada. Sheepherding had one other advantage: it did not interfere with small farmers as much as cattle driving did.

Commercial Farmers Subdue the Plains

Between 1860 and 1900, the number of farms in America nearly tripled, thanks largely to the economic development of the West. On the Great Plains and in the desert Southwest, farmers took up former Indian lands. In California, white settlers poached on the estates

>> Mining Camps in the West

Rosa Cassettari's mining camp experience had none of the glamour that mythology lends those farther West. The greatest strike came in 1848 when James Marshall found gold at John Sutter's mill site in the California foothills. In poured prospectors by thousands, creating boomtowns like Ophir and You-Be-Damned overnight—and ghost towns just as quickly, when the lode gave out. Findings actually peaked years after the "Forty-Niners'" gold rush. New discoveries pulled prospectors eastward, into Colorado in 1859, Idaho in 1862, and Montana in 1864. In Nevada, prospectors hit the largest vein of all, the Comstock Lode. It would yield 350 million dollars' worth of gold and silver over 20 years.

Western mining camps were raw, violent, male-dominated, and diverse. New England Yankees mingled with Australians, Mexicans, Chinese, and African Americans. Alone or in small groups, they panned for gold, squatting in icy stream beds. Once the surface gold had been captured, miners shoveled dirt into boxes or sluices to capture ore by running water over it. A few miners struck it rich. The biggest winners may have been the storekeepers who sold blasting powder, shovels, and groceries. Four became partners and built the western half of America's first transcontinental railroad. They had such a stranglehold on California's transit system that locals called their company "the Octopus." Levi Strauss, a German immigrant, came to sell canvas tents and made a fortune turning them into pants—one reason blue jeans are called Levis today.

Penniless Irish-born Marcus Daly did even better. Pooling resources, he and some San Francisco investors dug for silver in Montana and hit one of the world's largest veins of copper. The Anaconda mine made Daly millions. Its high-grade copper entered worldwide markets, wherever cities and industries needed copper wire to harness electricity's power. Partly due to Anaconda, by 1883 the United States led the world in producing copper.

Daly's venture represented the future. By the 1870s, gold veins ran too deep for lone prospectors to reach; heavy, costly machines were needed. Minerals like zinc and copper required a heavier initial investment that would take much longer to be repaid. Mine shafts needed timber supports in a treeless land, as well as blowers to cool the 130-degree temperatures deep underground. Deep mines needed constant pumping: 2 million gallons of water seeped into the Comstock every day. Copper or silver took smelting. Thus, corporations alone could tap most of the West's mineral wealth. Engineers and wage laborers, managed from boardrooms miles away, extracted, smelted, and shipped the ore. Even Comstock's 750 miles of tunnels 3,000 feet underground were corporation run. Companies built the railroads to carry ore to market, and the towns where miners lived. These were shabby, utilitarian places free from libraries, parks, schools—or the chance to strike it rich on one's own. The Comstocks had given way to the Cassettaris.

of Spanish-speaking landlords, stripping them of their natural resources and undermining their profitability. Over time, Hispanic ranchers gave way to European American farmers. The Hispanic population of Los Angeles fell from 82 percent in 1850 to 19 percent in 1880. A similar pattern occurred in New Mexico and Texas.

This ethnic shift signaled profound changes in the ecology and political economy of the West, driven by the exploding global demand for western products. Cattle ranchers were feeding eastern cities. Lumber from the Pacific Northwest found its way to Asia and South America. By 1890 western farmers produced half of the wheat grown in the United States, and they shipped it across the globe.

But farming in the arid West was unlike eastern farming. The 160-acre homesteads that lawmakers proposed were too small for the less well watered prairies. Farmers needed costly equipment and extensive irrigation to produce wheat and corn for international markets. To make these capital investments, they mortgaged their lands. For mechanized, commercial agriculture to succeed on mortgaged land, western farms had to be much bigger than 160 acres.

Government homesteads made up only a fraction of all the lands sold. Speculators may have bought up as much as 350 million acres from state or federal governments or from Indian reservations. Railroads were granted another 200 million acres by the federal government. They sold much of it at bargain rates. The more farmers the railroads could settle on their lands, the more customers they would have, and the more farm produce to ship. Railroads set up immigration bureaus and offered settlers cheap transportation, credit, and agricultural aid. The Great Plains filled with settlers from the East Coast and from Ireland, Germany, and Scandinavia. In 1890 the director of the Bureau of the Census reported that the frontier had at last been filled.

Changes in the Land

No Garden of Eden welcomed prairie farmers. "All Montana needs is rain," a promoter was said to have told one settler—who agreed: but that was also all that Hell needed. Rain fell rarely and in sparse amounts on the Great Plains and the desert Southwest. Howling blizzards, blistering summers that warped railroad track out of alignment, sky-blackening clouds of locusts, and loneliness meant ruin for some, despair for others. Yet settlers came, worked, endured, and improvised. With little wood or stone available, many farmers built

>> Time Line

▼1848
Taiping Rebellion spurs Chinese
    emigration to United States
Revolution in Austria-Hungary
Andrew Carnegie emigrates to
    United States

▼1851
Fort Laramie Treaty establishes
    Indian reservations

▼1857
Henry Bessemer develops
    process for making steel

▼1862
Pacific Railroad Act
Homestead Act

▼1864
Sand Creek Massacre

▼1865
First transatlantic telegraph cable
    begins operation

▼1867
Medicine Lodge Treaty

▼1868
Second Fort Laramie Treaty
Washita Creek Massacre

continued

sod houses—even sod schoolhouses. Joseph Glidden's invention, barbed wire, provided them fencing. Strong steel plows cut a sod so knotted with grass roots that hoes bounced off it like paving. Windmills rose from the prairie to pump water from hundreds of feet below ground and over time drain much of it dry. Mennonite settlers from Russia brought durum wheat, ideal for the harsh climate. Everywhere, families built schools, churches, and communities alongside the now-ubiquitous railroad stations.

The western environment was new-made. Wolves, elk, and bears were exterminated as farmers brought in pigs, cattle, and sheep. Tulare Lake, covering hundreds of square miles of California's Central Valley, was sucked dry by 1900. Mines sent tons of earth and rock down the rivers of the Sierra Nevada, threatening entire cities with flooding. The skies above Butte, Montana, turned gray from pollutants released by copper-smelting plants. Sheepherding destroyed the vegetation on the eastern slopes of the Rocky Mountains and the Sierra Nevada. But the West was also dotted with communities and railroad depots. California oranges found a market in New England, and Washington apple orchards filled the stalls in eastern markets.

By the turn of the century, states and reservations stood where the Cheyenne, Dakota, and Comanche nations had commanded vast domains. Settlers of many ethnicities—Swedish, Finnish, Hispanic, and others—experienced the bounty and hardship of what had once been Indian land. Corporate enterprises and mechanized farms now shared the West with the homesteaders and storekeepers. Farmers had connected to world markets. They were clothed and supplied by cities' industries. They owed eastern railroad corporations their access to the world, and they owed nearly everything else to eastern mortgage-holders. Mining and lumber corporations employed tens of thousands of wage laborers. Thanks to the gold rush, San Francisco rose from 5,000 inhabitants midcentury to 150,000 twenty years later. Denver was incorporated in 1861 with a population just below 5,000. By 1870, it had grown twentyfold.

Conclusion

Rosa Cassettari and Andrew Carnegie—two immigrants whom the new global economy of industrial capitalism helped draw overseas—met wholly different destinies. Not just their origins, but gender roles, opportunity, and good luck explained how they ended up. Yet

>> **Time Line** *continued*

▼**1871**
October: Great Chicago Fire

▼**1872**
Edgar Thomson Steel Works open near Pittsburgh

▼**1873**
Financial panic, followed by depression

▼**1876**
Custer's Last Stand at Little Bighorn

▼**1878**
American Bar Association founded

▼**1882**
John D. Rockefeller forms Standard Oil trust
Edison Electric Company lights up New York buildings

▼**1887**
Dawes Severalty Act

▼**1890**
Jacob Riis publishes *How the Other Half Lives*
Massacre at Wounded Knee, South Dakota
Director of US Census declares frontier "closed"

both shared the same striving spirit that held out at least the chance for them to better themselves (as Cassettari did, however modestly) and their adopted country. Cassettari's experience with failure impelled her to search for something better. Carnegie's success made him yearn for more than money. By 1900, having thrown his energies into getting, Carnegie threw them all into giving. He set up endowments, funded universities, and founded an institute for peace. He had helped create an industrial nation. Now he set out to re-create American culture. Ironically, the Rosa Cassettaris of the world had beaten him to it.

Who, What

Andrew Carnegie 517

Rosa Cassettari 511

Red Cloud 528

Jacob Riis 515

Tom Scott 518

Sitting Bull 530

Bessemer Process 519

Fort Laramie 527

Longhorn cattle 531

Overland Trail 526

Reservations 527

Scabs 525

Sharecropping 525

Tenement 523

Trusts 521

Review Questions

1. Define "industrial capitalism." How was industrial capitalism a global phenomenon in the late nineteenth century?

2. What were the differences in lifestyle and in opportunities for those in America's upper, middle, and lower classes, and how did those differences widen or narrow during the late nineteenth century?

3. How did western Indians respond to westward expansion?

4. How was the West absorbed into the national and international market?

Critical-Thinking Questions

1. How and why did the effects of industrial capitalism differ in the South, West, and North?

2. Historians often refer to this period as the "Gilded Age." "Gilded" refers to something of base or common substance coated with a thin layer of gold, so that it seems far brighter and more valuable than it is. In view of America's industrial development at this time, do you think the term "Gilded Age" is appropriate? Why or why not?

3. What factors aside from the expansion of industrial capitalism affected American development during this period? How important are those factors in comparison to capitalism's growth?

For further review materials and resource information,
please visit www.oup.com/us/ofthepeople

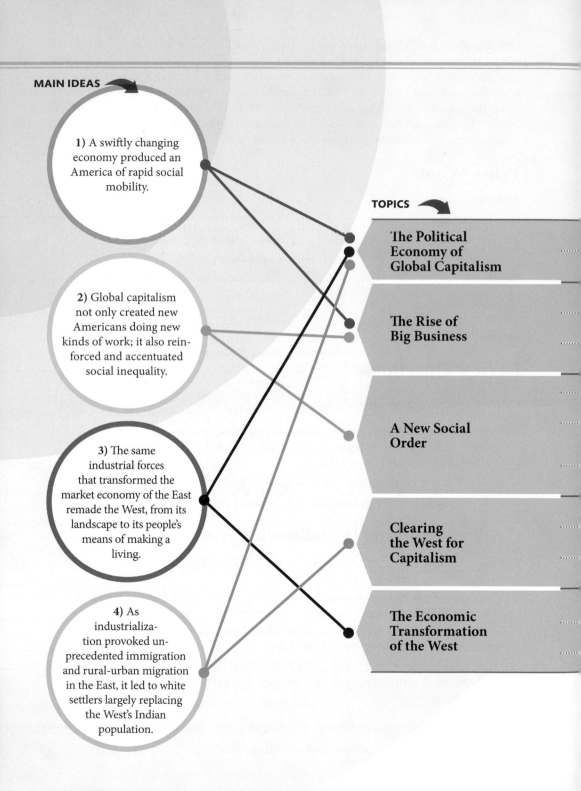

MAIN IDEAS

1) A swiftly changing economy produced an America of rapid social mobility.

2) Global capitalism not only created new Americans doing new kinds of work; it also rein-forced and accentuated social inequality.

3) The same industrial forces that transformed the market economy of the East remade the West, from its landscape to its people's means of making a living.

4) As industrializa-tion provoked un-precedented immigration and rural-urban migration in the East, it led to white settlers largely replacing the West's Indian population.

TOPICS

The Political Economy of Global Capitalism

The Rise of Big Business

A New Social Order

Clearing the West for Capitalism

The Economic Transformation of the West

THE TRIUMPH OF INDUSTRIAL CAPITALISM

1850–1890

EVENTS

The "Great Depression" of the Late Nineteenth Century Hard times and economic globalization led to upheaval, breaking people's ties to the land and accelerating US industrialization.

America Moves to the City Large numbers of Americans moved to cities, which offered perils and opportunities.

The Rise of Andrew Carnegie Scottish immigrant Carnegie used his railroad experience to become a wealthy industrialist.

Carnegie Dominates the Steel Industry Carnegie used modern management techniques to lead the steel industry.

Big Business Consolidates Businesses grew by vertical and horizontal consolidation to face competition and dominate industries.

Lifestyles of the Very Rich Upper-class families greatly increased their proportion of America's wealth.

The Consolidation of the New Middle Class A new class of professionals and white-collar employees developed between the wealthy and the working class. Its growth helped create the suburbs.

The Industrial Working Class Comes of Age Technological innovations reduced the number of skilled workers and increased the ranks of common laborers. The latter had little power to alter harsh working conditions.

Sharecropping Becomes Wage Labor In the South, tenant farming of cash crops benefited landowners but limited opportunity for white small farmers and former slaves.

The Overland Trail The creation of transcontinental railroads made the journey west faster and safer for family migrants.

The Origins of Indian Reservations US officials forced Indians onto reservations to prevent hostilities with whites.

The Destruction of Indian Subsistence The destruction of the buffalo opened the West to settlement by eastern farmers and herders at the expense of Indian nations.

Cattlemen: From Drovers to Ranchers The West became parceled out and permanently settled, as cowboys gave way to cattle companies, sheep herders, and farmers.

Commercial Farmers Subdue the Plains With government aid, a massive expansion of farming connected the West to the eastern market economy.

Changes in the Land Large-scale migration to the West had serious ecological consequences.

Cultural Struggles of Industrial America

1850–1895

>> Anthony Comstock's Crusade Against Vice

Beefy and belligerent, moral crusader Anthony Comstock devoted most of his adult life to "indecency": dance halls, abortion clinics, the lurid, the lewd. A New York City clerk raised in rural Connecticut, he took from his Protestantism a passion for cleansing a civilization he saw as alien and degraded. Fame came his way in 1873 when the United States Congress enacted the Comstock Law. This was the first federal law to ban the production, distribution, and public display of obscenity. The law also gave Comstock a lifelong cause: bringing pornographers, prostitutes, and strippers to justice. In a quarter of a century, he had 1,200 arrests to his credit.

With corrupt police lackadaisical about enforcing Comstockian morality, reformers established private organizations to smite smut with prosecutions and citizens' arrests. Comstock's own New York Society for the Suppression of Vice inspired many others. It deputized itself to enforce laws "for the suppression of the trade in, and circulation of, obscene literature and illustrations, advertisements, and articles of indecent or immoral use." As head of the society, Comstock himself acted as a special post office agent. "You must hunt these men as you hunt rats," Comstock declared, "without mercy." In many cases, that meant without respecting the rights of due process. Reformers used entrapment, enticing and then arresting perpetrators. Comstock himself caught America's most notorious abortionist that way. He felt no remorse when she cut her throat rather than go to trial.

Comstock's chief concern was the protection of children. In his book *Traps for the Young* (1883), he warned that obscenity was luring American youngsters into deviant ways by stoking youthful wants and passions until they had "a well-nigh irresistible mastery over their victim." For Comstock, the city included many evils. The relative anonymity of

continued

>> **AMERICAN PORTRAIT** *continued*

urban life and the cash value set on everything made sin pay better than ever before and perpetrators less fearful of being shamed for it. Workers had more leisure, and white-collar employees more still. With prostitutes renting their bodies for as little as fifty cents a trick and with saloon keepers doubling as brothel keepers (or tripling as aldermen), the SSV might win battles, but never the war.

While Comstock saw the cities' vice and corruption, linking both to immigrant slums, some of America's best artists were "realists," trying to make art reflect the gritty truths of everyday life and celebrating the cities' vitality. If Comstock's admirers defined "culture" no further than the great works in the Western European tradition (even suppressing some of those, including Voltaire, Walt Whitman, Aristophanes, and Ovid), city dwellers embraced a wider array of influences. Out of "Storyville," the red-light district in New Orleans, came the beginnings of jazz; out of the honky-tonks came the first great composers of ragtime. And a canny publicity agent knew how to sell a faintly risqué painting, *September Morn*: he got Comstock to arrest the gallery owner for indecency. Firms running off copies of it could not keep up with the demand.

Culture was contested ground, as much a part of urbanization as class conflict and political upheaval. Rural Americans were drawn by urban culture's freedom but troubled by its licentiousness. Native-born Protestants, often truly concerned with helping immigrants, were also suspicious of immigrant folkways. Defenders of high culture tried to contain or control popular culture. Amateur sportsmen sniffed at spectator sports. Victorian moralists assailed the collapse of traditional gender distinctions. All these struggles reflected the efforts of Americans to cope with dramatic social transformations. There were no clear winners—unless diversity and a wide array of choices made everyone a winner.

The Varieties of Urban Culture

Cities symbolized Americans' larger ambivalence about the social changes of the era. Boasting of how up-to-date their country was, Americans longed for a reassuring past. Tenement kids cheered Buffalo Bill Cody's romanticized re-creations of the plains wars and loved the chance to see Sitting Bull himself. (Sitting Bull liked "Buffalo Bill" more than he liked white civilization. He puzzled at how a society so rich could leave homeless children begging in the streets.) Yankees paid good money for tickets to minstrel shows about happy plantation life down South, and everybody read Joel Chandler Harris's "Uncle Remus" stories, recasting African folk tales with a kindly old slave as their narrator.

At the same time, city culture took on a life all its own. From the 1880s on, it meant bright lights: electricity, in place of dimmer gaslight, and a vigorous "night life." Electric trolleys and suburban rail networks drew tens of thousands downtown (see Figure 18–1), to department stores, firms, and factories by day and to theaters, music halls, and concert saloons by night. Big-city life meant baseball stadiums and teams like the Brooklyn "Trolley Dodgers." But it also stirred images of an alarming diversity: "Chinatowns" in San Francisco and Los Angeles, Polish Athletics Clubs and German *schutzenvereins* (shooting clubs), pushcart peddlers haggling in Yiddish, Irish Americans demanding that New

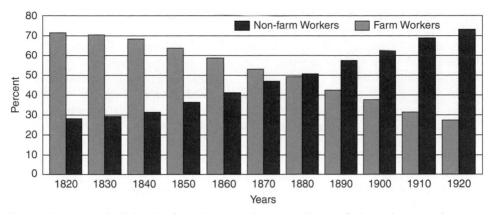

Figure 18–1 Growth of the Non-farm Sector Underpinning the rise of urban culture was the emergence of a wage-earning labor force. Concentrated in cities, wage earners had cash at their disposal to spend on the amusements cities had to offer.

York's City Hall fly the Irish flag on St. Patrick's Day, Catholics expecting a day off from school on Good Friday. Native-born Protestants fretted that "E Pluribus Unum" might no longer apply: How could we become one, out of so many?

Minstrel Shows as Cultural Nostalgia

Nowhere was nostalgia for a simpler way of life more obvious than in the minstrel shows. Minstrel shows may have been the century's most significant form of public entertainment—after politics. During the 1830s and 1840s, white performers in blackface dominated minstrel shows. Onstage, plantation slaves were shown as happy and carefree, free blacks as buffoons above their station in life. But the shows also mocked pretentious whites, do-gooders, and

BILLY KERSANDS.
CALLENDER'S (GEORGIA) MINSTRELS.

Billy Kersands African American minstrels such as Billy Kersands moderated the racism characteristic of white minstrelsy.

swells; they combined music, dance, and enduring popular songs. Even Mark Twain, sharply critical of racial prejudice, loved nothing better than a minstrel show.

In the 1870s minstrel shows grew larger and more elaborate, which naturally took a heavier capital outlay. There were fewer but bigger companies, and their appeal came from more than a muted defense of the Old South. With four touring comedy theaters and houses in four major cities, J. H. Haverly led the way. He toned down the emphasis on blackface singers and plantation themes and added scantily clad women and off-color routines. Of Haverly's three national minstrel troupes, two were white and one was black. Black performers there and elsewhere kept the plantation theme alive on stage, operating within the racial stereotypes established by prewar whites in blackface. The most famous black minstrel of the nineteenth century, Billy Kersands, drew huge audiences. Still, amid the stereotypes of foolish black people, black performers added hints that slavery itself was nothing to mourn.

The Origins of Vaudeville

If minstrel shows looked more like vaudeville, that was because the art form bred in the big cities was outdrawing them. Nostalgia played no part in vaudeville or in its cheaper cousins (concert saloons and dollar theaters). Even as elites worked for a clean break between serious theater and variety shows, working-class audiences flocked to the cheap theaters, where, for pennies, they could get music, singing, sketches, and variety acts. Rowdy and exclusively male crowds gave way to the family trade—though the only blacks visible were those onstage, like Bert Williams, with his hangdog expression and shabby costume. ("Bert Williams," a fellow performer on the circuit, W. C. Fields, once said, "was the funniest man I ever saw and the saddest man I ever knew.")

The respectability of a mixed-gender audience was one of the distinguishing signs of vaudeville, which featured a variety of acts appealing to a broad audience. Producers also began offering shows any time of the day or evening. These continuous performances kept prices down, increasing the size of the potential audience. Locating downtown in the heart of the city had the same effect. Theater owners also regulated smoking and banned alcohol consumption to promote the image of family entertainment. Finally, they booked great opera singers or distinguished musicians in an effort to upscale vaudeville's reputation. Starting in 1896, some of them added another novelty, the moving picture, recently developed by Thomas Alva Edison.

Growing audiences allowed vaudeville producers to construct ornate theatrical "palaces" that housed ever more elaborate productions. Higher costs meant that a handful of companies came to dominate the vaudeville theater industry, much as minstrel companies had become concentrated in the hands of a few owners. They did not stay on top for long. By 1903, "nickelodeons," storefront movie arcades, were popping up all through cities' working-class sections. Offering continuous film performances for a nickel, nickelodeons took little capital to found and proved that motion pictures were not the novelty act that vaudeville houses had taken them for. But Americans did not just go to shows in their leisure time.

Sports Become Professional

As growing numbers of Americans went to the theater to be entertained, still more went to the baseball park or sports arena. For much of the urban population, sports became something to watch, not just something to do.

AMERICA AND THE WORLD

....

>> **World's Fairs**

To celebrate the accomplishments of urban and industrial society, the city of London hosted a spectacular world's fair at the Crystal Palace in 1851. By 1900 there had been expositions in Paris, Vienna, Brussels— even Sydney, Australia. Most highlighted their own countries' technological accomplishments and cultural achievements while expressing the sponsoring cities' civic pride. All of them celebrated the new, a present far better than the past, and a future more wondrous still. So did American fairs.

The first major world's fair in the United States took place in Philadelphia in 1876, timed to commemorate the centennial of American independence. Machinery Hall occupied its spiritual center. There the tremendous Corliss steam engine stood, its 75 miles of belts powering 8,000 other pieces of machinery. Visitors (some 9 million) could see incredible inventions: linoleum, the Remington typewriter, canned foods, and, most impressive of all, Alexander Graham Bell's telephone, able to transmit the human voice across unimaginable distances. "My God! It talks!" Brazil's emperor cried, as he sat down to listen into the earpiece. What surprised nobody, though, was the assumption that various nations' pavilions made about the world's "races." France and its colonies, "representing the Latin races," were grouped together, as were England and its colonies, "representing the Anglo-Saxon races," and "the Teutonic races," represented by Germany, Austria, and Hungary. Native Americans appeared, but only as a relic of bygone days, and soon to disappear.

A very different hierarchy marked the next great fair, the Columbian Exposition in Chicago in 1893. Ethnographic exhibits based on the new supposedly scientific ideology of racism portrayed the "races" of the world in a scale ranging from the most civilized (Europeans) to the least (Africans and Asians). But the most noted distinction came between the high-minded, grandiose "White City" showcasing American might, industrial invention, and the latest consumer goods under brilliant electrical lighting, and the part that visitors thronged to see: the Midway Plaisance. The White City had all the lessons; the Midway had all the fun, the first Ferris wheel, games, sideshows, and "Little Egypt," a belly dancer whose movements were thought to be daring, if not erotic. (Comstock roared that it would be better to close the fair rather than let the dance go on, but when he did the dance himself to show its lewdness, reporters just giggled.) The White City offered an idealized vision of urban life, the inspiration for the "City Beautiful" movement to come. As the model for civilization, rural simplicity had given way to the majestic city. But the Midway showed how little visitors could be led where the cultural elite wanted them to go. The Women's Building got nowhere near the crowd that the World Congress of Beauty ("40 Girls from 40 Countries") got. Just as significant about the fair's meaning as a sign of the growing culture of leisure, the moralists' attempt to close the fair on the Sabbath or shut down the drinking saloons failed miserably. The fair's longest legacy, in fact, may have been the Pledge of Allegiance, first recited there and spread to every schoolroom in the land.

Prizefighting had long been a disreputable amusement of shady bars and lower-class streets, but during the 1880s it became an organized sport, attracting a national audience second only to that of baseball. Richard Kyle Fox, owner of the *National Police Gazette*, used his popular magazine and his wealth to transform boxing. Because Fox put up the prize money, he had the power to reform the sport. He made it both more profitable and more respectable, and he introduced standardized rules. Entrepreneurs sponsored matches at indoor rings where they could control unruly audiences with police and security guards.

By the 1860s baseball had become a major draw among city dwellers. Every neighborhood had a team. But not until 1869, when the Cincinnati Red Stockings went on tour and charged admission, did baseball become a professional spectator sport with standardized rules.

Within a decade the owners of eight baseball clubs had formed a National League with all the earmarks of a corporate cartel. It restrained the power of players, restricted the number of teams to one per city, prohibited Sunday games, banned the sale of alcohol at ballparks, hired umpires, and set schedules and admission prices. Chafing under these restrictions, many players jumped to a new American Association and later tried forming a league of their own. Neither alternative lasted. Until the American League was founded in 1901, the National League controlled professional baseball. (The first World Series came in 1903.)

Long before "Take Me Out to the Ball Game" was written (1908), the sport had become known as America's "national pastime." A model of ordered competition, baseball idealized the principle of success based purely on merit. Objective statistics identified the best players without respect to their personal background. Recruited from factories, farms, and slums, professional players with names like "Iron Man" Joe McGinty and John "Honus" Wagner became immigrant and working-class heroes. (Typically, the first mythological baseball hero was "Casey," a distinctly Irish surname, in the humorous poem "Casey at the Bat.") A Brooklyn promoter introduced the custom of starting the game with "The Star-Spangled Banner," one reason why the song eventually became the national anthem. But professional baseball reflected some of the less attractive realities of American society as well. The owners' cartel prevented players from taking advantage of the market. Nor did the players' association admit black players, however worthy. They had to form teams of their own. Even the seating arrangements in ballparks reflected social divisions: working-class fans in the bleachers, the middle class in the stands, and elites in the box seats.

As daily work became more sedentary, especially for white-collar workers, Americans spent more time in physical recreation. Within a decade of the invention of the modern "safety bike" in 1888, there were 10 million bicycles in the United States. At Harvard, Yale, and Princeton young men took up football, basketball, and rowing. At Smith, Vassar, and Berkeley young women played baseball, basketball, and tennis. As baseball and prizefighting became popular and professional, elites reacted by glorifying the amateur ideal, embracing athletic activity for its own sake rather than for monetary reward. By the turn of the century, the most exclusive colleges in the Northeast had formed football's Ivy League, a name that became synonymous with elite private universities.

The sports craze mirrored the diversity and anxieties of industrial America. Urban neighborhoods fielded Irish, Italian, and German baseball teams. Americans followed the annual America's Cup yacht race all the more passionately when Sir Thomas Lipton represented England, the nation's foremost rival. When, in the early 1900s, Jack Johnson, a black contender, made heavyweight champion, every contender was billed (wistfully) as "the Great White Hope." (Hope kissed the canvas every time.) A vocal segment of the elite saw athletic activities as an antidote to the supposedly feminizing tendencies of industrial capitalism. Boxing his way through Harvard and cowpunching on his Dakota ranch, Theodore Roosevelt praised bodily exercise and "the sports which develop such qualities as courage, resolution, and endurance" for building "the more virile virtues."

The Elusive Boundaries of Male and Female

Anthony Comstock saw the city as a place where traditional morality broke down, particularly standards of sexual propriety. In fact, the political economy of industrial capitalism and the triumph of wage labor helped men and women rethink traditional concepts of masculinity and femininity. As they did so, new cities and newfound leisure time offered unprecedented opportunities to test the conventional boundaries of sexual identity.

The Victorian Construction of Male and Female

Until the mid-1700s most European doctors believed that there was only one sex: females were simply inferior, insufficiently developed males. Sometime after 1750, however, scientists and intellectuals began to argue that males and females were fundamentally different, that they were "opposite" sexes. For the first time it was possible to argue that women were naturally less interested in sex than men or that men were "active" whereas women were "passive." Nature itself seemed to justify the infamous double standard that condoned sexual activity by men but punished it in women.

Nineteenth-century society drew even more extreme differences between men and women. Taking its name from the long reign of Britain's Queen Victoria, the Victorian era is often stereotyped as an age of sexual repression and cultural conservatism. So it was, up to a point. Boys reading moralistic stories of heroes who overcame their fears prepared for the competitive worlds of business and politics, both largely male preserves. To be a "man" in industrial America was to work in the rough-and-tumble world of the capitalist market. Men proved themselves by their success at making a living and therefore at taking care of a wife and children.

Victorian men defined themselves as rational creatures threatened by insistent sexual drives. Physical exertion was an important device for controlling a man's powerful sexual urges, just as masturbation was deemed an unacceptable outlet for these drives. Men were urged to channel their sexual energies into strenuous activities such as sports and, conveniently enough, wage labor.

Where masculinity became a more rigid concept, femininity became less certain. Women's schools established their own sports programs. Affluent women took up bicycling, tennis, swimming, and croquet. Yet the stereotype still persisted that women were too frail for the hurly-burly of business and enterprise. Lacking the competitive instinct of the male, the female was best fitted to become a wife and mother within the protective confines of the home. Just as men joined social clubs and sports teams, a "female world of love and ritual" developed. Middle-class women frequently displayed among themselves a passionate affection that was often expressed in nearly erotic terms. But genuinely passionate female sexuality disturbed the Victorians. Evidence of sexual passion among women was increasingly diagnosed, mostly by male doctors, as a symptom of a new disorder called "neurasthenia."

Over time the differences between men and women were defined in increasingly medical terms. Victorian doctors redefined homosexuality as a medical abnormality, a perversion, and urged the passage of laws outlawing homosexual relations. The new science of gynecology powerfully reinforced popular assumptions about gender differences. Leading male physicians argued that the energy women expended in reproduction left them unable to withstand the rigors of higher education. In extreme cases physicians would excise a woman's clitoris to thwart masturbation or remove her ovaries to cure neurasthenia.

On the assumption that motherhood was a female's natural destiny, doctors pressed to restrict women's access to contraception and to prohibit abortion. Before the Civil War many Americans tolerated abortion in the first three months of pregnancy, though they did not necessarily approve of it. This began to change as the medical profession laid claim to the regulation of female reproduction. The American Medical Association (AMA, founded in 1847) campaigned to suppress abortionists and criminalize abortion. The AMA also supported passage of the Comstock Law, which outlawed the sale of contraceptive devices. "Our Heavenly Father never sends more mouths than He can feed," one doctor explained. To hear Comstock tell it, the only naysayers were "long-haired men and short-haired women"—the unmanly and unfeminine.

To bolster traditional marriage, states passed laws raising the age of consent, forbidding common-law and interracial marriage, punishing polygamy, and making divorce more difficult. Only in the West did authorities make incompatibility grounds for ending a marriage. Many places set up family courts to handle desertion and juvenile delinquency. Congress passed several antipolygamy laws to protect Mormon wives and, as a fringe benefit, to take the vote away from a religious group known to lean Democratic.

Victorians Who Questioned Traditional Sexual Boundaries

All those changes could not reverse the underlying trends. Illegal contraceptive devices were widely known of and used. In major cities, abortionists charged $10 for their services. As for the divorce rate, it increased 15 times over. By 1915, the United States had the highest divorce rate in the world, affecting one marriage in seven.

In a new economy based on wage labor, single young men found the city ideal for cutting loose at comparatively little risk. Those looking for prostitutes found them readily available (see Map 18–1). In many towns, they had their own neighborhood, the "red-light district," and sometimes the "sporting trade" published guidebooks detailing different houses' specialties.

One did not have to venture far in the biggest cities to find shows flouting Victorian standards of propriety by using sexual titillation to entertain audiences. Can-can girls, off-color jokes, and comedy skits focusing on the war of the sexes played well in working-class districts. Even among the "respectable classes," both men's and women's clothing became simpler, looser, and more comfortable. Within limits, popular culture idealized the sensuous human body, while for the first time male sports heroes were openly admired for their physiques. Police cracked down on homosexual conduct more severely than before, but the old rules still applied: private and consensual behavior ran relatively little risk.

Map 18–1   Houses of Prostitution, 1850–1859 and 1900–1909 One measure of the sexual freedom characteristic of city life was the explosive increase in prostitution. As the demand for prostitution rose, so did attempts to suppress it. *Timothy J. Gilfoyle,* City of Eros *(New York: Norton, 1992), p. 33.*

Immigration as a Cultural Problem

When novelist Henry James returned to the United States in 1907 after a quarter of a century in Europe, he was appalled by the pervasive presence of immigrants in New York City. On the streetcars, he confronted "a row of faces, up and down, testifying, without exception, to alienism unmistakable, alienism undisguised and unashamed." James was one of the many native-born Americans who assumed that their culture was Protestant, democratic, and English speaking. They saw a threat in vast numbers of immigrants who were none of those things and in the roots that ethnic subcultures were setting down in the cities. Yet among immigrants and their children, an ethnic identity was often traded for a broader assimilation into American culture.

Josiah Strong Attacks Immigration

"Every race which has deeply impressed itself on the human family has been the representative of some great idea," clergyman Josiah Strong wrote in *Our Country*. Greek civilization was famed for its beauty, he explained; the Romans for their law; and the Hebrews for their purity. The Anglo-Saxons claimed two great ideas: the love of liberty and "pure spiritual Christianity." Strong was optimistic that as representatives of "the largest liberty, the purest Christianity, the highest civilization," the Anglo-Saxon race would "spread itself over the earth." Published in 1885, Strong's best-selling book went through many editions and was serialized in newspapers across America. Like him, many native-born Americans saw themselves as the defenders of Anglo-Saxon culture.

But there was a problem. Strong and his followers saw the arrival of millions of immigrants as a challenge to Anglo-Saxon America. By 1900 more than 10 million Americans were foreign born. The typical immigrant, he warned, was not a freedom-loving Anglo-Saxon Protestant but a narrow-minded "European peasant" whose "moral and religious training has been meager or false." Immigrants brought crime to America's cities and, voting in blocs, undermined the nation's politics. "[T]here is no more serious menace to our civilization," Strong warned, "than our rabble-ruled cities."

For Strong, the problem was that immigrants were coming in such huge numbers that assimilation was becoming impossible (see Map 18 2). Worst of all—in Strong's view—the Catholic Church held millions of immigrants in its grip, filling their heads with superstition rather than "pure Christianity." Through its parochial schools, the Catholic Church was training new generations to love tyranny rather than liberty.

Strong and his readers need not have worried (and to be fair, Strong himself saw the real solution in what came to be called the Social Gospel, the active involvement of Protestants in helping those less well off than themselves). Indeed, they misread their own evidence. By cultivating the German vote or the Irish vote, for example, politicians brought immigrants into American culture. Nor were immigrants as slavishly subservient to the Catholic Church as Strong thought.

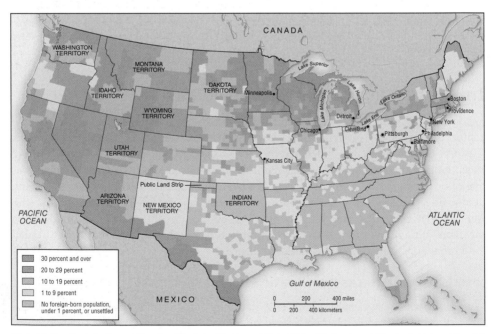

Map 18–2   Population of Foreign Birth by Region, 1880 Clifford L. Lord and Elizabeth H. Lord, Lord & Lord *Historical Atlas of the United States* (New York: Holt, 1953).

From Immigrants to Ethnic Americans

In the middle of the nineteenth century, most immigrants came with loyalties to their regions and villages, not to a nationality. German-speaking immigrants thought of themselves primarily as Bavarian or Prussian rather than German, just as Rosa Cassettari thought of herself as Tuscanese and did not count Sicilians as Italians at all. For many Slavs, identification went no further than the parish whose church bells they heard on Sunday morning.

Regional differences faded, an ocean away from home, but they would have done so anyhow. Nationalism as a self-identifying concept was spreading throughout the Western world. It was reflected in a unifying Italy, a consolidated German Reich, the czar's "Russification" program that laid the whip on Jewish backs and made Russian, not French, the language of the St. Petersburg elite. The patriotic fervor that the Civil War unleashed in the United States, liberal revolutions did in Paris and Berlin. Immigrants brought an increasingly robust sense of their ethnic identities with them. At the same time, in the United States secular fraternal organizations and mutual aid societies, designed to help newcomers find jobs and housing, forged wider ethnic identities. In 1893 mine workers formed the Pennsylvania Slovak Catholic Union to help cover burial expenses for those killed in the mines. Most often, however, middle-class immigrants or local priests took the lead in forming fraternal organizations, which eventually counted about half of all immigrants as members.

Immigrants Immigrants often crowded into "tenements," a new form of apartment building that actually improved living conditions for many of America's poor city dwellers.

Some immigrant businessmen led the drive toward larger ethnic definitions. Because regional loyalties among his workers hindered efficiency, Marco Fontana, who ran the Del Monte Company in California, encouraged the growth of an "Italian" identity.

The Catholic Church and Its Limits in Immigrant Culture

The Roman Catholic Church played a complicated role in the development of ethnic immigrant cultures. Many ethnic communities collected donations to build churches to preserve their Old World traditions. But the church also eased the transition into American life. Polish churches in Chicago and German parishes in Milwaukee used their women's groups and youth clubs as mutual aid societies for newcomers.

The church sometimes unintentionally sped the development of ethnic identities. The Irish became more devout in America as they came to rely on the church for help resisting an overwhelmingly Protestant culture. Through the church, Germans also overcame their regional differences. But the more they came to equate their German identity with Catholicism, the more they resented Irish domination of the church hierarchy. German Catholics worked to establish their own churches and parish schools or to have sermons preached in German. By contrast, the Italians were suspicious of and largely alienated from the official church, the hierarchy of which was largely Irish. By the late nineteenth century, North American bishops were trying to standardize Catholicism in America. They published uniform catechisms, established powerful bureaucracies, and tried to suppress the folk rituals of Italian Catholicism.

The church's power was reinforced by the struggle for control over the education of immigrant children. Throughout the nineteenth century, public schools were heavily Protestant. Shifting the focus away from the classics and toward "practical" education and language training, reformers hoped to shape reliable workers and patriotic citizens. But immigrants balked at "Americanization" efforts beyond providing them with skills they could use to get ahead, and the bulwark of their resistance was the church.

During the second half of the nineteenth century, both the Catholic and Lutheran Churches established parochial school systems to protect immigrant children from the biases of public education. By 1883, all but two Chicago parishes had their own parochial schools. Yet parochial education contributed to assimilation. Schools in Irish Catholic or German Lutheran parishes reinforced the growth of distinctively American ethnic identities tied to an increasingly standardized and Americanized Catholicism or Lutheranism.

Immigrant Cultures

Newcomers adjusted to American culture on their own terms. Some changed their names to English equivalents. Piccolo became Little, Wahlgren became Green, Schmidt became Smith. Even those who did not set out to assimilate found that the longer they stayed, the more their customs diverged from those of the Old World. Irish Americans fused together songs from various parts of Ireland and added piano accompaniment. Polish immigrant bands expanded beyond the traditional violin by adding accordions, clarinets, and trumpets. Hundreds of immigrant theaters offered productions that adjusted traditional plot lines to the New World. Jewish plays told of humble peddlers who outwitted their prosperous patrons. Italian folktales celebrated the importance of the family. In these ways distinctive ethnic identities adapted to urban and industrial America.

One of the most distinctive features of immigrant culture was family size. At a time when middle-class families had only two or three children, immigrant families remained large, for sound economic reasons: they often needed their children's income to survive. At the turn of the century, Italian mothers in Buffalo, New York, had an average of eleven children. Among Polish wives the average was closer to eight. In Pennsylvania's coal-mining district, working-class immigrant women had 45 percent more children than native-born women. But the death rate among immigrant children was also high. In 1900, one out of three Polish and Italian mothers had seen one of their children die before his or her first birthday.

As ethnicity developed in the late nineteenth century, class divisions were increasingly difficult to isolate from cultural distinctions. The middle class, for example, was overwhelmingly native born, white, Anglo-Saxon, and Protestant. The working class was, by contrast, African American, foreign born, Catholic, or Jewish. By 1900, 75 percent of manufacturing workers were immigrants or the children of immigrants, closer to 85 percent in large cities. In the South, wage laborers were overwhelmingly black sharecroppers. In this context, educated elites constructed a definition of high culture that distinguished the middle classes from the allegedly uncultivated and uncultured working classes.

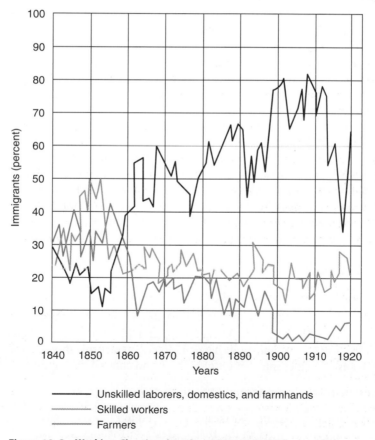

Figure 18–2 Working-Class Immigration, 1840–1920 *US Bureau of Census.*

The Creation of High Culture

During the late nineteenth century, many intellectuals sought to isolate and define a traditional high culture that stretched through Western history from ancient Greece and Rome to the present. By the 1890s, high culture embodied principles of social, cultural, and political hierarchy that found their clearest representation in museums, libraries, and universities across the United States. A "Western tradition" had been created as an antidote to the new forms of popular culture that had emerged in the same decades. In actuality, high culture served as a rarefied alternative to an equally vibrant and valuable popular culture.

High Culture Becomes Sacred

The leading advocate of high culture was an Englishman, Matthew Arnold. In *Culture and Anarchy*, published in 1869, Arnold promoted the study of "the best which has been thought and said in the world" as a source of stability amidst the "anarchy" of capitalist society. "Certain things are not disputable," *Harper's Magazine* declared in 1867, proclaiming that authors such as Homer, Shakespeare, and Dante "are towering facts like the Alps or the Himalayas. . . . It is not conceivable that the judgment of mankind upon those names will ever be reversed." American elites looking for firm moral guidelines were establishing a canon of great cultural achievements and turning to it the way earlier generations had looked to holy scripture. Secular culture took on the qualities of the sacred.

Beneath the sacred view of culture was the fear that the modern world had undermined traditional values, especially religious values. Particularly troubling was the apparent decline in religious fervor. Middle-class men and women occasionally confessed to a loss of their own faith, though they were much likelier to feel it dimming in intensity.

Those so troubled sometimes took solace in a more secular evangelism. A genteel few responded as Thomas Wentworth Higginson did. Nurtured in the reform movements of antebellum New England, Higginson had been an abolitionist and supporter of women's rights. During the Civil War he led a famed regiment of African American troops. Fully engaged in the politics of his day, Higginson was equally at home in the New England literary world, turning to culture for relief from the sordid realities of urban life and industrial capitalism.

In 1871, two years after Matthew Arnold published *Culture and Anarchy*, Higginson made a strikingly similar case. Culture, he explained, "pursues" art and science for their intrinsic worth. It "places the fine arts above the useful arts." It sacrifices "material comforts" for the sake of a "nobler" life. Like Matthew Arnold, Higginson saw culture as a defense against materialism.

Higginson shared the Victorian conviction that the middle classes made culture. At the top of the social order stood an increasingly dissolute and unrestrained capitalist class. At the bottom, poor working people lived lives devoid of gentility and refinement. Yet these very classes, the greedy capitalists at the top and the ignorant masses below, seemed to grow in influence as capitalism developed. To counteract this threat, American elites worked to transform cities into centers of high art and cultural distinction.

Cultural Establishment Versus Mass Culture

In the early nineteenth century, Shakespeare played to sellout crowds across America. Traveling through the country in the 1830s, Alexis de Tocqueville observed that "there is hardly a pioneer's cabin but that does not contain a few odd volumes of Shakespeare."

>> **The Modern University**

American elites endowed not just museums and libraries but distinguished private universities. Cornell, Johns Hopkins, Vanderbilt, Stanford, and the University of Chicago all appeared between the late 1860s and the 1890s. Some wealthy businessmen hoped to burnish their reputations or show off their generosity in monumental works, just as Renaissance princes had. Others may have seen that industrial capitalism rested on technological developments and management ability. Those in turn depended on the up-to-date scientific learning and professional skills that research universities could provide by training the new engineering and business elite. Others had more selfless motives, and many shared the general belief that a great nation deserved great universities.

The new universities transformed higher education's methods and purposes. Daniel Coit Gilman, the first president of the Johns Hopkins University in Baltimore, created specialized departments of history, English, and the various sciences. These departments were responsible for recommending faculty appointments and promotions and for developing courses. Gilman also encouraged the publication of academic journals and established the first American university press in 1878. Pioneers like Gilman changed the university from an institution intended to give a refined classical education to some and training for the ministry to others into one dedicated to research and the expansion of scholarly knowledge. Lectures replaced rote recitation, and PhD programs requiring a dissertation became essential for many professional degrees. The study of modern literature entered the college curriculum for the first time and became the preserve of specialists. Some professors, influenced by German scholarship, emphasized sentence structures, word roots, and forms of publication. This approach appealed to those who sought to make the study of literature into a science, but it was based on assumptions about the intrinsic superiority of western European languages. An Oxford scholar, Friedrich Max Müller, saw "an unbroken chain between us and Cicero and Aristotle." Müller and his American followers created a canon of great works they believed defined culture of the "West."

Leading scholars in the new "social sciences" of sociology, anthropology, and political science also divided the world into great and inferior nations. At the top stood the so-called Teutonic nations of western Europe and North America. This hierarchy, far from reflecting the biases of its creators, was grounded in the objective methods of pure science—or so anthropologists, sociologists, and professional economists claimed. But a vocal minority, just as well trained abroad, came back to apply objective standards to social Darwinism and expose its fallacies. In either case, science had become the model for producing human knowledge and professionalism the standard for specialized disciplines. Thanks in part to the educational revolution, lawyers needed to attend law school, just as would-be doctors did medical school. Becoming a dentist hereafter would require something more than a pair of pliers.

continued

AMERICAN LANDSCAPE *continued*

The modern university reflected the inequalities of the age—and the promise. Only a tiny fraction of Americans attended college, mostly native-born and well-to-do men. But it was a larger fraction than ever before. One reason was the first Morrill Land Grant Act of 1862, which had endowed the states with great tracts to fund institutions teaching "agriculture and the mechanic arts." Seventy "land grant" institutions were founded, including the major state university systems of New York, Illinois, Michigan, and California. Those in the Midwest admitted women as well as men. Women's colleges also opened their doors: six of the so-called "Seven Sisters" began after the Civil War. By 1910, two college students in five were women, though not many were allowed to go on to professional degrees. If blacks found themselves largely shut out of the elite schools (which also set quotas limiting Jewish admissions), they, too, had new opportunities in land grant institutions as well as in black colleges like Fisk University in Tennessee or Booker T. Washington's Tuskegee Institute in Alabama.

Shakespearean plays, and not only a few classics, were performed in theaters more than any others—which made sense, given that American drama was just beginning to develop.

A Shakespearean play often shared the bill with music, dancing, acrobats, magicians, and comedians—with a short humorous skit, or farce, to end the evening. Audiences yelled, cheered, whistled, demanded encores of death scenes, and sometimes tossed flowers or fruit. They generally preferred highly melodramatic renditions of Shakespeare with clean moral lessons, where the ending was always satisfying, and good always won out—in which, instead of committing suicide, Romeo and Juliet lived happily ever after. By 1850 Americans knew Shakespeare's plays so well that politicians spouted lines from them without fear of losing an audience.

Now all this changed. Shakespeare was redefined as high culture. Out went the skits and performing-dog acts. Theater audiences parted ways, the respectable classes retiring into decorous houses, with prices high enough to turn away roisterers and rowdies.

Opera, too, went through a status revolution. Italian immigrants noticed the difference. Back home, opera was widely popular. Certain composers, like Verdi, were national heroes. America had made opera too good for the average man, all dress suits and lavish gowns. The opening of the opera season began the "social season" for the very rich. Orchestral music went through the same cleansing. In the early nineteenth century, local bands across America (3,000 of them by 1860) regaled crowds with a repertoire mingling popular and classical pieces. Beginning in the 1840s, elite symphony orchestras took over classical music, purifying the programs so that a Beethoven symphony would never rub elbows with a popular tune like "Little Brown Jug."

Symphonies and opera companies cost a lot of money. Orchestras needed new halls. Opera companies needed endowments. Serious theater needed generous patrons. All

"Opera War" Cartoon, *Puck Magazine*, 1883 City life at its best allowed a rich cultural mix and a receptive paying audience unimaginable before the Civil War: in New York City's case, vying grand opera companies, bursting with Europe's star performers. As Joseph Keppler's cartoon in a middle-class humor magazine shows, high culture was not just the playground of the plutocracy.

these took massive infusions of private wealth. In effect, the rich, the leading performers, and intellectuals shaped a cultural establishment that still endures. Built with and sustained by the patronage of the wealthy, opera houses and symphony halls were the architectural embodiment of high culture.

Great cities required great museums as well. In the 1870s, Americans founded a stunning array of secular temples devoted to the world's great art, in New York, Boston, Philadelphia, and Chicago. Spectacular new public libraries appeared at the same time. By 1900, elite Americans had come to associate "culture" with impressive institutions in major cities. For them at least, Chicago's cultural life was embodied not in its immigrant neighborhoods or popular theaters but in the Art Institute, Symphony Hall, and the Chicago Public Library.

That elite culture was only part of the story. Alongside the massive mausoleums of books, Americans built thousands of smaller libraries. Andrew Carnegie alone paid for more than 1,600 of them. By 1900, a range of reading matter wider than ever before stood within the reach of more people than at any time in the past. Much of it comprised dime-novel thrillers about the shoot-'em-up West and the hundred or so Horatio Alger novels, in which plucky boys used pep and good moral values to rise from rags to respectability. (More Americans could read, too: 20 percent of Americans were illiterate in 1876 and only 6 percent by 1915.) New York had its symphony orchestra, but nearly every small town had its band, playing whatever it pleased. Within two generations, a still wider audience came to enjoy music from another source: Thomas Alva Edison's phonograph. Still in its earliest stages in the 1890s, it had already leaped beyond the limited purpose that Edison had intended, of being used by businessmen to dictate messages for their ste-nographers. Opera singers like Enrico Caruso sold well, but record buyers had their own ideas about culture. They also bought spirituals, vaudeville comedy routines, and songs like "Meet Me Under the Anheuser Busch." Thanks in part to Edison's invention, the great-est American advances in music at the turn of the century came not in classical imitations of European masters but in the "ragged time" works of honky-tonk performers like Scott Joplin, the showstoppers on the musical stage such as those written by George M. Cohan, and the stirring marches of John Philip Sousa, composer of "Stars and Stripes Forever." Even Charles Ives, the greatest American classical composer of his day, drew on folk songs for his symphonies—mixing together "Turkey in the Straw," "Columbia, the Gem of the Ocean," and a bugler's "Reveille."

Social Darwinism and the Growth of Scientific Racism

In 1859 Charles Darwin published his masterpiece of evolutionary theory, *On the Origin of Species*. Several scientists had already suggested that life had evolved over a long period of time, but Darwin offered the first persuasive explanation of how this had taken place. He argued that a process of "natural selection" favored those biological changes that were most suited to the surrounding environment. American scientists took readily to Darwin-ism. Asa Gray at Harvard and Joseph LeConte at the University of California spread the evolutionary word in their influential textbooks on botany and geology. By 1900 virtually all American high school science textbooks embraced evolution.

Darwin's influence did not stop with the natural sciences. Social scientists applied the theory of natural selection to social evolution. This combination of social theory with evo-lutionary science was known as social Darwinism. Social Darwinists argued that human inequality was the outcome of a struggle for survival in which the fittest rose to the top. This theory made the rich seem more fit than the poor; it made blacks seem less fit than whites. To social Darwinists, inequality was the natural order of things. In this way Dar-win's theory was hijacked to defend the new social order of industrial capitalism.

Natural selection was also invoked to show an inherent African racial inferiority. Rac-ists had argued that without slavery, freed blacks could not compete—or even survive. After the war, newspapers predicted the disappearance of African Americans by cen-tury's end. The 1890 census seemed to show a declining African American population, and racial theorists published influential studies "proving" that competition with whites was killing blacks off. Their only salvation, biologist Joseph LeConte argued, would come through permanent subordination. Only white overlordship could save blacks from their natural fate.

Far more influential than the LeConte article was statistician Frederick L. Hoffman's full-length treatise *Race Traits and Tendencies of the American Negro*, published in 1896. The book's many tables and figures gave the authoritative air of social science to Hoffman's conclusion: ever since leaving the shelter of slavery, blacks had been degenerating morally. Evolutionary theory doomed them to poverty and social inferiority.

Social Darwinism had plenty of defenders, notably Professor William Graham Sumner of Yale. "Before the tribunal of nature," he asserted, "a man has no more right to life than a rattlesnake." Any government intervention to help the unfortunate interfered with natural selection. It would be useless in the long run and a harmful interference with the rigid economic laws of supply and demand in the short run. But the Sumners of the world found themselves under increasing challenge as the century ended. Ministers, who saw man as a moral, rather than an economic, animal, rejected the concept of a natural selection process based on selfishness and scramble. Economist Richard T. Ely argued that even in economic decisions, self-interest did not play the all-controlling role that social Darwinism presumed. Success, a younger generation of economists and social scientists argued, depended not just on a person's natural gifts but also on the surrounding conditions. Change the conditions—replace a slum with clean and healthy apartments, an alley with a playground or a park, a pittance with a living wage—and the man or woman with abilities might have the chance to use them to rise.

Social scientists such as Ely and Hoffman prided themselves on their commitment to the truth as facts and statistics revealed it. Like advocates of high culture, sociologists and anthropologists claimed to have isolated the definitive truths of human society. But not all "realists" sought solace in statistics. Some of America's best artists responded to the realities of a diverse, urban, industrial America.

Artistic Realism Finds an American Voice

In the second half of the nineteenth century, artists and writers took in the world that Anthony Comstock wanted to control, that Matthew Arnold wanted to escape, and that Thomas Wentworth Higginson wanted to uplift. "This is the age of cities," writer Hamlin Garland declared, "and the problem of our artistic life is practically one of city life." Garland's own writing hardly showed it, but in his harsh view of farm life, Garland belonged with the "realists" who saw themselves as part of the first major artistic movement that was grounded in urban and industrial America. "The public demands realism and they will have it," the novelist Willa Cather declared.

The Advance of Literary Realism

In April 1861 the *Atlantic Monthly* published a powerful story called "Life in the Iron Mills" by a writer named Rebecca Harding. Her story created a sensation. Rarely had the dreary lives of ordinary workers been presented in such relentless detail. In the decades to come, the best writers in America joined the crusade to make fiction realistic. The leading spokesperson for realistic fiction was William Dean Howells, the author of one of the best-known realist novels, *The Rise of Silas Lapham*, and editor of the *Atlantic Monthly*, one of a few influential magazines that championed literary realism.

Realists and regionalists tried to bridge the gap between "high" and "popular" culture by making great literature out of the details of everyday life. To "enjoy the every-day life," Sarah Orne Jewett explained in *Deephaven*, one must "find pleasure in thought and observation of simple things, and have an instinctive, delicious interest in what to other eyes is unflavored dullness." Nobody could accuse Mark Twain of unflavored dullness. His cynical eye mocked Wild West myths, European high culture, politics, and respectability. "Civilization," he wrote, "is the limitless multiplication of unnecessary necessities." Bringing the colloquial language of the Mississippi River valley and the local color of mining camps and steamboat captains into literature, he joined a number of regionalists in giving literature a distinctly American idiom, just as O. Henry's short stories did for big-city life in the early 1900s. Twain's work shattered the genteel romantic conventions that depicted, for example, bad little boys being hit by lightning for fishing on Sundays. There was nothing dewy-eyed in cunning, adventurous Tom Sawyer, and the footloose Huckleberry Finn was unrespectability itself. In the same way, Ambrose Bierce's stories of the Civil War gave an unsparing view of the madness and horror of a struggle being sentimentalized as it receded into the past.

The characters in realistic novels were flawed people who struggled with moral dilemmas. Silas Lapham had to decide whether to mislead the men who wanted to buy his failing paint company. Huck Finn had to decide whether to turn in a runaway slave. Yet neither Lapham nor Finn was "heroic" in the way that earlier heroes were, and neither found it easy to do the right thing. Lapham would suffer by doing so. But in both cases, the author had created characters whose psychological complexity (and bad habits) made them more "realistic." For Henry James, psychological realism was the whole point, and his characters—Isabel Archer in *Portrait of a Lady* is a good example—are among the most vivid and compelling in all American literature.

The realist movement shocked the defenders of the genteel tradition of American letters. In 1885 the public library committee of Concord, Massachusetts, banned *The Adventures of Huckleberry Finn* from its shelves, denouncing it as "the veriest trash" and characterizing Twain's masterpiece as "rough, coarse and inelegant, dealing with a series of experiences not elevating, the whole book being more suited to the slums than to intelligent, respectable people."

Realists dismissed such criticism as evidence of the "feminine" taste that prevailed in American letters, and they saw realism as a "masculine" alternative to sentimental writing that appealed to women novel readers. But female realists also rejected the assumption, common to sentimental fiction, that women's lives should be bounded exclusively by the needs of their husbands and children. Realistic writers challenged the depiction of women as nervous, frail, and fit only for the domestic life. Louisa May Alcott wanted her female characters to be "strong-minded, strong-hearted, strong-souled, and strong-bodied."

Other authors, most notably Walt Whitman, pushed the radical possibilities of realism even further. Through his poems Whitman hoped "to exalt the present and the real, to teach the average man the glory of his daily walk and trade." He was the poet of the city, appreciating the "goodness," as well as the "wickedness," of modern urban America. Just as vaudeville flirted with sexual titillation, Whitman wrote openly about eroticism, as in this passage from *Leaves of Grass*:

Have you ever loved the body of a woman?
Have you ever loved the body of a man?
Do you not see that they are exactly the same to all in all nations and times
    all over the earth?

If anything is sacred the human body is sacred,
And the glory and sweet of a man is the token of manhood untainted,
And in man or woman a clean, strong, firm-fibred body, is more beautiful
    than the most beautiful face.

Walt Whitman One of America's greatest poets, Whitman was a champion of the diversity and excitement of city life.

Thus Whitman, like so many realists, fused the themes of popular culture with the forms of "high" art (and, incidentally, got the Comstocks to ban his *Leaves of Grass* from libraries and discourage publishers from issuing a new edition).

Painting Reality

In 1878 New York artist John Ferguson Weir declared that "art, in common with literature, is now seeking to get nearer the reality, to 'see the thing as it really is.'" Like the best writers of the era, the foremost painters rejected romanticism. Winslow Homer and Thomas

Eakins shifted the emphasis of American painting from sentiment to realism, from unspoiled nature to the facts of social life in postwar America.

Winslow Homer was, in the words of one critic, a "flaming realist—a burning devotee of the actual." A series of Civil War studies, notably *Prisoners from the Front* (1866), presented ordinary soldiers with ragged uniforms and worn, tired expressions. This was a sharp departure from a tradition of painting military men in heroic poses. As an illustrator for *Harper's Weekly*, one of the nation's first successful mass-circulation magazines, Homer also drew realistic scenes of factories, railroad workers, and other aspects of industrial life.

Two of Homer's most enduring contributions were his sensitive depictions of African Americans and his remarkable portrayals of seafaring men struggling against nature. At a time when intellectuals were perfecting theories of black racial inferiority and minstrel shows presented blacks in the grossest stereotypes, Homer represented blacks as varied men and women who worked hard and struggled with dignity against the difficulties of everyday life.

Thomas Eakins was even more determined to steer clear of romantic sentiment. He wielded his paintbrush with the precision of a scientist. Indeed, in his effort to represent the human body with perfect accuracy, Eakins attended medical school. After studying in Europe, Eakins returned to his native Philadelphia in 1870 and was soon shocking viewers with warts-and-all portraits of his own sisters. Eakins, one critic sniffed, "cares little for what the world of taste considers beautiful."

Eakins established his reputation with a series of lifelike paintings of rowers. A master at rendering scenes with startlingly three-dimensional effects, in 1875 he shocked the art world again with *The Gross Clinic*, a large canvas depicting the gruesome details of a surgical procedure. The selection committee for the 1876 Philadelphia Centennial Exposition rejected *The Gross Clinic* on the grounds that "the sense of actuality about it was . . . oppressive."

>> Time Line

▼**1851**
YMCA is founded

▼**1859**
Charles Darwin publishes *On the Origin of Species*

▼**1862**
Mathew Brady exhibits Civil War photos at his New York studio

▼**1869**
Cincinnati Red Stockings charge admission to watch baseball games

▼**1870**
Metropolitan Museum of Art and Boston Museum of Fine Arts are founded

▼**1870s**
National League is formed; baseball becomes professional

▼**1873**
New York Society for the Suppression of Vice (SSV) founded
Congress enacts the Comstock Law

▼**1875**
First Harvard-Yale football game is played
Thomas Eakins paints *The Gross Clinic*

▼**1876**
World's Fair held in Philadelphia
Philadelphia Museum of Art founded

▼**1878**
Johns Hopkins establishes the first American university press

Fascinated by the human form, Eakins photographed dozens of naked men and women and used some of them as the basis for full-scale paintings. *The Swimming Hole* (ca. 1884) was based on an Eakins photograph. By 1886 the directors of the Academy had had enough. Eakins was fired after he pulled the loincloth from a male model posing before a group of female students.

For Eakins, the exact details of the human body allowed a deeper exploration of character. Like Winslow Homer's portrayals of blacks, Eakins's women were thoughtful and dignified. *Miss Amelia C. Van Buren* (1891) conveys its subject's intelligence and complexity with no sacrifice of accuracy. Eakins did for painting what Henry James did for literature. Both demonstrated that distinguished works of art could be impressively realistic and at the same time deeply insightful. The one unspoken limitation was one that Comstock would have appreciated: unlike French impressionists, most American artists steered clear of painting nudes.

Is Photography Art?

As city life became the subject matter of painters and writers, a major technological development—photography—created a new medium of artistic expression. The camera had been invented scarcely a generation earlier, in 1839, by a Frenchman, Louis Daguerre. By the early 1860s, photographic technology had improved dramatically, and cameras had become more portable. Mathew Brady grasped the possibilities. In the fall of 1862 he mounted an exhibit of his Civil War photographs in his New York gallery. For the first time, a large viewing public could see realistic pictures of war at its grimmest. His exhibition had electrifying effects. By the 1880s, journalists used photographs to heighten the reality, the sense of "truth," conveyed by their stories. The effect of Jacob Riis's *How the Other Half Lives*, published in 1890, was enhanced with dramatic photographs documenting the misery of the urban poor. Photography had become part of the body of factual evidence.

▼1879
Art Institute of Chicago founded

▼1880s
Richard Kyle Fox professionalizes prizefighting

▼1881
Henry James publishes *Portrait of a Lady*

▼1883
Anthony Comstock publishes *Traps for the Young*

▼1884
Mark Twain publishes *The Adventures of Huckleberry Finn*
Thomas Eakins paints *The Swimming Hole*

▼1885
William Dean Howells publishes *The Rise of Silas Lapham*
Josiah Strong publishes *Our Country*

▼1888
Modern "safety" bike invented

▼1890
Jacob Riis publishes *How the Other Half Lives*

▼1891
Thomas Eakins paints *Miss Amelia C. Van Buren*

▼1893
World's Columbian Exposition held in Chicago

▼1894
Vaudeville producer B. F. Keith opens the New Theatre in Boston

The camera's eye inevitably fascinated realistic writers and artists. In the second half of the nineteenth century, photography set the standard for accurate representation. Thomas Eakins, for example, used the camera to freeze images, such as those of horses in motion, which he intended to paint on canvas. He soon became a skilled photographer, producing hundreds of portraits of his subjects. He took numerous photos of the naked human form and was one of the first artists to recognize the artistic element of photography itself. His work raised questions that remain unanswered: Is a painting based on a photograph a work of art? Is photography art?

Some writers applauded the camera's capacity to capture the "truth." Writers as varied as Walt Whitman and Harriet Beecher Stowe used photographic metaphors to describe the effects they hoped to achieve with their words. But others were not persuaded that the photograph could ever be a genuine work of art. The camera captures only "the external facts," *The Galaxy* magazine declared; it "does not tell the whole truth."

Anthony Comstock worried a great deal about the difference between art and photography. Millions of copies of great and not-very-great works of art flooded the market in the late nineteenth century. Photographs of naked men and women suddenly brought pornography within the means of all. Painters of nude portraits use artistry to divert viewers' attention from the nudity, Comstock protested. Photographers had no such artistic devices at their disposal, "or, anyhow, did not try to find any." "A photograph of a nude woman in a lewd posture, with a lascivious look on her face," was to Comstock no work of art, for it lacked "the skill and talent of the artist."

Comstock could make judgments, but he could not control photography. Industrial capitalism had made that impossible. Thanks to technological innovation and mass production, George Eastman's Kodak roll-film camera put the instant "snapshot" picture within the means of middle-class Americans. The Brownie, marketed for children, sold for just a dollar. Family events could be preserved forever at a fraction of the cost of hiring a professional photographer, and by 1910 newspapers themselves had begun capturing incidents and scenes on film for their teeming millions of readers.

Conclusion

When Comstock asked if photography could be art, he was joining a larger debate about what counted as culture in the new world created by industrial capitalism. Did it include the popular culture of the city, or was American culture restricted to great libraries, universities, museums, and opera houses? And what was culture supposed to do for people? Americans argued over whether culture should maintain traditional values or boldly face up to the realities of the new political economy.

Often these cultural struggles spilled into politics, especially when they came to upholding the moral values and behavior of a native-born Protestant middle class. But American politics was much more than a cultural struggle. Issues of economics, of race, of social justice, of national purpose stirred an increasingly diverse electorate with increasingly divergent desires. Just as American culture only partly reflected the problems of industrial capitalism, American politics only tentatively came to grips with them.

Who, What

Review Questions

1. How did the growth of cities affect American culture in the late nineteenth century?

2. Name some of the ways immigration affected American culture. How did native-born Americans react to immigrants and the cultural diversity they brought with them?

3. How did a many-cultured America reflect itself in the variety of American cultural expressions in this period?

4. What was "artistic realism"?

Critical-Thinking Questions

1. In what ways did American culture reflect the patterns of race relations in the late nineteenth century?

2. To what extent was American culture shaped and defined by economic and social elites in the late nineteenth century?

3. To what extent did race and class shape the evolution of American culture in this period? What other forces also played a role?

4. Did American culture become more repressed or more eroticized in the second half of the nineteenth century? Explain your answer.

For further review materials and resource information, please visit www.oup.com/us/ofthepeople

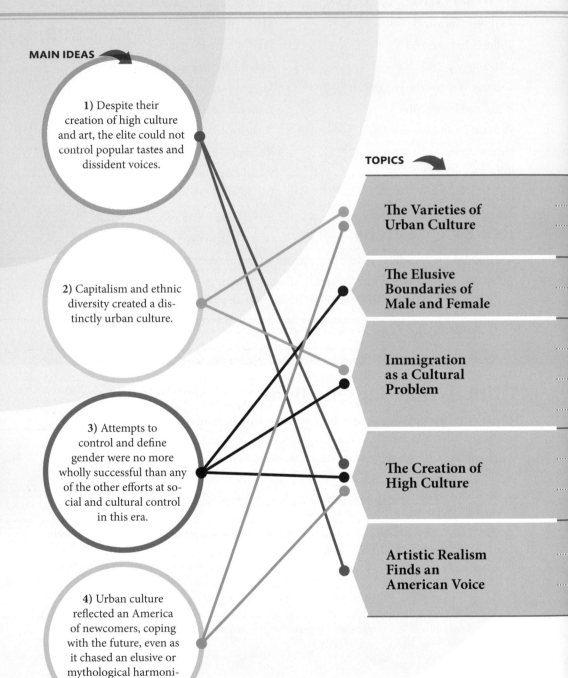

MAIN IDEAS

1) Despite their creation of high culture and art, the elite could not control popular tastes and dissident voices.

2) Capitalism and ethnic diversity created a distinctly urban culture.

3) Attempts to control and define gender were no more wholly successful than any of the other efforts at social and cultural control in this era.

4) Urban culture reflected an America of newcomers, coping with the future, even as it chased an elusive or mythological harmonious past.

TOPICS

The Varieties of Urban Culture

The Elusive Boundaries of Male and Female

Immigration as a Cultural Problem

The Creation of High Culture

Artistic Realism Finds an American Voice

CULTURAL STRUGGLES
OF INDUSTRIAL AMERICA

1850–1895

EVENTS

Minstrel Shows as Cultural Nostalgia Minstrel shows looked backward but reflected tensions of the time.

The Origins of Vaudeville Vaudeville reflected the diverse urban culture that was developing.

Sports Become Professional Physical recreation increased, and spectator sports became big attractions while undergoing economic professionalization and consolidation.

The Victorian Construction of Male and Female Victorians drew sharply differentiated gender roles and passed laws to enforce them.

Victorians Who Questioned Traditional Sexual Boundaries Urban Americans pushed the confines of Victorian sexual propriety.

Josiah Strong Attacks Immigration The influx of immigrants from many cultures alarmed many native-born Protestant Americans.

From Immigrants to Ethnic Americans Immigrants became members of ethnic groups based on national, rather than local, identities.

The Catholic Church and Its Limits in Immigrant Culture The Catholic Church failed to unite immigrant Catholic practice but successfully established schools to counter Protestant public education.

Immigrant Cultures Immigrants developed ethnic American cultures reinforced by class differences.

High Culture Becomes Sacred Secular culture took on the qualities of the sacred as elites sought to reassert traditional values.

Cultural Establishment Versus Mass Culture The "high culture" of theaters, museums, and libraries coexisted with a rich and varied popular culture.

Social Darwinism and the Growth of Scientific Racism Elites used the theory of natural selection to justify social inequality.

The Advance of Literary Realism Realists tried to shift literature away from the prevailing sentimentalism and romanticism, but met resistance.

Painting Reality Artists turned away from romanticized nature and toward unsparing depiction of everyday subjects, including urban themes.

Is Photography Art? Photography created a new medium of artistic expression, but its uses often shocked the elite.

COMMON THREADS

>> How did both culture and politics reflect sharp distinctions between men and women? How did culture and politics break those distinctions down?

>> What was the overriding issue of American politics in the late nineteenth century?

>> Was American politics headed for a crisis in the 1890s?

The Politics of Industrial America

1870–1892

>> Luna Kellie and the Farmers' Alliance

As a girl, Luna Kellie dreamed of raising a family on her own farm. Her father, a railroad worker on the Northern Pacific line, did try to make a go of farming in Minnesota, but when the farm failed he moved the family to St. Louis, Missouri. There Luna met and married James T. Kellie. At the age of 18, Luna moved with her husband and their infant to a homestead in Hastings, Kansas.

Life on the prairie fell far short of her dreams. The Kellies lived in an 8-by-12-foot sod house dug into a hillside. She gave birth to twelve children. Two died. Weakened by the strain of childbirth and constant toil, Luna dreamed of a brighter future, a holiday to Yellowstone's geysers. "Our trip never materialized," she recalled years later, "but we put in some happiest hours of life planning it."

The life of sturdy independence that farmers supposedly enjoyed turned out to be a pinched, isolated existence. Luna tried to connect with friends and neighbors, but there was not much choice. Her family attended a Methodist church until James quarreled with the pastor. Schools were even scarcer than churches, but Luna went out of her way to become active in the school district, where she took part in discussions over whether women should have the right to vote.

Like many rural women, Luna shared the responsibility for managing the farm. She kept a garden, which helped feed the family and brought in extra income from the sale of chickens and eggs. Luna also learned how to tend livestock and grow fruit trees. Her husband tried to grow spring wheat, but between falling prices and high interest rates, their work never freed them from debt. After seven years, the Kellies lost the farm. They struggled to survive by raising chickens, sheep, and livestock.

Like so many prairie farmers just barely scraping by, Luna Kellie turned to the Farmers' Alliance, the largest and most powerful association that coped with agricultural woes. She was not alone: 250,000 women joined the Alliance, making it the largest women's organization in the United States.

continued

For Kellie, the Alliance held out the hope of realizing the dreams of her youth. Its program could break down the isolation of rural life, bringing farmers together in cooperative enterprises while giving them the advantages that the "Money Power" had taken away. In 1892, when the Nebraska Farmers' Alliance affiliated with the National Farmers' Alliance and Industrial Union, Kellie was elected state secretary. She worked as tirelessly on Alliance business as she had on her own farm, writing countless letters. She edited and set the type for articles for the Alliance newspaper.

Without setting foot outside her home, Luna Kellie found herself at the center of a vast network of farmers who learned from each other by discussing key issues. Starting in efforts to improve rural Americans' lives, the movement quickly advanced into broader questions of political reform. By 1892 the Farmers' Alliance had fostered the most important political insurgency of the late nineteenth century, the Populist Party.

Two Political Styles

Politics came in two flavors in the Gilded Age: the male-dominated partisanship of voters, political operatives, and officeholders; and the voluntarism of those who put cause above party, from reform societies and women's organizations to labor unions and farmers' groups. The politicians had every advantage on their side. Because the "spoils system" let them appoint every official down to janitor when they took power, they could extort a share of government employees' wages to fund a campaign. They chose the candidates and counted the returns. In close elections, they had "soap" (payoffs to voters) to buy a winning margin. Most of the newspapers framed the news in one party's way. Political organizations became more sophisticated and much more centralized. This was the age when people began to speak of "bosses" and "political machines" in which, supposedly, the leader rallied his party followers like an army to carry every election and fill every office: the Democratic hordes in New York City that the Tammany Hall machine mobilized, for example. But time and again, politicians—even Tammany's—found themselves forced to accommodate outside pressures, and by the 1890s, those pressures had remade the very basis of the political game.

The Triumph of Party Politics

Ever since Lincoln's day, most Americans had voted the straight party line every time. Political parties printed and passed out their own ballots for loyalists to drop in the right box. Nobody needed to be literate to make his choice (no state gave women the vote until Wyoming's admission in 1889). Partisans could remove candidates' names from these ballots, and organizers often bribed voters. Intimidation also played a role. In much of the South, passing out Republican ballots was nearly as fatal as yellow fever. "Resurrectionists" voted in dead men's names, "colonizers" crossed state lines to vote in crucial elections, and political agents might even march their purchased public to vote in "blocks of five," as one Indiana Republican advised in 1888. But most voters cast honest ballots and cared so strongly that if they could have voted a dozen times they would have—as, in big cities, some did!

From the 1840s through the 1860s, an average of 69 percent of those eligible voted in presidential elections. During the final quarter of the century, the average rose to 77 percent. Southern figures lagged slightly: between 1876 and 1892, nearly two out of three southern men voted in presidential elections, compared with 82 percent of northern ones.

Newspapers played a critical role in maintaining this level of political participation. Much of the press acted as cheerleaders and opinion makers. Most papers survived with the help of party and government advertisements as well as contracts to print ballots and campaign documents. Papers slanted stories their party's way, and proudly. "Republican in everything, independent in nothing," the *Chicago Inter Ocean* boasted.

Campaign hoopla offered voters unrivaled spectacle. Political clubs and military companies paraded. Marchers rang bells, flew banners, and escorted floats with pretty girls representing Liberty, Columbia, or the various states. A good mass meeting combined barbecue, rousing oratory, band music, and fireworks. Together, they made politics America's most popular participatory sport.

However, politics was more than sport. Civil War veterans were reminded, "Vote as you shot!" Roused by the Union veterans' organization, the Grand Army of the Republic, and speeches that used the memory of the war to inflame sectional grievances, Union veterans typically backed the Republican Party. Black Americans also usually supported the party that had ended slavery. Confederates mostly voted Democratic. Democrats spoke for states' rights, small government, and white supremacy. In their eyes, Republicanism meant state and local laws telling people what to drink and how to use their Sundays. As Democrats saw it, "The Party of Moral Ideas" protected the national banker, the railroad tycoon, and the upstart Negro. To Republicans, Democrats were the party of "rum, Romanism, and Rebellion," of Catholics, saloon keepers, violence, and vice. They themselves spoke for the northern middle class, especially the better-educated ones. Government, local and national, had a duty to make Americans better off. As the Republicans told it,

Figure 19–1   Percent of Eligible Voters Casting Ballots Between 1840 and 1896 a huge proportion—often 80 percent—of those eligible to vote did so in presidential elections. In the 20th century, turnout dropped substantially.

their party's symbol was the schoolhouse while the Democrats' was the whipping-post of slavery. And each side knew that the republic's fate depended on its winning.

Masculine Partisanship and Feminine Voluntarism

The public sphere of campaigns and voting was a man's world; the private sphere of home and family was widely celebrated as a woman's. In practice, though, women shared in popular politics. They decorated the meeting halls, prepared the food, watched and sometimes joined the parades. By the end of the 1880s, both parties pitched part of their appeals to wives and families. Nevertheless, politically active women opted for a different style of politics.

A stereotype that had previously limited female political activity now gave women their chance to enter public debate. Seen as the special protectors of the family's values, women found that their views on marriage, morality, and the need to protect America's children would get a respectful hearing from lawmakers. Women's supposed superior virtue gave them a privileged position in moral reform movements. These included anti-alcohol temperance societies and campaigns for laws to keep the Christian Sabbath holy— by keeping barbershops, museums, and baseball parks closed on Sunday. To protect the private sphere, many women claimed the right to enter the public one.

Women could only pursue politics as representatives of voluntary associations dedicated to specific reforms. Voluntarism mostly recruited members from the educated middle class, who brought their class biases with them.

Sometimes women's associations copied the style of partisan politics, staging mass marches and rallies. But the marching, chanting, and military flavor of mass politics did not sit well with society's image of women's traditional role. So activists were likely to concentrate less on rousing voters than on educating them and lobbying elected officials. Men also joined voluntary associations, but they were dismissed by mainstream politicians as "namby-pamby, goody-goody gentlemen." In the late nineteenth century, voluntarism was associated with feminine politics, and party politics was associated with masculinity.

The Women's Christian Temperance Union

Still, voluntarism could do wonders, and over time the boundaries of the women's sphere became increasingly unclear. One of the most prominent female-backed political movements, the Women's Christian Temperance Union, emerged in 1873 to battle the ravages of alcohol. Led by Frances Willard from 1879 until her death in 1898, the WCTU built itself on women's calling as protectors of the home. A decentralized structure allowed groups to tailor their activities to local needs. Women found in the WCTU a source of camaraderie as well as political activism. They made it among the largest women's political organizations in the late nineteenth century, with 150,000 adult members. (The National American Woman Suffrage Association had only 13,000.) The WCTU convened huge rallies with none of the masculine rowdiness of party conventions. Willard and her associates gave speeches, wrote articles, published books and newspaper columns on the evils of drink, organized petition campaigns, and lobbied officeholders.

But under Willard, the crusade against alcohol broadened to tackle the problems of a new industrial society. The WCTU endorsed women's suffrage and formed an alliance with the country's largest labor union. Willard supported laws restricting the workday to

AMERICAN LANDSCAPE

>> **The "Crusade" Against Alcohol**

Just before Christmas in 1873, Dr. Diocletian Lewis arrived in Hillsboro, Ohio, to speak on the evils of alcohol. He had given the speech many times before, but this time the women who came proved unusually responsive. The next morning a group of Hillsboro women met for prayer and then marched through the town urging local merchants to stop selling liquor. Inspired by their success, the women kept up the pressure through the winter of 1873–1874. Neither jail nor a rain of curses, eggs, and sour beer could dampen their spirit.

The Crusade, as it came to be called, spread quickly into 31 states and territories. Druggists and hotel keepers promised to quit selling alcohol. Nearly 70 breweries closed. The women's fervor inspired crusaders to make a permanent organization, the WCTU. But Americans' drinking habits hardly changed at all. Cincinnati's distilleries, good for 30,000 jobs, kept running full-blast. Saloons thrived. People went there not just to drink but to find companionship and release. Italians went there to read

newspapers in their own language. Workers went there to find jobs listings, and foremen to do hiring. Bartenders knew everybody, one reason why saloons were tied closely to party machines. The fastest way to empty a Chicago council meeting, residents joked, was to shout, "Your saloon's on fire!"

Prayer was never enough to bring temperance. Reformers set up "temperance saloons" that served ice cream or coffee. They opened YMCA chapters with reading rooms and employment agencies to co-opt services that bars had provided. Sunday schools recruited children to break from their parents' habits and to parade, chanting, "Tremble, King Alcohol! We shall grow up!" In the end, lasting change took political action. So across the West, states and territories outlawed the sale of alcohol, and because women took leading roles in the cause, prohibitionists became the foremost advocates of woman suffrage. For good reason, Frances Willard was the first woman honored with a statue in the US Capitol.

eight hours and prohibiting child labor. By the 1890s Willard was treating drunkenness as a public health issue rather than a personal sin, a social problem rather than an individual failure. Temperance advocates supported reforms designed to relieve poverty, improve public health, raise literacy, alleviate the conditions of workers, reform prisons, suppress public immorality, and preserve peace.

The Critics of Popular Politics

The mix of partisanship and voluntarism made American politics more "popular" than ever before, attracting women and men, blacks and whites, immigrants and the native born, working class and middle class. But some Americans saw behind the spectacle to the games professional politicians played. After the Civil War, a small but influential group known as Liberals (and later as Mugwumps) challenged the party-run state. Alarmed at its selfishness, corruption, and incompetence, they called for government by professionals and independent agencies. Though some agreed with Charles Francis Adams that "universal suffrage can only mean in plain English the government of ignorance and vice," most believed that with a cleaner politics and "campaigns of education," the people would see where their true interests lay. A merit system must reward ability in the public service; a government-issued official (Australian) ballot distributed only at polling places must give every voter the chance to choose, in privacy, among all the possibilities. Tasks like setting a fair railroad rate or tariff duty, running a park system, or policing a great city should no longer be left to vote-getters. Education and expertise, not political pull, must drive policy.

Thanks to Liberals, the nonpartisan secret ballot was adopted everywhere. In 1881, supporters of good government organized the National Civil Service Reform League to prevent political parties from filling government positions. Victory came two years later with the establishment of a Civil Service Commission that would assign federal jobs on the basis of merit rather than patronage. Some states followed suit. But regarding the problems of rapid industrialization, Liberals' solutions fell short.

Most Americans approached their politics looking backward to the issues of the Civil War and Reconstruction. Every president but one between 1869 and 1901 had military service (and the one exception, Grover Cleveland, sent a substitute). But many Americans also came to feel deep concerns about a society becoming more diverse, urban, and industrial. Such issues would dominate public life by the close of the century.

The Enemy at the Gates

Political opposition to immigration, known as nativism, had enjoyed a brief success in the 1850s. Even foreign-born workers resented low-paid Chinese labor, and in 1882, Congress passed the first Chinese exclusion act. Not the least of the Tammany Hall political machine's sins, in New York reformers' eyes, was how Irish it was, and how public funds endowed Catholic schools there. Especially in the Midwest, anti-Catholicism drew on Protestant nightmares of the Inquisition and beliefs that the church's leaders combined religious intolerance with a hatred of free government. In the 1890s, the American Protective Association (APA) threw its weight behind candidates favoring Protestant interests.

As immigration increased, nativist rhetoric grew more racist and drew on the dubious sociology of social Darwinism (see Chapter 18). The threat was no longer merely from radicals and Catholics but also from darker-skinned peoples from Italy, Russia, and eastern Europe. Experts proclaimed the inherent intellectual inferiority of such peoples, giving the imprimatur of science to the most vicious stereotypes. Italians were said to be genetically predisposed to organized violence, Jews to thievery and manipulation. Anti-immigrant societies appeared across America. Mob violence sacked Chinese neighborhoods in Los Angeles in 1871, and 11 Italians were lynched by a New Orleans mob, on charges of having murdered the police chief.

But Protestant cultural politics failed to shut out immigration from southern and eastern Europe; the United States would not even require immigrants to pass a literacy test until 1917. The APA died quickly when politicians recognized that they did better by appealing to immigrant voters. They passed resolutions favoring Irish "home rule" (rather than English occupation), denounced the Russian czar's persecution of Jews, and made

As the Number of Immigrants to America Swelled, So Did Opposition to Them This 1891 cartoon blames immigration for a host of social and political evils.

Columbus Day a holiday. The real cultural fights came at the state level over issues like outlawing boxing, charging prohibitively high licenses on working-class saloons, making Jewish stores close on the Protestant Sabbath, requiring Protestant Bible reading in public schools, and forcing parochial schools to use Protestant state-mandated textbooks.

Cultural politics helps explain why temperance remained a middle-class reform movement concentrated in cities, especially northern ones. Immigrants steered clear of it. The WCTU's strongly evangelical Protestant identity and its association of saloons with aliens and Catholics spoke louder than its official policy of religious toleration. Irish Catholics and German Lutherans resented a campaign aimed to replace altar wine with grape juice in Christian services.

Economic Issues Dominate National Politics

By the late nineteenth century, Americans were used to the idea that government should oversee the distribution of the nation's natural resources. After the Civil War, federal officials distributed public lands to homesteaders and railroads and granted rights to mining, ranching, and timber companies. During those same decades, the rise of big business led many Americans to believe that the government should regulate the currency. Many others saw salvation in trade barriers to protect American commerce and workers from ruinous foreign competition. Because the two major parties commanded nearly even support at the national level, the outcome was that no issue could be finally settled. Shaped by clusters of special interests until they covered over 4,000 items, tariffs rose, fell, and rose again. Congresses tinkered with the currency, even while gold continued to hold a privileged place as backing for paper money. The bolder a policy initiative, the likelier it was to founder.

Greenbacks and Greenbackers

The money question demonstrated the inability of Gilded Age politicians to act decisively on major issues. To support the Union effort during the Civil War, the US government printed $450 million worth of "greenbacks," paper bills backed by the government's word but not by the traditional reserves of specie, meaning gold or silver. When the war ended, most Americans agreed that the greenbacks should be withdrawn from circulation until any paper dollar could be exchanged for a dollar in specie at the bank. But with the onset of the 1870s, wage cuts and tight money led to a debate. Resumptionists, those who wanted to return to the gold standard, found themselves battling debtors and industrialists who thought that a shrinking money supply would worsen the economy. Greenbackers went further. They called for issuing even more greenbacks, without any requirement that precious metals back the notes up. In the middle were many Republicans and Democrats who favored inflation, but by backing dollars in silver as well as gold. The currency had been backed in this way before Congress legislated silver out of its privileged place with the "Crime of 1873," as the Coinage Act of 1873 came to be called. Later reformers blamed a bankers' plot for the change: gold, in shorter supply, meant a smaller money supply, big enough for eastern needs and small enough to make every dollar more valuable. A dollar that could buy three times as much forced a farmer to work three times as hard to pay off debts contracted before the "Crime of '73." Holders of mortgages and bonds, agrarians shouted, had legislated themselves a bonanza.

To gold's defenders, any shift to silver or paper meant national dishonor. "Honest money," they cried, was morality itself. A flood of silver into Treasury vaults meant a flood of paper, with wild speculation, inflation out of control, and debts paid off in such depreciated currency that creditors would face ruinous losses. The Greenback-Labor Party peaked in 1878, when it garnered over a million votes and elected 14 congressmen. However, as economic skies brightened, its appeal dwindled. In 1879, resumption took place, with the $300 million in circulating greenbacks made convertible into gold. Support for silver did not die away, and every time the economy contracted, calls for limited silver coinage rose across the West and South. Farmers there found loans hardest to get, except at interest rates that (to their thinking) verged on extortion. Until times became better all over, neither side could win a final victory. They could only take half steps in one direction or the other.

Weak Presidents Oversee a Stronger Federal Government

Starting in the mid-1870s, the Democrats and Republicans had nearly equal electoral strength. From 1876 through 1896 no president took office with an overwhelming electoral mandate. The results of the 1880 election were typical of the era. Republican James A. Garfield won by a tiny margin. He received 48.5 percent of the votes, and Democrat Winfield Hancock received 48.1 percent. Grover Cleveland won a plurality in 1888, but lost the Electoral College. In both cases, the losers accused vote-buying Republicans of making the difference. But Republicans could reply that in the South, Republican votes never received a fair count. No president enjoyed a full term during which his own party controlled both houses of Congress. Reelected in 1872, Grant was the last president in the century to serve two consecutive terms.

In some cases, a president took office already discredited by the electoral process, as did Rutherford B. Hayes in 1877 (see Chapter 16). Furious that their presidential candidate, Samuel J. Tilden, had been "counted out" by three southern states juggling

Table 19-1 Razor-thin Electoral Margins in the Gilded Age

Year	Popular Vote	% of Popular Vote	Electoral Vote
1876	4,036,572	48.0	185
	4,284,020	51.0	184
1880	4,453,295	48.5	214
	4,414,082	48.1	155
	308,578	3.4	–
1884	4,879,507	48.5	219
	4,850,293	48.2	182
1888	5,477,129	47.9	233
	5,537,857	48.6	168

the returns to make Hayes the winner, Democrats threatened "His Fraudulency" with impeachment. Hayes's fellow Republicans protested his overtures to win over southern conservatives at the expense of protection for black voters, and guests resented his ban on liquor at state dinners. The party bosses raged at his steps toward a professional civil service. Hayes forbade his party to exact tribute from Republican officeholders. He fought Roscoe Conkling, New York's ruthless Republican boss, for control of the New York Customs House—the most lucrative source of patronage in America. When the English writer Samuel Johnson defined patriotism as the last refuge of a scoundrel, Conkling snarled, he little anticipated the possibilities of the word "reform." With cabinet officers controlling civil service appointments, improvements were patchier than Hayes would have liked, and civil service reformers were crestfallen.

By sending federal troops to suppress the 1877 railroad strike (see Chapter 17), Hayes set an important precedent for federal intervention in industrial disputes. He vetoed the Chinese immigration exclusion legislation passed by Congress in 1879. Troubled as he was by widespread suffering, Hayes had no cure for the economic slump of the 1870s. To protect the public credit, he opposed any steps to end the deflation of currency that had forced wages and prices down so sharply and brought ruin to farmers and industrial workers. In 1878, he vetoed the Bland-Allison Act, hailed as a way to modestly inflate the currency by coining silver in amounts tied to the amount of gold being minted. (It passed anyway, with little effect on the money supply.) Though prosperity returned soon after, Republicans felt as much relief to see his term end as he did. They did not protest his decision not to stand for reelection.

Economic, rather than racial, issues dominated the 1880 campaign although Democratic state governments were rolling back the gains blacks had made during Reconstruction. Both parties relied on the patronage system too much to press civil service reform. Democrats favored lower tariffs than the Republicans, though both parties had strong protectionist blocs (supporting high tariffs to protect American producers) as well as members who favored lower tariff rates. Neither party wanted free trade; the government needed the revenue from tariff duties. So Garfield's victory in 1880 did not foreshadow any major shifts in government policy. It took a national tragedy to bring that about.

On July 2, 1881, a neglected office-seeker shot the president. Garfield died two months later, and Chester A. Arthur, the product of Conkling's patronage machine, became president. The assassination made it dangerous for the new president to resist the swell of popular support for civil service reform. The Republicans in control of Congress did resist, however, and Democrats swept into office on a tide of resentment against Republican corruption and patronage. The following year Congress passed, and President Arthur signed, the landmark Pendleton Civil Service Act. The Pendleton Act prohibited patronage officeholders from contributing to the party machine that gave them their jobs. More important, the law authorized the president to establish a Civil Service Commission to administer competitive examinations for federal jobs. Before the century ended, the majority of federal jobs were removed from the reach of the patronage machines. The Pendleton Act was a major turning point in the creation of a stable and professional civil service.

Dying of a kidney disease, Arthur could not win renomination. The corrupt Republican candidate, James G. Blaine, offended Liberals and gave Democrats a chance. They nominated Governor Grover Cleveland, who was elected after a mud-spattered campaign, complete with anti-Catholic slurs and a scandal about Cleveland's illegitimate child. His slogan, "Public office is a public trust," expressed Liberals' ideal. However, Blaine would have won had he not alienated irate prohibitionists and had the black vote not been suppressed in the South.

Cleveland was upright, downright, and forthright. He carried out the Pendleton Act to the letter, though not much beyond it, and harried railroad interests that exploited public land, including some of his campaign contributors. Special veteran's pension bills met ringing vetoes. So did a bill to relieve drought victims on the plains. Union veterans shouted when he tried to return captured Confederate flags to the southern states, and for once Cleveland backed down. Believing in a cheap, limited national government, he offered no great programs, but neither did he thwart congressional moves to broaden government's scope. He signed legislation raising the Agriculture Department to cabinet status and the Dawes Severalty Act, parceling out a fraction of the Indians' land to them as private property (see Chapter 17). Equally important, he approved the Interstate Commerce Act creating an Interstate Commerce Commission with power to regulate the railroads. Ever since the 1860s, states had been creating similar commissions, some of them setting railroad rates and all of them able to investigate and publicize abuses. Although weak and sometimes captive to the interests they regulated, they represented a growing state role overseeing many activities. Like the state agencies, the ICC promised more in the way of controlling rates and unfair practices than it could deliver, especially with court decisions hobbling the regulators.

With few accomplishments beyond a White House wedding to Frances Folsom and ominous political rumblings at the midterm elections, Cleveland needed a stirring issue. He found it in the high protective tariff. The tariff had done its work too well. Government surpluses had been growing, tightening credit as Treasury vaults locked away more and more of the nation's money, and tempting politicians to spend the revenue for pensions and subsidies. Critics saw the tariff as taking money from consumers' pockets to fill those of the monopolists, who, safe from foreign competition, could keep their prices high. Cautious presidents like Arthur had left the tariff alone, but Cleveland devoted his annual message to Congress in December 1887 to tariff reform. Favoring free trade would be political suicide, but adjustments downward, especially for raw materials, might make American exports more competitive and drive prices down.

It might drive wages down, too; so Republicans warned. Shouting that rate reductions would shutter factories and flood America in cheaper British goods, they had the Senate

PUCK

THE OPENING OF THE CONGRESSIONAL SESSION.

Puck **Cartoon on the Surplus** By the mid-1880s, government took in more revenue than it needed, tightening the national money supply and creating a "monstrous" surplus. Tariff reformers urged a cut in duties on goods to minimize the intake. Notice how many congressmen appear in the cartoon: the fact that readers would recognize so many political players reveals the extent of their interest in politics.

vote to block any bill that the House passed. Even one less skewed to serve southern interests than the House-begotten Mills bill would have had no chance. Better in pointing the way than in working out the details of an actual measure, Cleveland did not push for the Mills bill or even for a strong endorsement of tariff reform in the 1888 Democratic platform. All the same, the issue dominated the campaign, with Republicans charging that free-trading England wanted a Cleveland victory. He won a majority of the popular vote but lost the Electoral College to Benjamin Harrison (see Map 19–1).

Having won House, Senate, and presidency on a protectionist platform, Republicans had two years to deliver. Under the forceful leadership of "Czar" Thomas Brackett Reed and with influence from President Harrison, the so-called "Billion Dollar Congress" put through the new, higher McKinley Tariff, named for Congressman William McKinley of Ohio. At the same time, Congress gave the president the authority to lower tariffs with nations opening their markets to American goods, granting him important new power in the conduct of foreign affairs. Congress also passed a lavish Dependents' Pension Law, subsidies to encourage shipping, and a silver-purchase act that westerners hoped would inject more coinage into the money supply. The Sherman Anti-Trust Act of 1890 outlawed "combinations" in "restraint of trade," though what precisely that covered was uncertain. Five years later the Supreme Court even ruled out most manufacturing. Republicans also introduced—but failed to pass—both a federal enforcement bill that might have protected black southern voters and the Blair Education Bill, which might have provided federal money to guarantee black southerners an adequate education.

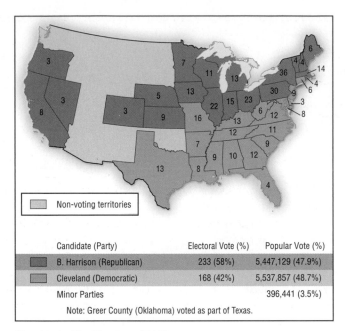

Candidate (Party)	Electoral Vote (%)	Popular Vote (%)
B. Harrison (Republican)	233 (58%)	5,447,129 (47.9%)
Cleveland (Democratic)	168 (42%)	5,537,857 (48.7%)
Minor Parties		396,441 (3.5%)

Note: Greer County (Oklahoma) voted as part of Texas.

Map 19–1   The Election of 1888

Nothing offends like success. Derided as a "human iceberg," Harrison lacked the common touch. But he was not the problem. Democrats blamed higher prices on the tariff. White southerners rose in alarm at the threat of a full and fair black vote. Reformers considered the pensions a steal, and in the Midwest, Republicans ran into trouble when they tried to regulate parochial and German-language schools—the first step, immigrants cried, to foisting their own values on Catholic children. In 1890 voters put the Democrats back in control of the House of Representatives. Two years later, Cleveland won the presidency, this time with an outright majority.

Government Activism and Its Limits

Two themes dominate the traditional impression of late nineteenth-century political history: first, brazen corruption and second, limited government that left the new industrial economy to develop as it pleased. The real heroes, according to this view, were those outside the party system, the Liberals and Populists, the moral crusaders and insurgents. While corruption was a problem, the above view falls short as a true picture of the age.

Only by later standards was the national government limited. When peace came, Congress cut taxes, trimmed the army to a mere 25,000 men, and virtually abandoned any oceangoing navy. Yet it never returned to its proportions or role in 1861. Civilian federal employees rose from 53,000 in 1871 to 256,000 30 years later. Congress created a Department of Justice in 1870 and a Department of Agriculture in 1888. The postal service tripled in size over a quarter of a century, delivering 7 billion pieces of mail in 1900. More than a quarter of the national budget in 1900 went for veterans' pensions, awarded to over a million veterans and their dependents.

AMERICA AND THE WORLD

>> # Foreign Policy: The Limited Significance of Commercial Expansion

Money was not everything: neither in domestic politics nor in foreign policy. In the 1860s, Secretary of State William Henry Seward shifted the emphasis of American foreign policy from the acquisition of territory to the expansion of American commerce. Working to open markets in the Americas and across the Pacific, Seward saw the nation's influence following its trade. He still dreamed of a nation extending beyond the water's edge. What he discovered was that, however adventurous American empire builders had been, the war had made them stingy in paying for new domains, either in money or in lives.

Seward's biggest success came in 1867, when the Senate ratified the treaty purchasing Alaska from Russia for $7.2 million. A few months later, however, the Senate rejected a treaty buying the Virgin Islands from Denmark and held off on leasing a naval base in Santo Domingo. Nor did a treaty with Colombia to give the United States exclusive rights to build a canal across the Isthmus of Panama come to anything. Despite some informal overtures, Canada showed no interest in joining the Union, either wholly or piecemeal. Instead, it forged a union of its own provinces and built a transcontinental railroad line.

Not all the wealth of the Indies (the West Indies, at any rate) could carry the United States beyond trade to the taking of territory. Slavery's end killed most of the zest for annexing Cuba. When a rebellion broke out there in 1868, congressmen mouthed sympathetic speeches but did nothing more. Grant's secretary of state Hamilton Fish had no intention of America absorbing half a million Cubans of "every shade and mixture of color." Similar inhibitions were among the reasons the Senate rejected President Grant's annexation treaty with Santo Domingo in 1870, but there were others: the stench of corruption around the scheme's chief promoters and the threat it posed to the country's black neighbor, Haiti.

Expansionism in the Gilded Age, then, meant expanding markets, and even then not always through government action. Between 1860 and 1897, American exports tripled, surpassing $1 billion per year. In 1874, for the first time, Americans sold more than they bought. Nearly 85 percent of those exports were farm goods, but the share of industrial exports grew prodigiously as the century closed. Between 1889 and 1898, iron and steel exports jumped by 230 percent.

Mexico provided a different example of commercial expansion: investment abroad. Political instability had hindered investment, but Porfirio Díaz's seizure of power in 1876 brought decades of reassuring autocracy—at least for investors. They rushed south to build railroads, dig oil wells, sell life insurance, and invest in commercial farming. By 1910 Americans owned 43 percent of all the property in Mexico; Mexicans owned rather less.

continued

AMERICA AND THE WORLD *continued*

Secretaries of state reaffirmed Seward's commitment to commercial expansion. Treaties with Japan and Korea opened new Asian markets. A treaty with King Kalakua of Hawaii gave the islands' sugar favored treatment on the American market, prompting a huge influx into the United States (along with a backlash by sugar producers on the mainland). Worried that European nations would divert Latin American commerce from the United States, Secretary of State James G. Blaine became the champion of "reciprocity," breaking down American trade barriers in return for special access to foreign markets. In 1889, he convened the first Pan-American conference. Concern for access to foreign markets pushed successive administrations to assert America's exclusive right to build a canal across Central America. But that motive never stood alone—not in a world that every year Americans could see being devoured by European empires, and where Britain's and Germany's flags (and artillery) so often followed where their loans and exporters had ventured first.

Beyond that, America steered clear of foreign entanglements. In the 1880s, the United States, Germany, and England rattled sabers over disputed claims in Samoa; a riot in Valparaiso led to threats of naval force against Chile; and "jingoes," as friends of an aggressive foreign policy were called, complained about English mistreatment of Irish patriots and British claims in Latin America. If they had gotten their way, America would have gone to war to punish Spanish "insolence" in stopping American gunrunners to Cuba and to punish Cana-

dian claims to sovereignty over the offshore fisheries and seal islands. They got no war.

Still, by the 1890s there were inklings of a new American assertiveness, mixing economic interest and a sense of America's mission to spread democracy. That showed itself most clearly in Hawaii. By 1886 two-thirds of the islands' sugar was produced on American-owned plantations. American power in Hawaii grew so great that it provoked a backlash among native Hawaiians. Queen Liliuokalani's ascension to the throne in 1891 meant trouble for sugar growers. Two years later, they helped Hawaiians dethrone the queen and appealed for the United States to annex the islands. Undeceived by white planters pretending to speak for a Polynesian people, the Cleveland administration refused, but McKinley's carried annexation through. Nobody dreamed of statehood for so dark-skinned and foreign an electorate.

Only in the late 1880s did America's hemispheric interests begin to shape military policy. In 1890 Congress approved the construction of the first modern warships, and the Supreme Court extended the president's control over "our international relations." The growing links between commercial and diplomatic interests were reviving the powers of the American presidency. But as the story of domestic politics has made clear, those links were never the whole story—nor did the scramble for markets make America forge a steel navy in a world grown different and more dangerous.

By the turn of the century, the rudiments of a modern federal government were in place. The Interstate Commerce Commission was able to compel safety machinery like automatic brakes and coupling devices on trains, but it lacked the power to enforce its own rulings, especially where unfair rates were concerned. It had to rely on courts friendly to government action protecting health, safety, and morals, but distrustful of any interference in the marketplace. Crippled by a damaging Supreme Court ruling in 1895, the weak Sherman Anti-Trust Act threatened few monopolies. In both cases, government action had not yet lived up to its potential. By comparison, state and municipal governments responded more aggressively to the problems of a transforming society.

States Discover Activism

Americans continued to clamor for state constitutions restricting government powers. They resented tax hikes and objected to bureaucrats. They had good reasons to distrust their officials. Lobbyists swarmed the capitols. Standard Oil did everything to the Pennsylvania legislators except refine them, a critic complained. Railroad tycoons, silver-mine owners, and copper kings bought themselves Senate seats, and the insurance lobby in New York spent tens of thousands of dollars making friends in Albany every year.

But lawmakers kept doing more every year—and that, contradictory as it might seem, was what Americans also seem to have wanted. In spite of lobbyists, corporation taxes went up. So did spending. Public school systems expanded. School years lengthened. In 20 years, spending per pupil doubled, and in almost every state outside the South, attendance became compulsory. "Tramp laws" jailed jobless workers for bad reputations or "criminal idleness." Upset that customers might buy "butterine," made from animal or vegetable fats, dairy farmers got legislatures to require the new name "oleomargarine" and, in some places, in unappetizing colors like pink. Unions put through laws establishing Labor Day and setting up fact-finding bureaus of labor statistics. Hundreds of laws went through to protect women workers or keep children out of the coal mines, to forbid employers paying their workers in company-issued paper money, "scrip," and even to set up arbitration machinery, so that industrial disputes could be settled by negotiation rather than confrontation. The laws promised more than they performed: enforcement was sometimes spotty or nonexistent—much less stringent than for laws forbidding boycotting of shop owners and picketing by strikers. The courts weakened or killed many statutes, especially the ones that regulated workers' hours.

Cities: Boss Rule and New Responsibilities

States also intervened to help govern the swelling municipalities. One reason for that was the cities' reputation for boss rule and control by party machines such as New York City's Tammany Hall. With urban services expanding so fast, the city government had more than enough jobs to do, and every job bought the machine a friend. Trading services for votes, the ward and precinct captains working for the "boss" made government matter in the most personal way. But as reformers pointed out, the money to do that had to come from somewhere: shakedowns and graft, perhaps; protection money from gamblers and saloon keepers; and forced donations from storekeepers afraid to have an enemy in City Hall. Government by two-bit politicians out to line their own pockets meant rotten government, and in many ways poorer neighborhoods suffered most. Boss rule meant garbage-choked streets, tenements that were firetraps, and police and fire chiefs turning their services into party armies.

Richard Croker as the Sun, by Udo J. Keppler, *Puck Magazine,* **March 30, 1898** Richard Croker, the boss of Tammany Hall, purportedly dominated New York City at the turn of the century. Police, gamblers, law-makers, and street sweepers all depended on him for contracts, jobs, or political protection.

Scandals and abuses gave legislatures the excuse to shift authority away from partisan elected officials to experts and specialists on unelected boards. Mayors, city council members, and aldermen lost much of their authority over budgets, schools, health, transportation, police, and parks to commissions generally staffed by middle-class professionals. The commissioners found help among city reformers, and in many cases, the bosses did not put up much of a fight. With competing private fire companies no longer rushing to a fire and beating each other up, with patrolmen no longer paying a kickback for their appointment and expected to take it out of saloons, prostitutes, and shopkeepers, the quality of the fire and police departments could only improve.

Bosses were never the uncrowned emperors reformers made them out to be. Nowhere, not even in Tammany's New York, did they have total power. They had to accommodate interest groups, including labor and reform organizations. That was one reason why, in the late nineteenth century, city governments provided broader social services than anywhere else and produced some of the century's great urban achievements: New York's Central Park, San Francisco's Golden Gate Park, and the Brooklyn Bridge. Chicagoans literally reversed the flow of the Chicago River.

Middle-Class Radicalism

In the late nineteenth century, middle-class radicals argued that economic development had undermined individual liberty and equality. Yet although their attacks on capitalism were severe, their assumptions were traditional. They often worried that without substantial reforms, a discontented working class would threaten private property and social order. Their radical critiques of industrial society exposed deep wells of discontent among Americans.

Henry George and the Limits of Producers' Ideology

Henry George was born in Philadelphia in 1839 to middle-class parents. Although his formal education was limited, George traveled and read widely. Shocked that as the nation grew richer its number of poor people grew as well, he published his conclusions in 1879 in a best-selling book called *Progress and Poverty*.

George's explanation rested on what historians have called producers' ideology. He assumed that only human labor could create legitimate wealth and that anything of value, such as food, clothing, or steel rails, came from the world's producing classes. By contrast, stockbrokers, bankers, and speculators made money from money rather than from the goods they produced. Their wealth was therefore illegitimate. From these premises, George divided the world into two classes: producers and predators.

The harmony of capital and labor was a central theme of producers' ideology. Henry George dreamed of a world in which working people owned their own farms and shops, making them both capitalists and laborers, a vision that recalled Thomas Jefferson's ideal society of small farmers and independent shopkeepers. America used to be that way, George believed, but as society "progressed," the land was monopolized by a wealthy few. Producers were forced to work for wealthy landholders. Employers invested in technology that increased the productivity of their workers but kept the added wealth for themselves. George's solution was a so-called Single Tax on rents. Because all wealth derived from labor applied to land, he reasoned, rents were an unnatural transfer of wealth from the producers to the landlords. To discourage the landowning class from accumulating land,

John F. Weir's 1877 Painting *Forging the Shaft: A Welding Heat* This painting graphically depicts the forms of industrial wage labor that Henry George feared. He advocated tax policies that would restore a Jeffersonian economy of small, independent producers.

George suggested prohibitively high taxes on rents and improvements on land. All other taxes would be abolished, including the tariffs protecting big business.

George was no socialist. He presented his Single Tax as an alternative to the dangerous radical doctrines he thought were spreading among the working class. But his work challenged social Darwinists' idea that those who were poor owed it to their own inadequacies, and that the rich owed their place to their superiority. George depicted a world in which the system itself had made a cluster of winners and a host of losers, and in which government policy could right the balance.

Edward Bellamy and the Nationalist Clubs

In 1888 Edward Bellamy, a Massachusetts editor, published a best-selling critique of capitalism even more powerful than Henry George's. Bellamy's *Looking Backward* was a utopian novel set in the future, where technology had raised the standard of living for all. Industrial civilization's problems had been solved by overcoming the "excessive individualism" of Bellamy's day. Progress came, not through social Darwinism's competition, but through its opposite: cooperation. Where *Progress and Poverty* proposed the restoration of the simple virtues of Jeffersonian society, *Looking Backward* imagined a high-tech future filled with consumer goods. In Bellamy's ideal world, production and consumption would no longer be subject to the whims of the market; instead, they would be harmonized by "nationalism," an obscure process of centralized planning. *Looking Backward* catered to a middle-class craving for order amidst the chaos of industrial society. Decisions about what to produce were made collectively, and society as a whole owned the means of production. Where Henry George reasserted the values of hard work and self-restraint, Edward Bellamy embraced the modern cult of leisure and looked to the day when there would be little need for government. This vision inspired thousands of middle-class Americans to form "Bellamy Clubs" or "Nationalist Clubs," particularly in New England.

Discontent Among Workers

Radicalized workers agreed that mainstream politics could not confront the problems of industrial capitalism. They questioned one of the premises of producers' ideology—that American democracy was secured by a unique harmony between capital and labor. Labor agitation often became violent. But if the harmony of capital and labor had been destroyed, advocates of the producers' ideology continued to hold faith in political solutions to the labor problem.

The Knights of Labor and the Haymarket Disaster

Between 1860 and 1890, wages overall grew by 50 percent, but elite skilled and semiskilled workers in a handful of industries, such as printing and metalworking, got the lion's share of the gains. The vast majority of workers suffered directly from deflation and economic instability. By 1880, 40 percent of industrial workers lived at or below the poverty line, and the average worker was unemployed for 15 to 20 percent of the year. To relieve their plight, American workers sought political solutions to economic problems.

Before the Gilded Age, labor organizations had never attracted many workers. The tradition of individuals lifting themselves up bred a suspicion of collective solutions. In 1869, some Philadelphia garment makers formed the Noble and Holy Order of the

Knights of Labor. The Knights was inspired by the producers' ideology and admitted everyone from self-employed farmers to unskilled factory workers. Stressing the need for uplift and temperance, the Knights advocated a host of reforms, including the eight-hour day, equal pay for men and women, the abolition of child and prison labor, inflation of the currency to counteract the deflationary spiral, and a national income tax.

By the late 1870s the union needed a strong national organization to hold various locals together. A new constitution required all members to pay dues and allowed the national organization to support local boycotts and thereby boost its credibility among workers. Open to women as well as men, skilled and unskilled, black and white (but not Chinese), the Knights grew rapidly, from 19,000 members in 1881 to 111,000 in 1885. Terence Powderly, leader of this largely working-class movement, believed in neither socialism nor the notion that there was any necessary conflict between labor and capital. Wage earners were "producers," and he meant to overthrow "wage slavery," not capitalism itself. Powderly favored arbitration and conciliation over confrontation, and the consumer boycott over the strike. Local assemblies struck anyhow. They even forced a settlement out of the railroads of the Southwest, including those of the notorious Jay Gould, who had bragged that he "could hire one half of the working class to kill the other half." The Knights' lobbying helped put through the Chinese exclusion act in 1882 and a federal law against imported contract labor three years later. By 1886 membership swelled to nearly a quarter of a million. Labor parties elected mayors and city councilmen; only vote fraud kept them from making Henry George mayor of New York. They even talked of fielding a presidential ticket.

But the more the Knights of Labor grew, the more the strains among its members showed. Shopkeepers and small-factory owners had very different interests from wage laborers, especially when it came to strikes. By 1886 work stoppages were twice what they had been the year before. The "Great Upheaval" had begun. The more Knights there were, the more militant they sounded.

The culmination came when trade unions called for a nationwide strike for the eight-hour day. On May 1, 1886, workers across the country walked off their jobs in one of the largest labor walkouts in American history. In Chicago 80,000 workers went out on strike. The Chicago strike was largely peaceful until May 4, when, at an anarchist rally at Haymarket Square, someone from the crowd tossed a bomb into a line of police. Eight policemen were killed. Police shot into the crowd. Four people died. Many more were wounded. The bomb thrower was never identified.

Anarchists—who questioned the legitimacy of all government power—had little influence on the labor movement, but their fiery rhetoric invoking the use of violence made them conspicuous. In a blatantly unfair trial with perjured testimony, eight of them were found guilty of inciting the "Haymarket riot." Four were hanged, one committed suicide, and the others went to prison. (In 1893, Governor Peter Altgeld pardoned the survivors. He knew it would doom him politically; it did.) Haymarket was a turning point in American labor politics. A wave of revulsion against labor agitation swept the country, and with it state antilabor laws. The Knights never recovered from the Haymarket disaster.

Agrarian Revolt

The late nineteenth century was a desperate time for American farmers in the grain and cotton belts of the West and South. To compete, they had to buy expensive agricultural equipment, often from manufacturers who benefited from tariff protection. Then they had to ship their goods on railroads that charged higher rates to small farmers than to big industrialists. At the market, they faced steadily declining prices.

A global economy put southern cotton in competition with cotton from India and Egypt. Western wheat competed with Russian and eastern European wheat. To keep up, farmers increasingly went into debt, and in a deflationary spiral the money they borrowed to plant their crops was worth more when it came time to pay it back, whereas their crops were worth less. The proportion of owner-occupied farms declined, and the number of tenants rose. A few years of drought meant ruin on the plains. "In God we trusted, in Kansas we busted," one departing farmer wrote on his wagon.

Scattered over large sections of the country, farmers were committed to an ideology of economic independence and cool to government intervention. The industrial transformation of the late nineteenth century taught many of them that they could no longer stand alone. One of the first attempts to organize farmers was the Patrons of Husbandry, generally called the Grange. The Grange claimed 1.5 million members by 1874. Consistent with producers' ideology, the Grange organized cooperatives to eliminate the role of merchants and creditors. By storing grain collectively, farmers held their products back from the market in the hope of gaining control over commodity prices. But inexperience made the Grange cooperatives difficult to organize and sustain. After 1875 their membership dwindled.

The National Farmers' Alliance and Industrial Union, known simply as the Farmers' Alliance, was much more effective than the Grange. Founded in Texas in 1877, the Alliance spread rapidly across the South and West. Its goal was not to restore rural Jeffersonian simplicity but to bring American farmers into the modern world of industry and prosperity. The Alliance focused above all on education, broadly conceived. That meant public schools and the spread of scientific agriculture and sound business practices. The Alliance also built its own network of newspapers and lecturers to free farmers from their isolation. For rural men and women alike, the Farmers' Alliance offered the chance to share in the progress and prosperity of American life.

At its core the Alliance was a reform organization calling for a specific set of economic policies. Above all, the farmers wanted to inflate the currency, whether by the circulation

>> Time Line

▼1867
United States purchases Alaska from Russia
Patrons of Husbandry (the Grange) founded

▼1869
Noble and Holy Order of the Knights of Labor founded
Suez Canal opened

▼1870
Department of Justice created

▼1872
Grant reelected

▼1873
"Crusade" against alcohol begins in Hillsboro, Ohio

▼1874
WCTU is formed

▼1876
Rutherford B. Hayes elected president
Porfirio Díaz seizes power in Mexico

▼1877
Farmers' Alliance founded

▼1878
Bland-Allison Act

▼1879
Frances Willard becomes president of the WCTU
Henry George publishes *Progress and Poverty*

▼1880
James Garfield elected president

▼1881
Garfield assassinated; Chester Arthur becomes president
WCTU endorses women's suffrage

of more silver currency or of more paper currency ("greenbacks") or a combination of the two. Inspired by the successes of highly organized corporations, especially railroads, the Alliance also supported a system of cooperative "subtreasuries" that would provide low-interest loans, backed by farmers' crops, held until the best prices were available.

By the late 1880s the Farmers' Alliance had drawn millions of members, concentrated in the southern, western, and plains states. Created at a huge meeting at Ocala, Florida, in 1890, the Ocala Platform supported a host of new policies that joined economic progress to democratic reform. The platform called for the free coinage of silver, lower tariffs, government subtreasuries, and a constitutional amendment providing for direct election of senators. Finally, the Alliance called for strict government regulation, and if necessary direct government ownership, of the railroad and telegraph industries.

The Farmers' Alliance steered clear of politics and instead judged political candidates by their support of the Ocala Platform reforms. They elected shoals of congressmen and even a few senators by cooperating with Democrats in the West and, where neither party gave satisfaction, by running independent candidates. Out of these efforts came the most significant third party of the late nineteenth century, the People's Party, otherwise known as the Populists.

The Rise of the Populists

On February 22, 1892, a coalition of reform organizations met in St. Louis, including representatives of the Knights of Labor and the Farmers' Alliance. Together they founded the People's Party. At Omaha on July 4, they nominated General James B. Weaver of Iowa for president and drew up the Omaha Platform, demanding an inflationary currency policy and a subtreasury system. The Populists also called for a graduated income tax, direct government ownership of railroads and telegraph lines, and the confiscation of railroad land grants. But they also spoke for a government restored to the people by a secret ballot, popularly elected senators, and the power of voters to make laws for themselves by initiative and referendum.

▼**1883**
Pendleton Civil Service Act

▼**1884**
Grover Cleveland elected president

▼**1886**
Nationwide strike for eight-hour day
Riot at Haymarket Square in Chicago

▼**1887**
Interstate Commerce Act
Four Haymarket anarchists executed
Dawes Severalty Act

▼**1888**
Benjamin Harrison elected president
Edward Bellamy publishes *Looking Backward*

▼**1889**
United States convenes first Pan-American Conference
Department of Agriculture created

▼**1890**
McKinley Tariff
Sherman Anti-Trust Act
Sherman Silver-Purchase Act
Ocala Platform

▼**1891**
Queen Liliuokalani assumes the Hawaiian throne

▼**1892**
Omaha Platform of the People's Party
Grover Cleveland reelected

▼**1893**
Queen Liliuokalani overthrown

▼**1898**
Frances Willard dies

Kansas Farmers Organizing to Attend a Populist Party Gathering

Populism took in more than wheat and cotton farmers. Small ranchers joined to fight the politically privileged cattle kings. Townspeople joined to oppose the railroads. Prohibitionists and woman suffragists found friends aplenty in the People's Party. Rallies took on the spirit of a revival, with speakers promising a return to the lost promise of the Revolution. In the 1892 elections Weaver won about 1 million votes, and the Populists elected several senators, representatives, governors, and state legislators. But wage earners in the industrial North and East still held back. The Populist platform, for all its talk of the unity of the toiling masses, offered industrial workers little. They depended on the protective tariff to shield them from cheap foreign labor. Higher prices for the farmer meant price hikes in the stores, when most workers had no hope of raising their wages to keep up. They knew how paper money worked: many were paid in company-issued "scrip," redeemable only at the company store at a steep discount. Conversely, farmers who hired workers had no zeal for an eight-hour day or laws restricting child labor. Wherever the Populists were strong, mainstream parties adopted their most popular causes.

Southern Populists faced a particularly difficult challenge. To win, they needed help from the largest class of impoverished farmers, black sharecroppers. Only by downplaying racial differences could they make such a coalition work. Not all whites could overcome their prejudices. The Farmers' Alliance had always been strictly segregated, with a separate Colored Farmers' Alliance. And in fact the economic interests of the two groups were not always compatible. Black leaders appreciated the limits of any alliance with white reformers, and most black southerners kept voting Republican. Coalitions between Republicans and Populists sometimes came about. But any multiracial alliance inspired the ugliest race-baiting that Democrats could devise, to break the partners apart and restore the color line. It gave them all the excuse they needed to stuff ballot boxes, count votes creatively, and remake the laws to cut as many Populists, white and black, out of the suffrage as possible—always in the name of reform.

Conclusion

Luna Kellie was not alone in seeing a nation on the edge of catastrophe by the early 1890s. Americans still went to the polls in record numbers, but the political system was showing serious strains. Strident voices rose, against Catholics, foreigners, Negroes, and Jews. Farmers cried out against the "Money Power." Bloody strikes convulsed the coalfields and Carnegie's mills. Culture wars disrupted politics in the Midwest, while southern Democrats fended off political challengers by invoking white supremacy in its rawest form. In big cities, reformers cried that boss rule had replaced government by the people. But Gilded Age politics offered more hope than it appeared. In its tumultuous variety, it showed a country bursting with reform impulses, and with the energy to regenerate a nation in crisis.

Who, What

Henry George 583

Luna Kellie 567

Terence Powderly 585

James B. Weaver 587

Frances Willard 570

Farmers' Alliance 586

Greenbackers 574

Knights of Labor 584

Mugwumps 572

Nationalist Clubs 584

Omaha Platform 587

Patronage 575

Pendleton Act 576

Political machine 568

Populism 588

Sherman Anti-Trust Act 577

Spoils system 568

Subtreasury 587

Tammany Hall 568

Temperance 570

WCTU 570

Review Questions

1. Describe the two major "styles" of politics in the late nineteenth century.

2. Describe the changes in the roles of national, state, and local government during this period.

3. What did Henry George, Edward Bellamy, and Frances Willard have in common? What did the Farmers' Alliance stand for?

Critical-Thinking Questions

1. Why did so many people participate in politics in the late nineteenth century? What did they expect to get out of it?

2. To what extent did the Industrial revolution described in Chapter 17 affect politics and the issues politicians discussed in this period?

3. What were the major challenges to "politics as usual" in this age, and where did those challenges come from? Why did they arise, and how successful were they in remaking American society?

For further review materials and resource information, please visit www.oup.com/us/ofthepeople

1) The exuberance and competitiveness of party politics created a stalemated national political system.

2) A fiercely competitive political system did not prevent a sharp increase in government activism during the Gilded Age.

3) Frustration at the pace of policy change made farmers, workers, and the middle class look for alternatives.

4) A relatively inactive national government coexisted with activist state and local governments.

TOPICS

Two Political Styles

Economic Issues Dominate National Politics

Government Activism and Its Limits

Middle-Class Radicalism

Discontent Among Workers

THE POLITICS OF INDUSTRIAL AMERICA

1870–1892

EVENTS

The Triumph of Party Politics Fiercely competitive party politics dominated the age.

Masculine Partisanship and Feminine Voluntarism Political activity came in two forms—the male politics of parties, elections, and street theater; and the female politics of persuasion and moral influence.

The Women's Christian Temperance Union The antialcohol WCTU showed how far women, even without the vote, could affect policy and define the issues.

The Critics of Popular Politics Liberal reformers sought government by experts who would be above partisan concerns.

The Enemy at the Gates Unable to curb European immigration, Protestants used cultural politics to control immigrants.

Greenbacks and Greenbackers Americans debated whether or not to back paper money with only gold reserves or with both silver and gold reserves.

Weak Presidents Oversee a Stronger Federal Government Presidents had trouble breaking the political stalemate in Washington.

States Discover Activism Even as voters put new limits on state governments, they expected more services from government—and got them.

Cities: Boss Rule and New Responsibilities Rapidly growing cities turned to political machines and independent commissions to cope with unprecedented demands.

Henry George and the Limits of Producers' Ideology Henry George imagined an ideal society with harmony between capital and labor.

Edward Bellamy and the Nationalist Clubs Edward Bellamy's book challenged the unregulated, competitive ideal of Gilded Age capitalism.

The Knights of Labor and the Haymarket Disaster Workers organized, but a nationwide strike led to violence that caused a backlash.

Agrarian Revolt Suffering from overproduction and deflation, farmers organized in their own defense.

The Rise of the Populists A coalition of reform organizations established a new political party but found a breakthrough elusive.

CHAPTER 20

Industry and Empire
1890–1900

>> J. P. Morgan

It was a short distance from the Arlington Hotel to the White House, and although it was icy and dark, J. Pierpont Morgan chose to walk. He pulled his scarf up around a scowling face known to millions of newspaper readers. He had not wanted to come to Washington. There were "large interests" that depended on keeping the currency of the United States sound, he told a Treasury official, and those interests were now in jeopardy. The commander in chief of the nation's bankers was going to meet the president to keep the United States from going bankrupt.

The events leading up to this meeting stretched back five years to 1890, when business failures toppled London's Baring Brothers investment house and triggered a collapse in European stock prices. Depression spread through Britain, Germany, and France. Anxious European investors began selling off their large American holdings. In early 1893 the panic reached the United States. The Philadelphia and Reading Railroad folded in February. Fourteen thousand businesses soon followed, along with more than 600 banks.

Summer brought more bad news from abroad. The government of India stopped minting silver, causing US silver dollars to lose one-sixth of their value. Wall Street went into another tailspin. In New York 55,000 men, women, and girls in the clothing industry were thrown out of work. Banks refused to cash checks, and coins vanished from circulation. Tens of thousands of homeless poor people filled the roads. Breadlines formed. "The world surely cannot remain as mad as it is," the historian Henry Adams observed.

For Grover Cleveland the madness was only starting. The anger of workers and farmers, simmering for decades, was boiling over. The president pledged to keep the dollar on the gold standard, but it was not enough. A wave of strikes swept the country. Unemployed workers battled police on the Capitol grounds. By January 1895 so many panicky investors

continued

were cashing government bonds that the Treasury's gold reserve was half gone, and it looked as if the remainder might last only two weeks. Reluctantly, Cleveland agreed to open negotiations with Morgan.

Admired and reviled, Morgan was known as the leading financial manipulator of the late nineteenth century. Born to wealth in Hartford, Connecticut, he had been a Wall Street fixture since before the Civil War. Like his contemporaries, steelmaker Andrew Carnegie and oil magnate John D. Rockefeller, Morgan's skill lay in organization. He restructured railroads, rooting out corruption, waste, and competition and driving down wages. Instead of taking risks, he eliminated them. He convinced leaders of warring firms to strike bargains and share the profits. Cleveland was about to place the Treasury in this man's hands.

The president opened the meeting by suggesting that things might not be so bad; a new bond issue might stabilize the Treasury. No, Morgan replied flatly, the run on gold would continue until European investors regained confidence. If the president agreed, Morgan would arrange a private loan and personally guarantee the solvency of the US Treasury. After a stunned silence, the two men shook hands. News of the deal instantly calmed the bond markets. The crisis was over. The *New York Sun* reported that the deal "revived a confidence in the wealth and resources of this country," but Populist newspapers denounced it as a conspiracy and a "great bunco game."

Culminating two decades of turbulence, the Panic of 1893 permanently transformed the American political economy. Businessmen such as Morgan created even larger corporate combinations and placed them under professional managers. They used technology and "scientific management" to control the workplace and push laborers to work faster and harder. Workers resisted, and the 1890s saw brutal clashes between capital and labor. Looking for jobs and schools, country people moved to the city and found both promise and danger. Social mobility among African Americans aroused fears in whites, and southerners created a system of formal segregation, enforced by law and terror. Amid growing violence, industrial workers, Native Americans, and African Americans debated how best to deal with the overwhelming forces ranged against them.

The 1890s were also a turning point in American political history. After the 1896 election, many Americans walked away from the electoral process. Others were removed from the voter rolls through a process known as "disfranchisement." African American leaders and union organizers urged their followers to turn away from politics in favor of "bread and butter" economic issues. The masculine, public spectacle of nineteenth-century politics with its parades and flag raisings died out. Patriotism, once synonymous with partisanship, now stood for America's global military and economic ambitions. Civic events featured army bands and cannon salutes. Newspapers conjured up foreign threats. As Americans became more conscious of their military power, they watched the horizon for threats to their well-being.

Americans began to feel that their economy's links to the world—and the changes wrought by manufacturing and rapid communications—separated their times from all that had happened before. Morgan's rescue required transactions on two continents, instantaneously coordinated by telegraph. The speed of industry, trade, and information, the way machines and technology spanned distance and time created a sense that the environment and the future could be controlled. Many felt that those who possessed this newfound control—citizens of modern countries—stood apart from those in other lands whose lives were not guided by science and information.

Between 1890 and 1900 Americans made their country recognizably modern. Those with the means to do so enlarged and refashioned many aspects of work and daily life. Financiers and giant corporations assumed control of the economy. Huge cities grew. The significance of voting declined, and a decade that opened with a global economic catastrophe ended with a dramatic display of the global reach of US power.

The Crisis of the 1890s

Financial convulsions, strikes, and the powerlessness of government against wealth rudely reminded Americans of how much their country had changed since the Civil War. When Illinois sent Abraham Lincoln to Congress, Chicago's population was less than 5,000; in 1890 it exceeded 1 million. Gone was the America of myth and memory, in which class tensions were slight and upward (or at least westward) mobility seemed easy. Many Americans foresaw the collapse of civilization. Others, however, felt that the United States was passing into a new phase of history that would lead to still greater trials and achievements.

Hard Times

Chicago in 1893 captured the hopes and fears of the new age. To celebrate the 400th anniversary of Columbus's discovery of America, the city staged the World's Columbian Exposition, transforming a lakefront bog into a gleaming vision of the past and the future. Just outside the exposition's gates was the city of the present. In December 1893 Chicago had 75,000 unemployed, and the head of a local relief committee declared that "famine is in our midst." In the nation's second-largest city, thousands lived in shacks or high-rise tenements with only a single bathroom on each densely packed floor. Jobs were scarce, and when men gathered at the exposition's gates to beg for work, the police drove them away.

As the depression deepened, the Cleveland administration ordered troops to guard Treasury branches in New York and Chicago. Jobless people banded together into "industrial armies," many with decidedly revolutionary aims. Hundreds heeded the call of Jacob Coxey, an Ohio landowner and Populist. In 1894 Coxey urged the unemployed to march on Washington and demand free silver and a public road-building program that would hire a half-million workers. When Coxey set out with 100 followers, reporters predicted the ragged band would disintegrate as soon as food ran out, but well-wishers turned out by the thousands to greet the Coxeyites with supplies for the trip.

Industrial armies set out from Boston, St. Louis, Chicago, Portland, Seattle, and Los Angeles. When Coxey arrived in Washington on May 1 with 500 marchers, Cleveland put the US Army on alert. The march ended ignominiously. In front of the Capitol, police arrested Coxey, and his disillusioned army dispersed. Still, no one could deny that something was seriously wrong and that, as Ray Stannard Baker, a reporter for the *Chicago Record*, noted, "the conditions in the country warranted some such explosion."

The Overseas Frontier

At noon on September 16, 1893, thousands of settlers massed along the borders of the Cherokee Strip, a 6-million-acre tract in northwestern Oklahoma. In the next six hours the last great land rush came to an end, and the line of settlement long marked on census maps ceased to exist.

Frederick Jackson Turner, a historian at the University of Wisconsin, described the implications of this event. Steady westward movement had placed Americans in "touch with the simplicity of primitive life," he explained, and helped renew the process of social development. The frontier furnished "the forces dominating the American character," and without its rejuvenating influence, democracy itself might be in danger. Turner's thesis resonated with Americans' fears that modernity had robbed their country of its unique strengths and that the end of free lands would put free institutions at risk. "There is no unexplored part of the world left suitable for men to inhabit," Populist writer William "Coin" Harvey claimed.

That assertion turned out to be premature. More homesteaders claimed more western lands after 1890 than before, and well into the next century new "resource frontiers"—oil fields, timber ranges, Alaskan ore strikes—were explored. Irrigation technology and markets for new crops created a boom for dry-land farmers. Nonetheless, the upheavals of the 1890s seemed to confirm Turner's contention that new frontiers lay overseas.

Whereas farmers had always needed to sell a large portion of their output abroad, until the 1890s the market for manufactured goods was almost exclusively domestic. As the volume of manufactured goods increased, the composition of exports changed. Oil, steel, textiles, typewriters, and sewing machines made up a larger portion of overseas trade. Americans still bought nine-tenths of domestic manufactures, but by 1898 the extra tenth was worth more than $1 billion (see Figure 20–1).

As American firms entered foreign markets, they discovered that other nations and empires also used restrictive tariffs to guard their markets and promote domestic manufacturing. Government and business leaders saw that the United States might have to use political or military leverage to open foreign markets to gain a larger share of world trade. Their social Darwinist view of the world—as a jungle in which only the fittest nations would survive—justified the global competition for trade and economic survival.

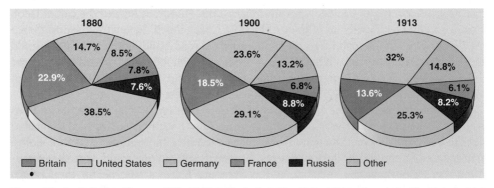

Figure 20–1   Relative Shares of World Manufacturing The United States was a significant industrial power by 1880, but by the turn of the century it moved into a position of dominance.

AMERICA AND THE WORLD

>> Singer Sewing Machine Company

Before the Russian Revolution, on St. Petersburg's grandest boulevard, the Nevskii Prospekt, the headquarters of the Singer Sewing Machine Company was Russia's tallest building. Completed in 1904, the six-story Kompaniya Singer tower was topped by an illuminated globe bearing the name "Singer" in gilded letters. It symbolized the global reach of one of America's preeminent manufacturers.

Isaac Merrit Singer did not invent the sewing machine; he invented a way to market it. Elias Howe, who applied for the first US patent in 1845, invented a device with an oscillating needle that made a locking stitch fed from spools turning on an overhanging arm. It seemed a practical, labor-saving device, but Howe found that tailors and shoemakers who made a living by hand sewing had no use for it. His principal customers viewed the gadget with hostility.

Singer, a machinist from Rochester, New York, made Howe's device smaller, added a decorative cabinet, and sold it as an article for the home. He employed young women to demonstrate the machine in shopfront "sewing centers." Salesmen went door to door, and in the 1880s, Singer introduced buying on the "installment" plan, whereby customers could purchase a new machine by putting down a dollar a week. It was a "psychological fact," he asserted, that "a woman would rather pay $100" in installments "than $50 outright." By 1867, Singer was the largest manufacturer of sewing machines in the world, producing 43,000 a year.

The federal government aided this growth in two ways. First, the need for military uniforms during the Civil War outstripped the capacities of hand tailors, and Singer promoted machine sewing as a woman's patriotic duty. "We Clothe the Union Army," the company proclaimed. Second, the government imposed a 35 percent tariff on imported sewing machines, preventing European makers from challenging Singer in its home market.

With its domestic base secure, Singer expanded. By 1890, it had an international merchandising network that sold three-quarters of the world's sewing machines. The sales formula did not work everywhere. In India, agents complained that they were not allowed to speak to women. Chinese merchants were suspicious of the "iron tailor." A Singer representative in Charkoff, Russia, was ordered to leave on the grounds that he was "a foreign Jew." In Japan, however, the adoption of Western-style military uniforms during the Sino-Japanese War (1894–1895) provided a ready market for the machines among Japanese outfitters. Europe, the Philippines, Mexico, and Russia all became significant markets.

Alarmed by Singer's success, European governments began protecting their colonial and home markets. In 1893, French courts ordered Singer to reveal information about its earnings and stock dividends. Other governments raised import taxes or set quotas to exclude American machines. Singer responded by forming separate national subsidiaries that could claim local, rather than American, origin. When the Spanish-American War broke out in 1898, the Singer offices in Madrid flew the Spanish flag and donated

continued

AMERICA AND THE WORLD *continued*

to the war fund. The locals were not fooled, however. The newspaper *El País* called Singer "an immense octopus whose tentacles encircle Spain and crush it" in order to "aggrandize the miserable, iniquitous, cowardly, disgusting North American nation."

The company prided itself on bringing democracy and fair dealing to the world. In the Middle East, Singer machines carried the brand *Hurriya*, Arabic for "freedom." By the turn of the century, the company had over 4,000 branch offices, located on every inhabited continent, and factories in Austria, Canada, Prussia, Russia, and Scotland.

Growth slowed in the tumultuous twentieth century. The agent in Teheran had to flee a revolution in 1907, and 10 years later Red Guards stormed the St. Petersburg office. The armies of World War I wore factory-made uniforms, and the postwar market for ready-to-wear clothing undercut demand. German bombers destroyed the Scotland plant in 1941, and four years later the Soviet army smashed the Prussian factory.

Singer was a forerunner of the global commerce in consumer goods that the United States would dominate in the late twentieth century. Portable and practical, the machine had universal appeal, and its marketing was infinitely adaptable. In 1891, Singer issued trading cards showing the peoples of the world in native costume. The images were strikingly different from racialized depictions common in that period. Although the fabrics and colors varied, the peoples of other cultures looked very much alike, each with their sewing machine, a global community of consumers.

Recognizing that a strong navy could extend America's economic reach, Congress authorized the construction of three large battleships in 1890. Four years later, an official commission investigated the feasibility of a canal across Central America. A newly organized National Association of Manufacturers urged the government to open foreign markets. The administration created a Bureau of Foreign Commerce and urged US consuls to seize opportunities to extend sales of American industrial products abroad.

Congress also knew that tariff rates could influence the expansion of trade. Before 1890, taxes on imports had been set high to raise revenue and to help domestic manufacturers by making foreign goods unaffordable. The Harrison-McKinley Tariff of 1890 did something different. It allowed the president to use the tariff to punish countries that closed their markets to US goods or to reward them for lifting customs barriers. This "bargaining tariff" used the weight of the US economy to open markets around the world.

The United States began reorganizing to compete in a global marketplace. The struggle required the executive branch to enlarge the military and take on additional authority. It also meant that domestic industries had to produce higher-quality goods at less cost to match those from Germany or Japan. Employers and workers had to gear up for the global contest for profits.

The Drive for Efficiency

In mines, factories, and mills, production relied on the knowledge of skilled workers. Laborers used their knowledge to set work routines, assure their own safety, and bargain with managers who wanted to change the nature of work. As profits stagnated and competition intensified, employers tried to prevent labor from sharing control over production. Employers relied on three allies: technology, scientific management, and federal power. Workers resisted, organizing themselves and enlisting the support of their communities.

Advances in management techniques enabled employers to dictate new methods. Frederick Winslow Taylor, the first "efficiency expert," reduced each occupation to a series of simple, precise movements that could be easily taught and endlessly repeated. To manage time and motion scientifically, Taylor explained, employers should convert traditional workplace skills and knowledge into "rules, laws, and formulae."

Taylor's stopwatch studies determined everything from how much pig iron a man should load into a boxcar in a day (75 tons) to how he should be paid (3.75 cents per ton). Even office work could be separated into simple, unvaried tasks. "Taylorism" created a new layer of college-educated "middle managers" who supervised production in offices and factories.

Although Taylorism accelerated production, it also increased absenteeism and worker dissatisfaction. Another new technique, "personnel management," promised to solve this problem with tests to select suitable employees, team sports to ward off boredom, and social workers to regulate the activities of workers at home.

As the nineteenth century ended, management was establishing a monopoly on expertise and using it to set the rhythms of work and play, but workers did not easily relinquish control. In the 1890s, the labor struggle entered a new phase. New unions confronted corporations in bloody struggles that forced the federal government to decide whether communities or property had more rights. Skilled workers rallied the labor movement to the cause of retaining control of the conditions of work.

Progress and Force

To accelerate production, employers aimed to seize full control over the workplace. They had private detective agencies, the courts, and federal troops on their side and ready to act. In Pennsylvania and Chicago this antagonism led to bloody confrontations.

The most modern steelworks in the world, Andrew Carnegie's mill at Homestead, Pennsylvania, made armor plating for American warships and steel rails for shipment abroad. In June 1892 Carnegie's partner, Henry Clay Frick, broke off talks with the plant's American Federation of Labor–affiliated union and announced that the plant would close on July 2 and reopen a week later with a nonunion workforce. The union contended that Frick's actions were an assault on the community, and the town agreed. On the morning of July 6, townspeople equipped with a cannon confronted 300 armed company guards and forced them to surrender.

The victory was short-lived. A week later the governor of Pennsylvania sent in the state militia, and under martial law strikebreakers reignited the furnaces. The battle at Homestead broke the union and showed that corporations, backed by government, would defend their prerogatives at any cost.

The Pullman strike, centered in Chicago, paralyzed the railroads for two weeks in the summer of 1894. It pitted the American Railway Union (ARU) against 24 railroads

Homestead Strike When Carnegie Steel locked out all 3,800 employees of the Homestead Steel Works, local citizens and police battled with Carnegie guards for control of the plant. They believed that as producers they had a right to work and profit from their labor. Carnegie believed that he had a right to hire and fire whom he pleased.

and the powerful Pullman Company over the company's decision to cut pay by 30 percent. Eugene V. Debs, the charismatic president of the ARU, urged strikers to obey the law, avoid violence, and respect strikebreakers. When Cleveland sent in the army over the governor's protests, enraged crowds blocked tracks and burned railroad cars. Police arrested hundreds of strikers. Debs went to jail for six months and came out a socialist. Pullman and Homestead showed that the law was now on the side of the proprietors.

Newspapers, magazines, and novels portrayed Pullman and Homestead as two more battles in an unending war against the savage opponents of progress, with the forces of government rescuing civilization from the unions.

The business elite's cultural influence allowed it to define the terms of this contest, to label its enemies as enemies of progress. Workers did not object to efficiency or modernization, but they wanted a share of its benefits and some control over the process of change. With state and corporate power stacked against them, their goals appeared beyond reach.

Just as the massacre at Wounded Knee in 1890 had ended the armed resistance of Native Americans, the violence at Homestead and Chicago marked a new phase in the struggle of industrial workers.

Corporate Consolidation

In a wave of mergers between 1897 and 1904, investment bankers consolidated leading industries under the control of a few corporate giants, and J. P. Morgan led the movement. His goal was to take industry away from the industrialists and give it to the bankers. Bankers, he felt, had better information about the true worth of an industry and so could make better decisions about its future. They could create the larger, leaner firms needed to take on foreign competitors.

Morgan's greatest triumph was the merger of eight huge steel companies, their ore ranges, rolling mills, railroads, and shipping lines into the colossal U.S. Steel. The 1901 merger created the world's largest corporation. Its capital amounted to 7 percent of the total wealth of the United States (by comparison, the largest US firm in 2008, Exxon Mobil, had assets valued at only six-tenths of 1 percent of gross domestic product). U.S. Steel's investors (Morgan especially) earned profits "greatly in excess of reasonable compensation," according to one government report.

Bankers outnumbered steelmakers on U.S. Steel's board, and they controlled the company. *McClure's* magazine reported that the new company was "planning the first really systematic effort ever made by Americans to capture the foreign steel trade."

A Modern Economy

Grover Cleveland's bargain with Morgan revived the industrial economy, but farm prices, wages, and the president's popularity remained flat. Cash-strapped farmers in the West and South disliked the president's hard-money policies and cozy relationships with plutocrats such as Morgan. Calling out troops to crush the Pullman strike cost Cleveland the support of northern workers. The escalating cycle of economic and political crises, farmer and labor insurgencies, middle-class radicalism, and upper-class conservatism fractured political parties. Democrats, Republicans, and Populists all called for stronger government action, but each party split over what action to take. In 1896 the "currency question" dominated a watershed election that transformed the two major parties and destroyed the third.

The year 1896 was the last time presidential candidates openly debated great economic questions in terms that had been familiar to voters since Thomas Jefferson ran for president in 1800; 1896 was also the first recognizably modern presidential election, the first time a successful candidate used the advertising and fund-raising techniques of twentieth-century campaigns.

Currency and the Tariff

The soundness of the dollar, which Morgan and Cleveland worked so hard to preserve, was a mixed blessing for Americans. Based on gold, the dollar helped sell American goods in foreign markets, especially in Europe, where currencies were also based on gold. The

United States traded on a much smaller scale with countries—such as Mexico and China—that used silver. Gold, however, was valuable because it was scarce, and many Americans suffered from that scarcity. The low prices and high interest rates Populists complained of were a result of the gold standard.

Increasing the money supply would reduce interest rates and make credit more available. There were two ways to put more money in circulation: the government could print paper greenbacks, or it could coin silver. "Free silver" advocates generally favored coining a ratio of 16 ounces of silver for each ounce of gold. Both Populists and western mining interests pushed silver. The Republican and Democratic Parties officially endorsed the gold standard, but by 1896 each party had a renegade faction of silverites. In the 1890s, the crucial political issues—jobs, foreign trade, the survival of small farms, and the prosperity of big corporations—boiled down to one question: Would the dollar be backed by gold or silver? The election of 1896 was "the battle of the standards."

The Cross of Gold

A dark mood hung over Chicago as delegates arrived at the Democratic convention in July 1896. They had come to bury Cleveland and the party's commitment to the gold standard along with him. The draft platform denounced Cleveland for imposing "government by injunction" during the Pullman strike. When the platform came before the full convention, delegates had to decide whether the party would stand for silver or gold and who would replace Cleveland as the candidate for president.

Both questions were decided when a former congressman from Nebraska, William Jennings Bryan, mounted the stage. He was an electrifying speaker. "You come and tell us that the great cities are in favor of the gold standard," he said. "Destroy our farms, and the grass will grow in the streets of every city in the country!" Bryan spoke in the rhythmic cadence of a camp preacher. "We will answer their demand for a gold standard by saying to them"—he paused, stretching out his arms in an attitude of crucifixion—"You shall not press down upon the brow of labor this crown of thorns. You shall not crucify mankind upon a cross of gold!" The hall exploded with cheers. Bryan won the nomination handily.

Two weeks later the Populists, meeting in St. Louis, also nominated Bryan. The Ocala and Omaha platforms, which imagined comprehensive changes in the money system and American institutions, had been reduced to a single panacea: silver. Republicans overwhelmingly adopted a progold plank, drafted with the approval of J. P. Morgan, and nominated William McKinley, the governor of Ohio and a supporter of industry. The parties could hardly have offered two more different candidates or two more different visions of the future.

The Battle of the Standards

In one of the most exciting electoral contests since the Civil War, the candidates employed new techniques in radically different ways. McKinley ran like an incumbent: he never left his home. Instead, delegations came to him. Some 750,000 people from 30 states trampled McKinley's grass and listened to speeches affirming his commitment to high tariffs and sound money. The speeches were distributed as newspaper columns, fliers, and pamphlets across the country. The campaign used public relations techniques to educate the electorate on the virtues of the gold standard. Posters reduced the campaign's themes to pithy slogans like "Prosperity or Poverty" and "Vote for Free Silver and Be Prosperous Like Guatemala."

The genius behind the campaign was a Cleveland coal-and-oil millionaire named Marcus Hanna who bankrolled his publicity blitz with between $3 million and $7 million raised from industrialists. The combination of big money and advertising revolutionized presidential politics.

With only $300,000 to spend, Bryan ran like a challenger even though his party occupied the White House. He logged 29,000 miles by rail and buggy and made more than 500 speeches in 29 states. Oratorical ability had won Bryan the nomination, but audiences were unaccustomed to hearing a candidate speak for himself, and many considered it undignified. "The Boy Orator has one speech," wrote an unsympathetic Republican, John Hay. "He simply reiterates the unquestioned truths that . . . gold is vile, that silver is lovely and holy."

Despite the scorn of eastern newspapers, industrialists feared the prospect of a Bryan presidency. Factory owners threatened to close shop if Bryan won. Just before Election Day, the global markets that McKinley praised returned the favor. Crop failures abroad doubled the price of wheat in the Midwest, raising farm incomes and alleviating the anxieties that drove farmers to Bryan. Bryan won the South and West decisively, but McKinley won the populous industrial Northeast and several farm states in the upper Midwest, capturing the Electoral College by 271 to 176 (see Map 20-1).

The election of 1896 changed the style of campaigns and shifted the political positions of both major parties. By pushing currency policies to improve the lives of workers and farmers, Bryan's Democrats abandoned their traditional Jacksonian commitment to

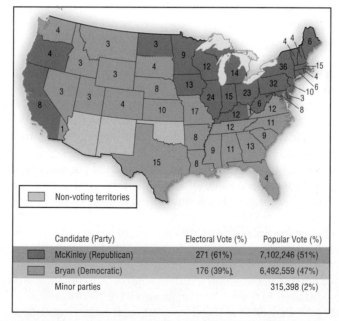

Candidate (Party)	Electoral Vote (%)	Popular Vote (%)
McKinley (Republican)	271 (61%)	7,102,246 (51%)
Bryan (Democratic)	176 (39%)	6,492,559 (47%)
Minor parties		315,398 (2%)

Non-voting territories

Map 20–1   The Election of 1896 William McKinley's "front porch campaign" carried the northern industrial states, along with the key farm states of Iowa and Minnesota, securing a narrow victory over Bryan.

minimal government. The Republicans recognized that voters would judge the president on his ability to bring them prosperity. Electoral democracy now had a distinctly economic cast. As president, McKinley asserted his leadership over economic policy, calling Congress into special session to pass the Dingley Tariff Act, which levied the highest taxes on imports in American history. He extended presidential power even more dramatically through an expansionist foreign and military policy.

In the election of 1896, basic economic questions—who is the economy supposed to serve? what is the nature of money?—were at stake in a closely matched campaign. No wonder voter turnout hit an all-time high. Administrative agencies took over those issues after the turn of the century, but Americans long remembered that raucous campaign when the nation's economic future was up for grabs. As late as the 1960s, schoolchildren still recited the Cross of Gold speech.

The Retreat from Politics

The economy improved steadily after 1895, but this latest business panic left lasting marks on corporate and political culture. Industrial workers made a tactical retreat in the face of a new political and legal climate. In the South, depression, urbanization, and the modernizing influence of railroads accelerated the spread of legalized racial segregation and disfranchisement. What was happening in the South and the nation was part of a nationwide decline of participatory politics. With the slackening of both agrarian unrest and resistance to corporate capitalism, politics lost some of its value. Voter participation declined, and Americans felt less of a personal stake in elections. Disaffected groups—such as labor and African Americans—had to devise new ways to build community and express resistance.

The Lure of the Cities

In the South as in the North, people left the countryside and moved to towns and cities. By 1900 one out of six southerners lived in town. Except for Birmingham, Alabama, southern cities were not devoted to manufacturing but to commerce and services. Doctors' offices, clothing and dry goods stores, and groceries could be found near warehouses in which cotton was stored, ginned, and pressed and near the railway station, from which it was shipped to textile mills.

The growth of villages and towns in the South was the product of rural decay. Crop liens, which gave bankers ownership of a crop before it was planted, and debt drove people from farms. The young and the ambitious left first, while older and poorer residents stayed behind.

While white newcomers settled on the outskirts of towns, African Americans moved into industrial districts along the railroad tracks. Cities grew more segregated, and by 1890 most blocks in the larger cities were either all black or all white. Still, towns offered things that were missing in the country, such as schools. A Little Rock, Arkansas, resident noted that newly arrived African American parents were "very anxious to send their children to school." Jobs were often available, too, although more frequently for women than for men. Men looked for seasonal labor at farms or lumber camps outside towns. This meant families faced a tough choice between poverty and separation.

AMERICAN LANDSCAPE
··

>> Galveston, Texas, 1900

Looking back, many survivors would re-member warning signs: an unusual still-ness in the Gulf of Mexico, lightning flashes in a clear sky. But when the winds began to pick up early in the morning on September 8, 1900, the residents of Galveston believed their solid slate-roofed homes would pro-tect them from what turned out to be the deadliest storm in American history.

Galveston was a Gilded Age boom-town, the "New York of the Gulf." Sited like Manhattan on an island at the mouth of a deepwater bay, it was Texas's principal port. Railroads brought cotton and cattle from San Antonio, Dallas, and Fort Worth to the wharves where they met steamships from Hamburg, Cartagena, and Marseille. Galveston was a major arrival point for im-migrants, who had their papers and throats checked at Pelican Island before setting foot in a land advertised as exuberantly fertile. Alongside hotels, offices, boutiques, and the Grand Opera House on the Strand were the consulates of 16 countries, includ-ing Russia and Japan.

Like many American cities, Galveston was ostensibly governed by a mayor and a council, comprised of aldermen elected by each of the 12 wards, but an elite of wealthy brokers and merchants maintained the city's dominance through private mo-nopolies. The Galveston Wharf Company charged outrageous port fees and steered trade into the hands of favored clients. The Cotton Exchange set prices for the region's principal crop. Economics and politics were a kind of competition; for boosters it was not enough for Galveston to be prosper-ous, it also had to trounce its rival, Houston. Traders on the powerful (and unelected) Deepwater Port Commission used their connections to get federal money to dredge the shipping canals, removing protective sandbars and sealing Galveston's lead. Even the weather bureau joined in, playing up the tornado threat to inland cities while dis-missing the danger from hurricanes as "an absurd delusion."

Galveston shared the confidence of the country at the dawn of a new century. Leaving the doldrums of the early 1890s, the national economy forged ahead. American armies were victorious in Cuba and Asia, and scien-tific advances—telecommunications, medicine, steam propulsion, and weather prediction—strengthened a sense that distance, disease, and nature itself could be tamed. Galveston was at the forefront of these changes, the first city in Texas with electric lights and tele-phones. Its streetcar line defied geography, traveling on elevated trestles over the Gulf itself. The city grew by 30 percent in the previ-ous decade, the Galveston *News* reported on September 7, and "the prospects are bright even to surpass it."

The 1900 storm was not unprecedented. In 1886 the coastal town of Indianola was wiped out by a hurricane. Still, when the red and black storm flags went up, Galvestonians and the thousands of tourists in town for a weekend at the beach sought shelter in the city rather than escaping to the mainland. It was a fatal choice. The storm surge pulver-ized the commercial district. The streetcar trestle, lifted by the flood, bulldozed through

continued

AMERICAN LANDSCAPE *continued*

neighborhoods, smashing houses in its path. Thousands were swept out to sea, while thousands more drowned in the wreckage. The clouds cleared over a ruined city. From one end to the other along the high-water mark stretched a ridge of broken timbers, masonry, furniture, and human and animal corpses.

With hospitals, churches, and city hall destroyed, the victims organized their own relief. Middle- and upper-class women distributed thousands of pounds of supplies from the Red Cross. An ad hoc Women's Health Protective Committee rallied survivors to care for the injured, clear debris, and set up tent cities. Meanwhile, the Deep Water Commission struggled to clear wrecked ships and reopen the port. Together, WHPC and port officials petitioned the legislature to replace the city's elected government with a board of appointed commissioners who would head departments of finance, fire, police, water, sewage, and streets. Democratic institutions were not up to the challenge, they agreed; this emergency required experts.

The commissioner system unmasked the control brokers and merchants had always had over Galveston's politics, but it also revealed the new power of educated women (who still lacked the vote) and reform groups. The commissioners launched an ambitious reconstruction scheme, beginning with data collection. They carefully mapped currents, wave patterns, and the debris wall, using it to mark the outer limits of new construction. Instead of relocating to the mainland, they laid plans for raising the city 17 feet and placing it behind a three-mile-long concrete seawall to hold back any future storm surge. The Women's Committee laid out lots for new houses separated by wide, well-drained streets and barriers of vegetation to disrupt flood currents.

Galveston lost the competition to become the state's largest city. The discovery of oil at Spindletop Dome a year later made Houston the next boomtown. But the commissioner system became a model of progressive reform imitated by over 500 cities, mostly in the Midwest. The "Galveston Plan" offered a cure for the corruption of urban machines. Commissioners agreed that "economy and business methods, not politics" should be the ruling principle. While efficient, it was also undemocratic. Only two members of the board were elected; the rest were appointed by the legislature. None were African American, despite black majorities in two of the wards. Residents were grateful for the speedy action, but uneasy about the new order. "Commission government is far from a perfect plan," wrote a journalist who survived the disaster; "it only marks a transition toward better things."

Despite setbacks, newcomers gained a place for themselves in urban life. By 1890 every southern city had an African American business district with churches, insurance companies, lawyers, doctors, undertakers, and usually a weekly newspaper. Benevolent and reform organizations, sewing circles, and book clubs enriched community life. African American professionals such as lawyers, doctors, and nurses were limited to working within

Mary Church Terrell (1863–1954) Activist, suffragist, and educator, Terrell tried to unite the struggles for women's rights and civil rights. "A white woman has but one handicap to overcome," she wrote. "I have two—both sex and race."

their community. Jobs on the bottom rung of the corporate ladder—clerk, salesman, telephone operator, stenographer, railroad conductor—were reserved for whites.

Inventing Jim Crow

In June 1892 Homer Plessy boarded the East Louisiana Railway in New Orleans for a trip to Covington, Louisiana. Having purchased a first-class ticket, he attempted to board the whites-only car and was arrested under a Louisiana law that required African Americans and whites to ride in "equal but separate accommodations." Before Judge John H. Ferguson could try the case, Plessy's lawyer appealed on the grounds that the separate-car law violated the Constitution's Fourteenth Amendment.

When *Plessy v. Ferguson* came before the Supreme Court in April 1896, the State of Louisiana argued that the law was necessary to avoid the "danger of friction from too intimate contact" between the races. In separate cars, all citizens enjoyed equal privileges. Plessy's lawyer, Albion Tourgée, replied that the question was not "the equality of the privileges enjoyed, but the right of the state to label one citizen as white and another as colored." In doing so, the government gave unearned advantages to some citizens and not to others. The issue for Tourgée was not racial conflict or even prejudice, but whether the government should be allowed to divide people arbitrarily. The court upheld the "separate but equal" doctrine, and the decision provided legal justification for the system of official inequality that expanded in the twentieth century. Informal segregation had existed since the Civil War, and unwritten local customs usually governed the public interaction of whites and African Americans—at work, in business, or when traveling. By the 1890s those informal customs were being codified in law. Railroads, as symbols of progress, were a chief point of contention.

The political and economic tensions created by the depression helped turn racist customs into a rigid caste division. Competition for jobs fed racial antagonisms, as did the migration into cities and towns of a new generation of African Americans, born since the war, who showed less deference to whites. New notions of "scientific" racism led intellectuals and churchmen to regard racial hostility as natural. Angry southern voters deposed the governing coalitions of landowners and New South industrialists and replaced them with Populist "demagogues."

Between 1887 and 1891, nine states in the South passed railroad segregation laws. Trains included separate cars for African Americans, called "Jim Crow" cars after the name

Lynchings Were Public Spectacles
When 17-year-old Jesse Washington was killed in Waco, Texas, in 1916, a crowd of several thousand, including the mayor, police chief, and students from Waco High, attended the event on the lawn of City Hall. Afterward, the murderers posed for a photograph and sold their victim's teeth for $5 apiece.

of a character in a minstrel show. Soon Jim Crow laws were extended to waiting rooms, drinking fountains, and other places where African Americans and whites might meet.

Segregation was also enforced by terror. The threat of lynching poisoned relations between the races, and African Americans learned that they could be tortured and killed for committing a crime, talking back, or simply looking the wrong way at a white woman. Between 1882 and 1903, nearly 2,000 African American southerners were killed by mobs. Victims were routinely tortured, flayed, castrated, gouged, and burned alive, and members of the mob often took home grisly souvenirs such as a piece of bone or a severed thumb.

Many African American southerners fought segregation with boycotts, lawsuits, and disobedience. Ida Wells-Barnett, a Nashville journalist, organized an international antilynching campaign (see Chapter 21). Segregation was constantly negotiated and challenged, but after 1896 it was backed by the US Supreme Court.

The Atlanta Compromise

When Atlanta invited African American educator Booker T. Washington to address the Cotton States Exposition in 1895, northern newspapers proclaimed a new era of racial progress. The speech made Washington the most recognized African American in the United States. Starting with 40 students and an abandoned shack, Washington had built Tuskegee Institute into the preeminent technical school for African Americans. Washington was a guest in the stately homes of Newport and at Andrew Carnegie's castle in Scotland. When Atlanta staged an exposition to showcase the region's industrial and social progress, the organizers asked Washington to speak.

Washington's address stressed racial accommodation. It had been a mistake, he argued, to try to attain equality by asserting civil and political rights, and he stated that progress "must be the result of severe and constant struggle rather than artificial forcing." He urged white businessmen to employ African American southerners "who have, without strikes and labor wars, tilled your fields, cleared your forests, built your railroads and cities." Stretching out his fingers and then closing them into a fist, he summarized his approach to race relations: "In all things that are purely social, we can be as separate as the fingers, yet one as the hand in all things essential to mutual progress." The largely white audience erupted into applause.

Washington's "Atlanta Compromise" stressed the mutual obligations of African Americans and whites. African Americans would give up the vote and stop insisting on social equality if white leaders would keep violence in check and allow African Americans to succeed in agriculture and business. White industrialists welcomed this arrangement, and African American leaders felt that for the moment it might be the best that could be achieved.

Disfranchisement and the Decline of Popular Politics

After the feverish campaign of 1896, elections began to lose some of their appeal. Attendance fell off at the polls, from 79 percent of voters in 1888 down to 65 percent in 1896. The public events surrounding campaigns also drew thinner crowds, and apathy seemed to have become a national epidemic.

In the South, the disappearance of voters was easy to explain. As Jim Crow laws multiplied, southern states disfranchised African Americans (and one out of four whites) by requiring voters to demonstrate literacy, property ownership, or knowledge of the Constitution in order to register. Louisiana added the notorious grandfather clause, which denied the vote to men whose grandfathers were prohibited from voting (see Table 20–1).

Whites saw disfranchisement and segregation as modern, managed race relations. Demonizing African Americans enforced solidarity among white voters otherwise divided by local or class interests.

No new legal restrictions hampered voting in the North and West, but participation fell there, too. This withdrawal from politics reflected the declining importance of political pageantry and the disappearance of intense partisanship. A developing economy with new patterns of social and cultural life undermined partisanship, but so did the new style of campaigns. For American men, the cliffhanger contests of the late nineteenth century had provided a sense of identity that strengthened ethnic, religious, and neighborhood identities.

The new emphasis on advertising, education, and fund-raising reduced the personal stakes for voters. Educated middle- and upper-class voters liked the new style, feeling that raucous campaigns were no way to decide important issues. They sought to influence

Table 20-1 The Spread of Disfranchisement

	State	Strategies
1889	Florida	Poll tax
	Tennessee	Poll tax
1890	Mississippi	Poll tax, literacy test, understanding clause
1891	Arkansas	Poll tax
1893, 1901	Alabama	Poll tax, literacy test, grandfather clause
1894, 1895	South Carolina	Poll tax, literacy test, understanding clause
1894, 1902	Virginia	Poll tax, literacy test, understanding clause
1897, 1898	Louisiana	Poll tax, literacy test, grandfather clause
1899, 1900	North Carolina	Poll tax, literacy test, grandfather clause
1902	Texas	Poll tax
1908	Georgia	Poll tax, literacy test, understanding clause, grandfather clause

policy more directly, through interest groups rather than parties. Unintentionally, they discarded traditions that unified communities and connected voters to their country and its leaders.

Organized Labor Retreats from Politics

Workers followed organized labor as it turned away from political activity and redefined objectives in economic terms. As traditional crafts came under attack, skilled workers created new organizations that addressed immediate issues: wages, hours, and the conditions of work. The American Federation of Labor (AFL), founded in 1886, built a base around skilled trades and grew from 150,000 members to more than 2 million by 1904. The AFL focused on immediate goals to improve the working lives of its members. Its founder, Samuel Gompers, was born in London's East End and apprenticed as a cigar maker at the age of 10. After his family moved to New York, Gompers joined the Cigar Makers' International Union.

Although affiliated with the Knights of Labor, the cigar makers were more interested in shortening work hours and increasing wages than in remaking the economy. High dues and centralized control allowed the union to offer insurance and death benefits to members while maintaining a strike fund. Gompers applied the same practices to the AFL. His "pure and simple unionism" made modest demands, but it still encountered fierce resistance from corporations, which were backed by the courts.

In the 1895 case of *In re Debs*, the Supreme Court allowed the use of injunctions to criminalize strikes. The court then disarmed one of labor's last weapons, the boycott. In *Loewe v. Lawlor* (1908), known as the Danbury Hatters case, the court ruled that advertising a consumer boycott was illegal under the Sherman Anti-Trust Act.

Gompers believed that industrial unions, which drew members from all occupations within an industry, lacked the discipline and shared values needed to face down corporations and government, whereas unions organized around a single trade or craft would be stronger. However, because the AFL was organized by skill, it often ignored unskilled workers, such as women or recent immigrants. Because employers used unskilled newcomers to break strikes or to run machinery that replaced expert hands, Gompers excluded a large part of the labor force. Organizers recruited Irish and German workers while ignoring Italian, African American, Jewish, and Slavic workers. The union attacked female workers for stealing jobs that rightfully belonged to men.

Other unions were built to represent the immediate interests of their members. Under Eugene V. Debs, railroad workers merged the old railroad brotherhoods into the ARU in 1893. The United Mine Workers (UMW), founded in 1890, unionized coal mines in Pennsylvania, Ohio, Indiana, and Michigan. The ARU and the UMW were industrial unions that tried to organize all of the workers in an industry. These new unions faced determined opposition from business and its allies in government. "Our government cannot stand, nor its free institutions endure," the National Association of Manufacturers declared, "if the Gompers-Debs ideals of liberty and freedom of speech and press are allowed to dominate."

American Diplomacy Enters the Modern World

The Republican victory in 1896 gave heart to proponents of prosperity through foreign trade. Before the turn of the century, the new president announced, the United States would control the world's markets. "We will establish trading posts throughout the world as distributing points for American products," Senator Albert Beveridge fore-cast. "Great colonies, governing themselves, flying our flag and trading with us, will grow about our posts of trade." McKinley sought neither war nor colonies, but many in his party wanted both. These "jingoes" included Assistant Secretary of the Navy Theodore Roosevelt; John Hay, the ambassador to London; and Senators Beveridge and Henry Cabot Lodge. Britain, France, and Germany were seizing territory around the world, and jingoes believed the United States needed to do the same for strategic, religious, and economic reasons. Spain was the most likely target, clinging feebly to the remnants of its once-vast empire in Cuba, the Philippines, Guam, and Puerto Rico. Under Cleveland, the United States had moved away from confrontation with Spain, but McKinley pushed for the creation of an American empire that stretched to the far shores of the Pacific.

Sea Power and the Imperial Urge

Few men better exemplified the jingoes' combination of religiosity, martial spirit, and fas-cination with the laws of history than Alfred Thayer Mahan. A naval officer and strategist, he argued that since the Roman Empire, world leadership had belonged to the nation that controlled the sea. Published in 1890, his book *The Influence of Sea Power upon History, 1660–1783* became an instant classic.

Mahan connected naval expansion and empire to the problem of overproduction that the United States faced. A great industrial country needed trade; trade required a mer-chant fleet; and merchant shipping needed naval protection and overseas bases. Colonies could provide markets for goods and congregations for Christian missionaries, but, more important, they allowed naval forces to protect sea lanes and project power in Asia, Latin America, and Africa.

Mahan urged the United States to build a canal across Central America for better access to Asian markets. He urged the building of naval bases along routes to Latin Amer-ica and the Far East. Congress and the Navy Department began implementing these rec-ommendations even before McKinley took office (see Figure 20–2).

Mahan was not the only prophet who recalled the Roman Empire. Brooks Adams's *The Law of Civilization and Decay* (1895) detailed the effects of the closed frontier: greater concentration of wealth, social inequality, and eventual collapse. To repeal this "law" the United States needed a new frontier in Asia, where it could regenerate itself through combat. Sharing the social Darwinist belief (see Chapter 18) that nations and races were locked in a savage struggle for survival, Mahan and Adams expected the United States to win the approaching conflict.

If subduing continents with the cross, Constitution, and Gatling gun appealed to anyone, it was Theodore Roosevelt. Roosevelt paid keen attention to the forces that were magnifying the power of some nations and diminishing others. Imperialism seemed to him the essential characteristic of modernizing countries. A frontiersman, writer, soldier, and politician, Roosevelt was acutely conscious of how modern forces—globalized trade, instant communications, modern navies, and imperialism—had altered the rules of do-mestic and international politics. He sought to position the United States at the center of these modernizing currents, a place that would have to be earned, he felt, both on foreign battlefields and at home, where the gains of the nineteenth century had not yet been trans-lated into the social and moral advancement that marked a true civilization.

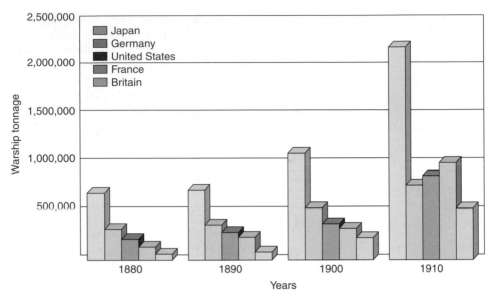

Figure 20–2   Warship Tonnage of the World's Navies Naval strength was the primary index of power before World War I. The United States held on to third place in the naval arms race, while Germany and Japan made significant gains. *Source: Paul Kennedy,* Rise and Fall of the Great Powers *(New York: Random House, 1987), p. 203.*

The Scramble for Empire

For jingoes, China was the ultimate prize in the global contest for trade and mastery. It had more people than any other country, hence more customers and more souls for Christ. The number of American missionaries in China doubled in the 1890s, many of them from the Student Volunteer Movement, which had chapters on nearly every college campus. Even though no more than 1 or 2 percent of US exports had ever gone to China, manufacturers believed that China could absorb the output of America's overproductive factories. James B. Duke founded the British-American Tobacco Company based on "China's population of 450 million people, and assuming that in the future they might average a cigarette a day." In 1890 Standard Oil began selling kerosene in Shanghai. Fifteen years later, China was the largest overseas market for American oil. Mahan had predicted that China would be the arena for the coming struggle for industrial and military supremacy, and by 1897 he seemed to be right.

In 1894 Japan declared war on China and soon occupied Korea, Manchuria, and China's coastal cities. When the fighting was over, Western powers seized slices of Chinese territory. In 1897, German troops captured the port of Qingdao on the Shandong Peninsula. An industrial area, Shandong was the center of American missionary activity, investment, and trade. To Americans, the invasion of Shandong presaged an imperial grab for territory and influence. In the 1880s European powers had carved up Africa. Now it appeared that the same thing was about to happen in China. The McKinley administration watched events in China carefully, but in the winter of 1897–1898 it had more pressing concerns closer to home.

Missionaries in China Thanks to the work of missionaries in China, Mark Twain observed, "the people who sit in darkness . . . have become suspicious of the blessings of civilization."

War with Spain

While other European powers were expanding their empires, Spain was barely hanging on to the one it had. Since the 1860s, its two largest colonies, Cuba and the Philippines, had been torn by revolution. Between 1868 and 1878, Cuban nationalists fought for independence. Spain ended the war by promising autonomy but not independence. US officials wanted an end to Spanish rule, but the McKinley Tariff and the Panic of 1893 ruined Cuba's chief export industry, sugar. Under a crushing debt, Spain reneged on its promise, and in 1895 the rebellion resumed. The rebels practiced a scorched-earth policy, dynamiting trains and burning plantations in an attempt to force Spain out.

Spain retaliated with a brutal campaign of pacification, killing nearly 100,000 civilians, but it was no use. The Spanish army was disintegrating. Cuban rebels, in control of the countryside, prepared a final assault on the cities. US officials, many of whom wanted to annex the island, now worried that Cuba would gain full independence. McKinley explored the options of either purchasing it from Spain or intervening on the pretext of ending the strife. William Randolph Hearst's *New York Journal* and other newspapers favored the latter, inciting readers with lurid stories of Spanish atrocities and Cuban rioting. Cuba sold newspapers. McKinley moved quickly toward confrontation. When riots erupted in the Cuban capital he ordered a warship to Havana. Theodore Roosevelt sent one of the newest battleships, the USS *Maine*. The arrival of the *Maine* reduced tensions for a while, but on February 15 an explosion ripped through the ship, killing almost the entire crew of 266. Navy investigators later concluded that boilers had exploded accidentally, but the newspapers blamed both Spanish and Cuban treachery. Hearst printed a full-page diagram of the ship being destroyed by a "sunken torpedo."

McKinley hesitated, mindful of the budget and events in China, but Roosevelt ordered Commodore George Dewey's Asiatic Squadron to ready an attack on the Philippines. Congress appropriated $50 million for arms. Spanish emissaries tried to gain support from other European countries, but they were rebuffed.

In March the economic picture brightened, and McKinley sent Spain an ultimatum demanding independence for Cuba. On April 11 he asked Congress for authorization to use force, and Congress passed a declaration of war. Expansionists such as Roosevelt, Mahan, and Adams would not have succeeded if war had been less popular. Corporate interests favored it, immigrants and southerners saw it as a way to assert their patriotism, and newspapers found it made good copy. "We are all jingoes now," declared the *New York Sun.*

Neither side had many illusions about the outcome. Fighting Spain, novelist Sherwood Anderson wrote, was "like robbing an old gypsy woman in a vacant lot at night after the fair," but the war opened with a cliffhanger that even Hearst could not have invented. On May 1 news arrived that Dewey's forces were fighting the Spanish fleet in Manila Bay in the Philippines. The war had begun, not in Cuba, but instead half a world away. There the information stopped. The telegraph cable from Manila had been cut. Official Spanish reports alleged that the Americans had suffered a "considerable loss of life." Dewey's squadron contained only two modern cruisers, but all of its ships were steel hulled in contrast to Spain's wooden vessels. For six anxious days Americans awaited word from the far edge of the Pacific.

It arrived early on May 7. The *New York Herald*'s Hong Kong correspondent had been at the battle. Dewey destroyed Spain's entire fleet of 12 warships without a single serious casualty. The country went wild with relief and triumph. New York staged a parade on Fifth Avenue. A Dewey-for-president movement began. In Washington, McKinley consulted a map to see where the Philippines were. Roosevelt quit his job and ordered up a uniform.

The war in Cuba unfolded more modestly. The navy bottled up Spain's ships in the Bay of Santiago de Cuba and American warships cut the fleet to pieces as it attempted to escape. "Don't cheer, men," an officer ordered the gun crews. "Those poor devils are dying."

In the years before the war, Congress had poured money into the navy but not the army, and it took some time before soldiers could be trained and equipped. Recruits were herded into camps in Florida without tents, proper clothing, or latrines. There were few medical supplies or doctors. In these unsanitary camps, soldiers died of dysentery and malaria. Of the 5,462 US soldiers who died in the war with Spain, 5,083 succumbed to disease, a scandal that forced the government to elevate the status of the surgeon general and to improve sanitation and disease prevention in the military.

The army landed on the Cuban coast and marched inland to engage Spanish defenders. Roosevelt came ashore with the First Volunteer Cavalry, known as the "Rough Riders." He recruited, trained, and publicized the regiment and wrote its history. An assortment of outlaws, cowboys, Ivy League athletes, New York City policemen, a novelist, and a Harvard Medical School graduate, its membership combined frontier heroism with eastern elite leadership. The regiment traveled with its own film crew and a correspondent from the *New York Herald.*

Spanish forces stubbornly resisted around the city of Santiago. At San Juan Hill, 500 defenders forced a regiment of the New York National Guard to retreat. The all–African American 9th and 10th Cavalry fought alongside the Rough Riders. "The negroes saved that fight," a white soldier reported. The capture of Santiago effectively ended Spanish resistance. When fighting ended in August, US troops occupied Cuba, Guam, Puerto Rico, and the city of Manila. The war had lasted only four months (see Map 20–2).

As American and Spanish diplomats met in Paris to conclude a peace treaty, McKinley had to decide which occupied territories to keep as colonies. Congress, not wanting to inherit the island's $400 million in debt, had already resolved not to annex Cuba. McKinley decided that Guam and Puerto Rico would make ideal naval bases.

The president also seized the opportunity to annex the island nation of Hawaii. In 1893 American sugar planters, led by Sanford Dole, overthrew the islands' last queen,

Map 20–2   Spanish-American War, Caribbean / Spanish-American War, Pacific

Liliuokalani, and petitioned for annexation (see Chapter 19). They were motivated by the Harrison-McKinley Tariff, which would ruin the planters unless they could reconnect Hawaii's trade to the United States. Annexation was their best chance, and they had a powerful ally in the US Navy. Mahan had identified Pearl Harbor, on Oahu, as a vital base. McKinley decided to take up Dole's annexation offer.

The Philippines were more of a problem. The 7,000 islands were far from the United States and had a population of several million. The United States needed a naval base and supply station close to the China coast, but holding just one island would be impossible if another power controlled the others. Shortly after Dewey's victory, British and German warships anchored in Manila Bay, clearly intending to divide up the territory the United States did not claim. McKinley felt trapped.

Spain recognized Cuban independence and surrendered most of its empire to the United States for free, but it gave up the Philippines only after the United States agreed to pay $20 million, or, as an American satirist calculated, $1.25 for every Filipino. The treaty was signed December 10, 1898.

McKinley did not take into account the fact that the Philippines had already declared independence. With Dewey's encouragement, rebels under the command of Emilio Aguinaldo had liberated the countryside surrounding Manila and laid siege to the city. At Malolos, north of Manila, a national assembly, including lawyers, doctors, professors, and landowners, issued a constitution. By the time the US Army arrived in 1899, Filipinos had overthrown the Spanish and rallied to their new government.

The Anti-Imperialists

Many prominent Americans opposed both the annexation of new colonies and the approaching war with the Philippines. During the treaty fight in Congress in January 1899, they tried to mobilize opinion against the treaty. The movement included ex-presidents Grover Cleveland and Benjamin Harrison; William Jennings Bryan; labor unionists, including Samuel Gompers and Eugene Debs; writers such as Mark Twain and Ambrose Bierce; and industrialists, including Andrew Carnegie. The anti-imperialists advanced an array of moral, economic, and strategic arguments. Filipinos and Hawaiians, they said, had sought American help in good faith and were capable of governing themselves. The islands could not be defended, and US forces would be exposed to attack at Pearl Harbor or Manila. Carnegie argued that imperialism took tax dollars and attention away from domestic problems. White supremacists asked whether Filipinos would become citizens or be allowed to vote and emigrate to the mainland.

The most moving objections came from those who believed imperialism betrayed America's fundamental principles. To Mark Twain imperialism was only the newest form of greed: "There is more money in it, more territory, more sovereignty, and other kinds of emolument, than there is in any other game that is played." Opponents of annexation organized an Anti-Imperialist League and lobbied for the rejection of the Paris Treaty.

Congress responded to anti-imperialist objections, banning Philippine immigration, placing the colonies outside the tariff walls, and promising eventual self-government. Jingoes had a military victory on their side. Anti-imperialists could not offer a vision comparable to naval supremacy, the evangelization of the world, or the China market. On February 6, 1899, the US Senate ratified the Paris Treaty and annexed the Philippines. A day earlier, on the other side of the world, the Philippine-American War began.

The Philippine-American War

McKinley believed he had annexed islands full of near savages "unfit for self-rule," but the Philippines by 1899 had an old civilization with a long tradition of resistance to colonialism. When Magellan discovered the islands in 1521, he found a literate population linked by trade ties to India, Japan, and China. The Spanish converted most Filipinos to Catholicism and established schools and a centralized government. Manila's oldest university was older than Harvard. By 1898 much of the upper class, the *illustrados*, had been educated in Europe.

Dewey gave Aguinaldo his word that America desired no colonies. Aguinaldo continued to trust the Americans despite the arrival of fresh US troops. On February 4 an argument between American and Filipino sentries ended in gunfire. Aguinaldo was despondent: "No one can deplore more than I this rupture. I have a clear conscience that I endeavored to avoid it at all costs."

Kansas volunteers drove the Filipino armies into the mountains. Aguinaldo adopted a guerilla strategy, which proved effective. Some 4,000 Americans were killed during the war and another 3,000 wounded out of a total force of 70,000. Frustrated by guerilla conflict, American soldiers customarily executed prisoners, looted villages, and raped Filipino women. An American general on the island of Samar ordered his soldiers to kill everyone over the age of 10. "No cruelty is too severe for these brainless monkeys," a soldier wrote home. "I am in my glory when I can sight some dark skin and pull the trigger."

The army's preferred mode of torture was "the water cure," in which water was forced down a prisoner's throat until the abdomen swelled, and then forced out again by kicking.

Military officials argued that Filipinos were "half-civilized" and that force was the best language for dealing with them.

Newspaper accounts of torture and massacres fueled American opposition to the war, just as US forces scored some victories. Recognizing that they were fighting a political war, US officers took pains to win over dissidents and ethnic minorities. In 1901 this strategy began to pay off. When American troops intercepted a messenger bound for Aguinaldo's secret headquarters, Brigadier General Frederick Funston devised a bold (and, under the rules of war, illegal) plan. He dressed a group of Filipinos loyal to the American side in the uniforms of captured Filipinos, and, posing as a prisoner, Funston entered Aguinaldo's camp and kidnapped the president.

After three weeks in a Manila prison, Aguinaldo issued a proclamation of surrender. When resistance continued in Batangas Province for another year, the US Army responded by herding people into concentration camps, a practice the United States had condemned in Cuba. It had the same tragic result. Perhaps a third of the province's population died of disease and starvation. On July 4, 1902, President Theodore Roosevelt declared the war over.

The American flag flew over the Philippines until 1942, but the colony never lived up to its imperial promise. Instead of defending American trade interests, US troops were pinned down in garrisons, guarding against uprisings and the threat of Japanese invasion. The costs of occupation far exceeded the profits generated by Philippine trade. The colony chiefly attracted American reformers and missionaries, who built schools, churches, and agricultural colleges. Some colonists sought statehood, but Americans liked their colonial experiment less and less. Labor unions feared a flood of immigration from the islands, and farmers resented competition from Philippine producers; in 1933 Congress voted to phase out American rule.

The Open Door

As Americans celebrated their victories, European powers continued to divide China into quasi-colonial "concessions." An alarmed imperial court in Beijing began a crash program of modernization, but reactionaries overthrew the emperor and installed the conservative "dowager empress" Ci Xi. In the countryside, Western missionaries and traders came under attack from local residents led by martial artists known as Boxers. Many Americans feared that the approaching disintegration of China would mean the exclusion of US trade.

Secretary of State John Hay watched events in China carefully. "The inherent weakness of our position is this," he wrote McKinley. "We do not want to rob China ourselves, and our public opinion will not allow us to interfere, with an army, to prevent others from robbing her. Besides, we have no army." Seeking some way to keep China's markets open, McKinley turned to William Rockhill, a legendary foreign service officer who had lived in China and had been the first Westerner to visit Tibet. He, in turn, consulted his friend Alfred Hippisley, an Englishman returning from service with the British-run Chinese imperial customs.

Rockhill, Hippisley, and Hay drafted an official letter known as the Open Door Note. Sent to each of the imperial powers, it acknowledged the partitioning of China into spheres and observed that none of the powers had yet closed its areas to the trade of other countries. The note urged the powers to declare publicly their intention to continue this policy. The Open Door was mostly bluff. The United States had no authority to ask for such a pledge and no military power to enforce one. The foreign ministers of Germany, Japan, Russia, Britain, and France replied cautiously at first, but Hay adroitly played one power off another, starting with Britain and Japan. Once the two strongest powers in China had agreed, France and then Russia and Germany followed. The United States had secured access to China without war or partition, but the limits of Hay's success soon became apparent.

In early 1900, the antiforeign Boxer movement swept through Shandong Province. Armed Chinese attacked missions and foreign businesses, destroyed railroads, and massacred Chinese Christians. Empress Ci Xi recruited 30,000 Boxers into her army and declared war on all foreign countries. The Western powers rushed troops to China, but before they arrived, Chinese armies attacked Western embassies in Beijing. A British, Russian, Japanese, and French force gathered at Tianjin to march to the rescue. European powers appeared all too eager to capture the Chinese capital.

Without consulting Congress, McKinley ordered American troops into battle on the Asian mainland. Five thousand soldiers rushed from Manila to Tianjin. Hay issued a second Open Door Note, asking the allies to pledge to protect China's independence. Again, the imperial powers reluctantly agreed rather than admit their secret plans to carve up China. On August 15, 1900, US cavalry units reached Beijing, along with Russian Cossacks, French Zouaves, British-Indian sepoys, German hussars, and Japanese dragoons. After freeing the captive diplomats, the armies of the civilized world looted the city. The United States was unable to maintain the Open Door in China for long. Russia and Japan established separate military zones in northeast China, but the principle of the Open Door, of encouraging free trade and open markets, guided American foreign policy throughout the twentieth century. It rested on the assumption that, in an equal contest, American firms would prevail, spreading manufactured goods around the world, and American influence with them. Under the Open Door, the United States was better off in a world with-

>> Time Line

▼1890

Global depression begins

United Mine Workers founded

Battle of Wounded Knee ends Indian wars

Harrison-McKinley Tariff passed

Alfred T. Mahan publishes *The Influence of Sea Power upon History, 1660–1783*

Standard Oil markets kerosene in China

▼1892

Homestead strike

▼1893

Financial crisis leads to business failures and mass unemployment

World's Columbian Exposition, Chicago

Cherokee Strip land rush

American sugar planters overthrow Queen Liliuokalani of Hawaii

▼1894

Coxey's Army marches on Washington

Pullman strike

US commission charts canal route across Nicaragua

▼1895

Morgan agrees to Treasury bailout

National Association of Manufacturers founded

Brooks Adams publishes *The Law of Civilization and Decay*

Booker T. Washington gives "Atlanta Compromise" address

Revolution begins in Cuba

Japan annexes Korea and Taiwan

▼1896

Plessy v. Ferguson declares "separate but equal" facilities constitutional

Mary Church Terrell founds National Association of Colored Women

William McKinley elected president

out empires, a world in which consumers in independent nations could buy what they wanted. Just one year after the Spanish-American War, Hay rejected imperial expansion in favor of trade expansion. This new strategy promised greater gains, but it placed the United States on a collision course with the empires of the world (see Map 20–3).

Conclusion

In the turbulent 1890s the social and economic divisions among Americans widened. The hope that a solution to these divisions could be found outside the United States was short-lived. Imperialism promised new markets and an end to the cycle of depression and labor strife. The United States conquered an overseas empire and challenged other empires to open their ports to free trade, but the goal of prosperity and peace at home proved elusive.

In many ways social Darwinism became a self-fulfilling prophecy, as competition rather than compromise prevailed. Workers and businessmen, farmers and bankers, middle-class radicals and conservatives, whites and African Americans saw each other as enemies. Racial segregation showed that middle ground, on which whites and African Americans could meet on equal terms, had disappeared. Americans now had to decide what was politically possible and devise new bargaining strategies.

Economic recovery and military victory closed the decade on an optimistic note. Prosperity, power, and technology seemed to have rewritten the rules of human affairs to America's advantage. In the American exhibit at the Paris Exposition of 1900, Henry Adams contemplated a 40-foot dynamo—a "huge wheel, revolving within arm's length"—and felt as if he had crossed a "historical chasm." The machine's mysterious silent force, emanating from "a dirty engine house carefully kept out of sight," seemed a metaphor for the modern age.

▼1897
Germany captures Qingdao on China's Shandong Peninsula
McKinley issues formal protest to Spain

▼1898
USS *Maine* explodes in Havana's harbor
United States declares war on Spain
Dewey defeats Spanish fleet at Manila Bay
In the Treaty of Paris, Spain grants Cuba independence, cedes Guam, Puerto Rico, and the Philippines to the United States

Aguinaldo proclaims Philippine independence

▼1899
Senate votes to annex Puerto Rico, Hawaii, and the Philippines
Philippine-American War begins
Hay issues first Open Door Note

▼1900
Hay issues second Open Door Note
US Army joins British, French, Russian, German, and Japanese forces in capture of Beijing

Great Exposition of Paris showcases American technology
Galveston destroyed by hurricane
William McKinley reelected

▼1901
Aguinaldo captured
McKinley assassinated; Theodore Roosevelt becomes president

▼1902
Roosevelt declares Philippine-American War over

Map 20–3 **The Imperial World** Modern imperialism reached its apex between 1880 and 1945. Most of Africa, the Middle East, and Asia, a third of the world's population, was absorbed into global empires linked by telegraph and steamship to centers of government and commerce in London, Paris, Tokyo, and Washington, DC.

Who, What

William Jennings Bryan 602

Samuel Gompers 610

William Randolph Hearst 613

Booker T. Washington 608

Crop liens 604

Gold standard 602

Jim Crow laws 608

Open Door 617

Separate but equal 607

Taylorism 599

Review Questions

1. What new techniques and practices made US industries more efficient?

2. What motivated Americans to seek an empire?

3. Why did the weather bureau discount the hurricane threat to Galveston?

4. Which cities were the main centers of industry and culture in the 1890s?

Critical-Thinking Questions

1. How did the concept of individual rights evolve in reaction to new economic conditions? Name key figures who articulated a concept of democratic rights, and describe their ideas.

2. Contrast the arguments for empire with the rhetoric of the anti-imperialists. Which dangers to the nation and democracy did each side stress?

3. Why was the issue of currency so important to Americans in 1896? What was at stake?

For further review materials and resource information,
please visit www.oup.com/us/ofthepeople

MAIN IDEAS

1) A corporate, industrial economy thwarted effective political action by potential opponents.

2) As American workers lost autonomy to machines and mass markets, so did the Chinese people.

3) Modernizing forces— global trade, technologies of communication and transport—fueled imperialism.

4) An increasingly power-ful president sent US troops to Chicago in 1894 and to Beijing in 1899, both times without declaring war or con-sulting Congress.

TOPICS

The Crisis of the 1890s

A Modern Economy

The Retreat from Politics

American Diplomacy Enters the Modern World

INDUSTRY AND EMPIRE

1890–1900

EVENTS

Hard Times A deepening depression left many Americans unemployed.

The Overseas Frontier As America increased exports, leaders promoted military might to ensure access to foreign markets.

The Drive for Efficiency Businesses sought improved management techniques to control labor and production.

Progress and Force Employers used government clout to break strikes and limit union growth.

Corporate Consolidation Bankers consolidated leading industries under the control of a few corporations.

Currency and the Tariff The choice of standard to back the dollar—gold or silver—would determine of the future of the US economy.

The Cross of Gold Political parties nominated candidates with two different visions of which standard to use.

The Battle of the Standards The election of 1896 changed the style of campaigns and shifted the political positions of both major parties.

The Lure of the Cities Large groups of people moved from the countryside to towns and cities in search of jobs and opportunities.

Inventing Jim Crow Segregation was established by law and enforced by terror.

The Atlanta Compromise Booker T. Washington offered a settlement between blacks and whites to ease racial tensions.

Disfranchisement and the Decline of Popular Politics New legal restrictions, apathy, and alternative forms of political participation led to a decline in voting.

Organized Labor Retreats from Politics Organized labor turned away from political demands as skilled workers created new organizations to address their issues.

Sea Power and the Imperial Urge Leaders urged naval expansion in order to capitalize on America's production effort.

The Scramble for Empire America competed with Japan and European powers for access to Chinese markets.

War with Spain America fought a declining Spanish Empire over its colonies in Cuba and the Philippines.

The Anti-Imperialists Anti-imperialists opposed both annexation of new colonies and war with the Philippines.

The Philippine-American War America fought and won a brutal war against Filipino guerillas.

The Open Door While European powers divided China into colonial concessions, America sought trade and access to overseas markets.

CHAPTER

21

A United Body of Action
1900-1916

>> Alice Hamilton

On an October morning in 1902, three friends, Maude Gernon of the Chicago Board of Charities, Gertrude Howe, kindergarten director at Hull-House, and Dr. Alice Hamilton, a professor of pathology at Northwestern University, stood over sewer drains catching flies. The prey was abundant, and the women trapped dozens in test tubes. Hamilton organized the expedition in the midst of a typhoid epidemic. The disease ravaged Chicago's 19th Ward, a working-class neighborhood where Hull-House stood. To find out why, Hamilton investigated the surrounding tenement houses, which often had illegal outdoor latrines rather than indoor plumbing. It was then that she noticed the flies. Army doctors in the Spanish-American War found a link between flies and poor sanitation and the spread of typhoid. Hamilton examined the insects under a microscope and confirmed that they carried the typhoid bacillus.

Her report in the *Journal of the American Medical Association* touched off a furor. Hull-House attacked the Board of Health for failing to enforce the sanitary codes, and an inquiry revealed that landlords bribed inspectors to overlook the outhouses. Investigations found that drinking water was pumped straight from Lake Michigan, without purification, and that broken pumps channeled raw sewage into the water mains. Through bribery and neglect, city government was responsible for an epidemic that killed hundreds of people.

Hamilton, who grew up wealthy in Fort Wayne, Indiana, attended medical school at the University of Michigan, later studying bacteriology and pathology at Leipzig and Munich. Despite her training, it was difficult for her to find work, but in Chicago she found support at Hull-House, a "settlement house" founded by women who wanted to live among the poor. Hamilton lived there for 22 years. A specialist in occupational health, she noticed a "strange silence on the subject" of job-related disease. Her early research linked the working conditions of Jewish garment workers to the tuberculosis that frequently claimed their lives.

continued

After the typhoid scandal, Hamilton began looking into stories of poisoning among workers at the National Lead Company. Clouds of metal dust filled the plant, and employees left work glistening with lead. The company refused to admit its high absenteeism had anything to do with the work. One foreman told Hamilton that lead workers "don't last long at it. Four years at the most, I should say, then they quit and go home to the old country." "To die?" she asked. "Well," he replied, "I suppose that is about the size of it." Using hospital records, she documented a pattern of chronic lead poisoning. Confronted with these findings, the company agreed to install ventilators and create a medical department. Hamilton pushed for state laws on occupational disease, and in 1911 Illinois became the first state to pass legislation giving workers compensation for job-related disability. Hamilton's activism was not unique. She was one of millions of people in the early twentieth century who reshaped democracy through a new type of politics. Responding to the challenges of immigration, industrialization, and urbanization, Americans agitated for change. They worked outside the two-party system, forming their own organizations. Women, who did not have the vote, took the lead and created a new style of activism.

Some activists feared the uncontrolled power of corporations, whereas others feared the uncontrolled passions of the poor. Both called themselves "progressives," and they shared certain ideas about democracy. They optimistically believed in people's ability to improve society, but they were pessimistic about the ability of people, particularly nonwhite people, to improve themselves. Science and religion, they felt, supported these beliefs and justified the supervision of human affairs by qualified experts.

Although reformers accepted modern industry, they were outraged by the trail of disease, waste, and corruption the factory system left behind. They sought a middle ground between revolutionary socialism and uncontrolled corporate capitalism. Finally, they belonged to a movement with national reach. Progressivism, as it came to be called, was the first and perhaps the only reform movement experienced by all Americans. Popular magazines carried its agitation into every town and county.

Toward a New Politics

Progressivism displaced the intensely partisan politics of the late nineteenth century. The political and economic crises of the 1890s left Americans disillusioned with traditional parties. A growing socialist movement threatened more radical action if moderate reform failed. Protestant churches spoke out against capitalism's abuses, and new interpretations of Christian ethics lent a moral urgency to reform. The dangers of urban life, some of which Alice Hamilton encountered, gave educated, affluent Americans a sense that civic problems needed to be dealt with immediately. Women took leading roles, using pressure groups to extend their influence while also seeking the vote.

Egged on by the press, progressives organized to solve the problems of the new industrial world. Although they sometimes idealized smaller towns and bygone eras, progressives recognized that large-scale industrial capitalism was here to stay. They worked as troubleshooters to make an erratic and brutal system more predictable, efficient, and humane. In pushing for reform, they were willing to enlarge the power of the state and to use it to tell people what was good for them. As reform gained momentum, mayors, governors, and presidential candidates identified themselves and their agendas as progressive.

The Insecurity of Modern Life

Most people who lived in cities at the turn of the century had grown up in the country (see Figure 21–1). They remembered living in communities where people knew each other, where much of what they ate and wore was made locally. In the modern city, water, fuel, and transportation were all supplied by large, anonymous corporations. Unknown executives made decisions that affected the livelihoods, savings, and safety of thousands of people. City dwellers felt more sophisticated than their parents but also less secure.

City living carried risks. Inspecting a Chicago market, journalist Upton Sinclair found milk laced with formaldehyde, peas colored green with copper salts, and sausage doctored with toxic chemicals. Dozens of patent medicines—including aspirin, cocaine, and heroin—were sold as remedies for everything from hay fever to cancer.

Tenement blocks housing hundreds of people often had no fire escapes or plumbing. Tragedy reminded New Yorkers of these dangers on March 25, 1911, when fire engulfed the Triangle Shirtwaist Company on the top three floors of a ten-story building. Five hundred Jewish and Italian seamstresses were trapped; many jumped from ledges in groups, holding hands. In all, 146 died. Such episodes demonstrated that an unregulated economy could be both productive and deadly.

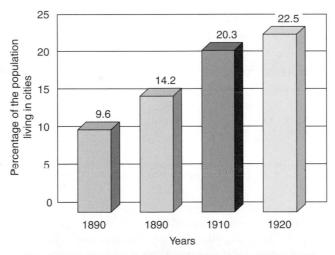

Figure 21–1   Percentage of the Population Living in Cities, 1890–1920 Cities and towns underwent dramatic growth around the turn of the century. Offices, department stores, and new forms of mass entertainment—from vaudeville to professional sports—drew people to the city center. Railroads and trolleys allowed cities to spread outward, segregating residents by class. *Kennedy,* Rise and Fall of the Great Powers, *p. 200.*

Triangle Shirtwaist Fire Disasters often galvanized support for new laws. After a fire at the Triangle Shirtwaist Company in Greenwich Village killed 146 young workers on March 25, 1911, New York finally enacted legislation on factory safety.

Government added to the problem. Regulation often created kickbacks and bribery. In 1904 and 1905, journalist Lincoln Steffens uncovered corruption in state after state. In New York, insurance companies paid off elected officials in return for favorable legislation. In San Francisco, boss Abraham Ruef ruled the city with a slush fund from public utilities. The Minneapolis police, along with the mayor's office, protected brothels and gambling dens in return for bribes. Elections made the system less accountable, not more. By creating a demand for campaign funds and jobs, elections became invitations to graft.

The rising middle class found public and corporate irresponsibility infuriating. In stately Victorian "streetcar suburbs," business managers, accountants, engineers, lawyers, and doctors became aware of themselves as a class, but one trapped between two groups, the rich and the masses of wage laborers. Because of education and experience, members of the middle class had their own ideas on how organizations, such as utility companies, cities, and states, should run. Modern corporations needed clear lines of authority, an emphasis on efficiency, and reliable sources of information. Yet these virtues were frustratingly absent from civic life.

The Decline of Partisan Politics

Participation in elections declined by choice and coercion. Nationally, 79 percent of the electorate voted in 1896, but four years later only 73 percent voted, and by 1904 the total fell to 65 percent (see Figure 21–2). Literacy tests accounted for much of the decline in the South, but in all regions the old spectacular style of electioneering, with parades and rallies, gave way to campaigns that were more educational and less participatory. Worse for the parties, the voters split their tickets. The ethnic and sectional loyalties that led to straight party ballots in the late nineteenth century seemed to be weakening.

Increasingly, Americans participated in politics through associations. Voluntary and professional societies took over functions that once belonged to the parties: educating voters and even making policy. These "interest groups" worked outside the system to gather support for a cause or proposal. Many were patterned after corporations, with a board of directors and state and local chapters. Built on the idea that reform was a continuous process, they strove for permanence. Some, such as the National Association for the Advancement of Colored People (NAACP), the Salvation Army, and the Sierra Club, are still prominent.

Social Housekeeping

The mounting clamor for change aroused political strength in unexpected places. Women's social clubs had been nonpolitical before the turn of the century. Dedicated to developing public talents such as art, speaking, reading, and conversation, they were highly

Figure 21–2   Voter Participation, 1896–1920 After the intense partisanship and high-stakes elections of the 1890s, campaigns became more "educational," and voters lost interest.

organized, with local, state, and national chapters. A General Federation of Women's Clubs was formed in 1890. Within 10 years the urgency of social problems led many clubs to campaign for free kindergartens, civil service reform, and public health.

A growing cohort of professional women energized reform. The first generation of graduates from the new women's colleges had reached adulthood, and some, like Alice Hamilton, had attained advanced degrees at a time when few men went to college. These "new women," as historians have called them, had ambitions and values different from those of their mothers' generation. About half did not marry. With career paths closed to them, educated women found careers by finding problems that needed solving. Florence Kelley, trained as a lawyer, became Illinois's first state factory inspector and later directed the National Consumers League. Margaret Sanger, a New York public health nurse, distributed literature on birth control and sex education when it was illegal to do so. Sophonisba Breckinridge, with a doctorate from the University of Chicago, led the struggle against child labor. Female activists discovered problems, publicized them, lobbied for new laws, and then staffed the bureaus and agencies administering the solutions.

Women's professional associations, unions, business clubs, ethnic and patriotic societies, and foundations changed the practice of democracy. What was once considered charity or volunteer work became political. Some groups, such as the Young Women's Christian Association (YWCA, 1894) and the International Council of Nurses (1899), had a global reach. The experiences of women's groups taught activists the importance of cooperation, organization, and expertise. When women's clubs built a playground and donated it to the city, they increased their stake in the political system. They gave themselves new reasons to demand full citizenship.

The women's suffrage movement grew quietly in the early years of the century. Women had gained the vote in four states—Colorado, Wyoming, Utah, and Idaho—but between 1896 and 1910 no other states adopted a women's suffrage amendment. The movement was stubbornly opposed by the Catholic Church, machine politicians, and business interests.

Competing suffrage organizations joined forces under the National American Woman Suffrage Association (NAWSA). Led by Carrie Chapman Catt and Anna Howard Shaw, NAWSA developed a strategy based on professional lobbying and publicity. Suffragists appealed to clubwomen and middle-class reformers by cultivating an image of Victorian respectability and linking suffrage to moderate social causes, such as temperance and education. At first, NAWSA's strategy paid off. After 1910, five states adopted suffrage amendments, but the opposition rallied and defeated referenda in three states.

Frustrated with the glacial pace of progress, Alice Paul's National Woman's Party adopted more radical tactics, picketing the White House and staging hunger strikes. Despite setbacks, women led the transformation of politics through voluntary organizations and interest groups and were on the threshold of even greater gains.

Evolution or Revolution?

Founded in 1901, the Socialist Party's swelling membership seemed to confirm its claims that the future would be revolutionary rather than progressive. In 1912, Eugene V. Debs, the party's candidate for president, won almost a million votes, or 6 percent of the total. "Gas and water" Socialists, who demanded public ownership of utilities, captured offices in many smaller cities. In the plains states, socialism drew strength from primitive Baptist and

Holiness churches and held revival-style tent meetings. In Oklahoma, almost one-quarter of the electorate voted Socialist in 1914.

Although tinged with religion, Socialists' analysis of modern problems was economic. They maintained that the profit motive distorted human behavior, forcing people to compete for survival as individuals instead of joining to promote the common good. Driven by profits, corporations could not be trusted with the welfare of consumers or workers. Socialists demanded the collective ownership of industries, starting with ones that most directly affected people's lives: railroads and city utilities. Socialists had faith that America could make the transition without violence and that socialism was surely "coming like a prairie fire," a Socialist newspaperman told his readers. "Social Gospel" clergymen preached this coming millennium. Washington Gladden, a Congregationalist pastor from Ohio; Walter Rauschenbusch, a Baptist minister from New York; William Dwight Porter Bliss, who founded the Society for Christian Socialists; and George Herron, an Iowa Congregationalist, were among the prominent ministers who interpreted the Bible as a call to social action. Their visions of the Christian commonwealth ranged from reform to revolution, but they all believed that corporate capitalism was organized sin and that the church had an obligation to stand against it.

When the Industrial Workers of the World (IWW) talked about revolution, they meant class war, not elections. Founded in 1905, the IWW (known as the "Wobblies") unionized some of the most rugged individuals in the West: miners, loggers, and even rodeo cowboys (under the Bronco Busters and Range Riders Union). Gathering unskilled workers into "one big union," the Wobblies challenged the AFL's elite unionism and the Socialists' gradualism. With fewer than 100,000 members, the union and its leader, William "Big Bill" Haywood, had a reputation for radicalism. In Lawrence, Massachusetts, and Paterson, New Jersey, IWW strikers clashed with police and paraded under red flags with thousands of marchers. To an anxious middle class, these activities looked like signs of an approaching conflict between rich and poor.

Conservatives and reformers alike felt the hot breath of revolution on their necks, and socialism's greatest influence may have been the push it gave conservatives to support moderate reform. Theodore Roosevelt warned that without reform the United States would divide into two parties, one representing workers, the other capital.

The failure of the two parties to deal with urgent problems created a chance to redefine democracy. As the new century began, Americans were testing their political ideals, scrapping old rules, and getting ready to fashion new institutions and laws to deal with the challenges of modern society.

The Progressives

Historians have found it difficult to define the progressives. They addressed a wide variety of social problems with many different tactics but appealed to a broad audience. A rally to end child labor, for instance, might draw out young lawyers, teachers, labor unionists, woman suffragists, professors, and politicians. A series of overlapping movements, campaigns, and crusades defined the era from 1890 to 1920.

Progressivism was a political style, a way of approaching problems. Progressives had no illusions that wage labor or industrialism could be eliminated or that it was possible to re-create a rural commonwealth. Big cities and big corporations, they believed, were permanent features of modern life, but progressives were convinced that modern institutions could be made humane, responsive, and moral.

In choosing solutions, progressives relied on scientific expertise as a way to avoid the clash of interests. Those raised during the Civil War knew democracy was no guarantee against mass violence. Rival points of view could be reconciled more easily by impartial authority. Like the salaried managers many of them were, progressives valued efficiency and organization. No problem could be solved in a single stroke, but only by persistent action.

Sure that science and God were on their side, progressives did not balk at imposing their views on other people, even if democracy got in the way. Such measures as naming "born criminals" to be put on probation before committing a crime were called "progressive." To southern progressives, "scientific" principles justified racial segregation. Progressives demanded more democracy when it led to "good government," but if the majority was wrong, in their view, progressives handed power to unelected managers. The basic structure of American society, they felt, should not be open to political debate.

Above all, progressives shared an urgency. "There are two kinds of people," Alice Hamilton learned from her mother, "the ones who say, 'Someone ought to do something about it but why should it be I?' and the ones who say, 'Somebody must do something about it, then why not I?'" Hamilton and other progressives never doubted which kind they were.

Social Workers and Muckrakers

Among the first to hear the call to service were the young women and men who volunteered to live among the urban poor in "settlement houses." Stanton Coit established the first on New York's Lower East Side in 1886, but the most famous was Hull-House, which opened in Chicago three years later. Its founders, Jane Addams and Ellen Starr, bought a run-down mansion at the center of an inner-city ward thick with sweatshops, factories, and overcrowded tenements. The women of Hull-House opened a kindergarten and a clinic, took sweatshop bosses to court, investigated corrupt landlords, criticized the ward's powerful alderman, and built the city's first public playground.

Addams drew together at Hull-House a remarkable group of women with similar backgrounds. Florence Kelley organized a movement for occupational safety laws. Julia Lathrop headed the state's Children's Bureau. All three women were raised in affluent Quaker homes during or shortly after the Civil War, and their parents were all abolitionists. Like Alice Hamilton, all three attended college and traveled or studied in Europe.

As the fame of Hull-House spread, women (and some men) organized settlement houses in cities across the country. By the turn of the century there were more than 100, and by 1910 more than 400. Reformers often began by using social science techniques to survey the surrounding neighborhoods, gathering information on the national origins, income, housing conditions, and occupations of residents. Addams released *Hull-House Maps and Papers*, a survey of the 19th Ward, in 1895. One of the most ambitious research projects was the Pittsburgh Survey, a massive investigation of city living and working conditions published between 1909 and 1914. Its data confirmed that the causes of poverty were social, not personal, contradicting a common belief that the poor had only themselves to blame. Settlements did "social work" rather than charity.

The Hull-House Choir in Recital, 1910 Chicago, according to Lincoln Steffens, was "loud, lawless, unlovely, ill-smelling, new; an overgrown gawk of a village." Addams and other settlement workers sought to tame this urban wilderness through culture and activism.

Surveys also used maps, photographs, and even three-dimensional models. In 1900, housing reformers exhibited a scale cutaway model of a New York tenement block, showing how airless, overcrowded rooms contributed to disease and crime. Shelby Harrison, director of surveys for the Russell Sage Foundation, explained that the survey itself was reform, stimulating popular action with "the correcting power of facts."

This statistical outlook motivated settlement workers to attack urban problems across a broad front. Social workers labored to make food safe, repair housing, and sponsor festivals and pageants. Working conditions, especially for women and children, drew special attention, but employers, landlords, and city bosses were not the only targets: working-class vices—gambling, saloons, and brothels—were also attacked. The loudest voice of progressivism came from a new type of journalism introduced in 1902. In successive issues, *McClure's* magazine published Lincoln Steffens's investigation of graft in St. Louis and Ida Tarbell's "History of the Standard Oil Company," sensational exposés of the crimes of the nation's political and economic elite. As periodicals competed for readers, the old partisan style of journalism gave way to crusades, celebrities, and "sob sister" features. The new 10-cent magazines, such as *Everybody's*, *Cosmopolitan*, and *McClure's*, had audiences and budgets big enough to pay for in-depth investigations. The result was a type of reporting Theodore Roosevelt disdainfully called "muckraking." Readers loved it, and an article exposing some new corporate or public villainy could easily sell half a million copies.

Muckrakers named names. Upton Sinclair described the grisly business of canning beef. Ray Stannard Baker investigated railroads and segregation. Samuel Hopkins Adams catalogued the damage done by narcotics in popular medicines. Tarbell exposed Standard Oil's camouflaged companies, espionage, sweetheart deals, and predatory pricing. Her series shattered the notion that industrial giants competed in a free market and pushed the Justice Department to sue Standard Oil in 1906 for conspiracy to restrain trade.

> I've come here to write the *Uncle Tom's Cabin* of the labor movement.
>
> UPTON SINCLAIR,
> CHICAGO, 1904

The 10-cent magazines projected local problems onto a national canvas. Newspapers had covered municipal corruption before, but Steffens's series in *McClure's* revealed that bribery, influence peddling, and protection rackets operated in nearly every major city. Magazines also reported on progressive victories, allowing solutions adopted in Toledo or Milwaukee to spread quickly. Muckraking declined after 1912, the victim of corporate advertising boycotts and declining readership, but while it lasted, "public opinion" became a force that could shake the powerful.

Dictatorship of the Experts

For doctors, lawyers, and engineers, reform offered a chance to apply their skills to urgent problems, and the Progressive Era coincided with the rise in influence of the social sciences and the professions. Experts could mediate potentially violent conflicts and eliminate the uncertainties of democracy. Scientific advances seemed to justify this faith. In just a generation, antiseptic techniques, X-rays, and new drugs created a new understanding of disease. Electric light, recorded sound, motion pictures, radio, and flight confirmed science's ability to shape the future.

Social workers copied doctors, diagnosing each case with clinical impartiality. Newly professionalized police forces applied the techniques of fingerprinting, handwriting analysis, and psychology to law enforcement. Dietitians installed bland but nutritionally balanced meals in school cafeterias. Reformers tried (but failed) to simplify spelling and bring "efficiency" to the English language.

Trust in science sometimes led to extreme measures. One was the practice of eugenics, an attempt to rid society of alcoholism, poverty, and crime through selective breeding. "If the knowledge [of eugenics] were applied, the defective classes would disappear within a generation," the president of the University of Wisconsin predicted. Persuaded that genetics could save the state money, the Indiana legislature passed a law in 1907 authorizing the forced sterilization of "criminals, idiots, rapists, and imbeciles." Patients with epilepsy, psychiatric disorders, or mental handicaps who sought help at state hospitals were surgically sterilized. Criminals received the same treatment. Seven other states also adopted the "Indiana Plan."

The emphasis on expertise hid a thinly veiled distrust of democracy. Professional educators, for example, took control of the schools away from local boards and gave it to expert administrators and superintendents. They certified teachers and classified students based on "scientific" intelligence tests. To reformers, education was too important to be left to amateurs, such as teachers, parents, or voters.

AMERICA AND THE WORLD

>> The Calorie

Just after breakfast on March 23, 1896, Professor Wilbur Atwater sealed a student in an airtight chamber in the basement of Wesleyan University's Judd Hall. The apparatus was described by the press as resembling a meat locker, lined with copper and zinc. Atwater carefully recorded the change in temperature inside the cell while the student, A. W. Smith, rested, lifted weights, and ate measured portions of bread, baked beans, hamburger, milk, and potatoes. The device was a calorimeter, a tool previously used to measure the efficiency of engines and explosives.

The press was riveted by the story of the "prisoner of science," but the results were even more startling. Atwater proved a theory European scientists had advanced 50 years earlier: that the human body had the thermodynamic properties of a machine. Both its intake (food) and its output (physical or mental exertion) could be measured in uniform units called *calories*. The discovery had immense military and industrial implications, allowing rations and wages to be calculated for maximum energy-producing efficiency. Congress voted funds to build a calorimeter in Washington, and government scientists proved another fact: all people, regardless of climate or race, need exactly the same number of calories to thrive. When it came to food, all men were created equal, after all.

Before the calorie, it was no more possible to measure appetite than to measure beauty or intelligence. Eating habits varied widely among cultures and individuals, and dietary knowledge was rudimentary. The calorie opened the way for the systematic study of nutrition.

World War I provided the first practical applications. After Germany's invasion of 1914 devastated Belgium, a wealthy mining engineer, Herbert Hoover, organized American charities to prevent famine. The Belgium Relief used the calorie to ration food supplies. When the United States entered the war, Hoover mobilized the country's food supply to feed the Allied armies. He prized wheat, "the largest supply of calories available" for the war effort. American families were told how to count calories and save wheat by cleaning their plates and avoiding "overeating." Restaurants listed calorie counts on their menus.

After victory in 1918, Europe's ports opened to American relief shipments, and Hoover's organization commanded the food supply from central Europe east to Moscow. The calorie briefly even became a unit of currency. Immigrants could send a check from New York to relatives in Poland or Lithuania to be cashed at food banks for a fixed number of calories. The newly formed League of Nations discussed using the calorie to rationalize the world's food supply, perhaps eliminating famines permanently.

Calorie consciousness revolutionized global cuisine in the interwar years. The discovery that Japanese sailors could eat just as much as their British counterparts prompted the Imperial Navy to provision its ships with high-calorie pork and chicken dipped in batter (tempura). These new recipes, popularized as the national cuisine, became what we know today as Japanese

continued

AMERICA AND THE WORLD *continued*

food. But while nationalists used calories to assert entitlement to a full plate, newspapers urged women to count calories to stay thin. Despite doctors' warnings, "dieting" became a global fad.

To many people, counting took the pleasure out of eating. Dutch historian Johan Huizinga saw the calorie as a peculiarly American "Taylorism of the mind." Indian leader Mahatma Gandhi rejected the calorie as another imperial ploy to control the world's hungry masses. He made hunger and self-denial into weapons in the independence struggle.

Nutrition was seen as a solution to economic and political problems. A 1936 League of Nations report proposed that the global agricultural depression could be solved if surplus calories in the industrial countries could be exported to countries, such as China, with caloric deficits. The proposal led in 1942 to the creation of the Food and Agriculture Organization, the first component of the United Nations system.

Since ancient times, societies have always kept a close eye on food supplies, but the calorie made food and nutrition an international concern. It implied that humanity had a single appetite and that those who had food had obligations to those who did not, even if they were on opposite sides of the world.

Progressivism created new social sciences and made universities centers of advocacy. Sociology was a product of the progressive impulse. The study of government became political science, and "scientific" historians searched the past for answers to modern problems. John R. Commons, Richard Ely, and Thorstein Veblen used economics to study how modern institutions developed and functioned. Legal scholars such as Louis Brandeis and Roscoe Pound called for revising the law to reflect social realities.

This stress on expertise made Progressive Era reforms different from those of earlier periods. Instead of trying to succeed at a single stroke—by passing a law or trouncing a corrupt politician—progressives believed in process and established organizations and procedures that would keep the pressure on and make progress a habit.

Progressives on the Color Line

In her international crusade against lynching, Ida B. Wells-Barnett pioneered some of the progressive tactics of research, exposure, and organization. A schoolteacher in Memphis, Wells-Barnett documented mob violence against African Americans and mobilized opinion in the United States and Britain. Cities that condoned extralegal executions soon faced a barrage of condemnation from church groups and women's clubs. As her Afro-American Council grew, Wells-Barnett joined forces with white suffragists, social workers, and journalists, but her cause was not fully embraced. Many reform groups sympathized with white southerners or wanted to avoid dividing their membership over race.

Reformers debated how much progress non-Anglo-Saxons were capable of, but they were inclined to be pessimistic. Eugenics gave white supremacy the endorsement of science.

Ida B. Wells-Barnett with Her Children Ida Wells-Barnett, journalist and activist, made lynching an international issue through her writing and speaking tours.

A new technology, the motion picture, showed its power to rewrite history from a racial viewpoint in D. W. Griffith's classic *Birth of a Nation* (1915), which romanticized the Klan's campaign of terror during Reconstruction. Policy was often based on racial assumptions. Trade schools, not universities, were deemed appropriate for educating Filipinos and Hawaiians. Progressives took Native American children from their families and placed them in boarding schools. Electoral reform in Texas meant disfranchising Spanish-speaking voters.

Wells-Barnett was not alone in finding doors through this wall of racial ideology. William Edward Burghardt DuBois documented the costs of racism in *The Philadelphia Negro* (1898). The survey spoke the progressives' language, insisting that discrimination was not just morally wrong but inefficient, because it took away work and encouraged alcoholism and crime. DuBois transformed the politics of race as profoundly as Addams transformed the politics of cities.

Raised in Massachusetts, DuBois learned Latin and Greek in public schools. At 17, he went to Fisk University in Tennessee, where he "came in contact for the first time with a sort of violence that I had never realized in New England." He also had his first encounter with African American religion and gospel music, which was "full of the voices of the past." DuBois later studied at Harvard and Berlin.

DuBois and Booker T. Washington espoused opposing visions of African Americans' place in the United States. Both emphasized the importance of thrift and hard work. DuBois, however, rejected Washington's willingness to accept legal inequality. DuBois came to believe that the Atlanta Compromise (see Chapter 20) led only to disfranchisement and segregation. He disliked the way Washington's influence with white philanthropists silenced other voices. Five years after the Atlanta speech he opened a sustained attack on Washington's "Tuskegee Machine."

In *The Souls of Black Folk* (1903), DuBois argued that the strategy of accommodation contained a "triple paradox": Washington had urged African Americans to seek industrial training, build self-respect, and become successful in business, while asking them to stop striving for higher education, civil rights, or political power. How could a people train themselves without higher education or gain self-respect without having any of the rights other Americans enjoyed—or succeed in business without the power to protect themselves or their property? Economic, political, and educational progress had to move together. Like other progressives, DuBois insisted on the importance of process and organization. African Americans could not stop demanding the vote, equality, or education.

In July 1905, DuBois and 28 African American leaders met on the Canadian side of Niagara Falls (no hotel on the US side would admit them) to organize a campaign against racial violence, segregation, and disfranchisement. The Niagara Movement was one of several such organizations. In 1909, Wells-Barnett, Addams, and other reformers created the National Association for the Advancement of Colored People to carry on the fight in the courts. In 1915 the NAACP won a Supreme Court decision outlawing the grandfather clause, which denied the vote to descendants of slaves; but another 40 years passed before it succeeded in overturning *Plessy v. Ferguson*.

Progressives in State and Local Politics

Progressives were of two minds about the public. Walter Lippmann, a journalist and reformer, could write fondly of "the voiceless multitudes" and contemptuously of the "great dull mass of people who just don't care." Progressives' tactics betrayed this split vision. Their reforms made city government less democratic and more "businesslike." Reforms at the state level, however, expanded voters' power to initiate legislation and remove officeholders. In both cases, the changes enlarged the influence of small-town and urban-middle-class reformers while reducing that of immigrants and the working class.

Redesigning the City

The machine politicians who ran American cities adapted well to change. To immigrants and factory workers, the local boss was one of the few people looking out for the average person. He rushed to fire scenes to aid homeless victims. He distributed turkeys in poor neighborhoods at Christmas. He could be counted on to post bail or find someone a job. Jane Addams acknowledged that she could not compete with Johnny Powers, the popular local ward boss, this "big manifestation of human friendliness, this stalking survival of village kindness."

Powers and other aldermen sheltered the brothels, saloons, and gambling dens that, in Addams's view, exploited honest workers. Hull-House organized to beat Powers in 1895, and in defeat the reformers revealed their frustrations with democracy. The reformers nominated an Irish bricklayer, William Gleeson, who they thought would appeal to the 19th Ward's working-class voters. But voters said they wanted someone grander to represent them, such as Powers, with his big house and diamond buttons. Gleeson was trounced. Addams was "puzzled, then astounded and indignant" at the outcome.

With officials like Powers in charge, corporations could do what they liked if they padded the right wallets. "If you want to get anything out of the council," the head of the Chicago Chamber of Commerce advised, "the quickest way is to pay for it—not to the city, but to the aldermen." City machines lost their appeal by providing not too few services but too many. As tax burdens grew, wealthier voters clamored for reform. Progressives set out to replace paternalism with efficient, scientific administration.

After the depression of 1893, many groups sprang up to criticize municipal government, which often resembled the federal system in miniature. A mayor, elected by the whole city, presided over a council of representatives from each neighborhood, or ward. This system diluted the influence of the "better classes" and allowed a few powerful wards to rule the city. In 1899, Louisville's Conference for Good City Government proposed a new model, later known as the "strong mayor" system. It gave more power to the mayor and required each council member to represent the whole city. Two years later, after the hurricane and tidal wave destroyed Galveston, Texas, the devastated city tried an even bolder plan (see Chapter 20). The recovery would be run by a commission of five elected officials, each managing a city department. Des Moines, Iowa, improved on Galveston's design, and by 1911 some 160 cities had commission governments.

The commission resembled a corporate board of directors. Professionalism and accountability, the keys to business success, could make a city run, too. This philosophy led Detroit voters to elect Ford Motor Company's chief efficiency expert, James Couzens, as mayor. Other cities, led by Dayton, Ohio, tried to improve on the city-commission plan by placing local government in the hands of an unelected "city manager."

Middle- and upper-class professionals led this revolution in city government, and they gained the most from it. The new officials could explain where tax money was spent, but there were no turkeys at Christmas. Getting a job from the city meant filling out the proper forms. Reform administrations targeted urban "vice," which included most working-class recreations. Voters also learned that efficiency did not lower taxes. Budgets grew along with the public's demand for services.

Reform Mayors and City Services

While commissioners rewrote the rules, a new breed of reform mayors cleaned up their cities. Samuel "Golden Rule" Jones, a Welsh immigrant who earned a fortune in the oil fields, won election three times as independent mayor of Toledo. He enacted the eight-hour day for city employees, pushed for public ownership of city utilities, and staged free concerts in the parks. Like Tom Johnson in Cleveland and Hazen Pingree in Detroit, Jones worried less about saloons and more about utilities. Milwaukee, Schenectady, and other cities bought or regulated the private monopolies that supplied lighting, garbage removal, water, and streetcars.

The reform mayors' efforts to humanize the city were supported by architects and engineers who looked to improve urban life through the arrangement of public space. A City Beautiful movement sought to soften the urban landscape with vistas, open spaces, and greenery. The District of Columbia, with its commission government, broad avenues, and parks, furnished a model of city planning, and Congress sought to make it a model of municipal reform as well by introducing a model child-labor law, slum-clearance plan, and school system. The new urban spaces performed social and educational functions as well, especially to Americanize and uplift immigrant city dwellers. New York enacted zoning laws in 1916, and "city planners" joined the ranks of specialists by organizing themselves as a profession.

Daniel Burnham's City Plan for Chicago, 1909 Through comprehensive planning, Burnham sought to save cities from "the chaos incident to rapid growth." He drafted designs for Washington, Cleveland, San Francisco, and Manila.

Progressivism and the States

State reform varied by region. The East mimicked the agenda of urban reform. New York's progressive governor, Charles Evans Hughes, passed laws prohibiting gambling and creating a state commission to regulate utilities. In southern states, progressivism often meant refining the techniques of segregation and disfranchisement. Lynching and mob assaults on African Americans were weekly occurrences in the Progressive Era. White leaders justified segregation and violence in terms used to justify urban reform in the North: the "better classes" had an obligation to rein in the excesses of democracy.

States in the West and Midwest produced the boldest experiments. Oregon introduced the secret ballot, voter registration, and three measures originally proposed by the Populists: the initiative, recall, and referendum. The initiative allowed voters to place legislation on the ballot by petition; the referendum let the legislature put proposals on the ballot; and the recall gave voters the chance to remove officials from office before the end of their terms. Other states soon adopted all or part of the "Oregon system."

The best known of the progressive governors was Robert M. "Fighting Bob" La Follette, whose model of state government came to be known as the "Wisconsin Idea." Elected in 1900, La Follette pushed through a comprehensive program of social legislation. Railways and public utilities were placed under public control. One commission designed a "scientific" distribution of the tax burden, including an income tax, whereas others regulated hours and working conditions and protected the environment. Wisconsin also implemented the direct primary, which allowed party nominees to be chosen directly by voters rather than by party caucuses.

Few machine politicians had as much personal power as the reform governors did. Wisconsin papers would call La Follette a "demagogue," but the reform governors brought policy making out of the "smoke-filled rooms." By shaking up city halls and statehouses, progressives made the public less cynical and government more responsive to reform. They knew, however, that social problems did not respect political boundaries: national corporations and nationwide problems had to be attacked at the federal level, and that meant capturing the White House.

The President Becomes "The Administration"

If Theodore Roosevelt stood at the center of the two great movements of his age, imperialism and progressivism, it was because he prepared himself for the part. The Roosevelt family was wealthy and one of the oldest in New York, but Theodore embarked instead on pursuits that were unusual for a man of his class. After graduating from Harvard in 1880, he married, started law school, wrote a history of the War of 1812, bought a cattle ranch in the Dakota Territory, and, most surprisingly, ran for the state legislature.

For Roosevelt's family and friends, government was no place for gentlemen. Roosevelt himself described his colleagues as "a stupid, sodden, vicious lot, most of them being equally deficient in brains and virtue." Avoiding the "rough and tumble," he argued, only conceded high offices to those less fit to lead. Roosevelt's flair for publicity got him noticed, and in 1886 the Republican Party nominated him for mayor of New York. He finished third, behind the Tammany nominee and the Socialist candidate.

A turn as head of New York's board of police commissioners from 1895 to 1897 deepened Roosevelt's commitment to reform. The commission supervised an army of 38,000 policemen. Roosevelt's crackdown on saloons and corruption in the police department earned him a reputation as a man who would not be intimidated, even by his own party's bosses, and when McKinley won the presidency he named Roosevelt assistant secretary of the navy. The Spanish-American War catapulted him to national fame, and in quick succession he became governor of New York, vice president, and then president of the United States.

Roosevelt believed that to restore democracy—"genuine democracy"—America needed a mission, "a genuine and permanent moral awakening." In the White House, he sought great tasks—duties to be carried out, principles to be upheld, isthmuses to be cut, and lands to be conserved—to inspire a common purpose and test the national will. In the process, he rewrote the president's job description, seizing new powers for the executive branch and turning the presidency into "the administration."

The Executive Branch Against the Trusts

Roosevelt approached politics the way Jane Addams approached poverty: studying it, living in its midst, and carefully choosing his battles. His fear of radicalism was borne out in September 1901. President William McKinley was shaking hands at the Pan

American Exposition in Buffalo, New York, when a man thrust a pistol into his chest and fired twice. The assassin, Leon Czolgosz, came from the Cleveland slums and claimed to seek vengeance for the poor.

At age 42, Roosevelt was the youngest man to attain the presidency. He was the first president to call himself a progressive, and the first, according to Lippmann, "who realized clearly that national stability and social justice had to be sought deliberately and had consciously to be maintained." Unsatisfied merely to lead his party, he set out to remake the executive as the preeminent branch of government, initiating legislation, shaping public opinion, and protecting the national interest at home and abroad. "I believe in power," he explained. Instead of asking Congress for legislation, he drafted bills and lobbied for them personally. He believed government should intervene in the economy to protect citizens or to save business from itself. McKinley had already planned against the trusts, but his plans were not as bold as his successor's.

> Theodore Roosevelt began the work of turning the American mind in the direction which it had to go in the Twentieth Century.
>
> WALTER LIPPMANN

Challenging the corporations would not be easy. Roosevelt took office less than a decade after J. P. Morgan rescued the federal Treasury. In 1895, the Supreme Court gutted the Sherman Act, one of the few laws allowing federal action against monopolies. The underfunded Interstate Commerce Commission possessed few powers. Roosevelt told Congress "publicity is the only sure remedy which we can now invoke." He used it to the limit, putting Wall Street on notice in his first inaugural when he asserted that trusts "are creatures of the State, and the State not only has the right to control them, but it is duty bound to control them." In 1903 Roosevelt established a Department of Commerce and Labor that required annual reports, making corporate activities transparent.

The Justice Department revitalized the Sherman Act with vigorous prosecutions, and Roosevelt selected cases for maximum publicity value. Attorney General Philander Knox filed suit against J. P. Morgan's holding company, Northern Securities. Morgan expected the matter to be settled in the usual way, and his attorney asked how they might "fix it up." "We don't want to fix it up," Knox replied. "We want to stop it." When the Court handed Roosevelt a victory in 1904, Americans cheered.

With this case, Roosevelt gained an undeserved reputation as a "trust buster." He did oppose serious abuses, but he distinguished between good and bad trusts and believed that government should encourage responsible corporations to grow. He agreed with such progressive writers as Herbert Croly, editor of the *New Republic*, who imagined a central government staffed by nonpartisan experts who would monitor big corporations to assure efficiency and head off destructive actions.

Not all progressives agreed. Louis Brandeis and Woodrow Wilson envisioned a political economy of small, highly competitive firms kept in line by regular use of the Sherman Act. To Roosevelt, there was no future in a small-business economy. Only large combinations could compete on a world scale, and government's obligation was not to break them up but to regulate them. He secured passage of the Hepburn Act (1906), which allowed the commission to set freight rates and banned "sweetheart" deals (of the kind Standard Oil enjoyed) with favored clients. The Mann-Elkins Act (1910) regulated telephone, telegraph, and cable communications. The Pure Food and Drug Act (1906) responded to Upton Sinclair's exposé of the meatpacking industry by making it a crime to ship or sell contaminated or fraudulently labeled food and drugs. Under Roosevelt, the federal government gained the tools to counterbalance the power of business. It grew to match its responsibilities. The number of federal employees almost doubled between 1900 and 1916.

The Square Deal

Roosevelt's exasperation with big business reached a peak during the coal strike of 1902. The United Mine Workers represented 150,000 miners in the coalfields of eastern Pennsylvania. The miners, mostly Polish, Hungarian, and Italian immigrants, earned less than $6 a week, and more than 400 died yearly to supply the coal to run railroads and heat homes. Seventy percent of the mines were owned by six railroads, which in turn were controlled by the usual financiers, including Morgan and Rockefeller. The owners refused to deal with the union, declaring it a band of outlaws. When the miners struck in May, they had the public's sympathy. Editorials, even in Republican newspapers, urged the president to take the mines away from the owners.

The "gross blindness of the operators" infuriated Roosevelt. Coal was the only fuel for heating, and a strike might cause hundreds to freeze. After failing to get the sides to negotiate, he invited union officials and the operators to Washington so that he could personally arbitrate. John Mitchell, head of the mine workers, eagerly accepted the offer, but the owners refused.

For Roosevelt this was the final straw. He prepared the army to move into the coalfields and put the mines under government control. The owners capitulated, agreeing to submit the dispute to a federal commission. The result was a compromise: miners received a 10 percent increase in pay and a nine-hour workday, but owners did not have to recognize the union.

Roosevelt's direct action made the federal government a third force in labor disputes. For the first time a strike was settled by federal arbitration, and for the first time a union had struck a strategic industry without being denounced as a radical conspiracy. The government would no longer automatically side with the corporations. "We demand that big business give the people a square deal," Roosevelt explained. "In return, we must insist that when anyone engaged in big business honestly endeavors to do right, he shall be given a square deal."

Conserving Water, Land, and Forests

When Roosevelt felt important issues were at stake, he pushed the limits of his office. He enraged Congress by stretching the definitions of presidential power, especially in the area of conservation (see Map 21–1). When Congress sent him a bill to halt the creation of new national forests in the West, Roosevelt first created or enlarged 32 national forests, then signed the bill. To stop private companies from damming rivers, he reserved 2,500 of the best hydropower sites by declaring them "ranger stations." Behind his program was Gifford Pinchot, the chief forester of the United States, who saw conservation as a new frontier. Unsettled, undeveloped lands were growing scarce, and Pinchot convinced the president of the value in managing resources more efficiently. Forests, deserts, and ore ranges were to be used wisely, scientifically, and in the national interest.

Map 21–1 Growth of Public Lands Responding to a national conservation movement, Roosevelt set aside public lands for use as parks and managed-yield forests. The National Park Service was founded in 1916.

One of Roosevelt's first victories was the Newlands Reclamation Act (1902), which gave the Agriculture Department authority to build reservoirs and irrigation systems in the West. In the next four years, 3 million acres were "reclaimed" from the desert and turned into farms. To prevent waste, Roosevelt put tighter controls on prospecting, grazing, and logging. Big lumber and mining companies accepted rationalized resource administration, but small-scale prospectors and ranchers were shut out of federal lands. Naturalists like John Muir also resisted, pointing out that nature was to be appreciated, not used.

By 1909, conservation had become a national issue and created a new constituency of hikers, sightseers, and tourism entrepreneurs. By quadrupling the acreage in federal reserves, professionalizing the Forest Service, and using his "bully pulpit" to build support for conservation, Roosevelt helped create the modern environmental movement.

TR and Big Stick Diplomacy

Imperial and commercial expansion put new strains on foreign and military policy after the turn of the century. US investors wanted Washington to protect their overseas factories and railroads against civil wars and hostile governments. Diplomatic and military budgets grew to meet these demands. Diplomats were no longer political cronies but trained professionals, and diplomacy was no longer a matter of weathering "incidents" but of making policy.

Roosevelt's view of world affairs flowed from his understanding of the past and the future. Global trade and communications, he believed, united "civilized" nations. His

AMERICAN LANDSCAPE

>> **The Hetch Hetchy Valley**

When landscape painter Albert Bierstadt visited in 1875, he saw a panorama of waterfalls. The canyon walls towered 2,500 feet above a wide, forested meadow populated by herds of elk. Twenty-five years later, San Francisco's mayor James Phelan beheld the cliffs and the pure glacier water pouring into the Tuolumne River and saw his city's answer to the problems of "monopoly and microbes."

The Hetch Hetchy Valley hypnotized naturalists and engineers equally because of its magnificence and its location. It was only 152 miles from San Francisco, close enough both to lure visitors and to channel its waters to the city. A village of less than a thousand in 1848, the City by the Bay was, by 1900, the nation's ninth largest, with 340,000 people. Only water kept it from growing larger.

Hemmed in by ocean on three sides, San Francisco faced a chronic scarcity of water. As the Gold Rush swelled the population, entrepreneurs bought up all available water supplies and formed the Spring Valley Water Company, which monopolized the city's water for 60 years. Water tycoons supported the political machine led by "Boss" Abe Ruef. The company's water was neither cheap nor safe, causing occasional outbreaks of cholera and typhus.

When voters elected Phelan and a reform ticket in 1897, they expected something to be done about water. The Republican mayor proposed to dam the Hetch Hetchy and build an aqueduct across the Central Valley, breaking the monopoly and making water an abundant, safe public utility.

Many obstacles stood in the way. The city's board of superintendents, controlled by Ruef,

sided with Spring Valley and blocked plans for a city reservoir. But it was even harder to get permission from the federal government. Hetch Hetchy was located in Yosemite National Park, one of the first nature preserves, created in 1890 to save its peaks and waterfalls. The parks system was new, and the philosophy of conservation—how to preserve natural resources, and for what purposes— was evolving rapidly. Phelan found an ally in Gifford Pinchot, who filled the newly created office of chief forester.

Pinchot's father had made millions in the lumber trade. Gifford argued that the job of forestry was "to grow trees as a crop." He and Phelan agreed that the two main threats to any resource were inefficient use and monopoly control. The few hikers who might enjoy Hetch Hetchy's magnificence were less important than the need "to supply pure water to a great center of population."

Natural and political disasters worked to Phelan's advantage. After the 1906 San Francisco earthquake and fire vividly demonstrated the need for a water supply, Congress allowed the city to apply to use part of Yosemite's land. The following year, a lurid scandal led to a bribery conviction for Ruef and disgrace for his followers. But just as the way seemed clear, a public outcry urged the secretary of the interior to save the Hetch Hetchy.

Behind the campaign was the 1,000-member Sierra Club and its ascetic founder, John Muir. A wilderness explorer and naturalist, Muir was popular for his writings on the transcendent, spiritual aspects of the *continued* natural world. "Dam Hetch Hetchy!" he re-monstrated. "As well dam for water tanks the people's cathedrals and churches." Historians have characterized the debate between Muir and Pinchot as a contest between rival concepts of environmentalism—conservation for use versus preservation for nature's sake—but the two men also represented opposing interpretations of democracy and the dangers it faced.

"Conservation is the most democratic movement this country has known for generations," Pinchot believed. The Hetch Hetchy project would replace unbridled corporate power with management of natural resources for the public good.

Democratic values were scientific values: efficiency, expertise, and "the greatest good, for the greatest number, for the longest time." For Muir, nature was a refuge where democratic values could survive amid the culture of self-interest and scientific progress. The valley had to be preserved not just to save the trees but also to "save humans for the wilderness." Only there could people share the nonmaterial values in which democracy took root.

The Sierra Club did not advocate leaving the area pristine. They imagined making Hetch Hetchy a retreat for harried city dwellers, managed by the park service. The public outcry surprised dam advocates, but they managed to cast the "nature lovers" as unwitting tools of the water and power monopolies.

The Roosevelt administration wavered, but in 1913, Phelan got his dam. Muir died a year later. Today the Hetch Hetchy aqueduct delivers 300 million gallons of water a day to San Francisco. But the battle for the valley gave birth to a modern environmental movement. When municipal and mining interests encroached on the Yosemite and Yellowstone preserves in the following decades, they were opposed by a national constituency that saw both activism and wilderness as national legacies.

foreign policy aimed to keep the United States in the mainstream of commerce, imperialism, and military (particularly naval) modernization. He felt a duty to interfere with "barbarian" governments in Asia, Latin America, or Africa that blocked progress. The United States was obliged, he felt, to overthrow governments and even to seize territory when it was acting in the interests of the world as a whole.

Building an interoceanic canal topped Roosevelt's list of foreign policy priorities. A canal would be a hub of world trade and naval power in the Atlantic and Pacific, and Roosevelt aimed to prevent France or Britain from building it. He negotiated a deal to buy out a failed French venture in the Colombian province of Panama.

A civil war in Colombia complicated his plans. In 1902 American diplomats brokered a peace between modernizers led by José Marroquín and traditionalists who fiercely opposed the canal. Marroquín favored it but knew war would erupt again unless the Americans gave Bogotá full control over the canal. For Roosevelt, control was not negotiable.

In the spring of 1903 Panamanian senators, upset by the rejection of the US offer, began planning to secede. Panama had had revolutions before, but the United States had always stepped in to preserve Colombia's sovereignty. Together with Philippe Bunau-Varilla, who represented the French company, the Panamanians lobbied US officials to support their plot. Bunau-Varilla predicted a revolution for November 3, thereby ensuring that the rebels, the Colombian army (which had been bribed into surrendering), and US warships would all be on hand.

The revolution went off without a hitch, and Roosevelt presented the new Panamanian government a treaty that gave less and took more than the one offered to Colombia. Congress launched an investigation. "I took the canal and let Congress debate," Roosevelt said, "and while the debate goes on the canal does also." The canal, a 50-mile cut built under the direction of George W. Goethals at a cost of $352 million and more than 5,600 lives, opened in 1914.

With construction under way, Roosevelt acted to protect the canal from other powers. Poverty in the region created opportunities for imperial governments to establish bases on Panama's doorstep. In 1902 Germany almost invaded Venezuela over an unpaid loan, but Roosevelt stepped in to mediate. When the Dominican Republic later reneged on its loans, four European nations laid plans for a debt-collecting expedition.

Roosevelt went before Congress in December 1904 and announced a policy later known as the Roosevelt Corollary. It stipulated that when chronic "wrongdoing or impotence" in a Latin American country required "intervention by some civilized nation," the United States would do the intervening. In Roosevelt's view, white "civilized" nations acted; nonwhite "impotent" nations were acted on. The next month, the United States took over the Dominican Republic's customs offices and began repaying creditors. The economic intervention turned military in 1916, when the United States landed marines to protect the customs from Dominican rebels. US troops stayed in the Dominican Republic until the early 1920s.

By enforcing order and efficiency in the Caribbean, Roosevelt extended progressivism beyond the borders of the United States. The movement spread to the Far East, too. In 1906 a US federal court was created in Shanghai, China, to control prostitution in the American community there.

Taft and Dollar Diplomacy

Enormously popular at the end of his second term, Roosevelt chose his friend, William H. Taft, to succeed him. Taft gained national attention as a circuit judge whose decisions enlarged federal power to regulate trusts. As governor general of the Philippines, he brought reform to Manila. Taft easily defeated William Jennings Bryan in the 1908 election, and as president he began consolidating Roosevelt's gains. He sent to the states constitutional amendments for the direct election of senators and for the income tax. He increased antitrust enforcement and levied the first tax on corporations. Satisfied that his legacy would continue, Roosevelt left for a tour of Africa.

In the Caribbean, Taft put the Roosevelt Corollary into action (see Map 21–2). The United States bought up the debts of Honduras and Nicaragua. Taft persuaded New York banks to refinance Haiti's debt to prevent German intervention there. Taft intended "dollar diplomacy" to replace force as an instrument of policy, but in most cases, dollars preceded bullets. For Caribbean nations, American protection meant high import taxes. A revolt usually followed. Marines went into Honduras and Nicaragua in 1912 and stayed until 1933.

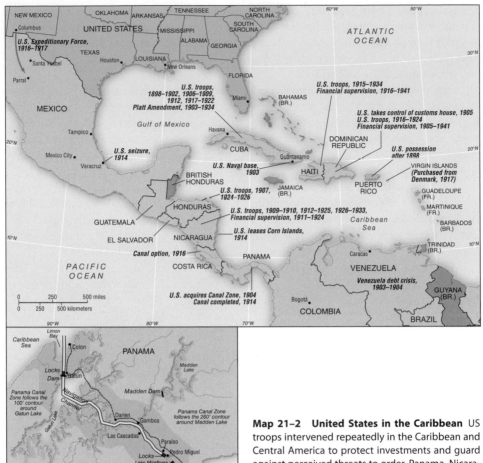

Map 21–2   United States in the Caribbean US troops intervened repeatedly in the Caribbean and Central America to protect investments and guard against perceived threats to order. Panama, Nicaragua, Haiti, and the Dominican Republic were under nearly constant US occupation until the mid-1920s. *Thomas Paterson et al.*, American Foreign Relations *(D.C. Heath, 1995), vol. 2, pp. 55, 40.*

Dollar diplomacy also aimed to harness economic power for diplomatic purposes. Taft mobilized a consortium to finance China's Chinchow-Aigun railway. Railroads were instruments of power in North China, and Taft felt he could drive a wedge between the imperial powers—Britain, Russia, and Japan—and compel them to resume open-door trade. Instead, they joined forces against the United States and the Open Door. Despite the setback, Taft still believed that economic power, not military force, was what mattered.

Taft disappointed both conservatives and progressives in his party. He first urged Congress to reduce the tariff, but then signed the Payne-Aldrich Tariff in 1909, which raised rates on key imports. Taft's secretary of the interior, Richard Ballinger, sided with ranchers and miners who opposed Roosevelt's resource-management policies. When Pinchot, the chief forester, fought back, Taft fired him. When the Ballinger-Pinchot affair revealed the party's divisions, Roosevelt felt his country needed him back.

Rival Visions of the Industrial Future

After Roosevelt returned from Africa in 1910, Pinchot, La Follette, Croly, and others trooped to his home at Sagamore Hill to complain about Taft. The former president denied any interest in the Republican nomination, but he could not keep his pledge. Roosevelt reentered politics because his views had evolved and because politics was what he knew best. Just 54 years old, his energy undiminished, he took more radical positions on corporations, public welfare, and labor than he had while president. The election of 1912 would define the future of industrial America.

The New Nationalism

At a sun-baked junction in Osawatomie, Kansas, in August 1910, Roosevelt declared that "the essence of any struggle for liberty . . . is to destroy privilege and give the life of every individual the highest possible value." He laid out a program he called the New Nationalism. It included the elimination of corporate campaign contributions, the regulation of industrial combinations, an expert commission to set tariffs, a graduated income tax, banking reorganization, and a national workers' compensation program. "This New Nationalism regards the executive power as the steward of the public welfare." The message drew cheers.

Roosevelt had the newspapers, whereas Taft had the delegates. The nomination fight tested the new system of direct primaries. Taft's control of the party machinery helped him in states that chose delegates by convention, but in key states Roosevelt could take his campaign to the voters. At the convention in Chicago in June 1912, Taft's slim but decisive majority allowed him to control the platform and win over undecided delegates. Grumbling that he had been robbed, Roosevelt walked out.

Roosevelt returned to Chicago in August to accept the nomination of the newly formed Progressive Party. The delegates were a mixed group. They included Hiram Johnson, the reform governor of California; muckraking publisher Frank Munsey; imperialist senator Albert Beveridge; and J. P. Morgan's business partner George W. Perkins. The party platform endorsed the New Nationalism, along with popular election of senators, popular review of judicial decisions, and women's suffrage. Women were delegates, and Jane Addams seconded Roosevelt's nomination. The gathering had an evangelical spirit. "Our cause is based on the eternal principles of righteousness," Roosevelt said. "We stand at Armageddon and we battle for the Lord."

The 1912 Election

In Baltimore the Democrats nominated a former college professor and governor of New Jersey. Like Roosevelt, the young Woodrow Wilson defied his family's expectations by pursuing a political career. He took an unusual route. Obtaining a doctorate in government from Johns Hopkins University in 1886, he published his first book, *Congressional Government*, at the age of 28. It advocated enlarging the power of the executive branch. As a professor and later president of Princeton University, he became a well-known lecturer and commentator for new national political magazines such as *Harper's* and the *Atlantic*

Monthly. In 1910 he was elected governor of New Jersey and enacted sweeping progressive reforms. For Democrats, smarting from losses under Bryan's leadership, Wilson offered a new image and the ability to unite the South and the East under a progressive program.

With Roosevelt in the race, Wilson had to stake his own claim to the progressive constituency. With the help of Louis Brandeis, Wilson devised a program called the New Freedom. It challenged Roosevelt on his approaches to the economy and politics. Simply regulating the trusts, Wilson argued, would not help consumers, workers, or small entrepreneurs. Instead, it would create a paternalistic bureaucracy. Wilson wanted a lean, strong government and antitrust laws to encourage a return to competition and economic mobility. Both agreed on the importance of a strong executive, but they had different economic formulas. Roosevelt appealed to a collective, national interest, whereas Wilson stressed the needs of individual consumers and investors. The New Nationalism was evangelical, aiming to inspire people to work for the common good. Wilson appealed to reason and self-interest.

On Election Day, the split in the Republican Party gave Wilson a plurality. He won 42 percent of the popular vote, compared with 27 for Roosevelt, 23 for Taft, and 6 for Debs (see Map 21–3). Although his margin was thin, Wilson could interpret Taft's loss and the large combined vote for the progressive candidates as a mandate for change. "What the Democratic Party proposes," he told his followers, is "to do the things the Republican Party has been talking about doing for sixteen years."

The New Freedom

Within a year and a half of his inauguration, Wilson produced one of the most coherent and far-reaching legislative programs ever devised by a president. Drawing on his long study of congressional politics, he seized the advantage of his party's majority and exercised an unprecedented degree of personal control through the majority leaders in both houses. The New Freedom advocated lower tariffs, increased competition, and vigorous antitrust enforcement. Three monumental bills passed through Congress in rapid succession.

The first bill was the Underwood-Simmons Tariff (1913), which made the first deep cuts in tariff rates since before the Civil War. The bill overturned a cornerstone of Re-

>> Time Line

▼1889
Hull-House founded

▼1890
General Federation of Women's Clubs founded

▼1893
Illinois passes eight-hour day for women

▼1895
National Association of Manufacturers organized

▼1900
Robert La Follette elected governor of Wisconsin

▼1901
Socialist Party of America founded

Galveston introduces commission government

McKinley assassinated; Theodore Roosevelt inaugurated president

▼1902
Newlands Reclamation Act funds construction of dams and irrigation systems

Alice Hamilton investigates Chicago's typhoid epidemic

McClure's publishes first episodes of Ida Tarbell's "History of the Standard Oil Company" and Lincoln Steffens's "The Shame of the Cities"

Roosevelt settles anthracite strike

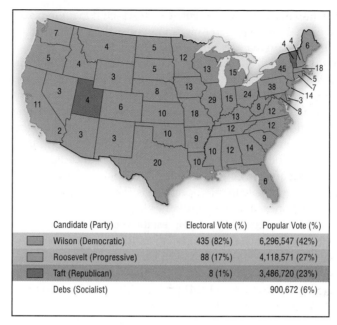

Candidate (Party)	Electoral Vote (%)	Popular Vote (%)
Wilson (Democratic)	435 (82%)	6,296,547 (42%)
Roosevelt (Progressive)	88 (17%)	4,118,571 (27%)
Taft (Republican)	8 (1%)	3,486,720 (23%)
Debs (Socialist)		900,672 (6%)

Map 21–3   The Election of 1912 The election pitted rival visions of progressivism against each other. The decentralized regulation of Wilson's "New Freedom" had more appeal than Roosevelt's far-reaching "New Nationalism."

publican economic policy, the protectionist tariff. It helped farmers and consumers by lowering prices and increasing competition, but Wilson argued that its real beneficiaries would be manufacturers. Lower tariffs would help persuade other countries to reduce taxes on imports from the United States, opening new markets for American-made goods. Wilson created an expert Tariff Commission in 1916 to improve tariff bargaining. The

▼1903

Roosevelt establishes Department of Commerce and Labor

Panama declares independence from Colombia

W. E. B. DuBois publishes *The Souls of Black Folk*

▼1904

Justice Department sues Standard Oil under the Sherman Anti-Trust Act

US Supreme Court orders Northern Securities Company dissolved as an illegal combination

Roosevelt reelected president

Roosevelt Corollary announced

▼1905

US takes over Dominican customs

Industrial Workers of the World founded

Roosevelt mediates end to Russo-Japanese War

▼1906

Hepburn Act passed, allowing the Interstate Commerce Commission to set freight rates

Pure Food and Drug Act requires accurate labeling

▼1907

Indiana passes forcible-sterilization law

continued

most-favored-nation policies it implemented (and which remain in place) induced European powers to open their empires to American goods. The Singer, Ford, and Camel brand names began appearing in markets from Caracas to Mandalay.

Wilson next targeted the banking system. When Steffens and Lippmann investigated banking for *Everybody's* magazine in 1908, they found that its structure was "strikingly like that of Tammany Hall," with a similar concentration of power, lack of accountability, and extralegal maneuvering. The Federal Reserve Act of 1913 set up a national board to supervise the system and created 12 regional reserve banks throughout the country. Banks were now watched to ensure that their reserves matched their deposits. The system's real advantage was the flexibility it gave the currency. The board could put more dollars into circulation when demand was high and retire them when it subsided. Regional banks could adjust the money supply to meet local needs. The system broke Wall Street's stranglehold on credit and opened new opportunities for entrepreneurship and competition.

Finally, Wilson attacked the trusts. He established the Federal Trade Commission (FTC), an independent regulatory commission assigned to enforce free and fair competition. It absorbed the functions of Roosevelt's Bureau of Corporations, but with more authority, including the right to subpoena corporate records and issue cease-and-desist orders. The Clayton Antitrust Act (1914) prohibited price fixing, outlawed interlocking directorates, and made it illegal for a company to own the stock of competitors. To enforce these provisions, citizens were entitled to sue for triple the amount of the actual damages they suffered. In 1916 Wilson produced more reform legislation, including the first national workers' compensation and child-labor laws, the eight-hour day for railroad workers, and the Warehouse Act, which extended credit to cash-strapped farmers.

These programs furthered Wilson's goal of "releasing the energies" of consumers and entrepreneurs, but they also helped business. Businessmen headed many of the regulatory boards, and the FTC and Federal Reserve Board helped stabilize unruly markets. The New Freedom brought reform without the elaborate state machinery of the New Nationalism or European industrial nations. The New Freedom linked liberal reform to individual initiative and free markets.

>> Time Line *continued*

▼**1908**
William H. Taft elected president
Supreme Court upholds maximum-hours laws for women in *Muller v. Oregon*

▼**1909**
Payne-Aldrich Tariff goes into effect
NAACP founded

▼**1910**
Taft fires chief forester Gifford Pinchot
Elkins Act authorizes Interstate Commerce Commission

to regulate electronic communications
Roosevelt announces the New Nationalism

▼**1911**
Triangle Shirtwaist Company fire

▼**1912**
US troops occupy Nicaragua
Woodrow Wilson elected president

▼**1913**
Federal Reserve Act reorganizes banking system

Underwood-Simmons Tariff

▼**1914**
Panama Canal completed
Clayton Act strengthens antitrust enforcement

▼**1916**
New York City enacts zoning laws
Federal workers' compensation, child-labor, and eight-hour-day laws passed

Conclusion

By 1900 America's political economy had outgrown the social relationships and laws that served the rural republic for most of the nineteenth century. Squeezed between corporate elites and the large, transient immigrant communities that controlled urban politics, middle-class reformers created a new style of political participation. They experimented with new forms of political decision making and vested the state with responsibility for the quality of life of its citizens. Progressives challenged but never upset the system. Science and the pressure of informed opinion, they believed, could produce managed, orderly change without open conflict.

The progressive presidents took this movement to the national stage. Roosevelt and Wilson touted their programs as attacks on privilege, but both presidents helped position the federal government as a broker among business, consumer, and labor interests. In less than two decades, the federal government overcame its reputation for corruption and impotence and moved to the center of economic and social life. The concept of a "national interest" greater than individual and property rights was now firmly ingrained; so, too, was the need to protect it. The president's leadership now extended beyond the administration to Congress and public opinion. These achievements created a modern central government just as military, diplomatic, and economic victories made the United States a global power. War and its aftermath would curtail the progressive movement, as support for a strong central government would be tested by events unfolding in Europe.

Who, What

Eugene V. Debs 630
W. E. B. DuBois 637
Theodore Roosevelt 641
Woodrow Wilson 649

Commission plan 639
Eugenics 634
Initiative, recall, and referendum 640
Interest groups 629

Review Questions

1. Why did reformers feel that privately owned utilities caused corruption?
2. What were the Oregon system and the Wisconsin Idea?
3. Choose one level of government—local, state, or federal—and describe three key progressive reforms.

Critical-Thinking Questions

1. Were the progressives' goals conservative or radical? What about their strategies? Explain your answers.
2. Theodore Roosevelt has been called the first modern president. In what ways did he change the presidency?
3. Did the progressives' emphasis on research and documentation indicate their respect for public opinion or not? Explain your answer.

For further review materials and resource information, please visit www.oup.com/us/ofthepeople

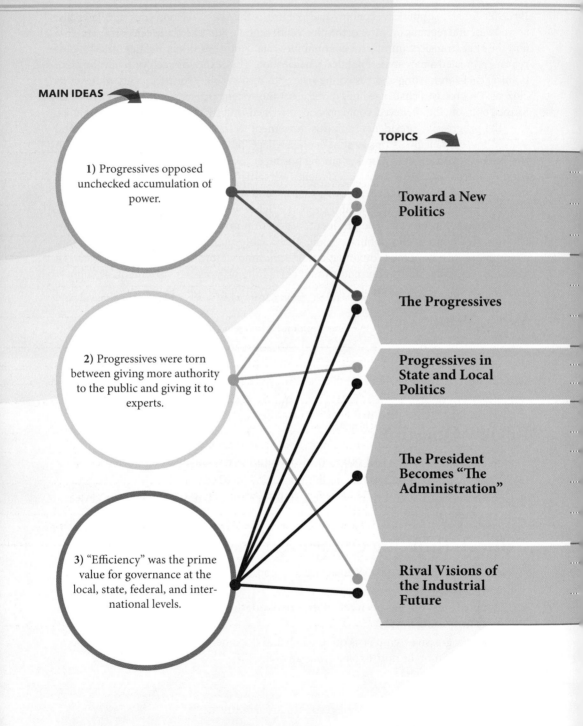

MAIN IDEAS

1) Progressives opposed unchecked accumulation of power.

2) Progressives were torn between giving more authority to the public and giving it to experts.

3) "Efficiency" was the prime value for governance at the local, state, federal, and international levels.

TOPICS

Toward a New Politics

The Progressives

Progressives in State and Local Politics

The President Becomes "The Administration"

Rival Visions of the Industrial Future

A UNITED BODY OF ACTION

1900–1916

EVENTS

The Insecurity of Modern Life City living included both severe health risks and political corruption.

The Decline of Partisan Politics Participation in elections declined by choice and coercion, but Americans formed associations to advance their political interests.

Social Housekeeping A growing cohort of women energized reform and changed the practice of democracy.

Evolution or Revolution? The failure of the two parties to deal with problems led to pressure for reform.

Social Workers and Muckrakers Social workers attacked urban problems, while muckraking journalists exposed corrupt practices.

Dictatorship of the Experts Reform offered opportunities for professionals to apply their technical skills to solve social problems.

Progressives on the Color Line African American leaders promoted a new strategy of legal equality for African Americans.

Redesigning the City Progressives reformed city government to improve accountability.

Reform Mayors and City Services Reform mayors improved public services and built public parks.

Progressivism and the States Progressive governors made state governments more responsive to reform.

The Executive Branch Against the Trusts President Theodore Roosevelt used federal power to counterbalance the power of the largest corporations.

The Square Deal For the first time, the president took direct action to arbitrate a labor dispute.

Conserving Water, Land, and Forests Roosevelt stretched presidential powers to conserve land and water.

TR and Big Stick Diplomacy The United States used military and diplomatic leverage to secure its preeminence in Central and South America.

Taft and Dollar Diplomacy William H. Taft was elected president and aimed to harness economic power for diplomatic purposes.

The New Nationalism Roosevelt endorsed a sweeping progressive agenda to prevent Taft's reelection.

The 1912 Election With the Republican vote split, Woodrow Wilson won the contentious 1912 presidential election.

The New Freedom Wilson produced a coherent and far-reaching legislative program to lower tariffs, increase competition, and regulate trusts.

CHAPTER 22

COMMON THREADS

>> As a progressive, Wilson was committed to order, efficiency, and gradual reform. How did his policies toward Mexico and Europe reflect this commitment?

>> Both the Philippine-American War of 1899 and US involvement in World War I in 1917 provoked dissent at home. Why did the government tolerate opposition in the first case but suppress it in the second?

>> How did the repression of the war years set the stage for the Red Scare?

>> Walter Lippmann

Walter Lippmann had just landed in Brussels in July 1914 when the trains stopped running. At the station, "crowds of angry, jostling people" were struggling to leave the city. This looked, he confided to his diary, like the beginning of a war. Four weeks earlier, Austria-Hungary's crown prince, Archduke Ferdinand, had been shot in the Serbian city of Sarajevo. Austria threatened to attack unless Serbia punished the terrorists. Russia mobilized to come to Serbia's defense. As stock markets tumbled and banks collapsed, Lippmann found himself caught in a conflict between the world's most powerful states: Austria and Germany on one side, Russia, France, and Britain on the other. As land borders closed, he escaped across the channel to England.

In the twilight of August 4, he stood with an anxious crowd outside the House of Commons, as Parliament passed a war resolution. In Berlin, the Reichstag declared war on France. "We sit and stare at each other and make idiotically cheerful remarks," Lippmann wrote, "and in the meantime, so far as anyone can see, nothing can stop the awful disintegration now."

Twenty-four years old, Lippmann had come of age in the Progressive Era. As a student at Harvard, he came to believe that reason and science would allow his generation to "treat life not as something given but as something to be shaped." After graduation, he set out to become a journalist, studying under the legendary investigator Lincoln Steffens and helping to start a magazine called the *New Republic*. "It was a happy time, those last few years before the First World War," he later remembered; "the air was soft, and it was easy for a young man to believe in the inevitability of progress, in the perfectibility of man and of society, and in the sublimation of evil."

The European war crushed those hopes. Just days after Lippmann left Belgium, German armies slashed through the neutral nation in a great maneuver designed to encircle the French army, but before the ring could be closed, reserve troops from Paris, many of them rushed to the front in taxicabs, stopped the German advance at the Marne River. By November, the western front had stabilized into the bloody stalemate that would last the next four

continued

years, taking between 5,000 and 50,000 lives a day. Two inventions first used in the American West, barbed wire and the machine gun, defeated all attempts to break through the enemy's trench lines. Colossal artillery, poison gas, submarine warfare, aerial bombardment, and suicide charges would each be used in desperate bids to break the deadlock, and all would fail.

The carnage horrified Americans. German soldiers terrorized Belgian civilians in retaliation for guerilla attacks, killing over 5,000 hostages and burning the medieval city of Louvain. The gruesome tragedy of modern war made Americans feel both fortunate and guilty to be so uninvolved. "We Americans have been witnessing supreme drama, clenching our fists, talking, yet unable to fasten any reaction to realities," Lippmann told his readers. For three years, Americans watched a civilization they had admired sink into barbarism. They recoiled from the war's violence and the motives behind it, and they debated what, if anything, they could do to stop it.

When the United States entered the fight in 1917, it mobilized its economy and society to send an army of a million to Europe. The war disrupted and culminated the progressive movement. In the name of efficiency, the state stepped in to manage the economy as never before, placing corporations under federal supervision but allowing them profits and some autonomy. The war transformed controversial items on the progressive agenda—women's suffrage, prohibition of alcohol, restrictions on prostitution—into matters of national urgency. The federal government punished political dissenters. On the battlefield, American forces brought swift triumph, but not a new stability. Defeated powers collapsed into revolution and anarchy. New ideologies threatened American ideals. The experience of war brought home the dangers of a modern, interdependent world, but it also revealed the United States' power to shape the global future.

The Challenge of Revolution

Like other progressives, Wilson saw threats to democracy arising from rapid change in industrial society. Revolution, militarism, and imperial rivalries threatened global stability just as surely as labor wars, reckless corporations, and corrupt officials endangered the republic. Wilson opposed radicalism at home and abroad, and he tried to foster orderly change. Stability, like reform, was a process not a goal, but Wilson believed it had to be forced on those who resisted.

Imposing order, the president believed, was both a duty and an opportunity. An expanding commercial power such as the United States had talent, technology, and capital to share. "Prosperity in one part of the world ministers to prosperity everywhere," he declared, but only in safe markets. Imperialism and revolution endangered the trade necessary for peace in the world and growth at home. It was the government's duty to safeguard goods and investments in order to secure American prosperity and its benefits for the world.

This combination of idealism and self-interest, humanitarianism and force, produced a seemingly contradictory policy. Wilson renounced "dollar diplomacy" only to use Taft's tactics himself in China. He atoned for US imperialism but intervened repeatedly in Central America. Secretary of State William Jennings Bryan negotiated a series of "cooling-off" treaties that required arbitration before resorting to war, but Wilson seldom submitted his own policies to arbitration. He believed the United States had a mission to promote democracy, yet he considered many peoples—including Filipinos—unready to govern themselves.

These contradictions arose from Wilson's view of history. As he saw it, modern commerce and communications were creating a global society with new rules of international conduct. Meanwhile, relics of the past—militarism and revolution—threatened to "throw the world back three or four centuries." Resolving the struggle between the past and the future would require "a new international psychology," new norms and institutions to regulate conflict. Wilson's sympathies lay with Britain and France, but with Europe aflame, the United States, the sole voice of reason, had to remain aloof. "Somebody must keep the great economic processes of the world of business alive," he protested. He was also preoccupied with matters closer at hand. In April 1914, American troops invaded Mexico in an attempt to overthrow its revolutionary government.

The Mexican Revolution

In May 1911, rebels took control of Mexico City, ending over three decades of enforced order and rapid industrialization under the dictatorship of Porfirio Díaz. Díaz and a clique of intellectuals and planners known as the *científicos* had made Mexico one of the world's leading oil exporters. They confiscated communal lands, forcing Indians to farm as tenants on commercial haciendas. Foreign investment poured in, and by 1911 Americans owned 40 percent of the property in the country. Mexicans grew to resent foreign business and the regime's taxes. When Francisco Madero's revolt broke out, the army folded, Díaz fled to Spain, and power changed hands in a nearly bloodless coup.

The fall of Díaz hardly troubled the United States: Madero held an election to confirm his presidency. But in February 1913, two weeks before Wilson's inauguration, General Victoriano Huerta seized power and had Madero shot. Mexican states raised armies and revolted against Huerta's regime, beginning one of the twentieth century's longest and bloodiest civil wars. In the mountains south of Mexico City, Emiliano Zapata led a guerilla resistance. Meanwhile, along Mexico's northern border, Venustiano Carranza organized a constitutionalist army.

Wilson denounced Huerta, gave arms to Carranza's soldiers, and sent 7,000 marines to occupy Mexico's largest port, Veracruz, in April 1914. The invasion radicalized the revolution, unifying all sides against the United States. When Carranza deposed Huerta a few months later, he promised to nationalize US oil fields. Wilson pressured Carranza to resign while providing arms to his enemy, Francisco "Pancho"

> We intend to teach the Mexicans to elect good men.
>
> WOODROW WILSON

Villa. Villa briefly seized the capital at the end of 1914, but Carranza drove Villa's army north toward the border. Reluctantly, Wilson recognized the Carranza government and cut ties to Villa. Stung by Wilson's betrayal, Villa crossed the border and attacked the 13th Cavalry outpost at Columbus, New Mexico, killing 17 Americans and stealing horses and guns.

Furious, Wilson sent 10,000 troops under General John J. Pershing into Mexico (see Map 22-1). Pershing never found Villa, but the invasion again unified Mexicans against the United States. Rather than declare war, Wilson ordered Pershing home. After three years of trying to bring democracy and stability to Mexico, Wilson had nothing to show for his efforts. He failed to tame nationalism and revolution in Mexico. The civil war still raged, and American property was more in danger than ever.

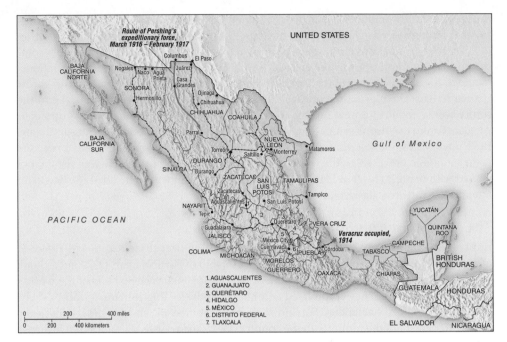

Map 22–1   Mexican Invasion Routes to Veracruz General John Pershing led 10,000 troops, together with observation aircraft and a convoy of trucks, 419 miles into Mexico on a fruitless hunt for Francisco Villa's band. Federal forces loyal to Carranza confronted Pershing near Parral, bringing the US advance to a halt.

Bringing Order to the Caribbean

In principle, Wilson opposed imperialism, but his desire to bring order to neighboring countries led him to use force again and again. He sent the marines into more countries in Latin America than any other president. Marines quashed a revolution in Haiti in 1915, then occupied the country. They landed in the Dominican Republic the following year to supervise an election and stayed to fight a guerilla war until 1924. Wilson kept marines in Honduras, Panama, and Nicaragua and briefly sent troops into Cuba.

Progressive senators wondered why Wilson busted trusts and reorganized banks at home but put the marines at their service abroad. Senators Robert La Follette and George Norris argued that revolutions might be necessary in some countries to protect the many against the few. On August 29, 1914, some 1,500 women, dressed in black, marched down Fifth Avenue in New York City to oppose wars in the Caribbean and Europe. Peace advocates, such as Jane Addams, saw signs of a country being drawn toward war.

A One-Sided Neutrality

As German armies crossed Belgium in August 1914, Wilson declared a policy of strict neutrality. The war took him by surprise, and like Addams he found it "incredible" that civilized nations could display such savagery. His first worry was that America's immigrant communities would take sides. Shortly after the crisis began, 450 steelworkers from

Gary, Indiana, enlisted in the Serbian army. Irish Americans, who wanted independence for their homeland, sided with Germany against England. The Allies (Britain, France, Italy, and Russia) and the Central powers (Germany, Austria-Hungary, and Turkey) each used propaganda to manipulate US opinion.

Wilson sent his closest aide, Colonel Edward House, to Europe with offers to broker a peace agreement. Privately the president believed that a German victory would be a catastrophe. Protected by Britain's control of the seas, the United States had expanded its influence during the previous century. In an Allied defeat, he said, "the United States, itself, will have to become a military nation, for Germany will push her conquests into South America." With Europe and possibly Asia controlled by a single power, the United States would be vulnerable and alone.

Modern warfare and commerce made true neutrality difficult. The belligerent powers desperately needed everything the United States had to export. As purchasing agent for France and Britain, J. P. Morgan's firm soon became the world's largest customer, buying more than $3 billion worth of armaments, food, textiles, steel, chemicals, and fuel. US loans to the Allies grew to $2.5 billion by 1917, but the Central powers received only $127 million in credit. Trade with the Central powers meanwhile sank from $170 million to less than $1 million by 1916. An Allied victory would make the United States the world's leading creditor, whereas defeat might mean financial collapse. The United States had not formally taken sides, but the American economy was already in the war on the side of the Allies.

Wilson's response to the British and German naval blockades reinforced the tilt toward the Allies. Both sides violated the "freedom of the seas," Britain with mines and warships, Germany with submarines. Wilson considered Britain's violation justifiable, but not Germany's. Britain's surface fleet was able to capture civilian ships as required by international law, but a German *Unterseeboot*, or U-boat—a small, fragile submarine—could not do that without giving up the stealth and surprise that were its only weapons.

The *Lusitania*'s Last Voyage

Germany used advertisements in American newspapers to warn against travel on ships bound for the war zone. The State Department was divided. Robert Lansing, the department's counselor, condemned submarine attacks as an offense against law and morality, but Bryan wanted to bar Americans from traveling on belligerent ships. Wilson sided with Lansing and declared that Germany would be held to "strict accountability" for American lives or property.

On the afternoon of May 7, 1915, submarine U-20 sighted the luxury liner *Lusitania* off the coast of Ireland and fired a torpedo that detonated against the starboard side. In 18 minutes the *Lusitania* broke apart and sank. Of almost 2,000 passengers aboard, 1,198 drowned, including 94 children and 124 Americans. The newspapers reacted with rage and horror, but Wilson's advisers again disagreed on how to respond. Bryan wanted to balance a protest with a denunciation of Britain's violation of neutral rights. Wilson ignored him and demanded that submarine warfare stop altogether. He hinted that unless his demands were met, the United States would break relations.

Public opinion was equally divided. Lippmann told a friend in England that "the feeling against war in this country is a great deal deeper than you would imagine by reading editorials." When Germany promised not to attack passenger liners without warning, Wilson accepted this pledge as a diplomatic triumph. It momentarily restored calm, but official and public opinion had turned against Germany. The *Lusitania* crisis, Lippmann predicted, "united Englishmen and Americans in a common grief and a common indignation" and might "unite them in a common war."

The Drift to War

The *Lusitania* disaster divided progressives on the issue of the war. Peace advocates such as Addams, Bryan, and La Follette urged a stricter neutrality. Others believed war, or preparations for war, were justified. Theodore Roosevelt clamored for it. He endorsed the preparedness campaign mounted by organizations such as the National Security League and the American Defense Society. Thousands marched down New York's Fifth Avenue under an electric sign declaring "Absolute and Unqualified Loyalty to Our Country."

Preparedness leagues, headed by businessmen and conservative political figures, called attention to the state of the armed forces, equipped only for tropical wars and lacking trucks, planes, and modern arms. The preparedness campaign appropriated patriotic rituals once reserved for elections. Wilson himself led the parade in Washington in 1916, wearing a red tie, white trousers, and a blue blazer. Hundreds of young Americans, positive that a German victory would mean the defeat of civilization, went to Paris to enlist. The French army soon had an American Volunteer Corps and a squadron of American fliers, the Lafayette Escadrille, whose exploits filled American newspapers. Magazines featured the poems of Alan Seeger, a Harvard graduate who joined the foreign legion. While Americans slept "pillowed in silk and scented down," Seeger wrote, "I've a rendezvous with death / At midnight in some flaming town." Wilson felt that to shape the world after the war, Americans would have to meet that rendezvous.

The Election of 1916

Although Wilson believed the United States would need to enter the fight, he campaigned for reelection under the slogan "He kept us out of war." The preparedness issue reunited Theodore Roosevelt and the Republicans behind Supreme Court Justice Charles Evans Hughes, who attacked Wilson for failing to defend American honor in Mexico and Europe. Woman suffragists campaigned against Wilson and picketed the White House with signs asking, "Mr. President? How long must women wait for liberty?" Although the Republicans remained dominant, Hughes was an inept campaigner. He won New York, Pennsylvania, and Illinois but lost in the South and West. Wilson won narrowly, whereas Republicans controlled the House and the Senate. Still, reelection freed Wilson to pursue a more vigorous foreign policy. As Lippmann realized, "What we're electing is a war president—not the man who kept us out of war."

The Last Attempts at Peace

After the election, Wilson launched a new peace initiative. Looking for an opening after years of stalemate, he asked each of the belligerent powers to state its war aims. Each insisted on punishing the other and enlarging its own territories. Before Congress in January

AMERICAN LANDSCAPE

···

>> Plattsburg Training Camp

Dawn rose over Lake Champlain as a special train pulled onto a siding near the old army barracks at Plattsburg, on the lake's New York side. The passengers, young men in their 20s and early 30s, some in civilian clothes, others already in uniform, filed from the cars and stood at attention on the platform. These were no ordinary recruits. They included diplomat and Morgan partner Willard Straight; congressman Thomas Miller; Raynal C. Bolling, a top executive at United States Steel; southern plantation owners; Ivy League professors; the editor of Vanity Fair; and the mayor of New York.

They were there for four weeks of push-ups, marches, and intensive military training, although none had actually enlisted in the army. Drill sergeants called them "tourists," but the recruits saw themselves as the bearers of a new martial spirit. The camp was conceived in New York's Harvard Club by an alliance of generals, businessmen, and professors. Leonard Wood, commander of the army's eastern division, wanted to create an army reserve that could be used in a foreign war. University presidents suggested that he organize a summer military camp for college students. Students needed the discipline and exercise, and the army needed educated commanders. Private businessmen provided funds, and the first college camps bivouacked at Gettysburg, Pennsylvania, and Monterey, California, in the summer of 1913.

When war erupted in Europe the following summer, young business leaders clamored for a camp of their own. Over a thousand people jammed the Harvard Club on June 14, 1915, five weeks after the *Lu-sitania* disaster, to hear Wood announce the Businessmen's Military Training Camp at Plattsburg. Word spread through alumni and professional societies, and 1,300 of "the best and most desirable men" signed up. Young men from the wealthiest and most prestigious families shelled out $30 for a khaki uniform and mess kit.

The press sniped at this new fashion for militarism, but Willard Straight replied that the camp's organizers "do not propose to militarize the American nation. They seek rather to civilize the American military." Harvard was out to show West Point how to run an army, but two weeks of close-formation drill was enough to give the "tourists" a new respect for professional soldiers. The recruits answered reveille at 5:55 a.m. Calisthenics and drill began at 7:25 and went until supper. Top college athletes found it grueling. Regular infantry marched 30 miles in a day, but at the end of four weeks the recruits could barely manage 10.

At evening campfires, recruits discussed politics and war. Theodore Roosevelt, who had three sons and a nephew at the camp, came one evening to denounce "the professional pacifist, the poltroon, and the college sissy" trying to keep the country out of war. Some recruits agreed with Roosevelt that the United States must be prepared for war, but others saw preparedness as a way to avoid war. They agreed that young Americans, and particularly the rich, could benefit from military drill.

Over the previous decades, the upper class had detached itself from American

continued

AMERICAN LANDSCAPE *continued*

··

society, retreating into exclusive schools, neighborhoods, and enclaves, a process known as "social closure." Aloofness undermined its claim to leadership in a democratic society, especially in the military. The regular army came from the rural South and West, from farming and working-class families. Few in the corporate elite sent their sons to West Point and almost none to the enlistment depots. The heroes of the coming war would become the elected leaders of the future, and Plattsburg was Wall Street's chance to claim a share of military glory.

Recruits talked about the wholesome, democratic influence of military training. It instilled "discipline, manliness, and that comradeship in a high common purpose," one observed. A millionaire looked like anyone else in uniform, and a journalist remarked that "each reservist left his worldly goods, his 'pull,' his record of past performances at home." Just as in sports, the only standard was how well one performed now, and the camp included a large number of college athletes. Not surprisingly, recruits saw what one described as the "obvious parallel between a football team and an army." War, he wrote, was the "real game."

In articles and memoirs, the recruits remembered the emotions stirred by watching the flag lowered at sunset to the strains of a bugle sounding retreat. "I do not believe that anyone in the camp," John J. McCloy, an Amherst College student who would become an adviser to five presidents, told a friend, "no matter how tired or blue he felt, ever 'stood retreat' without having a tiny thrill run up his spine." Like McCloy, many of the young men at Plattsburg fought in World War I, served the federal government in World War II, and ran law firms, industries, embassies, and government agencies during the cold war. For them, Plattsburg was the beginning of America's adventure in world leadership, a place where, as historian Kai Bird wrote, "the upper class elite underwent a conversion experience of patriotism."

1917, the president called for a "peace without victory," based on self-determination of all nations and the creation of an international organization to enforce peace.

Germany toyed with accepting Wilson's proposals but decided to wait. With the defeat of Russia in 1917, it could shift armies from the eastern front to France. U-boats again torpedoed British passenger liners and American merchant ships. In late February, British intelligence officers showed the US ambassador in London a telegram from the German foreign minister, Arthur Zimmermann, plotting an alliance with Mexico. With the Zimmermann Telegram revealed, if Wilson did not declare war now, Roosevelt declared, he would "skin him alive."

Americans disagreed then, as historians do today, on why the United States went to war. Critics pointed to the corporate interests that stood to gain. Publicly and in private, Wilson stressed two considerations: the attacks on American ships and the peace settlement. The treaty conference would settle scores of issues affecting American interests.

Unless it went to war, Wilson told Jane Addams, the United States would have to shout "through a crack in the door."

War Aims

Rain was falling on the evening of April 2, 1917, as Wilson went to ask Congress for war. Some on Pennsylvania Avenue cheered and waved flags, whereas others stared silently at the president's limousine. The war, Wilson told the assembly, was in its last stages. American armies could bring it to a merciful end. The United States had tried to stand apart, but it had failed. Neutrality had provided no safety for travelers or trade. The only hope for avoiding even more dangerous future wars was for the United States to dictate the peace, to establish a "concert of free peoples." This would be a war to end all wars, to make the world safe for democracy.

In urging the vote for war, the president explicitly rejected the aims of the Allies. "We have no quarrel with the German people," he said, but with the kaiser and all other emperors and autocrats who blocked his road to a new world order. Wilson realized, however, that imperial France and Britain did not stand for democracy or self-determination, either. The United States would fight with Britain and France as an "associated power."

Edward House assembled a secret committee, known as the Inquiry, to draft a peace proposal both generous enough to show "sympathy and friendship" to the German people and harsh enough to punish their leaders. Made up of economists, historians, geographers, and legal experts, with Lippmann as its secretary, the Inquiry produced a set of 14 recommendations that redrew the boundaries of Europe, created a league of nations, and based peace on the principles of freedom of the seas, open-door trade, and ethnic self-determination.

The Fight in Congress

During the ovation after Wilson's speech to Congress, one senator stood silently, his arms folded. La Follette told his colleagues that if this was a war for democracy, it should be declared democratically. The country had voted for the peace candidate for president, and there were strong reasons to suspect a declaration would fail a national vote. Representatives found that voters opposed American entry, often by two to one. Midwestern farmers, William Allen White reported from Iowa, "don't seem to get the war."

Prowar representatives blocked La Follette's move for a referendum and brought the declaration to a vote on April 6, when it passed 82 to 6 in the Senate and 373 to 50 in the House. Divisions resurfaced over questions of how to pay for the war and who would fight in it. Wilson wanted universal conscription, the first draft since the Civil War. The 1917 draft law deputized 4,000 local boards to induct men between 18 and 45. Both supporters and opponents believed the draft would mold citizens. It would "break down distinctions of race and class," said one representative, turning immigrants into "new Americans." La Follette countered that the new Americans would be like the new Germans, indoctrinated by the army.

Newspapers and politicians denounced the antiwar progressives as traitors. They had too few votes to stop conscription, but they did create an exemption for conscientious objectors and reduced some taxes used to pay for the war. Opposition voices were soon silenced by patriotic calls for unity. "I pray God," Wilson avowed, "that some day historians will remember these momentous years as the years which made a single people of the great body of those who call themselves Americans."

Mobilizing the Nation and the Economy

News of the war declaration, carried in banner headlines on Easter Sunday, 1917, set the nation abuzz with activity. Wilson recognized that he was asking for an unprecedented effort. Raising an army of over 3 million, supplying it with modern equipment, and transporting it across submarine-infested waters were herculean feats. By midsummer, there were more men at work building barracks than had been in both armies at Gettysburg. Americans would send to Europe 1.8 million tons of meat, 8.8 million tons of grain, and 1.5 million tons of sugar. Factories that produced sewing machines and automobiles would retool to make howitzers and tanks.

The strain war placed on the American people and economy was severe. Wilson and others feared that it could widen political divisions and destroy 15 years of progressive achievements. Others felt that sharing the sacrifices of war would consolidate the gains. "We shall exchange our material thinking for something quite different," the General Federation of Women's Clubs predicted. "We shall all be enfranchised, prohibition will prevail, many wrongs will be righted." Lippmann hoped war would bring a new American revolution.

THE NAVY NEEDS YOU! DON'T READ AMERICAN HISTORY— **MAKE IT !**

U·S·NAVY RECRUITING STATION

Enforcing Patriotism

Authorities dealt severely with dissent. Suspicions about the loyalties of ethnic communities and rumors of German saboteurs fed the hysteria. On July 30, 1916, across the river from New York City, the largest arms storage facility in the country blew up. The explosion destroyed thousands of pounds of shells and guns bound for Russia and tore away parts of the Statue of Liberty. Federal agents responded by rounding up aliens. However, domestic opinion posed a greater danger to the war effort than enemy agents. While initial enthusiasm ran high, the skepticism La Follette expressed

World War I Draft Registration Poster
All men between the ages of 18 and 45 were required to register for the draft. Almost 3 million men and women would serve during the war.

was just beneath the surface. Victories might not come quickly, and if the public should start to turn against the war, consent would have to be manufactured by propaganda or the police.

Congress gave the president sweeping powers to suppress dissent. The Espionage Act (1917) and the Sedition Act (1918) effectively outlawed opposition to the war and used the postal service to catch offenders. Although there was no link between the labor movement and sabotage, unions were the prime target. The Justice Department raided the Chicago offices of the Industrial Workers of the World and sent 96 leaders to prison on charges of sedition. William D. "Big Bill" Haywood was sentenced to 20 years. Eugene V. Debs, leader of the Socialist Party, received 10 years for telling Ohioans they were "fit for something better than slavery and cannon fodder."

States also passed laws criminalizing "unpatriotic" activity. Indiana's Council for Defense licensed citizens to raid German homes, prevent church services in German, and make sure German Americans bought war bonds. Towns, schools, and clubs with German-sounding names changed them. East Germantown, Indiana, became Pershing. Hamburgers became "liberty sandwiches." Schools in the Midwest stopped teaching German altogether. Americans who had once proudly displayed their ethnicity now took pains to disguise it.

Pacifist faiths had their own ordeals. Some sects had come to America to avoid conscription in Germany or Russia. Many could not comply with the conscientious objector statute, which required submission to military control. Fifteen hundred Mennonites fled to Canada to avoid being placed in camps. Thirty-four Russian Pentecostals were arrested in Arizona, turned over to the army, court-martialed, and sent to Leavenworth.

The government's propaganda effort was managed by the Committee on Public Information (CPI) under former muckraker George Creel. It made films, staged pageants, and churned out ads, billboards, and press releases. The CPI sold the war by telling Americans they were fighting to save their own homes. One poster showed German bombers over a shattered, headless Statue of Liberty. Like Wilson, propaganda distinguished between Germany and the German people. CPI leaflets in German offered "Friendly Words to the Foreign Born." It cast immigrants as potential patriots and women as symbols of progress and sacrifice. Creel drafted Charles Dana Gibson, whose "Gibson Girl" ads personified glamour, to depict women as mothers, nurses, and patriotic consumers. As advertising mobilized American thought for the war effort, it also advanced progressive agendas.

Regimenting the Economy

The first prolonged conflict between industrial nations, World War I introduced the term "total war." By 1917 all of the resources, manpower, and productive capacities of the combatants had been mobilized. It soon became clear that the economy of the United States would have to be organized in new ways.

The navy planned a vast shipyard on Hog Island, near Philadelphia, with 250 buildings, 80 miles of railroad track, and 34,000 workers. It would be larger than Britain's seven largest shipyards combined, but in April 1917, Hog Island was 847 acres of swamp. Steelmaker Charles M. Schwab, in charge of the project, signed contracts for machinery, cement, steel, and timber. Materials were loaded on trains headed east. The result was the Great Pile Up, the biggest traffic jam in railroad history. Without enough workers to unload, cars began to back up on sidings in Philadelphia and then all the way back to Pittsburgh and Buffalo, their loads dumped on the outskirts of cities. Schwab begged the

Hog Island Shipyard Building the massive shipyard at Hog Island was a major feat. The railroad network broke down under the strain, leading Wilson to nationalize the railroads.

railroads to cooperate, to no avail. The voluntary system had failed, and on January 1, 1918, Wilson nationalized the railroads.

The Hog Island fiasco demonstrated the need for supervision of the economy. Wilson created a War Industries Board (WIB) to regulate prices, manufacturing, and transport. The job was enormous, and Wilson found the overseer he needed in Bernard Baruch, a Wall Street financier, who believed in regulation by "socially responsible" businessmen. Baruch recruited corporate executives for top positions and paid them a dollar a year. The president of the Aluminum Company of America became chairman of the WIB's aluminum committee, and a former top executive of John Deere headed the agricultural implements section.

The dollar-a-year men regimented the economy and put business to work for government, but they also guaranteed profits and looked after their own interests. One of their innovations, the "cost-plus" contract, assured contractors the recovery of costs plus a percentage for profit. Under these arrangements, the Black and Decker Company made gun sights, Akron Tire made army cots, and the Evinrude Company stopped making outboard motors and turned out grenades. Each company built up revenues to launch new product lines after the war. Standardization also helped industry. The WIB set standard designs and sizes for everything from shirts to lug nuts. One steel executive observed, "We are all making more money out of this war than the average human being ought to."

Not all businesses submitted willingly to "war socialism." The Ford Motor Company had just set up a national dealer network, and it refused to stop delivering cars. When other automakers followed suit, the board threatened to cut off the industry's supply of coal and steel. After long negotiations, the automakers agreed to cut production by three-fourths. The delay hurt. When American troops went into battle, they had a grand total of two tanks.

The war economy was a culmination of two movements: Wall Street's drive for corporate consolidation and the progressives' push for federal regulation. Businessmen saw that the WIB could rationalize the economy. These "New Capitalists" wanted to end cutthroat competition and make business predictable. They encouraged workers to identify with the company through stock sharing and bonus plans. The WIB's example of government-industry cooperation would serve as a model in national crises to come.

The Great Migration

The war economy gave Americans new choices and opportunities. As factories geared up, they faced a shortage of labor. The draft took eligible employees from the cities, and the usual source of new workers—Europe—was sealed off by a screen of U-boats. Employers found eager workers in the South. In small towns and rural junctions, labor recruiters arrived offering free rides to the North and well-paid employment on arrival. Manufacturers came to rely on the labor of former sharecroppers. Westinghouse employed 25 African Americans in 1916; by 1918 it employed 1,500. The Pennsylvania Railroad recruited 10,000 workers from Florida and Georgia. Veterans saw no reason to go back to sharecropping after the war. In some northern cities, a thousand migrants were arriving each week. This massive movement from the rural South to the urban North and West came to be called the Great Migration.

Lynchings, intimidation, and a declining southern economy encouraged migration. Almost half a million people came north during the war years—so many that some counties emptied out, creating panic among whites left behind. Mississippi alone lost 75,000 workers. "We must have the Negro in the South," the Macon, Georgia, *Telegraph* pined. "It is the only labor we have. . . . If we lose it, we go bankrupt." Southern states banned recruiters. In some places violence provoked migration. "Every time a lynching takes place in a community down south," one observer noted, "you can depend on it that colored people will arrive in Chicago within two weeks."

African American workers moved into jobs at the bottom of the pay scale: janitors, domestics, and factory hands. Rent, groceries, and other necessities were substantially more expensive in the cities. Still, African American workers could earn wages 70 percent higher than what they were used to at home. Almost no one went back, and the new arrivals adapted to the rhythms of city life. "South State Street was in its glory then, a teeming Negro street with crowded theaters, restaurants, and cabarets," Langston Hughes wrote of Chicago in 1918. Housing was scarce, and African American renters were limited to overcrowded districts wedged between industrial zones and hostile white neighborhoods. W. E. B. DuBois noted that African Americans had lived in many neighborhoods of Philadelphia before the war, but by the end of the war they were concentrated in just one ward. Ghetto neighborhoods were both expensive and decrepit. On Chicago's South Side, rents were 15 to 20 percent higher than in white neighborhoods, and the death rate was comparable to that of Bombay, India. White property owners and real estate agents worked to create the ghettos, enforce their boundaries, and "Make Hyde Park White." A real estate agent said that African American homeowners "hurt our values." When discrimination failed, there was dynamite. From 1917 to 1919, whites bombed 26 African American residences in Chicago. On July 2, 1917, in East St. Louis, an arms manufacturing center in southern Illinois, competition for housing and political offices led a mob of white workers to attack "Black Valley," an African American neighborhood along the Southern Railroad track. Forty-seven people were killed and six thousand left homeless.

After East St. Louis, white mobs found black neighborhoods less easy to attack. When a mob invaded a Washington, DC, ghetto three years later, residents fought back with guns. The novelist Alden Bland wrote that the mood in Chicago's Black Belt, under attack in the hot summer of 1919, was "get them before they get you." An African American newspaper explained drily that "New Negroes are determined to make their dying a costly investment for all concerned." The New Negro, urban, defiant, often a war veteran who demanded rather than asked for rights, became the subject of admiring and apprehensive reports. Police kept files on suspected militants, but the mobility and anonymity of northern cities translated into freedom.

Reforms Become "War Measures"

On August 3, 1917, thousands of protestors marched in New York under signs demanding "Why not make America safe for democracy?" In the wake of the East St. Louis outrage, the NAACP urged Congress to outlaw lynching as a "war measure." African Americans were not alone in using the president's language to justify reform. Carrie Chapman Catt told Wilson that he could enact women's suffrage as a "war measure." Advocates of progessive change demanded that the United States practice at home the ideals it fought for abroad.

Suffragists hitched their cause to the national struggle. Catt's National American Woman Suffrage Association (NAWSA) abandoned its state-by-state lobbying to identify women with the national cause. Members sold liberty bonds and knitted socks for the Red Cross, making it clear they expected a constitutional amendment in return. Alice Paul's National Woman's Party (NWP) picketed the White House with signs quoting Wilson's demand for all peoples to "have a voice in their own governments." When Wilson announced his support in 1918, he cited women's war service as the reason. The Nineteenth Amendment was finally ratified in 1920, "so soon after the war," according to Jane Addams, "that it must be accounted as the direct result of war psychology."

As it had for African Americans, the labor shortage increased opportunities for women. Although most women workers were already in the labor force, many took jobs previously considered "inappropriate" for their sex. Women replaced men as bank tellers, streetcar operators, and mail carriers and in heavy-manufacturing firms. Many of these opportunities vanished when the war ended, but in expanding sectors such as finance, communications, and office work, women made permanent gains. By 1920, more than 25 percent worked in offices or as telephone operators, and 13 percent were in the professions. The new opportunities gave women a source of prestige and enjoyment. Alice

Hamilton remarked on the "strange spirit of exaltation among the men and women who thronged to Washington, engaged in all sorts of 'war work' and loving it." Army General Order 13 set standards for women's work, including an eight-hour day, prohibitions on working at night or in dangerous conditions, and provisions for rest periods, lunchrooms, and bathrooms. The government also empowered women consumers, encouraging them to report on shopkeepers who charged above the official price.

Wilson authorized a National War Labor Board to intervene in essential industries. The board set an unofficial minimum wage. For the first time, the federal government recognized workers' rights to organize, bargain collectively, and join unions. Unskilled workers earned higher real wages than ever before. When the Smith and Wesson Company refused to acknowledge its workers' right to bargain collectively, the army seized the factory and recognized the union. There were limits, however, for the administration. When skilled machinists at the Remington Arms plant made demands the board considered excessive, Baruch threatened to have them drafted and sent to France.

Prohibition did not please workers, either, but beer, wine, and spirits were early casualties of war. The Anti-Saloon League and the Woman's Christian Temperance Union had built a powerful antiliquor coalition by 1916. Congress would have passed Prohibition without war, but temperance became a patriotic crusade. Military regulations prohibited liquor near army camps. Finally, in 1919 the states ratified the Eighteenth Amendment, banning the "manufacture, sale, or transportation of intoxicating liquors." The Anti-Saloon League celebrated the dawn of "an era of clear thinking and clean living." America was "so dry it couldn't spit," according to Billy Sunday. He overstated the case. By some estimates, after the ban illegal speakeasies in New York outnumbered the saloons they replaced. Bootleggers and smugglers slaked American thirsts, but liquor prices rose and consumption declined. Americans never again drank anything like the average two and a half gallons of pure alcohol per person annually imbibed before Prohibition.

The war also lent patriotic zeal to anti-vice crusaders. During the Progressive Era, muckrakers exposed the police-protection rackets that allowed gambling dens and brothels to thrive. Within days of the declaration of war, reformers identified prostitutes as enemies of the health of American troops. Gonorrhea afflicted a quarter of the Allied forces in France, and middle-class Americans were appalled. Before 1917, reformers targeted commercial vice as a source of political and social corruption, but afterward they directed their efforts at women as carriers of disease.

The army acted against liquor and prostitution to protect the welfare of soldiers, but it did not challenge racial injustice, even when lives were at stake. At camps in the South, it was often unclear who had more authority, uniformed African American soldiers or white local officials. Clashes could easily turn violent. A riot in Houston in August 1917 began when soldiers from nearby Camp Logan rushed to the aid of an African American woman being beaten by police. Twenty policemen and soldiers were killed, and 54 soldiers received life sentences in the largest court-martial in US history.

After the Houston riot, African American units were dispersed across the country, and the army remained segregated. Worse, many southern communities used military discipline to strengthen their own Jim Crow laws. Encouraged by the army's "work or fight" order, which required draft-age men to either enlist or get a job, states and localities passed compulsory work laws that applied to women and older men. The laws were intended to keep laborers in the fields and servants in the kitchens at prewar wages.

In this "war welfare state," the government mediated among labor, industry, and other organized interests. Social activism became a matter of lobbying federal agencies that could either dictate sweeping changes or use wartime powers to maintain the status quo. Success required organization and an ability to tie one's goals to the government's ambitions.

Over There

When the Senate took up the enormous war budget Wilson submitted in April 1917, the finance committee questioned Major Palmer E. Pierce about what would be done with the money. "Clothing, cots, camps, food, pay," he replied, "and we may have to have an army in France." "Good Lord!" exclaimed Senator Thomas Martin of Virginia. "You're not going to send soldiers over there, are you?" After the horrors of the Somme and Verdun, where men were fed to machine guns by the tens of thousands, it hardly seemed reasonable to send Americans to such a place. "One would think that, after almost four years of war, after the most detailed and realistic accounts of murderous fighting, . . . it would have been all but impossible to get anyone to serve," one veteran later recalled. "But it was not so, we and many thousands of others volunteered."

Americans went to France optimistically believing they could change the war and the peace. Trench warfare was not for them. They planned to fight a war of movement, sweeping in formations across open fields, like those at Antietam and Gettysburg. To a remarkable degree, they got the war they wanted. Europeans watched their civilization destroy itself in the Great War, but Americans saw theirs rising. Soldiers, "doughboys," said so in their letters, echoing the words of their leaders, their newspapers, and the volumes of poetry they carried with them into battle.

Citizens into Soldiers

Enlisting, training, and transporting soldiers began in a rush. Camps housing 400,000 recruits went up in the first 30 days. Conscription went smoothly, and soon 32 camps were housing 1.3 million men. Commander John J. Pershing arrived in France in June with 40,000 men and the first of some 16,000 women who would serve in the American Expeditionary Force (AEF).

Neither the Wilson administration nor the Allies initially anticipated that soldiers would be the United States' main contribution to the war effort. Britain urgently needed financial support, and Wilson advanced $200 million immediately, the first of an eventual $10 billion in loans to the Allies. Funds, food, and ammunition were needed more urgently than men, but that changed in October 1917, when German and Austrian forces smashed through the Italian lines at Caporetto, capturing 275,000 men and finishing the war on that front. When the Bolshevik Revolution curtailed Russian resistance in the East in November, Britain and France saw that by the next spring Germany would be able to mass its armies on the line from Belgium to Switzerland and break through to Paris. The war became a race to the western front between the United States and Germany.

Getting troops to the war required ships, but the American merchant fleet was smaller in 1917 than it was during the Civil War. For a time the United States had to cut back draft calls because it lacked ships to transport soldiers. The navy, meanwhile, cured the U-boat problem. The American destroyer fleet drove submarines from the sea lanes with depth charges, allowing the Allies to convoy effectively for the first time. By July 18, some 10,000 troops a day boarded the "Atlantic Ferry" for the ride to France.

The Fourteen Points

In December 1917, the Inquiry sent the president a memorandum titled "The War Aims and the Peace Terms It Suggests." Wilson redrafted it and presented it to Congress on January 8, 1918. The Fourteen Points outlined US objectives, but more fundamentally they offered an entirely new basis for peace. Unlike nineteenth-century wars waged for limited territorial or political objectives, the Great War was a total war, fought for unlimited aims. The principal belligerents—Britain, France, Russia, Germany, and Austria-Hungary— were global empires. Germany hoped both to defeat Britain and to take its empire. France wanted to destroy Germany's future as a great power, economically and militarily. Wilson replaced these imperial visions of total victory with a peace based on limited gains for nations, not empires.

The Fourteen Points addressed four themes: national self-determination; freedom of the seas; enforcement of peace by a league of nations; and open diplomacy. The Inquiry's memorandum included maps marked with new European boundaries based on national, ethnic identities. The new state of Poland, for instance, should govern only territories with "indisputably Polish populations." Point three restated the Open Door, urging international free trade, reflecting Wilson's hope of eliminating what he saw as the two leading causes of war, imperial ambition and commercial rivalry. By calling for an end to secret diplomacy, he appealed directly to the people of Europe. The expectation was that the hope of a just peace would weaken the enemy nations' will and inspire the Allies to fight harder. Creel printed 60 million copies and had them distributed around the world. Planes dropped copies over Germany and Austria.

Wilson hoped the Fourteen Points would dispel both the old dream of empire and the new one of socialist revolution. On November 7, two months before Wilson presented the points to Congress, Russian workers overthrew the Provisional Government of Alexander Kerensky. The one-party regime of the Bolsheviks, led by Vladimir Lenin, summoned workers everywhere to rise against their governments and to make peace without indemnities or annexations. "The crimes of the ruling, exploiting classes in this war have been countless. These crimes cry out for revolutionary revenge." In December, Lenin revealed the contents of the secret treaties, unmasking the imperial ambitions of the Allies. He sued for peace based on the principle of self-determination. The Council of People's Commissars allocated 2 million rubles to encourage revolutions around the world and called "upon the working classes of all countries to revolt."

Two world leaders—Lenin and Wilson—now offered radically different visions of the new world order, and Lenin was putting his into effect. The Bolsheviks' contempt for democracy angered Wilson, but he hoped that Russia would stay in the war. Those hopes ended with the Treaty of Brest-Litovsk, signed by Russia and Germany in March 1918. The treaty showed the fearful price of defeat in modern war. Russia lost the Ukraine, Poland, and Finland, most of its iron, steel, and best farmland, and one-quarter of its population. Those assets went into the German war machine, which began transferring 10 divisions a month to the West, its eastern front now secure.

Wilson was the first, but not the last, American president to be haunted by the specter of a German-Russian alliance, uniting the immense war-making resources of Europe and Asia. In Wilson's strategic vision, the great land powers of Eurasia, not Alfred Thayer Mahan's sea powers, most threatened US security. He refused to recognize the Bolshevik government and sent 7,000 American troops to Russia to support anti-Bolshevik forces on the eastern front. US and Japanese forces invaded Siberia from the east. The Bolshevik government now counted the United States among its enemies. Meanwhile, the battle for the control of Europe was about to begin.

The Final Offensive

The German high command knew the spring offensive would be the last. Their exhausted economy no longer could supply food or ammunition for a sustained effort. Bread lines, strikes, and industrial breakdowns foreshadowed the chaos that would follow defeat. Risking everything, the German commander Erich Ludendorff launched his offensive on March 21, 1918 (see Map 22–2). Shock troops hurled the British Fifth Army back to Amiens. In May they penetrated French lines as far as Soissons, 37 miles from Paris. As gaps split the lines, French general Ferdinand Foch and General Douglas Haig of Britain appealed urgently to Pershing to put American troops under British and French command. Pershing opposed the idea. He wanted the American army to play its own part in the war.

Map 22–2 Western Front, 1918 On the western front, the opposing armies fought from trenches fortified with earthworks and barbed wire. The parallel trench lines stretched thousands of miles from the North Sea to Switzerland.

Pershing criticized European commanders for remaining on the defensive instead of "driving the enemy out into the open and engaging him in a war of movement." Trained at West Point in Civil War tactics, he imagined himself a General Grant replacing European McClellans and saw trenches as symbols of inertia. Pershing favored massed assaults in which the sheer numbers of American troops would overwhelm the Germans, rifles against machine guns. In seeing Europe's war as a replay of the US Civil War, Pershing revealed a habit of mind that would typify American geopolitical thinking for the next century: the belief that Americans could understand the world through the prism of their own experience. He was not alone in wanting a decisive alternative to trench warfare. Billy Mitchell, head of the army's aviation section, noted that "we could cross the lines of these contending armies in a few minutes in our aeroplanes."

On May 27, German divisions pierced French lines at Château-Thierry and began advancing on Paris at a rate of 10 miles a day. The French government considered whether to abandon the capital or surrender. Bowing to urgent requests, Pershing threw the AEF into the breach. Column upon column of fresh American troops filled the roads from Paris to the front. "We are real soldiers now and not afread [sic] of Germans," John F. Dixon, an African American infantryman from New York, wrote home. "Our boys went on the battlefield last night singing." Ahead lay five German divisions, poison gas, minefields, rolling artillery barrages, and machine guns in interlocking fields of fire. The Germans were stopped, but at a fearful cost. The marine brigade that took Belleau Wood suffered 4,600 casualties, half the force. Without artillery or tanks, they assaulted machine gun nests head-on, with rifles.

By mid-July, the initiative passed to the Allies. On September 12, Foch allowed Pershing to try his tactics against the St. Mihiel salient, a bulge in the French lines which, unknown to the Allies, the Germans had already begun to evacuate. The doughboys raced behind the retreating enemy past their planned objectives. Pershing was delighted. St. Mihiel had vindicated his strategy, and he yearned for another chance. It came two weeks later, at the battle of the Meuse-Argonne.

Ten miles northwest of Verdun, the Argonne Forest contained some of the most formidable natural and man-made defenses on the western front. Atop parallel ridges lay three fortified trench lines, *Stellungen*—barriers of concrete pillboxes, barbed wire, artillery, and observation posts. Half a million German troops had defended these fortifications for four years. Against this force, Pershing arrayed the American First Army, 1,031,000 men. The average doughboy at the Meuse-Argonne had a total of four months of training, and some had as little as 10 days. Pershing's battle plan called for overwhelming the German defenses with speed and numbers, reaching the second trench line, 10 miles inside the German front, the first day.

"Moving slowly forward, never heeding the bursting shells, nor gas, we followed a road forking to the left . . . into no man's land. It was soon noticed that we were in the bracket of a German barrage," a soldier wrote from the battlefield. They broke through the first line of German trenches after a day and a half; then the battle turned into a deadly crawl. In two weeks of fighting, 26,277 Americans died. French soldiers reported seeing the American dead lying in rows, cut down by machine guns as they marched in formation. Finally, on November 10, American troops reached their objective and dynamited the rail line connecting the cities of Metz and Sedan. Meanwhile, Germany announced that it would accept the Fourteen Points as the basis for an armistice and negotiations. At 11:00 a.m. on November 11, 1918, the guns fell silent.

The Western Front From 1914 to 1918, the western front was the largest metropolis on earth, in Robert Crowley's phrase, an "unreal city" whose inhabitants—8,000 of whom died each day—worked in an industry of destruction.

American intervention had been decisive. The American economy, two and a half times the size of Germany's, lent its industrial and agricultural strength to the Allies at a crucial moment. American military power also tipped the balance. Pershing failed to transform strategy—it remained a mechanized war of attrition until the end—but by striking the final blow, Americans had the illusion that their way of war had been triumphant. American losses, 116,516 dead, were smaller than those of the British (908,371), the French (1.4 million), or the Germans (1.8 million), but they still show the colossal destructiveness of industrial war. In just six months, the United States suffered twice as many combat deaths as it would in the Vietnam War and almost a third as many as in World War II.

Americans and Europeans fought two vastly different wars on the same battlefields. The Americans' war was swift and victorious, but the Europeans experienced a catastrophe that consumed an entire generation. For Europeans, their faith in modernity and in the ability of science and democracy to create a better future vanished forever. Confidence in the inevitability of progress became a distinctive feature of US culture in the postwar era. In much of the world, "American" became almost synonymous with "modern," but not everywhere. In the East another political and economic system shouted its claim to the future.

Revolutionary Anxieties

Americans celebrated the armistice with bonfires, church bells, automobile horns, and uplifted voices. Wilson told Congress that "everything for which America fought has been accomplished," but he observed that the situation in Russia cast doubt on the durability of peace. Even before the armistice, German revolutionaries took power in Bavaria. Over the next months, revolutions broke out throughout eastern Europe. From the trenches of Flanders to the Sea of Japan, not a single government remained intact, and in Moscow the new Soviet state towered above the ruins of the old regimes.

Wilson in Paris

For Wilson, the moment he had planned for in 1917 had arrived—the United States could help set the terms of peace—but war had exhausted the president. Confident that the public would view the nation's victory as his victory, he committed mistakes. Had he remained in Washington, some historians argue, he could have taken credit for the peace while keeping a close eye on his critics. Instead, he went to Paris, staking the treaty's success on his own popularity. He passed up a chance to include in the delegation a prominent Republican, such as Henry Cabot Lodge, who could guide the treaty through Congress.

In December 1918, Walter Lippmann, now an army captain, watched Wilson's triumphal entry into Paris. Crowds lined the streets, and as the procession crossed the Pont du Concorde, a great cheer echoed off the walls of the Chamber of Deputies. "Never has a king, never has an emperor received such a welcome," *L'Europe Nouvelle* declared. For the next month, Wilson toured France, Italy, and Britain to cries of "Viva Veelson." "They say he thinks of us, the poor people," a workingman remarked, "that he wants us all to have a fair chance; that he is going to do something when he

The Treaty of Versailles "There was just a little mass of black frock-coated figures under the vast decoration," wrote Sir William Orpen, who painted this image in 1919. "For the most part, they looked profoundly bored, yet they were changing the face of the map; slices were being cut off one country and dumped onto another."

AMERICA AND THE WORLD

>> The Influenza Pandemic of 1918

The 57th Vermont Pioneer Infantry marched for hours through the rain on the night of September 29, 1918, from Camp Merritt, New Jersey, to ferries that carried them down the Hudson to Hoboken, where they boarded the U.S.S. *Leviathan* for the trip to France. The 9,000 wet, tired soldiers and 200 nurses aboard the country's largest and fastest troop transport were nervous about U-boats in the Atlantic, but they had a deadlier enemy, one that came on board with the men of the 57th.

Within hours of embarkation, every bed in the ship's infirmary was full, and every patient had symptoms all too familiar to military doctors: aches in the legs and back, nosebleed, and, in extreme cases, the blue lips and ears, the thin, gasping breaths that indicated advanced pneumonia. But though doctors recognized the signs, they knew nothing about how to treat or prevent Spanish influenza. They could only comfort patients and try to separate the sick from the well on the overloaded ship. By the time it arrived in France, 1,700 passengers were down with "the flu." The disease would kill 290.

The 1918 pandemic affected nearly every spot on the globe, killing over 30 million people, far more than died in the world war. Called "Spanish" because the king of Spain was the first well-known figure to die, the flu was first observed at Fort Riley, Kansas, where the virus may have jumped from pigs to humans. War and commerce accelerated its spread. Men from all of Europe and colonial nations in Asia and Africa came together in the trenches and then carried the disease to every continent. In August the flu mutated into an exceptionally lethal strain. Patients showed signs of massive pneumonia and usually died within three days.

It spread westward across North America, following the railroads, and within weeks encircled the world in a fatal embrace, killing 6 million in India and 675,000 in the United States. In Cincinnati, Ohio, and Harbin, China, farmers noticed that the disease killed hogs in the same proportion that it killed humans, roughly one in ten. A steamer from San Francisco put in at Tahiti on November 16, and within the next three weeks 10 percent of the population died. Isolated habitations newly tied to global trade and communications were hit hardest. The virus arrived in Eskimo villages on postal dogsleds and by camel caravan to Arabian towns. Australia closed its ports in a vain effort to shut out the disease.

At the Paris Peace Conference, delegate and Plattsburg veteran Willard Straight died, and President Wilson, Walter Lippmann, Edward House, and the entire American delegation were sick. At the height of the pandemic in Philadelphia, churches, schools, saloons, and theaters were shut; San Francisco required everyone to wear surgical masks in public. Trolley cars were used as hearses, and the dead were interred in mass graves. Katherine Anne Porter, who nearly died, described the "noiseless houses with the shades drawn, empty streets, the dead cold light of tomorrow."

World war aroused a fervid nationalism, but the pandemic revealed that all nations were equally powerless in the face of catastrophe on this scale. Citizens accused their governments of apathy. The British Raj was in "a state of coma," the Bombay *Chronicle* complained. At Cartwright, on Canada's Labrador Coast, a minister wrote bitterly of his "resentment at the callousness of the authorities, who sent us the disease by mail-boat, and then left us to sink or swim." American soldiers in Brest mutinied, demanding to be released from flu-infested Camp Pontanezen.

One of the first acts of the new League of Nations in 1920 was to establish an international health organization to track epidemics. Agents at port cities collected reports of influenza, typhus, smallpox, cholera, and other plagues and sent them by telegraph to centers at Geneva and Singapore, allowing quarantines to be established or lifted when danger passed. Quarantines disrupted trade, and the League wanted to control panic as much as disease. In 1948, the service became the World Health Organization (WHO), an affiliate of the United Nations.

Nearly a century later, air transport and global food-supply chains have made every epidemic into a potential pandemic. Outbreaks of communicable disease—or livestock infections, such as mad cow disease—touch off a global response. In March 2003, a strange pneumonia appeared in China, Canada, Vietnam, and Singapore, reviving memories of the 1918 flu. A WHO doctor, an Italian tending an American patient in a Hanoi hospital, identified it as a new virus: severe acute respiratory syndrome (SARS). The WHO issued travel alerts, established quarantine procedures at airports, and sent epidemiological teams to trace the outbreak to its source. National governments tried to conceal the extent and danger of the disease from the media, but the WHO prevailed, and the outbreak was contained. Still, experts counted us lucky. No cure has yet been found for viral diseases, and had SARS spread at the rate of the Spanish flu, the toll would have numbered in the millions. In April 2009, a lethal flu virus—transferred, like the 1918 strain, from pigs—emerged in Mexico and spread through New York and Toronto to the rest of the world. Once again, the WHO mobilized a global response. For disease trackers, 1918 remains the standard for how destructive a modern plague can be—and might be again.

gets here that will make it impossible for our government to send us to war again. If he had only come sooner!"

By the time Wilson arrived for treaty talks at the Palace of Versailles, two of the Fourteen Points had already been compromised. Britain refused to accept the point on freedom of the seas, which would thwart the use of the Royal Navy in a future conflict. Wilson also undercut his own position on point six, respect for Russia's sovereignty, as American troops were occupying Russian Siberia. Wilson was unable to prevent Britain, France, and Japan from dividing Germany's colonies among themselves and imposing harsh peace terms. Germany had to sign a humiliating "war guilt" clause and pay $33 billion in reparations, enough to cripple its economy for decades. Wilson concentrated on the League of Nations, which might make up for the treaty's other weaknesses and provide some safety against the rising tide of revolution. He took the lead in drafting the League Covenant, which committed each member to submit disputes to arbitration and pledged them to take action against "any war or threat of war."

The Senate Rejects the League

To many observers in the United States the Treaty of Versailles betrayed the goals Americans had fought to attain. "This is Not Peace," declared the *New Republic*. Congress saw the League of Nations less as a way to prevent wars than as a guarantee that the United States would be involved. Americans were "far more afraid of Lenin than they ever were of the Kaiser," Lippmann wrote. To Republican leaders such as Henry Cabot Lodge, the United States' best bet was to look to its own security, keep its options open, and work out its international relations independently rather than as part of an alliance or league.

In March 1919, before the treaty was concluded, Lodge and 38 other senators—more than enough to defeat the treaty—signed a petition opposing the League of Nations. James A. Reed of Missouri said the covenant would turn American foreign policy over to foreigners. Editorials feared that American troops would be summoned to settle blood feuds in the Balkans. Wilson expected to fight, but he believed that the Senate would not reject the treaty.

In September, Wilson went "over the heads" of Congress and stumped for the treaty on a nationwide tour. He assured listeners in Sioux Falls that "the peace of the world cannot be established without America." He promised the citizens of Salt Lake City that China's independence would be respected. Traveling more than 8,000 miles and speaking before large audiences without loudspeakers took a toll on his health. After a speech in Pueblo, Colorado, he became so ill that he was rushed back to Washington, where he suffered a stroke that left him partially paralyzed and unable to concentrate for more than a few minutes a day. Mrs. Wilson and the president's physician kept his condition a secret and refused to allow anyone to see him.

With Wilson secluded in the White House, the Senate voted against ratification. To the end, Wilson refused to allow Senate Democrats to accept any modifications. Even Lippmann's *New Republic*, a mouthpiece for Wilson throughout the war, called the treaty's demise "desirable and wholesome." Lodge and the Republicans were not ready for isolation, but they preferred diplomatic strategies based on economic strength rather than a relatively

>> Time Line

▼1911
Mexican Revolution begins

▼1912
Woodrow Wilson elected president

▼1914
US troops occupy Veracruz, Mexico
World War I begins

▼1915
US troops occupy Haiti (until 1934)
Lusitania sunk

▼1916
US forces invade Mexico in search of Pancho Villa
US forces enter Dominican Republic
Woodrow Wilson reelected

▼1917
Russian czar abdicates; parliamentary regime takes power
US declares war on Germany
East St. Louis riot
Houston riot
October Revolution overthrows Russian government; Lenin takes power

weak military. They also saw Latin America as more critical than Europe to US security. Meanwhile, European governments organized the League of Nations without delegations from the United States or the Soviet Union.

Over the next decade, US influence abroad grew enormously. American automobiles, radios, and movies could be seen in far corners of the globe. The United States still practiced cautious diplomacy in Europe and Asia, to avoid being drawn into what the *New York Tribune* called the "vast seething mass of anarchy extending from the Rhine to the Siberian wastes."

Red Scare

On May 1, 1919, a dozen or more mail bombs were sent to prominent Americans: J. P. Morgan, John D. Rockefeller, senators, cabinet officials, and Supreme Court Justice Oliver Wendell Holmes. None of the packages reached its intended target, but one injured a maid in the home of Senator Thomas Hardwick and another exploded at the residence of Attorney General A. Mitchell Palmer in Washington, nearly injuring Franklin and Eleanor Roosevelt, who lived next door. Investigations later showed that the bombings were the work of lone lunatics, but many people quickly concluded that the United States was under attack. Since the Russian Revolution, newspapers, evangelists,

Wall Street Bombing On September 16, 1920, Mario Buda detonated a horse-drawn wagon filled with dynamite and scrap metal in front of the J. P. Morgan offices on Wall Street. It was the first use of a new technology of terror, the car bomb. Sending shockwaves through an America already anxious about revolutionaries, the blast intensified the hunt for radicals and "reds."

▼**1918**

Wilson announces US war aims: the Fourteen Points

Wilson nationalizes railroads

Sedition Act outlaws criticism of the US government

US troops stop German advance

Wilson sends troops to Siberia

Armistice ends fighting on the western front

Influenza pandemic peaks in September

▼**1919**

Eighteenth Amendment outlaws manufacture, sale, and transport of alcoholic beverages

Versailles Treaty signed in Paris

Mail bombs target prominent government and business figures

Gary, Indiana, steel strike

US Senate rejects Versailles Treaty

▼**1920**

Nineteenth Amendment secures the vote for women

Palmer raids arrest thousands of suspected Communists

Sacco and Vanzetti arrested on charges of robbery and murder and government officials had fed fears of Bolshevism. Revolution, Palmer alleged, was "licking at the altars of the churches, leaping into the belfry of the school bell, crawling into the sacred corners of American homes."

Revolutions in Europe terrified conservatives in the United States and led them to look for Soviet terrorists, particularly among immigrants and unionized workers. They drew no distinctions among Socialists, anarchists, Communists, and labor unionists; they were all "red." Seattle's mayor called in the army to break a dockworkers' strike. When steelworkers in Gary, Indiana, struck for higher wages and shorter hours in September 1919, Judge Elbert Gary, president of U.S. Steel, denounced them as followers of Russian "anarchy and Bolshevism." During the war they had worked 12 hours a day, 7 days a week, for an average wage of $28 a week. With the help of local loyalty leagues, Gary broke the strike.

Using the patriotic rhetoric of the war, industry leaders labeled strikers as dangerous aliens. They persuaded allies in the courts to take action, and a series of Supreme Court decisions made union activity virtually illegal. In 1919 the Court allowed antitrust suits to be filed against unions and later outlawed boycotts and picketing. Then, in January 1920, a series of crackdowns known as the Palmer raids rounded up and deported 250 members of the Union of Russian Workers. In one night, 4,000 suspected Communists were arrested in raids across the country.

> The Department of Justice has undertaken to tear out the radical seeds that have entangled American ideas in their poisonous theories.
>
> ATTORNEY GENERAL
> A. MITCHELL PALMER

The most notorious case associated with the "Red Scare" began in May 1920 when Nicola Sacco and Bartolomeo Vanzetti, a shoemaker and a fish peddler, were arrested for robbing a shoe company in South Braintree, Massachusetts. Two men died of gunshot wounds during the robbery, and ballistics experts claimed the bullets came from Sacco's gun. The trial, however, focused less on the evidence than on the fact that the defendants were Italian and anarchists. The state doctored evidence and witnesses changed testimony, but the judge favored the prosecution. The appeals lasted six years, as protests for their release mounted. With the execution approaching, labor parties organized worldwide boycotts of American products. Riots in Paris took 20 lives. Uruguayan workers called a general strike. Governments called on the president to intervene, but on August 23, 1927, Sacco and Vanzetti died in the electric chair.

Americans who had talked in 1917 about making the world safe for democracy now seemed ready to restrict their own freedoms out of fear. Lippmann found it "incredible that an administration announcing the most spacious ideals in our history should have done more to endanger fundamental American liberties than any group of men for a hundred years." By the end of 1920, the terror subsided, but labor unions and social radicals would have to fight the charge of Communism for decades to come.

Conclusion

Wilson tried to lead America toward what he called a new world order, in which nations and international law would count more than empires and in which the United States could light the way toward progress, stability, and peace. He failed to recognize that for many

Americans this future was filled with terrors, as well as promise. The strains of war had introduced new divisions into American society. Progressivism, which had given coherence and direction to social change, was a spent force. The growth of federal administration, the new powers of big business, internal migrations, and new social movements and values added up to what Lippmann called a "revolutionary world." Many of the changes that began during the war had not fully played out, nor were their consequences apparent, but Americans entered the 1920s with a sense of uneasiness. They knew that their nation was now the world's strongest, but they were unsure about what that might mean for their lives.

Who, What

Bernard Baruch 668

Carrie Chapman Catt 670

George Creel 667

Porfirio Díaz 659

Langston Hughes 669

John J. Pershing 659

Cost-plus contract 668

Neutrality 660

Propaganda 667

Red Scare 681

Suffrage 670

Review Questions

1. Wilson encouraged Americans to fight a war for democracy, but what other goals did US intervention serve?

2. How did mobilization for war advance the progressive agenda? In what ways did it set progressives back?

3. Where were the main battles in which US troops fought?

Critical-Thinking Questions

1. Allied commanders wanted to use American troops as a reserve, but Pershing wanted his soldiers to enter the battle as an army. Why was that so important to him?

2. Why did Senate Republicans reject the League of Nations? Did they want the United States to withdraw from the world, or did they want to deal with the world in a different way?

3. Managing the pace of change posed a tricky problem for leaders in the early twentieth century. How did Wilson try to control the dynamic of social and political change? What methods of change was he unwilling to accept?

4. Why were American leaders so much more concerned about sedition and dissent during World War I than they were during the Civil War or World War II?

For further review materials and resource information, please visit www.oup.com/us/ofthepeople

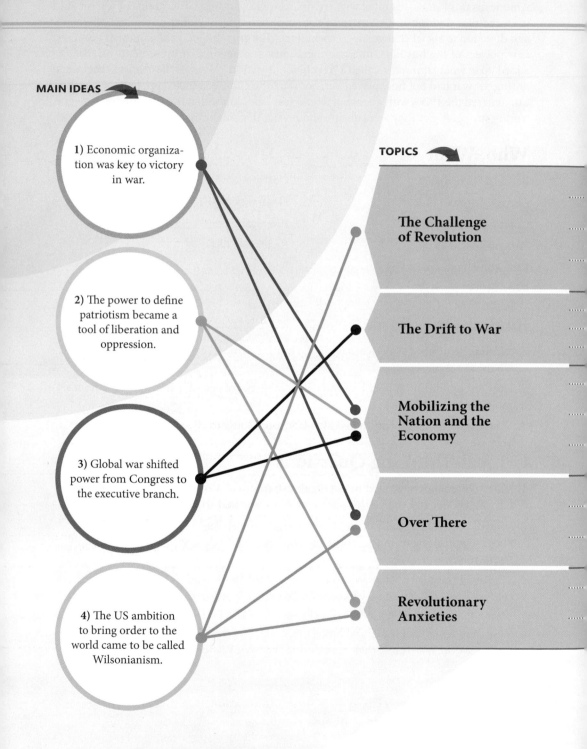

MAIN IDEAS

1) Economic organization was key to victory in war.

2) The power to define patriotism became a tool of liberation and oppression.

3) Global war shifted power from Congress to the executive branch.

4) The US ambition to bring order to the world came to be called Wilsonianism.

TOPICS

The Challenge of Revolution

The Drift to War

Mobilizing the Nation and the Economy

Over There

Revolutionary Anxieties

EVENTS

The Mexican Revolution Wilson sent troops into Mexico on behalf of US business interests, uniting all of the civil war factions against the United States.

Bringing Order to the Caribbean Wilson repeatedly intervened in Latin America and the Caribbean to bring "order" to the region.

A One-Sided Neutrality Despite a guiding principle of strict neutrality at the start of World War I, US policy favored the Allies.

The *Lusitania*'s Last Voyage Germany's sinking of the *Lusitania* stirred public opinion to enter the war against Germany.

The Election of 1916 Wilson's reelection allowed him to pursue a more vigorous foreign policy.

The Last Attempts at Peace Wilson's last attempt to end the war failed, almost guaranteeing US entry.

War Aims The US entered the war against Germany in order to set the terms of the peace.

The Fight in Congress Antiwar congressmen tried and failed to put the war to a national referendum.

Enforcing Patriotism Congress gave the president sweeping powers to suppress dissent.

Regimenting the Economy The United States imposed central regulation of the economy to meet production needs for a prolonged war.

The Great Migration Large numbers of African Americans left the rural South for manufacturing jobs in the urban North and West.

Reforms Become "War Measures" Advocates of progressive change demanded that the ideals fought for abroad be practiced at home.

Citizens into Soldiers The United States quickly enlisted, trained, and transported soldiers to meet the demands of combat in Europe.

The Fourteen Points Wilson presented new war objectives, offering a new basis for peace and addressing the potential causes of future wars.

The Final Offensive The American economy and military power tipped the balance toward the Allies at a crucial time.

Wilson in Paris Wilson went to Paris to negotiate a peace settlement.

The Senate Rejects the League After fierce debate, the Senate rejected the League of Nations and failed to ratify the peace treaty.

Red Scare Fearing Communist infiltration, conservative Americans denounced their political enemies as unpatriotic.

CHAPTER
....
23

The Modern Nation
1919-1928

>> "America's Sweetheart"

By the end of World War I, 26-year-old Mary Pickford had become "America's Sweetheart." After a decade in Hollywood, the diminutive, long-haired actress was one of the first and greatest stars of the movies. Fans flocked to her films, eagerly read news about her, and mobbed her in public. The actress, earning hundreds of thousands of dollars a year, was one of the richest women in the United States.

Mary Pickford's phenomenal success was certainly a product of her talent and good luck. But her career was also a product of increasingly important trends after World War I. A dynamic industrial economy, drawing on such rapidly developing technologies as motion pictures, seemed effortlessly to produce plenty of prosperity, leisure, and consumer goods. More than ever before, Americans had both the money and time to enjoy themselves, to consume a host of pleasures.

Pickford exemplified the new national culture that emerged from the needs of the booming consumer economy. Breaking with the past, this modern culture celebrated innovation, modernity, and the future. "One should always go forward," Pickford declared. "It isn't good to go back to anything, not even to the old home farm, or one's old loves." The new culture welcomed leisure, including movie going, spectator sports, and other diversions. Pickford worked hard but she entertained lavishly and took highly publicized vacations, too. The new culture also glorified conspicuous consumption. Living well, Pickford bought such indulgences as a miniature, glass-enclosed, two-seater Rolls-Royce automobile, one of only three in the world.

The movie star embodied still other aspects of the new culture—its fascination with youth and its infatuation with independent, nontraditional women. Well into her twenties, "Little Mary" still played plucky, playful young girls. Although married, Pickford focused on her career and increasingly took control of the production of her films. Like the new culture, Pickford broke free from old restraints. Americans, as she wrote, had seen divorce as a

continued

"dreadful disease," but even so, in March 1920, she divorced her first husband and married the star Douglas Fairbanks Sr. Her popularity did not decrease.

Going her own way so often, Pickford also exemplified a resurgent individualism that shaped the Republican-dominated politics of the 1920s. In the movies and real life, she seemed to prove that individuals, even immigrants and the poor, could still find opportunity and achieve great things in an increasingly corporatized and bureaucratized society. Born to poverty in Canada, Pickford had found success in America. Remaking her identity, she changed her name from Gladys Smith. In 1919, she escaped the control of the big movie studios by joining with Douglas Fairbanks Sr., comic actor Charlie Chaplin, and director D. W. Griffith to create their own distribution company, United Artists.

The new culture helped redefine the United States in the eyes of the world. Pickford's films were popular around the globe. When she and Fairbanks traveled to Europe in the 1920s, they met huge crowds and near riots. Even citizens of the communist Union of Soviet Socialist Republics lionized the visiting "Little Mary."

Amid all the trappings of Mary Pickford's popularity, it was easy to conclude that Americans loved the emerging cultural and political order as much as they loved "America's Sweetheart." In fact, many people were troubled by the changes of the 1920s. The modern order did not reflect the values of millions of Americans. For all the celebration of the individual, many Americans felt they did not have enough power over their lives. American democracy seemed too limited. As a result, the new cultural and political order faced a powerful backlash as the decade went on.

A Dynamic Economy

By and large, the 1920s were a prosperous time for America. After a recession during 1920 and 1921, the economy continued to grow. Consumer prices remained steady throughout the decade, and jobs were plentiful; the unemployment rate went as low as 1.8 percent in 1926. Wages jumped: the nation's net income—the value of its earnings from labor and property—leapt from $64.0 billion in 1921 to $86.8 billion in 1929. This prosperity was driven by a dynamically evolving industrial economy featuring new technologies, increased efficiency, a maturing automobile industry, and new businesses.

Despite general prosperity, the transformation of the economy involved defeats for organized labor and decline for many farmers. The relative weakness of agriculture and the strength of industry helped to turn the United States into a predominantly urban nation. In the prosperous 1920s, as always, industrial capitalism was a transforming force.

The Development of Industry

Several long-term factors shaped the development of American industry in the 1920s. Searching for more efficient production, businessmen used a flood of new technologies, other innovations, and new technical expertise. More patents were issued for new inventions—421,000 of them—than in any preceding decade. During the 1920s, the number of engineers in the country nearly doubled.

The switch from coal to electricity, under way since the 1910s, was a critical innovation. By the end of the 1920s, electricity powered more than two-thirds of American manufacturing plants. Henry Ford's car company pioneered another crucial innovation, the system that became known as Fordism, or mass production. By the 1910s, Ford, like other American manufacturers, used interchangeable parts, simple and accurate machine tools, and electric power to speed output at its Highland Park plant in Detroit. But traditional manufacturing practice slowed production. Frames, transmissions, and other key subassemblies waited on stands while teams of workers moved from one stand to another. Eager to meet the rising demand for the popular Model T car, Ford's managers reversed the process by "moving the work to the men." Beginning in 1913, conveyor belts and chains sent subassemblies past groups of stationary workers. Instead of making an entire engine, a worker might tighten a few bolts or install a single part. The results were astonishing: in 1914, Ford produced 300,000 Model Ts; in 1923, more than 2 million. Other manufacturers raced to copy Ford's techniques.

Mass production, electrification, and other innovations spurred an extraordinary increase in productivity for American industry. Output per worker skyrocketed 72 percent from 1919 to 1929.

Along with increased productivity, the rise of several industries drove the economy. Auto production now dominated as textiles, railroads, iron, and steel had earlier. In 1921,

Ford Assembly Line Mass production at work: the assembly line at the Ford Motor Company plant in Dearborn, Michigan, 1928.

there were 9.3 million cars on American roads; by 1929, there were 23 million. The manufacture of all those cars stimulated demand for plate glass, oil, gasoline, and rubber.

Other sectors of the economy also grew rapidly. The demand for processed foods, household appliances, office machinery, and chemicals increased dramatically. Emerging industries such as aircraft demonstrated their potential importance.

Arguably the first powered, fixed-wing flight had occurred in December 1903, when Wilbur and Orville Wright's "Flyer" flew 120 feet in 12 seconds over the beach at Kitty Hawk, North Carolina. But the civilian airplane industry did not take off until the 1920s. Aircraft production rose from less than 300 in 1922 to more than 6,000 in 1929. By then, fledgling airlines were flying passengers on scheduled flights.

The Trend Toward Large-Scale Organization

The development of industry reinforced the trend toward large-scale organization that was basic to US capitalism (see Chapter 17). Only giant corporations, with thousands of employees and hundreds of millions of dollars in capitalization, had the financial resources to pay for mass production. A wave of mergers meant that these big businesses controlled more factories and assets than ever. By 1929, corporations produced 92 percent of the nation's manufactured goods.

The largest firms also benefited from more efficient organization. When the recession of 1920 and 1921 left them with too many unsold goods, companies reorganized. Top managers, aided by financial, legal, and other experts, now oversaw semiautonomous divisions that supplied different markets. At General Motors, the Chevrolet division produced huge numbers of relatively inexpensive cars, while the Cadillac division turned out a smaller number of expensive cars. The new system made corporations more flexible, efficient, and responsive to consumer demand.

Corporate growth was not confined to industry. Chains such as A. & P. grocers and F. W. Woolworth variety stores increased their share of retail sales from 4 percent to 20 percent. One percent of the nation's banks managed nearly half of the country's financial assets. By 1929, just 200 corporations held about one-fifth of national wealth.

Giant firms and their leaders had often been targets of hostility and reform during the Progressive Era, but the decade's prosperity led many Americans to soften their attitude toward business. There were fewer calls to break up or regulate giant corporations. Big-businessmen had seemed to be selfless patriots during World War I. Now their companies were apparently creating a new period of economic well-being. To ensure a better image, businessmen paid for public relations campaigns that stressed their commitment to ethical behavior and social service. Basking in the glow of public approval, big business was confident about its role in the nation's destiny.

The Transformation of Work and the Workforce

The quest for productivity had dramatic consequences for American workers. Industrial efficiency was not just a matter of electricity and machines. To speed up production, the managers at Ford and other factories had to change the nature of work.

Accordingly, the spirit of scientific management continued to sweep across the factory floor. Under ever-tighter supervision, workers were pushed to work faster and harder. In textile mills, the "stretch-out" required workers to tend more looms than before. Ford's system of mass production shared Frederick Winslow Taylor's determination to simplify and regiment labor. The result was less-satisfying work. Instead of making a whole engine, a Ford assembly line worker might spend his day turning a few nuts on one engine after another. In 1913, Ford's labor turnover rate soared to 380 percent as unhappy workers quit their jobs.

As production grew more efficient, about a million workers lost manufacturing, mining, and railroading jobs. The growth of other kinds of employment more than compensated for this decrease, however. The ranks of white-collar workers increased 80 percent from 1910 to 1930, or nearly one worker in three. The nation had already begun to evolve from an industrial economy based on manual labor to a postindustrial economy based on sales and service.

Economic development also encouraged the gradual movement of women into the paid workforce. By the end of the 1920s, women, most of them unmarried, made up a majority of clerical workers. In 1900, 22 percent of women had worked for pay; by the 1940s, the percentage would reach 27.

Despite these changes, women still faced discrimination. Mary Pickford was exceptional. Overwhelmingly concentrated in low-wage occupations such as domestic service, factory work, and agriculture, they were paid less than men who did comparable work. Female sales workers earned between 42 and 63 percent of the wages paid to their male counterparts. Few women held high-level managerial jobs. Moreover, most people continued to believe that a woman's place was in the home, especially if she had children, and many men feared that paid labor would make women too independent. Only economic necessities reconciled American society to women's employment in the 1920s.

The Defeat of Organized Labor

The American labor movement did not respond effectively to the transformation of work and the workforce. In an age of increasing economic organization, workers became less organized. In 1920 nearly one nonagricultural worker in five belonged to a union. By 1929, little more than one in ten did. The labor movement was especially weak in such developing mass-production industries as automobiles and steel and barely addressed the growing ranks of clerks and other white-collar workers.

Prosperity also weakened organized labor. Earning relatively good wages, many workers were less interested in joining unions. To show that unions were unnecessary, corporations promoted welfare capitalism, highly publicized programs ranging from lunch-hour movies to sports teams to profit-sharing plans. Many firms created company unions, but when it became clear that they did not give employees a real voice in management, their membership dwindled.

Although some firms tried to win over their workers with baseball teams and company unions, many others used tougher tactics to battle the labor movement. Management crusaded for the "open shop"—a workplace free of labor organization—and found an ally in the judicial system. Rulings by the US Supreme Court, such as *Duplex Printing Press Co. v. Deering* (1921) and *Bedford Cut Stone Co. v. Journeymen Stone Cutters' Assn.* (1927), made it easier for state and federal courts to grant injunctions to stop unions from striking and exercising their rights. Businesses could sue unions for damages. They also demanded that workers sign "yellow-dog contracts" promising not to join a union.

The labor movement also hurt its own cause. The leadership of the major national organization, the American Federation of Labor, was increasingly conservative and timid. The heads of the AFL, mostly white males of western European extraction who represented skilled crafts, had little interest in organizing women workers and wanted nothing to do with socialists, radical unionists, or African American workers. The AFL was slow to acknowledge the Brotherhood of Sleeping Car Porters, the assertive union of African American workers organized in 1925 under socialist A. Philip Randolph. Despite pleas from Randolph and others, the AFL failed to organize unskilled workers, many of whom were African Americans or white immigrants from eastern and southern Europe.

Weakened by internal divisions, welfare capitalism, the open-shop crusade, and the courts, the labor movement did not effectively challenge the transformation of industrial labor. Nationwide, the number of strikes and lockouts dropped from 3,411 in 1920 to 604 in 1928. These labor actions often ended in defeat for workers.

The Decline of Agriculture

Despite national prosperity, American agriculture continued its long decline. Prices for basic crops such as cotton and wheat fell, and the number of farms dropped.

The larger story of decline obscured important signs of growth and health. Some agricultural sectors were as dynamic as industry and for the same reasons—increased efficiency promoted by new technologies and large-scale organization. Mechanization, including the introduction of powerful tractors, made farm labor more efficient. So did the development of irrigation systems. By the 1920s, the irrigated farms of the Southwest were producing bumper crops of cotton, fruits, and vegetables. The Southwest also witnessed the rise of huge mechanized farms with hundreds and even thousands of irrigated acres. These "factories in the fields" depended not only on size and technology but also on the old-fashioned exploitation of farm labor. In California's Imperial Valley and elsewhere, migrant workers labored in harsh conditions for low pay on modern farms.

Ironically, the dynamic agricultural economy created a problem for many farmers. Midsize farms, too big to be run by their owners alone and too small for mechanization, could not compete with the vast "factories in the fields." Increased efficiency, meanwhile, led to bumper crops that did not always find a good market price. Farmers were hurt by a changing American diet, with declining consumption of bread and potatoes, and by the rise of competitors overseas. Productive American farmers could no longer export enough of their surplus. The resulting glut reduced the price of farm products. As their incomes lagged behind those of urban workers, farmers yearned for the return of high pre–World War I agricultural prices to restore parity between city and country. As a Georgia farmer observed, "The hand that is feeding the world is being spit upon."

The Urban Nation

The woes of agriculture contributed to a long-term shift in the American population. For the first time, according to the census of 1920, a majority of Americans—54 million out of 105 million—lived in urban territory. The census defined "urban territory" as places with as few as 2,500 people, many of them small towns close to country life. Still, the population of the United States was no longer predominantly rural.

The decline of farming spurred this shift. As agricultural prices fell, millions of Americans fled the nation's farms. The total US population increased by 17 million during the 1920s, but the farm population declined by more than 1.5 million.

At the same time, the growth of the industrial economy swelled the population of towns and cities. In the 1920s, factory production was still centered in urban areas and gave many cities their identity. Detroit was becoming the "Motor City." Akron was the home of rubber production. Pittsburgh and Birmingham symbolized the steel industry. Most of the new white-collar jobs were located in cities. Corporations also put their headquarters in cities, especially the two largest, Chicago and New York.

The rise of the automobile further contributed to the emergence of the urban nation. The car made it practical for Americans to live in suburbs and drive into the city to work and shop. In the 1920s, the suburban lifestyle was still reserved mostly for the well-to-do. Elite suburbs, such as Grosse Pointe and Ferndale outside Detroit and Beverly Hills and Glendale outside Los Angeles, grew explosively. The transformation of farms into suburbs symbolized the new urban nation.

A Modern Culture

The 1920s saw the full emergence of a modern culture that had been taking shape for decades and that now surrounded Americans with something fundamentally new. Symbolized by Mary Pickford, the new culture extolled the virtues of modernity and pleasure. Rooted in the nation's economic development, the new culture reflected both the needs of businessmen with goods to sell and the desires of Americans with more money and free time than ever. Supported by advertising and installment buying, the culture of leisure and consumption offered movies, spectator sports, popular music, radio, and sex. It also offered new views of gender, family life, and youth and renewed old values of individualism in an increasingly organized society.

The Spread of Consumerism

Encouraged by big business, many Americans now defined life as the pursuit of pleasure and found happiness in leisure and consumption rather than in work. This philosophy of consumerism saturated society by the end of the decade.

Increased efficiency and profitability enabled American employers to allow their workers higher wages and more leisure hours. Some employers, notably Ford, also raised wages in order to hold on to workers alienated by the drudgery of mass production. And Ford himself increased workers' pay to enable them to buy the products of modern factories. The incomes of workers and other employees reached a new high in the 1920s. Factory workers' real wages rose 19 percent from 1914 to 1923.

Many workers had more time to enjoy their wages. For salaried, middle-class workers, the annual vacation had become a tradition by the 1910s. Although blue-collar workers seldom enjoyed a vacation, they spent less time on the job. Some employers, including Henry Ford, instituted a five-day workweek during the 1920s. More businesses shortened their workdays, and the average workweek fell from 47.4 hours in 1920 to 44.2 in 1929. "The shorter work day brought me my first idea of there being such a thing as pleasure," said one young female worker. "Before this time it was just sleep and eat and hurry off to work."

A change in attitude accompanied these changes in wages and workdays. The work ethic seemed less necessary in a prospering economy. Thanks to Fordism and Taylorism, work was also less satisfying, and people justified pleasure as an essential antidote to labor.

The advertising industry encouraged the new attitude toward pleasure. Although advertising agencies had first appeared in the 1850s and 1860s, the business did not mature until the 1920s. Now, ads appeared everywhere—in newspapers and magazines, on billboards and big electric signs. Major advertising agencies such as J. Walter Thompson and Batten, Barton, Durstine, and Osborn concentrated in New York City, home to so many corporations. Impressed by successful ad campaigns for Listerine mouthwash and Fleischmann's yeast, big business hired ad agencies to sell goods and services. Expenditures for advertising leapt from $682 million in 1914 to nearly $3 billion by 1929.

> Every morning,
>
> Every evening,
>
> Ain't we got fun? /
>
> Not much money,
>
> Oh but honey,
>
> Ain't we got fun?
>
> RICHARD A. WHITING,
>
> RAYMOND B. EGAN,
>
> AND GUS KAHN,
>
> 1921

Advertising, like the new culture, optimistically embraced change and trumpeted the new. In advertisements, purchasing the right products solved problems, made up for the drudgery of work, and brought fulfillment. To enthusiastic ad men, advertising was as important as the products it sold. In his best-selling book *The Man Nobody Knows* (1925), ad pioneer Bruce Barton portrayed Jesus Christ as a great advertiser, whose disciples "conquered the world" by selling a new product, Christianity. Along with advertising, business used installment loans to encourage Americans to buy goods and services "on time." Credit buying spread so rapidly that total consumer debt more than doubled from 1922 to 1929. The sales of such consumer goods as pianos, washing machines, and automobiles boomed. Americans bought 181,000 automobiles in 1910; they bought 4,455,000 in 1929. Thanks to the availability of another kind of loan, the mortgage, more Americans were able to invest in a home of their own. Spending on new private housing jumped from $2.0 billion in 1920 to $5.0 billion by 1924. Loan-driven spending helped power the economic prosperity of the 1920s.

New Pleasures

The culture of the 1920s offered many escapes, especially sports, movies, popular music, and radio. Although people still played games themselves, they also watched other people's games more than ever before. Tennis, boxing, and auto racing flourished as spectator sports during the decade. The American Professional Football Association, which became the National Football League, played its first season in 1920. Although crowds packed college football stadiums, baseball remained the most popular American sport. Minor-league baseball covered the nation. Meanwhile, the popularity of major-league baseball surged, thanks in part to the exploits of home run–hitting Babe Ruth and his New York Yankees.

Spectator sports enthralled millions, but another passive enjoyment, the movies, was the most popular consumer attraction of the 1920s (see Table 23–1). A novelty in the mid-1890s, silent films had become a big business. In city neighborhoods in the 1900s, crowds

Table 23-1 Spending for Recreational Services, 1909–1929

Year	Total (millions of dollars)	Motion Picture Theaters (millions of dollars)	Spectator Sports (millions of dollars)
1909	377	###	###
1914	434	###	###
1919	806	###	###
1921	911	301	30
1923	1082	336	46
1927	1405	526	48
1929	1670	720	66

Historical Statistics of the United States, Millennial Online Edition (Cambridge: Cambridge University Press, 2008), Table Dh309–318.

= No Data

packed into stuffy "nickelodeons"—storefront theaters showing short, silent one-reel films for the price of a nickel. The movies became longer and more sophisticated, and theaters became larger and more lavish. Nationwide, weekly attendance doubled from 40 million in 1922 to 80 million in 1929.

Booming attendance fueled the growth of a handful of corporate movie studios, including Warner Brothers and RKO, that dominated the film industry. By the 1920s, the center of movie production had shifted from New York to Hollywood, California. Now called "Hollywood," the film industry grew still bigger toward the end of the decade, when studios learned to synchronize sound and moving images in such films as *The Jazz Singer* of 1927.

It was fitting that one of the first "talking pictures" was about jazz. Popular music in general and jazz in particular played an important role in the new consumer culture. Created by African Americans in the 1910s, jazz was a rhythmically and harmonically innovative music that featured improvised solos and a hot beat. The new music emerged around the country, but its first great center was the streets, brothels, and dives of New Orleans. The Louisiana city was home to the first major jazz composer, Jelly Roll Morton, and to the first jazz superstar, trumpeter and singer Louis Armstrong. As jazz became nationally popular, Morton, Armstrong, and the focus of jazz moved on, as did so many African Americans, to Chicago and New York City (see Chapter 22).

The new music quickly attracted white Americans, especially the young, who yearned for something more daring than the relatively sedate popular music of the day. Even its name—a reference perhaps to speed or sexual intercourse—conjured up pleasure and liberation. Soon white musicians were contributing to the music. For many whites, jazz summed up a period marked by the pursuit of liberating pleasures. The 1920s became known as the "Jazz Age," after the title of a 1922 book of short stories by F. Scott Fitzgerald.

The great popularity of jazz and other musical genres was made possible by the phonograph, originated by Thomas Edison in the 1870s and modified by other inventors. In the 1920s, the electrical recording microphone dramatically improved sound quality and made the new music accessible to millions of Americans.

***The Jazz Singer* Premiere** The dazzling allure of a new pleasure—the "talking picture"—draws a big opening-night crowd to Warners' Theatre, New York City, October 6, 1927.

A newer technological innovation, the radio, also allowed Americans to hear popular music. In 1895, Italian inventor Guglielmo Marconi transmitted the first radio waves; by 1920, commercial radio broadcasting began in the United States. The federal government started licensing radio stations the next year.

Like the movies, radio quickly became corporatized big business. By 1923, there were more than 500 stations, and by 1926, the first permanent radio network, the National Broadcasting Company (NBC). Americans tuned in to broadcasts of live music, news, sports, and soap operas. By 1925, manufacturers turned out more than 2 million radios a year. Radio, like the movies, disseminated the values of consumerism, as corporations rushed to advertise their products by sponsoring radio programs.

A Sexual Revolution

Along with such new pleasures as radio and movies, the modern culture offered a new attitude toward an old pleasure, sex. By the 1920s, Americans' sexual attitudes and behavior were changing. People openly discussed sex and placed a new emphasis on the importance of sexual satisfaction, primarily in marriage. And there were signs of greater sexual exploration among unmarried young people.

In the nineteenth century, Americans, especially middle-class Victorians, had largely kept a discreet silence about sex. That silence gave way in the twentieth century.

Progressive Era reformers had forced public discussion of issues such as prostitution and venereal disease. The reformers, anxious to control extramarital sexual behavior, hardly wanted to glorify sexual pleasure. But they helped pave the way for an approving depiction of sexuality.

Popular amusements of the 1910s and 1920s were filled with sexual images. The movies explored sexual topics in such films as *The Anatomy of a Kiss* and *A Bedroom Blunder*. Popular music featured suggestive songs about sex, such as "It's Tight Like That" and "I Need a Little Sugar in My Bowl." Popular dances such as the grizzly bear and the turkey trot promoted close physical contact or sexually suggestive steps. As early as 1913, a magazine concluded that "Sex O'Clock" had struck in the United States.

The increased openness about sex reflected the growing belief that sexual pleasure was necessary and desirable, particularly within marriage. Married couples increasingly considered intercourse an opportunity for pleasure, as well as procreation. Experts insisted that healthy marriages required sexual satisfaction for both partners.

The new view of marital sexuality helped change attitudes toward contraception. By the 1910s, a grassroots movement, led by socialists and other radicals, promoted sex education and contraceptives, which were largely illegal. The crusade's best-known figure was the fiery former nurse and socialist organizer Margaret Sanger, who coined the term "birth control." Although Sanger once had to flee the country to avoid prosecution, birth control became respectable—and widely practiced—in the 1920s.

At the same time, most adult Americans still condemned premarital sex. Nevertheless, premarital intercourse apparently became more common. Many couples believed that intercourse was acceptable if they were "in love" and intended to marry. There was also an apparent increase in "petting"—sexual contact short of intercourse.

While changing some of their attitudes about sexual behavior, most heterosexual Americans still condemned homosexuality. Nevertheless, a sexual revolution was under way.

Changing Gender Ideals

Shifting sexual attitudes were tied to new gender ideals. By the 1920s, Americans' sense of what it meant to be female was changing. Since the late nineteenth century, Americans had been talking about the independent, assertive "New Woman" who claimed the right to attend school, vote, and have a career. The "New Woman" of the 1920s, exemplified by Mary Pickford, was now a sexual being, too, a fun-loving individual with desires of her own.

The sexual nature of women was central to a new movement, known as feminism, that had emerged in the 1910s. The feminists, like earlier female reformers, were generally white, well-educated, Protestant, urban women. Concentrated in New York's Greenwich Village, feminists broke with older reformers by insisting on sharing the sexual opportunities that men had presumably long enjoyed. Unlike the older generation of activist women, feminists were unwilling to give up marriage and children for careers outside the home. Feminism insisted on women's right to pleasure and satisfaction in all phases of life, from the most public to the most intimate.

Small in number, the feminists commanded a great deal of attention. Several of their ideas and practices were too radical for many American men and women, such as some feminists' decision to retain their maiden names in married life or to explore sexual relationships outside of marriage. Most fundamentally, many Americans were unwilling to accept the feminist insistence on full equality with men.

American culture proved rather open to a more liberated view of female sexuality. The most popular image of the American woman of the 1920s was the vivacious "flapper," with her short skirt, bound breasts, and bobbed hair. The flapper was likely to wear cosmetics and to smoke cigarettes—practices once associated only with prostitutes.

Notions of masculinity were also changing. With the growing emphasis on female needs and desires, men were urged to be attentive and responsive and to focus on the home. As the world of work became less satisfying, experts told men to look for fulfillment in family life. The family man of the 1920s was no longer to be a distant, stern patriarch but a companion to his wife and a doting friend to his children.

In practice, many men still defined themselves in terms of their work rather than their domestic life, and society still regarded women as the primary caretakers of children. Despite the change in domestic values, many men were still relative outsiders in the home.

The Family and Youth

Changing gender ideals were directly related to a reconsideration of family life and youth. Although whole families still labored together in fields and mills, most Americans no longer regarded the family as a group of productive workers. Child-labor laws increasingly made sure that boys and girls went to school rather than to work. The family became primarily a unit of leisure and consumption. The home was where men, women, and children, gathered around the radio, found pleasure and fulfillment.

Reflecting modern cultural values, parents became more likely to indulge their children, who enjoyed more toys, possessions, and spending money than had earlier generations. The automobile gave young people more mobility, too. With their new freedom, they began to create their own separate culture. One sign was the dramatic spread of petting among high school youth, newly free from parental control.

Most adults accepted this situation partly because they admired and envied youthfulness. The modern culture, unsatisfied with work and anxious for fun, glorified sexually adventurous, fast-living young people. The title of the 1923 novel *Flaming Youth* became a catchphrase for the youth culture of the 1920s.

The Celebration of the Individual

The emphasis on the individual, so evident in changing views of sex, gender, family, and youth, was fundamental to the modern culture. In addition to Babe Ruth, Americans admired a host of sports heroes and heroines, and the movie industry increasingly showcased the distinctive personalities of such stars as Mary Pickford and Douglas Fairbanks Sr. Individualism was basic to the "New Woman," too.

The resurgence of individualism was not surprising. The belief in the importance of the individual was deeply ingrained in American culture. Paradoxically, the development of industrial capitalism intensified the importance of both individuals and organizations. As corporations grew larger and produced more, they needed to stimulate consumerism, the gratification of individual needs and desires.

>> "Flaming Youth" on Campus

During the 1920s, college and university campuses were laboratories for "flaming youth," as male and female college students created a distinctive youth culture. Campus life reflected central features of the larger society: the desire for individual freedom and the need to cope with organization. The world of the "advance guard of the younger generation" also reflected the uneven development of American democracy in the Jazz Age.

Traditionally for the elite, higher education was anything but democratic. In 1899, only 238,000 students—some 2 percent of Americans ages 18 to 24—enrolled in colleges and universities. Only 85,000 of those students were women. But as the dynamic economy demanded educated white-collar workers, more middle-class families found the means to send their sons and daughters to college. By 1929, 1.1 million students—7.2 percent of 18- to 24-year-olds—were enrolled. Thanks to changing attitudes toward women, 480,000 of those students were female. The development of public-supported colleges and universities made this growth possible. From 1919 to 1922, enrollments doubled from 3,000 to 6,000 at the University of Illinois and from 4,000 to 8,000 at the Ohio State University. The public schools were at the forefront of a more democratic student culture.

That culture celebrated independence. "To me the Jazz Age signifies an age of freedom in thought and action," explained a female student at the University of Denver. Liberated from the traditional constraints of home and workplace, college students could pursue their desires. "We were big-eyed with wanting," said the songwriter Hoagy Carmichael, then a student at Indiana University, "with making fun."

Students held "petting parties." They forced college officials to tolerate racy new dances such as the toddle, the shimmy, the Charleston, and the black bottom. By the end of the decade, about two out of three students defied Prohibition (see Chapter 22) by drinking on and off campus. Public drunkenness was no longer a scandal. Women students engaged in the "unladylike," sexually suggestive practice of smoking. "College," sniffed a dean at Princeton, "has unfortunately become a kind of glorified playground . . . a paradise of the young."

Students' quest for pleasure shaped their politics. Although Carmichael and his friends cared little about most public issues, they believed strongly in individual rights. Students regarded sex and other satisfactions as a private matter. College newspapers criticized Prohibitionists and other reformers who wanted to regulate individual behavior.

Even as they reflected the individualist values of modern culture, college students adapted to the growing power of organization. Collegiate life became more crowded and more bureaucratic. Students turned to organizations in the 1920s, when the number of fraternities and sororities shot up. By 1930 about one student in three belonged to one; Hoagy Carmichael joined Kappa Sigma. Greek houses often included most student leaders and set the tone of campus fashion for the "barbs," the

continued

"barbarians" who made up the rest of the student body.

While fraternities and sororities offered spaces for freedom and expression, they also forced members to come to terms with organization. As the campus newspaper at Cornell University explained, the fraternity "crushes individuality." Initiation rites and hazing taught new members they were expected to conform to the norms of the group. The distinctive culture of "flaming youth," like the new national culture, embraced organization and freedom, conformity and individualism.

There were serious obstacles to true individualism in the 1920s. Powerful organizations, including corporations, controlled individual life. Even the most famous individual exploit of the decade depended on organization. On May 20–21, 1927, Charles A. Lindbergh flew the *Spirit of St. Louis* from New York City to Paris. This first nonstop solo crossing of the Atlantic made Lindbergh an international symbol of individual achievement, but his feat relied on businessmen who put up the money and a corporation that built the plane. So, too, Mary Pickford's individual success culminated in the creation of a corporation, United Artists. Organization and individualism, the new and the old, were interdependent in the 1920s.

The Limits of the Modern Culture

The modern culture had clear limits in the 1920s. For millions of Americans, much of the consumer lifestyle was out of reach. Many Americans, including artists and intellectuals, chose not to define themselves by the pursuit of pleasure, leisure, and consumption. For them modern society, with its emphasis on the new, including the "New Negro," the "New Woman," and the "New Era," represented an unwelcome abandonment of old values. In different ways, fundamentalist Christians, immigration restrictionists, and the Ku Klux Klan demanded a return to an earlier United States. Mexican Americans, African Americans, and others found that the new culture, like the old, treated them like second-class citizens.

The Limits of Prosperity

Despite the aura of prosperity, low incomes and poverty persisted in the 1920s. As late as 1928, six out of ten families made less than the $2,000 a year required for the "basic needs of life." Despite the housing boom, most American household heads did not own their own homes.

The towns and cities of the increasingly urban nation were still divided by social class. In *Middletown* (1929), their pioneering study of a small midwestern city in the 1920s, Helen and Staughton Lynd discovered that the "division into the working class and business class . . . constitutes the outstanding cleavage." The working class of "Middletown"—Muncie, Indiana—had less money and leisure to enjoy the new culture. About a third of the city still did not own automobiles.

The "Lost Generation" of Intellectuals

Many artists and intellectuals felt alienated from the United States of the 1920s. For white, mostly male writers and artists who came of age during World War I, the conflict represented a failure of civilization, a pointless exercise in destruction. Its aftermath left them angry, alienated, and rootless. In a nation supposedly devoted to individualism, they did not feel free. They were, as the writer Gertrude Stein described them, a "Lost Generation." Some of them, such as Stein and her fellow writer Ernest Hemingway, left the United States for Paris and other places in Europe.

However prosperous and peaceful, the postwar years did not reassure the Lost Generation that American life had changed much. In such works as *Winesburg, Ohio* (1919), novelist Sherwood Anderson portrayed a still-repressive society that denied people real freedom and individuality. The acid-tongued H. L. Mencken, editor of the *American Mercury*, condemned a provincial culture still dominated by the "booboisie" and its rural values.

Still other American artists and intellectuals feared their country had changed too much. Although excited by the potential of the machine, they criticized the routinized work and superficial pleasures of modern life. In his 1922 novel *Babbitt*, Sinclair Lewis satirized a midwestern Republican businessman whose consumerism made him a conformist, not an individualist. F. Scott Fitzgerald, in such fiction as *This Side of Paradise* (1920) and *The Great Gatsby* (1925), conveyed the sense of loss and emptiness in the lives of fashionable "flaming youth" in the "Jazz Age."

From a different angle, 12 southern intellectuals, including Allen Tate, Robert Penn Warren, Donald Davidson, and John Crowe Ransom, attacked the modern culture in *I'll Take My Stand: The South and the Agrarian Tradition* (1930). Their essays offered a defense of rural culture and a critique of a consumer society that demeaned work and exalted individualism.

Artists and intellectuals did not set off a mass rebellion against modern culture, but they did express a widespread ambivalence and uneasiness. In different and contradictory ways, they laid out an agenda for Americans as they came to terms with modern, consumer society.

Fundamentalist Christians and "Old-Time Religion"

For many Americans of faith, the modern culture promoted a sense of deep, unsettling change. "The world has been convulsed," declared *Presbyterian Magazine.* "The most settled principles and laws of society have been attacked." The new culture was troubling because it was so secular and seemed to define life in terms of material satisfaction rather than spiritual commitment. Many Protestants, feeling betrayed by their own churches, resented the influence of liberal Protestants who had tried to accommodate religion to science and scholarship.

Fundamentalists, the opponents of liberalism, took their name from *The Fundamentals*, a series of essays by conservative Protestant theologians that began to appear in 1909. Emerging across the continent, fundamentalists were strongest in the countryside and in the South and West. By the end of World War I, they dominated the Southern Baptist Convention and were fighting liberals for control of northern churches.

Fundamentalists rejected liberalism above all for its willingness to question the historical truth of the Bible. The fundamentalist movement urged a return to biblical, patriarchal,

Scopes Trial The battle between liberalism and fundamentalism: Clarence Darrow, lawyer for John Scopes in his 1925 trial for teaching evolution, confronts chief prosecutor William Jennings Bryan on the witness stand.

and denominational authority, to what came to be called "old-time religion."

The high point in the fundamentalist-liberal battle came in a courtroom in Tennessee in 1925. That year, a high school biology teacher, John Scopes, defied a new state law banning the teaching of "any theory that denies the story of the divine creation of man as taught in the Bible, and that teaches instead that man has descended from a lower order of animals." Scopes's trial became a national media event. The chief lawyer for the prosecution was William Jennings Bryan, the former Democratic presidential candidate and now a leading crusader for fundamentalism. While Bryan was a champion of rural America, Scopes's attorneys—Clarence Darrow and Dudley Field Malone—represented the city and modern culture. In a dramatic confrontation, Darrow called Bryan to the stand and forced him to concede that the Bible might not be literally accurate. Although Scopes was convicted and fined, the fundamentalists lost some credibility. Other southern and western states later passed antievolution laws, but similar measures failed in the more urbanized Northeast.

The Scopes trial did not end the war between fundamentalism and liberalism. Fundamentalists were numerous. Their hostility to liberal Protestantism and modern culture would affect American life for decades to come.

Nativists and Immigration Restriction

While fundamentalist Christianity sought a return to old-time religion, a resurgent nativist movement wanted to go back to a supposedly more homogenous America. As mass migration from Europe resumed after World War I, nativist feeling revived among Americans from western European backgrounds. Thanks to the Russian Revolution and the domestic Red Scare, they associated immigrants with anarchism and radicalism and derided Asians and southern and eastern Europeans as inferior races that would weaken the nation.

In response, Congress overwhelmingly passed the Immigration Act of 1921, which limited annual immigration from any European country to 3 percent of the number of its immigrants living in the United States in 1910. This quota sharply reduced the number of new immigrants from southern and eastern Europe, but nativists wanted tougher action. Congress responded with the Immigration Act of 1924, which reduced the annual intake from a European country to 2 percent of the number of its immigrants living in the United States in 1890, when there were far fewer southern and eastern Europeans in America. The

Table 23-2 The Impact of Nativism: Immigration, 1921–1929

	Arrivals (in thousands)		
Origin	**1921**	**1925**	**1929**
Eastern Europe and Poland	138	10	14
Southern Europe	299	8	22
Asia	25	4	4
Mexico	31	33	40
Total	805	294	280

Source: *Historical Statistics of the United States*, (Cambridge: Cambridge University Press), I, 401.

Itemized groups do not add up to totals.

act also effectively excluded Asian immigrants altogether. The legislation worked: immigration fell from 805,000 arrivals in 1921 to 280,000 in 1929 (see Table 23–2).

The Rebirth of the Ku Klux Klan

Nativism and fundamentalism helped spur another challenge to the new order of the 1920s. In 1915, the Ku Klux Klan, the vigilante group that had terrorized African Americans in the South during Reconstruction, was reborn in a ceremony on Stone Mountain, Georgia. It enjoyed explosive growth after World War I. The "Invisible Empire" borrowed the rituals of the nineteenth-century Klan, including its white robes and hoods and its symbol of a burning cross. The new Klan was still driven by a racist hatred of African Americans, but it took on new targets, including Jews, Roman Catholics, immigrants, religious liberalism, and change in general.

The Invisible Empire condemned big business and modern culture for valuing "money above manhood." The Klan condemned pleasure, "the god of the young people of America," and was hostile to the new gender ideals, birth control, freer sexuality, and the independence of youth. Klansmen and Klanswomen yearned for an earlier America in which white Protestant males controlled women, youth, and other groups and had nothing to fear from big business.

The Klan's tactics blended old and new. Seeing themselves as a secret army of vigilantes, some Klan members supported the age-old tactics of moral regulation—intimidation, flogging, and sometimes lynching—to scare people into good behavior. At the same time, much of the Invisible Empire repudiated violence and used the latest advertising techniques to boost its membership.

For several years, the Klan proved extraordinarily successful. Despite its extremist views, the Invisible Empire had a mainstream membership in every region, in cities and the countryside. At its peak, there were perhaps 3 to 5 million secret members. Because so many politicians and newspaper editors feared or sympathized with it, the Klan had considerable political influence. It helped to elect governors, senators, and other officials from both major parties.

The Klan collapsed, however, when its leaders were revealed to be caught up in financial scandal, alcohol, pornography, adultery, kidnapping, and murder. Most people realized they had nothing to fear from such Klan targets as Communists, unions, and Jews. Millions of Americans, however uneasy about the new culture, had no desire to support prejudice, lawbreaking, and violence in a futile attempt to go back to the past. The Klan's membership dropped precipitously in the late 1920s.

Mexican Americans

Despite the efforts of immigration restrictionists and the Klan, the United States became more diverse than ever. Up to a million and a half Mexicans entered the United States legally or surreptitiously between 1890 and 1929. Many left to avoid the upheaval of the Mexican Revolution of 1910 (see Chapter 22) and to escape the agricultural changes driving the rural poor from the land. The dynamic US economy created opportunities for impoverished Mexican immigrants, as did, ironically, the restrictionist immigration legislation of the 1920s. Unable to get enough European or Asian workers, employers turned eagerly to Mexico as a source of cheap seasonal labor. The Southwest's rapidly developing economy particularly needed Mexican workers for mines, railroads, construction gangs, and, above all, farms.

Like many immigrants from Europe, many Mexican migrants did not plan to stay in the United States. They traveled back and forth to their homeland or returned permanently. Gradually, many chose to stay as they developed economic and family ties in the United States. The National Origins Act, which made it costly, time-consuming, and often humiliating for Mexicans to cross the border, also encouraged migrants to remain in the United States. As a result, the official Mexican population of the United States rose from 103,000 in 1900 to 478,000 by 1920. At the turn of the century, the majority of immigrants lived in Texas and Arizona, but California, with its booming agriculture, rapidly became the center of the Mexican population. Los Angeles, growing phenomenally in the early twentieth century, attracted perhaps 190,000 Mexicans by 1930.

Mexican immigrants, like so many other ethnic groups in the United States, wrestled with questions about their national identity. Were they still Mexicans, or had they become Americans or some unique combination of the two nationalities? In varying degrees, the migrants clung to old identities and adapted to their new home. Mexican Americans, eager to hold on to the advantages they had won by birth and residence in the United States, feared that newcomers would compete for jobs and cause native-born whites to denigrate all Mexicans alike. The immigrants, in turn, often derided Mexican Americans as *pochos*—bleached or faded people—who had lost their true Mexican identity.

Nevertheless, ethnic Mexicans created a distinctive culture in the United States. For all their differences, they shared a sense of common origins and common challenges. In a white-dominated society, they saw themselves as *La Raza*—The Race—set apart by heritage and skin color.

Poverty and discrimination also contributed to a sense of common identity. In many towns and cities, ethnic Mexicans were effectively segregated in certain neighborhoods— *barrios*—in poor conditions. Largely ignored by national corporations, Mexican Americans supported their own businesses and listened to their own Spanish-language radio programs. Anglo-American prejudice also drove Mexicans together. Many whites stereotyped them as a lazy and shiftless race that would take jobs from native-born workers but could not be assimilated into American life. Still other white Americans, drawing on the reform agenda of the Progressive Era, wanted to "Americanize" ethnic Mexicans by teaching them English and middle-class values.

Mexican American Workers Mexican American women workers at the Gladding-McBean Pottery Company in Los Angeles, 1928.

Their sense of shared identity encouraged Mexican Americans to struggle for economic progress and equal rights. In 1928, farm workers in California created La Unión de Trabajadores del Valle Imperial (Imperial Valley Workers Union) in a successful fight for higher wages. A year later, Mexican American businessmen and professionals formed the League of United Latin American Citizens (LULAC) in Texas.

African Americans and the "New Negro"

Like Mexican Americans, African Americans found the new cultural terrain of the United States appealing but unsatisfying. They enjoyed and helped to create the new culture, but it did little to affect racial discrimination. South and North, African Americans still lived with economic and political inequality.

Although discrimination had not changed, many African Americans insisted that they had. It was the decade of both the "New Woman" and the "New Negro." In 1900, Booker T. Washington titled one of his books *A New Negro for a New Century*. By the 1920s, the increased use of "New Negro" reflected a fresh sense of freedom as African Americans left the rural South for cities. It was also the product of frustration as African Americans encountered inequality along with opportunity. The "New Negro" was assertive in the face of mistreatment. "The time for cringing is over," said an African American newspaper.

The "New Negro" was also defined by a deep sense of racial difference and pride. Applauding their distinctive life and culture, African Americans spurred the Harlem Renaissance. Harlem, the section of upper Manhattan in New York where many African Americans had moved, became a center of artistic and intellectual creativity. Novelists such as Zora Neale Hurston, Jessie Fauset, Claude McKay, Jean Toomer, and Dorothy West; poets such as Langston Hughes, Sterling Brown, and Countee Cullen; and artists such as Aaron Douglas and Augusta Savage produced a new birth of African American creativity. In different ways, these women and men explored and celebrated the nature of American blackness in 1920s America and its origins in Africa.

The militancy of the "New Negro" was reflected in the development of the NAACP, which turned increasingly to African American leadership. Its key figure, W. E. B. DuBois, became more critical of whites and more determined that white colonizers return Africa to Africans. The NAACP also pushed the cause of African American civil rights more aggressively and attacked the white primary system that denied African Americans any say in the southern Democratic Party. The NAACP continued a longtime antilynching campaign, which bore fruit in the 1920s, as southern whites were increasingly embarrassed by vigilante justice.

For a time, the NAACP's efforts were overshadowed by the crusades of Marcus Garvey. A Jamaican immigrant to New York City, Garvey founded the Universal Negro Improvement

Association (UNIA), which became the largest African American activist organization of the 1920s. Less interested in political rights and integration, Garvey focused on African American pride and self-help and on Africa. He exalted "a new Negro who stands erect, conscious of his manhood rights and fully determined to preserve them at all times." Garvey urged African Americans to develop their own businesses and become economically self-sufficient. Like DuBois, he insisted that the imperial powers give up their control of Africa. Sure that blacks could never find equality in a white-dominated nation, Garvey believed African Americans should return to Africa.

Unlike the mostly middle-class NAACP, Garvey's UNIA developed a vast following among the African American working class. In 1919, he launched an economic self-help project, the Black Star Line, which, he promised, would buy ships and transport passengers and cargo from the United States to the West Indies, Central America, and Africa. Many of his followers invested in the venture, but it collapsed due to mismanagement. Garvey was indicted for mail fraud in connection with the project. In 1927, he was deported to Jamaica, and the UNIA lost its mass following.

As the fate of the UNIA suggested, militancy could be costly for African Americans. The NAACP also saw its membership drop dramatically during the decade. Nevertheless, African Americans' struggles laid the groundwork for more successful struggles in the future.

A "New Era" in Politics and Government

The economic and cultural transformations of the 1920s shaped American democracy in important but contradictory ways. Modern culture helped empower ordinary people and transform the style of politics. But organized groups—big business above all—affected public life more decisively while a succession of conservative Republican presidents monopolized the White House during the decade. In a society fascinated by all things "new," the Republicans claimed to represent a "New Era" in politics and government. But the Republican ascendancy of the 1920s mostly meant the return of an older vision of minimalist government, individualism, and a less internationalist foreign policy. The mix of old ideology and new political styles failed to galvanize the democratic system: the prosperous 1920s became an age of apathy and low voter turnout.

The Modern Political System

In some ways, the cultural changes of the 1920s stimulated equality and reinforced the idea that the individual could make a difference in politics, too. The emphasis on female freedom and empowerment encouraged women to exercise their newly won right to vote.

The modern culture also hastened the emergence of a political style taking shape since the late nineteenth century. Copying big business, politicians used advertising to appeal to the electorate. In the Gilded Age, voters had been active participants in political campaigns. Now, citizens were political consumers choosing candidates just as they chose mouthwash or automobiles.

The shift to advertising was necessary, too, because the major parties' control over the media had dramatically decreased. Once partisan, many newspapers now took a more independent stand. The new radio stations and movie theaters had no political affiliations at all. With the decline of partisanship, political ad campaigns focused more on individual candidates than on their parties.

Economic and cultural change also benefited big business and other organized groups. Congress was besieged by lobbyists from corporations, business groups, professional organizations, and single-issue pressure groups such as the Anti-Saloon League. Organizations employed a political style that used supposedly objective facts to educate legislators and voters. Unorganized Americans had less chance of influencing the political process.

The new, less partisan politics did a poor job of mobilizing voters. Nationwide, voter turnout fell from 79 percent in the presidential election of 1896 to just 49 percent in 1920 and 1924 (Figure 23-1). A number of factors accounted for this drop-off: African Americans in the South had been effectively disfranchised, and newly enfranchised women were less likely to vote than men; but white male turnout dropped dramatically, too.

The Republican Ascendancy

The chief beneficiaries of the new politics were the Republicans. Determined to regain the White House in 1920, the Republican Party chose an uncontroversial, conservative ticket. Presidential nominee Warren G. Harding of Ohio, handsome and charismatic, had accomplished little during a term in the Senate. His running mate, Governor Calvin Coolidge of Massachusetts, was best known for his firm stance against a strike by the Boston police.

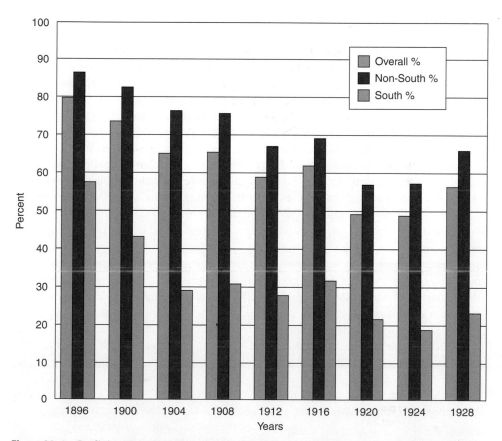

Figure 23–1   Declining Voter Turnout, 1896 to 1928 Why was turnout so much lower in the South?

AMERICA AND THE WORLD

>> **"Jazz-band partout!"**

Even as political leaders pulled back from an activist foreign policy, American culture spread across the world in new ways. Along with the wide appeal of Mary Pickford, the rapid diffusion of jazz epitomized the powerful global impact of the new, modern culture emerging in the United States. In 1920, a popular French song proclaimed *"Jazz-band partout!"*—"Jazz band everywhere!": "They're jazz bands by day, by night / They're jazz bands everywhere / It's all the rage in Paris, it makes men crazy."

Jazz itself was the product of globalization, of the encounter between the musical cultures that Europeans and Africans had brought to the Americas. As World War I ended, jazz became an agent of US musical globalization. African American musicians had been part of the American army sent to France in 1917. The pioneering "Hell Fighters" band of the 369th Infantry Regiment, led by Lt. James Reese Europe, helped introduce the French to the new music. After the war, American jazz groups and musicians began to tour overseas. Both the white musicians of the Original Dixieland Jazz Band and the African American musicians of Will Marion Cook's Southern Syncopated Orchestra visited England in 1919. Sam Wooding's band for the Chocolate Kiddies revue began a tour in 1925 that took African American jazz to Germany, Scandinavia, Spain, the Union of Soviet Socialist Republics, and South America. Meanwhile, phonograph records carried the excitement of this swinging, hot music throughout the world.

The new sounds from America had a strong but complicated impact overseas. Noble Sissle, one of James Reese Europe's musicians, described a jazz "spasm" at a Hell Fighters concert in France: "The audience could stand it no longer; the 'jazz germ' hit them and it seemed to find the vital spot, loosening all muscles and causing what is known in America as an 'eagle rocking fit.'" Jazz seemed at once primitive and modern to the French. On one hand, it conjured up fantasies about African American sensuality and the mysteriousness of the African jungle. On the other, jazz conveyed the excitement of modern life in the industrial age. "The jazz band is the panting of the machine," said a French critic. Above all, jazz seemed quintessentially American and, as a French writer observed, "helped us finally to discover and to understand the United States." After playing to enthusiastic French audiences, Noble Sissle happily predicted that "American music would one day be the world's music."

That was a worrisome prospect for some French musicians and writers. "[D]oes the whole world," one complained, "have to be American?" A number of French artists feared that jazz would silence French music, especially the French song, or *chanson*. But the chanson did not die. Just as white and black Americans had absorbed each other's music, so French musicians reinterpreted American jazz. By the mid-1930s, the greatest jazz-guitar player in the world was a French Gypsy, Django Reinhardt, whose many records incorporated French popular music, as well as the distinctive, traditional sounds of the Gypsies.

Jazz was indeed *partout*. The music was one sign of the internationalization of the new American culture in the 1920s. It was a reminder, too, that the United States could not simply remake the world in its own image, musical and otherwise.

The Republican ticket was not imposing, but neither was the opposition. The Democratic presidential nominee, Governor James M. Cox of Ohio, was saddled with the unpopularity of the Wilson administration. His running mate, Franklin Roosevelt of New York, was a little-known cousin of former president Theodore Roosevelt who had served as assistant secretary of the navy. While the Democrats ran an ineffective campaign, the Republicans made excellent use of advertising. Harding cleverly appealed to the reaction against Wilson's activist government, offering a return to "normalcy" after years of unsettling progressive innovations. Harding won a huge victory with 60.3 percent of the popular vote, a new record; he won 37 states for a total of 404 electoral votes. The Republican Party substantially increased its majorities in Congress.

The Harding administration was plagued by revelations of fraud and corruption, some involving the so-called Ohio Gang of cronies from Harding's home state. The director of the Veterans' Bureau, caught making fraudulent deals with federal property, went to prison. One of the Ohio Gang, fearing exposure of the group's influence-peddling schemes, committed suicide.

A shaken Harding died suddenly of a misdiagnosed heart attack in August 1923, but the troubles continued. Congressional hearings revealed that former secretary of the interior Albert B. Fall had apparently accepted bribes in return for leasing US Navy oil reserves at Teapot Dome, Wyoming, and Elk Hills, California. Teapot Dome, as the scandal came to be called, earned Fall a fine and a jail term. In 1924, Harding's attorney general resigned because of his role in the Ohio Gang.

The scandals damaged Harding's reputation but did not seriously harm his party or his successor, Calvin Coolidge. The former vice president—so reserved in public that he was called "Silent Cal"—was well suited to the political moment. The picture of rectitude, Coolidge restored public confidence in the presidency.

In 1924, Coolidge easily won the presidency against the Democrat John W. Davis, a colorless, conservative corporate lawyer from West Virginia, and Wisconsin's Senator Robert M. La Follette, the standard-bearer of the new Progressive Party. The choice, insisted Republicans, was either "Coolidge or Chaos." Holding on to the White House and to their majorities in Congress, the Republicans continued their ascendancy.

The Politics of Individualism

The Republicans practiced the politics of individualism. Eager to serve big business, they denounced the activist, progressive state and called for less government and more individual freedom. Coolidge declared, "The chief business of the American people is business."

Despite such slogans, Republicans sometimes used government power to spur economic development. The Federal Highway Act of 1921 provided federal matching grants to improve roads, and the Fordney-McCumber Tariff of 1922 restored high protective taxes on imports.

These measures were exceptions, however. Above all, the Harding and Coolidge administrations called for "economy"—reduced government spending and lower taxes. The Republicans also condemned budget deficits and pledged to reduce the national debt; they succeeded on all counts. Federal expenditures dropped from $6.4 billion in 1920 to $3.1 billion in 1924. Congress repeatedly cut income and other taxes, but the federal government still produced annual budget surpluses and reduced its debt.

Republicans' commitment to minimal government was obvious in their lax enforcement of Progressive Era legislation. Under Harding and Coolidge, the federal government made only weak attempts to carry out Prohibition. The Republicans also allowed regulatory commissions to atrophy. The Interstate Commerce Commission (ICC) and the Federal Trade Commission (FTC) were effectively controlled by the businesses they were supposed to regulate.

Herbert Hoover, the secretary of commerce for both Harding and Coolidge, had a more activist view of the government's role in the economy. Sensitive to business interests, Hoover used the Commerce Department to promote "associationalism"—organized cooperation among business trade groups. However, businessmen did not trust one another enough to make voluntary cooperation effective, and Hoover did not advocate federal action to force cooperation. Afraid of too much government, Hoover believed above all in what he called "American individualism."

Republican Foreign Policy

After America's intense involvement in international affairs during World War I, the 1920s were a period of relative withdrawal. But even without a foreign policy crisis, the United States, the world's greatest economic power, played an active role around the globe.

In the aftermath of World War I, Americans were eager to reduce the size of the military and to avoid new conflict. Horrified by the "Great War," women's groups and

>> Time Line

▼**1913**
Introduction of assembly line at Ford Motor Company

▼**1918**
End of World War I

▼**1919**
Mary Pickford, Douglas Fairbanks, Charlie Chaplin, and D. W. Griffith found United Artists

Black Star Line founded by Marcus Garvey
Original Dixieland Jazz Band and Will Marion Cook's Southern Syncopated Orchestra bring jazz to England

▼**1920**
Commercial radio broadcasting
Warren G. Harding elected president

▼**1922**
Fordney-McCumber Tariff
Sinclair Lewis, *Babbitt*

religious organizations joined a surging international peace movement. Activists' calls for disarmament helped push the Harding administration to organize the Washington Naval Conference of 1921–1922. In the first international arms-reduction accord, the United States, Great Britain, and Japan agreed to scrap some of their largest warships and, along with France and Italy, promised to limit the tonnage of their existing large ships, abandon gas warfare, and restrict submarine warfare.

The peace movement was less successful in its second goal, outlawing war. In 1928, the United States and 14 other countries signed the Kellogg-Briand Pact forswearing war as an instrument of national policy. Enthusiastically received, the measure lacked an effective mechanism to stop a nation from going to war. US membership in a world court, the third major goal of the peace movement, was not achieved in the 1920s. Too many Americans believed that the court, like the League of Nations, would undermine US sovereignty.

Meanwhile, the United States became an increasingly active member of the world economy. During the 1920s, Americans made investments and loans around the world. American corporations, including movie studios and automobile companies, exported their products. More US corporations became multinational firms by building plants overseas.

The growth of American economic activity abroad complicated the priorities of the Harding and Coolidge administrations. In the 1920s, the United States had more interests than ever to protect overseas, but Americans were wary of policies that might lead to war. Many were also uneasy about imperialism, the nation's military role in its own possessions and in supposedly sovereign nations.

The Harding and Coolidge administrations tried to pull back from some of the imperial commitments made by presidents Taft and Wilson in the 1910s. US Marines withdrew from the Dominican Republic in 1924. They also withdrew from Nicaragua in 1925 but returned the next year when the country became politically unstable.

The Harding and Coolidge administrations also attempted to promote a stable world for American business. During the 1920s, the United States helped negotiate an increase in Chinese sovereignty to reduce the chances of conflict in Asia. The United States also tried to stabilize Europe after World War I. With the quiet approval of Republican presidents, American businessmen intervened to help resolve the controversial issue of how much Germany should pay in reparation to the Allies.

▼**1923**
Calvin Coolidge succeeds
    Harding as president

▼**1924**
Teapot Dome scandal
Immigration Act of 1924

▼**1925**
Founding of the Brotherhood of
    Sleeping Car Porters
Bruce Barton, *The Man Nobody
    Knows*
Scopes trial

▼**1927**
Charles Lindbergh's solo
    transatlantic flight

▼**1928**
Kellogg-Briand Pact
Herbert Hoover elected
    president
Mary Pickford, Academy Award
    for *Coquette*

Extending the "New Era"

With their cautious foreign and domestic policies so popular, Republicans faced no serious challenge as the decade came to a close. The Democrats were also hurt by the backlash against modern culture. The Democratic Party depended on support not only from nativists, fundamentalists, and Klansmen but also from their frequent targets—urban Catholics and Jews. The antagonism among these constituencies helped doom the Democrats' chances in the 1924 and 1928 elections.

In 1928, the Democrats nominated Al Smith, the governor of New York, for president. The first Irish Catholic presidential nominee of a major party, Smith displeased fundamentalists and nativists. Moreover, his brassy, urban style—his campaign theme song was "The Sidewalks of New York"—alienated many rural Americans. Smith represented a new generation of urban, ethnic Democrats ready to use activist government to deal with social and economic problems. Their brand of urban liberalism would be influential in later years, but Smith could not galvanize a majority of voters in 1928.

Meanwhile, Herbert Hoover, the Republican nominee, polled 58.2 percent of the popular vote and carried 40 states for a total of 444 electoral votes—the Republicans' largest electoral triumph of the decade (see Map 23–1). Republicans also increased their majorities in the House and Senate. The New Era would continue.

Conclusion

The Republicans' victory in 1928 underscored the triumph of modern culture. The "New Era" had swept past the challenges of nativists, fundamentalists, and Klansmen. As Hoover prepared to take office, the appeal of the modern culture, rooted in the industrial econ-

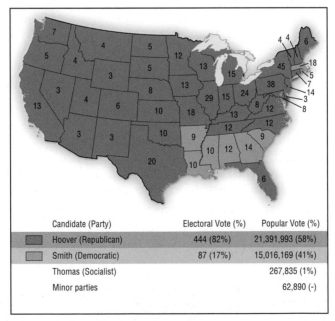

Candidate (Party)	Electoral Vote (%)	Popular Vote (%)
Hoover (Republican)	444 (82%)	21,391,993 (58%)
Smith (Democratic)	87 (17%)	15,016,169 (41%)
Thomas (Socialist)		267,835 (1%)
Minor parties		62,890 (-)

Map 23–1   The Election of 1928 Herbert Hoover's landslide victory extends the Republican "New Era."

omy, appeared undeniable. It offered a renewed sense of individual worth and possibility. It promised new freedom to women and youth. It held out an alluring vision of material pleasures—a life devoted to leisure and consumption—to all Americans. Mary Pickford still embodied the promise of the new culture and the "New Era." In 1929, moving with the times, she made her first "talking picture," *Coquette*. Her performance won her an Oscar, an award for the best performance by a female actor, from the American Academy of Motion Picture Arts and Sciences, which she had helped found.

Nevertheless, Pickford, the modern culture, and its Republican defenders were vulnerable. The political "New Era" of the 1920s was especially dependent on the state of the economy. Perhaps more than ever before in their history, Americans equated happiness with the capacity to pay for pleasures. What would happen if Americans lost their jobs and their purchasing power? What would happen when they began to wonder whether their country was really so democratic after all? The new culture and the "New Era" had survived the dissent of alienated and excluded Americans in the 1920s. It would not survive the sudden end of prosperity.

Who, What

Bruce Barton 694

Calvin Coolidge 709

Henry Ford 689

Marcus Garvey 707

Warren G. Harding 707

Herbert Hoover 709

Margaret Sanger 697

John Scopes 702

Fordism 689

Fundamentalism 702

New Era 706

New Negro 705

New Woman 697

Review Questions

1. What factors created the dynamic industrial economy of the 1920s?
2. What were the main values of the modern culture that emerged after World War I?
3. What groups opposed or resisted the modern culture?

Critical-Thinking Questions

1. Why was individualism such a powerful force in America despite the growing power of corporations? Did individuals really influence American life?
2. Why did the Republican Party dominate the emerging political system of the 1920s?
3. Did the United States become more or less democratic in the 1920s?
4. How would the emergence of consumer culture shape the United States beyond the 1920s?

For further review materials and resource information, please visit www.oup.com/us/ofthepeople

MAIN IDEAS

1) The impact of the dynamic industrial economy illustrated how economic change can lead to cultural change.

2) The modern culture did not transform the lives of all Americans—a reminder of the limited power of even the most sweeping change.

3) Because of continuing inequality and the power of individualist values, the Republican Party could successfully control the political system in a period of rapid change and popular discontent.

A Dynamic Economy

A Modern Culture

The Limits of the Modern Culture

A "New Era" in Politics and Government

THE MODERN NATION

1919–1928

EVENTS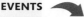

The Development of Industry Mass production, electrification, and other innovations spurred an extraordinary increase in productivity for American industry.

The Trend Toward Large-Scale Organization Increased productivity reinforced the central role of big corporations in American capitalism.

The Transformation of Work and the Workforce The quest for productivity required workers to work faster and harder and increased white-collar employment.

The Defeat of Organized Labor The labor movement failed to challenge the transformation of industrial labor effectively.

The Decline of Agriculture Increased efficiency contributed to the continuing decline in the number of farms and the importance of agriculture in the economy and culture.

The Urban Nation The decline of farming and the dynamism of industry shifted the population balance from rural to urban.

The Spread of Consumerism The philosophy of consumerism, defining life in terms of leisure and consumption, saturated society and helped create the new modern culture.

New Pleasures New pleasures such as spectator sports, movies, popular music, and radio contributed to the new culture.

A Sexual Revolution Freer sexual attitudes and practices contributed to the new culture.

Changing Gender Ideals The new culture rested on a more liberated view of women and a more family-oriented ideal for men.

The Family and Youth The new culture considered the family as a unit of consumption rather than production, and celebrated youth.

The Celebration of the Individual The new culture, despite its dependence on large-scale organizations, nevertheless celebrated the individual.

The Limits of Prosperity Despite general prosperity, many Americans faced low incomes and poverty.

The "Lost Generation" of Intellectuals Many artists and intellectuals felt alienated from the new modern consumer society.

Fundamentalist Christians and "Old-Time Religion" Fundamentalists, unsettled by the new culture, urged a return to older values.

Nativists and Immigration Restriction A resurgent nativist movement, wanting to return to a more homogeneous America, prompted Congress to enact legislation limiting immigration.

The Rebirth of the Ku Klux Klan The resurgent Klan also challenged the more permissive modern culture.

Mexican Americans The continuing migration of Mexicans frustrated the Klan and immigration restrictionists by helping to create a less homogeneous nation.

African Americans and the "New Negro" Although African Americans experienced a new sense of pride, the new culture did little to change their unequal status.

The Modern Political System The new culture helped create a new politics that was both more democratic (women could vote) and less democratic (large-scale organizations gained great power).

The Republican Ascendancy The Republican Party, capitalizing on the new culture's emphasis on individualism, dominated national politics during the decade.

The Politics of Individualism The Republicans, aiding large corporations, called for a less activist government in the name of individual freedom.

Republican Foreign Policy Despite a popular withdrawal from formal international involvement after World War I, the federal government supported the major role of American business in the world economy.

Extending the "New Era" The election of Herbert Hoover in 1928 confirmed the dominance of the Republican Party and the new culture.

CHAPTER

24

A Great Depression and a New Deal

1929–1940

>> Superman

Like many immigrants, Kal-El took a new name when he came to the United States. His origins were spelled out in the June 1938 issue of *Action Comics*: As his old world, Krypton, was blowing apart, the infant's parents sacrificed themselves to ensure his escape. Landing in the Midwest, he was raised as Clark Kent knowing he would one day seek his destiny in the faraway city of Metropolis. To the generation of comic-reading teenagers whose parents came from Europe between 1914 and 1920, it was a familiar story.

Superman was the creation of two Cleveland teenagers, Jerry Siegel and Joe Shuster. Jerry's father, Mikhel Segalovich, emigrated from Lithuania, renaming himself Mitchell Siegel. Shuster's parents fled the Ukraine as war, revolution, and anti-Semitic pogroms destroyed Jewish communities across eastern Europe. Seeking a new life in America, Mary Antin wrote, "with our despised immigrant clothing, we shed also our impossible Hebrew names."

For those looking to remake themselves, Cleveland must have seemed a city of possibility. Cleveland made oil, textiles, locomotives, and steel. Between 1890 and 1920, the city doubled in size twice to over a million. Offering refuge and prosperity, the city became an ethnic patchwork. Hungarians clustered along Buckeye Road, African Americans in Cedar Central, and Germans on Dutch Hill, while affluent, native-born whites retreated to Shaker Heights. Jewish immigrants built shops and homes along Kinsman Road.

Mitchell Siegel, owner of an upscale clothing store, embodied the promise that with hard work and luck anyone could succeed in Cleveland. But he also personified another American dream; at the end of the day he could retreat to a place where he fit in. By the time Jerry Siegel and Joe Shuster reached high school, Glenville was almost entirely Jewish. With their own schools, hospitals, movie theaters, and newspapers, communities of former outsiders lived separately but came together at work, on Election Day, and to root for the Indians, who won the World Series in 1920.

continued

When the stock market crashed in 1929, Cleveland's promises evaporated. In two years, a quarter of the city was unemployed. In March 1930, a crowd of 15,000 marched on city hall to plead for relief, only to be beaten by police. On the radio, Father Charles Coughlin denounced Jews as the culprits behind the financial collapse. Since the time of Andrew Jackson, Americans believed that democracy rested on individualism, private property, and a market economy. Now, with millions starving, Clevelanders began to turn on their institutions and each other.

Joe and Jerry found escape in "pulp" comics. *Buck Rogers*, *Tarzan*, and *Dick Tracy* imitated the movies in pacing, composition, and rippling sensuality. The first comic books, *The Shadow* and *Doc Savage*, featured loners who fought crime with the aid of hidden powers. Underlying these plots was anxiety about the limits of democracy. Citizens could be hardworking and decent, but in a real emergency they needed a hero.

At the Glenville High newspaper, Shuster and Siegel drew similarly dark urban landscapes in which chaos was held at bay by a muscled "superman." Adolf Hitler's propaganda about Aryan "supermen" had filtered into the politics of Cleveland. Jewish leaders protested in 1936 when Mayor Harold Burton attended a July 4 "German Day" celebration festooned with swastika flags and uniformed Nazi Party members shouting "Heil Mayor."

Siegel and Shuster crafted a different vision of human perfection. Superman, according to Siegel, was a champion who would "smack down the bullies of the world." Shuster gave him a cape and a uniform in the colors of the American flag. The first 13-page *Superman* episode changed the industry. Comics rarely sold more than 200,000 copies, but each *Superman* fetched over a million readers. By the end of 1939, Superman was syndicated in newspapers and on radio.

What set Superman apart was his double identity. For half of each issue he was Clark Kent, a junior reporter disdained by his alluring colleague, Lois Lane. He was what Vice President Henry Wallace called "the common man," the uncomplaining, hardworking citizen who embodied democratic virtue but had little power over his fate. With each trip to the phone booth, however, Kent revived the dream that an individual could transform society through his own inner strength.

In early issues Superman attacked the Depression itself, demolishing a slum with his bare hands. In place of the smashed tenements, the government built a gleaming public housing project. After thrashing unscrupulous stockbrokers, Superman assured readers that "the nation is once again returning to its march toward prosperity!" Kids without much money or hope could, for a mere 10 cents, escape into a world in which the common man could even the odds.

Like Captain America and the Green Lantern, Superman declared war on the Nazis before the United States did. In 1939 issues, he foiled the poison-gas plot of a Hitler-like nemesis and smashed the German war machine. Hitler's propaganda minister, Josef Goebbels, denounced Superman as a Jew. Writing in the newspaper of the Nazi SS, he accused the Man of Steel of perverting "the noble yearnings of American children" and sowing "hate, suspicion, evil, laziness, and criminality in their young hearts."

Superman's Metropolis, full of decent people who were helpless without super intervention, revealed Americans' ambivalent attitudes about individual responsibility and government power. For the first four years of the Depression, the federal government offered solutions that relied on individuals' willingness to help each other or themselves. But as the catastrophe deepened, the administration undertook a dramatic series of experiments to rescue suffering Americans. Known collectively as the "New Deal," these experiments changed the relationship between individuals and their government. Voters relied on elected officials not just to represent them but to protect their livelihoods. By the late 1930s, however, ingrained suspicions of big government revived and the New Deal ground to a halt.

The Great Depression

In the fall of 1929 declining confidence in the stock market shook the economy. By Thursday, October 24, panic had set in as brokers rushed to unload their stocks. Prices rallied briefly, but on October 29, "Black Tuesday," stock values lost over $14 billion, and within the month the market stood at only half its precrash worth. Hundreds of corporations and thousands of individuals were wiped out. On Wall Street, the symbol of prosperity in the 1920s, mounted police had to keep angry mobs away from the stock exchange. Although the crash did not cause the Depression, it did expose underlying weaknesses and shatter the confidence President Herbert Hoover relied on for recovery. His optimistic speeches would ring false over the years of unemployment, hunger, and homelessness.

Causes

No single factor explains the Great Depression. Politicians, bureaucrats, and business leaders had no clear idea why things had gone so wrong. Economists and historians still debate the issue today. Yet, even without a definitive account, it is clear that structural flaws in the national and international economies and ill-conceived government policies were at fault.

In the 1920s the base of the economy had begun to shift. No longer was it driven by steel, coal, textiles, railroads, and other heavy industries. New industries that sold complex consumer goods such as automobiles became the driving force. In addition to cars, sales of radios, clothing, processed foods, and a whole range of consumer products grew dramatically. This shift toward a new consumer-oriented economy was fueled by favorable business conditions, job growth, and plentiful consumer credit. The limits of this market had, however, been reached even before the great crash. When the stock market fell, the collapse of purchasing power caused by mass unemployment and the loss of savings slowed the transition to the new economy.

> Now everyone will get back to work instead of cherishing the idea that it is possible to get rich overnight.
>
> ALFRED P. SLOAN,
> CHAIRMAN,
> GENERAL MOTORS,
> OCTOBER 27, 1929

A rickety credit and financial system added to the problems of the late 1920s. Even in good times banks failed by the hundreds. For rural banks these failures could be traced to low farm prices, but financial institutions everywhere suffered from inept and even criminal management. Banks were virtually unregulated, and in the booming 1920s many bet depositors' money on stocks or large, risky loans. Bank failures magnified the impact of the crash; many thousands lost money they thought was safe.

Like banks, corporate finance was free from regulation and given to misrepresentation, manipulation, and corrupt insider deals. Few could be sure whether investments were going into sound companies or worthless paper.

Government missteps and poor policies also had a role. The Republican administrations of the 1920s reduced government interference in the economy, lowered taxes on the wealthy, and reduced spending. They failed to address the banking mess, the problems of farmers, or the growing reliance on credit. The Federal Reserve could have dampened speculation in stocks or, after the Depression began, expanded the currency to promote growth. Concerned more about a strong dollar than about stable employment, the Harding and Coolidge administrations cut spending and the money supply, worsening the eventual collapse.

The Depression was magnified by an international economy still reeling from the effects of World War I. Under the peace terms, Germany owed $33 billion in reparations to Britain and France, who in turn owed billions in debts to the United States. Only US bank loans to Germany made these huge payments possible, so throughout the 1920s, funds that could have created jobs and industries went instead into this financial merry-go-round. The cycle was broken by the depression in the United States. European nations tried to protect themselves by devaluing their currencies and raising trade barriers. The result was a steady economic decline that made payments on reparations or loans impossible. The cycle reached a breaking point in 1931, and the international financial system came crashing down, bringing with it many more American banks and further deepening the crisis.

Descending into Depression

The statistics describing the Great Depression were alarming. Between 1929 and 1933 every index of economic activity steadily worsened. The gross national product shrank from $104.4 billion in 1929 to $74.2 billion in 1933. The combined incomes of American workers fell by more than 40 percent. Bank failures increased, from 640 in 1928 to 2,294 in 1931. A *New York Times* index of business activity dropped from 114.8 in June of 1929 to 63.7 in March of 1933. Both exports and imports fell by more than two-thirds.

As business activity collapsed, joblessness skyrocketed. Periods of unemployment had always been a feature of capitalist economies, even in good times. What distinguished the Great Depression was the extent and duration of unemployment. At the lowest point of the slump, in the early 1930s, between 20 and 30 percent of wage earners were out of work (see Table 24–1). In some cities the jobless rate was much higher, with Chicago and Detroit near 50 percent, Akron 60 percent, and Toledo a crushing 80 percent. In 1933, the Bureau of Labor Statistics estimated that as many as one in three workers, more than 12,600,000 Americans, were unemployed.

Behind the grim statistics lay terrible human costs. In the spring of 1930, as the first Depression winter came to an end, breadlines appeared in major cities. The unemployed could be seen in the thousands, Sherwood Anderson wrote, "creeping through the streets

Table 24-1 Labor Force and Unemployment, 1929–1941
(Numbers in Millions)

| Year | Labor Force | Unemployment | |
		Number	% of Labor Force
1929	49.2	1.6	3.2
1930	49.8	4.3	8.7
1931	50.4	8.0	15.9
1932	51.0	12.1	23.6
1933	51.6	12.8	24.9
1934	52.2	11.3	21.7
1935	52.9	10.6	20.1
1936	53.4	9.0	16.9
1937	54.0	7.7	14.3
1938	54.6	10.4	19.0
1939	55.2	9.5	17.2
1940	55.6	8.1	14.6
1941	55.9	5.6	9.9

Source: United States Department of Commerce, *Historical Statistics of the United States
(1960)*, p. 70.

of American cities, eating from garbage cans." Unemployed men and women stood out-side factory gates desperately seeking work, at soup kitchens hoping for a meal, and at homeless shelters that were already overflowing.

Food, clothing, and shelter were suddenly hard to get. Schoolteachers reported that growing numbers of students were listless from hunger. Hospitals began receiving patients suffering from nutritional disorders, including children with rickets, a disease caused by a lack of vitamin D. *Fortune* magazine ran an article on Americans who had starved to death. Embarrassed mothers sent children to school in rags. Men wrapped newspapers beneath their shirts as protection from the cold. Desperate families, unable to pay the rent, "doubled up" with relatives. More and more tenants were evicted; more and more banks foreclosed on mortgages. Apartments stood vacant and homes went unsold, yet by 1932 more than a million homeless men, women, and children occupied shantytowns or slept in doorways and alleys. Hoboes were everywhere, searching for something to eat, some-where to live, someplace to work.

Farmers faced both economic and environmental disaster. Farmers in the plains states and the West aggressively increased production in the 1920s and then saw the mar-kets for corn, wheat, beef, and pork collapse. Between 1929 and 1932, farmers' income dropped by two-thirds. Then drought struck. Between 1930 and 1936, rains all but stopped in much of the South, the Southwest, and the Great Plains (see Map 24–1). Exposed by decades of wasteful farming practices, the earth dried up and blew away. Spectacular dust storms carried topsoil hundreds of miles through the air, giving a new name—the Dust Bowl—to much of the southern plains. Dust and depression ripped thousands of farm

Dust Storm Drought and modern agriculture churned the Great Plains into silica powder that was carried by windstorms. Over half the patients in Kansas hospitals in 1935 suffered from dust pneumonia.

families from the land in Texas, Kansas, Oklahoma, and Arkansas, sending these "Okies," "Arkies," and "Texies" off to California in search of work.

The Great Depression affected nearly everyone in America, but it was most severe for those already disadvantaged. Although the shock of the Dust Bowl affected many poor white farmers, the larger agricultural depression was even more devastating for sharecroppers on the southern cotton lands, workers in the wheat fields of the Midwest, and the vast migrant labor pools that traveled the East and West Coasts picking fruits and vegetables. In cities, African Americans, who held the least-secure jobs, found themselves pushed from menial service tasks and unskilled work by desperate white workers.

By 1932, private charities, the major social safety net, failed to meet the needs of desperate citizens. Ethnic organizations such as the Bohemian Charitable Association or Jewish Charities in Chicago found themselves overwhelmed. Arthur T. Burns, the president of the Association of Community Chests and Councils, flatly declared, "The funds we have are altogether inadequate to meet the situation."

Public monies were also scarce. Only eight states provided any form of unemployment insurance; most of it was meager. The few state welfare agencies were poorly funded and now stretched beyond their limits. Cities faced insolvency as their tax bases dwindled. Many states were forbidden by their constitutions to borrow for social welfare expenditures. Frustrated Americans looked to the federal government for a solution, but there was little help beyond pensions for veterans. There was no social security for the elderly and disabled, no federal unemployment insurance for those who lost their jobs, and no food stamp program to relieve hunger.

The federal government was under unprecedented pressure to do something, anything, to relieve the Depression. Even bankers and businessmen abandoned their resistance to a strong central government. The president of Columbia University suggested that a dictatorship might provide more effective leadership. Others warned of social revolution. Most of the pleas for action were aimed at the administration, and Herbert Hoover himself came to symbolize the failures of government. The newspapers that jobless men wrapped themselves in were called "Hoover shirts"; shantytowns were "Hoovervilles." In the popular imagination, Hoover and the Great Depression became inseparable.

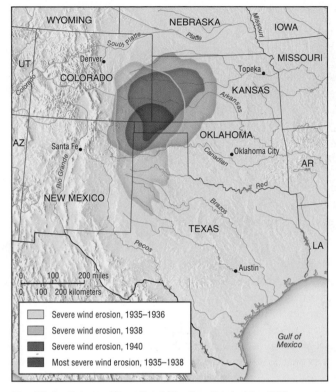

WYOMING

NEBRASKA

IOWA

South Platte

Platte

Missouri

UT

Denver•

MISSOURI

COLORADO

Topeka•

KANSAS

Arkansas

Colorado

AZ

Santa Fe•

OKLAHOMA

•Oklahoma City

AR

Canadian

Rio Grande

NEW MEXICO

Red

Brazos

TEXAS

LA

0   100   200 miles

0   100   200 kilometers

Pecos

•Austin

Gulf of
Mexico

☐ Severe wind erosion, 1935–1936

☐ Severe wind erosion, 1938

■ Severe wind erosion, 1940

■ Most severe wind erosion, 1935–1938

Map 24–1   Extent of Dust Bowl The Dust Bowl of the 1930s eventually spread across thousands of square miles of the southern plains.

Hoover Responds

In many ways, Hoover was ideally qualified to handle this emergency. He had experience with natural and human catastrophes. Orphaned at a young age, Hoover worked hard to educate himself. Trained as an engineer at Stanford University, he roamed the world building and managing mining operations and was a millionaire by his mid-20s. Like other young progressives, Hoover sought to use business skills to solve social problems. He won fame as an administrator of emergency relief, saving Belgium from starvation during World War I and overseeing rescue efforts during the Great Mississippi Flood of 1927.

He brought to the presidency a well-developed theory of the role of government in a modern economy. Hoover believed that complex societies required accurate economic information, careful planning, and large-scale coordination. His political philosophy, associationalism, envisioned a federal government that gathered information and encouraged voluntary cooperation among businesses but did not intervene further. He feared that an overbearing government would crush the creativity essential to a capitalist economy. This voluntarist dream fit well with America's dominant ideology, and Hoover easily won the presidency in 1928.

A Hooverville in Seattle, Washington As the Depression deepened, the homeless settled in "Hoovervilles" on the edge of city centers.

Hoover acted quickly. One of his first achievements was the Agricultural Marketing Act of 1929, designed to raise farm incomes and rationalize production. Since the turn of the century, farmers had been plagued by a "paradox of plenty." They produced more food and fiber than Americans could consume, so the more farmers grew, the less they earned. The bill established a Federal Farm Board to create cooperatives for purchasing and distributing surplus crops. It issued $500 million in loans to stabilize prices but did not limit production or dictate prices.

When the market crashed, Hoover's initial response reflected his overall vision. His goal was to get business to promise to cooperate to maintain wages and investment. In 1931, as 25 banks a week were failing, he encouraged formation of the National Credit Corporation, in which banks were urged to pool resources to stave off collapse. Rather than distribute unemployment insurance or poor relief, he tried to persuade companies not to lay off workers and to contribute to charities for the homeless and unemployed. But the breadth and depth of the Depression overwhelmed Hoover's schemes. Crop prices fell so low that farmers blockaded cities and demanded compensation for their crops.

Hoover had never failed before, and he worked tirelessly to fight the Depression. By 1932, he reluctantly agreed to more aggressive government action, even at the risk of deficit spending. He proposed a Reconstruction Finance Corporation (RFC) authorized to loan $2 billion to revive large corporations. Plans to increase government revenues and distribute farm surpluses to the needy were also enacted. But it was too little, too late. The Depression was three years old and showed no signs of lifting.

Hoover's policies increased the Depression's severity. Unable to control his own party, Hoover watched Congress pass the Hawley-Smoot Tariff in 1930. The tariff raised import duties to record levels, stifling hopes that international trade might help the economy and damaging the weak nations of Europe. Despite misgivings, he signed the bill into law. At the same time, Hoover opposed other measures that might have relieved poverty or stimulated recovery. He vetoed massive public works bills sponsored by congressional Democrats. Finally, Hoover's commitment to the gold standard and a balanced budget also prevented a potential turnaround.

Hoover, whose popularity had plummeted as the Depression deepened, reinforced his reputation as a protector of the privileged by his response to the Bonus Marchers in 1932. In 1924 Congress had issued the veterans of World War I a "bonus" to be paid in 1945. But as the Depression threw millions out of work, veterans asked to have their bonuses paid early. In the summer of 1932, veterans formed a "Bonus Expeditionary Force" to march on Washington. Arriving on freight cars and buses, over 20,000 Bonus Marchers and their families encamped on Capitol grounds. Hoover ordered the army to remove the marchers. Against orders, General Douglas MacArthur attacked with tanks and mounted cavalry. Major George S. Patton, saber drawn, galloped through the encampment, setting fire to its miserable tents and shacks. Among those he attacked was Joseph T. Angelino, who won the Distinguished Service Cross in 1918 for saving Patton's life. Photographs of government brutality shocked Americans. Hoover's silence solidified his reputation for callousness.

As Congress struggled to relieve unemployment and suffering, Hoover dismissed the "futile attempt to cure poverty by the enactment of law." He questioned the motives of everyone who disagreed with his policies. By the end of his term the "Great Humanitarian" had become sullen and withdrawn. It was a dispirited Republican Convention that met in Chicago to nominate Hoover for reelection in 1932.

The First New Deal

When the Democratic Convention chose a presidential candidate in 1932, Franklin Delano Roosevelt flew from Albany, New York, to Chicago to accept the nomination in person, a dramatic gesture in an age new to air travel and personal politics. "I pledge myself," he told the enthusiastic crowd, "to a new deal for the American people." The phrase stuck, and the reforms enacted between 1933 and 1938 have come to be known as the New Deal. The programs came in two great waves, the "first" and "second" New Deals. The first New Deal began with the Hundred Days, a burst of executive and legislative activity following FDR's inauguration, and continued through 1934.

The Election of 1932

The Depression reached its lowest depths as the 1932 election approached, and the Republicans seemed headed for disaster. Their inability to develop a legislative program to attack the Depression had already cost them control of the House. But to take advantage of the situation, Democrats had to overcome internal divisions.

Throughout the 1920s the Democratic Party had been split between the ethnically diverse, wet (anti-Prohibition), urban wing concentrated in the North and the East and the Anglo-Saxon Protestant, rural southern and western wings. Ideological divisions on many issues separated northeastern business Democrats from western populists and urban progressives from southern conservatives.

The leading candidate for the Democratic nomination, New York's governor Franklin D. Roosevelt, had the background to overcome many of these divisions. He came from an upstate rural district, and his interest in conservation endeared him to many westerners. He had built ties to southern Democrats while serving as Wilson's assistant secretary of the navy and as a sometime resident of Warm Springs, Georgia. As governor of New York his strong record of support for progressive social reforms appealed to urban liberals.

Roosevelt turned out to be the ideal candidate. As a distant cousin of Theodore Roosevelt, he had a recognizable name. FDR also had immense personal charm. Despite having been crippled by polio since 1921, he was a tireless campaigner and would become one of the most visible of modern presidents. Raised in wealth and educated at Groton and Harvard, he spoke in clear, direct language that ordinary Americans found reassuring.

During the campaign, Roosevelt simultaneously embraced old orthodoxies and enticed reformers with hints of radical changes. He promised to cut government spending and provide relief for the poor. FDR did not say how he would do both, but it hardly mattered. In November 1932, the Republicans were swept out of office in a tide of popular repudiation (see Map 24–2). FDR and the Democrats took control of the government with the promise of "a new deal" for the American people.

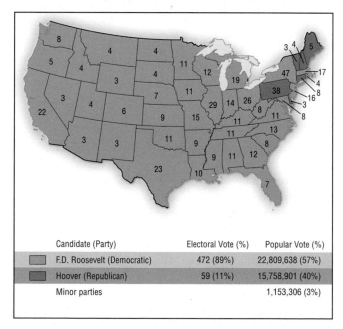

Candidate (Party)	Electoral Vote (%)	Popular Vote (%)
F.D. Roosevelt (Democratic)	472 (89%)	22,809,638 (57%)
Hoover (Republican)	59 (11%)	15,758,901 (40%)
Minor parties		1,153,306 (3%)

Map 24–2 The Presidential Election of 1932 By November 1932 most American voters blamed the Depression on Hoover and the Republicans. The Democrats, led by Franklin Delano Roosevelt, swept into office by huge electoral margins.

Roosevelt worked hard to develop a program to fight the Depression. While governor of New York, FDR had recruited intellectuals who provided him with an influential diagnosis of the Great Depression. Known as the "Brains Trust," they attempted to convince Roosevelt that the Depression was caused by the economy's fundamental defects. The core issue was the maldistribution of wealth. Because the rich held on to too large a share of the profits of American industry, the economy was producing much more than Americans could consume.

Roosevelt never fully bought the ideas of the Brains Trust nor allowed any one group to dominate his thinking. FDR's comfort with experimentation and chaos would hold his administration together and enable it to confront the complexities of the Depression. Where Hoover had retreated into dogmatism, FDR endorsed "bold, persistent experimentation." Above all, he ordered his officials, "try something." And rather than trying to unite his followers behind a single idea or policy, Roosevelt seemed to enjoy watching his advisers feud while he orchestrated their final compromises. The president, an adviser said, was "the boss, the dynamo, the works."

FDR Takes Command

In the weeks before the inauguration, the ailing American banking system took a sharp turn for the worse. In mid-February the governor of Michigan declared an eight-day bank holiday. In one of the most important manufacturing states, nearly a million depositors could not get their money. Stock prices dropped when the news came, and the rich began shipping their gold to safer countries. Panic struck, and funds flew out of bank tellers' windows. On the morning of the inauguration New York and Illinois joined most of the other states in calling a bank holiday. The New York Stock Exchange and Illinois Board of Trade also closed. To many, it seemed like the end of the American economy.

With commerce at a standstill, the nation turned to the new president, and Roosevelt did not disappoint. "First of all," he declared, "let me assert my firm belief that the only thing we have to fear is—fear itself, nameless, unreasoning, unjustified terror." In the midst of a frightening financial collapse, these words revitalized the nation almost overnight.

Roosevelt knew words alone would not end the crisis. On his first day in office, he declared a national bank holiday to last through the end of the week. He instructed his new secretary of the Treasury to draft emergency legislation and called Congress into special session. When Congress convened on March 9, the drafting team had barely finished the bill, but Congress was ready to act. Breaking all precedent, the House unanimously shouted its approval of the bill after less than a half hour of debate; the Senate voted to do the same with only seven dissents, and the president signed it into law that night. The Emergency Banking Act was a modest reform. It gave the Treasury secretary the power to determine which banks could safely reopen and which had to be reorganized. It also enabled the RFC to strengthen sound banks by buying their stocks.

On Sunday night, a week after taking office, FDR went on national radio to deliver the first of his many "fireside chats." Sixty million people tuned in to hear Roosevelt explain, in his resonant, fatherly voice, his response to the banking crisis. He assured Americans that their money would be "safer in a reopened bank than under the mattress." The government was not fully sure how solid most banks were, but the gamble worked. The next day, 12,756 banks reopened, the run stopped, and deposits started flowing into the system. The immediate crisis was over.

FDR Photographed During One of His Fireside Chats Hoover broadcast his speeches on radio, but Roosevelt's "fireside chats" took advantage of the intimacy of the new medium.

Once the banking crisis had been resolved in March 1933, Roosevelt wanted to ensure that the financial system would remain sound for the long run. He moved to restrict banks' speculations while guaranteeing their profitability. The Glass-Steagall Banking Act of 1933 imposed conservative banking practices nationwide. Chancy loans, stock investments, and shady business practices were outlawed, and close federal oversight guaranteed bank stability until Glass-Steagall was repealed in 1999. In addition, the new Federal Deposit Insurance Corporation protected deposits. The Banking Act of 1935 reorganized the Federal Reserve under more centralized and democratic control. Together, these laws established the credibility of the US banking system. One reason the banking system had become so vulnerable was its ties to the unregulated securities markets. So in 1933 the administration sponsored a Truth in Securities Act that required all companies issuing stock to disclose accurate information to all prospective buyers. In 1934 Congress passed the Securities and Exchange Act. Whereas the 1933 law regulated companies, the 1934 legislation regulated the markets, prohibiting inside trading and other forms of manipulation. It gave the Federal Reserve Board the power to control the supply of credit and established the Securities and Exchange Commission, which quickly became one of the largest and most effective regulatory agencies in the country.

Federal Relief

Roosevelt's unemployment programs departed sharply from Hoover's relief strategies. In May, Congress passed a bill providing a half-billion dollars for relief and creating the Federal Emergency Relief Administration (FERA) to oversee it. Local and state agencies dispensed the funds. Headed by Harry Hopkins, a shrewd social worker and Roosevelt confidant, FERA distributed money at a rapid rate. As winter came on, Hopkins convinced Roosevelt that only a massive new federal program could avert disaster. At FDR's request, Congress created the Civil Works Administration (CWA), which employed 4 million men and women. During the winter, the CWA built or renovated over half a million miles of road and tens of thousands of schools and other public buildings. The CWA was eliminated in the spring—Roosevelt did not want the nation to get used to a federal welfare program—but FERA continued to run programs on a smaller scale.

Of all the relief programs, Roosevelt was most enthusiastic about one, the Civilian Conservation Corps (CCC). FDR believed that life in the countryside and service to the nation would have a positive moral impact on the young men of the cities and on those

Depression "wild boys" roaming the nation. For the CCC, these young men built roads and trails in the national parks. By the time the program ended in 1942, it had transformed America's public lands and employed over 3 million teenagers and young adults.

The Farm Crisis

"I don't want on the relief if I can help it," a Louisiana farm woman wrote to the first lady, Eleanor Roosevelt, in the fall of 1935. "I want to work for my livin'." But she was desperate. She asked Mrs. Roosevelt to send money to save the family cow "for my little children to have milk." The doctor was no longer able to give her sick child medicine "unless we pay him some for he is in debt for it." The landlord was threatening to evict them. She had turned to the first lady because of Mrs. Roosevelt's reputation for caring about the poor, but political realities would limit what the first lady, or her husband, could do to help.

By the spring of 1933, farmers were desperate. Prices of commodities such as corn, cotton, wheat, and tobacco had fallen so low that it was not even worth the cost of harvesting. The banking crisis left farmers without access to necessary credit, and millions faced foreclosure, homelessness, or dust storms.

FDR saw a stark "imbalance" between city and country as a root cause of the Depression. While the land remained the only real source of wealth, modern cities absorbed all of the countryside's water, produce, talent, and people. The Dust Bowl was a result of this ecological distortion. His aim was to restore a more even pattern of development, with small manufacturing towns, suburbs, and farms linked to centers of culture and commerce. The New Deal program that came closest to fulfilling these goals was the Tennessee Valley Authority, or TVA. In his campaign, Roosevelt had endorsed a proposal to develop the Muscle Shoals property along the Tennessee River. Congress created the TVA within the first Hundred Days. The TVA was a "corporation clothed with the power of government but possessed of the flexibility and initiative of a private enterprise." According to its administrator, it aimed to change the environment, the economy, the way of life, and the "habits, social, economic, and personal" of a region that spanned nine states.

One of the most ambitious projects of the entire New Deal, the TVA was also astonishingly successful. The dams built by the TVA controlled flooding, created reservoirs for irrigation, and provided cheap hydroelectric power (see Map 23–3). Electricity improved life for millions of farm

Eleanor Roosevelt Eleanor Roosevelt wrote a syndicated newspaper column, personally inspected government projects, and acted as a presidential adviser, all new roles for a first lady.

Map 24–3   TVA Projects The Tennessee Valley Authority (TVA) was one of the most ambitious of all New Deal projects. A network of dams provided electricity, irrigation, and flood control to many of the poorest regions of the South.

families and made it possible for industry to move into new areas, bringing jobs to some of the poorest parts of the country. The TVA took responsibility for soil conservation, reforestation, improved navigation, and the manufacture of fertilizer and aluminum. During the Roosevelt administration, the poor Tennessee–North Carolina border region went from growing cotton to manufacturing aircraft and components for nuclear weapons. Average incomes in the area increased tenfold. As a comprehensive, centrally planned development scheme, the TVA came closest to the Brains Trusters' vision of how a modern "democracy on the march" should work.

Headed by Henry Wallace, founder of the Pioneer Hi-Bred Corn Company, the Agriculture Department was an idea factory in the first Hundred Days. An emergency farm bill gave Wallace powers to control production, buy up surpluses, regulate marketing, and levy taxes. Conservation and reclamation projects drained swamps, irrigated deserts, and sheltered the Great Plains from windstorms. The Agricultural Adjustment Act (AAA) turned agriculture into a regulated industry. After 1933, farmers, once fiercely independent, essentially worked for the federal government. The New Deal farm system permanently altered the American diet by making processed grains, grain-fed meat, sugar, and dairy products cheap and plentiful relative to unsubsidized fresh vegetables, fruits, and fish.

In many respects, however, the New Deal did little for the rural poor. Price supports and production controls helped farmers who owned their own land, whereas soil conservation, irrigation, and rural electrification tended to benefit independent commercial farmers. Subsistence farmers and the landless poor—Mexican migrant workers in the Far West and tenants and sharecroppers, black and white, in the cotton South—gained little. An unintended consequence of New Deal production limits was to take work away from the poorest Americans, pushing them to migrate from the country to industrial cities.

Native Americans suffered an especially severe form of rural poverty. Shunted onto reservations in the late nineteenth century, the majority of American Indians by 1930

AMERICAN LANDSCAPE

>> **Angola, Louisiana**

"Angola was a pleasant place to live back then," Patsy Spillman remembers of her childhood in the 1930s. "You could get inmates as cooks, yard boys, house boys; you could have two or three of them if you wanted." "It was wonderful," her sister JoAn agrees. "We had servants, and we didn't want for anything." There were occasional problems. Once, a convict put rat poison in the girls' milk. The Himel family down the road had their throats slit by a prisoner attempting to escape. JoAn and Patsy were the daughters of John Spillman, a guard "captain" at the Louisiana State Penitentiary at Angola. Their home was a plantation house inside the prison.

Apart from the striped uniforms, Angola in the 1930s resembled a pre–Civil War plantation, 18,000 treeless acres of cotton and sugarcane bounded on one side by the Tunica Hills and on the other three by levees holding back the Mississippi River. Inmates, organized into work gangs, slept in military-style "camps" and rose before dawn to chop cotton and cane and refine sugar in the prison's own mill. Guards, all of them white, flogged prisoners, most of them black, with a leather strap an average of three times a day between 1928 and 1940. "Angola was probably the closest thing to a feudal system in America," one warden observed, "the guard captains being the lordly aristocrats and the inmates as the downtrodden serfs."

The prison's main purpose was to turn a profit, not to reform prisoners or even to keep them alive. With the economy in crisis, voters and legislators wanted to lower property taxes while increasing state spending on roads, education, and jobs. To save money, Governor Huey Long demanded that the prison system be self-supporting, or even return revenue to the state. Democratic pressures created the system of convict slavery at Angola.

Before 1928, many southern states had a "convict lease" system that allowed planters and private businesses to rent chain gangs of prisoners. In the 1930s that system disappeared, as Long and other governors realized that the state could as easily reap the proceeds for itself. With two-thirds of American workers unemployed, convict laborers nationwide produced $75 million a year in shirts, shoes, cement, license plates, and other goods and services. Inmates at Angola were treated as state property and used to repair roads, tend gardens at the governor's mansion, and even to perform minstrel shows. Prisoners worked 60 hours a week for two cents a day. They grew their own food, slept in unheated barracks, used the same bucket for a toilet and to hold drinking water, and had no medical care. Epidemics regularly swept through the camps. In the 1930s, an average of 41 prisoners died each year.

No walls stood between the prisoners and the outside. The prisoners guarded themselves. Fewer than 20 free captains, along with 600 armed "trusty" convicts, guarded over 4,000 prisoners. Trusties were rewarded for shooting prisoners who stepped over the "deadlines" that surrounded work areas. Mounted teams hunted escapees with dogs. Survivors were "hotboxed" in airless cells at the notorious Red Hat camp, where they

continued

received only bread and water. Desperation drove prisoners to keep trying. On
September 10, 1933, 12 prisoners took
advantage of a Sunday baseball game to
shoot a captain and two trusties and steal
a car. They were captured in hours. The
next year, 15 Red Hats working an okra
field brandished wooden pistols and disarmed two trusties, but other guards shot
them down.

The system established in the 1930s has
proven surprisingly resilient. Voters continue to demand that prisons turn a profit.
When the population topped 4,000 inmates in the 1950s, the prison was deemed

overcrowded. Today it has 5,100; over half
are lifers, and 87 are awaiting execution.
Prisoners still work five days a week, raising soybeans and cattle instead of sugar, for
two cents an hour. The prison now serves
the local tourist economy. Vacationers
can explore a museum on the site of the
old Red Hat camp and attend an annual
rodeo, where convicts ride bulls. In 1976,
inmates started a newspaper, *The Angolite*,
which won a Pulitzer Prize for reporting on
prison life. Its editor likes to quote the es-
sayist William Hazlitt, who wrote, "We are
all, more or less, slaves of opinion."

were landless, miserably poor, and subjected to the corrupt paternalism of the Bureau of
Indian Affairs. Alcoholism, crime, and infant mortality plagued reservations. John Collier, FDR's commissioner of Indian affairs, was determined to correct the situation, and
the Indian Reorganization Act of 1934 gave him the power to try. Collier reversed decades
of federal attempts to assimilate Native Americans into the mainstream. Under the New
Deal, forced land sales ended, and reservations were enlarged. Tribal democracy replaced
bureaucratic authority. But congressional opponents, even western liberals, resented attempts to preserve traditional culture. Indians themselves were divided over policies and
goals, and what suited Pueblo communities might not work for the Navajo. As a result, although the New Deal relieved some poverty among Native Americans, it did not develop
a satisfactory long-term solution.

The Blue Eagle

FDR had no fixed plan for industrial recovery and preferred to wait for business interests
to agree on one before acting. Congress, however, moved independently to pass a bill
aimed at spreading employment by limiting the workweek to 30 hours. Heading off what
he thought an ill-conceived plan, Roosevelt offered his last proposal to become law in
the first Hundred Days: the National Industrial Recovery Act. It mandated that business,
labor, and government officials negotiate a "code" restructuring each industry into a national cartel. The code would set trade practices, wages, hours, and production quotas. The
hope was to raise prices by limiting production while protecting the purchasing power of
workers. The NIRA reversed decades of antitrust law. The act protected organized labor by

guaranteeing unions the right of collective bargaining. Finally, $3.3 billion was earmarked for jobs creation through a Public Works Administration.

The NIRA was a bold idea, but it suffered from many of the same problems as Hoover's earlier schemes. It brought together hundreds of industries to draw up their codes, but the process tended to be dominated by business. Few strong unions existed, and smaller businesses were shut out, leaving the largest corporations to write the codes in their interest. For a time in 1933 and 1934 the Blue Eagle banner, the symbol of compliance with the codes, flew proudly in the windows of shops and factories. Dissatisfaction with the program soon dampened enthusiasm, and by 1935 the eagle had come to roost atop a shaky and unpopular agency.

The Second New Deal

The first Hundred Days had been extraordinary by any standard. Congress had given the president unprecedented power to regulate the economy. The financial system had been saved from collapse. Federal relief reached the unemployed. The agricultural economy was given direct federal support. The TVA had created a yardstick for public utilities. A bold experiment in industrial planning had been attempted. Almost everyone was dazzled, but not everyone was pleased. Critics noted that much of this legislation was poorly drafted, overly conservative, or just self-contradictory. If Hoover had been too rigid, FDR struck even his admirers as hopelessly flexible. By 1935 the New Deal was besieged by critics from all directions. But Roosevelt responded to political criticism and judicial setbacks by keeping Congress in session throughout the hot summer of 1935. The result was another dramatic wave of reforms known as the second New Deal.

Critics Attack from All Sides

In May 1935 one of William Randolph Hearst's emissaries traveled to Washington to warn Roosevelt that the New Deal was becoming too radical. Hearst was one of the most powerful newspaper publishers in America and, like many businessmen, had "no confidence" in Roosevelt's advisers. But by 1935 Roosevelt was losing patience with the business community. Saving capitalism was always one of Roosevelt's goals, but shortsighted capitalists never appreciated his efforts. They had their own reasons for detesting the New Deal, and they proved more potent critics than all of Roosevelt's radical opponents combined.

The fate of the Communist Party illustrates the difficulties radicals faced during the New Deal. On the one hand, the 1930s were the "heyday of American Communism," as perhaps a quarter of a million disillusioned Americans joined the Communist Party (CPUSA). The Communists organized labor unions and took the lead in defending the Scottsboro Boys, nine young African American men falsely accused of raping two white women in Alabama. On the other hand, the party's appeal was greatest after 1935, when, on orders from the Soviet Union, it adopted a "popular front" strategy in support of the New Deal. The Communists were most popular when they surrendered their revolutionary aims. Most of those who joined had left the party by the end of the decade.

Populist radicals gave Roosevelt more trouble. Father Charles Coughlin was a Catholic priest in Detroit who attracted listeners to his weekly radio show by blaming the Depression on international bankers and Wall Street. His solution was to nationalize the banking system and inflate the currency. At first the radio priest defended Roosevelt and blamed the New Deal on Communist and Jewish influence. But by 1935 Coughlin turned on the president. He formed his own organization, the National Union for Social Justice, to pressure Congress for further reforms.

A California physician, Dr. Francis Townsend, offered an agenda appealing to older Americans devastated by the Depression. Through a transaction tax of 2 percent, the government would fund retirement pensions of $200 per month. By requiring elderly retirees to spend all of their pensions each month, the program was supposed to pump money into the economy and stimulate a recovery. Huey Long's "Share Our Wealth" program was more comprehensive than Townsend's and more popular than Coughlin's. As governor of Louisiana, Long slapped steep taxes on the oil industry that he used for roads, schools, hospitals, and Louisiana State University. In the process, he amassed nearly dictatorial powers, controlling the legislature and the state police. At first, Long was a loyal but critical supporter of FDR, but by 1934 he was proposing his own alternative to the New Deal.

Long believed the Depression was caused by the maldistribution of income. His program for recovery called for the radical redistribution of wealth through confiscatory taxes on the rich and a guaranteed minimum income of $2,500 per year. Townsend's, Coughlin's, and Long's plans all contained truths about the American economy. The currency did need to be inflated. Elderly Americans were indeed desperate, and wealth was unequally distributed. Roosevelt eventually defused these movements by adopting parts of their programs.

The business community's rising hostility concerned FDR as he prepared for his 1936 campaign. It would be years before bankers admitted that the New Deal had saved the financial system. Wall Street never admitted it. And most industrialists became vocal critics of the NIRA. As criticism grew, a conservative US Supreme Court moved to strike down many of the key laws of the first Hundred Days. On May 27, 1935, in *Schechter Poultry Corporation v. United States*, the Court invalidated the NIRA. The case had been brought by a small poultry company but was financed by larger companies out to kill the Blue Eagle. The justices ruled the NIRA unconstitutional in a way that made it difficult for Congress to regulate the national economy to any significant degree. Roosevelt feared the setback would undo most of his achievements, and his fears were borne out in January 1936, when the Court overturned the Agricultural Adjustment Act.

The Second Hundred Days

FDR loved a good fight. No longer concerned about attracting support from business, he welcomed criticism and shot right back. After 1935 the rhetoric became noticeably more radical. When the Supreme Court invalidated the NIRA, Roosevelt kept Congress in session through a sweltering summer and forced through a raft of legislation in a "second Hundred Days," which began the second New Deal.

A few of the new proposals were meant to salvage pieces of the NIRA and AAA or to silence radical critics. Hoping to undermine the "crackpot ideas" of Huey Long, Roosevelt proposed a Revenue Act to encourage a "wider distribution of the wealth." It raised estate and corporate taxes and pushed personal income taxes in the top bracket up to 79 percent. Despite the political motives behind the bill, it made economic sense. Before the 1935 Revenue Act, most New Deal programs had been financed by regressive sales and excise taxes.

Thereafter, programs were funded with progressive income taxes that fell most heavily on those best able to pay.

The first New Deal had been preoccupied with the emergency of 1933. The second New Deal left a more enduring legacy. The administration finished its program to ensure the long-term security of the financial system and extend the relief programs that had helped so many to survive. It created a social security system that anchored the American welfare state for the rest of the century. With organized labor it created a new and powerful Democratic Party coalition. By the time Congress adjourned in late August 1935, the most important achievements of the New Deal were in place.

Social Security for Some

Bolstered by big Democratic gains in the 1934 elections, FDR pursued a massive effort to fund work relief by sponsoring the Emergency Relief Appropriations Bill. Providing nearly $5 billion, more than the entire 1932 federal budget, the bill rejuvenated the relief programs of the first New Deal and created a new Works Progress Administration (WPA), headed by Harry Hopkins. The WPA lasted for eight years, employing as many as 3.3 million Americans. WPA workers built bridges, schools, libraries, sewer systems, the Blue Ridge Parkway, and more than 800 airports. The WPA commissioned artists to decorate post offices and historians to collect the stories of mill workers and former slaves. At Indiana University, the WPA paid undergraduates to build a student union. WPA lexicographers wrote a Hebrew-English dictionary. The program was hugely popular.

Critics of the WPA complained with some justice about meaningless "make-work" jobs and unqualified workers. Political corruption was a more serious problem. WPA officials, especially at the local level, often used the agency as a patronage machine, favoring loyal party regulars with contracts and jobs. In many states, particularly in the South, officials openly discriminated against African Americans. The WPA was never able to employ all those who needed work, but for millions of Americans it provided immediate relief from the very real prospect of hunger and misery.

The New Deal also created a permanent system of long-term economic security. In 1932 there were no national programs of unemployment insurance, workers' compensation, old-age pensions, or aid to needy children, and the states were only slightly more able to care for citizens. Most Americans had little or no protection from economic calamity.

The Social Security Act of 1935 took a critical first step toward providing such protection. It established matching grants to states that set up their own systems of workers' compensation, unemployment insurance, and aid to families with dependent children. More important, the federal government itself created a huge social security system that guaranteed pensions to millions of elderly Americans. FDR insisted that it be funded as an insurance plan, with payroll taxes paid by employees and employers. He hoped that this would protect the system from the political attacks that welfare programs typically encountered.

Most New Dealers hoped to go much further. Secretary of Labor Frances Perkins wanted to include agricultural laborers and domestic servants, mostly women and African Americans, in the new social security system. But that would have provoked enough opposition from southern conservatives to kill the entire program. The administration also preferred federal- rather than state-run programs. There was, however, no federal bureaucracy in place to run such programs, and there was fierce opposition to the idea of taking such programs away from the states.

Local and factional opposition limited the New Deal's plans for nationalized social welfare and economic security. Welfare and insurance programs were weaker in the South than in the North and weaker for women and African Americans than for white men. Despite such strong opposition, the New Deal accomplished many of its goals. By 1939 every state had a program of unemployment insurance and assistance to the elderly. Almost overnight the social security system became the federal government's first huge social welfare bureaucracy. More Americans than ever before were now protected from the ravages of unemployment, disability, poverty, and old age.

Labor and the New Deal

During the 1930s, unions took a new role in America's political and economic life. The number of Americans organized in unions leaped by the millions, and by 1940 nearly one in four nonfarm workers was unionized. Labor organizations were able to enroll workers in core industries, including steel, rubber, electronics, and automobiles. Unions also became key players in the Democratic Party. None of the leading New Dealers, Roosevelt included, had anticipated this in 1932, but in critical ways the New Deal fostered the growth of organized labor and its inclusion in the Democratic electoral coalition.

Unlike past administrations, Roosevelt's had never demonstrated outright hostility toward unions. Rather, through the 1930s FDR moved from grudging acceptance to open support for organized labor. Across the country, workers responded to the change. Unions were now allowed to run organizing drives, and labor began to flex its muscle with a spontaneous wave of strikes. Mill workers in the South launched brave, but doomed, strikes against textile manufacturers. Dockworkers in San Francisco organized a successful general strike throughout the city. At the same time, the NIRA inspired a talented group of national leaders, in particular John L. Lewis of the United Mine Workers, Sidney Hillman of the Amalgamated Clothing Workers, and David Dubinsky of the International Ladies' Garment Workers.

Employers fought back against this new militancy. They used all the methods to intimidate workers—espionage, blacklisting, and armed assault—that had once worked so well. But when it became clear that the federal government would now protect workers seeking to organize and bargain collectively, employers formed company unions to thwart workers' independent action. By 1935 the employers seemed to be winning, particularly when the Supreme Court declared the NIRA, and its protection of union rights, unconstitutional. In 1935 worker militancy declined, and the unionization drive seemed stalled. But the hopes of organized labor were kept alive by an influential and imaginative liberal senator from New York named Robert Wagner.

Wagner took the lead in expanding the NIRA's limited labor protections into the National Labor Relations Act, also known as the Wagner Act. Although he had few ties to organized labor, Wagner believed workers had a basic right to join unions. He also hoped that effective unions would stimulate the economy by raising wages, thereby building consumer purchasing power. Like the NIRA provisions, the Wagner Act guaranteed workers the right to bargain collectively with their employers, but it also outlawed company unions, prohibited employers from firing workers after a strike, and restricted many other antiunion tactics. Most important, the Wagner Act created the National Labor Relations Board (NLRB) to enforce these provisions. In the summer of 1935 FDR declared the Wagner Act "must" legislation, and the bill became law.

While Wagner and his colleagues moved in Congress, John L. Lewis and Sidney Hillman took another course. In 1935 they pressed the conservative leadership of the American Federation of Labor to accept the principle of industrial unions, which would organize workers in an entire sector of the economy, such as steel. AFL traditionalists rejected the idea and held fast to the notion that workers should be organized by their crafts, not by whole industries. Thwarted by AFL leadership, Lewis, Hillman, and their allies formed a rival organization that eventually became the Congress of Industrial Organizations (CIO).

The CIO began organizing some of the most powerful and prosperous industries in the country. The government's new attitude toward organized labor played an important role in the CIO's initial success. For example, when the United Automobile Workers initiated a series of sit-down strikes against General Motors, neither Roosevelt nor the Democratic governor of Michigan sent in troops to remove workers from the factories they were occupying. This clear message to the leaders of industry helped to win the strike against America's most powerful corporation. The NLRB also protected the new unions from an employer counterattack during the recession of 1937.

By the late 1930s a crucial political alliance had formed. A newly vigorous labor movement had become linked to a reinvigorated national Democratic Party. Thanks to this alliance, American industrial workers entered a new era. Having won the ability to organize with the help of the government, industrial workers used their power to increase wages, enhance job security, improve working conditions, and secure their retirements. Organized labor now had a stake in preserving the system from collapse. As much as the banking and financial reforms of the first New Deal, the successful unionization of industrial workers helped stabilize American capitalism.

The New Deal Coalition

Roosevelt believed that to overcome his varied opposition and win reelection he needed to create a coalition far broader than that of 1932. By 1936, the Democratic Party was transformed in fundamental ways. For the first time since the Civil War, a majority of voters identified themselves as Democrats, and the Democrats remained the majority party for decades to come. FDR achieved this feat by forging a powerful coalition between the competing wings of the party. In the end, however, the same coalition that made the New Deal possible also limited its progressivism.

The rural South had been overwhelmingly Democratic for a century, but urban voters in the North became the party's new base. This shift was well under way during the 1920s, when Al Smith's two presidential bids attracted ethnic blue-collar voters. FDR offered prominent ethnic Americans an unprecedented number of federal appointments. Jews and Catholics (Italian, as well as Irish) served Roosevelt as advisers, judges, and cabinet officers. More important, thousands of working-class city dwellers found jobs with the CWA, the WPA, or the CCC. Those New Deal programs generated a flood of patronage appointments that endeared Roosevelt to local Democratic machines. Finally, the unions reciprocated FDR's support for labor. The CIO alone poured $600,000 into Roosevelt's campaign, replacing the money no longer forthcoming from wealthy donors, and its members formed an army of campaign volunteers. By 1940, the Democratic Party became the party of the urban working class.

The New Deal's programs also explain a dramatic shift of allegiance among African American voters. Since Reconstruction, southern blacks had supported the party of Lincoln, but as they migrated to the urban North they gained voting strength and abandoned the Republican Party. By 1936 northern blacks voted overwhelmingly for FDR, even though the Democrats were weak on the issue of civil rights. The New Deal included no legislation against discrimination, and FDR silently allowed Congress to reject anti-lynching laws. New Deal agencies did offer more assistance to poor, unemployed African Americans than previous federal programs, and some leading New Dealers supported equal rights. Mary McLeod Bethune, a prominent African American educator and close friend of Eleanor Roosevelt, served the New Deal as director of the National Youth Administration's Office of Negro Affairs, which gave jobs and training to some 300,000 young African Americans. Besides controlling her own Special Negro Fund, Bethune convinced other New Deal administrators to open their programs to blacks. With perhaps a million African American families depending on the WPA by 1939, black voters had solid reasons for joining the New Deal coalition.

A similar logic explains why women reformers threw their support to the Democrats in the 1930s. Once again, FDR had no feminist agenda, and New Deal programs discriminated against women by offering lower pay and restricting jobs by sex. But women also benefited in unprecedented numbers from New Deal welfare and jobs programs. For the first time in American history, a woman, Frances Perkins, was appointed to the cabinet.

The most prominent female reformer associated with the New Deal was Eleanor Roosevelt. She was in many ways the last great representative of a woman's reform tradition that flourished in the Progressive Era. She had worked in a settlement house and campaigned for suffrage and progressive causes. Eleanor and Franklin made a remarkable political couple. Millions of Americans read Eleanor's opinions in her weekly newspaper column, "My Day." She became for many the conscience of the New Deal, the person closest to the president who spoke most forcefully for the downtrodden. Her well-deserved reputation for compassion also protected her husband. Liberals who might have been more critical of the New Deal instead relied on Eleanor Roosevelt to push the president toward more progressive reform. At the same time, conservatives who were charmed by FDR's personality blamed the faults of the New Deal on his wife. "It was very simple," one southern journalist explained. "Credit Franklin, better known as He, for all the things you like, and blame Eleanor, better known as She, or 'that woman,' for all the things you don't like."

Although four years of the New Deal had not lifted the Depression, the economy was making headway. Jobs programs had put millions of Americans to work; the banking crisis was over; the rural economy had been stabilized. Based on this record and the backing of his powerful coalition of southern whites, northern urban voters, the labor movement, and many other Americans, FDR won reelection by a landslide in 1936. He captured over 60 percent of the popular vote and, in the Electoral College, defeated his Republican opponent Alf Landon in every state but Maine and Vermont. Landon, the governor of Kansas, even lost his home state. The new Democratic coalition also won sweeping command of the Congress, and Roosevelt now stood at the peak of his power.

AMERICA AND THE WORLD

>> **The Global Depression**

In 1930, mulberry trees covered the hills of the Japanese islands of Hokkaido and Honshu. In parts of Japan, two-thirds of the cultivated land was fodder for the silkworms that produced Japan's leading export. Over 2 million families depended on silk, which went chiefly to the United States to be made into the fashionable stockings worn by American women.

The silk market was the one bright spot in Japan's economy after World War I. Chinese consumers had boycotted Japan to protest land grabs during the war. In 1923, an earthquake followed by fires and a tidal wave leveled Tokyo and Yokohama. Japan was not alone: in much of the world, economies stagnated in the 1920s under the burden of war reparations and war loans. One of the worst hit was Italy, where unemployment contributed to the rise of Benito Mussolini's fascist government in 1922. But the New York Stock Exchange crash triggered a global depression. As the world's leading creditor, producer, and consumer, the United States exported its financial disaster to the world.

Countries tied to a single commodity or to the American market suffered most. After the crash, American women stopped buying stockings, and the price of silk dropped by three-quarters. By 1931, Japanese silk farmers were broke; by 1932, they were starving. Similar catastrophes hit the rubber plantations of Malaya and the coffee farms of Guatemala. International prices for Australian wool, Cuban sugar, Canadian wheat, and Egyptian cotton plummeted. Brazil, unable to export coffee, used it to fuel locomotives. In Rwanda a famine aggravated by the loss of tin exports killed 40,000.

The disruption of trade intensified conflict in India, Africa, and other areas under imperial rule. Unable to collect taxes at the ports, colonial governments imposed taxes or monopolies that shifted burdens onto the rural poor. The distress of the peasantry intensified demands for independence in India, and Mohandas Gandhi's *satyagraha*, civil resistance, reached a peak in 1932, when 32,500 nonviolent protestors filled the jails. The French government of Indochina (Vietnam) forced rice farmers to pay taxes in gold. Uprisings against French rule increased as the Depression wore on, as did insurgencies against the US colony in the Philippines.

In the industrial countries, jobless people stood in breadlines and lived in shanties. More than 2 million workers were unemployed in Britain. When American loans to Germany dried up in 1930, two out of every five Germans were out of work. This catastrophe, the worst economic crisis in memory, silenced the voices of political moderates. Voters demanded extreme action. Each country now looked out for itself, marshaling scarce resources and forming self-contained economies known as autarkies. Brazil and Argentina restricted trade and steered investment into industry. The Soviet Union, already cut off from the capitalist world, built "socialism in one country." Japan merged Taiwan, Korea, and Manchuria into a "Greater East Asia Co-Prosperity Sphere." The 1932 Ottawa

continued

Accords merged Britain, its empire, Canada, and Australia into a self-contained economic bloc. In Germany autarky was the policy of the National Socialist (Nazi) Party led by Adolf Hitler.

Autarky exacted heavy demands on citizens, requiring them to sacrifice prosperity, liberty, and lives for the nation. Efficiency was more important than democracy, and regimes became more ruthless and less free. Even to Americans, dictatorships had a high-tech sheen. "If this country ever needed a Mussolini," Senator David A. Reed remarked, "it needs one now." FDR and other American leaders drew the connections between global trade, autarky, repression, and war. "If goods don't cross borders," Secretary of State Cordell Hull observed, "armies will." As another global war loomed, they recognized it as a contest between dictatorship and democracy, but also as a conflict between economic systems. The outcome would mean either autarky or a New Deal for the world.

Crisis of the New Deal

In 1937 it seemed as if Roosevelt was unbeatable, but within a year the New Deal was all but paralyzed. A politically costly fight to "pack" the Supreme Court at last gave FDR's conservative opponents a winning issue. A sharp recession encouraged the New Deal's enemies and provoked an intellectual crisis within the administration. In 1938, when the Republicans regained much of their congressional strength, the reform energies of the New Deal were largely spent. Within a year the nation turned its attention to rising threats from overseas.

>> Time Line

▼1929
Stock market crash

▼1930
Hawley-Smoot Tariff enacted

▼1931
National Credit Corporation authorized

▼1932
Franklin Roosevelt elected president

▼1933
FDR declares a bank holiday
First Hundred Days
Emergency Banking Act passed
Economy Act passed
Civilian Conservation Corps (CCC)

United States goes off the gold standard
Agricultural Adjustment Act (AAA)
Emergency Farm Mortgage Act
Tennessee Valley Authority (TVA)
Truth in Securities Act
National Industrial Recovery Act (NIRA)
Glass-Steagall Banking Act
Farm Credit Act

Conservatives Counterattack

With conservative opponents vanquished, it seemed as if New Dealers could finish the job begun in 1933. Administration progressives such as Frances Perkins hoped that existing legislation could now be strengthened.

FDR seemed poised to launch the next great wave of New Deal reforms, but one apparently immovable barrier stood in the way: the US Supreme Court. The Court had already struck down the NIRA and the AAA, and recent rulings made it seem that neither Social Security nor the Wagner Act were safe from the Court's nine "old men." Roosevelt wanted to change the Court. He had not yet had the opportunity to appoint any new justices, and pundits joked that the elderly judges refused to die. Sure that a constitutional amendment supporting his program would take too long or fail, FDR launched a reckless and unpopular effort to "reform" the Court. He proposed legislation that would allow the president to appoint a new justice for every sitting member of the Court over 70 years of age. This "court packing" plan, as opponents labeled it, would have given the president as many as six new appointments.

Conservatives had long complained of FDR's "dictatorial" powers, and the court plan seemed to confirm their warnings. They skillfully cultivated congressional allies, giving Democrats the lead in opposing the court reform. Even his allies refused to campaign for the president's bill, and it took all of FDR's political power and prestige to keep it before a hostile Congress. By the end of the summer of 1937, the bill was defeated.

Ironically, Roosevelt won his point. Several justices soon retired, giving FDR the critical appointments he needed, and the Supreme Court backed away from its narrow conception of the role of the federal government. Nevertheless, FDR's court plan proved a costly mistake, and its defeat emboldened his opponents. In November 1937 the administration's critics issued a Conservative Manifesto calling for balanced budgets, states' rights, lower taxes, and the defense of private property and the capitalist system, themes that would rally conservatives for the remainder of the century. Behind the manifesto lay some hard political realities that drove the conservatives into opposition.

▼**1935**
Second Hundred Days
NIRA declared unconstitutional
National Labor Relations Wagner Act
Social Security Act

▼**1936**
AAA overturned
FDR reelected

▼**1937**
FDR announces "court packing" plan
Economy goes into recession

▼**1938**
Second Agricultural Adjustment Act
Fair Labor Standards Act

Superman first appears in *Action Comics*
New Deal opponents win big in Congress

▼**1939**
Administrative Reorganization Act

Southern congressmen, for example, desired to preserve white privilege. The new federal programs disturbed entrenched systems of political and economic dominance. Southern conservatives blamed the New Deal. "You ask any nigger in the street who's the greatest president in the world. Nine out of ten will tell you Franklin Roosevelt," one white southerner declared. "That's why I think he's so dangerous."

In the rural South and West there were fears that the New Deal was growing too close to the urban working class in the Northeast. Against this trend, conservatives appealed to the deeply rooted American suspicion of central government. Still, conservatives were not strong enough to block all New Deal legislation. Farm-state representatives needed Roosevelt's support. In late 1937 the administration succeeded in passing housing and farm tenancy reforms. In 1938 Congress passed the Fair Labor Standards Act, requiring the payment of overtime after 40 hours of work in a week, establishing a minimum wage, and eliminating child labor. Even with flagging support, FDR could enact proposals blocked during the Progressive Era.

The 1938 congressional elections gave conservatives the strength they needed to bring New Deal reform to an end. The president campaigned against leading conservatives, but he failed. Republicans gained 75 seats in the House and were now strong enough in the Senate to organize an effective anti–New Deal coalition with southern Democrats. By then, a jolting recession had created a crisis of confidence within the New Deal itself.

The Liberal Crisis of Confidence

During the 1936 campaign Roosevelt was stung by conservative criticism of his failure to balance the budget. He had leveled the same charge against Hoover four years earlier, but the demands of the Depression made it difficult and dangerous to reduce government spending. Deficit spending seemed to help resuscitate the economy.

Hoping to silence conservative critics, Roosevelt ordered a sharp cutback in relief expenditures in 1937. On top of an ill-timed contraction of the money supply and the removal of $2 billion from the economy by the new Social Security taxes, the measure had a disastrous effect. Once again, the stock market crashed and industrial production plummeted. Even the relatively healthy automobile, rubber, and electrical industries were seriously hurt. Opponents carped about the "Roosevelt Recession" and accused the administration of destroying business confidence.

Among the president's advisers, the competition between the budget balancers and the deficit spenders intensified. This was an important turning point in the New Deal and in twentieth-century American politics. Until 1938, the orthodoxy that associated economic health with balanced budgets was entrenched in government and the business community. The recession of 1937–1938 converted young New Dealers to the newer economic theories associated with John Maynard Keynes, the great English economist. During periods of economic stagnation, Keynes argued, the government needs to stimulate recovery through deficit spending. The goal of fiscal policy was no longer to encourage production, but rather to increase the purchasing power of ordinary consumers. Roosevelt never fully embraced these theories, but more and more members of his administration did. Moreover, the breathtaking economic revival created by massive government expenditures in World War II seemed to validate Keynesian economics. Until the 1980s, presidents of both parties subscribed to Keynesian theory, although they differed on what kind of government programs federal spending should buy.

Conclusion

The New Deal did not bring an end to the Depression, and this was undoubtedly its greatest failure. Nevertheless, FDR achieved other important goals. "I want to save our system," he said in 1935, "the capitalistic system." By this standard, the New Deal was a smashing success. By allowing Americans to survive the worst collapse in the history of capitalism while preserving core freedoms, the New Deal reaffirmed democracy at a time when most of the industrialized world chose dictatorship. The New Deal also created a system of security for the vast majority of Americans. National systems of unemployment compensation, old-age pensions, and welfare programs were born during the 1930s. Farm owners received new protections, as did the very soil of the nation. Workers were granted the right to organize, hours of labor were limited, child labor ended, and wages were held above the bare minimum. The financial system was stabilized and strengthened. America was a safer place at the end of the 1930s, but the world had become more dangerous. After 1938 the Roosevelt administration was increasingly preoccupied with the threatening behavior of nations that had responded poorly to the challenge of the Great Depression.

Who, What

FDR 725

Herbert Hoover 719

Huey Long 734

Eleanor Roosevelt 729

Autarkies 739

CCC 728

The New Deal 725

Social Security 735

TVA 729

Wagner Act 736

Review Questions

1. Did the stock market crash cause the Great Depression?

2. How did Roosevelt's philosophy of government differ from Hoover's?

3. What setbacks caused FDR to launch a second New Deal?

Critical-Thinking Questions

1. Compare the American response to the Depression with that of Britain, Germany, and Japan. Why did other industrial countries choose different paths?

2. What were Franklin Roosevelt's attributes as a leader? What aspects of his style inspired confidence or animosity?

3. Histories of the Depression focus on national statistics and large-scale programs. How could you retell the story of the 1930s from a local, personal perspective?

For further review materials and resource information, please visit www.oup.com/us/ofthepeople

1) Disagreements on what caused the Depression stoked political feuds about solutions.

2) Economic collapse led to a new attention to the geography of growth and the natural environment.

3) Conservatives opposed government intervention as a solution to the crisis.

4) The New Deal redefined liberalism, giving government responsibility for the overall health of the economy.

The Great Depression

The First New Deal

The Second New Deal

Crisis of the New Deal

A GREAT DEPRESSION
AND A NEW DEAL

1929–1940

EVENTS

Causes Structural flaws in the national and international economies, plus ill-conceived government policies, caused the Great Depression.

Descending into Depression The collapse affected nearly all Americans, but especially those already disadvantaged.

Hoover Responds Hoover's reluctance to use aggressive government action increased the Depression's severity.

The Election of 1932 Roosevelt and the Democrats were elected to enact a "new deal" for the American people.

FDR Takes Command Roosevelt and Congress acted quickly to resolve the banking crisis and revive the financial system.

Federal Relief Roosevelt developed new federal programs to attack unemployment.

The Farm Crisis Roosevelt developed new federal agencies designed to relieve the financial and environmental crises faced by farmers.

The Blue Eagle Congress passed a bill mandating that business, labor, and government negotiate a set of trade practices, wages, and production quotas.

Critics Attack from All Sides Parts of the New Deal faced criticism from radicals, conservatives, and populists, while the Supreme Court struck down key components.

The Second Hundred Days The second New Deal ensured long-term security of the financial system and extended relief programs.

Social Security for Some The New Deal created a system for long-term economic security that included pensions for the elderly.

Labor and the New Deal Unions took on a new prominence in America's political and economic life.

The New Deal Coalition FDR forged a new political coalition including blue-collar workers, African Americans, and women to give the Democratic Party a national majority.

Conservatives Counterattack Conservatives criticized New Deal reforms, gaining the seats in Congress to block Roosevelt's agenda, while the Supreme Court invalidated several measures.

The Liberal Crisis of Confidence Young New Dealers subscribed to new economic theories that changed the philosophy of government spending.

CHAPTER
....

25

AMERICAN PORTRAIT

....

>> A. Philip Randolph

"**W**ho is this guy Randolph," Joseph Rauh wondered, and "what the hell has he got on the President of the U.S.?" It was June 1941 and Rauh, a government attorney, had just been instructed to draft a presidential order prohibiting discrimination on grounds of "race, color, creed, or national origin" in defense industries. It was a radical departure from decades of official support for legalized racism. It would use the economic muscle of the federal government to overturn job segregation and, in the process, make enemies for President Franklin Roosevelt. Rauh was enthusiastic, but he couldn't understand why FDR, with his reliance on southern votes, would even consider it. The president was bending to pressure, Rauh learned, from African Americans led by a charismatic organizer named A. Philip Randolph.

Raised in Florida and educated at New York's City College, Randolph had founded the largest African American labor union, the Brotherhood of Sleeping Car Porters, in 1925. Porters traveled the railroads as baggage handlers and valets, and during the Depression Randolph's influence extended into every station and depot reached by the Brotherhood's magazine, the *Messenger*.

In 1941, it looked to Randolph like only a matter of months before the United States entered the war raging in Europe and Asia. He believed, according to FBI informants, "that Negroes make most fundamental gains in periods of great social upheaval." War would create a chance to achieve equality, but only if African Americans demanded it. "The Negro sat by idly during the first world war thinking conditions would get better," he told an audience in Oklahoma City. "That won't be the procedure during the duration of this conflict."

In January 1941, Randolph called for African Americans to march to Washington to demand an end to job discrimination. Only 3 percent of workers in war industries were people of color. "The administration leaders in Washington will never give the Negro justice," he declared, "until they see masses, ten, twenty, fifty thousand Negroes on the White House

continued

lawn." The March on Washington Movement (MOWM) was largely bluff, but Roosevelt and the FBI believed it enough to try to head it off.

A protest march would embarrass the government, and Roosevelt had the power to accept Randolph's demands. Leveraging federal defense contracts, the president could desegregate a large portion of the economy without even asking Congress. He opened negotiations with Randolph through Eleanor Roosevelt. The organizers agreed to cancel the march in return for a presidential directive—Executive Order 8802—establishing a Fair Employment Practices Committee to assure fairness in hiring.

It was a victory for civil rights and for Randolph personally. If the Emancipation Proclamation had ended physical slavery, the New York *Amsterdam News* declared, E.O. 8802 ended "economic slavery." Within a year, thousands of African Americans would be working at high-tech jobs in aircraft factories and arms plants. Randolph had recognized that war created an opening for changing the economic and political rules of the game. War touched all Americans. Millions were sent to serve and fight everywhere from the Arctic to the tropics. Millions of others left home to work in plants producing war materiel. Government stepped in to run the economy and created new relationships with corporations, labor, the states, and universities. The war stimulated revolutionary advances in science, industry, and agriculture. The United States itself became the foremost military and economic power in a world destroyed by war.

These changes enlarged the discretionary powers of the presidency and the federal government. Americans willingly accepted personal sacrifices and greater federal authority as part of the price of victory. As the March on Washington Movement proved, the president's enhanced powers could enlarge freedom and opportunity—but they could also restrict individual liberties. Many Japanese Americans spent the war imprisoned in "relocation centers," and the FBI placed Randolph's name on a list of persons to be placed in "custodial detention" in the event of a national emergency. The war unsettled the economy and society, enlisting all Americans in a global crusade and arousing both idealism and fear.

Island in a Totalitarian Sea

Randolph's movement capitalized on a world crisis that reached back to the treaty that ended World War I. The Depression heightened international tensions, turning regional conflicts in Africa, Europe, and Asia into tests of ideology and power. In 1937 Japan attacked China. Two years later, when Germany invaded Poland, France and Britain declared war, beginning World War II in Europe. As with the previous war, Americans had time to reflect on the world crisis. Most blamed it on the failures of the Versailles Treaty and the desperation caused by the global Depression. Nations and empires were solving economic problems with military force.

Americans were divided, however, on how their country ought to respond, on its role in the world and responsibilities at home. Isolationists wanted to stay out of war and secure the Western Hemisphere against attack. But Roosevelt and other internationalists believed the United States had to support the nations fighting Germany and Japan. Internationalists saw a free-trading, open-door world economy as a solution to international conflict. Isolationists worried about growing federal power and the ambitions of Britain and the Soviet Union. The threat of fascism forced Americans to ask whether their economy and government could compete in the world.

Both camps knew war would change American society. The future of world politics and the world economy would be shaped by America's choice of allies and aims. In 1940, most Americans feared involvement and opposed aid to the enemies of fascism. When France's defeat left Britain to fight alone, more Americans saw aid to Britain as an alternative to US involvement. Japan's attack on Pearl Harbor ended a debate that divided the nation.

A World of Hostile Blocs

The Depression destroyed the liberal international order based on free trade. For a century, governments had favored policies that increased the movement of goods, people, and investment across borders. The steamship and telegraph accelerated that trend. Movement toward an open-door world slowed during World War I and the 1920s, and then stopped completely with the Depression. World trade shrank from almost $3 billion a year in 1929 to less than $1 billion in 1933. Empires and nations began to restrict the movement of goods, capital, and people and to regiment their societies for self-sufficiency. Everywhere, it seemed, governments became more ruthless and less free.

Dictators offered visions of imperial conquest and racial supremacy. Mussolini promised a new Roman Empire in Africa and the Mediterranean. Japanese schoolchildren learned they belonged to a "Yamato race," purer and more virtuous than the inferior peoples they would one day rule. Hitler urged Germans to defend themselves against the *Untermenschen*, subhumans, in their midst—Jews, Gypsies, homosexuals. He built a state based on racism, total control, and brutality, where secret police, the Gestapo, hunted down enemies of the regime, and a Nazi army, the SS, enforced party rule.

Jews were the main target of Nazi terror. In 1935, the Nuremberg Laws stripped Jews of citizenship and outlawed intermarriage with members of the "Aryan race." On the night of November 9, 1938, Nazi stormtroopers and ordinary citizens rampaged throughout Germany, burning synagogues and destroying Jewish shops, homes, and hospitals, killing 100 Jews and arresting 30,000 more. Until *Kristallnacht*, this "night of the broken glass," FDR thought international opinion would restrain Hitler. Now he was no longer sure.

Roosevelt grew apprehensive as Germany, Italy, and Japan, the Axis powers, sought to solve their economic problems through military conquest. Italy invaded Ethiopia in 1935. In July 1937, Japan attacked China. In 1938, Hitler's troops marched into Austria. Roosevelt worried that the Axis would soon control most of Europe and Asia, but American leaders had an even darker fear, one they scarcely breathed: that totalitarianism would outcompete democracy. America's free markets and free labor might be no

> If Hitler destroys freedom everywhere else, it will perish here. Ringed around by a world hostile to our way of life, we should be forced to become a great military power.
>
> *FORTUNE* MAGAZINE, JUNE 1941

match for the ruthless efficiency of the fascist states. The United States would have to regiment its own citizens just to keep up, and to enlist industry, labor, and agriculture into a "state system," *Fortune* magazine predicted, "which, in its own defense, would have to take on the character of Hitler's system."

The Good Neighbor

Some believed the United States ought to retreat into its own sphere. The Hawley-Smoot Tariff of 1930 blocked most imports, but within a year, FDR reversed course and began pushing trade as the answer to America's economic problems. He reacted mainly to the vision of his single-minded secretary of state, Cordell Hull. A conservative former senator from Tennessee, Hull believed that equal access for all to the world's markets was the cure for dictatorship and depression and the best way to ensure peace. In a world of empires and blocs, Hull turned an old foreign policy tradition, the Open Door, into a bold plan for peace and prosperity.

Roosevelt and Hull slowly began to reopen markets in Latin America. FDR expanded Hoover's "Good Neighbor" policy, encouraging trade and renouncing the use of force. A new Export-Import Bank financed transactions, and tariffs were lowered. Hull surprised the 1933 Pan-American Conference by approving a declaration that no nation had the right to intervene in the affairs of another. Good Neighbor policies undermined German and Japanese economic ventures, and Latin American governments invited the FBI to track down Axis agents on their soil.

In 1938, after absorbing Austria, Hitler demanded part of Czechoslovakia's territory. Fearing that a small war over the territory would escalate into a larger war, Czechoslovakia's allies, Britain and France, agreed to negotiations. In a meeting at Munich in September they yielded to Hitler's demands. FDR cabled Hitler a last-minute appeal for restraint but accepted the final decision. After World War II, the term "Munich" came to symbolize the failed attempts to appease aggressors, but in 1938 Americans were unsure how best to guard their freedoms in a hostile world.

America First?

As the Axis threat grew, Roosevelt pushed for a buildup of US forces, but Congress and the public disagreed. Disillusioned by the last war, the public wanted to stay out of the conflicts in Europe and Asia. Polls indicated that more than 70 percent believed the United States had been tricked into World War I. Half a million students pledged their refusal to serve in another war. Senator Gerald P. Nye charged that the munitions industry was lobbying for war. Pacifists, economic nationalists, and veterans groups, backed by the *Chicago Tribune* and the Hearst newspapers, composed a powerful isolationist constituency.

From 1935 to 1937, Congress passed annual Neutrality Acts prohibiting loans and credits to nations engaged in war. The action took place against the backdrop of the Spanish Civil War, in which Fascist forces, aided by Germany and Italy, fought against democratic Loyalist forces aided by the Soviet Union. Some 3,000 Americans volunteered to fight with the Loyalists. For that reason, Congress decided to stay out of the conflict; the Neutrality Acts also restricted the president's ability to aid the enemies of fascism.

In late 1939, Roosevelt's worst nightmare came true, as the United States became an island in a world dominated by force. The Soviet Union signed a nonaggression treaty with Germany. The full terms of the Nazi-Soviet pact were secret, leading diplomats to fear the worst, a totalitarian alliance stretching from the Rhine to the Pacific. In September, German armies struck Poland, using tanks and dive-bombers in a *Blitzkrieg*, or "lightning war." Hitler and Soviet leader Josef Stalin split Poland between them. Britain and France declared war on Germany.

The following April, Nazi armies invaded Denmark and Norway. On May 10, 1940, Hitler launched an all-out offensive in the West. Tank columns pierced French lines in the Ardennes Forest and headed toward the English Channel. France, Belgium, and the Netherlands were defeated; Britain faced the German onslaught alone. Roosevelt now had to consider the possibility of a British surrender, placing the Royal Navy, control of the Atlantic, and possibly even Canada in Hitler's hands. The German air force, the *Luftwaffe*, was already dueling for control of the skies over England.

Determined to shore up this last line of defense, Roosevelt used his powers as commander in chief to bypass the Neutrality Acts. In June 1940, he submitted a bill to create the first peacetime draft in American history. He declared army weapons and supplies "surplus" so they could be donated to Britain. In September 1940, he traded Britain 50 old destroyers for leases to naval bases in Canada, Bermuda, and the Caribbean.

The isolationists were now isolated. Sympathy for Britain grew as radio audiences heard the sounds of air attacks on London. Two-thirds of the public favored the draft, but isolationists were not finished. In September 1940, the America First Committee launched a new campaign that urged Americans to turn from Europe and prepare for their own defense. Charles A. Lindbergh and Senator Burton Wheeler headlined America First rallies. The only reason for United States involvement, Lindbergh argued, "is because there are powerful elements in America who desire us to take part. They represent a small minority . . . but they control much of the machinery of influence and propaganda."

Roosevelt worried that the 1940 election would become a referendum on intervention. Isolationist senator Robert Taft was a leading contender for the nomination, but the Republicans chose Wendell L. Willkie, an anti–New Deal internationalist who endorsed the draft and expressed sympathy for Britain. With defense and foreign policy off the table, FDR won an unprecedented third term by a 5 million–vote margin.

Means Short of War

British prime minister Winston Churchill could now broach the delicate but urgent issue of war finances. Britain had been buying arms on a "cash and carry" basis but was now out of funds. The Neutrality Act prohibited new loans, but without arms Britain would have to surrender. FDR gave his cabinet a weekend to devise a plan, and the following Monday he produced the answer himself. Instead of loaning money, the United States would lend arms and equipment. Roosevelt compared the idea to lending a garden hose to a neighbor whose house was on fire. "There would be a gentleman's obligation to repay," but because there would be no loans, it would not violate the Neutrality Act. Lend-Lease, as the program was called, put the US "arsenal of democracy" on Britain's side and granted FDR unprecedented powers to arm allies. The Lend-Lease bill, H.R. 1776, passed the Senate by a two-to-one margin in 1941.

Repayment took the form of economic concessions. Hull saw Lend-Lease as a chance to crack one of the largest autarkic blocs, the British Empire. He insisted that in return for aid, Britain had to discard the Ottawa Accords and open its empire's door to American trade. Churchill's economic adviser, John Maynard Keynes, reluctantly agreed. Later that year, Churchill and Roosevelt met aboard the cruiser *Augusta* to issue a declaration of war aims, the Atlantic Charter. It ensured all nations, "victor and vanquished," equal access to the trade and raw materials of the world.

In June 1941, Hitler stunned the world again with a lightning invasion of the Soviet Union. Three million men and 3,000 tanks slashed through Soviet defenses toward Moscow and Leningrad. Secretary of War Henry Stimson predicted that in three months the Axis would control Europe and Asia, but George C. Marshall, the army's chief of staff, saw that this might be a turning point. If the Soviet army could hold the area between Moscow and the Black Sea, the Germans would have a long winter. Roosevelt shared his optimism. The eastern front took pressure off Britain and gave the Allies a real chance to defeat Hitler. Roosevelt extended Lend-Lease aid to Moscow. The German columns advanced steadily, but they were no longer moving through Poland or France. "Even when encircled, the Russians stood their ground and fought," a Nazi general reported.

German U-boats worked to cut Britain's lifelines, sinking half a million tons of shipping a month. To help the British, Roosevelt fought an undeclared naval war against Germany in the western Atlantic. The US Navy convoyed merchant ships as far as Iceland, where British destroyers took over. FDR said he was offering "all aid short of war," but it was not far short. In September a U-boat fired torpedoes at the USS *Greer*, and the destroyer threw back depth charges. When Roosevelt ordered patrols to expel German and Italian vessels from the western Atlantic, he had crossed the line from neutrality to belligerency and seemed to be seeking an incident that would make it official.

Japan, meanwhile, moved into Southeast Asia. In 1939, the Japanese adopted a "go south" strategy to capture oil fields in the Dutch East Indies and encircle China. Because the Philippines, a US territory, blocked the invasion route, the question for the Japanese was not whether to declare war on the United States, but when. In July 1941, Japan established bases in French Indochina. Roosevelt saw this as a threat, but, preoccupied with Europe, he wanted to forestall war in the Pacific. US diplomats opened talks with Japan while Marshall dispatched a fleet of B-17s in an attempt to deter an attack. When Japanese troop convoys moved into the South China Sea, Hull ended negotiations and cut off US oil exports, Japan's only source of fuel. On November 27, Marshall warned commanders in Hawaii and the Philippines to expect "an aggressive move by Japan" in the next few days. The Philippines, Thailand, and Malaya were the likely targets.

On Sunday afternoon, December 7, Americans listening to the radio heard that aircraft "believed to be from Japan" had attacked US bases at Pearl Harbor in Hawaii. At 7:40 a.m. Hawaii time, 181 planes had bombed and strafed airfields on Oahu, destroying or damaging more than 200 planes on the ground. Bombers then attacked the 96 ships of the US Pacific Fleet anchored next to each other. Three torpedoes struck the battleship *Oklahoma*, capsizing it with 400 crew members aboard. Alongside her the *Maryland* went down. A bomb exploded in the *Arizona*'s forward magazine, breaking the ship in half and killing over a thousand men. In the Philippines, Japanese bombers also caught American planes on the ground. The following day, President Roosevelt appeared before

Pearl Harbor Japan's attack on the US Navy's principal Pacific base at Pearl Harbor brought the United States into World War II. For Japan, it was the opening phase of a campaign to capture European and American colonies in Southeast Asia.

Congress to ask for a declaration of war against Japan. Only one representative, Montana's Jeannette Rankin, voted no. On December 11, Germany honored its alliance with Japan and declared war on the United States.

Some historians have argued that Roosevelt knew of the approaching attack but withheld warnings in order to draw the United States into war. In fact, naval authorities at Pearl Harbor anticipated an attack but doubted that Japan could project air and sea power across the Pacific in secrecy. When Japanese planes destroyed American aircraft on the ground in the Philippines nine hours after the Pearl Harbor attack, Douglas MacArthur said Germans must have flown the bombers. Such preconceptions blinded commanders to the warning signs.

Turning the Tide

For the Allies there was only bad news in the first half of 1942. Japanese invaders walked over the larger British and Dutch armies in Southeast Asia and captured the American islands of Guam and Wake. In February, the "impregnable" fortress of Singapore surrendered with most of the Australian and Indian armies still inside. Japan's Combined

Fleet ruled the seas between Hawaii and India, striking at will. MacArthur abandoned Manila and staged an Alamo-style defense of the Bataan Peninsula and the fortress island of Corregidor.

But the tide was beginning to turn. The Soviets stopped the German advance outside Moscow. On April 18, Colonel James Doolittle's B-25 bombers raided Tokyo. Roosevelt wanted to hold the line in the Pacific while coming to the aid of Britain and the Soviet Union as soon as possible. This meant stopping Japan, creating an American army, and sending it to the other side of the Atlantic. None of those jobs would be easy.

Midway and Coral Sea

"We can run wild for six months or a year," Admiral Isoroku Yamamoto prophesied before the victorious attack on Pearl Harbor, "but after that I have utterly no confidence." Panic-stricken Americans imagined enemy landings in California, but Japan was never so ambitious. It called for fortifying a defensive screen of islands in the western Pacific (see Map 25–1) and holding the Allies at bay until they sued for peace. "The fact that the

Map 25–1 World War II in the Pacific, 1942–1945 Japan established a barrier of fortified islands across the western Pacific. US forces penetrated it westward from Hawaii and from Australia northward through the Solomon Islands to the Philippines.

AMERICA AND THE WORLD

>> **Carrier**

illiam Meredith, a navy pilot and later a poet laureate, wrote a sonnet in honor of his carrier, a craft as proud and majestic as an old queen: "The planes rise heavy from her whining deck. Then the bomb's luck, the gun's poise and chattering, the far-off dying are her near affair." Prior to World War II, admirals saw little grace in the new species of vessel they described as "a barn door laid atop a bathtub." Compared to the battleship, or even the destroyer, it lacked elegance and purpose.

The aircraft carrier joined the US Navy almost by accident. To head off a naval arms race after World War I, the Harding administration wanted to scrap the largest battleships, the dreadnought-class warships then being built in Virginia, Britain, and Japan. The problem was what to do with dreadnoughts already partially built. As a compromise, the Washington Naval Treaty of 1922 allowed each navy to place a flat deck atop the unfinished hulls to serve as a landing place for observation planes. In 1928 the Norfolk shipyard launched two ungainly "flattops," *Saratoga* and *Lexington*. "They are the weirdest ships in the Navy," noted the *Washington Post*, pointing out that their chief defense was speed—33 knots—which would enable them to escape enemy shells by running away.

Even after battleships' vulnerability to aerial bombing became apparent, naval strategists had difficulty envisioning a role for the carrier. Future battles, it was thought, would be slugfests between heavily armored gunships throwing shells at each other from a distance of up to 23 miles. Until the attack

on Pearl Harbor, the carrier's worth was unproven.

Meanwhile, the Japanese navy made the carrier the principal element of its battle plan. After destroying the ships at Hawaii, Japan's six-carrier Combined Fleet roved the Pacific and Indian Oceans from New Zealand to India virtually unchallenged. Pacific Commander Chester W. Nimitz, himself a former submariner, rebuilt US forces around the carriers *Enterprise*, *Hornet*, *Lexington*, and *Yorktown*.

The result was a new kind of warfare in which carrier battle groups struck each other across wide tracts of ocean using torpedo planes and bombers. The first such encounter came at the Coral Sea, where both sides displayed their inexperience. Signals intelligence revealed the target but not the location of the Japanese fleet, while Japanese submarines sent to scout for the American carriers missed them entirely. Groping toward each other, the two commanders struck blindly. Planes from the *Lexington* spotted one of the enemy carriers, the *Shoho*, and sank it. Meanwhile Japanese squadrons mistook a destroyer and an oiler for the US carriers and, after sinking the wrong ships, found the *Yorktown*, took it for one of their own carriers, and tried to land. The following day Vice Admiral Takeo Takagi had better luck, and each side lost one carrier before breaking off.

Success in this new type of battle required information, timing, and luck, but unlike the bloody land battles in New

continued

AMERICA AND THE WORLD   *continued*

Guinea and the Solomons, the result was quick and decisive. Since the beginning of the twentieth century, modern weapons and industrial mobilization had reduced the significance of battle; victory went not to the swift but to the side that could overwhelm its enemies with organization and materiel. Carrier war was different; an empire's fortunes could turn in a single day. Nowhere was this clearer than at the Battle of Midway. Outnumbered four carriers to three (including the badly damaged *Yorktown*), Nimitz was able to inflict a crushing defeat on the Combined Fleet. Navy code breakers had given him advance warning, but victory might not have been possible had Admiral Raymond Spruance not launched planes from *Hornet* and *Enterprise* at the right time and in the right direction, and had they not arrived above Admiral Nagumo Chuichi's fleet just when Japanese planes were refueling on deck.

A carrier was a small city, with its own telephone network, hospital, commissaries, crime, and residential districts. The crew of 3,000 men had one job, launching and landing planes, but between flights were long spells of idleness. "Most of them sleep, curled up on the naked deck; others sharpen their knives, write letters or read," Joseph Bryan, an officer on the *Yorktown*, wrote in his diary. "There is a man in the compartment at the foot of the Exec's ladder who is as expert and delicate an embroiderer as I've ever seen." Living quarters were strictly segregated by rank and race. Despite regulations, navy custom kept African Americans off carriers except as stewards. In 1945 veterans groups picketed the carrier *Croatan* after its commander refused to allow African American quartermasters to board.

The golden age of carrier warfare lasted just three years. After the last Japanese flat-top sank in the Battle of the Philippine Sea in 1944, American carriers provided air cover over invasion beaches as the navy closed the ring around Japan's home islands. Spruance's battle group at Okinawa contained 40 carriers and a "fleet train" of fuel and supply ships that enabled it to remain continually at sea.

Immense nuclear-propelled carriers later proved ideal for the containment and symbolic missions of the cold war. In 1968, Moshe Dayan, an Israeli general and hero of the Yom Kippur War, visited the *Constellation* off the coast of Vietnam. Its five-acre deck gave him a "breathtaking impression" of American power. The carrier, he said, was "not fighting against guerrillas, or against North Vietnamese leader Ho Chi Minh, but against the entire world. Their real aim was to show everybody—including Britain, France, and the USSR—their power and determination so as to pass this message: wherever Americans go, they are irresistible."

Japanese did not return to Pearl Harbor and complete the job was the greatest help for us," Chester W. Nimitz, the US Pacific commander, later remembered.

After the Doolittle raid, the Japanese realized their error and laid plans to lure the US Pacific Fleet into battle. The increase in radio traffic helped Commander Joseph Rochefort, who had already partly broken the Japanese codes. In late April, he was able to tell Nimitz that Japan was planning an attack on Port Moresby on the island of New Guinea. Nimitz dispatched two carriers, *Lexington* and *Yorktown*, to intercept the Japanese carrier force. The Battle of Coral Sea was the first between carrier task forces, an entirely new type of sea battle. Sailors never saw the enemy's ships, only their aircraft, which struck with devastating speed. Planes from *Yorktown* turned back the Japanese transports while Lexington's torpedo- and dive-bombers sunk the carrier *Shoho*. The Japanese fatally crippled *Lexington* and tore a hole in *Yorktown's* deck. The two sides pulled back after fighting to a draw.

Yamamoto next chose to attack the US fleet directly. Sending a diversionary force toward the Aleutians, he aimed his attack at Midway, the westernmost island of the Hawaiian chain. Yamamoto gambled that Nimitz would divide his forces, allowing the Combined Fleet to crush the remnant guarding Hawaii. But trusting Rochefort's code breakers, Nimitz knew the real target was Midway. He also learned from Coral Sea that aircraft, not battleships, were the winning weapons. He hastily assembled task forces around the carriers *Hornet* and *Enterprise* and reinforced airfields on Midway and Oahu. Crews worked night and day to repair *Yorktown*. The American fleet was still outnumbered, but surprise was now on its side.

When Japanese aircraft met stiff resistance from Midway's guns on the morning of June 4, they returned to their carriers and prepared for an unplanned second attack. With bombers, bombs, and fuel littering their decks, Japan's four carriers were vulnerable, their defending Zeros busy intercepting US torpedo bombers. At that moment dive-bombers from *Yorktown* and *Enterprise* burst out of the clouds. They destroyed three carriers in a matter of minutes. The mighty Combined Fleet ceased to exist. Midway put Japan on the defensive and allowed the United States to concentrate on building an army and winning the war in Europe.

Gone with the Draft

The German army that overran France in May 1940 consisted of 136 mechanized divisions of 17,000 men each. The United States had only five divisions and was still using horse cavalry. "Against Europe's total war," *Time* observed, "the U.S. Army looked like a few nice boys with BB guns." Military officials drew up plans for a 10 million–man force. As in World War I, the United States had to find ways to house, equip, and transport the army, but this time it would be five times larger. By December 1941, 2 million men and 80,000 women had enlisted. A year later the total exceeded 5 million.

Buses rolled into the new boot camps and unloaded recruits, called selectees, in front of drill instructors. Basic training aimed to erase the civilian personality and replace it with an instinct for obedience and action. Eugene Sledge left college to join the marines and found himself at a camp in San Diego. "Your soul may belong to Jesus," his drill instructor bellowed, "but your ass belongs to the Marines." After 13 weeks of calisthenics,

> Through the haze
> I saw Marines
> stumble and pitch
> forward as they got
> hit. I then looked
> neither right nor
> left but just straight
> to my front. The
> farther we went, the
> worse it got.
>
> ~~~~~~~~~~
>
> EUGENE B. SLEDGE,
>
> BATTLE OF PELELIU,
>
> SEPTEMBER 1944

close-order drill, marches, and rifle practice, Sledge was assigned to the infantry.

Recruits hungered for a weekend pass, but in the South and West, where many bases were located, there was little to do. The War Department joined several charities in creating the United Services Organization (USO) to provide a "home away from home" with meals, dances, and wholesome entertainment. Still, wherever they were on leave, soldiers often fought with each other and with the locals. Distinctions of apparel and race could stimulate violence. Southerners lynched African American soldiers for wearing their uniforms. In 1943, riots erupted in Harlem after police arrested an African American soldier in uniform. The same year, sailors in Los Angeles attacked Mexican American shipyard workers who wore distinctive "zoot suits." In both cases the clothes signified a disruption of the established social order, a process accelerated by the war.

Army leadership struggled to preserve racial traditions amid wartime changes. Like the multiethnic armies of Britain and France, the US Army consisted of segregated units, some with special functions. The Japanese American 442nd Regimental Combat Team and the marines' Navajo "code talkers" became well known. African Americans served in the army in segregated units and, until 1942, were excluded from the navy altogether. Roosevelt ordered the services to admit African Americans and appointed an African American brigadier general, Benjamin O. Davis, but injustices remained. Even blood plasma was segregated in military hospitals.

Two issues aroused the most anger among African Americans: exclusion from combat and the treatment of soldiers at southern bases. Many GIs in uniform experienced the indignity of being refused service at restaurants where German prisoners of war were allowed to eat. Mutinies and race riots erupted at bases in Florida, Alabama, and Louisiana, where African American soldiers were housed separately and denied furlough privileges. The army responded by sending African American GIs to the war theaters.

Though desperately short of infantrymen, the army kept African Americans out of front-line units and assigned them to menial chores. Combat symbolized full citizenship, and the NAACP pressed Roosevelt to create African American fighting units. An African American infantry division, the 92nd, fought in Italy; three air units—among them the 99th Pursuit Squadron, known as the Tuskegee Airmen—flew against the Luftwaffe; and one mechanized battalion, the 761st Tanks, received a commendation for action in the Ardennes. Most African Americans went into the line individually as replacements, and racially mixed units aroused few complaints in the field. Resistance to desegregation came mainly from Washington.

With manpower in short supply, the armed forces reluctantly enlisted women. The Women's Army Corps (the WACs) was created in 1942, while the navy signaled its reluctance in the title of its auxiliary, the Women Accepted for Volunteer Emergency Ser-

The 99th Pursuit Squadron Known as the Black Eagles, they trained at the Tuskegee Institute and engaged the Luftwaffe in the skies over North Africa.

vice (WAVES). Eventually more than 100,000 women served as mechanics, typists, pilots, cooks, and nurses, an unusually low rate of mobilization. Nearly every other warring country enlisted women for industry and combat, leaving the state to perform traditionally female jobs: caring for children, the sick, and the elderly. This government role came to be accepted in Europe, Canada, and Australia, but in the United States "welfare" continued to be associated with poor relief.

The Winning Weapons

During World War II, weapons technology advanced with blinding speed. Entering the war late, the United States gained a technological edge. American factories produced models using the latest innovations, but many of these would not see combat until 1943 or later.

Until then, troops had to make do with inferior weapons. Marines landed on Guadalcanal wearing World War I–era helmets and carrying the 1903 Springfield rifle. Japan's Zero was faster and lighter than any American fighter. After 1943, the advantage began to pass to the Americans. The M1 rifle was the finest infantry weapon in the war. Artillery was precise and lethal, and American crews were skilled in the devastating "time-on-target" technique, which delivered shells from several directions simultaneously. The elegant P-51 Mustang, a high-speed ultra-long-range fighter, could escort bombers from Britain to Berlin. It dominated the skies after D-Day. American four-engine bombers—the B-17 Flying Fortress and the B-24 Liberator—were superior to German or Japanese counterparts. In 1944, the B-29 Superfortress, with its 10-ton bomb load and unrivalled range, took to the skies over the Pacific and incinerated one Japanese city after another. American tanks, however, remained inferior to their German counterparts throughout the war, owing to the army's failure to recognize the importance of this weapon.

Quantity often trumped quality, however, and the results were impressive. When Allied troops landed in France in 1944, they enjoyed a superiority of 20 to 1 in tanks and 25 to 1 in aircraft. When Roosevelt set a production target of 50,000 aircraft in 1940, the Germans considered it a bluff, but American factories turned out almost 300,000 planes during the war (see Figure 25-1). Sometimes, sheer American numbers defeated Axis skill. An American soldier in Salerno asked a captured German lieutenant why he had surrendered. "The Americans kept sending tanks down the road," the German replied. "Every time they sent a tank, we knocked it out. Finally, we ran out of ammunition, and the Americans didn't run out of tanks."

Americans also developed secret weapons. The War Department funded defense laboratories at Johns Hopkins, MIT, Harvard, and other universities, forging a permanent link between government, science, and the military. American and British scientists invented one of the first "smart" bombs, the proximity fuse. American and British scientific collaboration also produced improvements in sonar and radar, penicillin, and the atomic bomb.

The Manhattan Project that produced the atomic bomb was the war's largest military-scientific-industrial enterprise. In 1939, Albert Einstein warned Roosevelt that the Germans might invent a nuclear weapon. The National Academy of Sciences concluded that a weapon of "superlatively destructive power" could be built, and General Leslie R. Groves was put in charge of the project, which eventually employed 600,000 people and

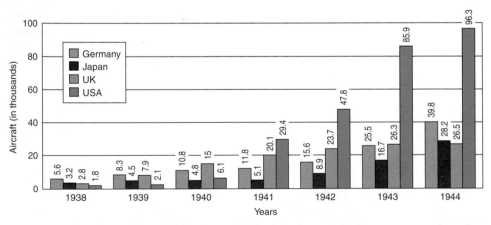

Figure 25–1   Number of Military Aircraft Produced US production of military equipment lagged at first, but once in high gear it dwarfed the rest of the world. *I. C. B. Dear,* The Oxford Companion to World War II *(Oxford University Press, 1995), p. 22.*

cost $2 billion. World War II's marriage of technology and war changed warfare, and it also changed science. Researchers and inventors had once worked alone on their own problems. Now they worked in teams at government-funded laboratories on problems assigned by Washington.

The Second Front

To reassure Britain and the Soviet Union, FDR adopted a "Europe First" strategy, holding the line against Japan while directing the main effort at Nazi Germany. The Allies had little in common except that Hitler had chosen them as enemies. Britain was struggling to preserve its empire. The Soviet Union had once been allied with Germany and had a non-aggression pact with Japan. Roosevelt needed to keep this shaky coalition together long enough to defeat Hitler. His greatest fear was that one or both of the Allies would make a separate peace or be knocked out of the war. Stalin and Churchill each had their own opinions about how to use American power, and their conflicting aims produced bitter disputes over strategy.

As the Nazis closed in on the Soviet oil fields during 1942, Stalin pleaded with Britain and the United States to launch an invasion of France. Roosevelt and Marshall also wanted a second front against Germany in northern Europe. But to the British, the idea of a western front evoked the horrors of the trench warfare of World War I and the losses it could no longer sustain. Instead, Churchill wanted to encircle the Nazis and attack the "soft underbelly" of the Axis from the Mediterranean.

Concerned about U-boats and the inexperience of American troops, FDR reluctantly accepted Churchill's plan (see Map 25-2). A month after Pearl Harbor he had promised Stalin a second front "this year." In late 1942, he postponed it to the spring of 1943. Finally, in June 1943, he told Stalin it would not take place until 1944. The delays reinforced Stalin's suspicions that the capitalist powers were waiting for the USSR's defeat.

Instead of invading Europe, the Americans chose a softer target, North Africa, where troops under Lieutenant General Dwight Eisenhower landed in Algeria and Morocco on November 8, 1942. As they moved east to link up with British forces attacking into Tunisia, German tank divisions under General Erwin Rommel burst through the Kasserine Pass and trapped American columns in high, rocky terrain. Panicky troops fled, blowing up their ammunition stores. Once through the pass, Rommel had a chance to encircle and defeat the Allied forces, but his Italian commanders ordered him to advance in another direction. The Americans and British regrouped for a counterattack.

Ernie Pyle, the popular war correspondent, reassured readers that despite the rout, "there was never at any time any question about the American bravery." Eisenhower was not so sure. He sacked the commander responsible for Kasserine and replaced him with Major General George S. Patton. The army increased basic training from 13 to 17 weeks and reviewed its doctrine and weapons. For Patton, Kasserine showed that firepower delivered by air, tanks, and artillery was more reliable than infantry. His preference for technology over bravery became ingrained in American strategy.

On May 7, Allied forces captured Tunis and Bizerte and took 238,000 German and Italian prisoners. Rommel escaped to fight again in France a year later. There he would encounter a different American army, larger, more experienced, and equipped with the newest weapons. As it mobilized, the United States was changing, too.

Map 25–2   World War II in Europe, 1942–1945 While the Soviets reduced the main German force along the eastern front, the British and American allies advanced through Italy and France.

Organizing for Production

To defeat totalitarian regimes, Americans had to gear their economy for war. Big government and corporations made possible the "miracle of production" that was winning the war and raising living standards. During the height of the Depression, FDR did not use deficit spending to stir the economy (a technique economists call a "Keynesian stimulus"), but during the war, half the money the federal government spent was borrowed, and nobody complained. The economy boomed. War contracts created 17 million new jobs. Industrial production doubled. The employment dial reached "full" in 1942 and stayed there until Japan surrendered.

War industries worked by a new set of rules. Contractors depended on the government for financing, materials, and labor. New war plants, built at taxpayer expense, went up in towns with little industry. As industry moved, workers moved with it into the new boomtowns, organizing themselves into a powerful political and economic force.

A Mixed Economy

The Roosevelt administration added new war agencies to control prices, assign labor, and gear up industry. It dusted off methods from World War I—dollar-a-year men and "cost-plus" contracts—and added new incentives, such as tax breaks, federal loans, and subsidies. "You have to let business make money out of the process," Secretary of War Henry Stimson explained, "or business won't work." Sometimes it didn't, and the government seized at various times the steel industry, the railroads, the coal mines, and a department store chain.

Output soared. A Ford plant at Willow Run, Michigan, turned out a fleet of B-24s larger than the whole Luftwaffe. Cargo ships, which took more than a year to build in 1941, were coming out of the Kaiser Shipyards in an average of 56 days. Entirely new industries such as synthetic rubber and Lucite (a clear, hard plastic used for aircraft windshields) appeared overnight. Industrial techniques applied to agriculture—mechanization and chemical herbicides and pesticides—raised output with fewer farmers. Corporations patriotically increased their market share. Coca-Cola's mobile bottling plants followed the front lines, creating a global thirst for their product. Wrigley added a stick of gum to each K ration and made chewing gum a national habit.

Business leaders regained the prestige lost during the Depression. Major corporations such as General Electric, Allis-Chalmers, and Westinghouse ran parts of the super-secret Manhattan Project. Edwin Witte, a member of the National War Labor Board, called this partnership "a mixed economy, which is not accurately described as either capitalism or socialism." Most business was still small; 97 percent of manufacturing came from firms with just a few hundred employees. During the war, Congress and the administration drew a line between large high-tech firms, its partners in defense, and "small business" that needed tax breaks and loans. Small business acquired its own federal agency and lobbying groups, while major corporations such as Boeing and General Electric negotiated long-term contracts with the federal government. World War II permanently divided the economy into separate "government" and "market" sectors, each with its own rules and ways of dealing with Washington.

Industry Moves South and West

Although Detroit got its share, the bulk of war contracts went to states in the South and Southwest and on the Pacific coast, shifting industry's center of gravity. Airplanes flown in World War I came from Dayton and Buffalo, but the B-29 Superfortress was made in Seattle, Omaha, Wichita, and Marietta, Georgia. The Manhattan Project's largest facilities at Oak Ridge, Tennessee, Hanford, Washington, and Los Alamos, New Mexico, also broke the historic concentration of industry in the Northeast and Midwest (see Map 25-3).

There were several reasons for this shift. Like other industries moving to the huge hydroelectric grids created by the New Deal, aluminum plants went up along the Tennessee and Columbia Rivers to tap abundant power from federal dams. The government also

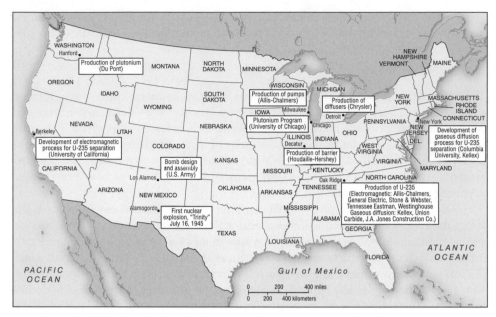

Map 25–3   The Manhattan Project The Manhattan Project created a new kind of collaboration between industry, government, and science. Much of the new infrastructure was located in the South and West.

encouraged construction in the middle of the country to lessen the danger of enemy attacks. Corporations moved south and west to find low-wage nonunion workers. Powerful southern and western senators, who controlled military appropriations, steered new development into their states.

The results were visible. The population of the West increased by 40 percent. San Diego doubled in size in 1942. Los Angeles, Houston, Denver, Portland, and Seattle, became boomtowns. Whereas "old" industries such as automobiles and steel remained strong above the Mason-Dixon Line, the Sunbelt states became home to the gleaming industries of the future: plastics, aluminum, aircraft, and nuclear power.

Few objected to government direction of the economy when it meant new jobs and industry in poor regions. A 1942 Gallup poll showed that two-thirds of Americans wanted the government to register all adults and assign them to war work as needed. The Office of Price Administration enlisted women consumers to enforce price ceilings by informing on their local grocers. Citizens started scrap drives, bond drives, blood drives, and victory gardens. The war effort was so popular that the administration did not worry much about propaganda. Roosevelt and other leaders—many of them former progressives—had learned a lesson from World War I: in gaining public support, inducements worked better than coercion.

New Jobs in New Places

As it had during World War I, the need for workers pushed up wages, added new employees to the workforce, and set people on the move. It also swelled the ranks of organized labor from 10 million to almost 15 million between 1941 and 1945. Enlisted as a partner in the war effort, unions grew because of a federally mandated "maintenance of membership" policy, by which new employees automatically joined the union. Through the National Defense Mediation Board (NDMB), the administration encouraged cooperation, a process begun by the New Deal. When wildcat locals of the United Auto Workers struck North American Aviation plants in Los Angeles in 1941, Stimson sent the army to break the strike, but the NDMB then forced management to accept the union's wage demands. Using carrots and sticks, federal administrators encouraged a more collaborative, managerial style of union leadership. Unions did not have to struggle for membership or recognition; in return, they curbed militant locals and accepted federal oversight. Decision making moved from one-story brick "locals" in factory towns to the marble headquarters of national unions in Washington, DC.

People moved to jobs, rather than the other way around, and some 4 million workers, and with them another 5 million family members, migrated to the new sites of war production. Some 200,000 Mexican *braceros* crossed the border to harvest crops. San Francisco's African American population doubled in a year. In Los Angeles, African Americans were arriving at a rate of 300 to 400 a day. By leaving Mississippi to take a factory job in California, a sharecropper could increase his salary six- or sevenfold.

Workers were generally happy with higher wages, but many lacked a decent place to live. New York, with plenty of housing, suffered from unemployment while new factories were located in places with no housing. There were no rooms to rent within miles of Willow Run. In many towns, workers "hot bedded"—slept in shifts in boardinghouses—or lived in cars. Frustrations over the housing shortage sometimes boiled over into racial conflict. In 1943, two days of mob violence erupted in Detroit over who would take possession of 1,000 new units of federal housing. Housing remained a chronic problem during the war and for several years afterward.

Women in Industry

"Rosie the Riveter," the image of the glamorous machinist laboring to bring her man home sooner, was largely a creation of the Office of War Information. Some 36 percent of the wartime labor force was female, but that was only slightly higher than the peacetime figure (see Figure 25-2). Few women left housework to take a job in a factory solely for patriotic reasons. Instead, the war economy shifted women workers into new roles, some from service jobs into industry and others from factory jobs to better-paid positions.

The number of manufacturing jobs for women grew from 12 million to 16.5 million, with many women moving into heavy industry as metalworkers, shipwrights, and assemblers of tanks and aircraft, jobs that had been off-limits before. Women worked coke ovens, blast furnaces, and rolling mills. For many women, the war and its demands offered the first real chance for mobility.

Even so, employers did not offer equal pay or help to women trying to juggle job and family. Unions either refused women membership or expelled them when the war ended. The Lanham Act provided the first federal support for day care, but the 2,800 government centers were not nearly enough. "Latchkey children," left home alone while their mothers worked, were said to be a major problem. Experts saw female labor as necessary during the war but dangerous in the long run. "Many of them are rejecting their feminine roles," a social worker complained. After the war, women were expected to yield their jobs to

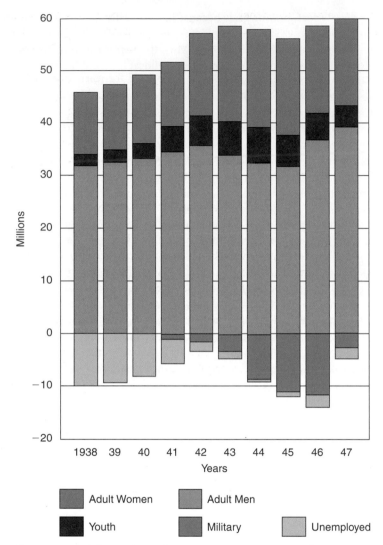

Figure 25–2   Makeup of US Labor Force, 1938–1947 *Dear,* Oxford Companion to World War II, *p. 1182.*

returning servicemen. They were also blamed for neglecting their duties and encouraging juvenile delinquency.

Between Idealism and Fear

In the movies, Americans marched to war (and war plants) singing patriotic tunes by George M. Cohan, but in real life this war was noticeably free of high-minded idealism. Americans had already fought once to end all wars and to keep the world safe for democracy. They were not ready to buy that bill of goods again. Journalist John Hersey asked marines on Guadalcanal what they were fighting for. "Scotch whiskey. Dames. A piece of blueberry pie. Music," they replied. Things were no clearer at home, where to writer Dwight Macdonald the war seemed to represent "the maximum of physical devastation accompanied by the minimum of human meaning."

If Americans weren't sure what they were fighting for, they knew what they were fighting against: totalitarianism, gestapos, and master races. Throughout the war and after, totalitarianism was a powerful symbol of what America and Americans ought to oppose. The president of the US Chamber of Commerce denounced the New Deal as "fascist" and "totalitarian." Labor unions and civil rights groups used the same words against their enemies, but wartime rhetoric also held Americans to a higher standard of tolerance. "All races and religions; that's America to me," sang Frank Sinatra in *The House I Live In* (1945).

Wartime leaders struggled to fill the inspirational vacuum with some of the century's most stirring restatements of the democratic creed. Winston Churchill spoke of protecting the liberty and culture of the "English-speaking peoples." In his State of the Union address in January 1941, Franklin Roosevelt aspired to a world based on the "Four Freedoms": freedom of speech, freedom of worship, freedom from want, and freedom from fear. A month later, *Life* magazine published an essay by its founder, Henry Luce, entitled "The American Century." It was a powerfully optimistic vision of globalized democracy and abundance, "a sharing with all people of our Bill of Rights, our Declaration of Independence, our Constitution, our magnificent industrial products, our technical skills." In response, Vice President Henry Wallace proclaimed that in the "Century of the Common Man," nations would "measure freedom by standards of nutrition, education and self-government." He equated democracy—as American leaders would do after the war—with schools, jobs, food, and a New Deal for the world.

African Americans sought their four freedoms in an atmosphere of increasing racial hostility. Detroit was just one city in which rapid growth touched off racial conflict. In Maryland, Michigan, New York, and Ohio, white workers engaged in "hate strikes" to prevent the hiring of African American workers. Over 3,000 white employees of a naval shipyard burned African American neighborhoods in Beaumont, Texas, in June 1943. Curfews, rumors of riots, and white citizens' committees kept many other cities on edge.

African Americans responded by linking their struggle for rights at home to the global war against fascism. Thurgood Marshall, chief counsel for the NAACP, compared the Detroit rioters to "the Nazi Gestapo." In 1942, the *Pittsburgh Courier* launched the "Double V" campaign to connect the fight against racism to the one against fascism. "Defeat Hitler, Mussolini, and Hirohito," it urged, "by Enforcing the Constitution and Abolishing Jim Crow." NAACP membership grew tenfold during the war. In Chicago, students and activists inspired by the nonviolent tactics of Mohandas Gandhi organized the Congress of Racial Equality (CORE), which desegregated restaurants and public facilities in the North. The NAACP won a legal victory in the Supreme Court case of *Smith v. Allwright* (1944), which invalidated all-white primary elections.

The experience of war may have been the greatest catalyst to change. Many African Americans returned from combat determined not to accept discrimination any longer. Amzie Moore came home to Cleveland, Mississippi, after serving in the army and was elected head of the local NAACP chapter. "Here I am being shipped overseas," he said of his service in the Pacific, "and I been segregated from this man who I might have to save or he save my life. I didn't fail to tell it." The war prepared Moore and his generation for the struggle ahead.

Japanese Internment

Idealism was no match for fear, and in the days after Pearl Harbor, panicky journalists, politicians, and military authorities perpetrated an injustice on American citizens of Japanese descent. Ominous signs reading "Civilian Exclusion Order" went up in California and the Pacific Northwest in February 1942. They instructed "Japanese aliens and non-aliens" to report to relocation centers for removal from the Pacific coast "war zone." The Western Defense Command of Lieutenant General John L. DeWitt and the *Los Angeles Times*, believing the Japanese planned to invade the West Coast, aroused the public against the Japanese "menace." FBI investigators found no suspicious plots and told the president so, but the press continued to print rumors. Responding to the press, DeWitt, and the California congressional delegation, Roosevelt ordered the relocation.

Internees and lawyers challenged the legality of confining American citizens without charge or trial. Fred Korematsu, a welder from San Leandro, California, took a new name

Hizako Hibi's *The Third Winter at Topaz* (1944) Topaz, where 110,000 people braved the desert in pine barracks, became Utah's fifth-largest city. California justified removing Japanese Americans on grounds that they posed a threat, but when the Supreme Court ruled the incarceration illegal in 1944, the state said they could not come back because they might be threatened by "unthinking people."

AMERICAN LANDSCAPE

....

>> **Manzanar**

Jeanne Wakatsuki's internment began with a Greyhound bus ride from Los Angeles across the Mojave Desert. A mile from her destination, she saw "a yellow swirl across a blurred, reddish setting sun. The bus was being pelted by what sounded like splattering rain. It wasn't rain. This was my first look at something I would soon know very well, a billowing flurry of dust and sand churned up by the wind through Owens Valley." Its lakes and rivers emptied by the Los Angeles Aqueduct, Owens Valley was a man-made desert.

Temperatures ranged from 115 degrees in summer to well below freezing in winter. On an alkali flat beneath the towering Inyo Range, workmen were building the Manzanar Relocation Camp, 600 wood and tar paper barracks that would soon house more than 10,000 people. Each family received 20 square feet of floor space and an iron cot and army blanket for each member. Prisoners made the other furnishings themselves, filling burlap bags with straw for mattresses, crafting chairs and tables from spare lumber.

The prisoners fed themselves. They planted tomatoes, turnips, radishes, watermelons, and corn. They raised cattle, pigs, and poultry, making the camp self-sufficient in both meat and vegetables. The flowers and greenery they planted softened the dry land. Prisoners opened shops, laundries, a newspaper, a clinic, and a cemetery. They practiced medicine and law. The Manzanar Co-Op sold $1 million of retail and mail-order goods in 1944.

Manzanar was like a small city, but one surrounded by wire and armed guards. Camp administrators created a network of informants to spy on inmates. In December 1942, four prisoners beat up a man suspected of being an informant. When one was arrested, a group of prisoners demonstrated to demand his release. Nervous guards fired into the crowd, killing two young men and wounding eight others. "You can't imagine how close we came to machine-gunning the whole bunch of them," a camp official explained. "The only thing that stopped us, I guess, were the effects such a shooting would have had on the Japs holding our boys in Manila and China."

It was the last "uprising" at the camp. Administrators censored the newspaper, prohibited expressions of Japanese culture, and required all meetings to be conducted in English. The community within the camp remained forever divided. Young men denounced their elders for respecting the law even when it was unjust. Administrators separated the angry from the docile and drew up blacklists.

Defiance was severely punished. Over 8,000 internees who would not renounce the emperor were sent to a camp at Tule Lake, California, and 263 men who refused military service went to federal prison. Still, the majority of draft-eligible men in the camps served in the armed forces, many in intelligence and combat roles. The separation of the loyal from the disloyal and the placement of so many in positions of trust removed all justification for continuing to hold loyal Japanese Americans, apart from the political embarrassment their sudden release would cause.

continued

Those who could leave—students admitted to universities, workers with contracts elsewhere, those who joined the armed forces—did so, leaving behind the very old and the very young. "What had to be endured was the climate, the confinement, the steady crumbling of family life," Wakat-suki wrote in her memoir, *Farewell to Manzanar.* "In such a narrowed world, in order to survive, you learn to contain your rage and your despair, and you try to re-create, as well as you can, your normality, some sense of things continuing."

and had his face surgically altered in a futile attempt to stay out of the camps. When he was arrested, the American Civil Liberties Union used his case to challenge the evacuation order. Supreme Court Justice Hugo Black upheld the policy as justified by "military necessity." In January 1947, the Western Defense Command praised the evacuation program and suggested that it could be used as a model for the treatment of suspect populations during the next national emergency.

No Shelter from the Holocaust

The United States might have saved more of the victims of Hitler's "final solution" had it chosen to do so. A combination of fear, anti-Semitism, and a desire to avoid unwanted burdens led American leaders to dismiss the Holocaust as someone else's problem. The State Department, worried that spies and saboteurs would sneak in with the refugees, erected a paper wall of bureaucratic restrictions. Refugees found it easier to get a visa from China than from the United States. In 1939, the *St. Louis* steamed from Hamburg with 930 Jewish refugees aboard. American immigration officials refused to let the refugees ashore because they lacked proper papers—papers that only their Nazi persecutors could have furnished. The ship and its passengers returned to Germany.

Nazi Germany's systematic extermination of the Jews made news in the United States. Stories in the *New York Times* as early as 1942 described the deportations and concluded that "the greatest mass slaughter in history" was under way. At Auschwitz, Poland, in the most efficient death camp, 2,000 people an hour could be killed with Zyklon-B gas. Jewish leaders begged the War Department to bomb the camp or the rail lines leading to it. The city of Auschwitz was bombed twice in 1944, but John J. McCloy, the assistant secretary of war, refused to target the camp, dismissing it as a humanitarian matter of no concern to the army. Roosevelt knew of the Holocaust, but his inaction, according to historian David Wyman, was "the worst failure of his presidency."

When American soldiers entered Germany in 1945, they saw clearly why they were fighting. On April 15, Patton's Third Army liberated the Buchenwald death camp. Correspondent Edward R. Murrow described the scene to radio listeners in the United States: the skeletonlike survivors, the piles of the dead, the ovens. "I pray you to believe what I have said about Buchenwald," he said. "I have reported what I saw." Eisenhower had photographs and films taken, and he brought German civilians from nearby communities to witness the mass burial, by bulldozer, of the corpses. Many GIs doubted anyone would believe what they had witnessed. "We got to talk about it, see?" one told reporter Martha Gellhorn. "We got to talk about it if anyone believes us or not."

Americans entered the First World War flushed with idealism and became disillusioned in victory's aftermath. The Second World War reversed this trajectory. Americans slowly came to see the power of their shopworn ideals against the hatred and bigotry that afflicted all nations, including their own. Rose Mclain wrote her husband in the Pacific to promise "that our children will learn kindness, patience, and the depth of love . . . that they shall never know hate, selfishness and death from such [a war] as this has been."

Closing with the Enemy

"The Americans are so helpless," Joseph Goebbels, Hitler's propaganda minister, said in 1942, "that they must fall back again and again upon boasting about their matériel." After the North Africa campaign, the United States made good on its boasts. The American army was small—only 5 million compared with Germany's 9 million—but it was amply supplied and agile, emphasizing speed and firepower. In 1944 and 1945 the United States carried the war to Japan and into the heart of Europe with a singular destructiveness. As the war drew to a close, Americans began to anticipate the difficulties of reconstructing the postwar world and to create institutions to structure a global economy at peace.

Taking the War to Europe

Using North Africa as a base, the Anglo-American Allies next attacked northward into Italy, knocking one of the Axis powers out of the war. In Sicily, where the Allies landed in July 1943, Patton applied the mobile, aggressive tactics he had advocated since 1940. Slicing the island in half and trapping a large part of the Italian army, he arrived at Messina too late to block the Germans' escape. The defeat shook Italy. Parliament deposed Mussolini and ordered his arrest. German troops took control and fiercely resisted the Allied landings at Salerno in September, and winter rains stopped the Anglo-American offensive south of Rome. American troops finally broke through to Rome on June 5, 1944.

The next day, D-Day, finally began the second front the Soviets had asked for. Early on the morning of June 6, 1944, the massive Allied invasion armada assembled off England's Channel coast and launched the assault on France's Normandy coast on beaches designated Juno, Gold, Sword, Utah, and Omaha. Hitler had fortified the beaches with an "Atlantic Wall" of mines, obstacles, heavy guns, and cement forts. Americans waded ashore on the lightly held Utah Beach without much difficulty, but on Omaha the small boats headed straight into concentrated fire. The boats unloaded too soon, and men with full packs plunged into deep water. Floating tanks overturned and sank with crews inside. Commanders briefly considered calling off the attack, but soldiers in small groups began moving inland to outflank German batteries. By the end of the day, they held the beach.

Eisenhower's greatest fear was another Italy. The hedgerow country behind the beaches contained the most defensible terrain between the Channel and Germany. Each field and pasture was protected by earthen mounds topped with shrubs, natural walls

Invasion of Normandy The failure to seize an intact port nearly foiled the Normandy invasion plans, but low-ranking boat pilots saved the Allies from disaster. They invented the technique of driving large landing ships onto shore at high tide and unloading directly onto the beach. When the tide came in, the now-empty ships would float off and return to England for another cargo.

that isolated troops. When GIs crossed a hedgerow, "the Germans could knock off the first one or two, cause the others to duck down behind the bank and then call for his own mortar support," according to one infantryman. "The German mortars were very, very efficient." However, just as had happened on Omaha Beach, the defects of the generals' strategy were compensated for by the initiative of ordinary soldiers. On their own, tankers hand built devices to help their tanks cut through the thick hedgerows. By the end of the month, the US advance broke through German defenses and captured the critical port city of Cherbourg.

Once in open country, highly mobile American infantry chased the retreating enemy across France to the fortified German border. There, in the Ardennes Forest, Hitler's armies rallied for a final desperate counterattack. Thirty divisions, supported by 1,000 aircraft, hit a lightly held sector of the American lines, broke through, and opened a "bulge" 40 miles wide and 60 miles deep in the Allied front. Two regiments were forced to surrender, but the 101st Airborne, encircled and besieged at Bastogne, held on to a critical road junction, slowing the German advance until Allies brought in reinforcements. The Battle of the Bulge lasted a month and cost more than 10,000 American dead and 47,000 wounded, but the German army had lost the ability to resist.

Island Hopping in the Pacific

To get close enough for a knockout blow at Japan, the United States had to pierce the barrier of fortified islands stretching across the western Pacific. The army and the navy each had a strategy and bickered over supplies and the shortest route to Tokyo. MacArthur favored a thrust from Australia through the Solomon Islands and New Guinea to retake the Philippines. Nimitz preferred a thrust across the central Pacific to seize islands as staging areas for an air and land assault on Japan.

By November 1943, MacArthur's American and Australian forces had advanced to Bougainville, the largest of the Solomon Islands and the nearest to the Japanese air and naval complex at Rabaul. Jungle fighting on these islands was especially vicious. Each side treated the other without mercy, killing prisoners, mutilating the dead, and fighting with "a brutish, primitive hatred," according to Eugene Sledge, whose marine comrades kept gold teeth and skulls as trophies. Air attacks pulverized Rabaul in early 1944, opening the way for an advance into the southern Philippines.

Meanwhile, Nimitz launched a naval attack on Japan's island bases. With 11 new aircraft carriers, the Fifth Fleet attacked Tarawa, a tiny atoll with 4,500 Japanese troops protected by bunkers and hidden guns. Coral reefs snagged landing craft, forcing troops to wade ashore under heavy fire. Americans were shocked by the losses, more than 3,000 dead and wounded, for such a small piece of territory, but it was only one of many island battles. "Island hopping" from Tarawa to the Marshall Islands and the Marianas, American forces bypassed strongly held islands and moved the battle closer to Japan.

The Allied capture of Saipan, Tinian, and Guam in July 1944 brought Japan within range of B-29 bombers. General Curtis LeMay landed his 21st Bomber Command on Saipan in January 1945 and began a new kind of air offensive, known as "city busting," against Japanese cities. LeMay experimented with low-level attacks using high explosives (to shatter houses) and incendiaries (to set fire to the debris). The proper mix could create a "firestorm," a flaming tornado hundreds of feet high. On the night of March 9, 1945, 334 bombers lit a fire in Tokyo that destroyed 267,000 buildings. The heat was so intense that the canals boiled and 83,000 people died from flames and suffocation. LeMay went on to burn more than 60 percent of Japan's cities. Americans felt the attacks justified, but, as historian Ronald Spector has written, bomber crews "realized that this was something new, something more terrible than even the normal awfulness of war."

Building a New World

As the war progressed across Europe and the Pacific, Allied leaders met to discuss their visions of the world after victory. In Casablanca in 1943, Roosevelt and Churchill agreed to demand the unconditional surrender of the Axis powers to give the Allies a free hand to set the terms of peace. No country planned for peace as thoroughly as the United States. The State, War, and Navy Departments undertook a comprehensive survey of the world, examining each country and territory to determine its importance to the United States. Planners had only sketchy ideas about future threats, but based on experience they believed that American security would depend on having a functioning international organization, a global system of free trade, and a worldwide network of American military bases.

The weak League of Nations stood little chance of maintaining the peace in the 1930s. Roosevelt envisioned a stronger organization led by regional powers acting as "policemen" within designated spheres of influence. The new organization would disband empires, placing "trusteeships" over colonial territories preparing for self-government. The world after victory would be a world of nations, not empires or blocs. In September 1944, delegates from 39 nations met at the Dumbarton Oaks estate in Washington, DC, and sketched out a plan for a United Nations (UN) organization comprising a general assembly, in which all nations would be represented, and an executive council made up of the United States, China, the Soviet Union, Britain, and France.

To American leaders, the lesson of the 1930s had been that without prosperity there could be no peace. They wanted to remove the economic conditions that caused desperate people to follow dictators into war. A true victory, they imagined, would create an open-door world, in which goods and money could move freely, eliminating the need or justification for conquest. In 1943, before the UN existed as an organization, the United States created the United Nations Relief and Rehabilitation Administration (UNRRA) to provide food and medicine to areas retaken by the Allies. The next year, the Bretton Woods Conference set conditions for a postwar expansion of trade with new institutions, the International Monetary Fund and the World Bank, to manage the flow of money in a global economy. The army established schools at universities, where officers studied languages and discussed strategies for instilling a democratic culture in enemy nations. The invasion of Italy provided a first test of these techniques, and the United States drew on its resources as an immigrant nation to staff units with Italian-speaking officers.

Military planners were not ready to stake America's future security entirely on trade or international organizations. Pearl Harbor had shown that oceans offered no protection against aggression. Military leaders could imagine aircraft and rockets striking deep into the American heartland without warning. Beginning in 1943, they laid plans for a global system of military bases from the Azores to Calcutta to Manila, encircling the vast Eurasian land mass. Planners could not say who the next enemy would be, but with such an extensive base network, the United States could act against any challenger before it could

>> Time Line

▼1933
Hitler becomes chancellor of Germany
President Roosevelt devalues the dollar
United States recognizes Soviet Union

▼1934
Reciprocal Trade Act passed
Export-Import Bank created

▼1935
Congress passes first Neutrality Act

▼1937
War begins in Asia

▼1938
Munich agreement gives Hitler Sudetenland

▼1939
War begins in Europe

▼1940
Germany defeats France, Netherlands, Belgium

Destroyers-for-bases deal between the United States and Britain

▼1941
Lend-Lease passed
Executive Order 8802 ends discrimination in defense industries
Roosevelt and Churchill sign Atlantic Charter
Germany invades Soviet Union

strike. Britain and the Soviet Union looked upon this plan warily, suspecting that they might be its targets, but American leaders were willing to take diplomatic risks to attain the security they felt they required.

The Fruits of Victory

Despite rumors of his failing health, Americans elected Franklin Roosevelt to a fourth term in 1944 by a margin of 53.5 percent to 46 percent for the challenger Thomas E. Dewey. On April 12, 1945, less than three months after his inauguration, Roosevelt died suddenly of a cerebral hemorrhage at Warm Springs, Georgia. "Mr. Roosevelt's body was brought back to Washington today for the last time," reporter I. F. Stone wrote on April 21, 1945. "The marching men, the solemn bands, the armored cars, the regiment of Negro soldiers, the uniformed women's detachments. . . . In that one quick look thousands of us said goodbye to a great and good man, and to an era." In Paris, French men and women offered condolences to American GIs. Flags flew at half-staff on Guadalcanal, Kwajalein, and Tarawa. Roosevelt died just days before Allied troops in Europe achieved the great victory for which he had struggled. On April 25, American and Soviet troops shook hands at Torgau in eastern Germany. On April 30, with Soviet soldiers just a few hundred yards away, Hitler committed suicide in his Berlin bunker. On May 8, all German forces surrendered unconditionally.

Harry S. Truman, the new vice president and former senator from Missouri, was now commander in chief. Shortly after he took office, aides informed him that the Manhattan Project would soon test a weapon that might end the war in Asia. The first atomic explosion took place in the desert near Alamogordo, New Mexico, on July 16, 1945. Truman, meeting with Churchill and Stalin at Potsdam, Germany, was elated by the news. He informed Stalin while Churchill looked on, watching the expression of the Soviet leader. The bomb had been developed to be used against the Axis enemy, but by the time Truman learned about it, American leaders already saw it as a powerful instrument of postwar diplomacy.

As American forces neared the Japanese home islands, defenders fought with suicidal ferocity. On Okinawa, soldiers and civilians retreated into caves and battled to the

Japan attacks United States at Pearl Harbor

United States declares war on Axis powers

▼1942

Philippines falls to Japan

Internment of Japanese Americans begins

Battles of Coral Sea and Midway turn the tide in the Pacific

Allies land in North Africa

▼1943

Allies land in Sicily

Churchill and Roosevelt meet at Casablanca

US troops advance to Bougainville

Marines capture Tarawa

▼1944

US troops capture Rome

Allied landings in Normandy

US troops capture Saipan

Bretton Woods Conference

Roosevelt reelected for fourth term

▼1945

Roosevelt dies

Harry S. Truman becomes president

Germany surrenders

Truman meets Churchill and Stalin at Potsdam

Atomic bombs dropped on Hiroshima and Nagasaki

Japan surrenders

death. GIs feared the invasion of Japan's home islands, where resistance could only be worse. Then, on August 6, a B-29 dropped an atomic bomb on Hiroshima. Two days later the Soviet Union declared war on Japan, and Soviet armies attacked deep into Manchuria. On August 9, the United States dropped a second atomic bomb, this time on Nagasaki. It detonated 1,900 feet above Shima Hospital. In a fraction of a second, the hospital and nearly a square mile of the city ignited. Bricks and granite melted in the nuclear fire. People were vaporized, some leaving shadows on the pavement. In the ruins of Hiroshima, a French Red Cross worker saw "not a bird or an animal. . . . On what remained of the station facade the hands of the clock had been stopped by the fire at 8:15. It was perhaps the first time in the history of humanity that the birth of a new era was recorded on the face of a clock."

Conclusion

Emperor Hirohito announced Japan's unconditional surrender on August 14. In New York, crowds celebrated, but everywhere there was silence and reflection. Thirty million people had been killed; great cities lay in ruins. At the end of the war, the United States' economic, scientific, and military mastery reached a pinnacle never attained by any of the great empires of history. Two-thirds of the world's gold was in American treasuries; half of the world's manufactured goods were made in the United States. At its height, imperial

V-J Day Jubilant crowds greeted V-J Day in New York. Many soldiers newly returned from Europe were on their way to the Pacific.

Britain controlled 25 percent of the world's wealth. In 1945, the United States controlled 40 percent. America's air force, almost 80,000 planes, dominated the skies; its fleet had more ships than the navies of all its enemies and allies combined. Then there was the atomic bomb. The rest of the world looked to see how the United States would use its formidable wealth and power.

The war's sudden end meant Americans had to reconvert to a peacetime economy, preferably one more stable and prosperous than the depression economy of the 1930s. A. Philip Randolph predicted government would have to take a larger role in raising wages and stimulating key industries, such as housing, if returning soldiers were to find jobs and goods to buy. The postwar future looked tenuous. America could either succumb to "a native variety of fascism" or open an era of expanding rights, democracy, and material abundance.

Who, What

Braceros 765

Benjamin O. Davis 758

Charles Lindbergh 751

Chester W. Nimitz 755

George S. Patton 761

Rosie the Riveter 765

Atomic bomb 760

City busting 773

Internment 768

Review Questions

1. Which was more important to victory at Midway, planning or luck?

2. Why did the population of the West grow so rapidly during the war?

3. According to American leaders, what caused World War II? How did their answers to that question affect their plans for the postwar world?

4. Thurgood Marshall worried about the emergence of "gestapos" in America. What did he mean?

Critical-Thinking Questions

1. Contrast isolationist and internationalist viewpoints. How did they imagine different futures for the United States?

2. The government used propaganda and repressive laws to control domestic opinion during World War I. Why was there no repeat of those policies in World War II?

3. Some historians blame Roosevelt for luring the United States into war. How might that historical view be rooted in the isolationist/internationalist debate?

For further review materials and resource information, please visit www.oup.com/us/ofthepeople

1) New technologies were
critical to victory.

2) Americans disagreed on the
causes and meaning of the war.

3) Global war transformed
American society.

4) American leaders used the
war to open foreign markets
to trade.

Island in a
Totalitarian Sea

Turning the Tide

Organizing for
Production

Between Idealism
and Fear

Closing with
the Enemy

THE SECOND WORLD WAR

1941–1945

EVENTS

CHAPTER
....

26

The Cold War
1945-1952

>> Matt Cvetic

It took a half hour for flashbulbs to stop popping when Matt Cvetic appeared as a surprise witness before the House Un-American Activities Committee (HUAC) in February 1950. Radio audiences had already heard of the FBI undercover agent who had penetrated the inner circles of the American Communist Party. Cvetic described his clandestine life, how he had been recruited by the bureau in 1942 and been admitted as a "card-carrying" member of the Communist Party the next year.

His language fascinated the congressmen. Communists in a factory were grouped in a "cell." A party-infiltrated ethnic club was a "front organization." Cvetic named places: a travel bureau at 943 Liberty Avenue in Pittsburgh was used as a safe house; the Heinz Ketchup factory and the Crucible Steel Works were targets. And he named names. "Paul Morrison, a chemist" was in the party, he told the committee. "Jack Shore, a student at Carnegie Tech, was a member, as was his wife, Barbara Shore; Abe Franks and his wife, Nancy Franks, were members; and Ann Lipkind was a member."

Cvetic exposed the workings of a secretive, radical faction Americans had begun to identify as "the enemy within." Communists had never had real influence in elections or American political life. Party membership reached only about 100,000 at its peak in 1939 and fell off rapidly after that. But a series of sensational spy scandals, the Soviet Union's demonstration of a nuclear weapon, and disturbing setbacks for American policy in Europe and Asia convinced the Truman administration and J. Edgar Hoover, the powerful head of the FBI, that American Communists posed a danger far out of proportion to their numbers.

The committee thanked Cvetic for his "personal bravery" and "clear insight into the conspiratorial depths of the Communist Party." He left the room a celebrity. Within weeks he signed contracts for a magazine biography, a radio show, and a Hollywood movie, all titled *I Was a Communist for the FBI*. Conspiracy is the dark side of democracy, and Americans have always feared that customs of political participation—association, speech, and belief—if used

continued

secretly and maliciously, might threaten freedom. Suspicions of plots against liberty become more pronounced in times of rapid change, and in 1946 a sociologist, Karl Popper, defined the tendency, which he called "conspiracy theory," as the opposite of social science, a belief that history is shaped not by many actors, contingencies, and circumstances but by a single hidden power.

Cvetic had not told the committee everything. A few months earlier, he had been fired because the FBI deemed him unreliable. The bureau recruited him in 1942 after alcoholism and an assault and battery charge brought him to the attention of the police. He was turned away by army recruiters even after Pearl Harbor, but he had a Slovene surname, and the FBI wanted information on the Slavic social clubs that thrived around Pittsburgh's steel plants. He was one of an army of paid informants Hoover used to keep tabs on foreign influences and the Communist Party. Cvetic proved eager. His reports alleged Communist control of veterans groups, labor unions, youth clubs, and high schools. Slowly, agents began to notice exaggerations and fabrications. His personal behavior jeopardized security. He demanded more money, and he bragged about his undercover work to bartenders, newspaper reporters, and "more than one girl." When Hoover gave the order to cut off contact, Cvetic chose to go public.

Cvetic's testimony cast the party as a disciplined, ruthless clique dedicated to espionage, sabotage, and "the overthrow of the United States Government." But his FBI reports often depicted a bookish debating society targeted for persecution. Known Communists could not get jobs. Their homes were vandalized. Church leaders denounced "Christ-baiting Communists." Soviet occupation of Eastern Europe stoked hostility in Pittsburgh's Slavic neighborhoods. At one meeting in 1947, hundreds of anti-Communist demonstrators broke into the hall. "We were hit by pop bottles, our clothes fouled by spittle, and we were shoved around," Cvetic complained.

The crackdown on domestic dissent—later called McCarthyism—served a variety of purposes. In the South, charges of "red" infiltration were used against anyone who challenged segregation. In the Midwest, it expressed a conservative frustration with federal interference in school boards and local governance. In Washington, DC, it was fueled by anxieties about sexual roles and identity. More government officials were dismissed because of sexuality than for political reasons. In Pittsburgh it drew strength from Catholic, Eastern European immigrants eager to assert their loyalty, and from opponents of labor unions. It was an antiunion judge, Blair Gunther, who first put Cvetic on the radio as part of his reelection campaign.

Shot like a gangster film, *I Was a Communist for the FBI* depicted Cvetic as a tormented lawman who brings down "a vast spy system" made up of "American traitors whose only purpose is to deliver the people of the United States into the hands of Russia as a colony of slaves." Warner Brothers was surprised at the FBI's unwillingness to help with the film, but Hoover promoted his own undercover hero, Herbert Philbrick, star of *I Led Three Lives*. Celebrity Communist hunters such as Cvetic and Philbrick appeared as star witnesses at trials and loyalty hearings. Max Mandel, a violinist, was fired by the Pittsburgh Symphony after Cvetic labeled him a Communist. Dorothy Albert, a high school English teacher, denied Cvetic's charges but was fired anyway. Martin Sumrak, a park custodian, was suspended "until such time as he clears himself."

The McCarran Act of 1950 stripped citizenship from immigrants suspected of subversive activities. Cvetic testified at numerous deportation hearings, even as his own problems with alcohol and the police escalated. The act also required "subversive" organizations to register with the attorney general. Forty-two states criminalized subversive groups. The Supreme Court later threw out many of these laws and restricted the practice of using paid, confidential witnesses. "The government of a strong and free nation," Justice Earl Warren ruled in 1957, "does not need convictions based on such witnesses."

Origins of the Cold War

In a span of two years, the United States and the Soviet Union went from a wartime alliance to the protracted rivalry known as the cold war. The sweeping, long-term consequences of the cold war made it particularly important for Americans to understand the origins of the conflict. From the outset, the United States and the Soviet Union tried to pin the blame for the cold war on each other. For a long time, Americans wanted to believe that the Soviet Union, authoritarian and expansionist, was solely responsible. However, historians have gradually offered a more critical perspective, and they generally agree that actions by both countries caused the cold war.

Ideological Competition

There is less agreement about the precise sources of the conflict. Ideological, political, military, and economic factors all clearly played a role. Ever since the founding of the Soviet Union toward the end of World War I, Soviets and Americans were ideological adversaries with different political systems. The Soviet Union was committed to communism and socialism, the United States to democracy and capitalism. Despite their differences, the two countries fought as allies in World War II. Wartime decisions, especially about the postwar world, laid the groundwork for animosity after 1945. In peacetime, the Soviet Union and the United States were the only countries strong enough to threaten each other, and World War II showed that with modern arms both sides could strike with devastating suddenness. Moreover, they had different political, military, and economic ambitions. By 1947 those different goals produced open antagonism. With the United States' vow to combat the spread of communism, the cold war was under way.

The Union of Soviet Socialist Republics (USSR) emerged from the Russian Revolution of 1917 and the civil war that followed. Vladimir Lenin's Bolshevik Party introduced a socialist economy in which the state—the government—owned factories and farms. At home, the Soviet Union practiced forms of economic and social regimentation Americans recognized from Nazi Germany and imperial Japan, limiting individual rights, including freedom of speech and religion, and achieving a self-contained autarkic economy. Abroad, the new nation endorsed the revolutionary overthrow of capitalism.

The Soviets' Marxist ideology obviously set them at odds with American ideals. The vast majority of Americans favored a capitalist economy, in which private citizens owned property. They celebrated individualism, freedom of speech, freedom of religion, and democratic government based on free elections. Communists believed all modern societies would eventually eliminate religion and private property and set the collective good over the rights of the individual.

Nevertheless, open conflict was not inevitable. Although American leaders hated communism, the USSR was weak and hemmed in by powerful neighbors, Germany in the West and Japan in the East. It posed no military threat to the United States in the 1920s and 1930s and could even be helpful to American interests. President Franklin Roosevelt, eager to promote trade and restrain Japanese expansion, officially recognized the Soviet Union in 1933.

Uneasy Allies

World War II demonstrated that, despite differences, the United States and the Soviet Union could become allies. After the German invasion of the USSR and the Japanese attack on Pearl Harbor, the United States and the Soviets were thrown together in the war against fascism. They were uneasy allies at best. For many Americans, the lesson of the war was that the United States could not tolerate aggression. No new dictator should ever be able to take over other European countries unopposed, as Hitler did, nor should any single power be allowed to dominate Eurasia. By 1945 some Americans already equated the Soviets with the Nazis by denouncing "Red Fascism."

Different experiences drove each country to protect itself from future disasters. American leaders believed autarkic trade blocs had caused both the Great Depression and the war that followed, and they resolved to rebuild the world economy as a single system, with reduced trade barriers and uniform rules. Soviet leaders feared a repeat of the last two wars, when Poland and Eastern Europe had been staging areas for invasions that claimed millions of Russian lives. But the lessons they drew from war led to opposite solutions: American leaders favored an interdependent system, with open borders allowing goods, information, and people to move freely; Soviet leaders felt only a closed system and tight controls would give it real protection.

Wartime decisions also aggravated tensions. In 1943 the American government created ill feeling by excluding the Soviets from the surrender of Italy. The delay of the Allied invasion of France until 1944 embittered the Soviets, who were desperately resisting the Germans at the cost of millions of lives. The American government further strained relations by sharing news of its secret atomic bomb project with the British but not with the Soviets.

Decisions about the postwar world led to trouble as well. At a conference in Yalta in the Soviet Union in February 1945, Franklin Roosevelt, Josef Stalin, and British prime minister Winston Churchill proposed a self-contradictory vision of the postwar world. The "Big Three" supported national self-determination, the idea that countries should decide their own futures. They agreed that countries should act collectively to deal with world problems and laid plans for the United Nations, which would encourage states to cooperate for security. But they also believed powerful nations should dominate other nations within a "sphere of influence." In these areas—Latin America and the Pacific for the United States; Africa and the Middle East for Britain; and Eastern Europe for the Soviet Union—each power could act independently and limit the self-determination of smaller states. Clearly, spheres of influence and unilateral action conflicted with democracy, self-determination, and collective action.

The conflict was made apparent when the three leaders dealt with the future of Poland, the Soviets' neighbor to the west. Despite talk of self-determination and democracy, Stalin wanted to install a loyal Polish government that would not become a gateway for another invasion. Churchill and Roosevelt favored a self-governing Poland under its prewar leaders. Stalin agreed to elections but believed that Roosevelt had given him a free hand in Poland. This lack of clarity set the stage for future misunderstandings.

From Allies to Enemies

The United States' ambitions for global security appeared threatening to the Soviet Union. To prevent a future Pearl Harbor, the Pentagon erected a circle of air and naval bases around Europe and Asia. Thanks to the Bretton Woods agreement, the United States led a global economy that worked to the disadvantage of controlled, socialist economies. To Roosevelt these steps were not antagonistic, but to Stalin their effect was to block his ambitions with bombers and dollars.

Disagreements over Germany sharpened these suspicions. The United States wanted defeated Germany to rejoin the world economy. The Soviets wanted the country that attacked them twice in 50 years divided and weakened forever. In the end, the Big Three agreed to split it into four zones of occupation. The United States, the USSR, Great Britain, and France would each administer a zone. Although Berlin lay within the Soviet zone, the four powers would each control a section of the capital. The Big Three also agreed that eventually Germany would be reunified but did not indicate when or how.

The uncertainties and contradictions of Yalta led to disagreements even before the war ended. When Vice President Harry Truman succeeded Roosevelt in April 1945, he objected to the Soviets' attempt to take tight control of Poland. Promising to "stand up to the Russians," the new president met in Washington with the Soviet foreign minister, V. M. Molotov. Truman "gave it to him straight 'one-two to the jaw.'" "I have never been talked to like that in my life," Molotov answered. "Carry out your agreements," snapped Truman, "and you won't get talked to like that."

When Truman met with Stalin and the British prime minister in Potsdam in July, relations were more cordial. Because Soviet troops occupied most of Eastern Europe and much of Germany, Truman could do little about Stalin's actions there. There was no progress on planning the future reunification of Germany. But Truman learned during the meeting of the successful test of the atomic bomb in New Mexico. The new weapon would increase US influence everywhere in the world.

National Security

After the war, relations between the United States and the Soviet Union deteriorated. Although Stalin was still committed to overthrowing capitalism, his immediate concerns were in Eastern Europe and along the southern border with Turkey and Iran. The Soviet leader also wanted to keep Germany and Japan from menacing his country again. As an added measure of security, the USSR built a completely self-reliant economy. The United States, by contrast, did not have to worry about securing its borders or supplies. Armed with nuclear weapons, it was stronger than any rival. But American leaders feared that impoverished and vulnerable states would voluntarily align themselves with Soviet power. Every election in Europe, coup in the Middle East, or uprising in Asia had the potential to build a Communist war machine. Recalling the collapse of empires and alliances in the late 1930s, they could imagine the United States suddenly alone and vulnerable.

The Truman Doctrine

To avoid this scenario, American leaders favored the quick reconstruction of nations, including Germany and Japan, within a world economy based on free trade. They also needed military bases to keep future aggressors far from American shores. The opposing interests of the Soviet and US systems soon translated into combative rhetoric. In February 1946 Stalin declared capitalism and communism incompatible. A month later, Winston Churchill, the former British prime minister, spoke at Fulton, Missouri. Introduced by Truman, Churchill ominously declared that "an Iron Curtain has descended across the Continent" of Europe. Central and Eastern Europe, he warned, "lie in the Soviet sphere." Churchill called for an alliance against this menace.

In February 1946, George Kennan, an American consul in Moscow, sent the State Department a long telegram. The Soviet leadership, he wrote, believed "there can be no permanent peaceful coexistence" between capitalism and socialism. Stalin's regime was sure that capitalist nations, beset by internal problems, would attack socialist nations. Acting on this fear, the USSR would, Kennan insisted, try to destabilize other nations and align them with the Communist bloc. The Communist system had to expand to survive.

More concerned than ever, Truman took aggressive steps to counter apparent Soviet expansion in the Mediterranean. The USSR had been pressing Turkey for control of the Dardanelles, a key waterway. Meanwhile, in Greece, a civil war pitted Communist guerrillas against a monarchist government backed by Britain. By 1947 the British could no longer afford the war and wanted to pass the burden to the Americans. Truman told Congress on March 12, 1947, that the world faced a choice between freedom and totalitarianism. He announced what became known as the "Truman Doctrine." The United States must "support free peoples who are resisting attempted subjugation by armed mi-

norities or by outside pressures." The speech, said *Life* magazine, was "a bolt of lightning." Congress voted overwhelmingly to send aid to Greece and Turkey.

The crisis marked a turning point. In 1947, Walter Lippmann coined the term "cold war" to describe the American-Soviet confrontation. There was no formal declaration of war, but with the Truman Doctrine, confrontation had certainly begun. Dividing the world into good

Iron Curtain In Winston Churchill's image, an "iron curtain" divided Europe, but soon similar barriers would mark the frontiers of containment in Asia and the Middle East.

and evil, the United States would support "free peoples" and oppose Communism. Former allies were now bitter antagonists.

Was the confrontation inevitable? There is no way for historians to prove it was, but the United States and the Soviet Union realistically could not have avoided friction. They had a history of hostility, and both possessed great military power. It is also not clear that the form confrontation took—the cold war—was inevitable. It was the product of choices, such as Truman's decision to aid Greece, and perceptions, such as Kennan's judgment about Soviet expansion. Those choices and judgments were not the only ones that could have been made, and Americans, with good reason, would wonder for decades whether the cold war could have been different.

Containment

As the United States implemented diplomatic, economic, and military strategies for containing Soviet expansion, the scope of the confrontation widened to include the entire world. In 1949 China's civil war ended in a Communist victory. In 1950, five years after the end of World War II, the United States went to war again, this time to save a non-Communist regime in South Korea. The cold war spread and became more dangerous. When the Soviets exploded their atomic bomb, the United States also increased military spending and built a hydrogen bomb. As the arms race spiraled, the cold war seemed out of control.

Committed to opposing Soviet and Communist expansion, the Truman administration had to learn just how to fight the cold war. It would be, in George Kennan's words, "a long-term, patient but firm and vigilant containment of Russian expansive tendencies."

The term *containment* aptly described American policy for the cold war. The United States worked to hold back the Soviets for the next 40 years, but "containment," as Kennan described it in 1947, was still a vague concept. Truman and his successors had to decide where and when to contain the Soviet Union and what combination of diplomatic, economic, and military programs to use.

Containment would not, however, rely primarily on the United Nations. Like the United States, the Soviet Union had a veto over actions by the United Nations Security Council and used it to frustrate American efforts. The United Nations would become another arena for rivalry, not an instrument of American policy.

Truman and his advisors revolutionized American policies on foreign aid, overseas alliances, and national defense. Fearing a ruined and impoverished Europe would embrace Communism, they were determined to help rebuild. In June 1947, Truman's new secretary of state, General George C. Marshall, proposed a "European Recovery Plan" to combat "hunger, poverty, desperation and chaos" and to promote "political and social conditions in which free institutions can exist." The Soviets declined to join and refused to allow Eastern European countries to participate, but 16 nations eagerly supported what became known as the "Marshall Plan."

"The Marshall Plan saved Europe," Truman boasted. From 1948 to 1952, $13 billion went to boost agricultural and industrial output, increase exports, and promote economic cooperation. Whole cities were rebuilt. By 1950, participating countries had already exceeded prewar production. Prosperity helped stabilize Western European governments, bind them to the United States, and weaken Communist parties. Containment required more than aid. It also demanded the kind of military alliances that the United States had historically avoided as dangerous entanglements. But, challenged by the cold war, leaders now saw alliances as a way of preventing, rather than provoking, armed conflict. In 1949, the United States joined 10 Western European nations and Canada to form the North Atlantic Treaty Organization (NATO) (see Map 26–1). Under NATO, an attack on any member nation would be treated as an attack on all. To strengthen the American commitment to Western Europe, Congress appropriated $1.3 billion in military aid for NATO countries, and Truman ordered American troops to the Continent. General Dwight D. Eisenhower, the commander of the Allied invasion of France in World War II, became the supreme commander of NATO forces.

Map 26–1   Cold War in Europe, 1950 Five years after World War II, the cold war had divided Europe into hostile camps, with NATO members allied to the United States and Warsaw Pact signers tied to the Soviet Union.

AMERICAN LANDSCAPE

>> Dhahran

In the years after World War II an American city grew in the Arabian Desert. Starting with just 92 pioneers in 1942, Dhahran grew into a city of over 5,000 Americans, working and living in air-conditioned offices, clubhouses, movie theaters, and homes that looked, according to the *New York Times*, as if they had been lifted from Florida by magic carpet.

The clean, modern facilities inside the American zone contrasted sharply with the ragged tents and desert heat outside. Dhahran was like thousands of compounds built all over the world during the cold war to house the expatriates who staffed the corporate headquarters, military bases, and embassies that looked after America's interests.

America's interest in Arabia was oil. In the 1930s, US companies struck a bargain with Ibn Saud, patriarch of a nomadic clan, securing rights until 2005 to any petroleum found in an area twice the size of Texas. When a huge reserve was found near Dhahran in 1938, pipelines and refineries sprang up overnight, making the oil consortium, known as ARAMCO, into the largest US private overseas investment And as the company grew, so did the power of its partner, Ibn Saud. By the late 1940s, Americans began to refer to the territory as "Saudi Arabia."

Before World War II, the Saud family was one of several Bedouin clans vying for control over the Arabian Peninsula. With oil wealth, Saud created a centralized monarchical state, using radio to spread Wahabism, a puritanical faith that rejected liberal, pluralist Islamic practices in favor of Koranic literalism and a strict, punitive code of Sharia justice. Saud permitted no labor unions, prohibited music and the education of women, and forced nomadic Arabs into settlements.

Oil money financed these policies, but ARAMCO officials refrained from criticism. The king's relationship with the company was, the crown prince explained, "founded on mutual profit, with both parties respecting the rights of the other."

In the cold war, security for the company and the Saudi regime became vital US interests. The US Pacific Fleet consumed nearly three-quarters of ARAMCO's oil, and the remainder fueled European construction under the Marshall Plan. If rebels or the Soviets cut off Saudi oil, Defense Secretary James Forrestal warned, Americans would be reduced to driving four-cylinder cars. With its tennis courts and ranch homes, Dhahran looked like a suburb of Houston or Miami. It had its own PTA and scout troop, a country club, libraries, and television station. It resembled American cities in another way, too. It was racially segregated. Outside the American colony, ARAMCO built an "intermediate camp" for 2,000 Italian and Palestinian skilled workers. Beyond lay the "coolie camp," a squalid settlement of huts housing the 14,000 Arabs who drilled the oil, laid the pipe, and paved the roads.

Each settlement had its own electrical and water systems, schools, and clinics, except for the Arab camp, which had none of those things. The American colony had the country's only swimming pools and *continued*

AMERICAN LANDSCAPE *continued*

hospitals—no Arabs allowed. Americans could live, work, and shop entirely in air-cooled surroundings, but Arabs dug ditches and hauled loads in temperatures averaging 120 degrees in the shade for a starting wage of 90 cents a day. Friendships between Arabs and Americans were few.

Arabs resented being third-class citizens in their own country, but complaints were not tolerated in Saud's kingdom. Americans drank liquor and appeared in public unveiled, flouting Sharia laws that Saud's religious police sternly enforced in the Arab community. Bedouin shepherds complained that pipelines fenced them in. Literate Arabs resented United States support for Israel. By the early 1950s, occasional flashes of violence unsettled the community. In 1953, Dhahran erupted in a general strike as 13,000 Arabs walked off the job to protest the arrest of workers attempting to organize a union. Americans met the challenge and kept the oil flowing. Together with Saud's US-trained police they broke the strike.

ARAMCO and the king responded to the strike with paternalism and force. The company raised wages to over a dollar a day and built a hospital and concrete dormitories for Arab workers. Saud built a modern military equipped with US jets and tanks. More Saudis took white-collar positions in the company, but the number of Americans living in the country grew. Executives hoped the American example would make Saudi society more tolerant, progressive, and democratic, but the company adapted readily to the kingdom's autocratic customs. ARAMCO refused to hire Jews for fear of offending their hosts. It helped the king seize lands from rival tribes and from neighboring Yemen.

An opportunistic partnership between an American industry and an antidemocratic monarchy had become a permanent alliance. The cold war created many such relationships, and US officials worried that so many of America's allies were dictators and kings. But the Soviet threat, they believed, did not allow the United States to choose its friends. That time would come when the danger had passed.

Containment also required vigilance. In 1947 Congress passed the National Security Act, creating a Central Intelligence Agency (CIA) to gather and assess information for the president and a National Security Council (NSC) to advise him on military and political threats. The act placed the army, navy, and air force under a single command, the Joint Chiefs of Staff, and a single cabinet secretary, the secretary of defense. The term "national security" provided a blanket justification for responses to all kinds of threats—for actions such as election rigging, proxy wars, and other "covert operations." Congress passed a new Selective Service Act creating a draft for men between 19 and 25.

Taking Risks

Containment entailed risks. There was always the chance that simmering conflict could boil over into world war. One particularly dangerous hot spot was Berlin. In 1948, the

Americans, British, and French began to unify their zones of occupation in Germany into a single unit under a new currency, the deutschmark. Faced with an anti-Communist western Germany, Stalin sealed off his own German zone of occupation. On June 24, the Soviets cut road and rail transport into Berlin, the jointly occupied German capital. "We stay in Berlin, period," Truman snapped, calling what he felt was Stalin's bluff. But 2.5 million Berliners were at risk of running out of food and coal. Sending an armed supply convoy through the Soviet blockade could provoke a shooting war.

Instead, Berlin was supplied by air. American transport planes carried 2,500 tons of food and fuel a day. Along with this massive airlift, the Truman administration sent to Britain two squadrons of B-29 bombers, the kind that dropped the atomic bombs on Japan. In May 1949 the Soviets ended the blockade. Tested, the strategy of containment had worked: Soviet expansion had seemingly been deterred. But the risks were clear.

Those risks became even clearer later that year. In early September, American planes found radioactivity in the air over the Pacific, evidence that the Soviet Union had exploded an atomic bomb. The US nuclear weapon monopoly was over. Suddenly, confrontation with the Soviets had potentially lethal consequences. It was now, a Republican senator somberly observed, "a different world."

Global Revolutions

The cold war soon spread from Europe to shape the politics of the world. Civil and postcolonial strife in Asia, Africa, the Middle East, and Latin America came to be seen as part of the conflict between the nuclear superpowers.

In China, the nationalist government of Jiang Jieshi had waged a civil war against Mao Zedong's Communist rebels since the 1920s. Both sides joined forces to fight the Japanese in World War II, but whereas combat strengthened the Communists, it weakened Jiang's corrupt and unpopular regime. When Japan surrendered, US forces helped Jiang regain control of Chinese cities. Truman urged a permanent settlement, but the civil war resumed. Congressional Republicans saw China as a key cold war battleground, but Truman doubted the United States could influence the outcome. He sent the nationalists $2 billion in aid but refused to send troops. In December 1949 the defeated nationalists fled the Chinese mainland for the island of Taiwan, and Republicans angrily blamed the administration for the "loss" of China.

With most of Asia now in Communist hands, American strategists began to rethink containment. Before 1949, the danger zones were in the world's industrial heartlands, Europe and Japan. Now it seemed brushfire wars could spread nearly anywhere. Peasants had manned Mao's armies, and the rural "third world" seemed especially vulnerable. To contain Latin America, Truman organized the Rio Pact, through which the United States would provide training, weapons, and advisors for Latin American militaries. The Organization of American States (OAS), created in 1948, promoted stability and economic development from its headquarters in Washington.

Territories formerly of little strategic interest, such as Southeast Asia and Africa, became vital to security. Although the Truman administration favored self-determination, it tolerated Latin American dictatorships, European colonial dominion, and South Africa's white supremacist rule because these undemocratic regimes opposed Communism.

>> Underdevelopment

As the cold war unfolded, a second global drama, in some ways more consequential, played out in Asia, the Middle East, and Africa. Subjugated peoples struggled for and claimed independence, and European colonial systems crumbled. By the end of the 1940s, for the first time in history, a majority of the world's people lived in nations instead of empires.

Decolonization ripped apart systems of authority and trade. After years of conflict, new nations often gained little but freedom. They inherited economies without industry or markets, governments with no schools, roads, or tax collectors, and restless citizens living in deep poverty. The Truman administration recognized the need to help manage this movement toward nationalism.

In the fourth point of his 1949 inaugural address, Truman announced a "bold new program for making the benefits of our scientific advances and industrial progress available for the improvement and growth of underdeveloped areas." The "Point Four" program was the United States' first global foreign aid program, but Truman's real innovation was in redefining terms. By calling the new nations "underdeveloped," he asserted that nations were entitled to growth, that all nations would one day be fully developed.

National leaders eagerly accepted the new terms and sent delegations to ask for technical assistance. "America's attitude is our salvation," an Afghan prince declared. "We are free of the threat of great powers using our mountain passes as pathways to empire. Now we can concentrate our talents and resources on bettering the living conditions of our people."

While nationalists struggled for freedom from outside interference, development obliged every responsible government to open the door to foreign experts. Countries that had earlier expelled foreign advisers welcomed economists from the World Bank and the Ford Foundation. UN commissions on food, health, and education measured each nation's progress toward the universal benchmarks of a fully modern state. Development directed nationalist energies into economic channels and away from political actions that might endanger US interests. Nationalist leaders remarked on how material changes altered the spiritual and cultural outlook of people. Hydroelectric dams were the temples of modern India, declared Prime Minister Jawaharlal Nehru at the dedication of an enormous water project modeled on the TVA: "When we undertake a big work, our minds open out a little." Some contended that development might replace the cold war with a peaceful competition to modernize the world under rival economic theories.

Others argued that poverty went beyond aid, technical knowledge, or even states of mind. A Brazilian delegate at the first Point Four conference explained that poverty was caused by the terms of trade: Latin American agricultural exports declined in value, while manufactured imports from the United States increased in price. Economies advanced, in other words, by pushing others into backwardness. Development created underdevelopment.

But the success of the Marshall Plan and Japan's reconstruction gave Americans tremendous confidence in their ability to make over whole societies. In the 1950s, social scientists devised theories of "nation building." For their own convenience, specialists divided the world into three parts, each with its set of problems: a democratic, developed "first world," a Communist "second world," and the underdeveloped "third world," with most of the nations and two-thirds of the people on earth.

If the United States could ease the third world's ascent, it could strengthen its own security. Military strategies against guerilla insurgencies increasingly employed development techniques to stabilize governments and win (in Mao Zedong's phrase) the "hearts and minds" of the people.

Aid officials often said that development and democracy went together. As peasants became consumers and workers, they would demand more choice in their lives and their leaders. By giving of its resources and know-how, America could "export democracy." But development programs seldom asked ordinary people what kind of progress they wanted. Aid reinforced a centralized state, channeling funds to unelected commissions and experts who made decisions that affected millions of people.

By the 1960s, "nation building" had become central to US containment strategy. The long US struggle in Vietnam, which began with military aid in 1950 and ended with defeat in 1975, would test the theory that stimulating development would increase democracy and security. That idea, Henry Kissinger later concluded, was "clearly wrong."

But by then, a system of national and international institutions to guide the development of nations was already in place. Around the world, national success was judged by the statistical yardstick of economic growth. Although few fully accepted Truman's hunch that prosperity would guarantee peace, even fewer were ready to reject it entirely. Underdevelopment had taken a permanent place on the agenda of global problems.

Korea

Working to hold off Communism at so many points, it was probably not surprising that the United States was eventually drawn into war. Nevertheless, the news that US troops were fighting in Korea startled Americans in 1950, because the conflict was so far from areas considered strategically important. But the Korean War was firmly rooted in the logic of the cold war.

Korea, a peninsula bordering China and the Soviet Union, had been liberated from the Japanese in 1945. American and Soviet troops jointly occupied the territory, splitting it into two zones at the 38th parallel. The United States opposed the popular nationalist Kim Il Sung, a Communist, and acted unilaterally to install a regime in the South under Syngman Rhee, an anti-Communist. By 1948, Korea had two governments, each claiming jurisdiction over the whole. In June 1950, after incidents along the 38th parallel, Kim's army, led by Soviet-made tanks, invaded the South (see Map 26–2).

Truman responded boldly. By itself, South Korea was not important, but the administration believed the Soviet Union was behind the North Korean attack. After the "loss" of China, Truman could not afford another Communist victory in Asia. He secured United Nations approval for international action. Troops from 15 countries eventually fought in the UN force, but nine-tenths came from the United States. Was America at war, then? Claiming the conflict was only a "police action," Truman never asked Congress for a dec-

Map 26–2   The Korean War, 1950–1953 The shifting lines of advance mark the back-and-forth struggle that would end with stalemate and the permanent division of Korea.

laration of war. For the first time, but not the last, a president sent troops to battle in the cold war without regard for the Constitution.

At first, the fighting did not go well. Ill-prepared US troops fell back toward the coast. But in the summer, General Douglas MacArthur used the US Navy's control of the seas to put troops ashore at Inchon, deep behind enemy lines. North Korea's main armies were cut off and destroyed. Within weeks, the South had been reclaimed.

Then Truman and his advisers made a fateful decision. Rather than just contain Communism, they wanted to roll it back. Truman gave the order to invade North Korea and reunify the peninsula. MacArthur, who privately wanted war with the Chinese Communists, pushed ever closer to China. Fearing an invasion, the Chinese issued warnings, sent their forces into North Korea, and, on November 25, unleashed a massive attack on UN troops. MacArthur's shattered army pulled back to defend South Korea.

The Korean "police action" became a stalemate. A frustrated MacArthur wanted to fight aggressively, but the chastened Truman administration gave up reunification and accepted the 38th-parallel division. That was too much for MacArthur, who broke the military's unwritten rule against public criticism of civilian leaders. "There is no substitute for victory," MacArthur lectured in 1951. Fed up, Truman fired his popular general in April as the war dragged on.

The Korean stalemate underscored hard truths of the cold war. Containment could mean sacrificing American lives in minor, indecisive wars. As nuclear war was not an option, US troops had to be prepared, as the saying went, to "die for a tie"—to fight for something less than victory. In this kind of conflict, leaders had to convince allies, undecided nations, and citizens at home that, despite setbacks, the West would eventually win. Psychology was more important than territory.

NSC-68

Before Korea, the Truman administration tried to balance its international and domestic agendas. But by the 1950s, containment became the first priority. The administration escalated efforts against revolutionary movements even in peripheral areas, such as Southeast Asia. Colonial struggles, such as the Vietnamese rebellion against their French overlords, were seen as critical challenges.

In April 1950, the National Security Council approved a secret guideline known as NSC-68. Citing a growing list of threats and the "possibility of annihilation," it called for the United States to triple defense spending, impose order in postcolonial areas, and seek more powerful weapons. Truman worried about the cost, but the Korean War convinced him. By 1952, defense expenditures had nearly quadrupled, to $44 billion. Meanwhile, the armed forces grew—to 3.6 million by 1952—along with the list of combat theaters, now including Vietnam. Truman ordered the building of "the so-called hydrogen or superbomb." Successfully tested in November 1952, the thermonuclear bomb was far more powerful than the atomic bomb, but it did not stop the arms race. Less than a year later, the USSR had its own "H-bomb."

Although it remained top secret until the 1970s, NSC-68 profoundly changed the US economy and political system. The military buildup was paid for with deficit financing, and federal borrowing generated jobs and growth, particularly in the South and West.

To fight the cold war, Americans accepted things they had long feared: secrecy, debt, alliances, a massive standing army, and centralized direction of the economy. Each of these magnified the role of the federal government.

The Reconversion of American Society

While the cold war intensified, domestic policy focused on restoring the economy and society to a peacetime footing. "Reconversion" was welcomed by a nation tired of war, but it was also a cause for worry. Americans feared a return to the desperate conditions of the 1930s. Labor, women, and African Americans, especially, wanted to hold on to and extend wartime gains.

The Postwar Economy

As World War II ended, the economy threatened to slide back into depression. Millions of unemployed servicemen came home at a time when government was cutting spending. The disaster never happened. Unemployment did rise in 1946 but never approached the double-digit rates of the 1930s. Despite brief downturns, the economy was vibrant. Its resilience reflected several factors, including veterans' choices, the federal role, the transformation of industry, and US economic dominance. Returning veterans did not strain the economy, partly because half of them went to school rather than work. Under the GI Bill of 1944, the federal government paid veterans for up to three years of education. Federal

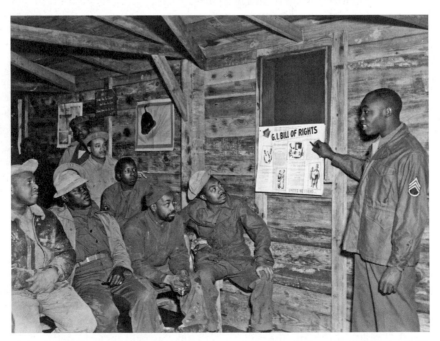

Officer Explaining GI Bill Over 1 million veterans enrolled in college in 1946 under the GI Bill. Veterans' benefits helped to democratize higher education and home ownership.

spending also helped prevent a return to the economic troubles of the 1930s. With World War II over, federal expenditures decreased dramatically, but spending was still far greater than it was during the 1930s. The GI Bill showed how spending stimulated the economy. Pumping nearly $14.5 billion into education, the bill encouraged colleges and universities to expand. As veterans swelled enrollments, institutions hired new faculty, and entire new systems, such as the State University of New York, were created.

Reconversion accelerated the economic change started by World War II. In the late 1940s, industrial production was still concentrated in the Northeast and Midwest, but new military spending was helping to shift factories and population south and west. In the 1940s, the population of the western states grew by 50 percent, compared with 10 percent in the East. The nature of the economy was changing, too. Oil and natural gas replaced coal as the chief source of power. New industries, such as plastics, electronics, and aviation, were growing rapidly.

Finally, the dominance of the United States in the world economy helped reconversion. At the end of World War II, the US economy was roughly the size of the European and Soviet economies combined. As late as 1950, America, with only 6 percent of the world's population, accounted for 40 percent of the value of all the goods and services produced in the world. Demand for American exports created jobs but also stoked inflation. Production caught up, and in the late 1940s, the economy began a prolonged peacetime boom.

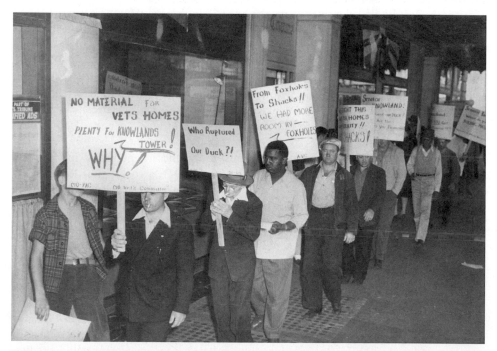

Veterans Demand Housing As millions of holders of the "ruptured duck"—the honorable service medal for World War II—were mustered out of the armed forces, the domestic economy struggled to keep up. Congress declared the housing shortage a national emergency and offered loans to entice developers to close the gap.

The Challenge of Organized Labor

Organized labor had never been more powerful than at the end of World War II. One-third of nonagricultural civilian workers belonged to unions. The Democratic Party paid attention to influential unions, such as the Congress of Industrial Organizations (CIO), and after pledging not to strike during World War II, organized labor was eager to test its clout. Workers wanted wage increases to cope with inflation and as a reward for their contribution to wartime profits. In Europe and Japan, unions were gaining control over the way corporations did business, and some American unions also wanted a role in management. Not surprisingly, corporations were reluctant to give up any of their power or profits. Along with conservatives in Congress, they branded the unions as agents of Communism.

The result was a huge wave of strikes as soon as the war ended in August 1945. In 1946, 2 million machinists, longshoremen, and other workers around the country called a record 4,985 strikes. "[L]abor has gone crazy," an anxious Truman told his mother.

Significant work stoppages hit automobile factories, coal mines, and railroad yards. Late in 1945, the United Auto Workers (UAW) struck General Motors (GM) for a 30 percent raise in hourly wages, access to the company's books, and more say in company decisions. GM rejected union interference in management decisions. When the strike finally ended after 113 days, the UAW won only some of its wage demands. It marked a turning point for labor. Unions never again demanded to participate in management, but instead focused on pay and benefits.

The coal and railroad strikes were even more contentious. Members of the United Mine Workers (UMW) and the railway unions refused to accept federal arbitration. As the coal supply dwindled, power systems suffered "brownouts," and railroad passengers were stranded. The situation tested the strong relationship, forged in the New Deal, between the Democratic Party and organized labor. Truman ordered federal takeovers of the mines and the railroads. "Let Truman dig coal with his bayonets," snarled John L. Lewis, leader of the UMW. But the strikes ended in May. Many Americans applauded the president's action and believed that Lewis and other union leaders had become too powerful and demanding.

Counting on this unhappiness with unions, probusiness Republicans in Congress soon moved to limit the power of organized labor. In 1947, a coalition of Republicans and conservative, mostly southern Democrats passed the Taft-Hartley Act, a sweeping modification of federal labor law. The bill made it easier for employers to hire nonunion workers and to oppose the formation of unions. It also limited unions' right to organize and engage in political activity. Most humiliating, it compelled union leaders to swear that they did not belong to the Communist Party.

Despite these setbacks, workers and unions prospered. Landmark contract negotiations between the UAW and GM offered a model of labor relations. In 1948 the UAW won guaranteed cost-of-living adjustments, known as COLAs, and an annual wage increase tied to rises in worker productivity. In the so-called Treaty of Detroit, signed in 1950, the UAW won other increases and a pension plan in a long five-year contract. In return for pensions and protection against inflation, autoworkers gave management stable, predictable labor relations over the long term.

The Treaty of Detroit ended a difficult period for organized labor. Thanks to lucrative contracts, many workers were more secure than ever before, but reconversion also limited the power of organized labor and the support of the Democratic Party. Aggressive strikes produced mixed results, public hostility, and government interference. With the end of the strike wave, unions effectively abandoned their demand to participate in management.

Opportunities for Women

Reconversion also posed special challenges to the status of American women. During World War II, the shortage of male labor had expanded women's opportunities for employment. Working women prized the income and the sense of satisfaction they gained from performing jobs traditionally monopolized by men. But employers and government officials encouraged the belief that women should surrender jobs to returning veterans. The number of women in the labor force dropped 13 percent from 1945 to 1946, but reconversion did not send female workers home for good. Three-quarters of the women who wanted to stay at work after the war managed to find jobs.

Most women, of course, needed to earn a living for themselves or their families. By 1953 the number of women in the workforce matched the level of 1945. The number in nontraditional jobs increased, too. More women than ever before were skilled craftspersons, forepersons, physicians, and surgeons.

The number of married women in the postwar labor force was especially notable, as economic necessity overcame cultural prejudice against working mothers and married women. By 1947 there were more married women than single women in the wage labor force.

The armed forces, like civilian employers, initially cut back the number of women in the ranks when the war ended, but Congress granted women permanent status in the armed forces and merged the separate women's military organizations, such as the Women's Army Corps, into the regular armed services.

Despite these gains, women still faced discrimination. The majority had to settle for traditionally female, low-paying jobs in offices, stores, and factories. Women's hourly pay rose only half as much as men's pay in the first years after the war. In the military, women were largely confined to noncombatant roles such as nursing. There were no women generals.

In the larger society there was little interest in women's rights. After a meeting with female activists, Truman dismissed a constitutional amendment guaranteeing equal rights for women as a "lot of hooey."

Despite the lack of support for women's rights, women's opportunities were gradually expanding in the postwar years; the combination of women's desires and the economy's needs was slowly promoting the feminization of the labor force.

Civil Rights for African Americans

Like women, African Americans had made significant gains during World War II. They filled new roles in the military and higher-paying jobs in the civilian economy and pushed their demand for civil rights. Like women, African Americans sought to preserve and extend these rights and opportunities in the face of substantial resistance.

Several factors, including economic change, legal rulings, and wartime experiences, stimulated the postwar drive for equal rights and opportunities. By the end of the war, the transformation of the southern economy was undermining the system that segregated

African Americans and denied them the right to vote. As mechanization reduced the need for field hands, African Americans left for the region's growing cities and for the North and West. One of the basic rationales for segregation—the need for an inexpensive, submissive labor force in the fields—was disappearing. The developing southern economy also attracted whites from other regions who were less committed to segregation and disfranchisement. Meanwhile, by migrating to northern and western cities, African Americans increased their votes and political influence.

In fighting the Nazis during the war and the Communists afterward, the United States dedicated itself to universal freedoms. The United Nations Declaration on Human Rights committed member states to guarantee rights to education, free movement, assembly, and personal safety. African Americans appealed to the UN, the courts, and the press to have the United States recognize these commitments.

During the 1940s, a series of US Supreme Court decisions struck at racial discrimination and encouraged African Americans to challenge inequality. In *Smith v. Allwright* in 1944, the Court had banned whites-only primary elections. In *Morgan v. Virginia* in 1946, the Court ruled that interstate bus companies could not segregate passengers. In *Shelley v. Kraemer* in 1948, the court banned restrictive covenants, the private agreements between property owners not to sell houses to African Americans and other minorities. These and other court decisions weakened discriminatory practices and suggested that African Americans might have a judicial ally in the struggle for justice.

African Americans' war experiences also encouraged them to demand more and to expect justice from the country they fought for. "Our people are not coming back with the idea of just taking up where they left off," an African American private wrote. "We are going to have the things that are rightfully due us or else."

That kind of determination spurred civil rights activism after the war. In the South, African Americans increasingly demanded the right to vote after *Smith v. Allwright*. The National Association for the Advancement of Colored People (NAACP) set up citizenship schools in the South to show African American voters how to register. The campaign was driven, too, by individual actions. In July 1946 Medgar Evers, a combat veteran who had just reached his 21st birthday, decided to try to vote in the Democratic Party's primary election in Decatur, Mississippi.

Such activism was resisted by whites deeply committed to disfranchisement and segregation. A white mob kept Evers from voting in 1946. In Georgia, whites killed an African American voter. More often, they manipulated registration laws to disqualify voters. A voter seeking to register might have to answer such questions as "How many bubbles are there in a bar of soap?" Still, African American voter registration in the South, only 2 percent in 1940, rose to 12 percent by 1947. The result was the election of a few African American officials and improved service from local government.

Alongside the campaign for voting rights, civil rights activists fought segregation across the country. The interracial Congress of Racial Equality (CORE) took the lead in protesting public discrimination. To test the Supreme Court's decision in *Morgan*, CORE sent an integrated team on a bus trip through the upper South, where they met with violence and arrests. Activists hardly dented segregation in the South in the 1940s but had more success promoting antidiscrimination laws in the North. By 1953, fair-employment laws had been adopted in 30 cities and 12 states.

Activists also pressured Truman to support civil rights. In the spring and summer of 1946, picketers marched outside the White House with signs that read, "SPEAK, SPEAK, MR. PRESIDENT." Racial discrimination was an embarrassment for a nation claiming to represent freedom and democracy in the world, but support for civil rights was a risk for a politician dependent on white support. Nevertheless, Truman took significant steps.

In the fall of 1946, Truman supported a presidential committee report, *To Secure These Rights*, that called for strong federal action against lynching, vote suppression, job discrimination, and civil rights violations, including segregation in the armed forces. Furious white southern politicians and newspapers said Truman was "stabbing the South in the back."

African Americans, meanwhile, kept the heat on Truman. To protest discrimination in the military, A. Philip Randolph, the head of the Brotherhood of Sleeping Car Porters, proposed a boycott of the draft. In July 1948 Truman responded with Executive Order 9981, creating a committee to phase out discrimination in the military. He also established the Fair Employment Board, which moved more slowly against discrimination in federal hiring.

During the Truman years, the most publicized blow to racial inequality came not from the White House but the baseball diamond. When the Brooklyn Dodgers called up infielder Jackie Robinson from the minor leagues in 1947, he became the first African American to play in the major leagues since the late nineteenth century. A strong, self-disciplined former soldier, Robinson took taunts and beanballs on the field and death threats in the mail. Fast, powerful, and exciting, he finished the season as the National League's Rookie of the Year. Robinson's success paved the way for increasing numbers of African American players in the majors over the next several years.

Robinson's success also spelled the end of the Negro Leagues, created when African Americans were banned from the major leagues. Integration would sometimes undermine distinctly African American institutions. Nonetheless, the achievements of Robinson, Larry Doby, and other pioneering African American players sent a powerful message for civil rights and underscored the limits of reconversion. On the whole, African Americans preserved and sometimes expanded their wartime gains while still encountering injustice and inequality. In one respect, African Americans, women, and organized labor shared a common experience in the first years after World War II. For each of these groups, struggling for rights and opportunities, reconversion turned out to be better than feared and worse than hoped. They all confronted the limits of their power to change the society around them.

The Frustrations of Liberalism

During the Great Depression, New Deal liberalism had reshaped American democracy, thrusting the federal government more deeply than ever into economic and social life. But the liberal Democratic agenda of federal activism, which stalled during World War II, met more frustration afterward. Liberals and the Democratic Party strained to provide answers for a nation no longer facing an economic or military emergency. Harry Truman struggled to prove that he was a worthy successor to Franklin Roosevelt.

The Democrats' Troubles

Many Americans were skeptical about their accidental president. Liberals who wondered whether Truman shared their ideals were incensed when he fired FDR's trusted aide Henry Wallace after Wallace criticized Truman's policy toward the USSR. Conservatives and moderates also had their doubts. During the Depression, Americans had been willing to endorse government interventions in the economy, but they felt less need for government and more need for individual freedom in a prosperous peacetime.

The president was more liberal than the liberals expected. Shortly after he took office in 1945, he presented a legislative program that included proposals on education, employment, insurance, social security, and civil rights. Yet a full-employment bill, giving the federal government responsibility for securing jobs and prosperity, met overwhelming conservative and moderate opposition. Watered down by Congress, the resulting Employment Act of 1946 created a presidential Council of Economic Advisors but did nothing to increase the economic role of the federal government.

Truman and the liberals suffered an even sharper defeat over the president's sweeping proposal for a national health insurance system that would guarantee medical care to all Americans. Under the plan, the federal government would manage the insurance system and set doctors' and hospitals' fees. Conservatives and the medical profession promptly condemned the proposal. The bill failed, and so did most of Truman's domestic proposals.

Nevertheless, the federal role in national life continued to grow. Medical care offered a notable example. The Veterans Administration established a vast network of federal hospitals to care for returning soldiers. In 1946, the Hill-Burton Act appropriated federal money for new hospitals. That same year, Congress created a research lab in Atlanta, later called the Centers for Disease Control, to monitor infectious diseases. Congress also established the National Institute of Mental Health in 1949.

As Truman struggled with domestic and foreign policy, he became increasingly unpopular. "To err is Truman," went the joke. "Had Enough?" asked Republicans. Many had. In the 1946 congressional elections, the voters gave the Republicans a majority in the House of Representatives and the Senate for the first time in 16 years.

Truman's Comeback

The 1946 elections seemed to presage a defeat for Truman in two years, but the president managed a stunning comeback. It began with the Republican majority that took control in Congress in 1947. Led by Senator Robert Taft of Ohio, they hoped to replace New Deal liberalism with a different understanding of American democracy. Refuting "the corrupting idea" that prosperity, equality, or opportunity can be legislated, Taft wanted "free Americans freely working out their destiny." The Taft-Hartley Act was a blow to liberals and the administration, but Republicans found themselves trapped by Americans' ambivalence about liberalism. Few were enthusiastic about such innovations as national health insurance, but there was little sentiment to roll back the New Deal and its benefits. Besides Taft-Hartley, the Eightieth Congress did not accomplish much, and soon Truman was campaigning against a "do-nothing Congress."

Still, things looked bad for Truman. By March 1948 his approval rating was 35 percent. His party was also splitting apart. On the left, his former secretary of commerce Henry Wallace was running for president as a "Progressive." On the right, Democratic governor Strom Thurmond of South Carolina was running as a "Dixiecrat," appealing to white supporters of segregation. Truman seemed certain to lose in November. Or so his Republican opponent, Governor Thomas E. Dewey of New York, thought. Dewey believed an uncontroversial campaign would do the trick, but Truman pulled the New Deal majority back together. The president reached out to African Americans, labor, farmers, senior citizens, and other beneficiaries of New Deal liberalism. "Give 'em hell, Harry," the crowds shouted, and he did, driving home his vision. "The Democratic Party puts human rights and human welfare first," he declared. "These Republican gluttons of privilege . . . want a return of the Wall Street economic dictatorship."

On Election Day, Wallace and Thurmond received only a million votes each. Dewey attracted fewer votes than he had four years before. Leading Roosevelt's coalition, Truman won the presidency with only 49.5 percent of the vote (see Map 26–3). The Democrats recaptured the House and the Senate, but the triumph did not last long. Like Taft two years before, Truman soon discovered that a victory did not mean a mandate. In his State of the Union address in January 1949, Truman declared that "every individual has a right to expect from our Government a fair deal." But his "Fair Deal" legislation stalled in Congress. Despite Truman's comeback, the liberal vision could not dominate the politics of cold war America.

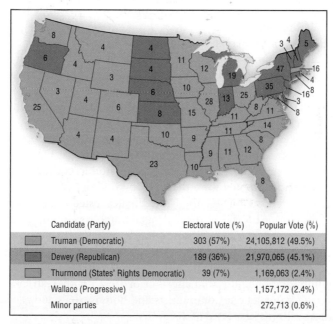

Candidate (Party)	Electoral Vote (%)	Popular Vote (%)
Truman (Democratic)	303 (57%)	24,105,812 (49.5%)
Dewey (Republican)	189 (36%)	21,970,065 (45.1%)
Thurmond (States' Rights Democratic)	39 (7%)	1,169,063 (2.4%)
Wallace (Progressive)		1,157,172 (2.4%)
Minor parties		272,713 (0.6%)

Map 26–3 The 1948 Presidential Election Segregationist and progressive candidates were expected to undermine the Democratic majority, but the Roosevelt coalition returned Truman to the White House for a second term.

Fighting the Cold War at Home

Beyond the battles over domestic policy, the cold war increasingly intruded into every aspect of life. Billions of dollars in defense expenditures stimulated economic growth, but fear, doubt, and insecurity pervaded the late 1940s. Americans added a new fear of nuclear weapons to their old fear of immigrants, and society succumbed to a largely irrational dread of hidden traitors in Hollywood, Washington, the universities, and the public library. To fight the cold war at home, anti-Communist crusaders such as Joseph McCarthy hunted for disloyal Americans. By the 1950s, McCarthyism was capable of destroying the lives of thousands of Americans.

Doubts and Fears in the Atomic Age

Despite triumph in World War II, American culture was dark and pessimistic in the late 1940s. The rise of fascism, the Holocaust, and the bombings of Hiroshima and Nagasaki raised questions about the direction of progress and the goodness of humankind. The cold war did nothing to calm those concerns. Even the welcome prosperity of the reconversion period did not soothe this sense of doubt. People felt small and powerless in an age of big corporations, big unions, big government, and superbombs.

Americans revealed their unease in a variety of ways. Not long after the announcement of the Truman Doctrine in 1947, people began seeing lights in the sky, and "flying saucers" were reported over 35 states and Canada. In a nuclear-armed world, columnist Joseph Alsop observed, the saucer scare was a reminder that "man-made horrors are quite real, quite imminent possibilities."

Meanwhile, Hollywood films explored popular fears. In 1946, *The Best Years of Our Lives* traced the difficult, sometimes humiliating readjustment of three returning veterans. The same year, *It's a Wonderful Life* told the story of a small-town banker forced to accept the disappointment of his unfulfilled dreams. Both films expressed reservations about the morality of capitalism and the chances of achieving happiness in the modern world. A new genre, film noir, offered an even darker view of individuals trapped in a confusing, immoral world.

As the greatest source of fear, nuclear weapons dominated the popular imagination. Many Americans dealt with their anxiety about the Atomic Age in a variety of ways, including dark attempts at humor. Americans drank "atomic cocktails" and danced the "atomic polka." American women wore the new "bikini," the explosively scanty bathing suit named for the Pacific atoll where the United States tested the H-bomb. The Soviets' development of the atomic bomb and the hydrogen bomb was impossible to laugh away.

Americans' fear was also reflected in the hardening of attitudes toward foreigners. In 1945, the nation welcomed the foreign wives of American servicemen by passing the War Brides Act, but as the cold war intensified, other potential migrants met a hostile reception. The Immigration and Nationality Act of 1952 tightly restricted immigration, particularly from Asia. It kept out Communists and homosexuals and allowed the deportation of American citizens suspected of disloyalty.

The Anti-Communist Crusade

Americans may have feared disloyalty most of all. Many believed the real Communist threat came from within. Historians debate the origins of this second "Red Scare." Some trace the anti-Communist crusade to a conservative reaction against the rise of labor,

George Tooker, *Government Bureau* (1956) Modernist painter George Tooker captured the claustrophobic anxiety of the McCarthy era in paintings like *Government Bureau* and *The Subway* (1950). In popular fiction and noir films, social conformity thinly concealed a mounting hysteria.

African Americans, women, and other disempowered groups. Others blame the Truman administration for using fear to justify unprecedented military activity and spending. Although anti-Communism had deep roots in American culture, politicians in both parties gave domestic anti-Communism its particularly dangerous form.

The crusaders had to search hard for local Communists. The Communist Party of the United States of America (CPUSA), a legal political party, was tiny and losing followers. Infiltrated by FBI and police informants, it never received more than 0.3 percent of the popular vote. Just to be sure, the Truman administration charged 12 party leaders with violating the Smith Act, which criminalized membership in "a group advocating . . . the overthrow of the government by force." In 1949, 11 were convicted and sent to jail.

Open Communists posed less of a threat than secret ones, and in fact, self-professed former Communists and spies were considered the most reliable informants on America's presumed hidden network of traitors. The hunt for these "subversives" was led by the House of Representatives' Un-American Activities Committee (HUAC). In 1947, HUAC held hearings on supposed Communist plots in Hollywood. The film industry cooperated, but eight screenwriters, a producer, and a director cited their First Amendment rights and declined to testify. The "Hollywood Ten" were convicted of contempt of Congress and sent to jail for up to a year. Film studios got the message and "blacklisted"—refused to hire—writers, directors, and actors even remotely suspected of Communist ties. Avoiding controversial subjects, studios put out overwrought anti-Communist movies such as *The Red Menace* and *I Was a Communist for the FBI*.

Afraid of looking "soft" on Communism, the Truman administration declared there was a real problem with domestic Communism. "Communists," said Truman's attorney general, Tom Clark, "are everywhere . . . and each carries with him the germs of death for society."

In 1947, the president created an "employee loyalty" program. Any civil servant could lose his or her job by belonging to any of the "totalitarian, Fascist, Communist or subversive" groups listed by the attorney general. The program had little regard for due process. People accused of disloyalty could not challenge evidence or confront their accusers and were presumed guilty until they proved their innocence. Although only about 300 employees were discharged, the loyalty program helped create the impression of a serious problem in Washington.

The Hunt for Spies

There was, in fact, spying going on inside the government. The Soviet Union, like the United States, carried out espionage abroad. The Canadian government found evidence of a spy ring that had passed American atomic secrets to the Soviets during World War II. Through interceptions of Soviet communications, the CIA knew about the spy ring but chose not to share this information with Congress, prosecutors, or even the president.

Thanks to the Canadian evidence, the FBI began to suspect that Alger Hiss, an aide to the secretary of state, was a Soviet agent. Hiss was quietly eased out of his job. Then, in 1948, HUAC took testimony from Whittaker Chambers, a *Time* magazine editor who claimed to have been a Soviet agent in the 1930s. Chambers accused Hiss of passing secret documents. The patrician Hiss denied the charges and said he had never even met Chambers. He seemed more credible than the rumpled Chambers, an admitted perjurer, but Congressman Richard Nixon of California, a Republican member of HUAC, forced him to admit that he had known Chambers under an alias. With help from the FBI, Chambers charged that Hiss had given him secret information in the 1930s. When Chambers produced microfilmed photographs of the secret documents, Hiss could not

>> Time Line

▼1945
Yalta conference
Harry S. Truman inaugurated
Potsdam Conference
Industrial strikes break out

▼1946
Winston Churchill's "Iron
    Curtain" speech
George Kennan's "long telegram"
    on Soviet expansionism

Employment Act of 1946
Morgan v. Virginia
Election of Republican majorities
    in House and Senate

▼1947
Announcement of Truman
    Doctrine
Beginning of Federal Employee
    Loyalty Program
CORE's "Journey of
    Reconciliation"

Integration of major league
    baseball by Jackie Robinson
HUAC Hollywood hearings
Rio Pact
Taft-Hartley Act
National Security Act
Presidential commission reports
    on civil rights

▼1948
Shelley v. Kraemer
Congressional approval of
    Marshall Plan

explain them. Under the statute of limitations, it was too late to try Hiss for spying, but not too late to indict him for lying to Congress. Hiss's perjury trial ended in a hung jury in 1949, but a second jury convicted him in 1950, and he served almost four years in federal prison. The case was a triumph for Republicans and conservatives and a blow to Democrats and liberals.

As the Hiss case ended, another scandal stoked Americans' fears. In early 1950, British authorities arrested Klaus Fuchs, a physicist who had worked at the US nuclear research facility in Los Alamos, New Mexico. The investigation led to David Greenglass, who worked on the atomic bomb project, and his brother-in-law, Julius Rosenberg. Julius, a former member of the CPUSA, and his wife Ethel were convicted of conspiring to steal atomic information in a trial controversial for its anti-Semitic overtones and because the act protecting atomic secrets became law after the spying allegedly took place. Though they had two young sons, both Rosenbergs were sentenced to death. Ignoring appeals for clemency, the federal government electrocuted the Rosenbergs in 1953.

There now seems little doubt that the USSR obtained American nuclear secrets, but the impact was probably not as great as conservatives feared or as small as liberals insisted. Most likely, espionage sped up work on an atomic bomb the Soviets would have eventually produced anyway.

The Rise of McCarthyism

Two weeks after Hiss's conviction, one week after Truman's announcement of the decision to build the hydrogen bomb, and days after the arrest of Klaus Fuchs, Senator Joseph McCarthy of Wisconsin spectacularly took command of the anti-Communist crusade. Speaking to the Republican Women's Club of Wheeling, West Virginia, the previously obscure senator claimed to have names of 205 Communists working in the State Department. In fact, McCarthy had no new information, only a handful of old accusations.

Nevertheless, McCarthy was instantly popular and powerful. Frightened by new dangers, many people wanted to believe in a senator bold enough to fight back. Some shared

Truman's Executive Order 9981
Beginning of Berlin crisis
Selective Service Act
Truman elected president

▼1949
Formation of North Atlantic
  Treaty Organization
Communist takeover of
  mainland China

▼1950
NSC-68
Alger Hiss's conviction for
  perjury
Joseph McCarthy's speech in
  Wheeling, West Virginia
Treaty of Detroit
Beginning of Korean War
Internal Security Act of 1950

▼1951
Truman fires General Douglas
  MacArthur

▼1952
Immigration and Nationality Act
Test of hydrogen bomb

▼1953
Execution of Ethel and Julius
  Rosenberg

▼1954
Army-McCarthy hearings

McCarthy's resentment of privileged elites—New Dealers, diplomats, scientists—whom he derided as "egg-sucking phony liberals" and "bright young men . . . born with silver spoons in their mouths." For some Americans—immigrants, midwesterners, Catholics, and fundamentalists—support for McCarthy was a way to prove their patriotism. Even Democratic legislators voted for the Internal Security Act of 1950, which forced the registration of Communist and Communist-front groups, provided for the deportation of allegedly subversive aliens, and barred Communists from defense jobs. Refusing to "put the Government of the United States in the thought control business," Truman vetoed the bill, but Congress overrode his veto.

Eventually, McCarthy went too far. Angry that one of his aides, David Schine, had not received a draft deferment, he launched an investigation of the army. The secretary of the army, Robert T. Stevens, refused to cooperate and claimed McCarthy had tried to get preferential treatment for Schine. In April 1954, before a television audience of 20 million people, McCarthy failed to come up with evidence of treason in the army. When he tried to smear an army lawyer as a Communist, the senator was exposed. "Have you no sense of decency, sir, at long last?" asked the army's chief counsel, Joseph Welch. It was an electric moment. The Senate hearings came to no judgment, but Americans did. McCarthy's popularity plummeted. By year's end, the Senate condemned him for "unbecoming conduct."

The fall of McCarthy did not end McCarthyism. Schools forced teachers to sign loyalty oaths. Faculty members at several universities lost their jobs, and deans gave the names of suspect students to the FBI. Communism had become a useful charge to hurl at anything that anybody might oppose—labor unions, civil rights, even modern art. To protect themselves, groups policed their own membership. Labor unions drove out Communist leaders and unions. The Cincinnati Reds renamed their team the "Redlegs."

Americans became more careful about what they said out loud. Many had come to believe, along with McCarthy, that the civility of democracy, the attention to rights and fairness, exposed America to a ruthless adversary not bound by similar codes of conduct. Even as the Senate was censuring McCarthy, James Doolittle, the heroic World War II aviator, handed the CIA a report on counterespionage and countersubversion. It explained that the goal of America's enemy is "world domination by whatever means and at whatever cost." "If the United States is to survive," it concluded, "long-standing American concepts of 'fair play' must be reconsidered."

Conclusion

To contain Communism, the United States had transformed its economy. American society dealt with the unfinished business of reconversion, including the role of government and the rights and opportunities of labor, women, and African Americans. Despite these changes, the cold war had widened and intensified. Just seven years after dropping the first atomic bomb on Japan, Americans were again at war in the Far East and were forced to live with the threat of nuclear annihilation. They lived, too, with the frenzied search for subversives. America seemed to be out of control.

As Cvetic pursued his war against hidden enemies, other Americans longed for peace. They wanted the fighting in Korea to end. Anxious to avoid a nuclear holocaust, they wanted the confrontation with the Soviets to stabilize. Meanwhile, American society adjusted to a postwar economy, sorting out the role that government, labor, race, and gender would have in the new cold war order.

Who, What

Alger Hiss 765

Douglas MacArthur 795

Jackie Robinson 801

38th parallel 793

Central Intelligence Agency 790

Conspiracy theory 782

NSC-68 795

Taft-Hartley Act 798

Review Questions

1. How did the National Security Act change the executive branch?

2. Why did Truman see Korea as important enough to defend?

3. Why were struggles in the workplace more intense in the late 1940s than during the Depression or World War II?

Critical-Thinking Questions

1. McCarthyism attacked government, science, education, theater, and Hollywood. What does this pattern reveal about the nature of American anxiety in the 1950s?

2. Two-thirds of the world's peoples gained their independence between 1945 and 1961. How did the cold war affect this movement toward nationhood?

3. In the 1950s and 1960s, historians debated the question of who started the cold war. In the 1990s, it became more interesting to ask when it started. Why the change, and what questions might historians today ask?

For further review materials and resource information, please visit www.oup.com/us/ofthepeople

MAIN IDEAS

1) The cold war inspired more fear and anxiety than World War II had.

2) Actions by both the United States and the Soviet Union caused the cold war.

3) Military industries drove industrial growth.

4) The New Deal coalition began to disintegrate.

TOPICS

Origins of the Cold War

National Security

The Reconversion of American Society

The Frustrations of Liberalism

Fighting the Cold War at Home

THE COLD WAR

1945–1952

EVENTS

Ideological Competition Despite ideological, economic, and political differences between the United States and the Soviet Union, the cold war was not inevitable.

Uneasy Allies Wartime and postwar decisions heightened suspicions between the United States and the Soviet Union.

From Allies to Enemies Disagreements over Germany and the threat of nuclear attack increased conflict between the United States and the Soviet Union.

The Truman Doctrine President Truman took aggressive steps to counter Soviet expansion.

Containment US leaders devised a strategy to limit Soviet expansion and influence.

Taking Risks The Berlin airlift revealed the dangers of the containment strategy.

Global Revolutions Revolutions in Asia, Africa, the Middle East, and Latin America threatened US designs for the postwar order.

Korea The Korean stalemate revealed that the cold war would be long and difficult.

NSC-68 Deficit spending fueled the arms race and US economic growth.

The Postwar Economy Despite fears of a new Depression, the United States developed a resilient and vibrant postwar economy.

The Challenge of Organized Labor Stronger than ever, unions demanded higher wages and a role in management.

Opportunities for Women Opportunity and necessity brought women into the skilled workforce.

Civil Rights for African Americans African Americans sought to make wartime pledges to human rights a reality.

The Democrats' Troubles Truman lost popularity as he struggled with domestic and foreign policy.

Truman's Comeback Truman pulled together a splintered party to win an upset reelection.

Doubts and Fears in the Atomic Age Popular culture expressed the anxiety of living in this new age.

The Anti-Communist Crusade Politicians launched a crusade against domestic Communists.

The Hunt for Spies Spy scandals intensified Americans' fears.

The Rise of McCarthyism The crackdown on Communist sympathizers targeted labor unions, professors, and artists.

The Consumer Society
1945–1961

>> Gene Ferkauf

At the end of World War II, Harry Ferkauf owned two luggage stores in Manhattan in New York City. A Jewish immigrant from Eastern Europe, he haggled with customers over prices in the old way and made a decent living. Having barely kept his business alive during the Depression, he did not want or expect much more.

Harry's son, Eugene, who managed one of the stores, did not accept the old limits. After the war, Gene began offering discounts on luggage, watches, and other goods. Father and son argued frequently over Gene's strategy. In 1948, Gene quit and put his savings into his own discount store on East 46th Street. Gene envisioned a new kind of store, where customers could buy appliances and other goods, without haggling, at low, fixed prices. Heavily discounting his merchandise, Gene could not make much from a single sale. But if he sold enough televisions and refrigerators, he would earn more than his father ever had. On opening day, crowds filled the small shop and spent $3,000. Harry, who usually took in about $50 a day, was impressed.

In a few years, Gene had five successful discount stores in and around New York City. The business was called "E. J. Korvettes"—E for Eugene, J for his partner Joe Zwillenberg, and Korvettes after the quick Canadian warships of World War II. Korvettes appealed to a new, more optimistic generation than the one that had survived the Depression. Eager to buy televisions and other appliances, these younger people were unafraid to go into debt. Prosperous, they were leaving their parents' neighborhoods in the city for new suburbs. Gene Ferkauf understood these people; he was one of them. He, too, moved from his small $75-a-month apartment in Brooklyn to a $75,000 "mansion" in Jamaica, Queens.

Gene had made it big. Adding to the New York stores, Korvettes built suburban stores in several states. In 1955, the partnership became a corporation. Gene had left his father's world behind.

continued

>> **AMERICAN PORTRAIT** *continued*

Gene Ferkauf's success reflected one of the central developments in American society after World War II. Along with the cold war, economic prosperity transformed the nation. Just as Gene left his father's world behind, American society left behind the economic limits and constraints of the Depression and the war. The 1950s marked the culmination of the nation's emergence as a full-fledged consumer society. Gene Ferkauf profited because mainstream culture celebrated consumption and pleasure above work and self-restraint and because televisions and suburbs defined the consumer lifestyle.

The emergence of the consumer society powerfully affected American politics and culture. The prosperous 1950s produced a more homogeneous and apparently harmonious nation, with decreasing class differences, changing gender relations, and a baby boom. Enjoying consumerism, Americans redefined democracy and demanded less from government. As the nation fought the cold war, consumerism became an economic and cultural weapon against Communism. In later years, American culture would look back nostalgically at the 1950s as a prosperous golden age. Consumer society did not benefit every group, end racial inequality, or win the cold war. By the decade's close, Americans worried about the inadequacies of the consumer society, even as they enjoyed its benefits.

Living the Good Life

Much of the consumer lifestyle was in place by the 1920s (see Chapter 23), but only in the 1950s did consumer values and habits finally dominate the American economy and culture. Never before had so many Americans had the chance to live the good life.

They tended to define that "good life" in economic terms. A dynamic, evolving economy offered more leisure and income. Sure of prosperity, Americans confidently spent more of their time and money in the pursuit of pleasure. Millions lived the dream of a home in new suburbs, bought flashy automobiles, purchased their first televisions, and enjoyed a new openness about sex.

> See the USA in your
> Chevrolet
>
> America is asking
> you to call
> Drive your Chevrolet
> through the USA
> America's the
> greatest land
> of all.
>
> ~~~~~~~~~~~~~~
>
> CHEVROLET COMMERCIAL
> JINGLE, 1950

Economic Prosperity

Consumerism could not have flourished without prosperity. Despite short recessions, the 1950s were a period of economic boom. The gross national product—the value of all the country's output of goods and services—grew solidly at an average of 3.2 percent a year.

Several major factors spurred this economic growth. Because of the cold war, federal spending for defense and foreign aid stimulated demand for American goods and services. The shortage of consumer goods during and just after World War II left Americans with money to spend. Robust capital spending by businesses helped ensure economic growth. The industrial economy was also evolving. Traditional heavy manufacturing—steel and automobiles—was still crucial to prosperity, but newer industries, such as electronics, chemicals, plastics, aviation, and computers, became increasingly important.

The emergence of computing was especially significant for the long run. In 1946, engineers at the University of Pennsylvania, J. Presper Eckert Jr. and John William Mauchly, completed the first fully electronic digital computer. The Electronic Numerical Integrator and Computer (ENIAC) weighed over 30 tons and filled a large room. Then Eckert and Mauchly produced the more advanced UNIVAC 1 (Universal Automatic Computer), which counted census data in 1951 and presidential election returns in 1952.

As tiny solid-state transistors replaced bulky vacuum tubes, computers became smaller, more powerful, and more common. By 1958, American companies were producing $1 billion worth of computers annually. Still large and expensive, computers were used mostly by universities, corporations, and the federal government. With about 10,000 computers in use by 1961, the nation was on the brink of the digital age.

As industry evolved, the nation's distribution and service sectors played a larger role than ever. While the number of manufacturing jobs barely changed, employment in retail stores such as E. J. Korvettes increased 19 percent. Jobs in the service sector, such as restaurants, hotels, repair shops, hospitals, and universities, jumped 32 percent. The nation had begun to develop a postindustrial economy, less dependent on production and more dependent on service and consumption.

Economic prosperity greatly benefited big business. New corporations such as E. J. Korvettes emerged and grew. Thanks to a wave of mergers, established corporations became still larger. By 1960, corporations earned 18 times as much income as the rest of the nation's businesses combined.

Prosperity boosted corporations' confidence and popularity. Even liberals, once critical of corporate power, now celebrated the benefits of large-scale enterprise. "What is good for the country is good for General Motors, and vice versa," Charles Wilson, the head of GM, supposedly declared.

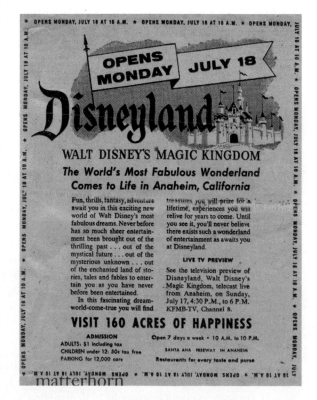

"**160 Acres of Happiness**" This ad for the opening of Disneyland in 1955 embodies the promise of pleasure for Americans in the consumer society.

American workers enjoyed high employment, low inflation, and rising incomes. Less than 5 percent of the workforce was unemployed at any one time. Factory workers' average hourly pay more than doubled between 1945 and 1960, while consumer prices rose less than 2 percent per year. The percentage of Americans living in poverty fell from as much as 30 in the late 1940s to 18 in 1959.

Americans also had more leisure time. By the 1950s, the 40-hour workweek was commonplace. Many workers now looked forward to two- or three-week paid vacations. As life expectancy increased and the economy boomed, more Americans expected to retire at age 65 and live off pensions and social security.

Workers' well-being produced labor peace, which in turn stimulated prosperity. After the contentious 1940s, workers and employers were more likely to resolve differences without strikes and lockouts. When the relatively aggressive Congress of Industrial Organizations (CIO) merged with the American Federation of Labor (AFL) to become the gigantic AFL-CIO in 1955, the union movement became more bureaucratic and complacent. "American labor never had it so good," crowed a union leader.

The Suburban Dream

For growing numbers of people, the good life meant a house in the suburbs. Most Americans had never owned their own homes. Suburbs had been mainly for the well-to-do. But entrepreneurship, new construction methods, cheap land, and federal aid made possible affordable housing outside the nation's cities. Along with Gene Ferkauf, much of America moved to the suburbs in the 1950s.

William J. Levitt's pioneering development, Levittown, illustrated the suburban housing boom. Back from World War II, Levitt optimistically believed he could make houses affordable for middle- and working-class people. Drawing on his military experience and Henry Ford's assembly line techniques, Levitt intended to build houses so efficiently that they could sell at remarkably low prices. He put up simple houses, with prefabricated parts, no basements, and low price tags, on 1,000 acres of cheap farmland near a Korvettes on New York's Long Island. Levitt's original Cape Cod–style house cost $7,990, ideal for young couples financing their first home.

Like Korvettes, Levittown quickly became a huge success. Buyers contracted for 1,400 houses on one day in 1949. The development grew to 17,500 dwellings housing 82,000 people. Levitt soon built more Levittowns, as did imitators all around the country.

The federal government made those suburbs more affordable by allowing buyers to deduct mortgage interest payments from their federal income taxes and by guaranteeing loans to military veterans. To make commuting practical, the Federal-Aid Highway Act of 1956 encouraged the construction of interstate freeways connecting cities and suburbs.

Under such favorable conditions, the United States quickly became a nation of suburban homeowners. As home ownership increased 20 percent between 1945 and 1960, nearly one-third of Americans lived in places like Levittown. The suburban dream had become an everyday reality.

The Pursuit of Pleasure

The consumer society depended on Americans' eagerness to pursue pleasure. Businesses made sure that nothing prevented people from buying. If their wages and salaries were not enough, consumers could borrow. In 1950, the Diners Club introduced the credit card for

AMERICAN LANDSCAPE

....

>> Levittown, New York

For many Americans, the first Levittown epitomized the virtues and defects of suburbia, consumerism, and democracy in post–World War II America. The new community seemed to be a democratic triumph, a visual reminder of equality and upward mobility. The male heads of Levittown households tended to be prosperous blue-collar workers, veterans of World War II seeking middle-class status for their growing, baby boom families. As an observer noted, Levittown was a "one-class community," where most households had an annual income of about $3,500 to $4,000.

From another angle, Levittown seemed less democratic, notable for who didn't live there. Amid the young families, there were few teenagers or senior citizens. There were hardly any African Americans, either.

Levittown's homogeneity was no accident. The developer, William Levitt, had planned it that way. Its first four-room Cape Cod houses came in only five very similar models. All the houses and streets appeared to be the same. Even Levitt admitted that he had once gotten lost in the look-alike streets of his suburb. The uniform style and cost of the houses attracted only one class of residents. So-called restrictive covenants—special clauses in housing deeds—ensured that those residents would be white.

Levitt also tried to impose uniform behavior on his residents. Community rules forbade putting up fences or hanging out the wash on weekends. Some residents helped promote conformity. They wrote the local newspaper to attack neighbors who broke the rules. A nonconformist could expect to be labeled a "commie" or a "Russkie."

The design of the community and its houses reflected the domestic values of the period. The small Cape Cod homes encouraged family "togetherness." With so little private space, family members congregated around the kitchen table or in front of the TV. Wives were expected to spend weekdays doing tasks at home, rather than working at a paying job. Because it was supposed to be the center of women's lives, the kitchen was placed at the front of the house.

Levittown's design also supported men's domestic role. Former apartment dwellers found they had to spend time at home mowing their new lawns. With few traditionally masculine public places—bars, firehouses, and ball fields—the child-centered community promoted family togetherness away from home with plenty of playgrounds and swimming pools. Despite the power of conformity, Levittown demonstrated the strength of individuality in America. Over time, the suburb became less homogeneous, and Levitt offered houses with more variety. In 1949, new ranch-style houses replaced the Cape Cod model. New features were added, including carports. Residents remodeled their houses to express individual tastes. They built garages and patios and added rooms, gardens, signposts, and distinctive paint jobs. They put up fences. "The houses take on the personalities of their owners," wrote a suburban resident.

Levittown was a product of 1950s America. This pioneering suburb revealed the power of domesticity and conformity, but it also demonstrated the limits of democracy and the persistence of individuality in the consumer society.

New Yorkers. By 1960, Sears Roebuck credit cards allowed more than 10 million Americans to spend borrowed money. In 1945, Americans owed only $5.7 billion for consumer goods other than houses. By 1960, they owed $56.1 billion.

In the 1950s, discount stores such as Korvettes made shopping simpler and more attractive. So did another new creation, the shopping mall. In 1956, Southdale, the first enclosed suburban mall, opened outside Minneapolis. Consumers ate more easily, too. The first McDonald's fast food restaurant opened in San Bernardino, California, in 1948. Taken over by Ray Kroc, McDonald's began to grow into a national chain in the mid-1950s.

To get to McDonald's, Southdale, Korvettes, or Levittown, Americans needed cars. In the 1950s, automobiles reflected a new sense of affluence and self-indulgence. Big, high-compression engines burning high-octane gasoline powered ever-bigger cars stuffed with new accessories—power steering, power brakes, power windows, and air conditioning. Unlike the drab sedans of the Depression, the new models featured "Passion Pink" and "Horizon Blue" interiors and two- and even three-tone exteriors studded with shiny chrome.

Automakers used that chrome to solve one of the problems of a consumer society—getting people who already had plenty to buy even more. How could Detroit persuade Americans to trade in cars that were running just fine for new ones? The answer was what General Motors' chief designer called "dynamic obsolescence," the feeling that last year's model was somehow inadequate. So automakers changed chrome, colors, and tailfins from year to year (see Table 27–1).

Icons of the Consumer Society The first enclosed mall in the United States—Southdale, outside Minneapolis, Minnesota.

Table 27-1 Automobiles and Highways, 1945–1960

Year	Factory Sales (in 1,000s)	Registrations (in 1,000s)	Miles of Highway Completed (in 1,000s)
1945	69.5	25,796.9	3,035
1946	2,148.6	28,217.0	5,057
1947	3,558.1	30,849.3	15,473
1948	3,909.2	33,355.2	21,725
1949	5,119.4	36,457.9	19,876
1950	6,665.8	40,339.0	19,876
1951	5,338.4	42,688.3	17,060
1952	4,320.7	43,823.0	22,147
1953	6,116.9	46,429.2	21,136
1954	5,558.8	48,468.4	20,548
1955	7,920.1	52,144.7	22,571
1956	5,816.1	54,210.9	23,609
1957	6,113.3	55,917.8	22,424
1958	4,257.8	56,890.5	28,137
1959*	5,591.2	59,453.9	32,633
1960	6,674.7	61,682.3	20,969

*Denotes first year for which figures include Alaska and Hawaii.

Source: *Historical Statistics of the United States, Millennial Online Edition* (Cambridge University Press, 2008), Table Df347–352 and Table Df213–217

The cars of the 1950s reflected a driver's identity and affluence. General Motors' line rose up the socioeconomic ladder, from the ordinary Chevrolet to the more prosperous Pontiac, Oldsmobile, and Buick, and up to the sumptuous success symbol Cadillac.

Automobiles also spoke to gender identities. To appeal to women, car interiors seemed like living rooms. The exterior offered men power and sexuality. While the back of a 1950s car could look like a jet's afterburner, the front might evoke the female body. A car, as a Buick ad promised, "makes you feel like the man you are."

In the 1950s, television became central to the consumer society. As TV sets became less expensive and sales boomed, broadcasters seized opportunity. By 1950, the Federal Communications Commission (FCC) had licensed 104 TV stations, mostly in cities. As television undermined the popularity of radio and movie theaters, the three major broadcasting companies quickly created TV networks and dominated the new industry. By 1960, 90 percent of the nation's households had a television (see Table 27–2). In 15 years, TV had become part of everyday life.

From its early days, television reinforced the consumer society's values. Advertisements for consumer products paid for programming. There were operas, documentaries, and live dramas in what critics consider television's golden age, but variety shows, sports, westerns, and situation comedies filled most of the broadcast day. Nightly national news broadcasts lasted only 15 minutes.

Table 27–2 Television, 1941–1960

Year	Television Stations	Households with Television Sets (in 1,000s)
1941	2	–
1945	9	–
1950	104	3,875
1955	458	30,700
1960	579	45,750

Source: George Thomas Kurian, *Datapedia* (Lanham, MD: Bernan Press, 1994), pp. 299–300.

Sexual openness also defined consumer society. Dr. Alfred C. Kinsey commanded enormous public attention with two pioneering academic studies—*Sexual Behavior in the Human Male* (1948) and *Sexual Behavior in the Human Female* (1953). Kinsey surprised Americans by reporting more sexual activity outside of marriage than had been thought. The Supreme Court contributed to sexual openness by overturning a ban on a film version of D. H. Lawrence's often erotic novel, *Lady Chatterley's Lover*, in 1959. *Playboy* magazine, first published by Hugh Hefner in December 1953, epitomized the new sexual candor. Featuring bare-breasted women, *Playboy* blended sex into a hedonistic lifestyle of flashy cars, expensive stereos, and fine liquor.

A Homogeneous Society?

The spread of consumerism reinforced a sense of sameness in America. The United States seemed a homogeneous society whose people bought the same products, watched the same TV shows, worked for the same corporations, and dreamed the same dreams. Critics worried that Americans had sacrificed individuality for conformity. Declining class differences and renewed emphasis on religion and family strengthened the feeling that people were becoming more alike.

Nevertheless, the United States remained a heterogeneous society. Although class and ethnic differences among whites decreased, race remained a powerful divider. Despite fears of conformity, the nation still encouraged difference and individuality.

The Discovery of Conformity

After World War II, sociologists and other writers discovered an increasing uniformity in American society for a variety of reasons. During the frenzied search for domestic Communists, people did not want to risk accusations by appearing different or unusual. As corporations merged and small businesses disappeared, more Americans worked for the same giant companies. Levittown and the other new suburbs intensified the sense of sameness. In 1957, one writer described suburbanites as "people whose age, income, number of children, problems, habits, conversations, dress, possessions, perhaps even blood types are almost precisely like yours."

Some observers believed that Americans actually wanted to be like one another. In *The Lonely Crowd* (1950), sociologist David Riesman argued that instead of following their own internal values, Americans adjusted their behavior to meet the expectations of other people. In *The Organization Man* (1956), William H. Whyte Jr. suggested that conformist white-collar workers in big corporations were making the United States more like the Soviet Union.

The Decline of Class and Ethnicity

The apparent decline of social class differences reinforced the sense of homogeneity. By the 1950s, the old upper class—the families of the Gilded Age—no longer ran American industry and finance. Thanks to taxes and the Depression, the largest American fortunes were smaller than at the beginning of the twentieth century. The corporate leaders of the 1950s did not have the swagger, the palaces, or the dynastic ambitions of the Gilded Age robber barons.

Meanwhile, the ranks of American farmers continued to shrink. As agriculture became more efficient and corporatized, the number of farms fell from over 6 million in 1944 to 3.7 million in 1959. Although manual and service workers remained the largest occupational group, they seemed a less distinctive social class. In an era of labor peace, well-paid blue-collar workers appeared content with American society. Labor leaders endorsed consumerism and anti-Communism. Some observers argued that American workers had become middle class in their habits and values. The middle class itself was burgeoning. By 1960, the white-collar sector made up 40 percent of the workforce.

Even ethnic differences no longer seemed significant. Whites from different national and religious backgrounds mixed together in the new suburbs. The rate of intermarriage between ethnic groups increased. Anxious to prove their loyalty during the cold war, newer Americans avoided emphasizing their origins. Ethnicity apparently disappeared in the consumer society's melting pot.

Many Americans, especially powerful ones, had long wanted to believe theirs was a unified society devoted to middle-class values. In the 1950s, there was more basis for this belief than ever before.

The Resurgence of Religion and Family

A renewed emphasis on religion and family contributed to social homogeneity. Political leaders, fighting the cold war, encouraged religiosity. Freedom of religion, they insisted, set the United States apart from allegedly godless Communist nations. To underscore this commitment to religion, the federal government put the words "In God We Trust" on all currency. Meanwhile, religion adapted to the consumer society. Charismatic preachers such as Roman Catholic bishop Fulton J. Sheen and Protestant evangelist Billy Graham now brought religion to Americans by television.

People participated more in organized religion. In 1945, 45 percent of Americans belonged to a religious denomination; by 1960, that figure had reached 61 percent. Weekly church attendance increased to a peak of 49 percent in 1958. By 1960, there were 64 million Protestants, 42 million Roman Catholics, and fewer than 6 million Jews (see Table 27–3).

American culture also celebrated what *McCall's* magazine christened family "togetherness." Manufacturers promoted TV viewing as a way of holding families together. Detroit called its big automobiles "family" cars.

"Togetherness" meant the nuclear family, with a mother, a father, and plenty of children. After decades of decline, the birthrate rose in the 1940s. Beginning in 1954,

Table 27-3 Religious Revival and Baby Boom, 1945–1960

Year	Membership of Religious Bodies (in 1,000s)	Live Births (in 1,000s)
1945	71,700	2,858
1946	73,673	3,411
1947	77,386	3,817
1948	79,436	3,637
1949	81,862	3,649
1950	86,830	3,632
1951	88,673	3,823
1952	92,277	3,913
1953	94,843	3,965
1954	97,483	4,078
1955	100,163	4,104
1956	103,225	4,218
1957	104,190	4,308
1958[1]	109,558	4,255
1959[2]	112,227	4,245
1960	114,449	4,258

[1]Includes Alaska.

[2]Denotes first year for which figures include Alaska and Hawaii.

Source: George Thomas Kurian, *Datapedia* (Lanham, MD: Bernan Press, 1994), pp. 37, 146.

Americans had more than 4 million babies a year. Thanks to new drugs, nearly all these infants survived. Antibiotics reduced the risk of diphtheria, typhoid fever, and other infections. The Salk and Sabin vaccines virtually wiped out polio. As a result, the average number of children per family went from 2.4 in 1945 up to 3.2 in 1957, and the population grew by a record 29 million people to 179 million.

Like the religious revival, the "baby boom" is somewhat difficult to explain. For over a century, Americans had reduced the size of their families to ease financial and personal burdens. Prosperity may have persuaded couples that they could afford more children. But affluence alone did not explain why American culture became more child centered in the 1950s. In his *Common Sense Book of Baby and Child Care* (1946), pediatrician Benjamin Spock urged parents to raise their children with less severity and more attention, warmth, tenderness, and fun. It outsold every other book in the 1950s except the Bible.

Maintaining Gender Roles

As many social differences decreased, American culture nevertheless reemphasized the distinctions between the sexes. During the baby boom, women were expected to be helpful wives and devoted mothers. Men were encouraged to define themselves primarily as family providers.

The 1950s underscored the differences between genders in a variety of ways. Blue became the color for boys and pink the color for girls. Standards of beauty highlighted physiological differences between women and men. Voluptuous actresses such as Jayne Mansfield and Marilyn Monroe defined femininity.

Nevertheless, gender roles grew more similar during the 1950s. Society stressed a man's domestic role more than before. Husbands were urged to do housework and spend more time nurturing their children, although few men lived up to the new ideal.

Female roles evolved more dramatically. To help pay for the consumer lifestyle, many wives had to find jobs. In 1940, 15.6 percent of married women were in the paid workforce. By 1960, that percentage had nearly doubled to 31.0, and women made up more than one-third of the labor force, mostly in clerical and sales positions. In the cold war competition with the Soviets, Americans celebrated the supposedly greater freedom and opportunity for women in the United States. Nevertheless, women had little help coping with their jobs and bigger families. Congress voted an income tax deduction for child-care costs in 1954, but little first-class child care was available. At work, women were expected to watch men get ahead of them. Women's income was only 60 percent of men's in 1960.

American culture strongly condemned women and men who strayed outside conventional gender norms. *Modern Woman: The Lost Sex*, a 1947 best seller by Marynia Farnham and Ferdinand Lundberg, censured feminism as the "deep illness" of "neurotically disturbed women" with "penis envy." Psychologists and other experts demonized lesbians and gay men. As police cracked down on gay bars, unmarried men risked accusations of homosexuality. In 1950, a small group of gay men formed the Mattachine Society to work for homosexual rights. Five years later, a group of lesbians formed a counterpart organization, the Daughters of Bilitis. But there were no large protests against the treatment of gays and lesbians. The dominant culture expected males to be heterosexual husbands and fathers and women to be heterosexual wives and mothers.

Persisting Racial Differences

Despite pressures toward conformity, American society remained heterogeneous. Although suburbanization broke down ethnic differences among whites, it intensified the racial divide. The suburbs were 95 percent white in 1950. As whites left for the suburbs, African Americans took their place in cities. By 1960, more than half of the black population lived in cities, where they were typically barred from white neighborhoods.

Living on reservations, Native Americans were also set apart. In 1953, Congress tried to "Americanize" the Indians by terminating their special legal status as sovereign groups and, with it, the traditional rights and reservations of more than 11,000 Native Americans. Termination was intended to turn them into members of the consumer society.

It did not turn out that way. As reservations became counties in the 1950s and early 1960s, Indians had to sell valuable mineral rights and lands to pay taxes. Tribes still faced poverty, unemployment, and social problems. Encouraged by the federal government's new Voluntary Relocation Program, about one in five Native Americans moved to the city. Some tribes, including the Catawba, the Coquille, and the Klamath, began legal fights to reclaim tribal status. But whether they lived on reservations or on crowded city blocks, a quarter of a million Indians remained largely separate and ignored.

The increasing migration of Puerto Ricans reinforced the nation's multiracial character. Beginning in the 1940s, a large number of Puerto Ricans, who were US citizens, left their island for more economic opportunity. By 1960, 887,000 Puerto Ricans lived on the mainland, two-thirds of them in the East Harlem section of New York City. They found opportunities but also separation and discrimination in their new homes. Mexican immigration also added to racial diversity. After 1945, increasing numbers of Mexicans left their impoverished country for the United States, particularly the booming Southwest. Congress, bowing to southwestern employers, continued the Bracero Program, the supposedly temporary agreement that had brought hundreds of thousands of laborers, or *braceros*, to the wartime United States. Meanwhile, illegal Mexican migration increased dramatically.

Like other Mexican migrants before them, the newly arrived met a mixed reception. As in the years before World War II, Mexicans already living in the United States worried that the new migrants would compete for jobs, drive down wages, and feed American prejudice. Many white Americans indeed derided them as *mojados*, or "wetbacks," because so many had supposedly swum the Rio Grande River to enter the country illegally. Mexican Americans feared that the federal government would use the Internal Security Act of 1950 and the Immigration and Nationality Act of 1952 to deport Mexicans and break up families. The government's intention became clear in 1954 with Operation Wetback, which sent more than 1 million immigrants back to Mexico in that year alone.

The Plight of Mexican "Wetbacks" Illegal immigrants taken off freight trains in Los Angeles, after two days without food or water, in 1953. They were probably sent back to Mexico.

About 3.5 million Mexican Americans were living in the United States by 1960. The great majority worked for low wages in the cities and on the farms of the Southwest. Many lived in *barrios* apart from whites. Because of Operation Wetback and other instances of prejudice, some Mexican Americans became more vocal about their rights. The League of United Latin American Citizens denounced the impact of the Immigration and Nationality Act. More outspoken was the American GI Forum, an organization of Mexican American veterans formed when a Texas funeral parlor would not bury a deceased comrade. Such assertiveness made it harder to ignore the presence of Mexican Americans in the consumer society.

The experiences of Hispanics, Mexican Americans, Native Americans, and African Americans underscored the continuing importance of race in the United States. Mostly living apart, whites and nonwhites faced different conditions and different futures. Prosperity and consumerism did not change that reality. As long as race was so potent a factor, the United States would never be a homogeneous society.

The Survival of Diversity

Along with race, other forces ensured the survival of diversity, especially regional differences. As in the past, internal migration and the expansion of national boundaries promoted change. During the 1950s, more than 1.6 million people, many of them retired, moved to Florida. As a result, the state increasingly played a distinctive national role as a center for leisure and entertainment.

Other Americans headed westward. During the 1950s, over 3 million people moved to California, which earned a reputation as the pioneer state of the consumer society, home of the first Disney amusement park and the first McDonald's.

The admission of two new states highlighted the nation's continuing diversity. In 1959, Alaska and Hawaii became, respectively, the 49th and 50th states in the Union. Racially and culturally diverse, climatically and topographically distinctive, they demonstrated that America was not simply a land of corporations and Levittowns.

Popular music also exemplified this continuing diversity. Big swing bands gave way to such popular singers as Frank Sinatra and Patti Page. Jazz split into different camps—traditional, mainstream, and modern. Country music featured cowboy songs, western swing, honky-tonk, bluegrass, and the suburbanized "Nashville sound." A range of African American musical forms, including blues, jazz, and vocal groups, became known as "rhythm and blues" (R & B). Gospel music thrilled white and black audiences. Mexican Americans made Tejano music in Texas, and Polish Americans danced to polka bands in Illinois.

R & B collided with country music to create rock and roll. By 1952, white disc jockey Alan Freed was playing R & B on his Cleveland radio show, "Moondog's Rock 'n' Roll Party." In 1954, a white country group, Bill Haley and the Comets, recorded the first rock-and-roll hit, "Rock Around the Clock." Early rock and roll produced both African American and white heroes—Chuck Berry, Fats Domino, Jerry Lee Lewis, and Buddy Holly, among others.

The biggest rock-and-roll sensation was a young white singer and guitar player, Elvis Presley. Born in Mississippi and raised in near poverty in Memphis, Presley drew on a variety of genres to create a distinctive personal style. "Who do you sound like?" he was asked. "I don't sound like nobody," he said.

Because of Presley and other musicians, the sound of America was anything but homogeneous. Because of Florida, California, Alaska, Hawaii, and other states, the United States hardly looked monolithic. In these ways, American society avoided uniformity after World War II.

The Eisenhower Era at Home and Abroad

Prosperity subtly changed Americans' understanding of democracy. On one hand, they expected more from politics and government. Along with guarantees of national security and civil rights, people wanted government to assure their opportunity to consume. The good life became the test of democracy. On the other hand, people expected less from politics and government in the 1950s. Since the country was so prosperous and middle class, democracy must be working. As long as the federal government maintained the economy and national security, Americans did not demand dramatic, new liberal programs. The politics of the decade were dominated by President Dwight D. Eisenhower, whose middle-of-the-road domestic program, "Modern Republicanism," appealed to a prosperous electorate wary of government innovation. But Eisenhower's anti-Communist foreign policy did little to diminish popular anxieties about the cold war and laid the groundwork for future trouble in the Middle East and Southeast Asia.

"Ike" and 1950s America

Eisenhower, a charismatic military hero with a bright, infectious grin, would have been an ideal public figure in almost any era of American history, but the man known as "Ike" was especially suited to the 1950s. The last president born in the nineteenth century, he had successfully accommodated the changes of the twentieth. Raised on the individualism of the rural Midwest, Eisenhower adopted the bureaucratic style of modern organizations. He succeeded in the military not because he was a great fighter but because he was a great manager, a classic "organization man." As a commander in World War II, Eisenhower worked to keep fractious allies together. After the war, he deepened his organizational experience as president of Columbia University and as the first commander of NATO armed forces. Just as he adapted to big organizations, Eisenhower accommodated America's expanding commitment abroad. Raised among people who often feared American involvement in the world's problems, Ike had made his career in the world.

Eisenhower easily fit the dominant culture of the 1950s. He was an involved, loving husband and father. In a society pursuing pleasures, he was famous for his hours on the golf course. His wife, Mamie, wore the "New Look" fashions inspired by designer Christian Dior and avidly watched television soap operas.

Nominated for president by the Republicans in 1952, Eisenhower ran against Adlai Stevenson, the liberal Democratic governor of Illinois. Running a moderate campaign, Eisenhower avoided attacks on the New Deal and promised to work for an end to the Korean War. Meanwhile, his tough-talking running mate, Senator Richard Nixon of California, accused Stevenson of being soft on Communism. Eisenhower handily won 55 percent of the popular vote and 442 electoral votes. The Republicans took control of the White House and both houses of Congress for the first time in 20 years.

Modern Republicanism

Eisenhower's Modern Republicanism steered a middle course between traditional Republican conservatism and Democratic liberalism. With a conservative's faith in individual freedom, the president favored limited government and balanced budgets, but Eisenhower the organization man believed that Washington had an important role in protecting individuals. He also knew that most Americans wanted to keep such liberal programs as Social Security and farm subsidies.

Accordingly, his administration limited government by decreasing regulation of business and cutting taxes for the wealthy. The Submerged Lands Act of 1953 turned over offshore oil resources to the states for private exploitation. The Atomic Energy Act of 1954 allowed private firms to sell power produced by nuclear reactors.

Nevertheless, the administration left the legacy of the New Deal and the Fair Deal intact. Eisenhower accepted increases in Social Security benefits and farm subsidies. In some cases, the president wanted the government to take a more active role. The expansion of the interstate system was largely his initiative, which he justified as a matter of national defense. Despite his belief in balanced budgets, Eisenhower's administration produced several budget deficits. Federal spending helped fuel the consumer economy.

Modern Republicanism frustrated liberals, as well as conservative "Old Guard" Republicans, but "the public loves Ike," a journalist observed. "The less he does the more they love him."

Eisenhower's popularity was confirmed at the polls in 1956. Repeating 1952, Eisenhower and Nixon again defeated Stevenson, this time with a bigger victory—58 percent of the popular vote and 457 electoral votes.

An Aggressive Cold War Strategy

Like Truman, Eisenhower opposed Communism at home and around the world. The president helped the crusade against alleged Communist subversives and tolerated its excesses. He refused to criticize publicly Senator Joseph R. McCarthy and declined to stop the execution of the convicted spies, Julius and Ethel Rosenberg, in 1953. Eisenhower denied the security clearance that J. Robert Oppenheimer, the former director of the Manhattan Project, needed to work on federal nuclear projects. Thousands of other alleged security risks also lost their federal jobs during the Eisenhower era.

Whereas Truman had pledged only to contain Communist expansion, Eisenhower and his advisers talked of rolling back Soviet power in Europe and freeing "captive peoples" from Communism. Secretary of State John Foster Dulles threatened "instant, massive retaliation" with nuclear weapons in response to any Soviet aggression. To support this threat, the US military adopted the "New Look" strategy, named after Mamie Eisenhower's favorite fashions, that de-emphasized conventional armies and increased the nuclear arsenal with long-range bombers, missiles, and nuclear-powered submarines.

The president also used the CIA to counter Communism by stealthier means. At his direction, the CIA carried out secret activities once considered unacceptable. At home, the agency explored possible uses of lysergic acid diethylamide—the dangerous hallucinogenic drug known as LSD—by testing it on hundreds of unwitting Americans. Abroad, the agency secretly aided pro-American regimes and ran programs against uncooperative governments.

The "New Look" of Defense in the Eisenhower Era A ceremony honors the production of the 1,000th B-47 Stratojet, the long-range bomber capable of delivering nuclear weapons in an attack on the Soviet Union.

In August 1953 a covert CIA operation, code-named Ajax, orchestrated a coup that removed Mohammad Mossadeq, the nationalist prime minister of oil-rich Iran. Eisenhower and Dulles feared that this "madman," who had nationalized Iran's oil fields, would shut out US business in favor of Communism and the Soviet Union. Mossadeq's successor, the young monarch, Shah Mohammad Reza Pahlavi, accepted $45 million in US aid, turned his back on the Soviets, and made low-priced oil available to American companies.

In 1954, PBSUCCESS, a secret CIA operation modeled on Ajax, overthrew another foreign leader. Eisenhower and Dulles worried that a "Communist infection" in the Central American nation of Guatemala could spread to the United States–controlled Panama Canal and to Mexico. In fact, the Soviet Union had made no effort to help Guatemala's new president, Jacobo Arbenz Guzmán, who supported redistribution of land and threatened the interests of a powerful American corporation, United Fruit. In June, PBSUCCESS used misleading "disinformation," a force of Guatemalan exiles, and CIA-piloted bombing raids to persuade Arbenz Guzmán to resign.

More openly, Eisenhower intensified efforts to shape perceptions of American culture and values abroad. In 1953, the administration created the United States Information Agency (USIA), overseen by the State Department. Active in 76 countries by 1960, the agency published pamphlets, promoted the exchange of visitors with other nations, broadcast Voice of America radio around the world, and worked with the CIA on propaganda and psychological warfare.

Avoiding War with the Communist Powers

Despite tough talk, the Eisenhower administration avoided direct confrontation with the two major Communist powers, the People's Republic of China and the Soviet Union. Eisenhower knew he had to end the Korean conflict. As he promised in his 1952 campaign, Eisenhower traveled to Korea to end the military stalemate that ultimately killed 33,629 Americans. A cease-fire agreement in July 1953 left North and South Korea divided and the United States without a victory. It was, Eisenhower declared, "an acceptable solution." In October 1956, Hungarians, spurred on by American broadcasts, rose up against their pro-Soviet government. The Soviet Union sent troops to break the rebellion, but Eisenhower did not intervene with "massive retaliation," after all.

Fundamentally, Eisenhower maintained Truman's policy of containment. Cautious about military confrontation with the Soviets and the Chinese, Eisenhower declined to unleash nuclear weapons that would "destroy civilization." Although he sent CIA agents to conduct covert operations, the president was more reluctant than Truman to send American soldiers into open battle.

At the same time, Eisenhower, like Truman, knew the cold war was an economic, political, and cultural war, waged by foreign aid and propaganda. The Eisenhower administration took modest steps to improve relations with the Soviets. Responding to the Soviets' interest in "peaceful coexistence," Eisenhower told the United Nations that he wanted disarmament and the peaceful use of atomic power. He proposed the "Atoms for Peace" plan in which an international agency would explore nonmilitary uses for nuclear materials. The Soviets dragged their feet.

In 1955 Eisenhower took another step when he joined Khrushchev in Geneva for the first meeting between an American president and a Soviet leader since World War II. Eisenhower's proposal for "Open Skies"—a plan to allow each side to fly over the other's territory—sparked optimism about better relations. In 1958, the United States and the Soviets also agreed to a program of cultural exchanges. But in May 1960, optimism plummeted when the Soviets downed an American U-2 spy plane over the USSR. After the United States denied the affair, Khrushchev triumphantly produced the captured pilot, Francis Gary Powers, along with pieces of the plane. The rivalry would continue.

Crises in the Third World

Although Eisenhower worried most about Western Europe, his administration increasingly focused on the threat of Communist expansion in Africa, Asia, Latin America, and the Middle East. These relatively rural, unindustrialized regions, which made up the "third world," were enmeshed in the confrontation between the "first world" of industrialized non-Communist nations and the "second world" of industrialized Communist countries. Plagued by poverty, violence, and civil war, many third world societies struggled against imperial domination.

Under Khrushchev, the Soviet Union tried to exploit third world discontent and conflict. Anxious to preserve America's influence and access to natural resources, the Eisenhower administration countered Soviet moves with the tools of containment—aid, trade, and alliances. Eisenhower offered increased foreign aid and trade opportunities to third world countries. He pursued closer military ties, including defense pacts with the Philippines, South Korea, and Taiwan.

AMERICA AND THE WORLD

>> **Consumerism and the Cold War**

In July 1959, the American National Exhibition, part of the cultural exchange agreement with the Soviet Union, opened in Moscow. The event underscored that the cold war with the Soviets was an economic and cultural battle as well as an arms race. The exhibition also revealed that consumerism, pervasive at home, increasingly defined America to the world.

Organized by the USIA and other federal agencies, the exhibition intended to create "a corner of America"—an outpost of democracy, technology, consumerism, and culture—in the midst of Communism. The theme, according to the State Department, was "freedom of choice and expression and unimpeded flow of diverse goods and ideas as sources of American cultural and economic achievement."

The exhibition's centerpiece was a modernistic geodesic dome of steel and glass. Inside, a Disney movie, *America the Beautiful*, played in dazzling 360-degree "Circarama" around the ceiling. An IBM computer, RAMAC, answered visitors' questions about America. "The American dream," the massive, one-ton computer typed in Russian, "is the fundamental belief by Americans that America has meant and shall always mean that all men shall be free to seek for themselves and their children a better life. Americans interpret this in terms of a demand for freedom of worship, freedom in the expression of belief, universal suffrage, and universal education."

The exhibits made clear that the American dream was also about the freedom to consume. There were fashion shows, cooking demonstrations, free Pepsi-Cola, fancy automobiles, books, art, color televisions, free makeovers for women, and a model American suburban house. "It was a blatantly materialistic exhibit with all sorts of glitzy, glitzy stuff," an American worker admitted, "but it was pretty impressive." On the way out, visitors used American voting machines to cast secret ballots for their favorite exhibit, their favorite American writer, and so forth.

When Vice President Nixon opened the exhibition on July 24, a predictable formality became a surprising confrontation over consumerism. His host, Soviet premier Khrushchev, already angry over US foreign policy, became combative about the American display. At a demonstration of color television and taping technology, Khrushchev suddenly predicted that the USSR, more than a century younger than the United States, would catch up and surpass the American economy in seven years.

From there, the day became a debate between the two leaders. Nixon suggested that the Americans might trail the Soviets in rockets but led in color televisions. Khrushchev insisted the Soviets were ahead in televisions, too. At the model kitchen exhibit, Nixon defended planned obsolescence and celebrated Americans' fascination with the new. "This theory does not hold water," Khrushchev sneered. Then the Soviet went after all the supposed labor-saving technology of the American home. "Don't you have a machine that puts food into the mouth and pushes it down?" he taunted his guest. "Many things you've shown us are interesting but they are not needed in life. They have no useful purpose."

In turn, Nixon defended consumerism as a form of democratic freedom. "To us, diversity, the right to choose, the fact that we have 1,000 builders building 1,000 different houses is the most important thing," he maintained. "We don't have one deci-

sion made at the top by one government official."

"You think the Russian people will be dumbfounded by this?" Khrushchev challenged Nixon at the model kitchen. When the exhibition closed six weeks later, 2.7 million Russians had visited. Time would tell whether they were dumbfounded or not.

This approach was sorely tested in Southeast Asia. When Eisenhower took office in 1953, the United States supported France's war to hold on to Vietnam and its other Southeast Asian colonies. Despite vast American aid, the French could not defeat the nationalist forces of the Viet Minh, led by the Communist Ho Chi Minh and helped by the mainland Chinese. By 1954, the Viet Minh had surrounded French troops at Dien Bien Phu. Unwilling to fight another land war in Asia, Eisenhower refused to send American troops and rejected the use of atomic bombs. France surrendered in May.

In 1954, peace talks at Geneva produced an agreement to cut Vietnam, like Korea, in half. Ho Chi Minh's forces would stay north of the 17th parallel; his pro-French Vietnamese enemies would stay to the south. The agreement called for a popular election to unite Vietnam in 1956. Certain that Ho Chi Minh and the Communists would win the election, the United States refused to sign the agreement. The president feared that a Communist Vietnam would deprive the West of raw materials and encourage Communism elsewhere. Comparing the nations of Asia and the Pacific to "a row of dominoes," Eisenhower explained that the fall of the first domino—Vietnam—would lead to the fall of the rest, including Japan and Australia.

Instead, the Eisenhower administration worked to create an anti-Communist nation south of the 17th parallel. To protect South Vietnam, the United States joined with seven nations to create the Southeast Asia Treaty Organization (SEATO) in 1954 (see Map 27–1). To ensure South Vietnam's loyalty, the Eisenhower administration backed Ngo Dinh Diem, an anti-Communist who established a corrupt, repressive government, with military advisers and hundreds of millions of dollars.

By thwarting the Geneva Accords and installing an unpopular regime in the South, Eisenhower ensured that Vietnam would be torn by civil war. In the short run, however, he had avoided war and seemingly stopped the Asian dominoes from falling.

Eisenhower soon confronted another crisis in the Middle East. Gamal Abdel Nasser, who had seized power in Egypt in 1954, emerged as a forceful spokesman for Arab unity and nationalism. Fearing that Nasser would open the way for Soviet power in the region, John Foster Dulles withdrew an offer to aid the Egyptians. Nasser struck back by taking over the British- and French-owned Suez Canal in 1956. In retaliation, Britain and France, with Israel's cooperation, moved against Nasser. As Israeli troops entered Egypt in October, Britain and France prepared to take back the Suez Canal. Eisenhower, fearing the

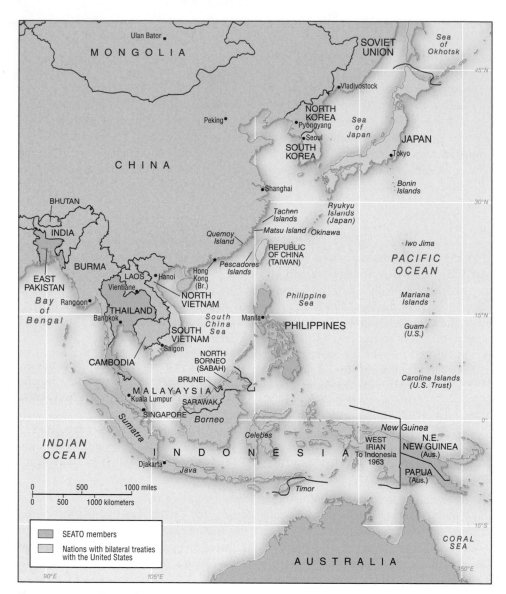

Map 27–1 America's Cold War Alliances in Asia Members of SEATO (the Southeast Asian Treaty Organization) and signers of other treaties with the United States. Through these pacts, the Eisenhower administration hoped to hold back the threat posed by Communist mainland China.

invasion would give the Soviets an excuse to move into the Middle East, threatened the British, French, and Israelis—US allies—with economic sanctions. They soon withdrew.

The Suez crisis was a pivotal moment. Before a joint session of Congress in January 1957, Eisenhower promised that the United States would intervene to protect any Middle Eastern nation threatened by "power-hungry Communists." He implemented this "Eisen-

Map 27–2   America's Cold War Alliances in the Middle East Located between the members of NATO and SEATO, the members of CENTO (the Central Treaty Organization) joined with the United States to deter the threat of international Communism sponsored by the Soviet Union to the north.

hower Doctrine" by sending troops to Lebanon the next year. In 1959, the United States joined with Turkey and Iran to create a Middle Eastern defense alliance known as the Central Treaty Organization (CENTO) for its geographical position between NATO and SEATO (see Map 27–2).

Eisenhower had helped to stabilize the Middle East and Southeast Asia temporarily, but he had also drawn the United States more deeply into these crisis-prone regions and increased the odds of future trouble. In the 1960s and 1970s, the United States would have to deal with this legacy.

Challenges to the Consumer Society

Along with crises abroad, American society confronted challenges at home. In different ways, a rebellious youth culture, the alienated beat movement, a nascent environmental movement, and the divisive civil rights struggle upset the stability of the Eisenhower era. Consumerism had not solved all the nation's problems or won over all of its citizens. Moreover, despite prosperity, Americans worried about a crisis of power in the nation.

Rebellious Youth

"Never in our 180-year history," declared *Collier's* magazine in 1957, "has the United States been so aware of—or confused about—its teenagers." In the 1950s, the emergence of a distinct youth culture, built around rock and roll, cars, comic books, and premarital sex, troubled many adults. The youth culture culminated a trend apparent since the 1920s and 1930s. As more and more teenagers attended high school, they were segregated in their own world and developed their own values and practices. In the 1950s, young people claimed rock and roll as their music. They wore blue jeans; they read comic books and teen magazines. Expressing their individuality, boys modified cars into customized "hot rods." Teens were attracted to alienated and rebellious movie characters, such as the troubled son played by James Dean in *Rebel Without a Cause* (1955) and the motorcycle-gang leader played by Marlon Brando in *The Wild One* (1953). Adults worried about teenage defiance and juvenile delinquency.

Many young people were rebellious, but not nearly as much as adults feared. Juvenile delinquency did not actually increase after World War II, and neither did rates of sexual intercourse among teenagers. Girls never played a strongly visible role in male-dominated youth culture. Most young people never questioned the political system, and youth culture exaggerated rather than rejected the values of the adult consumer society.

The early career of Elvis Presley illustrated the boundaries of youthful rebellion. Presley's appeal rested on an unsettling combination of rock-and-roll music and open sexuality. Presley's style—his sensual mouth, disheveled "duck's ass" haircut, and gyrating hips—amplified the music's sexuality.

Despite his appeal to teenagers, Presley was always polite, soft spoken, and devoted to his parents. Buying a pink Cadillac and other luxury cars, he was caught up in the consumer culture. Like millions of other Americans, Presley joined the suburban migration when he bought his house, Graceland, on the outskirts of Memphis. He was a new version of the old American dream of upward mobility.

Still, many adults blamed Presley, rock and roll, and mass media for the spread of violence, lust, and degeneration among young Americans. One popular television program showed Presley only from the waist up. To get rid of blue jeans and other teenage fashions, high schools imposed dress codes. There was a crusade against comic books, teen magazines, and movies. In well-publicized hearings from 1954 to 1956, the Senate's Subcommittee to Investigate Juvenile Delinquency focused attention on the corrupting power of the mass media.

The campaign against youth culture had little impact in a society of free speech and consumerism. Mass culture did not stop catering to teenagers with spending money. Many adults found youth culture appealing.

The Beat Movement

A smaller and older second group of rebels was much more critical of American society. The beat movement, which emerged in New York City in the 1940s, expressed a sense of both alienation and hope. The term "beat" referred to a feeling of exhaustion and also to a state of transcendence, the "beatific." Worn down by contemporary culture, the beats searched for a way beyond it.

Uptown at Columbia University and downtown in Greenwich Village, Allen Ginsberg, Jack Kerouac, John Clellon Holmes, William Burroughs, and others wanted, as one of them put it, "to emote, to soak up the world." Beats explored their sexuality, sampled mind-altering drugs, and pursued Eastern religions. In a society of bright colors, "beatniks" declared their alienation from consumerism by wearing black. Kerouac captured their spirit in his novel about a trip across America, *On the Road* (1957). In San Francisco, another center of beat culture, Allen Ginsberg published his long poem, "Howl" (1956), which gave voice to alienation: "I saw the best minds of my generation destroyed by madness, starving hysterical naked. . . ."

Though few in number, the beats attracted a great deal of attention. Their movement signaled a new dissatisfaction with consumer society, conventional sexual mores, and politics as usual.

The Rebirth of Environmentalism

A rebirth of environmental consciousness was also evidence of concern about consumerism. By the late 1950s, Americans were more concerned about the environment than at any time since the beginning of the twentieth century. The environmental threat was obvious in the cities. A well-publicized pall of smog seemed to hang perpetually over car-choked Los Angeles. Americans could no longer ignore the fact that their automobiles, the symbol of the consumer society, were polluting the air.

The environmental threat was obvious in the countryside, too. Even as they filled new suburban developments built on old farms, some Americans lamented the disappearance of open land. They began to criticize society's attitude toward the natural world. In the mid-1950s, environmentalists, led by the Sierra Club and the Wilderness Society, blocked construction of the Echo Park Dam in the upper Colorado River because it would have flooded a national park, the Dinosaur National Monument. A new environmental movement to protect wilderness lands emerged from the battle.

The Struggle for Civil Rights

The African American struggle for civil rights also challenged the Eisenhower era. By the 1950s, segregation was under increasingly effective attack in the courts and on the streets. Focusing on public schools (see Map 27–3), the NAACP assaulted the discriminatory legacy of the Supreme Court's *Plessy v. Ferguson* ruling of 1896 (see Chapter 20). In 1951 the NAACP's special counsel, Thurgood Marshall, combined five school lawsuits, including Oliver Brown's challenge to the constitutionality of a Kansas state law that allowed cities to segregate their schools. Because of the law, Brown's eight-year-old daughter, Linda, had to ride a bus 21 blocks to a "colored only" school, even though there was a "white only" school just three blocks from home. When the Brown case reached the Supreme Court in December 1952, Marshall attacked the *Plessy* argument that justified "separate but equal" facilities for whites and African Americans. Because of segregation, Marshall argued, Linda Brown and other African Americans received both an inferior education and a feeling of inferiority. He concluded that segregation violated the citizenship rights guaranteed by the Fourteenth Amendment.

In May 1954, the Court, led by new Chief Justice Earl Warren, handed down its ruling in *Brown v. Board of Education, Topeka, Kansas*. Overturning *Plessy*, the justices ruled unanimously that public school segregation was unconstitutional under the Fourteenth Amendment. "Separate but equal has no place," Warren announced. African Americans and white liberals were jubilant over what an African American newspaper called "a second emancipation proclamation." Marshall foresaw the end of school segregation before the close of the decade.

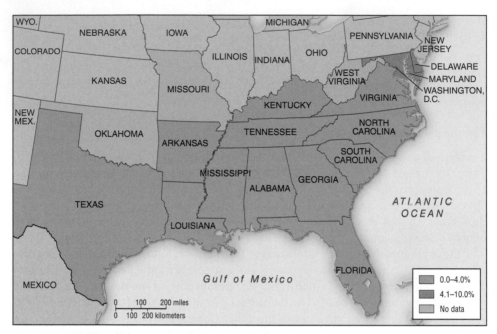

Map 27–3 African Americans Attending Schools with White Students in Southern and Border States, 1954 The small percentages indicate just how successfully segregation had separated the races before the Supreme Court ruled in *Brown v. Board of Education, Topeka, Kansas* in 1954.

It did not work out that way. When the Supreme Court ruled on the enforcement of its decision in 1955, the justices turned to local school boards, dominated by whites, to carry out integration. Federal district courts were to oversee the process, which should occur with "all deliberate speed." School segregation would have to end, but not right away.

Taking heart from the enforcement ruling, many whites refused to give up Jim Crow. As one white southerner put it, a "reasonable time" for the end of segregation would be "one or two hundred years." In 1956, 101 congressmen signed a "Southern Manifesto" calling on their home states to reject the *Brown* ruling. Amid calls for massive resistance to desegregation, White Citizens' Councils formed to resist desegregation in southern states, some of which passed laws intended to stop school integration. There was violence, too. In October 1955, white Mississippians brutally killed Emmett Till, a 14-year-old black boy from Chicago, who had supposedly whistled at a white woman.

African Americans were ready to fight even harder against segregation. In Montgomery, Alabama, the NAACP wanted to test the state law that segregated the city's buses. On December 1, 1955, Rosa Parks, a 42-year-old African American tailor's assistant and NAACP official, boarded a bus. Local custom required her to give her seat to a white passenger and move to the back of the bus, but when the bus driver told her to move, Parks refused. As she said, "my feet hurt." More than that, she wanted to find out "once and for all what rights I had as a human being and a citizen." The angry driver thought she had none; he had Parks arrested.

Seizing on Parks's arrest, African Americans began to boycott the bus system. Twenty-six-year-old Martin Luther King Jr., pastor of the Dexter Avenue Baptist Church, agreed to

An Unlikely Criminal Arrested for refusing to give up her bus seat to a white passenger, Rosa Parks poses for her official "mug shot" in December 1955.

lead the boycott. The son of a noted Atlanta preacher, King was already developing a brilliant oratorical style and a philosophy of nonviolent protest against segregation.

The boycott met immediate resistance. The city indicted the leaders, and African American homes and churches were bombed. In November 1956, however, the US Supreme Court ruled Alabama's bus-segregation law unconstitutional. By then, the boycott had cost the city dearly, and the white community had lost the will to resist. The city settled with the boycotters and agreed to integrate the buses. "We just rejoiced together," one of the boycotters remembered. "We had won self-respect."

Montgomery showed that a combination of local activism and federal intervention could overcome Jim Crow. It established a charismatic new leader with a powerful message and brought forward a new civil rights organization, the Southern Christian Leadership Conference. To one journalist, Montgomery "was the beginning of a flame that would go across America."

The flame did not travel easily. In 1957, the school board of Little Rock, Arkansas, accepted a federal court order to integrate Central High School, but in September the state's segregationist governor, Orval Faubus, called out National Guard troops to stop black students from enrolling. Even after meeting with Eisenhower, Faubus would not remove the troops. When he finally did, an angry mob of whites made it impossible for the African American students to stay. "Two, four, six, eight," cried the mob, "we ain't going to integrate."

Little Rock created a dilemma for the president. Not a believer in racial equality, Eisenhower wanted to avoid the divisive issue of civil rights. He privately opposed the *Brown* ruling and gave only mild support to the weak Civil Rights Act of 1957, which did not protect African Americans' right to vote. The president knew, however, that his government was being defied in Little Rock and humiliated around the world. So Eisenhower sent in troops of the army's 101st Airborne. With that protection, nine African American students went to Central High.

Like Montgomery, Little Rock demonstrated that a combination of federal action, however reluctant, and African American courage could triumph. The Central High crisis showed, too, how the cold war helped tip the balance against segregation. Competing with the Soviets for support from the multiracial third world, no president could afford the embarrassment of racial inequality at home. Segregation and discrimination were, the president concluded, "troublesome beyond imagination."

The Crisis of "Misplaced Power"

Youth culture, the beat movement, the environmental movement, and the civil rights struggle contributed to an uneasy mood by the end of the 1950s. Many people, worrying that the consumer society was flawed, blamed the nature of power in post–World War II America.

To some observers, corporations had become too powerful. In his best seller *The Hidden Persuaders* (1957), Vance Packard argued that advertisers manipulated Americans into buying corporate products. In 1958, the public got two object lessons in apparent corporate manipulation. That year, Americans learned about "payola," record companies' practice of paying disc jockeys to play particular records on the radio. Americans were shocked, too, by revelations that contestants on popular TV quiz shows had secretly been given the answers to questions in advance.

Other observers believed that not only corporations, but large institutions generally, had too much power. Conservatives such as Republican senator Barry Goldwater of Arizona decried what they saw as the excessive activism of the federal government. Sociologist C. Wright Mills argued in *The Power Elite* (1956) that an interlocking group of military, political, and economic managers ran the nation's institutions. In the age of nuclear weapons, still other Americans feared that scientists had too much power. Such movies as *The Day the Earth Stood Still* (1951) and *It Came from Beneath the Sea* (1955) exploited fears that scientific innovations would lead to disaster.

At the same time, Americans feared, too, that the nation might not be powerful enough. Such films as *The Deadly Mantis* (1957) and *Invasion of the Saucer Men* (1957) showed American science and technology unable to stop the destruction of the earth.

>> Time Line

▼**1947**
Levittown suburban development
Announcement of Truman Doctrine

▼**1948**
First McDonald's fast food restaurant
Alfred Kinsey, *Sexual Behavior in the Human Male*

▼**1950**
Diners Club credit card

▼**1951**
UNIVAC 1 computer

▼**1952**
Dwight D. Eisenhower elected president

▼**1953**
First suburban E. J. Korvettes store
Korean cease-fire

▼**1954**
"Baby boom" birthrate over 4 million per year

Supreme Court school desegregation decision, *Brown v. Board of Education, Topeka, Kansas*
Army-McCarthy hearings
Creation of divided Vietnam in Geneva peace talks

▼**1955**
Formation of AFL-CIO

▼**1955–56**
Montgomery, Alabama, bus boycott

"The Helicopter Era" Cartoonist Herblock lampoons President Dwight Eisenhower's apparent lack of involvement in the nation's problems.

There was also a sense in the age of conformity that ordinary Americans lacked the will-power to face the challenges of the twentieth century.

In October 1957, worries about American power went from science fiction fantasy to cold war reality. That month, the Soviet Union launched Sputnik, the world's first satellite, into orbit. The result was a wave of fear in the United States. If the Soviets could send

up a satellite, they could be ahead in nuclear weapons and economic growth, too. Americans felt suddenly vulnerable.

Sputnik intensified concerns about American education. A diverse and growing student population and rising parental demands had strained the nation's schools. Now Americans worried that the schools were not preparing children to compete with the Soviets in science and technology. In 1958, Congress passed the National Defense Education Act.

▼**1956**
National System of Defense
   Highways Act
William H. Whyte Jr., *The
   Organization Man*
Suez crisis
Reelection of President
   Eisenhower

▼**1957**
Eisenhower Doctrine
School desegregation crisis, Little
   Rock, Arkansas

Jack Kerouac, *On the Road*
Soviet Sputnik satellite launch

▼**1958**
National Defense Education Act
TV quiz show scandals

▼**1959**
Alaska and Hawaii statehood
Nixon-Khrushchev "Kitchen
   Debate" in Moscow

▼**1960**
President Eisenhower's
   Commission on National Goals
Soviet downing of US U-2 spy
   plane
John F. Kennedy elected
   president

▼**1961**
Eisenhower's farewell address on
   "military-industrial complex"

The measure promoted instruction in science, math, and foreign languages, supported construction of new schools, and offered loans and fellowships to students.

Sputnik forced Washington to accelerate the space program. The first US satellite launch collapsed in flames—Flopnik, the press called it. In January 1958 the government successfully launched its first satellite, Explorer I. Later that year, Congress created the National Aeronautics and Space Administration (NASA) to coordinate space exploration. These initiatives did not completely wipe away Americans' worry that, as one magazine railed, "the whole kit and caboodle of our American way of life—missiles and toasters, our freedoms, fun, and foolishness—is about to go down the drain."

Eisenhower did little to calm the anxiety about American power. Slowed by poor health, he seemed old and out of ideas. In 1960, the president even created a Commission on National Goals to help figure out what the country should do. At the end of his term in January 1961, Eisenhower fed anxiety with a somber farewell address about the problem of "misplaced power" in the nation. Noting that cold war spending had built up the military and the defense industry, he warned against allowing this "military-industrial complex" to gain too much power or "endanger our liberties or democratic processes." Eisenhower also warned that universities, fueled by federal money for research, might become too powerful. The president's farewell was a stunning admission that the cold war could destroy rather than save democracy in America. The speech contributed to the sense of uncertainty: Was America too powerful, or not powerful enough?

Conclusion

Along with the cold war, the triumph of consumerism dramatically affected the United States in the 1950s. The booming consumer economy gave Americans a new sense of security and affluence during the unsettling confrontation with Communism. Breaking with the past, they moved to the suburbs, had record numbers of children, bought televisions at E. J. Korvettes, and defined life as the pursuit of material pleasures. Consumerism helped promote homogeneity and conformity and spurred the victory of Dwight Eisenhower and his moderate approach to government. For a moment, it seemed as if America had achieved stability and harmony in a dangerous world, but that feeling did not last. By the close of the 1950s, many Americans wanted more for themselves and their country. They worried that power was "misplaced." They questioned whether consumer society could provide prosperity, democracy, and security for all its citizens. The next decade would offer a dramatic answer.

Who, What

John Foster Dulles 827

Dwight Eisenhower 826

Alfred Kinsey 820

William J. Levitt 816

Richard Nixon 826

Rosa Parks 836

Domino theory 831

Dynamic obsolescence 818

Massive retaliation 827

Modern Republicanism 827

Review Questions

1. What were the basic components of "the good life" in the 1950s?

2. What factors made American society more homogeneous in the 1950s? What factors kept the nation diverse?

3. What was Eisenhower and Dulles's strategy for fighting the cold war?

Critical-Thinking Questions

1. How did the emergence of consumer society affect democracy in the United States? Did the nation become more or less democratic during the 1950s?

2. Why did so many Americans believe there was a crisis of power by the end of the 1950s? Had the nation, in fact, become less powerful?

3. Was the United States winning the cold war in the 1950s?

For further review materials and resource information,
please visit www.oup.com/us/ofthepeople

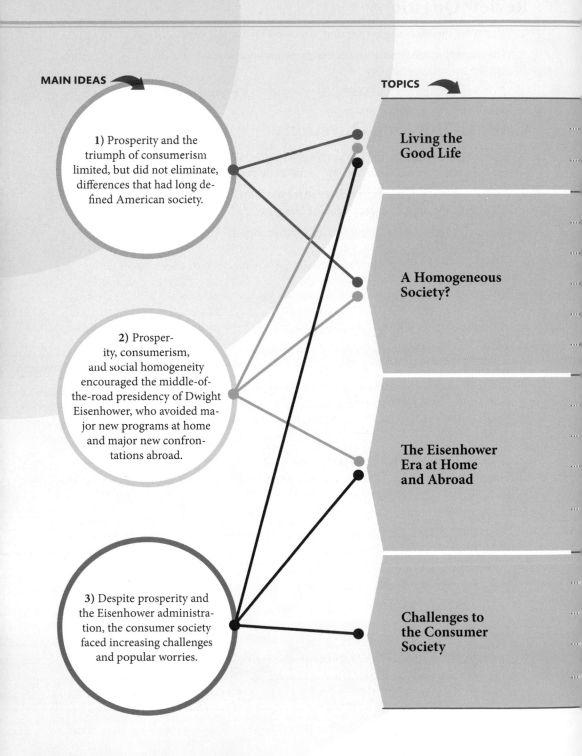

MAIN IDEAS

1) Prosperity and the triumph of consumerism limited, but did not eliminate, differences that had long defined American society.

2) Prosperity, consumerism, and social homogeneity encouraged the middle-of-the-road presidency of Dwight Eisenhower, who avoided major new programs at home and major new confrontations abroad.

3) Despite prosperity and the Eisenhower administration, the consumer society faced increasing challenges and popular worries.

TOPICS

Living the Good Life

A Homogeneous Society?

The Eisenhower Era at Home and Abroad

Challenges to the Consumer Society

THE CONSUMER SOCIETY

1945–1961

EVENTS

Economic Prosperity The emergence of the consumer society rested on economic prosperity and labor peace.

The Suburban Dream The increase of homeownership in the suburbs was a chief benefit of the consumer society.

The Pursuit of Pleasure The consumer society offered Americans such pleasures as automobiles, shopping malls, television, and a more open sexual culture.

The Discovery of Conformity The spread of consumerism reinforced an idea that Americans were too much like one another and too ready to conform to social expectations.

The Decline of Class and Ethnicity Declining class and ethnic differences supported the feeling of sameness in American society.

The Resurgence of Religion and Family Increased participation in organized religion and the baby boom strengthened the sense of a uniform society.

Maintaining Gender Roles Despite some evolution of gender roles, American culture reemphasized the differences between the sexes.

Persisting Racial Differences The continuing importance of racial differences undercut the homogeneity of society.

The Survival of Diversity Migration, the statehood of Alaska and Hawaii, and the varieties of popular music contributed to continuing social diversity.

"Ike" and 1950s America Elected president in 1952, Dwight Eisenhower reassured Americans that they could cope with sweeping changes after World War II.

Modern Republicanism Eisenhower's administration steered a middle course between traditional Republican conservatism and Democratic liberalism.

An Aggressive Cold War Strategy In some ways, Eisenhower adopted a more forceful policy against Communism, including support for covert coups against possibly hostile governments.

Avoiding War with the Communist Powers Despite tough talk, the Eisenhower administration ended the Korean War and avoided direct confrontation with the People's Republic of China and the Soviet Union.

Crises in the Third World The Eisenhower administration increasingly focused on the threat of Communist expansion in Africa, Asia, Latin America, and the Middle East and supported the new anti-Communist nation of South Vietnam.

Rebellious Youth A new youth culture, built around rock and roll, challenged the values of traditional society.

The Beat Movement A small group of artistic rebels offered a pointed critique of the values and politics of the consumer society.

The Rebirth of Environmentalism A rebirth of environmental consciousness promoted concerns about the consumer society.

The Struggle for Civil Rights The surging African American civil rights movement, aided by the Supreme Court decision in *Brown v. Board of Education, Topeka, Kansas*, unsettled the stability of 1950s America.

The Crisis of "Misplaced Power" Concerns about the consumer society fed worries that the nation was either too powerful or not powerful enough.

CHAPTER 28

AMERICAN PORTRAIT

>> The A&T Four

Franklin McCain and Joseph McNeill were scared. On the afternoon of February 1, 1960, the two African American college students had done the unthinkable at the Woolworth's in Greensboro, North Carolina: they had sat down at the lunch counter and asked for donuts and coffee. When the white waitress refused to serve them, they persisted. By arrangement, two friends from North Carolina Agricultural and Technical College, Ezell Blair and David Richmond, joined them at the counter. All four waited to see what would happen to them for challenging segregation, the policy of the Woolworth's lunch counter and the basic principle of the twentieth-century South.

Some white customers insulted the four students; but other whites even encouraged them. A white policeman stood behind them, McCain recalled, "with his club in his hand, just sort of knocking it in his hand, and just looking mean and red and a little bit upset and a little bit disgusted." Were the four students about to get beaten? Then McCain realized with surprise that the policeman "didn't know what the hell to do." The four African Americans had effectively disarmed this representative of white authority. "You had the feeling that this is the first time that this big bad man with the gun and the club has been pushed in a corner, and he's got absolutely no defense, and the thing that's killing him more than anything else—he doesn't know what he can or what he cannot do," McCain observed. "He's defenseless."

McCain and his friends stayed at the lunch counter until closing time. They did not get service. But they did get something important. For months they had talked about the frustration and humiliation of segregation; for months they had debated what to do. Now, they had confronted injustice. "I felt," McCain admitted, "as though I had gained my manhood."

The A&T Four, as they became known, also made a critical discovery: they had power. A group of unarmed African Americans, polite and persistent, could challenge authority and get away with it. Their nonviolent protest, inspired mainly by Christianity and the example

continued

845

of the Indian activist Mohandas Gandhi, actually empowered them. "To me," Blair said, "we were sitting down at the table of democracy."

That night, back on campus, the discovery of the A&T Four inspired fellow students. The next day, Blair, McCain, McNeill, and Richmond returned to the Woolworth's. This time, more than 20 other black students went with them to contest segregation and to test the power of ordinary people.

The story of the A&T Four both inspired and reflected the experience of their country in the 1960s. In different ways, the crisis of "misplaced power" came to an end as many people, like the A&T Four, discovered that they and their society could confront the problems that plagued the nation. In the 1960s, Americans demanded to sit at "the table of democracy" and offer new solutions for the problems of consumerism, civil rights, and the cold war. In the process, the nation turned to a new form of liberalism that pledged to confront Communism abroad and reform life at home. The result was a decade of remarkable change and conflict, both at home and abroad.

New Approaches to Power

The discontents at the close of the 1950s created an opportunity for new ideas and new strategies at the start of the 1960s. In a nation worried by insufficient or "misplaced power," four groups, in particular, became energized and empowered. Across the political spectrum, civil rights activists, new liberals, new conservatives, and the New Left offered fresh approaches to domestic and international problems. All these groups were driven by the participation of young people. But the four had different and often conflicting views of power and democracy in America.

Grassroots Activism for Civil Rights

The A&T Four were part of a new generation of African Americans impatient with the slow "deliberate speed" of the desegregation ordered by the Supreme Court in *Brown v. Board of Education* (see Chapter 27). Young blacks were ready to go beyond court cases and boycotts to try new tactics. As the Greensboro protests continued, hundreds of African American students, along with some white students, besieged lunch counters. Under pressure, Woolworth's and other large stores agreed to serve African Americans.

The Greensboro sit-in, as it was called, quickly inspired grassroots civil rights activism in other communities in both the South and the North and the formation of a new national civil rights organization. There were wade-ins at whites-only beaches, kneel-ins at whites-only churches, and even paint-ins at whites-only art galleries. The demonstrations forced whites to open up facilities to black patrons and spawned the Student Nonviolent Coordinating Committee (SNCC). The SNCC (pronounced "Snick") brought together white and African American young people. Demonstrating that ordinary people could confront the powerful, the sit-ins energized the civil rights movement and inspired Americans to confront other problems.

The New Liberalism

Defeated by Eisenhower and the Republicans in the 1950s, liberal intellectuals and politicians, mostly Democrats, had been forced to reconsider their ideas and plans. By the 1960s, the liberals were offering a fresh agenda in response to the civil rights movement, consumerism, and the cold war confrontation with Communism.

Faith in economic growth drove the new liberalism. To meet its domestic and international challenges, the United States, liberals believed, had to expand its economy more rapidly. By manipulating its budget, the federal government could keep the economy growing. The right amount of taxes and expenditures would ensure full employment, strong consumer demand, and a rising gross national product.

Growth alone would not make America great, liberals cautioned. A society devoted mainly to piling up personal wealth and spending it on consumer goods was fundamentally flawed. As the liberal historian Arthur M. Schlesinger Jr. argued, the nation needed now to focus on the "quality" of life and on the broader "public interest." Economic growth should create a better life for all Americans. Because the private sector could not solve pressing problems, the federal government had to deal actively with poverty, racial inequality, pollution, housing, education, world Communism, and other problems. Unimpressed with warnings about the excessive power of big institutions, the new liberals believed that the solution to the nation's woes was a still more powerful federal government.

In this respect, 1960s liberalism was much like the New Deal liberalism of the 1930s and the Fair Deal liberalism of the 1940s (see Chapters 24 and 26), both of which argued that government could and should correct problems created or ignored by the private sector. Nevertheless, the new liberalism differed from the old in important ways. New Dealers had worried most of all about restoring prosperity in the Great Depression; the new liberals almost took prosperity for granted. The old liberals had feared big business and class conflict. Their successors generally saw racial divisions and civil rights as the country's greatest domestic problems.

The New Conservatism

As in the past, conservatives differed fundamentally with liberals over power: the conservatives believed the federal government was already too big and active. But the conservatives, like the liberals, had been unhappily out of power for quite a while. In the 1930s, Herbert Hoover's failure to halt the Great Depression had discredited the conservative faith in minimalist government; then Hitler's aggression had undercut the conservative belief in isolationism.

By 1950, conservative ideas had already begun a quiet resurgence. In 1951, conservative intellectual William F. Buckley's book *God and Man at Yale* attacked his alma mater for its liberalism and denial of individualism. Two years later, Russell Kirk published *The Conservative Mind* to prove that there was a living conservative tradition in America. In 1955, Buckley and Kirk founded the magazine *National Review* as a forum for conservative ideas, especially vigorous anti-Communism.

The leading conservative political hero was outspoken Republican senator Barry Goldwater of Arizona. With a western belief in individual freedom and hostility to federal power, Goldwater was a blunt opponent of liberalism. A major general in the Air Force Reserve, he also advocated a more aggressive stance toward Communism.

By 1960, the growing conservative movement had its own younger generation of activists. That year, the Young Americans for Freedom gathered at Buckley's estate in Sharon, Connecticut, to adopt a manifesto. The Sharon Statement called for government to protect individual liberty by preserving economic freedom and maintaining a strong national defense.

The New Left

At the opposite end of the political spectrum, another young group, inspired by civil rights activism and troubled by life on campus, rejected both conservatism and liberalism. By the early 1960s many students felt confined and oppressed in overcrowded and impersonal colleges and universities, where their lives were regulated by rules that governed eating in dining halls, drinking alcohol, keeping cars on campus, and socializing in dorm rooms. Female students were subject to particularly strict rules, including curfews.

Some of these youth formed the New Left, a radical movement that attempted to create a more democratic nation. The key organization of the New Left was Students for a Democratic Society (SDS), which emerged in 1960 to produce "radical alternatives to the inadequate society of today." During its national convention at Port Huron, Michigan, in 1962, SDS approved an "Agenda for a New Generation." An answer to the Sharon Statement, the Port Huron Statement argued that American society denied people real choice and real power in their lives. The answer, SDS claimed, was "participatory democracy." The members of SDS did not believe that liberalism would promote real democracy in America. SDS did not expect much help from the old Left of socialists and Communists, with their Marxist faith in the revolutionary power of the working class. Instead, students would lead the way by fighting for control of their schools. The message began to resonate: SDS membership rose from 2,500 to 10,000 in late 1965.

The Presidential Election of 1960

As so often in American politics, new ideas did not immediately transform mainstream politics. The presidential election of 1960 offered a choice between a vaguely liberal Democratic future and a moderate Republican status quo. The Democratic nominee, Senator John F. Kennedy of Massachusetts, was open to the liberals' agenda and shared their optimism. Only 42 when he announced his candidacy, Kennedy was energetic and charismatic. Although he had an undistinguished record in Congress, he exuded an enormous sense of promise.

Kennedy gave voice to that promise during the campaign. Americans, he explained, stood "on the edge of a New Frontier—the frontier of the 1960s—a frontier of unknown opportunities and paths, a frontier of unfulfilled hopes and threats." The United States needed to foster economic growth, rebuild slums, end poverty, improve education, and enhance retirement.

In contrast, Kennedy's Republican opponent, Vice President Richard Nixon of California, favored balanced budgets, limited government, and the qualified acceptance of New Deal programs that marked the Eisenhower administration's "Modern Republican-

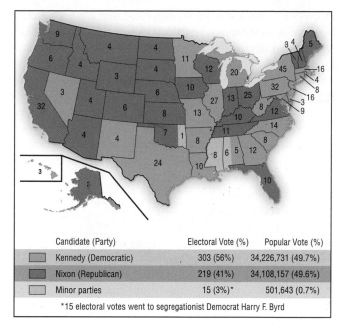

Candidate (Party)	Electoral Vote (%)	Popular Vote (%)
Kennedy (Democratic)	303 (56%)	34,226,731 (49.7%)
Nixon (Republican)	219 (41%)	34,108,157 (49.6%)
Minor parties	15 (3%)*	501,643 (0.7%)

*15 electoral votes went to segregationist Democrat Harry F. Byrd

Map 28–1   The Presidential Election, 1960 Democrat John F. Kennedy's clear margin in the electoral vote belies just how narrowly he outpolled Republican Richard M. Nixon in the popular vote.

ism." Nixon embraced neither the bold programs and dynamic economic growth of the new liberalism nor the soaring individualism and strident anti-Communism of the new conservatives.

Despite Kennedy's stirring rhetoric and apparent triumph in televised debates, the election was the closest in history. Kennedy managed to keep much of the Democratic New Deal coalition of liberals, workers, and African Americans together, but he won by less than 120,000 votes (see Map 28–1). However narrowly, the voters had turned to a Democrat, influenced by liberal ideas, who was eager to explore the New Frontier.

The New Frontier

Style and Substance

Kennedy voiced the confident liberal faith in America's unlimited power and responsibility. "Let every nation know," he declared in his inaugural address in January 1961, "that we shall pay any price, bear any burden, meet any hardship, support any friend, oppose any foe to assure the survival and the success of liberty. This much we pledge—and more." He perfectly captured the optimistic spirit of the early 1960s.

So did the president's space program. The exploration of space, the ultimate frontier, seemed like an ideal occupation for confident Americans in the 1960s. Moreover, the space race allowed Kennedy to reject cautious Eisenhower policies and confront the Soviet challenge. In April 1961 the Soviet Union sent up the first astronaut to orbit Earth.

The next month, NASA managed only to launch astronaut Alan Shepard for a brief, sub-orbital flight. Once again Americans feared "that the wave of the future is Russian."

Insistent on "beating the Soviets," the president boldly pledged to land "a man on the moon before the decade is out." Apollo, the moon project, got under way with 60,000 workers and billions of dollars. Meanwhile, in February 1962 astronaut John Glenn became the first American to orbit Earth. That year the United States launched Telstar, the first sophisticated communications satellite. The space program mixed practical achievements such as Telstar with more symbolic gestures such as manned space flights.

That mixture of style and substance epitomized the administration. The president maintained a dynamic image, but his administration, hampered by a weak mandate, did not venture too far out onto the liberal New Frontier.

For liberals, the persistence of poverty amid prosperity was a chief failure of the consumer society. Liberals argued that the government had to help the poor become productive workers; they contended that the battle against poverty should include improved housing, education, health, and job opportunities, as well as job training.

Kennedy supported some modest antipoverty measures. In 1961 he signed into law the Area Redevelopment Act to help revive depressed areas. He also signed the Omnibus Housing Act to clear slum housing and renew inner cities. But these measures were not enough to wipe out poverty.

Civil Rights

Grassroots activism for civil rights posed a critical challenge for the Kennedy administration. In one place after another, attempts to break down segregation and promote African American voting met with resistance.

After the Supreme Court outlawed the segregation of interstate bus terminals, a small group of African American and white "Freedom Riders" traveled south on buses to test the decision in the spring of 1961. The Freedom Riders met with beatings from white citizens and harassment from local authorities. Only then did the Kennedy administration send federal marshals to protect them.

In 1961, when SNCC started a voter-registration drive in Mississippi, white people struck back. SNCC workers were beaten and shot. When SNCC tried to register black voters in Albany, Georgia, members of this Albany Movement were beaten and arrested. Martin Luther King Jr., leader of the Southern Christian Leadership Conference (SCLC), came to Albany and was arrested, too, but segregation still ruled in the city.

SNCC activists resented the lack of presidential support. Kennedy understood that racial inequality damaged the United States' image abroad, but he also knew that the civil rights issue could split the Democratic Party.

The defiance of southern whites gradually pushed Kennedy toward action. In 1962 the governor of Mississippi, Ross Barnett, disregarded a federal court order by preventing a black student from enrolling at the University of Mississippi. When federal marshals escorted the student, James Meredith, to school, white students pelted them with rocks and Molotov cocktails. After the rioting killed two people and wounded more than 100 marshals, Kennedy called in federal troops to stop the violence and allow Meredith to enroll.

Two confrontations in Alabama forced the president's hand in 1963. In April, Martin Luther King Jr. and the SCLC tried to end segregation in Birmingham, perhaps the most segregated city in America. The city's public safety commissioner, Eugene "Bull" Connor, was a stereotypical racist white southern law enforcement officer. King and local allies planned to boycott department stores and overwhelm the jails with arrested protestors. In the next days, Connor's officers arrested demonstrators by the hundreds. Ignoring a judge's injunction against further protests, King ended up in solitary confinement. In a powerful statement, "Letter from Birmingham Jail," he rejected further patience: "We must come to see . . . that 'justice too long delayed is justice denied.'" Once King was out on bail, the SCLC pushed harder, with demonstrations by thousands of African American students.

Goaded by the new protests, Connor turned fire hoses on demonstrators, set dogs on them, and hit them with clubs. Shocking pictures of the scenes increased the pressure on the white leadership of Birmingham and on President Kennedy. The Justice Department arranged for a deal in which the SCLC gave up the demonstrations and local businesses gave up segregation and promised to hire African Americans. However, soon thereafter the Ku Klux Klan marched outside the city, and bombs went off at the home of King's brother and at SCLC headquarters. After African Americans rioted in the streets, Kennedy was forced to send federal troops to keep the peace.

A second confrontation in Alabama drew the president still deeper into the civil rights struggle. The segregationist governor, George Wallace, defied federal officials and tried to stop two black students from enrolling at the University of Alabama. In an eloquent televised address, Kennedy finally admitted that there was "a moral crisis" and called for sweeping civil rights legislation.

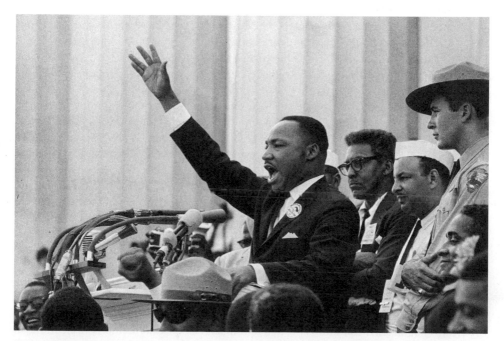

"I Have a Dream" Martin Luther King Jr. addresses the crowd at the Lincoln Memorial, Washington, DC, August 28, 1963.

On August 28, the March on Washington brought together a crowd of nearly 200,000 people, including 50,000 whites, at the Lincoln Memorial to commemorate the 100th anniversary of the Emancipation Proclamation and to demand "jobs and freedom." Demonstrators joined hands to sing the stirring civil rights anthem, "We Shall Overcome." Martin Luther King Jr. moved the nation with his vision of racial harmony. "I have a dream," he said, "that one day . . . little black boys and black girls will be able to join with little white boys and white girls as sisters and brothers." King looked forward to "that day when . . . black men and white men, Jews and Gentiles, Protestants and Catholics, will be able to join hands and sing . . . 'Free at last! Free at last! Thank God Almighty, we are free at last!'"

Kennedy's address and the March on Washington marked a turning point. The surging grassroots movement for racial equality had created broad-based support for civil rights and finally forced the federal government to act.

Flexible Response and the Third World

Like Eisenhower, Kennedy supported the containment of Communism. The new president believed the nation could afford to increase military spending. He also abandoned the doctrine of massive retaliation, Eisenhower's threat to use nuclear weapons against any Soviet aggression. Kennedy preferred the strategy of flexible response—the threat of different military options, not just nuclear weapons, to counter the Soviets. While spending generously on nuclear weapons, the Kennedy administration also built up conventional ground forces and Special Forces—the highly trained troops, known as Green Berets, who could fight in guerilla wars.

Kennedy was more willing than Eisenhower to intervene in the third world. This was partly a reflection of Kennedy's confidence about American power and partly a response to Soviet actions. In January 1961 Nikita Khrushchev announced Soviet support for "wars of national liberation," insurgencies against established governments in Asia, Africa, and Latin America.

To counter the appeal of Communism, Kennedy supported modernization for Africa, Asia, and Latin America; that is, the development of capitalist, democratic, independent, and anti-Communist regimes along the lines of the United States. In 1961, his administration created the Peace Corps to send young volunteers to promote literacy, public health, and agriculture around the world. The Peace Corps reflected not only the importance of the young in the new movements of the 1960s, but also the idealism, anti-Communism, and arrogant sense of superiority of the Kennedy years. Not surprisingly, the organization was not always welcomed by the people it was supposed to help. To promote the modernization of Latin America, Kennedy announced the formation of the Alliance for Progress in 1961. Over the next eight years, this venture provided $20 billion for housing, health, education, and economic development in the Western Hemisphere.

The Kennedy administration sometimes helped to thwart third world independence and democracy in the name of anti-Communism by intervening in the domestic affairs of supposedly independent countries. In the Republic of the Congo, the CIA engineered the election of an anti-Communist leader, and it secretly tried to manipulate elections in Chile, as well. The United States also backed antidemocratic, but anti-Communist, regimes in Argentina, Guatemala, Haiti, and Honduras.

Similarly, Kennedy wanted to bring down Fidel Castro, whose Cuban revolution was an example for the rest of Latin America. The president inherited a plan from the Eisenhower administration for a CIA-directed invasion of the island by anti-Communist Cuban exiles. To conceal US responsibility, Kennedy canceled air cover to protect the invaders. As a result, nearly all 1,500 exiles who landed at the Bay of Pigs in April 1961 were killed or captured. Embarrassed, Kennedy turned to the CIA, which launched "Operation Mongoose," an unsuccessful secret campaign to kill or depose Castro. The Cuban leader, aware of the plot, declared himself a Communist and turned to the Soviets for help.

Two Confrontations with the Soviets

Kennedy faced two direct confrontations with the Soviet Union. In 1961, Khrushchev threatened to stop Western traffic into West Berlin, which was surrounded by Soviet-dominated East Germany. In response, Kennedy called up reserve troops, asked Congress to increase defense spending, and hinted at a preemptive nuclear strike against the Soviets. Khrushchev backed down, but the East German government built a barbed-wire and concrete fence between East Berlin and West Berlin. By halting the embarrassing flight of East Germans to freedom in West Berlin, the Berlin Wall defused the crisis and became a symbol of cold war Europe, a visible "iron curtain" that separated Communists and non-Communists.

In 1962 Kennedy entered a more dangerous confrontation with the Soviet Union. On October 15 photos from a spy plane showed that the Soviets were building launch sites in Cuba for nuclear missiles that could strike the United States. On October 22, after tense secret meetings, Kennedy put ships in place to intercept Soviet vessels bound for Cuba. That night, a somber Kennedy told a television audience about the missiles and demanded their removal. Fearing a nuclear war, Americans waited for the Soviets' response. Khrushchev, unable to confront the United States in its own hemisphere, backed down.

Trying to Laugh About Nuclear War President Kennedy and Soviet Premier Khrushchev arm wrestle and threaten to push the buttons unleashing hydrogen bombs during the Cuban Missile Crisis, October, 1962.

The Soviets withdrew the missiles in exchange for the removal of obsolete American missiles from Turkey.

The Cuban Missile Crisis both eased and intensified the cold war. Faced with a nuclear conflict, neither side found the prospect appealing. To ensure communication in a crisis, a teletype hotline was installed between the White House and the Kremlin. In 1963 the two powers also approved a Limited Test Ban Treaty halting aboveground tests of nuclear weapons, even as the Soviets and the Americans remained more determined to stand firm against each other.

Kennedy and Vietnam

Kennedy inherited a deteriorating situation in South Vietnam in 1961. Ngo Dinh Diem's anti-Communist government faced increasing attacks from the Viet Cong guerillas determined to overthrow his regime. Diem also faced the Viet Cong's new political organization, the National Liberation Front, which was trying to mobilize his Communist and non-Communist opponents. In addition, he faced the continuing hostility of Ho Chi Minh's Communist government in North Vietnam, which was secretly sending soldiers and supplies into South Vietnam.

Like Eisenhower, Kennedy tried to shore up the Diem government with financial aid and advisers. This included sending the Special Forces to train the South Vietnamese army. Before Kennedy took office, there were 900 American troops filling noncombat roles in South Vietnam. By late 1963, there were more than 16,000. Despite this support, Diem's regime spiraled downward. His army could not stop the Viet Cong. A cold, unpopular ruler, he alienated his people. Losing confidence in Diem, the Kennedy administration did nothing to stop a military coup that resulted in his murder in November.

What Kennedy would have done next will never be known. On a trip to Dallas, Texas, on November 22, 1963, the president was shot while riding in an open limousine at 12:33 p.m. Two bullets tore through Kennedy's throat and skull, and doctors pronounced him dead half an hour later. That afternoon, police arrested Lee Harvey Oswald for the shooting. A quiet former Marine, Oswald had spent time in the Soviet Union. Two days later, as police transferred him from a jail, Oswald was shot and killed by Jack Ruby, the troubled owner of a local nightclub.

Americans were shocked and numbed. Some could only believe the assassination was the product of a dark conspiracy, but there was never proof of such a plot. The presidency of John Kennedy, little more than 1,000 days long, left a sad sense of unfulfilled promise. To many Americans, Kennedy's White House seemed like "Camelot," the seat of the mythical English King Arthur. The reality was less magical. Kennedy gave voice to the new liberalism, but he seldom translated liberal ideas into action. Some wanted to believe that Kennedy, if he had lived, would not have escalated the Vietnam War. Yet there was no compelling evidence that he intended to withdraw American troops.

The Great Society

After Kennedy's death, Lyndon B. Johnson and the Democratic-controlled Congress carried out most of the liberal agenda. A flood of new laws addressed poverty, race relations, consumer and environmental protection, education, and health care. At the same time, the liberal majority on the Supreme Court afforded new protections for individual rights. By the mid-1960s, the principles of the new liberalism, turned into law, were transforming American government and society.

Lyndon Johnson's Mandate

The new president, Lyndon Johnson, seemed far different from his slain predecessor. Born to modest circumstances in rural Texas, he had made his fortune largely through political connections. Never an eloquent public speaker or a charismatic figure, he was an especially effective legislator who knew how to bully and cajole Senate colleagues into a deal.

Still, there were fundamental similarities between Johnson and Kennedy. Both were products of the Democratic Party that had engineered the New Deal, won World War II, and fought the cold war. Both shared the liberals' expansive sense of American might. "Hell, we're the richest country in the world, the most powerful," Johnson declared. "We can do it all."

Johnson stressed continuity with his predecessor. Yet the situation had changed: Kennedy's death left Americans more willing to accept innovation. The presidential election of 1964 strengthened Johnson's mandate. The contest offered voters a clear choice between competing visions. Embracing the new liberalism, Johnson stood for activist government, growth economics, and civil rights. His Republican opponent, Barry Goldwater, stood unequivocally for the new conservatism. "We have gotten where we are," he declared, "not because of government, but in spite of government."

It was no contest. Democrats painted Goldwater as a dangerous radical who would gut popular programs and perhaps start a war. Appearing as a statesman and man of peace, Johnson won 61.1 percent of the popular vote, 44 states, and 486 electoral votes. Moreover, the Democrats increased their majorities in the House and Senate. It was a greater victory than Johnson's hero, Franklin Roosevelt, had ever enjoyed.

"Success Without Squalor"

With his mandate, Johnson moved to enact a legislative program that rivaled Roosevelt's New Deal. In May 1964, he had called for the creation of the "Great Society"—"a society of success without squalor, beauty without barrenness, works of genius without the wretchedness of poverty." To create that society, his administration pushed through liberal laws to wipe out poverty, end segregation, and enhance the quality of life for all Americans.

Johnson, like many Americans, was disturbed by the persistence of poverty: nearly one in five Americans was poor. Declaring "unconditional war on poverty," the administration won congressional approval in 1964 of the Economic Opportunity Act, which created an independent federal agency, the Office of Economic Opportunity (OEO), to spend nearly $1 billion on antipoverty programs. The OEO managed Volunteers in Service to America (VISTA), whose workers taught literacy and other skills in impoverished areas. It ran the Job Corps, which taught job skills to poor youth, and implemented Community Action Programs (CAPs), which encouraged the urban poor to organize themselves. By supporting the "maximum feasible participation" of the poor, the CAPs, unlike other poverty programs, had the potential to redistribute power away from local officials.

In 1965 and 1966 Congress continued the war on several fronts. It established an expanded food stamp program and created Head Start, which provided early schooling, meals, and medical exams for impoverished preschool-aged children. To protect the rights of the poor, the Legal Services Program brought lawyers into slums. To improve urban life, the Model Cities Program targeted 63 cities for slum clearance and redevelopment. Congress also created the Department of Housing and Urban Development in 1965 and the Transportation Department in 1966 partly to help manage antipoverty programs.

To improve the quality of life, the Great Society took a major step toward national health insurance when Congress created Medicare in 1965. This program provided the elderly with coverage for doctors' bills, surgery, and hospitalization. Congress also created Medicaid to help the states provide medical care to the nonworking poor.

The Johnson administration confronted the growing issue of consumer protection. In 1965, Ralph Nader published a disturbing book, *Unsafe at Any Speed*, charging that car manufacturers cared more about style and sales than about safety and that executives at General Motors had ignored safety defects in the Chevrolet Corvair. General Motors attempted to discredit Nader rather than promise to improve the Corvair. In response, Congress passed the National Traffic and Motor Vehicle Safety Act of 1966, which set the first federal safety standards for automobiles, and the Highway Safety Act, which required states to establish highway safety programs.

The president and Congress adopted the liberals' belief in using the federal government to support education. The Elementary and Secondary School Act of 1965 channeled $1.3 billion into school districts. The Higher Education Act of 1965 offered federally insured student loans.

The Great Society included programs for cultural enrichment. In 1965 Congress established the National Endowment for the Arts to fund the visual and performing arts and the National Endowment for the Humanities to support scholarly research. The Public Broadcasting Act of 1967 established the nonprofit Corporation for Public Broadcasting, which would support such commercial-free cultural and educational television shows as *Sesame Street*.

Protection of the environment was a natural issue for liberals. In 1962, the best-selling book *Silent Spring* sensitized Americans to the ecological threat posed by the consumer economy. The author, marine biologist Rachel Carson, warned that, like nuclear weapons, environmental contamination from pesticides threatened human survival.

During Johnson's presidency, more than 300 pieces of legislation led to the expenditure of more than $12 billion on environmental programs. In 1963 the Clean Air Act encouraged state and local governments to set up pollution control programs. Two years later, amendments established the first pollution emission standards for automobiles. The Air Quality Act of 1967 further strengthened federal authority to deal with air pollution. Meanwhile, the Water Quality Act of 1965 and the Clean Waters Restoration Act of 1966 enabled governments to fight water pollution. The Wilderness Act of 1964 created a system of lands protected from development.

Preserving Personal Freedom

The new liberalism contained a paradox: liberals wanted both to enhance the power of the federal government and to expand individual rights. Their concern for individual rights was apparent in their support for civil rights for African Americans and in a series of decisions by the Supreme Court, led by Chief Justice Earl Warren.

In *New York Times v. Sullivan* in 1964, the Supreme Court encouraged free speech by making it more difficult for public figures to sue news media for libel. In addition, two decisions protected the rights of people accused of crimes. In 1963 the court ruled in *Gideon v. Wainwright* that governments had to provide lawyers to poor felony defendants. Three years later, *Miranda v. Arizona* required police to inform individuals of their rights when they were arrested, including the right to remain silent and the right to an attorney.

The Warren Court also protected sexual and religious freedom. Throwing out a state law that banned the use of contraceptives in *Griswold v. Connecticut* in 1965, the court affirmed individuals' right to privacy and in effect kept government out of the bedroom. In *School District of Abington Township v. Schempp* (1963), the court prohibited state and local governments from requiring public school students to say the Lord's Prayer or read the Bible.

The Supreme Court's rulings were controversial. Some people charged that the court was "driving God out" of the classroom. Others believed that the court had gone too far to protect the rights of alleged criminals. Some conservatives demanded the impeachment of Chief Justice Warren. Through its rulings, the liberal majority on the court substantially increased individual freedom, but few people had yet thought much about the tension caused by expanding both individual rights and government power.

By 1967 the Great Society's programs added up to a major change in American democracy. Government claimed more authority than ever to manage many Americans' daily lives. The Great Society brought a massive expansion of the size, cost, and power of the federal government (see Table 28–1).

That expansion would be controversial for years to come. Some measures—Medicare in particular—proved to be enormously expensive. Conservatives did not welcome an enlarged federal government, and some corporations resented the regulation of business in the name of consumer protection. Despite these concerns, the attempts to improve the quality of life represented some of the major accomplishments of the new liberalism. The war on poverty was at least a partial success. Mainly because of an economic boom, the percentage of people living in poverty decreased to 13 percent by 1970. But 25 million Americans were still poor. Moreover, poverty was unevenly distributed. About a third of African Americans and a quarter of Americans of Hispanic origin were impoverished as the 1970s began.

Table 28–1 Expanding the Federal Government, 1955–1970

Year	Civilian Employees (thous.)	Total Spending (millions)	Defense (millions)	Space (millions)	Health (millions)	Education and Manpower (millions)
1955	2,397	$68,509	$40,245	$74	$271	$573
1960	2,399	$92,223	$45,908	$401	$756	$1,060
1965	2,528	$118,430	$49,578	$5,091	$1,704	$1,284
1970	2,982	$196,588	$80,295	$3,749	$12,907	$1,289

Source: *Historical Statistics of the United States* (1976), II, 1102, 1116.

The Death of Jim Crow

Meanwhile, the battle for civil rights had become still more intense. In the 10 weeks after the Birmingham confrontation in 1963, 758 demonstrations led to 14,733 arrests across the United States. When a bomb killed four African American girls in a Baptist church in Birmingham in September, some African Americans rioted, and the police killed two more children.

The violence continued in 1964: CORE, SNCC, SCLC, and the NAACP had created the Council of Federated Organizations (COFO) to press for African American voting rights in Mississippi. Robert Moses, an African American schoolteacher, led the COFO crusade uniting young African American and white activists to register black voters and start "Freedom Schools" for African American children. The effort, known as Freedom Summer, met hostility from whites. Two white activists, Michael Schwerner and Andrew Goodman, and one African American activist, James Chaney, were found shot to death near Philadelphia, Mississippi. Eventually, a white deputy sheriff, a local Klan leader, and five other whites were convicted of "violating the rights" of Chaney, Goodman, and Schwerner. The violence continued in Mississippi throughout Freedom Summer. Homes and churches were burned, and three more COFO workers were killed.

Lyndon Johnson could not escape the events in Mississippi. In the summer of 1964, the Mississippi Freedom Democratic Party (MFDP) sent a full delegation to the Democratic National Convention in Atlantic City, New Jersey. The MFDP delegates, including the eloquent Fannie Lou Hamer, hoped at least to share Mississippi's convention seats with the whites-only delegation. Hamer, the daughter of sharecroppers, had been jailed and beaten for trying to register African American voters. Afraid of alienating white southerners, Johnson offered the delegates two seats in the convention. "We didn't come all this way for no two seats," Hamer retorted. The MFDP delegation went away empty-handed.

Johnson and the Democratic Party were clearly not ready to share power with African American activists, but they were ready to end legalized segregation. In July, Congress adopted the Civil Rights Act, which outlawed racial discrimination in public places and also set up an Equal Employment Opportunity Commission (EEOC) to stop discrimination in hiring and promotion. Even the schools gradually became integrated. In 1964 hardly any African American students attended integrated schools; by 1972 nearly half of African American children did.

However, across the South, most African Americans still could not vote. In January 1965 the SCLC and SNCC tried to force the voting rights issue with protests in Selma, Alabama. Predictably, the demonstrations produced violent opposition and helpful publicity. The sight of state troopers using tear gas, cattle prods, and clubs on peaceful marchers built support for voting rights.

Seizing the moment, Johnson called for the end of disfranchisement, and Congress passed the Voting Rights Act of 1965. This powerful measure forced southern states to give up literacy tests used to disfranchise black voters and empowered federal officials to make sure that African Americans could register to vote. In three years, Mississippi saw African American registration increase from 6 percent to 44 percent of eligible voters.

Together with the Civil Rights Act of 1964, the Voting Rights Act transformed the South. These twin achievements of the civil rights movement and the Great Society effectively doomed Jim Crow and laid a foundation for African American political power. However, the struggle for racial equality was far from over.

AMERICAN LANDSCAPE

···

>> "The Long Cool Summer" of Greenville, Mississippi

The dramatic pictures of brave march-ers, menacing dogs, ominous police, and murdered activists can make the civil rights movement seem like a continuously violent confrontation. But civil rights, like much social change, was also a more quiet process, a slow dance in which blacks and whites gradually, haltingly created and ac-cepted a new, more democratic order. That was the case in Greenville, Mississippi, in the "Freedom Summer" of 1964, when civil rights workers fanned out across the state to ensure the voting rights of African Amer-icans. Although there was turbulence and violence in much of the state, Greenville witnessed what the local newspaper, the *Delta Democrat-Times,* described as "The Long Cool Summer."

Like the rest of Mississippi, Greenville, a city of 41,000 in the rich cotton-growing delta, was segregated. Although African Americans made up half the population, they faced second-class social and economic status. "I don't like it," a young black man de-clared, "when the white man works an easy job for $25 a day and I work a mean one for $3." African Americans lived with second-class political status, too: thanks to literacy requirements and poll taxes, black voters had long been effectively disfranchised. Few African Americans were registered to vote; the city had no black elected officials.

Freedom Summer—the voting rights drive led by the Council of Federated Or-ganizations (COFO), a coalition of leading civil rights groups—was intended to change that. In the spring of 1964, COFO's white

and black activists moved into Greenville. The arrival of these outsiders, mostly in their 20s, touched off a wave of speculation and anxiety among the city's whites. The enact-ment of the federal Civil Rights Act of 1964, banning segregation, intensified fears of demonstrations, confrontations, and blood-shed. "There are many of us . . . who are today dismayed by the attitude, actions and statements of some of the young men and women who are temporarily within the state," declared the *Democrat-Times.* "At times it would appear that nothing less than a calculated attempt to provoke wholesale violence is their aim."

Despite these fears, local officials urged "patience and self-control." In fact, COFO's strategy focused not on demonstrations but on voter registration. "If you get the vote you don't have to shoot a gun," a COFO leader insisted. "You can pull a trigger with a vote and kill off a politician." To encourage black activism, COFO set up two summer "freedom schools" in Greenville.

In July, COFO began to bring African Americans to the county courthouse to register to vote. The first day, 100 took the preliminary registration test; the turnout was so large that 35 would-be voters were still outside when the office closed for the day. The next day, another 45 began the registration process. And so the COFO drive went on. "There was no sustained violence, no bombings, no riots, no murders and no unruly mass demonstrations," the *Democrat-Times* reported, ". . . rowdies of both races *continued* never felt free to follow the course tolerated in other state communities."

Why were the African Americans of Greenville able to begin reclaiming their democratic rights with so little upheaval? Certainly, the nonconfrontational tactics of COFO made a difference. The city's growth and relative prosperity probably made whites more secure about sharing power. At least some whites accepted that American democracy demanded the registration of African Americans. "This is their undeniable right," the *Democrat-Times* conceded, "and what they seek is entirely within the American political pattern." The paper also pointed out that southern whites faced "in-

evitable changes" because of the federal government and the national civil rights movement; for many whites, it probably seemed pointless to disrupt the quiet lines of would-be black voters.

There was one final, ironic explanation for the long cool summer of Greenville. As the editor of the *Democrat-Times* noted, most of the city's whites didn't care enough to exercise their right to vote. The paper suggested that Greenville also needed a voting drive for whites "to make our democratic republic more truly democratic." Paradoxically, blacks won the vote in Greenville because whites cared so little about their own rights.

The American War in Vietnam

The war in Vietnam was the decisive event for the new liberalism and the nation in the 1960s. American participation in the conflict reflected the liberals' determined anti-Communism and their boundless sense of power and responsibility. Driven by these beliefs, Johnson made the fateful decision to send American troops into battle in 1965. When the war did not go according to plan, Americans divided passionately over the conflict, and the economy faltered. By the end of 1967 the war was destroying the Great Society.

Johnson's Decision for War

Like Kennedy, Johnson was a committed cold warrior with an optimistic view of American power. He kept flexible response in place and was equally willing to undermine the independence of third world countries. In 1965, Johnson sent 22,000 troops to the Dominican Republic to stop an increasingly violent struggle for political power. He violated the sovereignty of this Caribbean nation without obtaining evidence of a Communist threat and without consulting Latin American countries as required by treaty.

At first, Johnson followed Kennedy's policy in Vietnam. The new president believed in the domino theory, the idea that the fall of one country to Communism would lead to the fall of others. The president also felt he could not turn his back on commitments made by Kennedy, Eisenhower, and Truman. As one weak government followed another,

Johnson sent more aid and advisers to South Vietnam and stepped up covert action against the North.

This secret activity helped Johnson get congressional approval to act more aggressively. On August 2, 1964, a US destroyer, the *Maddox*, was cruising a few miles off the coast of North Vietnam in the Gulf of Tonkin. When three North Vietnamese torpedo boats unsuccessfully attacked the *Maddox*, the American ship sank two of the boats and damaged a third. Two days later, the *Maddox*, along with a second US destroyer, fired at a nonexistent North Vietnamese attack. Johnson ordered retaliatory air strikes and asked Congress for the power to protect American military personnel. With only two dissenting votes, Congress approved what became known as the Tonkin Gulf Resolution, which gave the president the authority, without a declaration of war, to use military force to safeguard South Vietnam. Even though Johnson knew there had been no real threat to the United States, he had misled Congress to obtain a "blank check" to fight in Southeast Asia.

He soon cashed it. After American soldiers were killed in a Viet Cong attack on a US base in February 1965, Johnson authorized air strikes against North Vietnam itself. In March the United States began Operation Rolling Thunder, a series of bombing raids on military targets in North Vietnam.

When the raids failed, Johnson had a disagreeable but clear choice. If he wanted to save both South Vietnam and his reputation, he had to commit ground troops to battle; otherwise, he would be blamed for the loss of South Vietnam to Communism. In July 1965, Johnson gave the order to send 180,000 soldiers to fight in South Vietnam without a declaration of war.

Johnson's decision was the ultimate expression of the new liberalism. The president went to war not only because he opposed Communism but also because he had faith that American wealth and wisdom could transform a weak, divided South Vietnam into a strong, united, modern nation. Although cautious about going to war, Johnson believed that the United States could afford to fight, and win, a war abroad and still build the Great Society at home. It was a fateful choice.

Fighting a Limited War

Johnson and his advisers believed the United States did not need all its power to save South Vietnam (see Map 28–2). Instead of another total war like World War II, Vietnam was to be a limited war in which the US forces, led by General William Westmoreland, would use conventional weapons against military targets. The goal was not to take over territory through "unconditional surrender" but rather to kill enough enemy soldiers to persuade the North Vietnamese and the Viet Cong to give up. Relying on superior technology, Westmoreland expected the United States to prevail by the end of 1967.

Westmoreland's strategy turned out to be poorly suited to the realities of Vietnam. As the United States discovered, the North Vietnamese and the Viet Cong usually escaped by hiding in tunnels, fleeing through the jungle, fighting mainly at night, or retreating into Cambodia, Laos, and North Vietnam. Their strategy was to live long enough for a frustrated US military to leave South Vietnam.

American troops fought well. Yet at the close of 1967, too many North Vietnamese and Viet Cong were still alive and committed to the overthrow of South Vietnam.

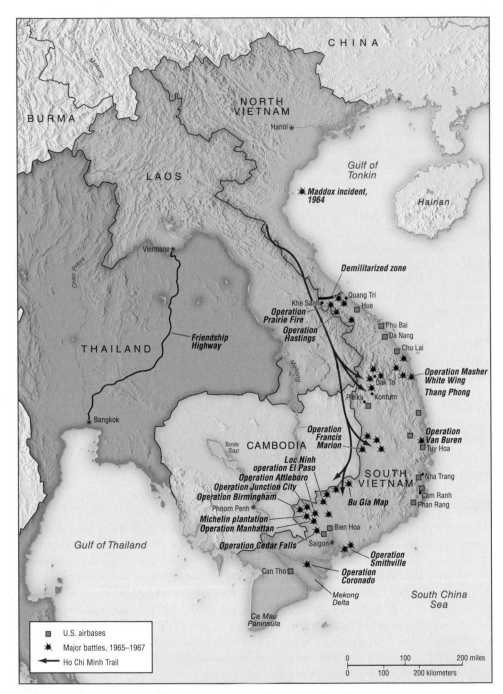

Map 28–2   America's War in Vietnam, 1965–1968 The many military bases suggest how much power the United States had to commit to South Vietnam; the many major battles show how hard American troops had to fight to protect the South Vietnamese regime from the Viet Cong and from the North Vietnamese soldiers who traveled the Ho Chi Minh Trail.

Table 28-2 The Escalating War in Vietnam, 1960–1968

Year	U.S. Troops	U.S. Battle Deaths	S. Vietnamese Battle Deaths	N. Vietnamese and Viet Cong Battle Deaths (estimated)
1961	3,164	11	(three-year	12,000
1962	11,326	31	total =	21,000
1963	16,263	78	13,985)	21,000
1964	23,310	147	7,457	17,000
1965	184,000	1,369	11,403	35,382
1966	385,000	5,008	11,953	55,524
1967	486,000	9,378	12,716	88,104
1968	536,000	14,589	27,915	181,149

Sources: Michael Clodfelter, *Vietnam in Military Statistics*, 46, 57, 209 and 258; Fox Butterfield, ed., *Vietnam War Almanac*, 50, 54, 57, 64, 102, 132, 158, 192; Shelby Stanton, ed., *Vietnam Order of Battle*, 333.

Meanwhile, 9,000 US troops died in 1967 alone. Even with half a million troops in his command, Westmoreland had not won the war on schedule. He had not lost the war, either. But the United States was running out of time to win (see Table 28–2).

The War at Home

The war in Vietnam had a divisive impact back home. An impassioned antiwar movement, led by SDS and other student radicals, emerged to condemn American policy. Communism in Southeast Asia, they believed, did not pose a real threat to the United States. But the misguided cold war had led liberals to support an antidemocratic regime. The war also revealed how undemocratic America had become. Johnson, the New Left pointed out, had ignored the Constitution by sending troops into battle without a declaration of war. In addition, the selective service law was forcing a repugnant choice on young men: they could either fight this illegal war or obtain deferments to stay in school and prepare for empty lives as corporate employees in the consumer society.

A growing number of liberals and Democrats shared part of the radicals' analysis. These "doves" acknowledged that the United States was backing an antidemocratic government in a brutal and apparently unnecessary war. The conflict appeared to be a civil war rather than some plot to expand Soviet or Chinese influence. Meanwhile, the war had shattered many liberals' and Democrats' overconfident view of the Great Society. The United States, confessed Senator J. William Fulbright of Arkansas in 1966, was a "sick society" suffering from an "arrogance of power."

Some African Americans viewed the conflict as a painful illustration of American racism. A disproportionate number of poor African Americans, unable to go to college and avoid the draft, were being sent to kill nonwhites abroad on behalf of a racist United States. First the SNCC and then Martin Luther King Jr. condemned the war. Refusing to be drafted, boxer Muhammad Ali was sentenced to jail and stripped of his championship in 1967.

The growing opposition to the war produced large, angry demonstrations. In 1965 students and faculty staged "teach-ins" at college campuses to question American policy in Vietnam. In April, 20,000 people gathered at the Washington Monument to protest the war. Some young men risked jail by returning or burning their draft cards. On campuses, students protested the presence of recruiters for defense contractors. In October 1967 during Stop the Draft Week, radicals in Oakland, California, tried to shut down an army draft induction center, fought with police, and briefly took over a 25-square-block area of the city. Meanwhile, nearly 100,000 people rallied in Washington, DC, to protest the war.

Despite the protests, most Americans supported the war. To many people, the demonstrators were unpatriotic. "America—Love It or Leave It," read a popular bumper sticker. "Hawks," mostly conservative Republicans and Democrats, wanted Johnson to fight harder. Nevertheless, by October 1967 support for the war in one public opinion poll had fallen to 58 percent, while only 28 percent approved of Johnson's conduct of the war.

Bad economic news contributed to the public mood. Massive government spending for the war and the Great Society had overstimulated the economy. With jobs plentiful, strong consumer demand drove up prices, which in turn put upward pressure on wages. Anxious about inflation, the Federal Reserve shrank the money supply, making it harder for businesses to get loans. When interest rates reached their highest levels since the 1920s, there were fears of a financial panic.

By the end of 1967 the war had put enormous stress on the Great Society. It undermined liberals' commitment to anti-Communism and their confidence in American power and wisdom. By dividing the nation, the conflict also undermined support for the Great Society. By weakening the economy, furthermore, the Vietnam War made it harder to pay for the Great Society. The United States could not, as Johnson believed, "do it all." The new liberalism had reached its crisis.

The Great Society Comes Apart

Even as Congress enacted the liberals' agenda, many Americans were expressing new dissatisfactions that liberalism could not accommodate. New forms of activism—the Black Power movement, the youth rebellion, and a reborn women's movement—exposed the limits of the liberal vision. In 1968 the strain of new demands, the Vietnam War, and economic realities tore apart the Great Society and destroyed the fortunes of Lyndon Johnson, the Democratic Party, and the new liberalism.

The Emergence of Black Power

For many African Americans, the Great Society's response to racial inequality was too slow and weak. Even as the civil rights movement reached its climax, a wave of more than 300 race riots from 1964 to 1969 dramatized the gap between the promise of the Great Society and the reality of life in black America. When a white policeman shot a 15-year-old African American in Harlem in July 1964, angry African Americans burned and looted buildings. In August 1965, friction between white police and African American citizens touched off a riot in the poor Watts section of Los Angeles. In five days more than 1,000 fires burned, and 34 people died. The wave of riots peaked in Detroit in July 1967 when 43 people died (see Map 28–3).

To many, the riots were, in the words of an official report on Watts, "senseless," but the disturbances flowed from real frustrations. Despite successful challenges to legalized segregation in the South, African Americans still lived with poverty and discrimination all across the country. Northern cities, the center of the riots, had been largely ignored by Martin Luther King Jr. and other civil rights leaders. The riots signaled that the civil rights movement and the new liberalism, for all their accomplishments, had not addressed some of the most difficult problems of racial inequality.

For years King and other activists had relied on nonviolent demonstrations and ties to white liberals to achieve integration, but that approach proved ineffective in the North. In 1965, King joined marches in Chicago protesting the de facto segregation of the city's schools. King faced the determined opposition of Mayor Richard Daley. Reluctant to challenge the powerful political boss, the Johnson administration did not give King real support. In 1966, King returned to lead the "Chicago Movement" to wipe out slums and win access to better housing in white neighborhoods. "Go back to Africa," white demonstrators chanted. Daley accepted a compromise on fair housing but repudiated it as soon as King left town. Under the leadership of 24-year-old Jesse Jackson, Operation Breadbasket threatened demonstrations and boycotts against businesses that refused to hire African Americans. The project produced few results; King's nonviolent tactics had failed.

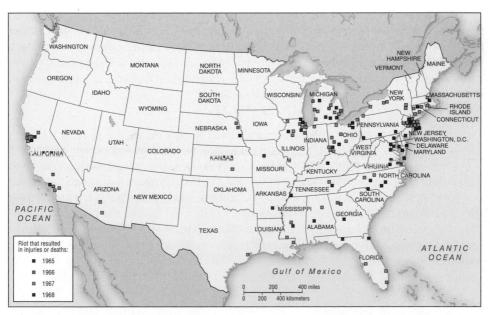

Map 28–3   Race Riots, 1965–1968 The clusters of riots in the Northeast, Midwest, and California emphasize that race was not just a southern issue in the 1960s. *Mark C. Carnes et al.,* Mapping America's Past, *p. 217.*

African Americans already had the example of a different approach to the problem of black-white relations. The Nation of Islam believed that whites were devils and African Americans were God's chosen people. The Black Muslims, as they were known, preached separation of the races and the self-reliance of African Americans. One of the Muslims' most powerful preachers was Malcolm X, a former pimp, drug pusher, and convict who angrily rejected integration and nonviolence. Malcolm X moderated his views before being gunned down, apparently by Muslims, in 1965. But he was best known for his militant call "for the freedom of the 22 million Afro-Americans by any means necessary."

By the mid-1960s, many African Americans were willing to follow at least some of Malcolm X's example. Rejecting integration, they now asserted a separate African American identity that declared, "Black is beautiful." Some African Americans wore African robes and dashikis, explored African language and art, and observed the holiday of Kwanzaa, based on an African harvest festival. Instead of working with white liberals and depending on the federal government, some African American activists insisted that blacks create their own institutions. In 1966, SNCC ousted its white members.

In rejecting nonviolence and integration, a number of African American activists adopted a more militant stance. "What we gonna start saying now is Black Power!" Stokely Carmichael told a rally in Mississippi. The new slogan had different meanings for different people. The most radical interpretation came from the Black Panthers, who were first organized in Oakland, California, by Huey P. Newton and Bobby Seale. Dressed in black clothes and black berets, the Panthers armed themselves to protect their neighborhoods from white police. Newton, admiringly described by an associate as "the baddest motherfucker ever to step foot inside of history," went to jail after a shootout with police. The Panthers also founded schools and promoted peaceful community activism, but they were best known in the media for their aura of violent militance.

Particularly because of the violent image of the Panthers, many people, African American and white, were hostile to the new slogan. For King and his allies, Black Power all too obviously meant repudiation of nonviolent integration. For many whites, Black Power stirred fears of violence. For white leaders such as Richard Daley, Black Power meant giving up political authority to African Americans. For Lyndon Johnson, Black Power obviously meant a rejection of his Great Society.

The Youth Rebellion

The anti-Vietnam War movement was part of a broader rebellion against adult authority and expectations. The battle began at the University of California at Berkeley in 1964. That fall, the university's administration banned political speaking and organizing at the one street corner where it had been allowed. When a civil rights activist was arrested for defying the ban in October, hundreds of students sat down around the police cars, trapping the officers for 32 hours. After the stand-off, students created the Free Speech Movement (FSM) to pursue greater student involvement in the educational process. When the university refused to accept that demand, students took over the main administration building. Speaking that day, the student leader Mario Savio reflected the ideas of the New Left. "We have an autocracy which runs this university," he exclaimed. "[W]e're a bunch of raw material[s] that . . . don't mean to end up being bought by some clients

AMERICA AND THE WORLD
···
>> **International Student Protest, 1968**

The unrest had built on campus almost from the moment it opened in 1964. Many students hated the sterile, modern buildings, erected in the midst of a big-city slum. They also chafed at the many rules: no cooking in the dorms, no changes to the furniture, no males in females' rooms. The campus represented, one student critic complained, "an assembly-line conception of educational organization." As the student body grew from 2,000 to more than 12,000 by the fall of 1967, the Vietnam War escalated half a world away. When six local leaders of the antiwar movement were arrested, radical students rushed into the university administration building and occupied the dean's office.

The protest took place not in the United States but on the suburban Nanterre campus of the University of Paris. The student movement of the 1960s was, in fact, a global phenomenon. In Europe, Asia, and Latin America, as well as the United States, mostly middle-class students criticized the authority of universities and governments, demanded more freedom, and condemned the Vietnam War. The wave of protest surged and reached its crest in the spring of 1968. In Western Europe, even in authoritarian, pro-Soviet Eastern Europe, students protested against universities and police. In Japan, students protested the Vietnam War. In Brazil, students confronted their universities' rigid governance and the nation's repressive military regime.

There were significant differences among these protest movements. In the United States, the New Left rejected the old Left and did not see organized labor as an ally. In Western Europe, students were influenced by socialism and eager to make common cause with workers and unions. In France, the result was a general strike of students and workers unlike anything seen in the United States. While American protestors seldom criticized the Soviet Union, East European students condemned their own Communist governments and the USSR.

Nevertheless, important commonalities united the movements. They generally shared origins in uneasiness about the cold war and the repressiveness of modern, bureaucratized society, dominated by big organizations. The movements reflected a powerful yearning for freedom and free expression. The simultaneity of these largely separate national protests was a product of rapid communication in this age of satellites and television: students learned quickly what was going on elsewhere around the globe. The rise of student movements was a reminder, too, of the global influence of the United States: America's war in Vietnam angered students abroad, and America's student movement set the example for protest around the world.

Finally, the international protests produced a common reaction—a frightened backlash from educators and other authorities. Tear gas, water hoses, and clubs were common sights in 1968. As in the United States, the result of protest was often the triumph of conservatism and the *continued*

AMERICA AND THE WORLD *continued*

status quo. The harshest backlash came in Czechoslovakia: the Soviets invaded, killed and wounded more than 700, and ended any loosening of authority. But in the long run, the international student movements also signaled a persisting, even growing, demand for freedom and democracy in the face of great organizations and worldwide superpower competition.

of the University, be they the government, be they industry, be they organized labor, be they anyone! We're human beings!" The administration eventually succumbed to faculty protests and a student boycott of classes and agreed to new rules on free speech.

Americans had never seen anything quite like the Berkeley protests. Here were privileged students condemning society, storming a building, and being dragged off by the police. Many people were infuriated; some younger Americans were inspired.

As campus activism flourished, young people were also creating the rebellious lifestyle that became known as the "counterculture." Less politically oriented than the New

The New Left in Action, University of California at Berkeley, 1964 Student radical Mario Savio stands on top of a police car to address a crowd of protesting students while two policemen sit uncomfortably inside the vehicle.

Left, the counterculture challenged conventional social values. By the mid-1960s, many younger Americans were condemning conformity, careerism, materialism, and sexual repression as they groped toward an alternative lifestyle.

The counterculture rested on the enjoyment of rock music, drugs, and sexual freedom. Beginning in 1964, the sudden popularity of the Beatles, the Rolling Stones, and other British bands brought back a rebellious note to rock and roll. The Beatles' irreverent attitude toward authority, symbolized by their long hair, helped create "Beatlemania" in the United States. Rock also became more socially and politically conscious in the 1960s. Bob Dylan, Simon and Garfunkel, and other musicians rooted in folk music sang about racism, nuclear weapons, and other issues.

Rock music often sang of the virtues of drugs and sex. The use of marijuana, the hallucinogen LSD, and other drugs increased during the 1960s as a way of flouting adult convention and escaping everyday reality for a more liberated consciousness. Sex offered a similar mix of pleasure and defiance. On campuses across the country, students demanded greater freedom, including the repeal of rules that restricted the mixing of male and female students in dorms. By the end of the decade, many students were living together before marriage.

Many young people hoped that the counterculture would weave sex, drugs, and rock into a new lifestyle. Novelist Ken Kesey joined with his followers, the Merry Pranksters, to set up a commune, complete with "Screw Shack," outside San Francisco. By 1965 Kesey had created the "acid test," which fused drugs, rock, and light shows into a multimedia experience and helped establish the popularity of "acid rock," the "San Francisco sound" of the Jefferson Airplane and the Grateful Dead.

The purest form of the countercultural lifestyle was created by the hippies, who appeared in the mid-1960s. Hippie culture centered in the Haight-Ashbury section of San Francisco. Rejecting materialism and consumerism, hippies celebrated free expression and free love. They wanted to replace capitalism, competition, and aggression with cooperation and community. One group of hippies, the Diggers, gave away clothes and food and staged the first "Human Be-In" at Golden Gate Park "to shower the country with waves of ecstasy and purification."

The power of youth rebellion was easy to exaggerate. There were not many full-time hippies. The countercultural lifestyle quickly became conformist consumerism, defined by the right clothes and records.

The counterculture also had roots in the orthodox culture it attacked. By the close of the 1950s, adults themselves had become ambivalent about consumerism, conventional morality, and institutional authority. Sexual freedom for youth was encouraged partly by the greater sexual openness of mainstream culture, the Supreme Court's *Griswold* decision, and the introduction of the oral contraceptive (the "pill") in 1960. Americans chafed at the authority of religious denominations. The "pop art" paintings of Andy Warhol and Roy Lichtenstein, the productions of the Living Theater, the essays of Susan Sontag, and the novels of Thomas Pynchon broke with formal, artistic conventions.

Nevertheless, the counterculture was a disruptive force in the 1960s. Like the Black Panthers, hippies deeply influenced young people and adults and encouraged Americans to question conventional values and authority and seek a freer way of life.

The Rebirth of the Women's Movement

By the 1960s American women were reacting against the difficult social roles enforced on them after World War II. More women than ever went to college, but they were not expected to pursue long-term careers. More women than ever worked outside the home, but they were still expected to devote themselves to home and family. Women also had to put up with the continuing double standard of sexual behavior, which granted men more freedom to seek sexual gratification outside marriage. Women began to question their second-class status. In part, they were inspired by the example of the civil rights movement.

Two best-selling books reflected these complaints. In *The Feminine Mystique* (1963), Betty Friedan described "the problem that has no name," the growing frustration of educated, middle-class wives and mothers who had subordinated their own aspirations to the needs of men. Meanwhile, Helen Gurley Brown rejected unequal sexual opportunities in *Sex and the Single Girl* (1962). Neither Friedan nor Brown challenged male sexual ethics or male careerism. Instead, both wanted equal opportunity for women, in and out of marriage. Brown explained, coyly, that "nice, single girls do."

Women's complaints received attention but little action from men. In 1961 Kennedy appointed the Presidential Commission on the Status of Women, chaired by Eleanor Roosevelt. The commission's cautious report, *American Women*, documented gender discrimination but reaffirmed women's domestic role. In 1963 Congress passed the Equal Pay Act, which mandated the same pay for men and women who did the same work, but the measure, full of loopholes, had little impact. A year later, Title VII, a provision of the Civil Rights Act of 1964, prohibited employers from discriminating on the basis of sex in hiring and compensation. Yet the EEOC did little to enforce the law.

In 1966 Betty Friedan and a handful of other women, angry at the inaction of the EEOC, formed the National Organization for Women (NOW). Although frustrated with the Great Society, Friedan and the founders of NOW expressed essentially liberal values. They saw NOW as "a civil rights organization" and wrote a women's "Bill of Rights" that focused on government action to provide rights and opportunities. NOW also demanded access to contraception and abortion.

NOW's platform was too radical for many women and not radical enough for others. Some younger women, particularly activists in the civil rights movement and the New Left, wanted more than liberal solutions to their problems. By the fall of 1967, activists were forming new groups dedicated to "women's liberation." Influenced by the New Left, radical feminists blamed the capitalist system for the oppression of women, but a growing number of radicals saw men as the problem. Like African Americans in the Black Power movement, radical women talked less about rights and more about power. Their slogan was "Sisterhood Is Powerful!" Radical feminists also rejected collaboration with male liberal politicians.

Few in number, radical feminists nevertheless commanded public attention. In September 1968 New York Radical Women organized a protest against the annual Miss America pageant in Atlantic City, New Jersey. The pageant, they said, was an act of "thought control" intended "to make women oppressed and men oppressors; to enslave us all the more in high-heeled, low-status roles." The protestors threw bras, girdles, makeup, and other "women-garbage" into a "Freedom Trash Can." Then they crowned a sheep "Miss

America." Not surprisingly, men and many women were generally uncomfortable with radical feminism. Onlookers at the Miss America protest called the women "lesbians" and "screwy, frustrated women."

Conservative Backlash

The rebellions against the Great Society strengthened the conservative movement. Just two years after humiliating defeat in the presidential election of 1964, conservatives won new national prominence. Two politicians became focal points for many Americans' resentment against feminism, civil rights and Black Power, the counterculture and the antiwar movement, and the new liberalism.

George Wallace, former governor of Alabama, increasingly combined his hostility to civil rights and federal power with a populist appeal to working-class and middle-class whites. In 1964, he ran for the Democratic presidential nomination, calling for "law and order." Encouraged by his success in northern primaries that year, Wallace prepared to mount an independent campaign aimed at the "average man—your taxi driver, your steel and textile worker" in 1968. Now he played on anger over the youth rebellion and the antiwar movement, as well as the civil rights movement. "If I ever get to be President and any of these demonstrators lay down in front of my car," Wallace vowed, "it'll be the last car they ever lay down in front of."

Meanwhile, former actor Ronald Reagan became a major conservative force in the Republican Party. A lifelong liberal Democrat, he had moved to the right and supported Goldwater in 1964. Two years later, Reagan ran for governor of California, vowing to "clean up the mess at Berkeley" with all its "Beatniks, radicals and filthy speech advocates" and its "sexual orgies so vile I cannot describe them." He opposed high taxes, Medicaid, and other liberal activism and favored escalation of the war in Vietnam.

1968: A Tumultuous Year

In 1968 the stresses and strains of the Great Society produced the most tumultuous year in the United States since World War II. In January, the Viet Cong and North Vietnamese launched bold, sometimes suicidal attacks all over South Vietnam on the first day of Tet, the Vietnamese new year. Although US and South Vietnamese forces inflicted punishing losses on the attackers, the Tet Offensive shocked Americans. If the United States was winning the war, how could the North Vietnamese and the Viet Cong have struck so daringly? More Americans now began to believe the war was unwinnable.

The Tet Offensive doomed Johnson's increasingly troubled administration. The president needed to send reinforcements to Vietnam, but he knew public opinion would oppose the move. As it was, he could not even pay for more troops. The economy would no longer support both the war and the Great Society. The political situation was bad, too. On March 12, Senator Eugene McCarthy of Minnesota, a longshot antiwar candidate with little money, nearly beat Johnson in New Hampshire's primary. Four days later, Senator Robert Kennedy of New York, the younger brother of John Kennedy, announced his own candidacy for the nomination. The charismatic Kennedy, opposed to the war, would be a formidable opponent. Besieged by the war, the

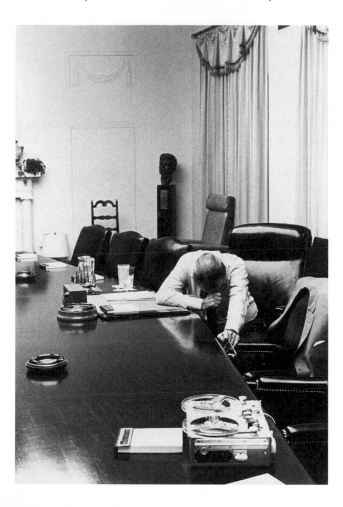

The Anguish of Vietnam President Lyndon Johnson listens to a tape-recorded report on the state of the American effort in South Vietnam, 1968.

>> Time Line

▼**1955–56**
Montgomery, Alabama, bus boycott

▼**1957**
Soviet Sputnik satellite launch

▼**1960**
Greensboro, North Carolina, lunch counter sit-in
Sharon Statement
John F. Kennedy elected president

▼**1961**
First US suborbital space flight, by Alan Shepard
Freedom Rides

▼**1962**
Port Huron Statement
Integration of University of Mississippi
Cuban Missile Crisis

▼**1963**
Birmingham, Alabama, civil rights protests
Civil rights march on Washington, DC
Assassination of John F. Kennedy

▼**1964**
Civil Rights Act of 1964
Lyndon Johnson's "War on Poverty"

economy, and the campaign, Johnson went on television the night of March 31. He announced a halt to the bombing of much of North Vietnam and indicated his willingness to talk peace with the North Vietnamese. He then announced that he would not run again for president.

Johnson painfully accepted new limits to the Great Society. Despite liberal pressure, Johnson did not have the money or the clout for new welfare programs, new initiatives to improve race relations, or even much of the space program, that symbol of liberal dreams. The Great Society was coming back down to earth.

Meanwhile, upheaval and violence tore the nation. In the first six months of 1968, students demonstrated at 101 colleges and universities. On April 4, a white man assassinated Martin Luther King Jr. in Memphis, Tennessee, where he had gone to support striking sanitation workers. King's assassination set off riots in more than 100 cities. Forty-one African Americans and five whites died.

The violence soon spread to the presidential campaign. After winning the California Democratic primary on the evening of June 5, Robert Kennedy was shot in a Los Angeles hotel by Sirhan Sirhan, a troubled Palestinian. Kennedy's death the next morning left McCarthy to contest the nomination with Vice President Hubert Humphrey, who still supported the Vietnam War. Humphrey won the nomination at the Democratic convention in Chicago in August, but the party was deeply divided. Outside the convention hall, Mayor Daley's police battled in the streets with antiwar demonstrators.

The Republican Party nominated Richard Nixon, who had lost to John Kennedy in 1960. A critic of the Great Society, Nixon promised to end the war and unify the country. Like the more conservative Reagan and Wallace, Nixon tried to exploit social divisions with promises to speak for "the forgotten Americans, the nonshouters, the nondemonstrators."

Unlike 1960, Nixon won this time. Although Humphrey made it close by repudiating Johnson's Vietnam policy, the vice president could not overcome the troubles of the Great Society. Nixon, running strongly in every region, attracted 43.4 percent of the popular vote to Humphrey's 42.7 percent and Wallace's 13.5 percent. Although the

Free Speech Movement
Tonkin Gulf incidents
Lyndon Johnson's landslide
    election as president

▼**1965**
US escalation of Vietnam War
Voting Rights Act of 1965
Water Quality Act
Watts race riot

▼**1966**
National Organization for
    Women (NOW)

▼**1967**
Air Quality Act
Stop the Draft Week

▼**1968**
Tet Offensive in Vietnam

Assassinations of Martin Luther
    King Jr. and Robert F. Kennedy
Richard Nixon elected president

▼**1975**
Surrender of South Vietnam to
    North Vietnam

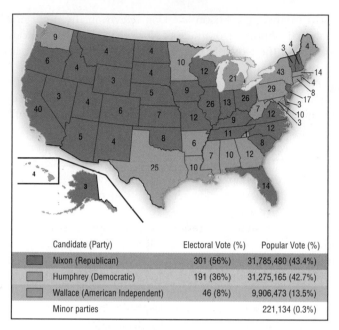

Candidate (Party)	Electoral Vote (%)	Popular Vote (%)
Nixon (Republican)	301 (56%)	31,785,480 (43.4%)
Humphrey (Democratic)	191 (36%)	31,275,165 (42.7%)
Wallace (American Independent)	46 (8%)	9,906,473 (13.5%)
Minor parties		221,134 (0.3%)

Map 28–4   The Presidential Election, 1968 Like the 1960 election, this was another close contest with widespread consequences. But this time, former vice president Richard M. Nixon was the winner.

Democrats retained control of Congress, the party's eight-year hold on the White House had been broken.

Conclusion

The upheavals of 1968 marked the end of illusions about limitless American power. John Kennedy's confident nation—able to "pay any price, bear any burden, meet any hardship, support any friend, oppose any foe"—had vanished. By 1968 the economy could no longer "pay any price." The United States could not support its friends in South Vietnam. The government could not extend the Great Society. Instead, generation, race, and gender deeply divided the nation. The assassinations of King and Robert Kennedy threatened democratic politics.

Nevertheless, the nation had changed in other ways in the 1960s. Americans did not enjoy unlimited power, but across the political spectrum they had found creative ways to change their nation. In critical respects, the United States was more democratic than ever before: African Americans and other Americans had new rights and new power. More people than ever sat, as Ezell Blair put it, at "the table of democracy." The New Frontier and the Great Society had established new protection for the poor, senior citizens, consumers, and the environment, as well as new precedents for supporting health and education.

So the 1960s fostered simultaneously a pessimistic sense of defeat and a triumphal claim to rights and empowerment. The nation would have difficulty coming to terms with these conflicting legacies.

Who, What

Review Questions

1. What were the tactics of the civil rights movement in the 1960s?

2. What were the key programs of the Great Society?

3. What was the US strategy for winning the Vietnam War?

Critical-Thinking Questions

1. Why did the Great Society come apart? Was it a success or a failure?

2. Compare liberal and radical feminism. Were these movements incompatible with each other?

3. Did the struggles and changes of the 1960s make the United States more or less democratic?

For further review materials and resource information, please visit www.oup.com/us/ofthepeople

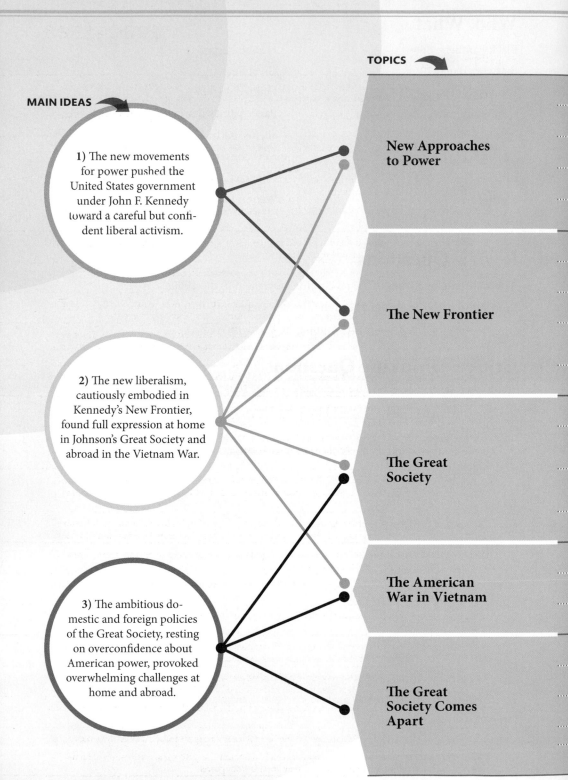

TOPICS

MAIN IDEAS

1) The new movements for power pushed the United States government under John F. Kennedy toward a careful but confident liberal activism.

2) The new liberalism, cautiously embodied in Kennedy's New Frontier, found full expression at home in Johnson's Great Society and abroad in the Vietnam War.

3) The ambitious domestic and foreign policies of the Great Society, resting on overconfidence about American power, provoked overwhelming challenges at home and abroad.

New Approaches to Power

The New Frontier

The Great Society

The American War in Vietnam

The Great Society Comes Apart

"THE TABLE OF DEMOCRACY"

1960–1968

EVENTS

Grassroots Activism for Civil Rights At the start of the 1960s, young African Americans became empowered by the discovery that grassroots tactics could effectively challenge segregation.

The New Liberalism Liberals wanted to use government power to deal with the problems of the 1950s, including race and the cold war.

The New Conservatism A young generation of activists demanded less government, more individual freedom, and a more aggressive anti-Communism.

The New Left Rejecting both liberalism and conservatism, some young activists offered a more radical demand for a more democratic nation.

The Presidential Election of 1960 John F. Kennedy's narrow victory in the 1960 presidential election signaled a turn toward the new liberalism.

Style and Substance Although Kennedy voiced the new liberals' expansive faith in American power and responsibility, his administration moved cautiously.

Civil Rights The grassroots movement for racial equality created new support for civil rights and forced the federal government to act.

Flexible Response and the Third World The Kennedy administration crafted a new strategy to counter the Soviet Union and contain Communism, particularly in Africa, Asia, and Latin America.

Two Confrontations with the Soviets Tense confrontations between the US and the Soviet Union over West Berlin and Cuba made nuclear war less likely but also left the superpowers determined to stand firm against each other.

Kennedy and Vietnam Kennedy's assassination in 1963 left unclear whether he would have continued to increase American support for the deteriorating regime in South Vietnam.

Lyndon Johnson's Mandate Kennedy's assassination and Johnson's landslide election in 1964 gave the new president a mandate to pursue the activist new liberal agenda.

"Success Without Squalor" Johnson's ambitious "Great Society" legislative program, embodying the new liberalism, included measures to eliminate poverty and segregation and to enhance the quality of life for all Americans.

Preserving Personal Freedom Reflecting the new liberalism's paradoxical commitment to individual rights, the Supreme Court issued a series of decisions that expanded civil rights, freedom of speech, and freedom of religion.

The Death of Jim Crow Driven by the intensifying struggle over civil rights in the South, the Johnson administration won legislation that ended legal segregation and secured African American voting rights.

Johnson's Decision for War Reflecting expansive liberal assumptions about American power, Johnson committed ground troops to battle in Vietnam in 1965.

Fighting a Limited War The Johnson administration decided to make the Vietnam conflict a limited war fought with conventional weapons.

The War at Home The escalation of the Vietnam War spurred an impassioned antiwar movement and divided the nation.

The Emergence of Black Power A new, more confrontational African American movement for racial equality posed challenges the liberal Great Society could not meet.

The Youth Rebellion The Great Society also faced challenges from a new youth revolt, which rejected consumerism, conventional morality, institutional authority, and the Vietnam War.

The Rebirth of the Women's Movement Liberal and radical feminist demands for equality also disrupted the Great Society.

Conservative Backlash The rebellions against the Great Society strengthened the conservative movement.

1968: A Tumultuous Year Military disappointment in Vietnam and political assassinations at home destroyed Johnson's presidency and drove the new liberals from power.

CHAPTER

29

Living with Less
1968–1980

>> "Fighting Shirley Chisholm"

At the end of the 1960s, Shirley Chisholm, an African American congresswoman from Brooklyn, New York, worried about her country. Amid the upheaval of the Great Society, the United States "sometimes seemed to be poised on the brink of racial and class war." Blacks, women, the poor, and the young demanded change, but the political system resisted. "Our representative democracy is not working," Chisholm declared. "It is ruled by a small group of old men."

It was not in Chisholm's nature to give in. Born to working-class West Indian immigrants, she had pushed her way to a master's degree and a career as an educator. Running as "Fighting Shirley Chisholm," she won election to Congress from a poor, mostly black and Puerto Rican district in 1968. In January 1972, she became the first black and first female candidate for the Democratic presidential nomination. "You've never had anyone looking like me running for President," Chisholm declared. "Other kinds of people can steer the ship of state besides white men."

Chisholm's campaign continued the 1960s battle for rights. She wanted to create a coalition of African Americans, women, and the young "to get their share of the American dream and participate in the decision-making process that governs our lives."

Chisholm campaigned hard in several primaries. But with little money and organization, she had little chance. She had to fight to win equal time on television. Black male politicians withheld their support, and black voters wondered whether an African American could really win. Her female and black supporters squabbled.

The campaign ended in defeat in California, but it enhanced her reputation. In November, she won reelection to Congress with a huge majority. An exhausted Chisholm did not regret her presidential bid. "I ran for the Presidency in order to crack a little more of the ice which has congealed to nearly immobilize our political system and demoralize people," she explained.

continued

Shirley Chisholm's failed campaign was part of a collision between Americans' aspirations for equality and new political, economic, and cultural realities. As the struggle for rights and opportunities expanded in the 1970s, the nation's economy and global influence continued to weaken. The United States no longer seemed a land of unlimited possibilities. Americans worried whether the nation could afford to meet everyone's needs in an age of dwindling jobs and resources. As a magazine concluded, Americans were "Learning to Live with Less."

The result was not the "racial and class war" that Chisholm feared. But neither did the liberal Great Society give way to a stable new order dominated by one party or ideology. Instead, workers, employers, politicians, and families struggled with the consequences of limited resources and power. While Americans puzzled over the relationship between the economy and government and between the nation and the world, the political system broke down in scandal and failure.

A New Crisis: Economic Decline

During the social, political, and military crises of the 1960s, Americans had largely taken the economy for granted. Prosperous and growing, the United States had seemed destined to remain the world's preeminent economic power. But the economy had faltered as the Great Society came apart. The failings of business, government, and economists, a shortage of oil, intensifying foreign competition, and the multinational strategies of giant corporations combined to weaken the foundations of prosperity. By the end of the 1970s, the United States seemed to be in critical economic decline.

Weakness at Home

Signs of economic weakness were almost everywhere in the 1970s. Although the economy continued to grow, corporate profits and workers' productivity fell off. Unemployment increased; inflation, which usually dropped when unemployment rose, also increased. At best, the economy seemed stagnant. The unprecedented combination of high unemployment and high inflation led to the coining of a new word—*stagflation*—to describe the nation's predicament (see Table 29–1).

Corporations were partially responsible for the weak economy. Corporate leaders had tended to maximize short-term profits at the cost of the long-term health of their companies. Some companies had not put enough of their earnings into research, development, and new equipment. As a result, some American products seemed less innovative and reliable. Detroit's automobiles, so attractive and advanced in the 1950s, now struck consumers as unglamorous, inefficient, and poorly made. Ford's new Pinto sedan had to be recalled because its fuel tank was prone to explode.

Long an emblem of security and stability, corporations now appeared as vulnerable as the Pinto. In 1970, the Penn Central Railroad became the largest corporation in American history to go bankrupt. That year, only federal aid saved Lockheed Aircraft from also going under. The federal government also played a part in the nation's predicament. Mas-

Table 29-1 Stagflation in the 1970s

Year	Inflation % Change	Unemployment % Change	Combined* % Change
1970	5.9	4.9	10.8
1971	4.3	5.9	10.2
1972	3.3	5.6	8.9
1973	6.2	4.9	11.1
1974	11.0	5.6	16.6
1975	9.1	8.5	17.6
1976	5.8	7.7	13.5
1977	6.5	7.1	13.6
1978	7.7	6.1	13.8
1979	11.3	5.8	17.1
1980	13.5	7.1	20.6

*"Combined" means annual percentage changes of inflation and unemployment.

Source: *Statistical Abstract of the United States*, 1984, pp. 375–76, 463; tables 624–25, 760. (1971 inflation data from *Statistical Abstract*, 1973, p. 348, table 569.)

sive federal spending had stimulated the economy from the 1940s to the 1960s but did not have the same effect in the 1970s. Some analysts claimed that Washington had diverted too much of the nation's talent and resources from the private sector to military projects during the cold war. In addition, the government's huge expenditures for the Vietnam War promoted inflation.

Economists did not give federal policy makers much help. In the 1960s, liberal economists had been sure they understood the secret to prosperity. The new problem of stagflation left them baffled. "The rules of economics," admitted the chairman of the Federal Reserve, "are not working quite the way they used to."

The Energy Crisis

An emerging energy crisis intensified economic problems. By 1974, the nation had to import over a third of its oil, particularly from the Middle East. The energy needs of the United States and other western countries empowered the Organization of the Petroleum Exporting Countries (OPEC), a group of third world nations that had joined together to get higher prices for their oil. In October 1973, war broke out between Israel and a coalition of Arab nations, including Egypt and Syria. Arab members of OPEC refused to send petroleum to the United States and other nations that supported Israel in the conflict. OPEC soon raised oil prices nearly 400 percent.

The effect of the oil shortage spread well beyond gas stations. In some states, truck drivers blockaded highways to protest the high cost of fuel and low speed limits. Lack of fuel grounded some airline flights. Heating oil for homes and businesses was in short supply. Some people could not afford to heat their homes. Although the Arabs ended the oil embargo in March 1974, the underlying energy problem remained.

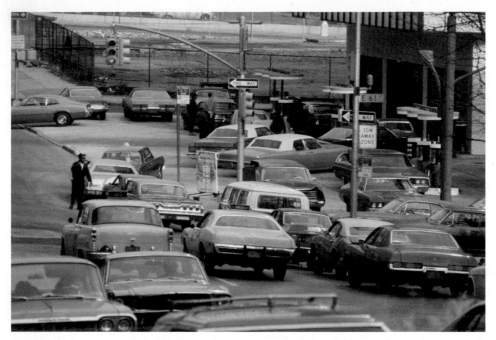

The Energy Crisis Motorists crowd around an open gas station, New York City, December 1973.

Competition Abroad

Weakened by trouble at home, the United States was vulnerable to increasingly tough competition from abroad. Thanks to American aid after World War II, Japan and Western European countries rose to create efficient, up-to-date industries. By the 1970s, these nations rivaled the United States, even in the American market.

The rise of Japan was the most dramatic. For decades, Americans had derided Japanese goods. By the 1970s, Japan's modern factories turned out high-quality products. Japanese televisions and other electronic goods filled American homes. Japanese cars—small, well made, and fuel efficient—attracted American buyers worried about the high price of gas.

Because of such competition, the United States fell back in the global economic race. In 1950, the nation had accounted for 40 percent of the value of all the goods and services produced around the world. By 1970 that figure was down to 23 percent. By the end of the 1970s, the United States imported more manufactured goods than it exported.

The Multinationals

Multinational corporations—firms with factories and other operations in several nations—played a key role in the economic crisis. Taking advantage of new technologies and lower trade barriers, US and West European corporations had moved aggressively into global markets after World War II. Multinationals accounted for about 15 percent of the world's annual gross product, and the biggest had annual sales larger than the annual product of some countries.

AMERICA AND THE WORLD

>> **Carl Gerstacker's Dream**

In February 1972, Carl A. Gerstacker, chairman of the multinational Dow Chemical Company, confessed his secret fantasy to an audience of executives, economists, and policy makers at a White House conference. "I have long dreamed of buying an island owned by no nation," Gerstacker revealed. But this sober executive did not plan to escape to his island for a life of leisure. Instead, Gerstacker wanted to take Dow Chemical along. "If we were located on such truly neutral ground," he explained, "we could then really operate in the United States as US citizens, in Japan as Japanese citizens, and in Brazil as Brazilians." The multinational would effectively be on its own, free to do as it pleased without interference from the US government.

Gerstacker's audience probably agreed. By the 1970s, the leaders of American multinationals felt surprisingly few ties to their home country. "We are not an American company," a US oil executive told a congressional committee. So unattached to the United States or any other country, multinational leaders did not believe their companies should let patriotism interfere with business. As Carl Gerstacker concluded, giant corporations were becoming not so much multinational or international as "anational" and "nationless."

Multinational leaders seemed to prefer a world with no nations at all. Eager for a unified global economy, they felt that governments only got in the way. They imposed tariffs, limited trade, taxed profits, dictated working conditions, nationalized resources, and started wars. "The world's political structures are completely obsolete," fumed Jacques Maisonrouge, a French-born vice president of IBM. "The multinational corporation today is a force that can serve global needs of mankind far better than the medieval concept of nation states," proclaimed José Béjarano, vice president of the Latin American division of Xerox. Of course, heads of the multinationals conveniently forgot how often their firms had turned to the US government for diplomatic and military support when other nations threatened their investments.

Few Americans shared the vision of men like Béjarano. The United States and other nation-states, all fueled by intense patriotism, were not about to disappear—or leave the multinationals alone. As Gerstacker acknowledged, US tax laws made it impossible for Dow Chemical to move to its island paradise. For their impact on the world around them, the multinational executives were ahead of their time. With the certainty of a prophet, John J Powers, president of the drug company Pfizer, insisted a unified global economy "is no idealistic pipe dream but a hard-headed prediction." Time would tell.

US firms made up the majority of the largest multinationals in the 1970s. As Americans struggled, US multinationals still earned large profits because of their lucrative overseas units. Not surprisingly, these American firms rapidly expanded abroad. In 1957, just 9 percent of American investments went abroad; by 1972, the figure had reached 25 percent.

The multinationals' most controversial foreign investment was the transfer of manufacturing from the United States to nations with lower wages and less restrictive labor laws. As corporations shifted production to plants in Mexico or Asia, American plants closed, with stunning job losses. The combination of overseas production and foreign competition was devastating. In 1954, US companies had made 75 percent of the world's televisions. Twenty years later, they produced less than 25 percent—and almost all of that production took place in Mexico and overseas.

Multinational executives argued that investment abroad increased jobs and prosperity in the United States. Capital invested in Mexico and Asia came back home, they insisted, as dividends to stockholders and tax payments to the government.

The Impact of Decline

Economic decline began to reshape life in the United States in the 1970s. It seemed as if the Industrial Revolution were being reversed. As factories closed, Americans witnessed the deindustrialization of their country. Huge steel plants, the symbol of American industrial might, stood empty. In the 1970s, most new jobs were in the sales and retail sectors, intensifying a 20-year trend toward a service-centered economy. America, a union official lamented, was turning into "a nation of hamburger stands."

For workers, the effects of deindustrialization were crushing. Heavy industry had been the stronghold of the labor movement. By the late 1970s, less than one in four workers belonged to a union, and organized labor lost power and influence.

The loss of unionized industrial jobs eroded workers' incomes. After rising from the 1950s into the 1960s, workers' spendable income began to drop. To keep up, more and more women took full-time jobs outside the home: the percentage of women in the workforce, 36 percent in 1960, rose to 50 percent in 1980—the highest level in American history to that time. Many Americans could not find work, however. As the huge baby boom generation came of age, the economy did not produce enough jobs. The unemployment rate, as low as 2.8 percent in 1969, jumped to a high of 9 percent in 1975.

> All I want is my
> damn job back.
>
> MARY FARMER KINNEY,
> A LAID-OFF
> AFRICAN AMERICAN
> AUTOWORKER IN
> HAMTRAMCK, MICHIGAN,
> 1979

Economic decline accelerated the transformation of America's regions. The energy crisis and deindustrialization sped up the shift of people and power from north to south and east to west (see Map 29–1). With its cold, snowy winters, the North was especially vulnerable to the oil embargo and higher energy prices. America's Snowbelt now seemed a less attractive place to live and do business. In the 1970s, empty, decaying factories made the Northeast and the Midwest America's "Rustbelt."

Fleeing deindustrialization and high prices, many northerners moved south to the band of states ranging from Florida to California. As this Sunbelt boomed, farms became suburbs, and cities such as Orlando, Houston, Phoenix, and San Diego boomed. Texas

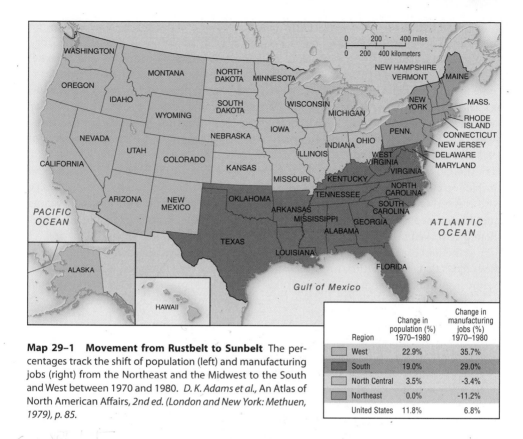

Map 29–1   Movement from Rustbelt to Sunbelt The percentages track the shift of population (left) and manufacturing jobs (right) from the Northeast and the Midwest to the South and West between 1970 and 1980. *D. K. Adams et al., An Atlas of North American Affairs, 2nd ed. (London and New York: Methuen, 1979), p. 85.*

Region	Change in population (%) 1970–1980	Change in manufacturing jobs (%) 1970–1980
West	22.9%	35.7%
South	19.0%	29.0%
North Central	3.5%	-3.4%
Northeast	0.0%	-11.2%
United States	11.8%	6.8%

and the southwestern states, rich in oil and natural gas reserves, profited from the energy crisis. The Sunbelt was home to new high-technology businesses: aerospace firms, electronics companies, and defense contractors. The Sunbelt was also at the cutting edge of the service economy, which was focused on leisure and consumption. More retirees moved to Florida than to any other state. Tourists flocked to California's Disneyland and Florida's Disney World. They gambled their money in Las Vegas.

Confronting Decline: Nixon's Strategy

Richard Nixon was the first president to confront the decline of America's prosperity and power. He recognized that the failed war in Vietnam marked the end of America's cold war pretensions and that the American economy had weakened. Despite his long opposition to Communism and the New Deal, Nixon was a pragmatist, open to new realities and approaches.

A New Foreign Policy

The president and his national security advisor, Henry Kissinger, still regarded Communism as a menace and saw the cold war rivalry between the United States and the Soviet Union as the defining reality of the modern world. However, Nixon and Kissinger understood that the relative decline of American power dictated a new approach to the cold war.

The twin pillars of the new foreign policy were the Nixon Doctrine and détente. In July 1969, the president announced that the United States "cannot—and will not— conceive all the plans, design all the programs, execute all the decisions and undertake all the defense of the free nations of the world." America would continue to provide a nuclear umbrella, but its allies would have to defend themselves against insurgencies and invasions. This Nixon Doctrine was a repudiation of the interventionist Truman Doctrine of 1947 (see Chapter 26).

The United States also pursued a new relationship with the Soviet Union and the People's Republic of China. Nixon and Kissinger wanted to lessen the cost of the rivalry with these two Communist nuclear powers. Separate agreements with the two nations might keep them from combining forces against the United States. Nixon and Kissinger therefore worked to establish *détente,* the relaxation of tensions.

At the start of Nixon's presidency, the United States had not recognized the legitimacy of the People's Republic of China. Instead, America supported the Communists' bitter foes, the Nationalist Chinese regime on Taiwan. In February 1972, Nixon became the first American president to go to mainland China. He gave the Chinese leaders what they most wanted—a promise that the United States would eventually withdraw its troops from Taiwan. The two sides also made clear they opposed any Soviet attempt to dominate Asia.

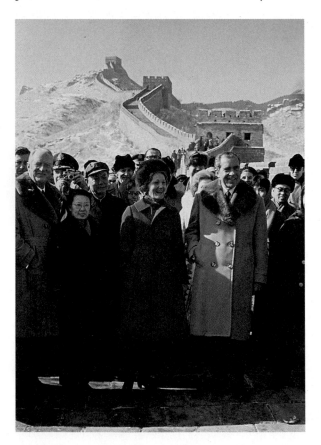

Nixon's trip brought American policy in line with the reality of the 1970s and underscored the gradual end of anti-Communist hysteria in America. By design, the trip also left the Soviets with the frightening possibility of a Chinese-American alliance.

Nixon did not want a confrontation with the Soviets, the only power that could destroy America with nuclear weapons. The United States no longer had clear military superiority. Instead, he sought détente. Above all, he wanted the Soviets to agree to limit their long-

Détente at the Great Wall of China, 1972 President Nixon, with his wife, Pat, became the first American president to visit mainland China.

range or strategic nuclear arsenals. The Soviets also wished to reduce the cost and danger of the cold war and to counter Nixon's overture to the Chinese. Moreover, the Soviets needed American grain to feed their people.

The two sides began talks on the Strategic Arms Limitation Treaty (SALT I) in 1969. In May 1972, three months after his trip to China, Nixon became the first American president to travel to Moscow, where he signed the SALT treaty, limiting for five years the number of each nation's nuclear missiles. An Anti–Ballistic Missile (ABM) treaty sharply limited the number of defensive missiles the two sides could deploy. Although they did not stop the arms race, the treaties symbolized the American and Soviet agreement that "there is no alternative to . . . peaceful coexistence."

Ending the Vietnam War

Nixon and Kissinger sought better relations with the Soviet Union and the People's Republic of China in part to pressure the North Vietnamese to accept a peace agreement and end the Vietnam War. Nixon knew the United States could not win the war. Meanwhile, the war divided the American people and undermined American prestige and power around the world. But Nixon did not want to the United States to look weak.

To appease public opinion, Nixon began to bring American soldiers home in 1969. With US forces reduced, Nixon needed a new strategy to persuade North Vietnam to accept the existence of South Vietnam. He turned to a policy known as "Vietnamization," in which the South Vietnamese were encouraged to defend themselves. But the South Vietnamese military alone could not beat back the Communists.

Accordingly, Nixon turned to US airpower to support South Vietnamese troops and intimidate the North Vietnamese. In March 1969, he authorized B-52 raids on North Vietnamese sanctuaries in Cambodia. Because bombing this neutral country might outrage American and world opinion, the raids were kept secret. Neither raids nor secret negotiations with North Vietnamese diplomats succeeded. Meanwhile, news of the secret bombings leaked out. In October, millions of Americans participated in Moratorium Day, a dramatic break from business as usual, to protest the war. In November, more than 250,000 people staged a "March Against Death" in Washington. That month, Americans learned about one of the most troubling episodes of the war. On March 16, 1968, US soldiers had killed between 200 and 500 unarmed South Vietnamese women, children, and old men in the hamlet of My Lai. This atrocity led to the 1970 court-martial and eventual conviction of Lieutenant William Calley Jr. for mass murder.

Demonstrations did not stop the president from using violence to force a peace agreement. When General Lon Nol, the new pro-American leader of Cambodia, appealed for aid to stop a Communist insurgency, a joint United States–South Vietnamese force invaded Cambodia to look for North Vietnamese troops in April 1970. The Cambodian invasion sparked demonstrations on campuses across the country. On May 4, National Guard troops fired at unarmed protestors at Kent State University in Ohio. Four students died. Ten days later, state police killed two African American students at Jackson State College in Mississippi. These deaths intensified the outrage over Cambodia. Students went out on strike at about 450 campuses.

Some Americans, angered by these protests, mobilized in support of the president and the war. In New York City, construction workers attacked student demonstrators.

Nixon Expands the Vietnam War US soldiers and helicopters operate in Cambodia in the spring of 1970.

"The country is virtually on the edge of a spiritual—and perhaps physical—breakdown," New York's mayor lamented.

As American troop withdrawals continued, the war and the peace negotiations dragged on. Meanwhile, the *New York Times* began publishing the so-called Pentagon Papers, a secret government history of American involvement in Vietnam. The documents, which revealed that the Johnson administration had misled the country, further undermined support for the war. The Nixon administration tried unsuccessfully to persuade the Supreme Court to block publication of the papers.

Unable to secure a peace agreement, Nixon pressed North Vietnam harder for a settlement. When the North Vietnamese army invaded South Vietnam in March 1972, the president ordered Operation Linebacker, an aerial attack on North Vietnam. When negotiations stalled, he intensified the air raids in December. On January 27, 1973, negotiators signed a peace agreement in Paris. For the United States, at least, the Vietnam War was over.

Nixon had promised "peace with honor," but the agreement did not guarantee the survival of South Vietnam. The cease-fire came at a heavy cost. Twenty thousand Americans and more than 600,000 North and South Vietnamese soldiers had died since Nixon took office in 1969. The number of civilian casualties will never be known. Nixon had ended US participation in the Vietnam War, but his critics asked whether so flawed an agreement had been worth four years of fighting.

Chile and the Middle East

Détente, a practical accommodation with Soviet power, did not mean that the Nixon administration accepted the rise of potentially hostile regimes. To stop the spread of socialism and Communism, Nixon, like the presidents before him, was willing to subvert a democratically elected government and tolerate an authoritarian one. In 1970, he ordered the CIA to block the election of Salvador Allende, a Marxist, as president of Chile. Allende was elected anyway. "I don't see why we need to stand by and watch a country go communist due to the irresponsibility of its own people," Kissinger fumed. The CIA then helped destabilize Allende's regime by aiding right-wing parties, driving up the price of bread, and encouraging demonstrations. When a military coup deposed Allende in 1973, the United States denied responsibility and offered financial aid to the new military dictator, General Augusto Pinochet.

In the Middle East, the Nixon administration also displayed both its hostility to Communism and its inability to shape events decisively. In October 1973, on Yom Kippur, the holiest day of the Jewish calendar, Egypt and Syria attacked Israel in revenge for their defeat in the Six-Day War of 1967, when Israel occupied territory in Egypt, Syria, and Jordan. After the United States sent critical supplies to Israel, Arab countries responded with the oil embargo. Meanwhile, the Soviets supplied the Arabs and pressed for a role in the region. Determined to keep out the Soviet Union, Nixon put American nuclear forces on alert. Kissinger mediated between the combatants, who agreed to pull back their troops in January 1974. The embargo ended, but American weakness was obvious. Supporting Israel, the United States still needed the Arabs' oil. Nixon and Kissinger held back the Soviets but could not bring peace to the Middle East.

Taming Big Government

The problem of decline, addressed in Nixon's foreign policy, proved more difficult to handle at home. Nixon took office with the conventional Republican goals of taming big government. He wanted a balanced budget and a reduction in federal power.

So Nixon cut spending for programs, including defense. The fate of the space program epitomized the new budgetary realities. On July 20, 1969, a landing module touched down on the moon. When astronaut Neil Armstrong set foot on the surface, the United States had beaten the Soviets to the moon, as President John F. Kennedy had vowed. There still seemed no limit to what Americans could do. There were, however, limits to what the space program could do. Congress slashed NASA's budget.

In 1969, Nixon called for a New Federalism, which would return "a greater share of control to state and local governments and to the people." Three years later, the administration persuaded Congress to pass a revenue-sharing plan that allowed state and local governments to spend funds collected by the federal government.

Nixon took the same pragmatic approach to domestic problems that he did to foreign affairs. He left popular New Deal and Great Society programs largely intact. Despite his budget cuts, the government kept spending vast amounts of money. By 1971, the cost of big government, combined with the unsettled economy, had produced a huge, unRepublican budget deficit.

The president did try to reform the federal welfare system put in place by the New Deal. Like many Republican conservatives, Nixon believed that welfare made the federal bureaucracy too large and the poor too dependent. His administration tried to replace the largest federal welfare program, Aid to Families with Dependent Children, with a controversial system inspired by presidential aide Daniel Patrick Moynihan, a Harvard sociologist. Moynihan's Family Assistance Plan would have provided poor families a guaranteed minimum annual income, but it also would have required the heads of poor households to accept any jobs available. Opposed by both liberals and conservatives, the program failed to pass Congress.

Meanwhile, the administration went along with several liberal initiatives expanding federal regulatory powers. By the 1970s, many Americans worried that corporations did not protect workers, consumers, or the environment. A grassroots environmental movement grew rapidly, particularly on college campuses, and on April 22, 1970, tens of millions of Americans celebrated the first Earth Day with teach-ins, demonstrations, and cleanup campaigns. Liberals in Congress responded to popular opinion with three new federal regulatory agencies: the Environmental Protection Agency (EPA), the Occupational Safety and Health Administration (OSHA), and the Consumer Product Safety Commission. These agencies enhanced the government's power over corporations, as did laws to safeguard coastlines and endangered species and limit strip-mining of coal, air and water pollution, and pesticide use.

An Uncertain Economic Policy

Nixon believed government should not interfere much in the economy. But high inflation, rising unemployment, and falling corporate profits tested his commitment to Republican orthodoxy. He was unable to persuade business to control price increases and organized labor to limit wage demands.

Meanwhile, the US dollar was in crisis. Since the Bretton Woods conference (see Chapter 25), many nations had tied the value of their currencies to the dollar. The value of the dollar, in turn, had been supported by the US commitment to give an ounce of gold in return for 35 dollars. This commitment to the gold standard had stabilized the international financial system and helped spur global economic development for decades. But by the 1970s, the weakening US economy had undermined the dollar: strong European economies had too many dollars and too little confidence in the United States, and the US government didn't have enough gold. If other countries demanded gold for their dollars, Washington would be unable to pay, and panic would follow.

Confronting inflation, monetary crisis, and economic weakness, Nixon announced his New Economic Policy in August 1971. To prevent the breakdown of the monetary system, the president took the United States off the gold standard by ending the exchange of gold for dollars. To strengthen US producers against foreign competitors, Nixon lowered the value of the dollar and slapped new tariffs on imports; now American goods would sell more cheaply abroad and foreign goods would cost more in the United States. To slow inflation, he authorized a freeze on wages and prices.

The New Economic Policy did strengthen the international monetary system and help US producers. But wage and price controls did not solve the underlying problems that caused inflation. The cost of the Vietnam War and the Arab oil embargo continued to drive up prices. Deindustrialization continued, too.

Refusing to Settle for Less: Struggles for Rights

Despite the troubled economy, many Americans, like Shirley Chisholm, refused to settle for less. In the late 1960s and 1970s, African Americans and women continued their struggles for the rights and opportunities they had long been denied. Their example inspired other disadvantaged groups to demand recognition. Mexican Americans, Native Americans, and gays and lesbians organized and demonstrated for their causes. But other Americans, worried about preserving their own advantages in an era of limited resources, were often unwilling to support these new demands. At times, the result was almost the "racial and class war" that Chisholm dreaded.

African Americans' Struggle for Racial Justice

As the civil rights struggle continued, attention focused on two relatively new and controversial means of promoting racial equality—affirmative action and mandatory school busing. First ordered by the Johnson administration, affirmative action required businesses, universities, and other institutions receiving federal money to provide opportunities for women and nonwhites. Supporters viewed the policy as a way to make up for past and present discrimination. Opponents argued that affirmative action was itself a form of discrimination that reduced opportunities for whites, particularly white men.

Nixon, despite his commitment to limited government, generally supported affirmative action. His administration developed the Philadelphia Plan, which encouraged the construction industry to meet targets for hiring minority workers. In 1978, the Supreme Court offered qualified support for affirmative action with its decision in *Regents of the University of California v. Allan Bakke*. The justices ruled that the medical school of the University of California at Davis could not deny admission to Bakke, a white applicant with better grades and test scores than some minority applicants accepted by the school. Although the court barred schools from using fixed admissions quotas for different racial groups, it did allow race to be used as an admissions criterion. By the end of the 1970s, affirmative action had become an important means of increasing diversity in schools and other institutions.

School busing was more controversial than affirmative action. By the late 1960s, the Supreme Court had become impatient with delays in integrating the nation's schools. Even in the North, with no *de jure*, or legal, segregation, there was still extensive de facto segregation. In *Swann v. Charlotte-Mecklenburg Board of Education* in 1971, the court upheld the mandatory busing of thousands of children to desegregate schools in the Charlotte, North Carolina, area. But many Americans opposed busing, because they did not want integration or did not want children taken out of neighborhood schools.

Nixon sided with the opponents of busing. Privately ordering his aides to enforce busing less vigorously, he publicly called for a "moratorium" on new busing plans. Some communities implemented busing peacefully. Others faced protest and turmoil. In 1974, a federal court ordered busing in Boston. When the white-dominated local school committee refused to comply, a federal judge imposed a busing plan on the community. Working-class and lower-middle-class whites formed Restore Our Alienated Rights (ROAR) and other organizations to protest plans to bus students between the predominantly African American neighborhood of Roxbury and the largely Irish American neighborhood of South Boston. In "Southie," whites taunted and injured black students. Although violence spread through the fall, the busing plan went into effect. With busing and affirmative action, the civil rights movement seemed to have reached its limits: many Americans were unwilling to go any further to ensure racial equality.

Women's Liberation

By the 1970s, the movement for women's liberation was flourishing. Many women came together in "consciousness-raising" groups to discuss a broad range of issues in their lives. To commemorate the 50th anniversary of the women's suffrage amendment to the Constitution, thousands marched in the Women's Strike for Equality on August 26, 1970.

AMERICAN LANDSCAPE

>> City Hall Plaza, Boston

On Monday morning, September 9, 1974, 8,000 to 10,000 whites gathered in the barren red brick plaza flanked by two drab, hulking structures of concrete and glass—Boston City Hall and the John F. Kennedy Federal Building. It was a stark setting for a rally that dramatized equally stark divisions of race, class, and politics in 1970s America.

The crowd, mostly working- and lower-middle-class white ethnic women, had come from Boston neighborhoods to protest the court-ordered busing due to start with the new school year in three days. As many as 1,500 protestors had come from South Boston, the predominantly Irish American center of opposition to the busing plan.

Crowd members were angry that their children would be bused to black-majority schools in Roxbury while black pupils would come into white-majority neighborhoods. Like the civil rights activists of the 1960s, these whites felt strongly that their own rights had been denied. The sponsor of the rally was the group Restore Our Alienated Rights—ROAR. "With Liberty and Justice for ALL?" one banner asked pointedly. Some protestors, evoking the Boston Tea Party of the Revolutionary era, threw teabags into the plaza's fountain and called for "the Second Revolution." "We're not ready to quit," insisted the moderator, Rita Graul of South Boston.

The protestors, most of them Democrats, were also angry at their own party and its leadership. They blamed the activist liberalism of the Democratic-sponsored Great Society for this intrusion of federal power into their neighborhoods. The crowd's anger even extended to one of their own, Senator Ted Kennedy, who, despite his Irish American heritage and long-time family ties to Boston, supported civil rights and busing. There were "Impeach Kennedy" signs in the crowd. One of the speakers wore a chicken mask representing "the white chicken, Sen. Kennedy."

To everyone's surprise, the "white chicken" suddenly turned up on the platform. But the protestors would not let Kennedy speak. One of the organizers pulled the plug on his microphone. Some crowd members turned their backs on him. "Give us our rights back," the protestors demanded. "God Bless America," they sang. "You're a disgrace to the Irish," some people yelled. "Why don't you put your one-legged son on a bus for Roxbury," one crowd member called. "Yeah, let your daughter get bused there so she can get raped." A crowd member even shouted, "Why don't you let them shoot you like they shot your two brothers."

"Why won't they listen?" Kennedy asked. One of the organizers, Thomas O'Connell, answered that "maybe now he knew what it was like to be deprived of his rights—the way we've been deprived of our rights." Stone-faced, Kennedy left the platform and headed toward his office in the building named for his brothers. Security held back angry protestors, who heckled him, turned thumbs down, and threw eggs and tomatoes. As he entered the building, crowd members banged on the big plate glass windows until one of them shattered.

Later, Kennedy told reporters, "They're not bigots." "We mourned President Kennedy," a woman declared outside the building. "We won't mourn this one." Three days later, whites began to boycott the schools.

The women's liberation movement, like the struggle for African American equality, was diverse. Liberal feminist groups, such as the National Organization for Women (NOW), concentrated on equal public opportunities for women. Radical feminists focused on a broader range of private and public issues. Oppression, they insisted, took place in the bedroom and the kitchen, as well as the school and the workplace. Some radical feminists, influenced by the New Left, blamed women's plight on capitalism; others traced it to men. Cultural feminists insisted that women's culture was different from and superior to male culture and felt that women should create their own separate institutions. Some lesbian feminists went further to argue that women should avoid heterosexual relationships.

Linking the private and personal with the public and political, the women's movement fought on many fronts. More women who married decided to keep their own names rather than adopt their husbands'. Rather than identifying themselves by marital status, many women abandoned the forms of address "Miss" or "Mrs." for "Ms." Women's liberation made its mark on the media. In 1972, Gloria Steinem began the feminist magazine *Ms*. On television, popular sitcoms portrayed independent women.

In the 1970s, feminists focused especially on three public issues—access to abortion, equal treatment in schools and workplaces, and passage of the Equal Rights Amendment (ERA) to the Constitution. Long effectively outlawed, abortions were generally unavailable or unsafe. In *Roe v. Wade* in 1973, the Supreme Court ruled a Texas antiabortion law unconstitutional on the grounds that it violated the "right to privacy" guaranteed by the Ninth and Fourteenth Amendments. With this decision, abortion became legal and widely available.

Like the civil rights movement, the women's movement demanded equal treatment in schools and workplaces. At first reluctant, the Nixon administration opened up federal employment to women and pressed colleges and businesses to end discriminatory practices. In 1972, Congress approved Title IX of the Higher Education Act, which required schools and universities receiving federal funds to give equal opportunities to women and men in admissions, athletics, and other programs.

The women's movement also continued the struggle to enact the ERA. "Equality of rights under the law," the amendment read, "shall not be denied or abridged by the United States or by any State on account of sex." In 1972 Congress passed the ERA. If 38 states ratified the amendment within 7 years, it would become law. But after 28 states ratified within a year, the ERA met heavy opposition. To male critics, feminists were a "small band of braless bubbleheads." Fearing that equal rights would end their femininity and their protected legal status, conservative women, such as activist Phyllis Schlafly, campaigned effectively against the ERA. Although more states ratified the amendment, some rescinded their votes, and the ERA never became law (see Map 29-2).

The ERA's defeat underscored the challenges to the women's movement. Women still did not have full equality, but they had more control over their bodies, more access to education, and more opportunity in the workplace.

Mexican Americans and "Brown Power"

In the 1960s and 1970s, Mexican Americans, the nation's second largest racial minority, developed a new self-consciousness. Proudly identifying themselves as Chicanos, they organized to protest poverty and discrimination.

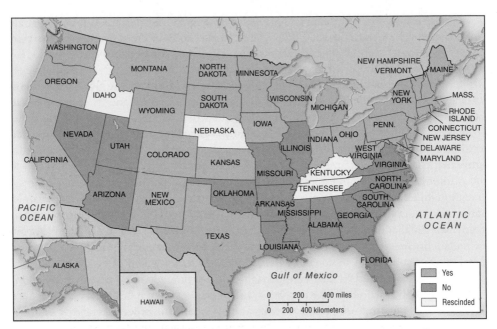

Map 29–2   The Equal Rights Amendment (ERA) Despite substantial support in state legislatures across the country, the ERA faced crippling opposition in the mountain West and the South.

Despite efforts to keep out Mexican immigrants, the Mexican American population grew rapidly. By 1980, at least 7 million Americans claimed Mexican heritage. The great majority lived in Arizona, California, Colorado, New Mexico, and Texas, most in urban areas and more than 1 million in Los Angeles. Winning more skilled and white-collar jobs, Mexican Americans still earned much less as a group than did Anglos (white Americans of non-Hispanic descent). One in four Mexican American families lived in poverty in the mid-1970s.

Stereotyped as lazy and shiftless, Mexican Americans faced racism and discrimination. Schools in their neighborhoods were underfunded. In some California schools, Mexican American children could not eat with Anglo children. California and Texas prohibited teaching in Spanish.

Gerrymandering diluted the political power of Mexican American voters. Despite its large Mexican American population, Los Angeles had no Hispanic city council member at the end of the 1960s. The justice system often treated Mexican Americans unfairly.

Poverty and discrimination marked Mexican American life. In cities, many Mexican Americans crowded into *barrios*, run-down neighborhoods. In the countryside, many lived without hot water or toilets. Infant mortality was high and life expectancy low. Nationwide, almost half the Mexican American population was functionally illiterate.

Encouraged by the civil rights movement, Mexican Americans protested against poverty and injustice for migrant farm workers. In the fertile San Joaquin Valley of California, the Mexican Americans who labored for powerful fruit growers earned as little as 10 cents an hour and lived in miserable conditions. César Chávez, a former migrant worker influenced by Martin Luther King Jr.'s nonviolent creed, helped them organize what became the United Farm Workers of America. In 1965 the union went on strike. The growers, accusing Chávez of Communist ties, called for police, strikebreakers, intimidation, and violence. Chávez's nonviolent tactics, which included a 25-day hunger strike in 1968, gradually appealed to liberals and other Americans. He also led a successful nationwide consumer boycott against grapes. Under this pressure, the growers began to settle with the union.

While King inspired Chávez, the nationalism of the Black Power movement spurred other Mexican Americans. In New Mexico, Reies López "Tiger" Tijerina, a former preacher, created the Alianza Federal de Mercedes (Federal Alliance of Land Grants) to take back land that the United States had supposedly stolen from Mexicans.

Mexican American activism flourished in the late 1960s. In East Los Angeles, the Brown Berets, a paramilitary group, showed the influence of the Black Panthers. In California in 1969, college students began the Movimiento Estudiantil Chicano de Aztlán (Chicano Student Movement of Aztlán, known by its initials, MEChA, or the word for "match" in the Spanish of Mexican Americans). MEChA was meant to kindle social change for Chicanos. In Crystal City, Texas, a boycott of Anglo businesses led to the formation of La Raza Unida ("The Unified Race"), a political party that won control of the local school board in 1970. These protests and organizations reflected a strong sense of pride and a powerful desire to preserve the Mexican American heritage. Activists asserted group identity by referring to Mexican Americans as "Chicanos." "A Chicano," said reporter Rubén Salazar, "is a Mexican-American with a non-Anglo image of himself."

Demanding bilingual education, Mexican American studies, equal opportunity, and affirmative action, activists fought for empowerment, for what some called "Brown Power." On the whole, white Americans paid less attention to Chicano activism than to African Americans' struggles. But Mexican American activists made important gains, including the end of state bans on teaching in Spanish.

Asian American Activism

Asian Americans also pressed for rights and recognition. Like Mexican Americans, they confronted a history of discrimination in the United States and faced denigrating stereotypes and hurtful epithets.

The small size of the Asian American population limited organization and protest, but the Immigration Act of 1965 made possible waves of new Asian immigration. By 1980 America was home to more than 3 million Asian immigrants, including 812,000 Chinese, 781,000 Filipinos, and 716,000 Japanese. Overall, there were 3.7 million Americans of Asian descent, mostly in the Pacific states and in cities.

Asian American activism followed the pattern of other minority movements. By the late 1960s, Asian Americans demonstrated a new ethnic self-consciousness and pride. Many Asian Americans saw themselves not only as Chinese or Japanese but also as members of a broader, pan-Asian group.

In 1968, the Asian American Political Alliance (AAPA) emerged on the campus of the University of California at Berkeley to unite Chinese, Japanese, and Filipino students. In response to demands by Asian American students, colleges and universities established

Asian studies courses and programs by the end of the 1970s. Beyond campuses, in 1974 protests forced the hiring of Chinese American workers to help build the Confucius Plaza housing complex in New York City's Chinatown. In San Francisco, activists brought suit against the public school system on behalf of 1,800 Chinese pupils. In *Lau v. Nichols* in 1974, the Supreme Court declared that school systems had to provide bilingual instruction for non-English-speaking students.

In the 1970s, Japanese groups demanded compensation for the US government's internment of Japanese Americans during World War II. In 1976 Washington rescinded Executive Order 9066, the 1942 directive that led to internment, but did not make a more comprehensive settlement until 1988.

Asian Americans, like Chicanos, made only limited gains by 1980. However, with a new consciousness and new organizations, Asian Americans had also forced real social change.

The Struggle for Native American Rights

After many years of decline and stagnation, the Indian population had grown rapidly since World War II (see Map 29–3). By 1970, there were nearly 800,000 Native Americans, half of whom lived on reservations. Divided into about 175 tribes and other groups, Native Americans were united by poverty and persistent discrimination. They had the lowest average family income of any ethnic group and faced high unemployment rates and substandard schools.

Native American life was shaped by the unique relationship with the federal government. Many resented the Bureau of Indian Affairs (BIA) for patronizing and exploiting tribes. Like African American and Mexican American separatists, some Native Americans saw themselves as a nation apart. Calling themselves "prisoners of war," they struck an aggressive stance, expressed in such slogans as "Custer Had It Coming" and "Red Power."

Beginning in the 1960s, a Native American movement emerged to protest federal policy, combat stereotypes, unite tribes, and perpetuate their cultures. Native Americans called for an end to employment discrimination and to the sale of Indian lands and resources to corporations. Activists staged "hunt-ins" and "fish-ins" to protest lost hunting and fishing rights. They also condemned the use of Indian symbols by schools and sports teams and demanded Indian-centered school curricula.

Some Indians favored more radical action. Copying the Black Panthers, a group of red-beret-clad Native Americans in Minneapolis formed an "Indian Patrol" to defend against the police. The patrol evolved into the American Indian Movement (AIM), which spread to other cities. In 1969, AIM activists occupied the abandoned federal prison on Alcatraz Island in San Francisco Bay. They unsuccessfully offered the government "$24 in glass beads and cloth" for the prison, which they planned to convert into a Native American center. In 1972 and 1973, AIM took over BIA headquarters in Washington and the BIA office in Wounded Knee, South Dakota, where federal troops had massacred Indians in 1890.

The Native American rights movement made few gains. The Indian Self-Determination Act of 1975 did allow Native Americans more independence on the reservations, but Native Americans were still divided about their relationship to the government. Many tribal leaders wanted to continue selling off their lands through the BIA but were assailed by AIM for accepting bureau authority. Despite such divisions, the movement had forced

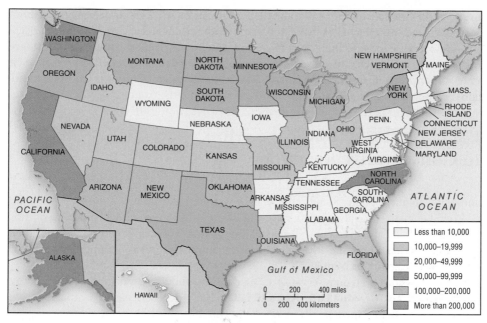

Map 29–3   Native American Population, 1980 After rapid growth in the years following World War II, the Native American population remained largest west of the Mississippi River and, above all, across the Southwest. But there were substantial numbers of Native Americans in every region. *Data from* Statistical Abstract of the United States, *1973 (Washington, DC: US Bureau of the Census, 1973), p. 348; and* Statistical Abstract of the United States, *1984 (Washington, DC: US Bureau of the Census, 1984), pp. 375–376, 463, 760.*

Americans to confront the inequitable treatment of Indians more directly than at any time since the Great Depression.

Homosexuals and Gay Power

Singled out for persecution in the McCarthy era, most homosexual men and women had learned to conceal their sexual identity in public. Mainstream American culture ridiculed homosexuals as "faggots," "queers," and "dykes," and the medical profession treated homosexuality as an illness. Despite the founding of the activist Mattachine Society in 1950, most homosexual men and women still maintained closeted identities into the 1960s.

During the decade, that began to change. In 1961, Frank Kameny, essentially fired from a federal job for being gay, unsuccessfully took his case to the federal courts. Another catalyst for change was the struggle of women, racial minorities, and students. Inspired by the chant "Black is Beautiful," Kameny offered the slogan "Gay is Good" in 1968. A decisive spur to the gay rights movement was a police raid on the Stonewall Inn, a gay bar in New York City's Greenwich Village, in June 1969. Such raids were commonplace, but this time gay men resisted. The next night, the police beat and arrested gay protestors, who yelled, "Gay Power!"

Stonewall became a rallying cry for gay activism. The Gay Liberation Front, the Student Homophile League, and other organizations appeared. Activists picketed companies that discriminated against gays, and homosexuals socialized more openly. On the first anniversary of Stonewall, 10,000 gay men and lesbians paraded up New York's Sixth Avenue. "Two, four, six, eight!" marchers chanted. "Gay is just as good as straight!" The gay movement began to have an effect. In 1974, the American Psychiatric Association decided that homo-sexuality was not a "mental disorder" and that homosexuals deserved equal rights.

The emerging gay, Native American, and Chicano movements, along with the ongoing crusades of women and African Americans, made a deep impact on American society. Women, gays, African Americans, Native Americans, and Chicanos did not win full equality, but these groups made important gains despite the troubled economic climate.

Backlash: From Radical Action to Conservative Reaction

By the close of the 1960s, American society shook with demands for peace in Vietnam and equal rights at home. Some activists believed the United States would be torn apart and remade by the "racial and class war" that Shirley Chisholm feared, but the revolution never came. Radical movements fell apart. Many Americans abandoned activism for their private concerns; others angrily rejected protest movements. Encouraging this backlash, President Nixon won reelection in 1972.

"The Movement" and the "Me-Decade"

By the end of the 1960s, women, minorities, student protestors, and antiwar activists seemed to be creating a single coalition, known simply as "the Movement." In August 1969, a crowd of nearly half a million mostly young people gathered for a music festival on a dairy farm near Woodstock in upstate New York. For three days, they created a temporary utopia dedicated to love, equality, and an end to the Vietnam War. What activist Abbie Hoffman called the "Woodstock Nation" briefly symbolized the possibility of a true mass-based coalition for radical change.

Nevertheless, the Movement stalled. "We had the dream and we are losing it," an activist lamented the same year. The different protest groups never merged and were often hostile to each other. Black activists, for instance, criticized white activists for neglecting poverty and other working-class problems.

In addition, Movement groups fell apart. Plagued by internal divisions, SDS held its last convention in 1969. The violent Weathermen called for "Days of Rage" in the "pig city" of Chicago in October 1969, but only a few hundred protestors showed up. Transient radical groups bombed or burned corporate headquarters and other "establishment" targets but succeeded only in giving the New Left and the Movement a bad name. The FBI infiltrated Black Panther chapters to discredit the organization. Panther leaders fled the country, went to jail, or died at the hands of police. Radical feminist groups also declined as women focused on liberal demands, such as the ERA.

Some protest movements lost their targets. After the demonstrations of 1970, the antiwar movement declined as the United States pulled out of Vietnam. The student movement declined as young people lost some of their grievances. In 1971, the voting age was lowered to 18, after ratification of the Twenty-sixth Amendment.

The revolution also failed because many people turned away from activism and political engagement. Some were disillusioned by the failure of the Great Society and the duplicity of the Johnson and Nixon administrations. Others were disappointed by radicalism's limited victories. Still others joined therapeutic and religious movements concerned with inner needs rather than political change.

To the writer Tom Wolfe, the 1970s were the "Me-Decade," a time in which Americans had become self-absorbed and narcissistic. The cause, explained the historian and social critic Christopher Lasch, was the crisis of capitalism in "an age of diminishing expectations." Fears about the self-absorbed Me-Decade were as exaggerated as hopes for the revolutionary Movement. People did not stop working for change, but in a time of economic decline and political disappointment, many Americans felt they could not afford the expansive liberal dreams of the 1960s. They had to look out for themselves.

The Plight of the White Ethnics

The "new American revolution" was a victim of anger, as well as apathy. Most lower-middle-class and working-class whites rejected the Movement. They decried radical feminism and resented the students and protestors who had avoided serving in Vietnam. They also rejected the new liberalism of the 1960s. Feeling threatened by urban renewal, welfare, and court-ordered busing, many whites believed the Great Society did too little for them and too much for minorities and young radicals. Most of all, they feared lost jobs and a lower living standard amid deindustrialization. "I work my ass off," said an ironworker. "But I can't make it."

The media painted an unflattering portrait of these Americans as frustrated racists and reactionaries. In reality, they were not all so racist or forlorn. They took renewed pride in the ethnic heritage that set them apart from other Americans. "White ethnics" were self-consciously German American or Irish American, like the opponents of busing in Boston. They were "PIGS"—Poles, Italians, Greeks, and Slavs.

White ethnics tapped their heritage to affirm an alternative set of values—their own counterculture. For them, ethnicity meant a grounding in family, neighborhood, and religion in place of the individualistic American dream and the centralizing federal government. In response, some colleges and universities created ethnic studies programs. In 1972, Congress passed the Ethnic Heritage Studies Act to "legitimatize ethnicity" and promote the study of immigrant cultures. Most important, white ethnics formed a large potential voting bloc, attractive to politicians.

The Republican Counterattack

Nixon tried to join white ethnics and white southerners in a Republican counterattack against radicalism, liberalism, and the Democratic Party. The president condemned protestors and demonstrations. "Anarchy," he said, "this is the way civilizations begin to die." Nixon ordered IRS investigations to harass liberal and antiwar figures. He used the FBI to infiltrate and disrupt the Black Power movement, the Brown Berets, and the New Left. He made illegal domestic use of the CIA against the antiwar movement.

Nixon also called for support from "the great silent majority of my fellow Americans." With his "southern strategy," the president reached out to Sunbelt voters by opposing busing, rapid integration, crime, and radicalism. He also tried to create a more conservative, less activist Supreme Court. In 1969, he named the cautious Warren Burger to succeed Earl Warren as chief justice. To fill another vacancy, Nixon nominated first a conservative South Carolina judge, Clement Haynsworth, who had angered civil rights and union leaders, and then Judge G. Harrold Carswell of Florida, a former avowed white supremacist. Both nominations failed, but Nixon had sent an unmistakable message to the "silent majority" and to white southerners.

The counterattack paid off in the 1972 presidential election. The Republican ticket of Nixon and Vice President Spiro Agnew benefited from unforeseen occurrences. Only George Wallace, the segregationist governor of Alabama, rivaled Nixon's appeal to the "silent majority." But Wallace's campaign for the Democratic nomination ended when a would-be assassin's bullet paralyzed him from the waist down. In addition, the Democratic vice-presidential nominee, Senator Thomas Eagleton of Missouri, had to withdraw after revelations about his treatment for depression.

Nixon did not really need good luck in 1972. The Democrats chose a strongly liberal senator, George McGovern of South Dakota, for president. McGovern's running mate was another liberal, Sargent Shriver, a brother-in-law of the Kennedys. The Democratic ticket—which endorsed busing and affirmative action and opposed the Vietnam War—alienated white ethnics, white southerners, and organized labor.

Nixon won 49 out of 50 states and nearly 61 percent of the popular vote, but the victory was deceptive: the Democrats still controlled both houses of Congress.

Nevertheless, the 1972 election was a sign that the traditional Democratic coalition was breaking up. Nixon's triumph, along with the failure of the Movement, the rise of the white ethnics, and the self-absorption of the Me-Decade, showed that the glory days of liberalism and radicalism were over.

Political Crisis: Three Troubled Presidencies

Nixon's triumph turned out to be his undoing. The discovery of illegal activities in his campaign led to the revelation of other improprieties and, finally, to his resignation. Nixon's successors, Gerald Ford and Jimmy Carter, could not master the problems of a divided nation discovering the limits of its power. Unable to handle the conflicting issues of rights and economic decline, the three troubled presidencies of the 1970s intensified the sense of national crisis. At the decade's end, Americans wondered whether their democracy still worked.

Watergate: The Fall of Richard Nixon

Nixon's fall began when five men were caught breaking into the offices of the Democratic National Committee in the Watergate complex in Washington, DC, just before 2:00 a.m. on June 17, 1972. The five burglars had ties to Nixon's campaign organization, the Committee to Re-Elect the President (CREEP). They were attempting to repair an electronic eavesdropping device that had been planted in the Democrats' headquarters.

At first, Watergate had no impact on the president. He won reelection easily, but a disturbing story gradually emerged. Two reporters for the *Washington Post*, Bob Woodward and Carl Bernstein, revealed payments linking the five burglars to CREEP and to Nixon's White House staff. The burglars went on trial with two former CIA agents, who had directed the break-in for CREEP. Facing heavy sentences, the burglars admitted in March 1973 that "higher-ups" had planned the break-in and orchestrated a cover-up. One of those higher-ups, presidential counsel John Dean, revealed his role in the Watergate affair to a grand jury. By the end of April, the president had to accept the resignations of his most trusted aides, H. R. "Bob" Haldeman and John Ehrlichman. To investigate Watergate, Nixon named a special federal prosecutor, Archibald Cox.

In the end, the president was trapped by his own words. A Senate committee, chaired by Sam Ervin of North Carolina, began hearings on Watergate in May 1973. A White House aide told the committee that conversations in the president's Oval Office were routinely recorded on secret tapes. Claiming "executive privilege," Nixon refused to turn over tapes of his conversations after the break-in. When Archibald Cox pressed for the tapes, Nixon ordered him fired on Saturday, October 20, 1973. Attorney General Elliot Richardson and a top aide refused to carry out the order and resigned. A third official finally fired Cox. Nixon's "Saturday Night Massacre" set off a storm of public anger. Nixon had to name a new special prosecutor, Leon Jaworski. The Democratic-controlled House of Representatives began to consider impeachment against the president. "I am not a crook," Nixon insisted.

By 1974, it became clear that the Nixon administration had engaged in a shocking range of improper and illegal behavior. Infuriated by news leaks in 1969, Henry Kissinger had ordered wiretaps on the phones of newspaper reporters and his own staff. Two years later, the White House had created the "Plumbers," an inept group of operatives to combat leaks such as release of the Pentagon Papers. In 1972, Nixon's men had also engaged in dirty tricks to sabotage Democratic presidential aspirants. Nixon's personal lawyer had collected illegal political contributions, "laundered" the money to hide its source, and then transferred it to CREEP.

Nixon himself had ordered the secret and illegal bombing of Cambodia. He had impounded (refused to spend) money appropriated by Congress for programs he disliked. He had secretly approved the use of federal agencies to hurt "political enemies."

As a result of Watergate and other scandals, many of Nixon's associates had to leave office. No fewer than 26, including former attorney general John Mitchell, went to jail. Vice President Spiro Agnew was found to have accepted bribes as the governor of Maryland in the 1960s. In 1973 Agnew accepted a plea bargain deal and resigned. He was replaced by Republican congressman Gerald R. Ford of Michigan.

Under pressure to release his tapes, Nixon tried to get away with publishing edited selections. Revealing a vulgar, rambling, and inarticulate president, the transcripts only fed public disillusionment. In July 1974 the House Judiciary Committee voted to recommend to the full House of Representatives three articles of impeachment—obstruction of justice, abuse of power, and defiance of subpoenas.

Nixon wanted to fight the charges, but the Supreme Court ruled unanimously that he had to give his tapes to the special prosecutor. They showed that Nixon himself had participated in the Watergate cover-up as early as June 23, 1972. The president had conspired to obstruct justice and had lied repeatedly to the American people. Almost certain to be impeached, Nixon agreed to resign rather than face a trial in the Senate. On August 9, 1974, he left office in disgrace. "My fellow Americans, our long national nightmare is over," the new president, Gerald Ford, declared. "Our constitution works."

Gerald Ford and a Skeptical Nation

At first, Gerald Ford was a welcome relief for a nation stunned by the misdeeds of Richard Nixon. Modest and good-humored, the new president seemed unlikely to abuse authority. But Ford also seemed stumbling and unimaginative in the face of declining prosperity and power. Moreover, he had no popular mandate. Ford was the first unelected vice president to succeed to the presidency. His vice president, former New York governor Nelson Rockefeller, had not been elected, either.

Ford had to govern a nation skeptical about politicians. Johnson's deceitful conduct of the Vietnam War and Nixon's scandals raised fears that the presidency had grown too powerful. To reestablish its authority, Congress passed the War Powers Act of 1973, which allowed the president to send troops to hostilities overseas for no more than 60 days without congressional consent. In 1975 Congress held hearings on CIA secret operations. Amid revelations about the agency's improper roles in domestic spying and the assassination of foreign leaders, Congress created permanent committees to oversee the agency. Ford had to ban the use of assassination in American foreign policy.

Soon after taking office, Ford himself fed the public's skepticism about the presidency by offering Nixon a full pardon for all crimes committed as president. Ford's popularity dropped immediately, and his presidency never fully recovered.

Ford's handling of economic issues did not help his popularity. A moderate Republican, he preferred a less active federal role in managing the economy. But, like Nixon, he could not stop some liberal initiatives, as Congress strengthened the regulatory power of the Federal Trade Commission and extended the 1970 Clean Air Act.

Ford had no solutions for deindustrialization and stagflation. Believing inflation was the most serious problem, he did little to stop rising unemployment, which topped 9 percent. His anti-inflation program, known as WIN for "Whip Inflation Now," mainly encouraged Americans to control price increases voluntarily, but inflation continued.

In foreign affairs, Ford had to accept limits on American power. Despite the 1973 cease-fire, the fighting continued in Vietnam. Ford promised to protect South Vietnam, but Congress cut his requests for monetary aid to Saigon. Sending American troops back to South Vietnam was out of the question. When the North Vietnamese invaded early in 1975, panicked civilians fled southward. As Saigon was overrun, the last Americans evacuated in helicopters. Thousands of loyal South Vietnamese fled with them, but many more were left behind. On April 30, 1975, South Vietnam surrendered. There was nothing Ford could do to prevent the final, ignominious failure of America's 20-year-long Vietnam policy.

The president could also do nothing to save the pro-American government of Cambodia from Communist insurgents, the Khmer Rouge, in April 1975. Ford did act the next month when the Khmer Rouge captured an American merchant ship, the *Mayaguez*, off Cambodia. At the cost of 41 deaths, United States marines rescued the 39-man crew. Despite the rescue, the United States no longer wielded much power in Southeast Asia.

The policy of détente with the Soviet Union, meant to help America cope with its limited power, was also in trouble. The United States and the Soviets failed to agree to a second Strategic Arms Limitation Treaty (SALT II). Critics of détente, including Democratic Senator Henry Jackson of Washington, claimed that the policy sapped American defenses and overlooked human rights violations by the Soviets. In 1974, Jackson added to a trade bill an amendment linking commerce to freedom for Soviet Jews to emigrate. The Jackson-Vanik Amendment helped sour the Soviets on détente. Ford further alienated conservatives when he signed an agreement in Helsinki, Finland, accepting the post–World War II boundaries of European nations.

Ford's troubles affected the polls. The Democrats made large gains in the 1974 congressional elections. Two years later, Ford won the Republican nomination for president, replacing Rockefeller with a more conservative vice-presidential nominee, Senator Robert Dole of Kansas. The Democrats chose former Georgia governor Jimmy Carter, a moderate promising efficiency rather than liberal reform.

With low turnout, Carter took 50.1 percent of the vote to Ford's 48 percent. The Democrat won an Electoral College majority by carrying the Northeast and taking back almost all the South from the Republicans (see Map 29–4). The outcome was less an endorsement

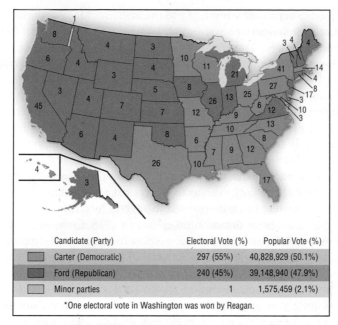

Candidate (Party)	Electoral Vote (%)	Popular Vote (%)
Carter (Democratic)	297 (55%)	40,828,929 (50.1%)
Ford (Republican)	240 (45%)	39,148,940 (47.9%)
Minor parties	1	1,575,459 (2.1%)

*One electoral vote in Washington was won by Reagan.

Map 29–4   The Presidential Election, 1976 Jimmy Carter managed to reestablish the Democratic Party's appeal to white southerners.

of Carter than a rejection of Ford, who became the first sitting president to lose an election since Herbert Hoover during the Great Depression in 1932.

"Why Not the Best?": Jimmy Carter

As he took office in 1977, Jimmy Carter seemed capable and efficient. A graduate of the Naval Academy, he had served as an engineer in the nuclear submarine program and successfully managed his family's peanut farm before entering politics. Carter's perfectionism was captured in the title of his autobiography, *Why Not the Best?*

Carter responded more energetically and imaginatively than Ford to the nation's problems. But Carter came to be seen as a weak, uncertain leader. More important, he faced the same intractable problems that had bedeviled Ford.

Like his predecessor, Carter had trouble putting to rest the recent past. He met angry criticism when he pardoned Americans who had resisted the draft during the Vietnam War.

Carter also faced increasing popular resentment of government. Many Americans believed that regulation and taxation had gotten out of hand. When the Endangered Species Act of 1973 forced a halt to the construction of a Tennessee dam because it threatened the survival of the snail darter, a small local fish, it seemed as if the federal government worried more about fish than about people's need for electricity and recreation.

The West was the stronghold of antigovernment sentiment in the 1970s. Assailing Washington bureaucrats, the Sagebrush Rebellion demanded state control over federal lands in the West. Businessmen in the West also wanted more exploitation of oil, forests, and other resources on federal lands. Meanwhile, California became the center of an anti-tax movement in 1978. Angered by high taxes and local government spending, California voters passed Proposition 13, which sharply reduced property taxes.

As always, antigovernment sentiment was inconsistent. Many of the same people who attacked taxes and regulation expected aid and benefits from Washington. When Chrysler faced bankruptcy in 1979, the government saved the automaker with a $1.5 billion loan guarantee. When Carter moved to cancel federal water projects in the West in 1977, he faced protest from the heart of the Sagebrush Rebellion.

Carter was most successful when he moved to limit government. By the 1970s, some economists were advocating deregulation of businesses as a way to lower costs, increase competition, and improve services. In 1978, the government removed price controls on the airline industry. In the short run the move lowered fares, but in the long run it drove some airlines out of business.

Deregulation marked a changing balance of political power. Big business, under attack since the 1960s, now lobbied effectively against regulation, organized labor, and taxes. Liberals, meanwhile, failed to convince Congress to create the Consumer Protection Agency or to make labor organization easier. In 1978, Congress diluted the liberal Humphrey-Hawkins Bill asserting federal responsibility for full employment. When Carter tried to raise business taxes, Congress instead cut taxes on capital gains and added more tax loopholes.

Carter attempted, with mixed results, to adjust the economy to the realities of living with less. His voluntary wage and price controls did not stop soaring inflation. After fuel shortages forced schools and businesses to close in the harsh winter of 1976–1977, Carter addressed the energy crisis. The president told Americans that "the energy shortage is permanent" and urged them to conserve. His energy plan included a new Department of Energy, taxes on gas-guzzling automobiles and large consumers of oil, tax incentives to stimulate oil and gas production, and development of nuclear power. Conservatives complained the program expanded government authority, whereas liberals and environmentalists objected to its support for nuclear power and oil-company profits. A weakened plan, passed in 1978, did encourage conservation.

Nuclear power, a key part of Carter's energy plan, lost much of its appeal. In March 1979 a nuclear reactor at Three Mile Island, Pennsylvania, nearly suffered a catastrophic

>> Time Line

▼1968
Assassinations of Martin Luther King Jr. and Robert F. Kennedy
Election of Richard Nixon

▼1969
Secret bombing of Cambodia
Stonewall Riot in New York's Greenwich Village
Apollo 11 moon landing
Nixon Doctrine

▼1970
First Earth Day
Invasion of Cambodia

▼1971
United States off gold standard
Ratification of Twenty-sixth Amendment, lowering voting age to 18
Supreme Court busing decision, *Swann v. Charlotte-Mecklenburg Board of Education*

▼1972
President Nixon's trips to People's Republic of China and Soviet Union

Strategic Arms Limitation Treaty (SALT I) and Anti–Ballistic Missile (ABM) Treaty
Congressional passage of Equal Rights Amendment
Watergate burglary
Reelection of President Nixon

▼1973
Peace agreement to end Vietnam War
Supreme Court ruling to legalize abortion, *Roe v. Wade*

meltdown. As 100,000 frightened residents fled their homes, the reactor had to be permanently closed. Around the country, utilities scrapped plans for new nuclear power plants.

Three Mile Island fed broader anxieties about the environmental damage of industrial capitalism. Americans wondered whether their neighborhoods would suffer the fate of Love Canal, near Niagara Falls, New York. There, hazardous waste buried by a chemical company caused so many cases of cancer, miscarriages, and other health problems that residents had to move away. Despite business hostility to regulation, Washington had to create a "Superfund" of $1.6 billion to clean up hazardous-waste sites. The administration also took control of 100 million acres of Alaska to prevent damage from economic development.

At first, Carter had success with foreign policy. Continuing Nixon's deescalation of the cold war, Carter announced that "we are now free of the inordinate fear of Communism." Without abandoning détente, he focused on building harmony and supporting human rights and democracy around the world. In 1978, Carter won Senate approval of a treaty yielding ownership of the Panama Canal to Panama at the end of the century, representing a new, more respectful approach to Central and Latin America.

In 1978, Carter also mediated the first peace agreement between Israel and an Arab nation. Bringing together Israeli and Egyptian leaders at the Camp David presidential retreat, Carter helped forge a framework for peace that led to Israel's withdrawal from the Sinai Peninsula and the signing of an Israeli-Egyptian treaty. The agreement did not settle the fate of the Israeli-occupied Golan Heights and Gaza Strip or the future of the Palestinian people, but it did create a basis for future negotiations.

Carter viewed a commitment to human rights and democracy as America's way of recapturing the international respect lost during the Vietnam War. In practice, however, Carter supported authoritarian American allies, such as the rulers of Iran and the Philippines, who abused human rights in their own countries.

Carter's foreign policy suffered from the collapse of détente. The president did reach an agreement with the Soviets on the SALT II treaty, but the Senate was reluctant to ratify it. Then, in December 1979, the Soviet Union invaded its southern neighbor, Afghanistan. In response, Carter withdrew the SALT II treaty, stopped grain shipments to the Soviet

▼1973-74
OPEC oil embargo

▼1974
Boston busing struggle
Resignation of President Nixon

▼1975
Surrender of South Vietnam to
   North Vietnam
Helsinki Agreement

▼1976
Announcement of the "Me-
   Decade" by Tom Wolfe
Jimmy Carter elected president

▼1977
Carter's energy plan

▼1978
Camp David peace accords
Supreme Court affirmative
   action decision, *Regents of the*
   University of California v. Allan
   Bakke

▼1979
Accident at Three Mile Island
   nuclear power plant

▼1979-81
Iranian hostage crisis

▼1980
Ronald Reagan elected president

Union, forbade American athletes to compete in the 1980 Olympics in Moscow, and increased military spending. These moves did not affect the Soviets' invasion, but détente was over, and the direction of American foreign policy was unclear.

By 1979, Carter was deeply unpopular. He had not stabilized the economy or forged a coherent foreign policy. After pondering the situation at Camp David for 11 days in July, he told a television audience that the nation was suffering a "crisis of spirit." The president offered proposals to deal with the energy crisis but spoke most strongly to the state of the nation. "All the legislation in the world can't fix what's wrong with America," Carter said. "What is lacking is confidence and a sense of community." The speech only seemed to alienate more Americans.

Carter became still more embattled when the Shah of Iran was overthrown by the followers of an Islamic leader, the Ayatollah Ruholla Khomeini, early in 1979. The Shah had long received lavish aid from the United States. Now, Iranian revolutionaries, eager to restore traditional Islamic values, condemned America for imposing the Shah and modern culture on their nation. In the wake of the revolution, oil prices rose. Americans had to contend again with gas lines and inflation.

The situation worsened when Khomeini condemned the United States for allowing the Shah to receive medical treatment in New York. On November 4, students loyal to Khomeini overran the United States embassy in Teheran, the Iranian capital, and took 60 Americans hostage. Carter froze Iranian assets in the United States but could not compel the release of the hostages. The United States seemed helpless. In the spring of 1980, a frustrated Carter ordered a secret military mission to rescue the hostages. On April 24, eight American helicopters headed for a desert rendezvous with six transport planes carrying troops and supplies. When two helicopters broke down and another became lost, the mission had to be aborted. An accident left eight soldiers dead. The hostages remained in captivity. And the limits of American power seemed more obvious than ever.

Disaster in the Iranian Desert, April 1980 The wreckage of this army helicopter, part of the failed attempt to free American hostages in Iran, symbolizes the weakness of the United States at the start of the 1980s.

Conclusion

As the 1970s ended, Shirley Chisholm was still deeply worried about her nation. The congresswoman feared that "there was a real crisis . . . in this country. . . . Government was being conducted by crisis." The mixture of economic decline with movements for rights and opportunity had proved too much to handle. To Chisholm, even the changes of the liberal 1960s seemed at risk. "Lots happened in the '60s," she noted sadly. "What's happening today? Every gain has been eroded."

As always, Chisholm refused to give in to pessimism. "I will continue to do what I'm doing—fighting, fighting, fighting," she vowed, "because I realize that this country is moving to the right." As the 1980s would reveal, Chisholm was correct. After the political uncertainty of the 1970s, the nation would finally deal with economic decline and the other challenges of the decade by embracing a new conservatism. The future lay to the right.

Who, What

Jimmy Carter 902

César Chávez 894

Gerald Ford 901

Henry Kissinger 885

Richard Nixon 885

Affirmative action 891

Busing 891

Deindustrialization 884

Détente 886

Multinational 882

New Federalism 889

Roe v. Wade 893

Watergate 900

Review Questions

1. What were the chief causes of American economic decline in the 1970s?

2. What were the main concerns of the white ethnics?

3. What were the key foreign policies of the Nixon administration?

Critical-Thinking Questions

1. Why did the demands of the African American civil rights movement become more controversial in the 1970s?

2. Did the upheavals of the 1970s strengthen or weaken democracy in America?

3. Analyze the troubled presidencies of Nixon, Ford, and Carter. Did these leaders create their own problems, or did they face impossible situations?

For further review materials and resource information, please visit www.oup.com/us/ofthepeople

MAIN IDEAS

1) The decline of American economic and military power fundamentally shaped the presidency of Richard Nixon.

2) The atmosphere of economic decline and political conservatism did not prevent more groups from demanding rights and opportunity.

3) Demands for peace in Vietnam and equal rights at home produced a conservative backlash that helped reelect President Nixon in 1972.

4) Economic weakness, new demands for rights, and declining power abroad helped undermine three successive presidents and contributed to doubts about the democratic political system.

TOPICS

A New Crisis: Economic Decline

Confronting Decline: Nixon's Strategy

Refusing to Settle for Less: Struggles for Rights

Backlash: From Radical Action to Conservative Reaction

Political Crisis: Three Troubled Presidencies

LIVING WITH LESS

1968–1980

EVENTS

Weakness at Home A weakening economy faced the new problem of stagflation—simultaneous high unemployment and high inflation.

The Energy Crisis Dependence on foreign oil intensified the nation's economic problems.

Competition Abroad Japan and Western Europe provided tough competition for the weakening US economy.

The Multinationals The rise of multinational corporations channeled American investment and manufacturing jobs to other countries.

The Impact of Decline Economic decline reshaped society by decreasing high-paying, unionized factory jobs and shifting income and population to the South and West.

A New Foreign Policy President Nixon pursued a less confrontational strategy toward the Soviet Union and the People's Republic of China.

Ending the Vietnam War The Nixon administration ended the US role in the Vietnam War, but not without new casualties and new division at home.

Chile and the Middle East Despite his support for détente with the Soviet Union, Nixon still pursued an anti-Communist agenda abroad, but faced limits on American power.

Taming Big Government Nixon wanted to pursue a more conservative domestic agenda, but had to compromise with the continuing influence of the new liberalism.

An Uncertain Economic Policy Nixon's economic policy, a compromise with liberalism, did not solve the most basic problems of American decline and deindustrialization.

African Americans' Struggle for Racial Justice African Americans pursued two controversial strategies for racial equality: affirmative action and mandatory school busing.

Women's Liberation The movement for women's equality made significant progress but also faced the defeat of the Equal Rights Amendment to the Constitution.

Mexican Americans and "Brown Power" Mexican Americans, developing a new self-consciousness, organized to demand power and equal rights.

Asian American Activism Asian Americans organized against discrimination and pressed for compensation for Japanese internment during World War II.

The Struggle for Native American Rights Native Americans, also reflecting a new consciousness, protested federal policy.

Homosexuals and Gay Power Like racial minorities, homosexual men and women also organized to claim equal rights and power.

"The Movement" and the "Me-Decade" Hopes for a mass coalition of youths, women, and African Americans for radical change gave way to disillusionment with political engagement and a new narcissistic preoccupation with individual well-being.

The Plight of the White Ethnics Many lower-middle-class and working-class whites, believing that the liberal Great Society did little for them, expressed a new sense of their own rights.

The Republican Counterattack Nixon won reelection in 1972 by uniting white ethnics and white southerners against radicalism, liberalism, and Democrats.

Watergate: The Fall of Richard Nixon Watergate, Nixon's self-inflicted scandal, forced the president to resign.

Gerald Ford and a Skeptical Nation Ford's inability to counter decline at home and abroad made him a one-term president and reinforced public concerns about the political system.

"Why Not the Best?": Jimmy Carter Like Ford, Jimmy Carter proved unable to solve the problem of limited economic, military, and political power.

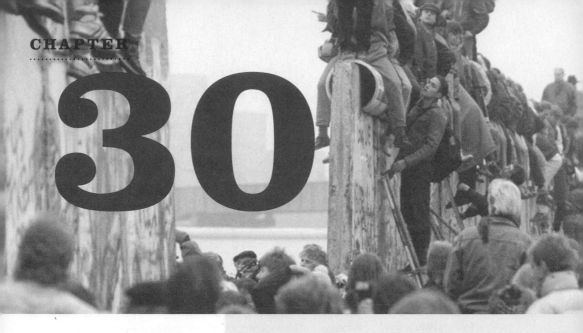

CHAPTER

30

The Triumph of Conservatism

1980–1991

AMERICAN PORTRAIT

>> Linda Chavez

"On Election Day 1980," Linda Chavez recalled, "I did something I had never imagined I could do: I voted for a Republican for president." A lifelong Democrat, she rejected her party's nominee, incumbent Jimmy Carter, and pulled the lever instead for the conservative Ronald Reagan.

Chavez admitted she made "an unlikely conservative." The daughter of an Anglo mother and a Mexican American father, Chavez had grown up in the Mexican American neighborhoods of Albuquerque and Denver. Her father, like most Mexican Americans, was a Democrat. Chavez herself was drawn to the party and its causes. As a girl in the early 1960s, she joined the civil rights organization CORE and demonstrated against racial discrimination. Chavez then worked for the Democratic National Committee, a liberal Democratic congressman, two liberal teachers unions, and the Carter administration.

Despite her partisan commitments, Chavez had been changing. As a student at the University of Colorado at Boulder in the late 1960s, Chavez discovered that she did not have to settle for her parents' working-class world. "For the first time," she said, "I realized that I could control my own destiny." Chavez also felt that the university's affirmative action programs shortchanged Mexican Americans by admitting unqualified students, allowing them to founder, teaching them to blame their problems on racism, and then leaving them to drop out.

Those realizations helped Chavez develop a new political outlook in the 1970s. She believed that individuals should take responsibility for their lives. She also rejected affirmative action programs, race-based hiring quotas, busing, and bilingual education as misguided liberal attempts to create equality.

Meanwhile, her stint in the Carter administration left her skeptical about another liberal article of faith. "The federal government was not at all what I expected," Chavez confessed. "Nothing—and almost no one—worked." She was troubled, too, that Carter and the Democrats did not support anti-Communism and a strong defense.

continued

>> **AMERICAN PORTRAIT** *continued*

In some ways, Chavez felt that she was not the one who had changed. It was her party that had changed by adopting controversial solutions to racial and gender inequality and by abandoning its pledge to contain Communism. In 1976, Chavez stayed home rather than vote for Carter. By 1980, she was ready to vote for Reagan, another longtime Democrat who felt his party had changed.

Linda Chavez was an unusual figure: there were hardly any prominent Mexican American conservatives, male or female. But her change from liberal Democrat to conservative Republican typified a basic shift in the 1980s. Still dealing with economic and political decline, a new majority of Americans, including businesspeople, evangelical Christians, and "Reagan Democrats" like Chavez, adopted a conservative vision of the country. Rejecting the pessimism of the 1970s, they wanted to believe that individual and national success was still possible. The new conservative majority was open to materialism and to a government that left people free to succeed or fail.

The trend toward conservatism had many consequences. Eager to restore old values, Reagan cut taxes, reduced government regulation, and diminished union power to restore economic growth. The president also embraced a conservative social agenda, including attacks on affirmative action and abortion. His foreign policy was dedicated to confronting Communism. Despite scandals, setbacks, and compromises, Reagan and the new conservatism arrested fears of decline and altered America's politics and culture for a generation.

Creating a Conservative Majority

In the 1970s and 1980s, the conservative movement continued its rise to power. The New Right drew strength from the transformation of the economy, the changing reputation of big business, and the growth of evangelical Christianity. Conservative power became clear in the 1980 presidential election, when voters sent Ronald Reagan to the White House.

The New Economy

Conservatism benefited from the emergence of a postindustrial, computer-centered economy. As deindustrialization continued, technological change pointed the way to national economic revival. Along with other innovations, semiconductors—transistorized integrated circuits attached to small silicon crystals—allowed manufacturers to shrink the computer. By the late 1970s they could put the power of a room-sized mainframe computer into a box that fit on a desktop. In 1981, IBM introduced its first personal computer, or PC. By the end of the 1980s, Americans were buying 7 million PCs a year (see Figure 30–1).

Computers seemed a way out of national economic decline. The microcomputer bolstered older companies such as IBM and created new firms such as Apple and Dell; it enriched new entrepreneurs such as Steve Jobs, a founder of Apple, and Bill Gates, a founder of Microsoft. Asian manufacturers built most consumer-electronics products, but American companies dominated computer hardware and software.

The growth of the computer industry inspired utopian dreams of a high-technology society built on the production of knowledge rather than things. Promoting literacy and education, the computer would lift up the poor and disadvantaged. Unlike the old indus-

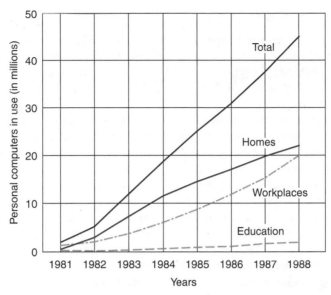

Figure 30–1   The Rise of the Personal Computer The rapid rise in the number of microcomputers in use in homes, workplaces, and schools in the 1980s inspired hopes that the nation's economic decline had ended. *Statistical Abstract of the United States, 1989 (Washington, DC: US Bureau of the Census, 1990), p. 743;* Statistical Abstract, 1993 *(Washington, DC: US Bureau of the Census, 1994), p. 761.*

trial economy, a computerized economy would cut pollution and the consumption of raw materials. Enabling people to work at home, the microcomputer would eliminate commuting and relieve urban congestion.

The promise of the computer-driven economy helped conservatism. New industries, new companies, and new jobs seemed to confirm conservatives' faith in capitalist free enterprise, unaided by government. The new economy also benefited conservatism by stimulating the flow of people, jobs, and political power from the North and East to the South and West. Computing did revive parts of the Rustbelt. In Massachusetts, computer companies sprang up around Boston along Route 128 to replace long-gone textile mills and shoe factories. But computing most benefited the Sunbelt, birthplace of the new conservatism in the 1950s and 1960s. Dell's headquarters were in Texas. Apple was one of many computer firms clustered in the area called Silicon Valley, outside San Francisco. Rustbelt cities such as Pittsburgh and Detroit lost population, while

A Revolution on a Desktop In 1981, the new IBM PC, or personal computer, conveniently offered the power of an old room-filling mainframe computer.

AMERICAN LANDSCAPE

>> **Silicon Valley**

It was, wrote a reporter, "an unlikely place to start a revolution." The Santa Clara Valley, south of San Francisco Bay, was a thin strip of lush orchards and conventional suburbs in the decades after World War II. Yet the region had long inspired a sense of promise and optimism. To farmers, it had been the "Valley of the Heart's Delight." By the 1980s, the area was the heart of "Silicon Valley," a much drier name, but just as full of promise and optimism. Silicon Valley, stretching from the mushrooming city of San Jose north through "intellectual boom-towns" on either side of San Francisco Bay, epitomized the hopes and accomplishments of the computer-centered new economy.

Like most revolutions, the rise of Silicon Valley was in fact the result of a long-term process. In the 1890s, the founding of Stanford University in Palo Alto established an engine for creativity and western economic development. In 1939, two Stanford graduates founded a pioneering electronics company, Hewlett-Packard, in Palo Alto. After World War II, new companies sprang up: Shockley Semiconductor Laboratory and Fairchild Semiconductor in the 1950s; National Semiconductor and Integrated Electronics Corporation (Intel) in the 1960s. Computing took center stage in the 1970s. In 1971, Intel marketed the first commercial microprocessor, the 4004 chip. In 1976, Steve Jobs and Steve Wozniak started Apple Computing on a shoestring budget in Cupertino.

By the 1980s, Apple and other companies had created a distinctive regional culture of innovation and entrepreneurship. Hundreds of small start-up companies encouraged the unconventional. "Silicon Valley rewards people who don't fit in," said a businessman. "It allows very bright and creative minds to innovate. Steve Jobs would have been beaten into submission in the East." Instead, Jobs and other entrepreneurs found success and riches in Silicon Valley. "This is the modern gold rush," declared a therapist in Palo Alto. "There is a strike-it-rich phenomenon, a feeling that 'I can do it as well as anybody else.'"

By the end of the decade, "Silicon Valley" meant even more than a cluster of companies and a culture. The term stood now for the whole range of computer-based technology business in the United States, just as "Detroit" stood for the nation's automobile business.

For all the promise of Silicon Valley, the comparison with Detroit was telling. The Michigan city had remained affordable for the working class. Silicon Valley in contrast, had become a crowded, expensive place that catered to the educated elite. For decades, the automobile industry had provided high-wage jobs and a middle-class standard of living for working-class Americans. Yet in the 1980s, companies tended to put research facilities and corporate headquarters in the valley—but not their factories, which were moving overseas. "Now, this has become a place for corporate brain trusts, for research and development and marketing activities, not a place for production lines," the city manager of Sunnyvale observed wistfully in 1988. "Most of the production lines are gone. People can't afford to live here anymore."

Perhaps Silicon Valley did not point to such a rosy future, after all. Could the region remain the "Valley of the Heart's Delight"?

some Sunbelt counties more than doubled in population. These regional shifts had direct political effects. Reapportionment in 1980 gave more congressional seats and electoral votes to the more conservative states of the Sunbelt.

The Rehabilitation of Business

While the 1980s pointed to a utopian future, the decade also recalled the cutthroat capitalism of the turn of the twentieth century. A wave of corporate takeovers and mergers swept the economy. Aggressive investment bankers and entrepreneurs such as Michael Milken and Ivan Boesky used junk bonds—high-risk, high-paying securities—and other techniques to finance takeovers. Executives took golden parachutes, huge payments for selling their companies and losing their jobs. Enormous deals merged some of the largest American corporations. In 1985 General Electric bought RCA for $6 billion. In 1986 alone there were more than 4,000 mergers worth a total of $190 billion. The biggest deal came in 1988 when RJR Nabisco was sold for $25 billion, and the company's president and CEO received a $53 million golden parachute.

The takeover wave and the growth of the computer industry helped rehabilitate business and its values, under attack in the 1960s and 1970s. Although some observers criticized the concentration of so much economic power, others saw the takeovers as a sign of economic vitality. They argued that the mergers created larger, more efficient, more competitive companies, and praised takeover artists as models of energy and creativity. The media enthusiastically reported on Milken, Boesky, Jobs, and Gates. *Dallas, Dynasty,* and other popular television shows celebrated the fictional sagas of wealthy, freewheeling families. Business was more respectable than at any time since the 1950s.

So were materialism and the pursuit and enjoyment of wealth. "Everybody should be a little greedy," Boesky advised. "Thank goodness it's back," gushed the *New York Times,* "that lovely whipped cream of a word—luxury."

The baby boom generation reflected the new appeal of business. Former 1960s radicals such as Yippie (Youth Independent Party) leader Jerry Rubin took up business careers. By 1983 the media were talking about the emergence of yuppies, young urban professionals in their 20s and 30s. Uninterested in social reform, these optimistic, self-centered baby boomers were supposedly eager to make lots of money and then spend it on BMW cars, Perrier water, and other playthings. Although the transition from Yippies to yuppies was exaggerated, the yuppie stereotype underscored American aspirations to a more conservative, money-centered way of life.

The Rise of the Religious Right

As American culture celebrated materialism, many Americans still turned to spirituality to find meaning in their lives. Their choice of denominations reflected the trend to conservatism. Such mainline Protestant denominations as the United Methodist Church, the Episcopal Church, and the Presbyterian Church, USA, had been losing their share of church members since at least 1940. Meanwhile, evangelical churches boomed (see Map 30–1). By the 1980s, the Southern Baptist Convention was the largest American Protestant denomination. Such smaller evangelical bodies as the Assemblies of God more than doubled in size from the 1960s to the 1980s.

This changing denominational balance had social and political consequences. The mainline churches often took moderate or liberal positions on such issues as civil rights

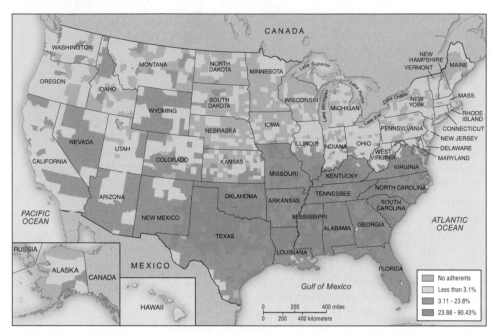

Map 30–1   The Growth of Evangelical Christianity The Southern Baptist Convention's share of the population, by county, reveals its gradual spread beyond its traditional base in the South by 1990. *Peter L. Halvorson and William M. Newman, Atlas of Religious Change in America, 1952–1990 (Cincinnati, OH: Glenmary Research Center, 1994), p. 120.*

and abortion, but the evangelical churches more often supported conservative positions. Troubled by social change and emboldened by their own growth, evangelicals wanted to spread a conservative message across American culture and politics.

The emergence of "televangelists" was the most obvious result of this impulse. From 1978 to 1989 the number of Christian television ministries grew from 25 to 336. The most successful televangelists also had their own networks, colleges, political groups, and even an amusement park. Pat Robertson, a born-again Baptist from Virginia, hosted *The 700 Club* and ran the Christian Broadcast Network. Jerry Falwell, a fundamentalist who believed in the literal interpretation of the Bible, hosted the *Old Time Gospel Hour* and founded Liberty Baptist College in Virginia. He also organized the Moral Majority, a political pressure group. Deeply conservative, the televangelists condemned women's liberation, abortion, gay rights, and liberal Great Society programs. They wanted prayer in public schools. Earning millions of dollars, they praised low taxes, limited government, and financial success. Determined to win what Falwell called the "war against sin," the televangelists were the spearheads of a religious Right ready for politics.

The 1980 Presidential Election

The new conservative majority came together in the presidential election of 1980. Former California governor Ronald Reagan continued his political rise by winning the Republican nomination. Although he chose a moderate running mate, George H. W. Bush of Texas, Reagan ran a conservative campaign. His vision of less government, lower taxes,

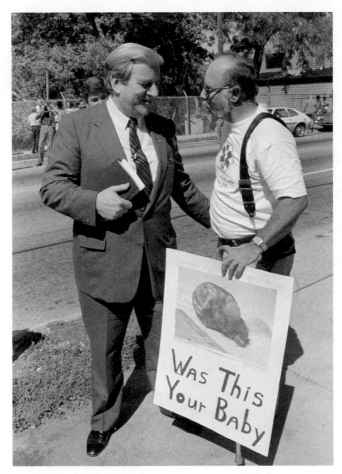

The Reverend Jerry Falwell Jerry Falwell (left), fundamentalist and leader of the religious Right.

renewed military might, and traditional social values appealed to business and evangelicals. His genial optimism suggested that the political system could be made to work. As a former Democrat, Reagan reassured Democrats and independents that they too could find a home in the Republican Party.

Meanwhile, the Democratic nominee, incumbent president Jimmy Carter, struggled with a weak economy and the ongoing hostage crisis in Iran. His moderate, sometimes conservative policies had alienated liberal Democrats. His poor economic record had alienated the party's white ethnics. Moderate Republican congressman John Anderson of Illinois, who ran as an independent, drew voters away from Carter. Meanwhile, Reagan focused relentlessly on America's decline during Carter's presidency. In the last presidential debate before Election Day, Reagan told the audience, "I think . . . it might be well if you would ask yourself, are you better off than you were four years ago?"

Americans answered that question by giving Reagan the presidency. Reagan carried all but four states and the District of Columbia (see Map 30–2). He managed only 50.7 percent of the popular vote, but with Anderson's 6.6 percent, the tally suggested the extent

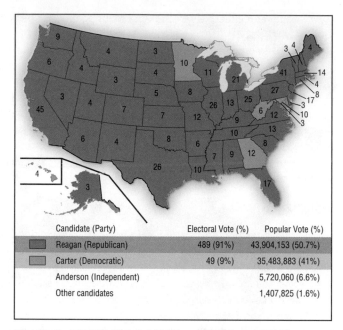

Candidate (Party)	Electoral Vote (%)	Popular Vote (%)
Reagan (Republican)	489 (91%)	43,904,153 (50.7%)
Carter (Democratic)	49 (9%)	35,483,883 (41%)
Anderson (Independent)		5,720,060 (6.6%)
Other candidates		1,407,825 (1.6%)

Map 30–2   The Presidential Election, 1980 As in other elections, a narrow victory in the popular vote translated into a landslide in the Electoral College.

of popular disaffection with Carter and the Democratic Party. The Democrats held on to the House of Representatives, but Republicans won the Senate for the first time since 1962. Sixteen years after the defeat of Barry Goldwater's conservative candidacy, the nation had turned sharply to the right.

The Reagan Revolution at Home

Ronald Reagan shaped American life more decisively than any president since Franklin Roosevelt. Reagan's folksy optimism made him popular, but the Reagan years were more than a triumph of style. With some justice, his supporters believed that his "Reagan Revolution" spurred a sweeping conservative transformation of American economic and political life.

The Reagan Style

The Reagan Revolution was partly a matter of style. Despite the frustrations of the 1960s and 1970s, Reagan exuded optimism. Rather than ask Americans to live with less, he embraced luxury. Reagan's presidency signaled a confident, even opulent, new era. On Inauguration Day, as if to mark the end of the frustrating 1970s, the Iranian government finally released its American hostages. In his inaugural address, Reagan firmly rejected pessimism. "We are not," the new president declared, "doomed to an inevitable decline." The Reagan inaugural cost five times more than Jimmy Carter's had four years earlier.

Even while Ronald and Nancy Reagan lived lavishly in the White House, the president retained a popular, common touch. After his career in movies and television, he knew how to speak simply and effectively to the American people. He became known as the "Great Communicator."

Reagan also appeared to enjoy and master his job. Although he took office as America's oldest president at the age of 69, he projected vigor and energy. After the troubled presidencies of the 1970s, Reagan made the presidency—and democracy—seem workable again.

The president even managed to survive an assassination attempt. On March 30, 1981, John W. Hinckley, a troubled loner, shot and wounded Reagan, his press secretary, and a policeman. Reagan's chest wound was more serious than his spokesmen admitted, but he met the situation with good humor. "Honey," he told his wife, "I forgot to duck." The president's popularity soared.

Shrinking Government

Reagan offered a clear alternative to the New Deal and the Great Society. Above all, he denied that a large, activist federal government could deal with the challenges of American life in the 1980s. So Reagan vowed to reduce the government's size and power.

The president's efforts to shrink the federal government met with mixed success. In his 1982 State of the Union address, Reagan, like the previous Republican president, Richard Nixon, endorsed the New Federalism, a plan to transfer federal programs and tax revenues to the states. Reagan insisted the New Federalism would promote efficiency and economic growth, but governors worried that their states would be saddled with expensive responsibilities. In the end, only a few programs were transferred.

Congress also rebuffed administration plans to save money with tighter qualifications for government benefits and with a line-item veto permitting the president to reject specific spending programs.

Reagan had more success when he attacked social welfare programs. Like other conservatives, Reagan condemned antipoverty programs as a waste of federal resources that sapped the work ethic and the morals of the poor. He wanted reductions in food stamps, school meal programs, and aid to cities. In response, Congress cut funding for urban public housing and ended job training for the unemployed.

Reagan found it nearly impossible to touch Medicare and Social Security, two expensive and popular programs that benefited most Americans. By the 1980s there was concern that workers' Social Security payments would eventually not be enough to cover the cost of benefits to retirees. After a long struggle, Congress produced the Social Security Reform Act of 1983, which raised the minimum age for full benefits from 65 to 67 and taxed some benefits. The measure did little to reduce program costs. By 1984, Reagan promised not to cut Social Security.

Although expenditures for welfare programs continued to rise, the Reagan administration managed to slow the growth of such spending. Benefits did not expand dramatically; there were no costly new programs. Reagan did not reduce the federal government overall, but he did shrink the relative size of some parts of it that he disliked.

Reaganomics

For Reagan and his followers, shrinking the government also meant decreasing Washington's role in the economy. As conservatives, they argued that the nation prospered most when Americans were left free to manage their own businesses and keep their own earnings. The Reagan administration worked to lower taxes, deregulate business, and cut federal support for unions.

"Reaganomics" drew on a new theory known as supply-side economics. In the 1970s, economist Arthur Laffer had offered an alternative to the liberal, Keynesian economics that had guided federal policy since the New Deal. While Keynesians believed that increased consumer demand would spur economic growth, Laffer contended that an increased supply of goods and services was the key to growth. He rejected the Keynesian idea that more government spending put more money in the hands of consumers. To promote prosperity, he believed government should cut, rather than raise, taxes. Leaving more money in the hands of businesses would allow them to produce more goods and services. The increase in supply would stimulate prosperity and increase, rather than decrease, tax revenues.

Supply-side economics was controversial. Liberal critics called it an excuse to let the rich keep more of their money. Even some Republicans doubted that a tax cut would produce more tax revenues. But the supply-side approach fit neatly with conservative dislike for high taxes and big government.

Following supply-side principles, Reagan asked Congress in 1981 to cut taxes dramatically. Impressed by Reagan's popularity and the electorate's conservatism, the Democratic-controlled House joined the Republican-dominated Senate to pass the Economic Recovery Act of 1981 (the Kemp-Roth Bill). An important victory for Reagan, it cut federal income taxes 5 percent the first year and 10 percent in each of the next two years. It benefited the wealthy by making the tax structure less progressive and by reducing the tax rates on the highest incomes and on large gifts and estates.

Like other conservatives, Reagan believed that federal regulations hamstrung American business and prevented economic growth. Accordingly, his administration stepped up the campaign for deregulation begun by Jimmy Carter. The budgets of such key regulatory agencies as the Environmental Protection Agency and the Occupational Safety and Health Administration were cut. The administration also made sure that officials did not strictly enforce regulatory rules and laws. In addition, the administration deregulated the telephone industry. In 1982 the giant American Telephone and Telegraph Company was broken into smaller regional companies, and new firms such as Sprint and MCI were allowed to compete for AT&T's long-distance business.

Reagan moved to lift environmental restrictions on business. His administration made it easier for timber and mining companies to exploit wilderness areas and for oil companies to drill off the Pacific coast. It also opposed environmentalists' demands for laws to protect against acid rain—industrial air pollution that harmed lakes, forests, and crops. Reaganomics also weakened organized labor, already suffering from deindustrialization. Ironically, Reagan, once the head of the Screen Actors Guild, was the first former union official to serve as president. Like most conservatives, Reagan believed that unions obstructed business and limited workers' freedom. He believed the federal government had done too much for organized labor since the New Deal.

Reagan took a strong antiunion stance during a strike by the Professional Air Traffic Controllers Organization (PATCO) in 1981. Despite a law banning strikes by federal workers, PATCO walked out to protest unsafe conditions in the air traffic control system. Reagan fired the striking controllers, refused to hire them back, and replaced them with nonunion workers. His action encouraged business to take a hard line with employees. By the end of the 1980s, unions were weaker than at any time since the Great Depression.

Reaganomics did not quite have the effect its supporters anticipated. Reagan's measures did not prevent a sharp recession, which began in the fall of 1981. As the Federal Reserve Bank fought inflation by raising interest rates, the economy slowed and unemployment increased. Reaganomics also increased the federal budget deficit. The supply-side theory that tax cuts would boost tax revenues and balance the budget proved incorrect.

By the spring of 1984, the recession had ended. Thanks largely to the Federal Reserve's monetary policy, "stagflation," the combination of stagnant economic growth and high inflation, was over. As employment increased, Reagan's supporters gave the president credit. His critics charged that the deficit, not Reaganomics, had produced the boom and that the deficit would ultimately hurt the economy. In the mid-1980s, however, Reaganomics seemed to be a success.

The 1984 Presidential Election

The changing impact of Reaganomics affected national politics. In the depths of the recession, the Republicans lost 26 House seats in the midterm elections of 1982. But with the return of prosperity, the president was easily renominated in 1984. Reagan ran against a liberal Democratic nominee, former vice president Walter Mondale of Minnesota. Against a popular incumbent, Mondale made bold moves. He chose the first female vice-presidential nominee of a major party, Representative Geraldine Ferraro of New York. To prove his honesty and openness, Mondale made the politically foolish announcement that he would raise taxes as president. The Democrat was also saddled with the record of the Carter administration and the alienation of white working- and middle-class Democrats.

Reagan ran an optimistic campaign emphasizing national renewal. "It's morning again in America," Reagan commercials announced. "And people have a sense of pride they never felt they'd feel again." Mondale would jeopardize all that, the Reagan campaign charged, with tax increases and favors to such "special interests" as labor unions, feminists, and civil rights groups.

Election Day revealed both the strength and the weakness of the Reagan Revolution. With his conservative message Reagan won 58.8 percent of the popular vote and lost only the District of Columbia and Mondale's home state of Minnesota. But his personal triumph did not translate into one for his party. Holding on to the Senate, the Republicans lost control of the House of Representatives.

The Reagan Revolution Abroad

Reagan's foreign policy, like his domestic policy, rested on old conservative values. The president rejected the main diplomatic approaches of the 1970s—Nixon's détente with the Soviet Union and Carter's support for international human rights. Instead, the Reagan Revolution revived the strident anti-Communism of the 1940s and 1950s. The president moved to restore the nation's military and economic power to challenge the Soviet Union and stop Communism in the Western Hemisphere. Communism, however, had little to do with such difficult international issues as conflict in the Middle East, terrorism, and global economic competition. Nevertheless, the Reagan Revolution refocused American policy on the cold war confrontation with Communism.

Restoring American Power

After losing the Vietnam War, the United States had reduced both its armed forces and its willingness to risk military confrontations abroad. Reagan set out to restore American power in the 1980s—and the will to use it.

Like most conservatives, the president did not believe that cutting government spending meant cutting the armed forces. Under Reagan, defense spending more than doubled, from $134 billion in 1980 to more than $300 billion by 1989. Reagan also ordered development of controversial weapons systems. Construction of the B-1 strategic bomber, stopped by Carter, resumed, while development of the B-2 Stealth bomber began. Reagan won congressional approval for the MX Peacekeeper, a nuclear missile with multiple warheads, and for work on the neutron bomb, a nuclear weapon. As he built up the military, Reagan faced a growing mass movement against nuclear weapons. In Europe and the United States, millions of people, frightened by nuclear war, called for a halt to new nuclear arms. In June 1982, a crowd of 700,000 in New York's Central Park demanded a nuclear freeze. The National Conference of Catholic Bishops supported the freeze and declared nuclear war immoral. But Reagan rejected the movement as naive and Communist-infiltrated. Peace, he believed, depended on developing more weapons.

The military buildup was also a matter of changing attitudes. In the wake of the Vietnam War, many Americans were reluctant to endorse intervention abroad. They feared

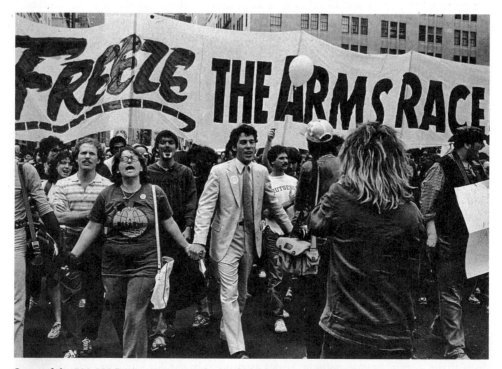

Some of the 700,000 Demonstrators at the Nuclear Freeze Rally in New York City's Central Park, June 1982 For a time, the movement to halt the introduction of new nuclear weapons challenged President Reagan's plans for an arms buildup.

becoming entrapped in another costly, losing, possibly immoral battle. This "Vietnam syndrome" threatened Reagan's foreign policy. The president could not afford to let other countries think he would not back up his words with action. Accordingly, Reagan used his speeches to stir up patriotic emotion and to persuade Americans that the Vietnam War had been "a just cause" worth supporting.

By the mid-1980s, Reagan had restored much of America's military power. It remained to be seen, however, whether Americans were willing to use that power abroad.

Confronting the "Evil Empire"

The main purpose of the buildup was to contain the Soviet Union. Suspicion of the Soviets and their Communist ideology was the heart of Reagan's diplomacy. In the early 1980s, Reagan called the USSR the "evil empire" and insisted that failing economies and unpopular regimes doomed the Soviets and their Communist allies. Communism, he predicted, would end up "on the ash heap of history."

Reagan avoided cooperation with the Soviet Union and held no summit meetings during his first term. His administration openly supported the *mujahedeen*, the Afghan rebels who were resisting the Soviets. More important, he avoided arms-control agreements with the Soviets during his first term. Instead, he used the military buildup to pressure the USSR. Reagan refused to submit the second Strategic Arms Limitation Treaty, signed by Jimmy Carter, to the Senate for ratification. In response to the United States' deployment of new nuclear missiles in Western Europe, the Soviets walked out of arms-control talks in 1983.

That year, Reagan put even more pressure on the USSR by announcing plans for the Strategic Defense Initiative (SDI), a space-based defense system of lasers and other advanced technology designed to shoot down enemy missiles. Funded by Congress, SDI was such a long way from reality that critics, sure it was science fiction, called the plan "Star Wars," after the epic space movie.

SDI doubly threatened the Soviets. It seemingly made the USSR vulnerable to attack. Since the 1950s, the Americans and the Soviets had relied on the theory of mutual assured destruction as a deterrent to war: because a nuclear war would destroy both sides, there was no incentive for either to start one. Now SDI raised the possibility that because the United States could survive a nuclear attack, it might be willing to start a war with the Soviets. The Soviets would then need to develop their own SDI. There was the second threat: the USSR would have to divert scarce resources and perhaps weaken their economy in order to compete with the United States.

While the United States pressed the Soviets, Reagan wanted to avoid open confrontation with the major Communist powers. In 1983, a Soviet fighter plane shot down an unarmed Korean airliner, killing all 269 aboard. Although a US congressman was one of the victims, Reagan responded with restraint. A year later, Reagan traded visits with the premier of the People's Republic of China and encouraged stronger relations and a nuclear-weapons agreement.

The Reagan Doctrine in the Third World

The Reagan administration also changed American foreign policy toward the third world. Reagan and other conservatives had been impatient with the Carter administration's attempts to promote human rights abroad. The United States, they believed, needed to back anti-Communist, pro-American governments, whether or not they respected human rights. Jeane J. Kirkpatrick, who became Reagan's ambassador to the United Nations, distinguished between totalitarian regimes hostile to the United States and authoritarian governments friendly to American interests. Critics claimed this distinction was meaningless and insisted the nation not support antidemocratic governments. The administration adopted Kirkpatrick's view, which became known as the Reagan Doctrine.

The administration applied the Reagan Doctrine aggressively in Central America and the Caribbean (see Map 30–3). Determined to keep Communism out of the Western Hemisphere, the United States opposed the Marxist Sandinista government of Nicaragua and supported the repressive anti-Communist government of neighboring El Salvador.

Encouraged by the Carter administration, the Sandinistas had come to power in the late 1970s by overthrowing the dictatorship of Anastasio Somoza. The Reagan administration believed the Sandinistas were too friendly to the Soviet Union and to leftist rebels in El Salvador. Reagan halted aid to Nicaragua in April 1981 and directed the CIA to train, arm, and supply the Contra rebels, who opposed the Sandinistas. Many of the Contras had ties to the oppressive Somoza regime, but Reagan praised them as "freedom fighters." Meanwhile, the president strongly backed the right-wing military government of El Salvador, locked in a civil war with pro-Sandinista and pro-Cuban rebels. Employing infamous "death squads," the military government engaged in kidnapping, torture, and murder. Some 75,000 people died in the conflict. Still, Reagan did not want this brutal, undemocratic regime to fall.

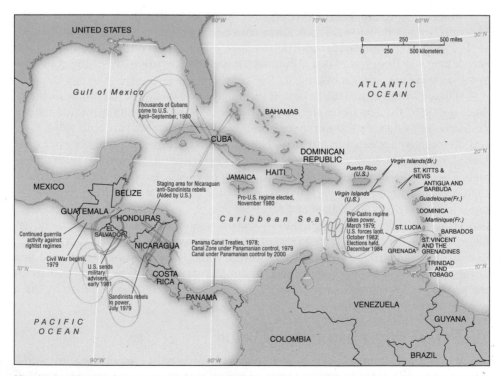

Map 30–3   The Reagan Doctrine in Central America and the Caribbean Events that shaped Reagan's anti-Communist initiative in the Western Hemisphere.

Reagan's Central American Policy The president holds up a T-shirt summing up his approach to the region: "STOP COMMUNISM CENTRAL AMERICA."

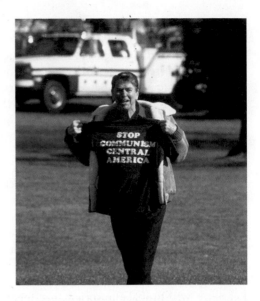

El Salvador, he explained, was "a textbook case of indirect armed aggression by Communist powers."

Despite such rhetoric, the administration could not persuade Congress to support its Central American policy. Congressional Democrats, like many Americans, did not want war in Central America. They were skeptical about the Communist threat and troubled by the antidemocratic character of the Salvadoran regime and the Contra rebels. In 1983 Congress approved Reagan's Caribbean Basin Initiative, an economic development package, but not military aid for the Salvadoran government. Instead, Congress passed the Boland Amendment, which restricted aid to the Contras and banned efforts to topple the Sandinista regime.

Reagan applied the Reagan Doctrine more successfully in the Caribbean. On October 25, 1983, US troops invaded the small island of Grenada, supposedly to protect about 1,000 Americans, mostly medical students, from a Marxist regime. Reagan feared Grenada would become a Cuban or Soviet base close to US shores. The invading force quickly secured the island and replaced the government with a pro-American regime. Critics charged that Reagan had violated the sovereignty of another state for an easy military victory. To his supporters, the invasion was a welcome demonstration of the Reagan Doctrine and an antidote to the Vietnam syndrome.

The president also applied the Reagan Doctrine in Africa. The Carter administration had condemned the long-standing policy of *apartheid*—racial separation—pursued by the white government of South Africa. Reagan, despite America's struggle with racial segregation, would not take such a strong stance. Rather than impose economic sanctions on South Africa, he endorsed mild diplomatic discussions known as "constructive engagement" while South Africa suffered violence and near civil war. Reagan held back because the South African regime was an ally against Communism in the region. During the 1980s, the United States supported South African military intervention in Angola, Mozambique, and Namibia against groups aided by Cuba and the Soviet Union. More than a million people died in these conflicts.

The Middle East and Terrorism

The Reagan Doctrine was not much help in dealing with the Middle East and the growing problem of terrorism. Communism and the Soviet Union had little impact on Middle Eastern issues in the 1980s. As before, the United States wanted to ensure its supply of oil and to support its longtime ally, Israel. There was no new Arab oil embargo during the

Reagan years, but the administration could not bring peace to the Middle East or end the threat of terrorism.

Reagan found it difficult to build on the Camp David Accords between Israel and Egypt, which were supposed to lead to self-government for the Palestinian Arabs living in the Israeli-occupied West Bank and Gaza Strip. Israel and the Palestine Liberation Organization (PLO), the official representative of the Palestinians, remained at odds. The PLO continued to threaten Israel from bases in neighboring Lebanon. In the spring of 1982, the Israelis invaded Lebanon, which was already convulsed by a civil war between Muslims and Christians.

To end the invasion and stabilize Lebanon, the United States sent marines to join an international peacekeeping force. On October 23, 1983, a terrorist bomb killed 241 Americans at marine headquarters at Beirut. The shocking attack marked a low point of Reagan's administration. The president did not retaliate. He did not want to reward terrorism by withdrawing from Lebanon. Nevertheless, he pulled out the soldiers in 1984, even though there was no peace in Lebanon and no agreement between the Israelis and the PLO.

The attack on the marine headquarters illustrated the growing threat of terrorism. Reagan vowed to make terrorists "pay for their actions," but terrorism proved hard to stop. Acts of terrorism by Palestinians and Libyans drew quick American reprisals in the 1980s. After Palestinians murdered an American passenger on a cruise ship in the Mediterranean in 1985, US planes forced down the Egyptian airliner carrying the escaping terrorists. The Reagan administration believed that Muammar Qaddafi, leader of the North African nation of Libya, supported terrorism. In 1982 US Navy fighter planes shot down two Libyan fighters. After American soldiers died in a terrorist bombing in West Germany in 1986, US jets bombed targets in Libya, among them military barracks and Qaddafi's personal residence, killing one of his daughters. Qaddafi seemed to become less critical of the United States, but the threat of terrorism did not go away.

Reagan also acted to safeguard America's oil supply. During a war between Iran and Iraq, the United States sent warships to protect oil tankers in the Persian Gulf. American intervention was costly. In May 1987, Iraqi missiles struck the US destroyer *Stark*, killing 37 of its crew. Unwilling to help Iran, Reagan accepted Iraq's apology. In July 1988, the US missile cruiser *Vincennes* accidentally shot down an Iranian airliner, killing 290 passengers. An American apology did not quell Iranian anger, but the Iran-Iraq war soon ended, and with it the threat to America's oil supply.

The United States and the World Economy

Middle Eastern oil was only one economic factor shaping Reagan's foreign policy. The president had to deal with strains on the world economy. Like presidents before him, Reagan believed strongly that free trade would boost national economies. He believed, too, that other nations would benefit from cutting taxes, government spending, and regulation. But after years of economic decline, the United States could not always impose its will on other nations.

Reagan did force his views on weak, debt-ridden third world countries. By the end of the 1980s, developing nations owed foreign banks more than $1.2 trillion. Mexico

AMERICA AND THE WORLD

>> **Japanese Management, American Workers**

Until the 1980s, most American workers had missed one of the basic experiences of globalization—management by foreigners. But with the weakening of American industry and the rebirth of the Japanese and West European economies, foreign firms began to set up operations in the United States in the 1970s and 1980s.

Japanese firms rushed to invest. By 1988, more than 300,000 Americans worked for Japanese companies in the United States. The most publicized Japanese ventures came in the auto industry, long dominated by US manufacturers. In the 1980s, leading Japanese auto manufacturers set up factories in such places as Marysville, Ohio, Smyrna, Tennessee, and Fremont, California. In these and other facilities, Japanese companies set about teaching Americans new ways to work.

The Japanese approach emphasized the importance of the group over the individual and the company as a harmonious family whose members had the same interests. To foster harmony, the Japanese eliminated reserved parking spaces for management and time clocks for labor. At the Nissan plant in Smyrna, managers and workers wore the same blue uniform. The Japanese also tried to improve communication with workers and draw them into decision making. To empower workers and increase efficiency, Japanese companies often gave workers the means to stop production to eliminate a problem—something US firms seldom did.

Japanese companies tried to improve factory life. Plants were clean and efficient. At the Nissan factory in Smyrna, workers had basketball hoops and Ping-Pong tables for use during breaks. But the Japanese also banned smoking and radios. Management pushed workers to speed up production and wanted workers to be flexible enough to do different jobs in a plant.

Some workers enthusiastically accepted the new approach. "I love it," gushed Nancy Nicholson, a laid-off factory worker who found a job in a Japanese plant in Virginia. "They make you feel like a part of a family." Workers appreciated that Japanese managers put in long hours and seemed devoted to efficiency and quality.

Laboring harder than before, many American workers were not quite so enthusiastic. They felt the Japanese were hostile to unions, African Americans, and women. Some American managers charged that Japanese employers would not promote them to top jobs. But most employees were glad to have a well-paying job that might last. Japanese executives had their own criticisms. They felt that American workers needed too many instructions and too much motivation. Individualistic Americans were not "team players" ready to admit mistakes or work outside their job descriptions. "Americans are too sensitive about fairness," complained Kosuke Ikebuchi, after years in the United States. Japanese managers generally concluded that their American subordinates were less productive than Japanese workers.

Despite such criticism, Japanese companies seemed successful in the United States
continued

in the 1980s. Their units made gains in productivity and quality. The General Motors–
Toyota plant in Fremont, California, turned
out a car in 20 hours, compared with 28

hours at another GM plant. That car was
more likely to satisfy buyers than one from
an American-run company.

was more than $100 billion in debt. American banks would lose heavily if those nations
defaulted on loans. American producers stood to lose if those countries could not afford
to buy US goods. The Reagan administration refused to protect American banks from
defaults, instead forcing debtor countries to adopt freer trade, deregulation of business,
and austerity programs in return for new loans.

The Reagan administration had much less power to dictate trade policy with Japan.
As Japanese exports flowed into the United States, Americans increasingly resented Japan's control of its home market. Congress, believing Japan discriminated against American goods, pushed for retaliation. Japan placed voluntary quotas on its export of steel
and automobiles to the United States. Although the United States devalued the dollar
to make American goods cheaper, the trade imbalance continued. In 1988 the president
signed the Omnibus Trade and Competitiveness Act, which allowed the government to
place high tariffs on Japanese goods if Japan discriminated against American goods. But,
as long as Americans wanted Japanese products, retaliation was unlikely. In 1989 a Japanese car, the Honda Accord, was the first international model to become the best-selling
automobile in America.

Many Accords had been made in the United States. Even as the administration struggled to open Japanese markets to American goods, Japanese firms increased their direct
investment in the United States. Honda built a new factory in Marysville, Ohio, to produce Accords for the American market. As Japanese companies built or took over other
facilities, many Americans wondered whether the global expansion of trade really benefited their country after all.

The Battle over Conservative Social Values

For all of Ronald Reagan's success in the early 1980s, the new conservatism met with
important opposition. The conservatives' social values were especially controversial. Angered by the changes of the 1960s, many conservatives, like Linda Chavez, wanted to restore supposedly traditional values and practices. The conservative agenda collided head-
on with one of the chief legacies of the 1960s—disadvantaged groups' demands for equal
rights and opportunities. Many Americans were also unwilling to abandon the social
changes of the last generation. Faced with such opposition, conservatives failed to achieve
much of their vision.

Attacking the Legacy of the 1960s

The new conservatism was driven by a desire to undo the liberal and radical legacies of the 1960s. Conservatives blamed federal courts for much of the social change over the last generation. In the 1960s and 1970s, liberal, activist justices had supported defendants' rights, civil rights, affirmative action, busing, and abortion while rejecting such conservative causes as school prayer.

Determined to take control of the courts, Reagan appointed many staunch, relatively young conservatives to the federal bench and the Supreme Court. In 1981 Sandra Day O'Connor, a fairly conservative judge from Arizona, became the Court's first woman justice. Reagan replaced retiring Chief Justice Warren Burger with conservative William Rehnquist. The appointments of two more conservatives, Antonin Scalia and Anthony Kennedy, seemed to push the Supreme Court away from liberalism.

It did not quite work out that way. In the 1980s the Court followed conservative views in limiting the rights of defendants. Rulings in *United States v. Leon* and *Nix v. Williams* in 1984 made it easier for prosecutors to use evidence improperly obtained by police. However, on other issues, the court took a moderate stance. In *Wallace v. Jaffree* in 1985, the Court invalidated an Alabama law that allowed schools to devote a minute each day to voluntary prayer or meditation.

Prayer was part of the conservatives' plan to reform public education. They believed that the federal government had played too large a role in the schools since the 1960s. Parents, meanwhile, had too little say in the education of their children. Preferring to use market forces rather than government to reform the schools, conservatives wanted to abolish the federal Department of Education. They also wanted to let parents choose the best schools—public or private—for their children and cover part of the cost with federally funded vouchers or tax credits.

Because many Americans worried about the quality of the schools, conservatives had a golden opportunity. But Congress refused to adopt vouchers or abolish the Department of Education.

Drug use was another issue conservatives linked to the 1960s. In the early 1980s, drugs again became a major concern with the spread of crack, a cheap, addictive form of cocaine. The sale and use of crack, especially in the cities, led to crime and violence. In 1986 the president and his wife, Nancy, announced a "national crusade" for a "drug-free" America. Their campaign encouraged young people to "Just Say No" to drugs, implemented drug testing for federal employees, and imposed mandatory minimum sentences for some drug use. The "war on drugs" was controversial. Critics called its rhetoric naive and ineffective. They also condemned new sentencing laws, which put millions in jail, as unfair to African Americans and expensive to taxpayers. Despite the crusade, drug use did not decrease appreciably.

Women's Rights and Abortion

One of the chief legacies of the 1960s was the women's rights movement. The new conservatism condemned feminism and deplored the changing role of women in America. Many conservatives, especially evangelical leaders, blamed feminists and liberal government for encouraging women to abandon their traditional family role for paid jobs. The conservative movement was especially determined to halt federal initiatives, such as affirmative action programs and the Equal Rights Amendment (ERA), that protected women's rights (see Chapter 29).

The conservative agenda on women's rights met with mixed results. The campaign for the ERA, lagging since the 1970s, ended unsuccessfully, but affirmative action programs to promote the hiring of women continued. So did women's push into the workplace and public life as more families needed two incomes. By 1983 women made up half of the paid workforce. As their economic role expanded, so did their political visibility. Ironically, Reagan gave women new public prominence by choosing Jeane J. Kirkpatrick and Sandra Day O'Connor for important offices.

Women still did not enjoy equality in America. They were generally paid less than men doing the same sort of work, and they had less opportunity to break through the "glass ceiling" and win managerial jobs. Commentators noted the feminization of poverty. Unmarried or divorced women, many with children, made up an increasing percentage of the poor. This unequal suffering, liberals and feminists argued, disproved the conservative claim that women did not need special protection.

For many conservatives, the right to abortion, guaranteed by the Supreme Court in *Roe v. Wade* in 1974, was the most troubling change in the status of women. A growing Right to Life movement passionately denounced abortion as the murder of the unborn, practiced by selfish women who rejected motherhood and family.

Conservatives failed to narrow abortion rights significantly in the 1980s (see Map 30–4). Reagan persuaded Congress to stop the use of federal funds to pay for abortions, but a constitutional amendment outlawing abortion stalled in the Senate. Supreme Court rulings made in 1983 and 1986 upheld *Roe v. Wade*.

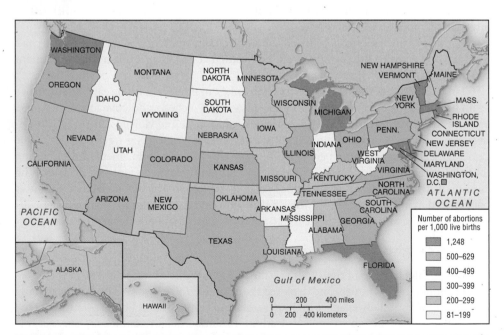

Map 30–4 Abortion in the 1980s The rate of abortions across the United States 14 years after the Supreme Court's decision legalizing abortion in *Roe v. Wade*. *Timothy H. Fast and Cathy Carroll Fast,* The Women's Atlas of the United States, *rev. ed. (1995), p. 166.*

Gays and the AIDS Crisis

The gay rights movement was another legacy of the 1960s that troubled conservatives. Evangelical leaders such as Jerry Falwell condemned homosexuality on religious grounds. Some people believed that equal rights for gay men and women would promote immorality and corrupt children. In 1977 Anita Bryant, a former Miss America, launched a national crusade, Save Our Children, to protest the passage of a gay rights ordinance in Florida. Voters soon repealed the measure. In San Francisco in 1978, Harvey Milk, the first avowedly gay member of the city's board of supervisors, was assassinated, along with the mayor, by a former supervisor. Many were shocked when the assassin received only a short jail sentence.

Despite such opposition, the gay rights movement made progress in the 1980s. In 1982 Wisconsin became the first state to pass a law protecting the rights of gay men and women. By the end of the decade, most states had repealed sodomy laws that criminalized gay sex. In *Bowers v. Hardwick* in 1986, however, the US Supreme Court dismissed a gay man's right to sexual privacy as "facetious."

The battle over gay rights took place against a tragic backdrop. In 1981 the Centers for Disease Control began reporting cases of acquired immune deficiency syndrome (AIDS), a disease that destroyed the body's immune system and left it unable to fight off infections and rare cancers. By the mid-1980s, researchers had traced AIDS to different forms of the human immunodeficiency virus (HIV) that were transmitted in semen and blood. But no cure had been found. By 1990 there were nearly 100,000 recorded deaths from the AIDS epidemic in the United States (see Figure 30–2).

Because 75 percent of the first victims were gay men, Americans initially considered AIDS a homosexual disease. Some people, including evangelical leaders, believed this "gay cancer" was God's punishment for the alleged sin of homosexuality. It became clear,

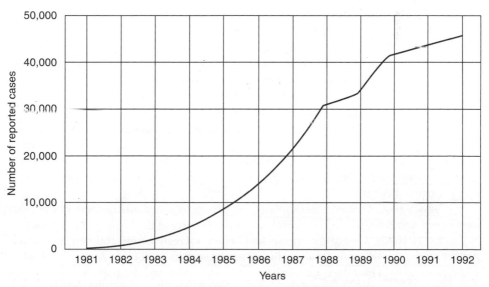

Figure 30–2   The Rapid Rise of AIDS Statistical Abstract of the United States, 1989, *p. 111;* Statistical Abstract, 1993, *p. 203.*

however, that AIDS could also be transmitted by heterosexual intercourse, by intravenous drug use with shared needles, and by tainted blood transfusions.

Although understanding of AIDS and HIV increased, the specter of "gay cancer" promoted homophobia and slowed the response to the disease. The AIDS Coalition to Unleash Power (ACT UP) and other organizations staged demonstrations and acts of civil disobedience to call attention to the crisis and push for government action. Nevertheless, the Reagan administration did not fund research on AIDS for several years, and the disease continued to spread.

The AIDS epidemic complicated the struggle over gay rights. For some Americans, the disease reinforced the conservative condemnation of homosexuality. For others, the suffering of victims evoked sympathy and compassion. As the 1980s ended, the conservative backlash against gay rights had failed, but the epidemic continued.

African Americans and Racial Inequality

Conservatives were uneasy with another legacy of the 1960s, the expansion of African American civil rights and benefits guaranteed by the federal government. They believed that the liberal policies of the Great Society hurt, rather than helped, black people and argued that individual initiative, not government action, would promote racial equality. Reflecting these ideas, Reagan opposed renewal of the Voting Rights Act and condemned busing and affirmative action. Like many Republicans, he opposed the creation of a national holiday marking the birthday of Martin Luther King Jr.

The conservatives' tough stance came at a difficult time for racial equality. African Americans' crusade for justice and opportunity generally slowed in the 1970s and 1980s. Despite legal equality, African Americans faced persistent racism and discrimination. Disproportionately clustered in manual occupations, they were particularly hurt by deindustrialization and economic decline. After years of improvement, African Americans' economic status relative to whites stagnated or declined during the Reagan era. African Americans still made less money than whites did for comparable work and had much less chance to attain managerial positions. All African Americans were not affected equally. In the 1980s the African American middle class continued to thrive. Among college-educated Americans, the incomes of black men rose faster than those of whites into the mid-1980s. Middle-class African Americans could afford to move to better housing, often in suburbs and integrated areas. Meanwhile, working-class African Americans found their wages stagnating or falling compared with those of white workers. In the 1970s and 1980s, poverty rates rose faster among African Americans than among whites. In 1985, 75 percent of poor African American children lived in families headed by a single female. Observers feared there was now a permanent African American underclass segregated in inner-city neighborhoods with poor schools and widespread crime.

As in the past, African American culture, driven by the distinctiveness of the black experience, was dynamic and controversial. In the poverty of the Bronx in New York City in the 1970s, young African Americans had begun to create a powerful new music, rap. Reflecting the city's diversity, pioneering rap artists such as Kool Herc, Afrika Bambaataa, and Grandmaster Flash drew on Caribbean musical styles and the popular dance music disco, as well as on African American expressive traditions. Rap typically featured spoken lyrics over a driving percussive "break" beat, often sampled from other music. Along with graffiti and break dancing, the new sound made up a loose African American cultural movement known as "hip-hop."

Rap was the first new musical form to rival the impact of jazz in the 1920s and rock and roll in the 1950s. Spreading rapidly, rap crossed boundaries of race, class, and nation to appeal to middle-class, white, and international audiences. Commercially successful, rap was also controversial for its often raw look at ghetto life. The subgenre of gangsta rap, with its celebrations of gang life, violence, and misogyny, was especially provocative to conservatives and other Americans. Rap also deeply influenced other genres of music—another instance of the powerful impact of African Americans on American culture.

African Americans also mobilized to fight for equality and opportunity. Across the nation, the number of African American elected officials increased markedly. The Reverend Jesse Jackson, a protégé of Martin Luther King Jr., won wide attention. Preaching self-esteem and economic self-help for African Americans, Jackson was the leader of Operation PUSH—People United to Save Humanity. In 1984 Jackson challenged Walter Mondale for the Democratic presidential nomination. His campaign suggested how far American society had come in accepting African American political participation.

African American activism and the persistence of inequality made it difficult to undo the civil rights revolution. Most Americans seemed to accept that some federal action was essential to redress the imbalance between races. Despite Reagan's opposition, in 1982 Congress voted to extend the Voting Rights Act for 25 years. In 1983 the Supreme Court ruled that Bob Jones University, an evangelical institution, could not retain its tax-exempt status while it prohibited interracial dating and practiced other forms of discrimination. The Court also rejected the Reagan administration's bid to set aside affirmative action programs.

The battles over the rights of African Americans, gays, and women underscored the limits of conservatism. Many Americans were not ready to undo the social and cultural legacies of the 1960s. New cultural expressions, such as rap, clashed with conservative values. The result was a stalemate. Disadvantaged groups made relatively little political progress in the 1980s, but conservatives also made little progress in their social and cultural agenda.

"The Decade of the Hispanic"

After the changes of the 1960s and 1970s, the Hispanic experience in the United States became quieter and more confident in the 1980s. Hispanics were not a homogenous group but a diverse population defined by geographical, cultural, and even linguistic differences. In New York City, Puerto Ricans predominated; in South Florida, Cubans; and in the long arc from South Texas to Southern California, Mexican Americans. In 1980 Hispanics were the nation's fastest-growing minority group, with a birthrate 75 percent higher than the national average. Most immigrants to the United States were Hispanic, and demographers predicted that Hispanics would replace African Americans as the nation's largest minority group within a generation.

These growing numbers created a new sense in the 1980s that Hispanics mattered and could not be ignored. "We are," a Hispanic Roman Catholic priest declared, "the future."

In this consumer society, the increasing importance of the Hispanic population could be measured in goods and services. Hispanic culture affected the nation's foodways. From the 1970s into the 1980s, more and more Americans discovered "Tex-Mex," the distinctive cuisine of the Tejanos, the Mexican Americans of South Texas. By the 1990s, salsa had passed catsup as the best-selling condiment in the United States.

Meanwhile, American business moved to attract Spanish-speaking consumers. The Coors brewery enthusiastically declared the 1980s "The Decade of the Hispanic." By 1983, Coors and other companies could advertise in the expanding Spanish-language media, including newspapers, magazines, and 67 television stations.

For politicians, the 1980s were also "The Decade of the Hispanic." Republicans, long unable to attract a majority of African Americans, hoped that Roman Catholic Hispanic voters, like Linda Chavez, would respond to the new conservatism's emphasis on values, family, and religion. Reagan's anti-Communism did attract Cuban Americans, so many of whom were refugees from the regime of Fidel Castro. However, most Hispanics, including Mexican Americans, emphasized economic issues. They continued to fight poverty and struggle for opportunity. Unlike Linda Chavez, the Hispanic majority preferred the more activist economic and educational policies of the Democrats.

The increasing importance of Hispanic voters also affected the response to the perhaps 3 million illegal immigrants who had crossed the border from Mexico into the United States. The Immigration Reform and Control Act of 1986, known as the Simpson-Mazzoli Act, penalized Americans who knowingly brought illegal aliens into the country and hired them. But the measure also reflected the sentiments of Mexican Americans and other Americans by offering amnesty to illegal aliens who had arrived since 1981.

From Scandal to Triumph

The stalemate over social values was not the only sign that there were limits to conservatism in the 1980s. Scandals plagued business and religious figures who had helped create the conservative agenda. Policy setbacks, economic woes, and scandals plagued the Reagan administration. For a time, the conservatives' triumph was in doubt, but then the cold war began to end.

Business and Religious Scandals

By the mid-1980s the new conservatism was suffering a series of business and religious scandals. In 1986 Ivan Boesky, the swaggering Wall Street deal maker, was indicted for insider trading, the illegal use of secret financial information. Rather than go to trial, he agreed to give up stock trading, inform on other lawbreakers, spend two years in jail, and pay a $100 million fine. In 1987 Michael Milken, the junk bond king, was indicted on fraud and racketeering charges. His plea bargain agreement included a 10-year jail sentence and a $600 million fine, the largest judgment against an individual in American history.

Such scandals provoked second thoughts about the celebration of business and materialism. Critics pointed out that Boesky's and Milken's business methods had hurt the economy by saddling corporations with a great deal of debt and little cash to pay for it. Lavish lifestyles no longer seemed so attractive.

Scandal also touched religion. In 1987 Americans learned that televangelist Jim Bakker had defrauded investors in his theme park, Heritage USA, and paid hush money to hide an adulterous liaison with a church secretary. In 1988 Jerry Falwell had to resign from his Moral Majority. That year, televangelist Jimmy Swaggart admitted he "had sinned" with prostitutes.

Political Scandals

The Reagan administration had its own scandals. Before the end of the first term, more than 20 EPA officials resigned or were fired over charges of favoritism toward lobbyists and polluters. In 1985 Secretary of Labor Raymond Donovan resigned after becoming the first cabinet officer ever indicted. In 1988 Reagan's friend and attorney general, Edwin Meese III, resigned amid questions about his role in the corrupt awarding of government contracts. To critics, the administration's "sleaze factor" stemmed from the president's contemptuous attitude toward government and his eagerness to please business.

In his second term, Reagan faced much more damaging accusations. In October 1986, Sandinista soldiers in Nicaragua shot down a plane attempting to supply the Contra rebels. The plane had been part of a secret effort by the administration to violate the Boland Amendment's ban on aid to the Contras. Then, a Lebanese magazine reported that the United States had traded arms to Iran. Despite Reagan's denials, the government had sold arms to win the release of American hostages held by terrorists in Lebanon. The administration had broken the president's pledge not to negotiate with terrorists and had violated a ban on arms sales to Iran. The arms deal and the Nicaraguan plane crash were connected: the government had illegally used proceeds from the arms sale to pay for supplying the Contras.

> At its best, the Reagan Presidency provided a tonic of self-confidence that helped to restore vigor to the national economy and psyche; at its worst, it fostered greed, chauvinism and intolerance.
>
> R. W. APPLE,
>
> 1989

The scandal that became known as the Iran-Contra affair had the potential to drive Reagan from office. If the president had ordered or known about the arms deal and the supply effort, he might have faced impeachment. Three separate investigations made clear the president's probable involvement in the Iran-Contra affair, but none turned up enough evidence to impeach him.

Nevertheless, Reagan's reputation was badly damaged. Several of his associates left office and faced jail sentences. Former national security adviser Robert "Bud" McFarlane pleaded guilty to withholding information from Congress. His successor, Rear Admiral John Poindexter, was allowed to resign. Poindexter's aide, Marine Lieutenant Colonel Oliver North, had to be fired. Meanwhile, the director of the CIA, William Casey, died in 1987, the day after he was implicated in the Contra affair. Much of the country concluded that Reagan must have known about his associates' dealings; his popularity dropped.

Setbacks for the Conservative Agenda

Amid the scandals, conservatives faced a series of policy setbacks. The Democratic-controlled House of Representatives was less cooperative during Reagan's second term. Democrats became even more combative after winning majorities in the House and Senate in the congressional elections of 1986.

As a result, Reagan had to compromise more with Congress. In 1985 he called for a Second American Revolution, a comprehensive overhaul of the income tax system. But the Tax Reform Act Congress passed in 1986 did not lower and simplify income taxes nearly as much as the president had wanted.

Reagan also met outright defeat in Congress. In 1988, a coalition of Democrats and Republicans passed a bill compelling large companies to give workers 60 days' notice of plant closings and layoffs. Reagan opposed this liberal measure, but he allowed the bill to become law without his signature.

The president was often defeated on environmental policy at a time of growing concern about environmental hazards. In December 1984 the subsidiary of a US corporation accidentally allowed toxic gas to escape from a pesticide plant in Bhopal, India. The emission killed more than 2,500 people and injured 200,000. In April 1986 an explosion and fire released radioactive material from a nuclear power plant at Chernobyl in the Soviet Union. The accident killed more than 30 people, injured more than 200, and exposed countless others to radioactivity. Suddenly, Reagan's hostility to environmentalism was no longer so appealing. The president had to accept the 1986 extension of the federal Superfund program to clean up hazardous waste. The next year, Congress overrode his veto of a bill renewing the Water Quality Control Act. In 1988 the Reagan administration signed an international agreement setting limits on emissions linked to acid rain.

A Vulnerable Economy

Even the economy, the centerpiece of the Reagan Revolution, became a problem in the president's second term. During the 1980s the gap between rich and poor widened sharply. From 1977 to 1980, the average family income of the highest-paid tenth of Americans rose 27 percent, whereas that of the poorest tenth fell 11 percent (see Figure 30–3). In the 1980s only the rich earned more and kept more. Other Americans faced economic stagnation or decline.

In 1980, 29 million Americans lived below the poverty line. Ten years later, that figure had grown to almost 37 million. Despite Reaganomics, the United States had one of the highest poverty rates among industrialized nations.

One of the most visible consequences of poverty was homelessness. In the 1980s the number of homeless Americans increased markedly. The sight of men and women sleeping on sidewalks was common during the Reagan years.

Homelessness, poverty, and inequality produced a spirited debate in the 1980s. Democrats and liberals blamed these problems on Reaganomics. The president, they charged, had done nothing to stop the erosion of high-paying factory jobs. His welfare, housing, and job-training cuts hurt the poor, while his tax cuts and deregulation helped the rich. Conservatives and Republicans maintained that activist, liberal government had hurt manufacturing and weakened the economy. Moreover, welfare programs caused poverty by destroying poor people's work ethic and making them dependent on handouts.

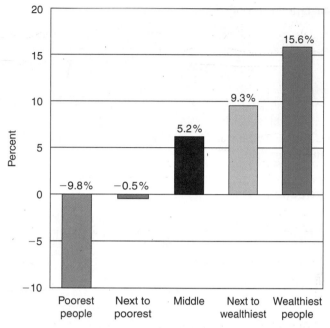

Figure 30–3 Changes in Families' Real Income, 1980–1990 The Reagan Revolution had very different consequences for rich and poor. *Copyright © 1989 by the New York Times Co. Reprinted by permission.*

In reality, both liberal and conservative policies had produced flawed economic results. Lyndon Johnson's spending for the Great Society, along with the cost of the Vietnam War, had begun to undermine the economy in the 1960s. His antipoverty programs had been less effective than liberals wanted to admit, but the Reagan Revolution did not end poverty, either. Reaganomics did not reinvigorate manufacturing or boost middle-class incomes.

There were other signs of economic vulnerability by the mid-1980s. Despite Reaganomics, the federal budget deficit did not disappear. Instead, between 1981 and 1986, tax cuts and increased defense spending drove the deficit from $79 billion to $221 billion—a staggering new record.

Like poverty and inequality, the deficit was controversial. Some economists believed the deficit was a sign of great economic weakness; others believed it did not matter. Democrats and liberals blamed Reagan for the red ink. Reagan's supporters blamed Congress for failing to cut the budget.

In fact both the president and Congress were to blame. Neither Republicans nor Democrats wanted to reduce Medicare and Social Security. Congress enacted the Balanced Budget and Emergency Deficit Control Act of 1985 (the Gramm-Rudman Act), which promised to balance the budget by 1990, but a Supreme Court ruling critically weakened the measure. During Reagan's last years in office, the national debt—the total amount owed by the federal government to its creditors—reached $2.6 trillion.

Along with burgeoning debt, the Reagan years produced a growing international trade deficit. In 1980 the annual value of imports was $25.4 billion greater than the value of the nation's exports. By 1986 that gap had grown to $145.1 billion, as American business lost out to foreign products both at home and abroad. Reaganomics had not solved the problem of America's relative decline in the world economy.

Doubts about Reagan's economic policy increased when the stock market fell unexpectedly on Monday, October 19, 1987, losing 508 points, or 23 percent of its value. It was the biggest one-day decline since "Black Tuesday" in October 1929. The market drop reflected underlying economic problems, including the federal budget deficit, the trade deficit, and deindustrialization, plus lax government regulation of Wall Street. The crash seemed to be a mortal blow to what a journalist called "the Reagan Illusion: the idea that there could be a defense buildup and tax cuts without a price, that the country could live beyond its means indefinitely."

Reagan's Comeback

Remarkably able to withstand defeat, Reagan began his comeback from scandals and economic troubles. Opponents dubbed him the "Teflon president" because nothing seemed to stick to him. That was a tribute to his political skills, as well as many Americans' real affection for him. After a series of disappointing presidencies, Americans seemed unwilling to let Reagan fail.

The economy also helped the president. The stock market crash did not, as feared, lead to depression or recession. The market soon recovered and the economy grew.

Reagan's comeback was probably helped most by the transformation of the Soviet Union. By the mid-1980s the Soviets suffered from a weakening economy, an unpopular war in Afghanistan, and a costly arms race. Mikhail Gorbachev, dynamic and charismatic, became General Secretary of the Communist Party and signaled a new era with a series of stunning reforms. At home, he called for restructuring the economy (perestroika) and tolerating more open discussion (glasnost). Abroad, he sought to ease tensions with the United States and the West.

Gorbachev's reforms gave the United States an opening to thaw cold war tensions. Reagan met with the Soviet leader in a series of summits beginning in November 1985. Visiting West Berlin in June 1987, the president challenged Gorbachev to "tear down" the Berlin Wall, which had symbolized the cold war division of Europe. Meanwhile, it became apparent that the Soviets were changing their foreign policy, as they withdrew their troops from Afghanistan and eased their control over Eastern Europe.

>> Time Line

▼1980
Ronald Reagan elected president

▼1981
IBM personal computer
Air traffic controllers' strike
Economic Recovery Act

▼1982
Nuclear-freeze rally in New York City
Boland Amendment

▼1983
Strategic Defense Initiative
US invasion of Grenada

Terrorist attack on US Marines in Lebanon

▼1984
Reelection of Ronald Reagan

The United States and the Soviets also made real progress on arms control. In December 1987 Reagan and Gorbachev signed the Intermediate-Range Nuclear Forces Treaty (INF), promising to destroy more than 2,500 intermediate-range missiles. For the first time, the two powers had agreed to give up a weapon altogether.

The INF treaty permanently eased tensions. The cold war suddenly ended. Reagan's presidency ended in 1989; a year later, the United States and the Soviet Union agreed to end production of chemical weapons and reduce existing stockpiles. In 1991, the two nations signed the START (Strategic Arms Reduction Talks) Treaty, which called for each side to reduce its nuclear arsenals as much as 30 percent.

Meanwhile, the Soviet Union weakened. In 1989, Gorbachev could do nothing to stop the collapse of its repressive allies in Eastern Europe, as regimes toppled in Bulgaria, Czechoslovakia, Hungary, Poland, and Rumania. Most dramatically, a new East German government agreed in November to allow travel through the Berlin Wall. As jubilant Berliners dismantled it, the wall's fate epitomized the collapse of Communism. Accepting the transition to democracy, the Soviets withdrew their troops from Eastern Europe.

Powerless to save its allies, the Soviet leadership soon could not save itself. Despite Gorbachev's efforts, the low standard of living, Communist repression, and the unpopular war in Afghanistan made many unhappy. Estonia, Latvia, Lithuania, and other republics chafed under Russia's domination of the USSR. In 1990 Russia chose a charismatic president, Boris Yeltsin, who quit the Communist Party, supported independence for the republics, and challenged Gorbachev. The next year, Gorbachev resigned as party leader and president, and the Soviet parliament suspended the Communist Party. As one republic after another declared its independence, the USSR ceased to exist.

With the collapse of the Soviet Union, the United States and its allies had won the cold war. Conservatives insisted that Reagan's overpowering defense buildup had forced the Soviets to surrender. Democrats maintained that the buildup and the president's harsh rhetoric had actually slowed the thaw in US-Soviet relations and that America won the cold war because of its long-term strength and strategy. Typically modest, Reagan himself gave credit to American policies reaching back to the 1940s.

Meanwhile, Americans did not celebrate very much as the Berlin Wall came down and the Soviet Union collapsed. The cold war had cost a great deal in money and lives. Many Americans wondered whether Communism had posed a mortal danger to the United States in the first place.

▼1985
General Electric purchase of RCA
Gramm-Rudman Act

▼1986
US bombing of Libya
Tax Reform Act

Revelation of Iran-Contra
   affair

▼1987
Stock market crash
Intermediate-Range Nuclear
   Forces Treaty

▼1988
Omnibus Trade and
   Competitiveness Act

▼1991
Collapse of the Soviet Union

The Fall of the Berlin Wall Residents celebrate the fall of the Berlin Wall and the collapse of Communist rule in East Berlin and East Germany, November 1989.

Conclusion

Reagan left office with the highest popularity rating of any president since the beginning of modern polling in the 1930s. His comeback culminated the triumph of the new conservatism, but the nature of that triumph would be debated for years to come. The Reagan Revolution did not solve such basic economic problems as poverty and even worsened some problems, such as inequality and the budget deficit. Much of its conservative social agenda failed to take hold.

Nevertheless, Reagan successfully combated the sense of national decline that had pervaded America in the 1970s. After the troubled presidencies of that decade, Reagan's confident leadership made the democratic system seem viable again. His presidency re-invigorated faith in capitalist innovation, minimal government, and American military power. At the end of the 1980s, business values and evangelical religion claimed a more prominent place in American culture.

The accomplishments of the new conservatism, as Reagan's troubled second term indicated, were fragile. The nation's economic revival was shaky, and Americans were still worried about the future. "I think," a businessman concluded, "the '90s are going to be much trickier than the 1980s."

Who, What

Ivan Boesky 915

Sandra Day O'Connor 929

Rev. Jerry Falwell 917

Mikhail Gorbachev 938

Ronald Reagan 916

Yuppies 915

Reagan Doctrine 923

Reaganomics 919

Religious Right 915

Review Questions

1. What were the main values and goals of the new conservatism in the 1980s? What role did business and religion play in the conservative movement?

2. What was the Reagan Revolution in domestic policy? How did Reagan's domestic programs reflect conservative values?

3. What were the aims of the Reagan Revolution abroad?

Critical-Thinking Questions

1. What groups resisted the conservative social agenda in the 1980s? Did the desire for equal rights and opportunities conflict with conservatism?

2. What factors limited the triumph of the new conservatism? Did conservatives really succeed in the 1980s?

3. How did the conservatism of the 1980s differ from earlier forms of conservatism in the twentieth century?

For further review materials and resource information, please visit www.oup.com/us/ofthepeople

1) The rise of the conservative majority enabled President Reagan to attempt the "Reagan Revolution," a dramatic remaking of American government and society.

2) Reagan attempted to promote conservative values and confidence about America abroad as well as at home.

3) Reagan and conservatives' success in shaping economic and foreign policy was not duplicated in battles over social policy.

4) The "Reagan Revolution" and Reagan's popularity survived scandal because of economic growth and victory in the cold war.

Creating a Conservative Majority

The Reagan Revolution at Home

The Reagan Revolution Abroad

The Battle over Conservative Social Values

From Scandal to Triumph

THE TRIUMPH OF CONSERVATISM

1980–1991

EVENTS

The New Economy The rise of the postindustrial, computer-centered economy helped revive economic growth and strengthen conservatism.

The Rehabilitation of Business Corporate takeovers and growth of the technology industry helped rehabilitate business and its values.

The Rise of the Religious Right The growth of evangelical churches and the influence of televangelists created new support for a conservative social agenda.

The 1980 Presidential Election The new conservative majority came together to elect Ronald Reagan.

The Reagan Style Reagan's confidence and optimism helped reassure Americans that the presidency and the broader political system could still work.

Shrinking Government Turning the nation away from activist liberalism, Reagan pressed, with mixed results, for a smaller federal government that spent less.

Reaganomics The Reagan administration enacted a conservative economic agenda to lower taxes, deregulate business, and weaken unions.

The 1984 Presidential Election With the return of prosperity after a brief recession, Reagan easily won reelection.

Restoring American Power Reagan's anti-Communist foreign policy required increased military spending and new confidence about American power.

Confronting the "Evil Empire" The Reagan administration avoided direct confrontation but used increased military spending to put pressure on the Soviet Union.

The Reagan Doctrine in the Third World Reagan supported antidemocratic, pro-US regimes in order to keep Communism out of Central America, the Caribbean, and Africa.

The Middle East and Terrorism The Reagan administration could not thwart terrorism and end conflict in the Middle East.

The United States and the World Economy Reagan pushed for freer trade and conservative economics in the third world but could not stop a trade imbalance that produced increasing Japanese sales and investment in the United States.

Attacking the Legacy of the 1960s The Reagan administration appointed conservative judges, but the conservative movement did not undo much of the liberal and radical legacy of the 1960s in such areas as defendants' rights, school prayer, drugs, and education.

Women's Rights and Abortion Although conservatism condemned feminism and the changing role of women, conservatives could not stop the continuing movement of women into the workforce or end abortion rights.

Gays and the AIDS Crisis Against the tragic backdrop of the AIDS epidemic, the gay rights movement made some progress.

African Americans and Racial Inequality As in other areas of social policy, the Reagan administration could not undo the 1960s legacy of African American civil rights.

"The Decade of the Hispanic" Dramatic population growth spurred Hispanics' confidence and political and economic importance.

Business and Religious Scandals A series of business and religious scandals tarnished the image of the new conservatism.

Political Scandals Scandal, including the Iran-Contra affair, also damaged the reputation of Reagan and his administration.

Setbacks for the Conservative Agenda In Reagan's second term, the Democratic Congress challenged his agenda on taxes, labor, and the environment.

A Vulnerable Economy Inequality, poverty, the federal budget deficit, and a stock market crash sharpened partisan debates and threatened the Reagan administration.

Reagan's Comeback Economic growth and the collapse of the Soviet Union bolstered Reagan's popularity and strengthened his record.

COMMON THREADS

>> How did deindustrial-
ization continue to affect
the United States?

>> How did the new con-
servatism of the 1980s continue to influence American
politics and culture?

>> How did the African
American civil rights movement continue to influence
the nation into the twenty-
first century?

"A Nation Transformed"
1989-2012

>> Lt. Craig Mullaney

In 2003, Lieutenant Craig Mullaney of the 10th Mountain Division, like so many American soldiers before him, went overseas to serve his country. A year and a half earlier, the United States had invaded Afghanistan in retaliation for a devastating attack on American soil by the transnational terrorist group Al Qaeda on September 11, 2001. So, Lt. Mullaney found himself in this rugged country at the crossroads of the Middle East and Asia to battle Al Qaeda fighters and their local Taliban protectors.

In critical respects, America's global war on terror was a product of globalization, the complex web of economic, technological, social, and political ties that bound the United States to the world in fresh ways. So was Lt. Mullaney. A graduate of the United States Military Academy, he had studied at Oxford University in England. His fiancée, a doctor, was the daughter of Indian immigrants.

As in past wars, Americans enjoyed economic and technological advantages over their enemies. Satellite telephones and global positioning satellites, devices of globalization, allowed instant communication and sure navigation for Lt. Mullaney's squad around the ancient city of Gardez and then Shkin, the isolated spot his colonel called "the evilest place in Afghanistan." Humvees carried the Americans over the rough terrain. Under attack, they could quickly call support from rocket-firing Apache helicopters and formidable A-10 attack planes. "I was energized by the power I commanded through the radio," Mullaney admitted. "It was like an incantation, like casting a spell, like summoning a demon."

The Americans also enjoyed the comforts of communications and information technology basic to globalization: computers, the Internet, DVDs, iPods, satellite television, and phone calls home. There was plenty of food and plenty of air conditioning, too.

For all their advantages, the Americans struggled. They did not have enough soldiers, Humvees, or heavy weapons. And they did not have enough armor on their vehicles to protect them from homemade bombs. "I felt as though I were riding in a death trap," Mullaney

continued

945

confessed. He and his men did not know enough of Afghan language and culture. Driving through Gardez, he saw men raise their index fingers. So, thinking it was "a number one gesture," he held out his index finger, too. "Yes, America is number one!" Afterwards, his interpreter revealed that the men had been making an obscene gesture at the Americans.

Mullaney and his men inflicted far greater casualties than they suffered. He himself won promotion to captain. Yet the United States was not clearly triumphing. "We were never really sure whether we were winning," Mullaney admitted. "But we had been transformed."

His experience reflected American life in the two decades after the cold war. As globalization and technological innovation reshaped American life, the nation struggled with the consequences. It was not clear that the economy was strong enough to enable Americans to live the good life at home and to project American power abroad. The nation adjusted to increasing social and cultural diversity, but American democracy seemed less able to confront economic dislocation and increasing inequality. The nation seemed perpetually at war. Echoing Craig Mullaney, the commission investigating the September attacks agreed that Americans lived in "a nation transformed." But the outcome of that transformation, abroad and at home, was not clearly a victory.

The Age of Globalization

By the end of the twentieth century, Americans increasingly felt enmeshed in global forces. America, of course, had long been defined by its relationship to the world. But this global connection entered a new, more self-conscious phase in the 1980s. During the decade, the term *globalization* first came into use to describe the web of technological, economic, military, political, and cultural developments binding people and nations ever more tightly together. The cold war's end, technological advances, the spread of multinationals and other organizations, the creation of transnational economic alliances, and a new wave of immigration all drew the United States deeper into globalization.

> Globalization is not just a trend, not just a phenomenon, not just an economic fad. It is the international system that has replaced the cold-war system.
>
> THOMAS L. FRIEDMAN, 1999

The Cold War and Globalization

For two generations, the cold war had both facilitated and hindered globalization. In some ways, the confrontation between the United States and the Soviet Union linked the world more closely together. Each power had a host of ties to other nations. The United States had established regional military alliances around the world and helped rebuild Asian and European economies through lower trade barriers, the World Bank, and the International Monetary Fund.

Still, the cold war inhibited globalization, too. The United States and the Soviet Union had largely avoided trading with each other. Each power had discouraged its allies from ties with the other side. The collapse of the Soviet Union in 1991 opened the way to further globalization. Now nations and companies could forge new ties more freely across the old cold war divide.

New Communications Technologies

New communications technologies sped up the global flow of news, ideas, and money. The Internet, a product of the cold war, emerged from a Department of Defense search for a means of maintaining communications in the event of a nuclear attack. Aided by the development of the telephone modem and fiber-optic cable, the Internet spread quickly in the 1990s and 2000s. At first, people used it to send and receive electronic messages, but by the middle of the 1990s, computer users also explored the World Wide Web, a rapidly expanding segment of the Internet that blended text, graphics, audio, and video. By 2000, some 304 million people from more than 40 nations already used the global information superhighway to do research, create and exhibit art, listen to music, share photographs and films, and buy and sell online.

Communications satellites also played a critical role in globalization. Following the US deployment of Telstar and other satellites in the 1960s, several other nations launched their own. In the 1990s, global satellite communications revolutionized the news business. Cable News Network (CNN), founded in 1979 by the entrepreneur Ted Turner, used satellite uplinks to provide live televised coverage of events around the world. Turner wanted CNN to be a "positive force in the world, to tie the world together." Satellite news organizations soon appeared in other countries.

Meanwhile, mobile and cellular telephones spread especially quickly in many countries outside the United States. In Africa, there were already more than 15 million cell telephone subscribers in the early 2000s. Before the decade was out, social networking—such Internet services as Facebook and Twitter—connected people rapidly in still more ways.

Multinationals and NGOs

Connecting businesses across national borders, communications advances helped stimulate an astonishing increase in the number of multinational corporations. In 1990, there were 3,000 multinationals worldwide. By 2003, the number had mushroomed to 63,000. With some 821,000 subsidiaries, multinationals employed about 90 million people and accounted for perhaps one-fourth of the world's economic output.

Long a leader in creating multinationals, the United States remained home to many of the largest and wealthiest. By 2003, Wal-Mart was Mexico's largest private-sector employer, with 100,000 workers. But America now faced intense competition from Japan, China, European nations, and others. In 1962, nearly 60 percent of the top 500 multinationals were American; by 1999, the percentage had declined to 36, and by 2011 it was 27 (see Map 31–1).

Along with multinational companies, private nongovernmental organizations—NGOs—also fostered globalization. Some NGOs, such as the International Red Cross, dated to the nineteenth century. The World Economic Forum, which brought leaders and experts together annually in Davos, Switzerland, was a product of the 1970s. So were the environmentalist Greenpeace and the humanitarian Doctors Without Borders. By the 2000s, there were more than 10,000 NGOs worldwide.

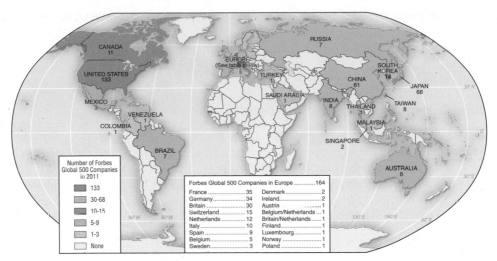

Map 31–1 A Global Economy In 2011, the United States still remained home to more multinational corporations than any other nation, as measured by the number of Fortune 500 Global companies. But Europe, Japan, and China were increasingly important competitors to the US. *http://money.cnn.com/magazines/fortune/global500/2011/countries/Australia.html*

Expanding Trade

Along with peace and communication, the most basic necessity for globalization was the easy movement of goods, services, and capital across national boundaries. After the cold war, nations, eager to seize their share of the global market, aggressively removed barriers to trade and investment. America established economic relationships with the former republics of the USSR, the European countries of the Soviet bloc, the Socialist Republic of Vietnam, and the People's Republic of China. By 1996, Wal-Mart had a store in Beijing, and McDonald's had restaurants in Russia.

To spur international trade and investment, nations also created regional economic alliances that guaranteed member states trading and investment privileges and lowered or abolished tariffs. In 1991, the member states of the European Economic Community, a pioneering regional trade alliance, signed the Maastricht Treaty to create a single vast unit, the European Union (EU), with its own currency, the euro. With 6.4 percent of global population, the EU produced a third of the world's goods and more than a third of its trade.

The 1990s also witnessed the transformation of the General Agreement on Tariffs and Trade (GATT). A US cold war–era creation, GATT had drawn together over 100 nations. Its efforts to increase trade through agreements known as "rounds" culminated in 1993 when the Uruguay Round produced a dramatic victory for free-trade policies. GATT was then reborn as a more powerful global body, the World Trade Organization (WTO), whose decisions would be binding on member nations. The United States joined the WTO in 1995.

Moving People

The movement of human beings was critical to globalization. Thanks to regional economic agreements and the end of the cold war, people could cross national borders more easily. Between 1990 and 1994, 4.5 million immigrants came to the United States. By 2000

AMERICA AND THE WORLD

··

>> **Globalization's Final Frontier**

After covering the earth, globalization also reached into space. Like the United States and the Soviet Union in the cold war, more and more nations translated their hopes, ambitions, and fears into space programs. Like America, other countries found satellites an indispensable part of globalization: they were critical to communications and information gathering and essential to building economies, spying on enemies, and positioning soldiers. A secure military foothold in space might even ensure survival on earth. Outer space became globalization's final frontier.

Dozens of countries had space programs by the 2000s. Reflecting the economic and political integration of Europe, 13 West European nations had formed the European Space Agency in 1975. By the end of the twentieth century, ESA was using the Ariane launch vehicle to send satellites and probes into space. By then, India, Israel, and Japan were also launching satellites, and Brazil was working to develop a launch capability.

The People's Republic of China had the most ambitious of the newer space programs. Despite its developing economy and limited investment in science, China wanted to rival the United States not only in the exploration of space but also perhaps in the development of space-based military capabilities. The Chinese had launched satellites in the 1970s, developed a successful launch vehicle in the 1980s, and begun a manned space program in the 1990s. In October 2003, China became the third nation to put a man in space when the vehicle Shenzhou ("Sacred Vessel"), based on old Soviet technology, carried an astronaut on a 21-hour flight. Meanwhile, the original space powers struggled. The Russians, inheriting the remnants of the Soviet space program, could barely afford to keep it going. Desperate for money, the Russians auctioned space memorabilia and signed up wealthy civilians as the first space tourists.

For most Americans, space no longer seemed exciting or important. With the Soviet Union gone, NASA faced even leaner budgets. In February 2003, the explosion of the shuttle *Columbia*—the second such tragedy—left Americans unsure about the safety and value of the space program.

In space, the United States pursued friendly collaboration with other countries. After partnering with the Soviets on space flights in the 1970s, the American space program joined Canada, Japan, Russia, and other nations in an often troubled effort to build the International Space Station in the 1990s.

The United States also unilaterally pursued its own interests in space. In the 2000s, George W. Bush, like Ronald Reagan before him, favored the development of a space-based system to defend against missile attack. Warily eying the People's Republic of China, policy makers feared an assault on American satellites and potential space weaponry. The globalization of space, like the globalization of the world, was both exhilarating and frightening.

Making Economic Policy in a Global Age World leaders, including President George W. Bush (sixth from the left, front row), meet in Washington, DC, in the midst of a developing economic crisis, November 2008.

the immigrant population had reached 26.3 million, about 11 percent of the national total population, the largest percentage since before World War II.

Travel also facilitated globalization by exposing people to other nations and cultures. Thanks to low-cost jet flights and improved living standards, tourism was possibly the largest single global industry by the 1990s.

The Politics of a New Economy

Globalization combined with technological change to create a new, information-centered American economy. This transformation produced a record economic boom in the 1990s; it also produced new insecurity and inequality. The political system responded with generally conservative solutions emphasizing individual responsibility and limited government. Despite unrest over immigration and trade, American leaders remained firmly committed to globalization. But democratic institutions often became deadlocked amid deep partisan divisions.

The Information Economy

As global competition closed American factories, the nature of the postindustrial economy became clearer. By the 1990s, factories employed fewer production workers than in 1955; meanwhile, the service sector accounted for about 70 percent of America's economic activity. The rise of services using sophisticated communications, computing, and biomedical technology encouraged the belief that information would define the twenty-first-century economy.

In the 1990s and 2000s, innovations in electronics continued to transform communications. High-speed fiber-optic cables, cell phone towers, and satellite dishes expanded the power and reach of telephone and television systems. By 1999 more than half of the nation's households had at least one computer. The new information economy spurred the hope that Americans would process data instead of coal and produce knowledge instead of steel.

Advances in genetics and medical technology further sparked hopes for an information-centered economy. At the close of the twentieth century, scientists made rapid advances in understanding animal and human genomes. Corporations soon began applying this genetic knowledge to agriculture, medicine, and other fields. The result was biomedical technology—the use of organisms and their products to alter health and the environment. By 2000, about one-third of the US corn, cotton, and soybean crops were products of genetic engineering. By then, over 125 genetically engineered drugs had been approved for the treatment of cancer and other diseases.

A Second Economic Revolution?

The information and industrial economies were fundamentally quite different. Manual, blue-collar labor tended the machines of smokestack America; white-collar, well-educated labor tended the computers of information America. The industrial economy had eaten up fossil fuels, minerals, and other exhaustible resources and produced substantial pollution; the information economy promised less damage to the earth.

In some ways, however, the rise of the information economy repeated the Industrial Revolution. As in the late 1800s and early 1900s, technological change pushed new corporations to the forefront of American capitalism: e-commerce pioneers such as Amazon.com and eBay, the search engine giant Google, and the social-networking leader Facebook. Like the Industrial Revolution, the information revolution spurred a wave of corporate consolidation. In 1989, media company Time, Inc. merged with entertainment conglomerate Warner Communications; in 1995, Time Warner then gobbled Turner Broadcasting.

The information revolution also paralleled the Industrial Revolution by producing a wealthy elite. The most famous of the new multibillionaires was Bill Gates, cofounder of Microsoft, who became the richest American since John D. Rockefeller, the cofounder of Standard Oil nearly a century before.

Just as the appearance of trains, planes, and machines stimulated artists and intellectuals in the nineteenth and twentieth centuries, so did the appearance of computers a century later. Digital technology made it easy to copy and manipulate text, images, and sounds, a development that encouraged collage and undermined linear narratives. More broadly, some thinkers believed a new, postmodern culture was replacing the modern culture inspired by industrialism. Hard to define, postmodern culture embraced a more skeptical view of accepted truths and dominant ideologies.

Despite parallels to the Industrial Revolution, the information economy was not as potent a revolutionary force in critical ways. Machine tools, railroads, and electricity had greatly boosted workers' productivity in the industrial era. Computers, the Internet, and biotechnology did not do the same in the 2000s. Moreover, factories had generated the need for additional jobs in supporting businesses, such as mining and transportation. Information-centered businesses did not have the same effect. Despite the glamour of information and biotechnology, most service jobs required little education, used limited technology, and paid less than the best blue-collar jobs of the old economy. By the 2000s, the biggest employer in America was not an information company but rather a low-wage retail store, Wal-Mart.

Boom and Insecurity

For most of the 1990s, globalization and the information revolution seemed to benefit the economy. Productive American workers and a vital service sector produced economic growth for nearly the entire decade, a record. Because of global competition, corporate cost cutting, and low oil prices, inflation was negligible. Interest rates stayed low; unemployment dropped to record lows. Excitement about information-related companies drove the stock market to one record high after another. After passing 3,000 for the first time ever in 1991, the Dow Jones industrial average soared past 11,000 in 1999. As memories of the 1987 market crash faded, many Americans no longer felt the need to live with less. Congress repealed the federal 55-mile-per-hour speed limit for interstate highways in 1995, and gas-guzzling sport utility vehicles (SUVs) became popular.

Nevertheless, most Americans faced economic challenges in the 1990s and 2000s. Confronting global competition, companies now "downsized" by laying off white-collar as well as blue-collar workers. Firms also "outsourced" jobs to other countries, where wages were lower. Outsourcing jolted Americans who believed that college degrees and corporate employment guaranteed middle-class status.

The increasing costs of health care also troubled Americans. In the 1990s, the United States spent a greater proportion of its gross domestic product on health care than did other developed nations. Still, 14 percent of Americans had no health insurance in 2000. The United States, almost alone among developed nations, had no national health insurance plan for its citizens. As employers cut costs, they decreased medical benefits for employees. The need for costly medical care would only increase as life expectancy continued to rise and the huge baby boom generation aged.

Americans feared, too, that they could not afford retirement. With the aging of the baby boom generation, there were more Americans over 65 and eligible for Social Security benefits than ever before (see Map 31–2). Many people believed there would not be enough money to pay pensions in the twenty-first century. Private employers, meanwhile, reduced pension benefits for many retirees.

The Return of Inequality

The insecurities of many working- and middle-class Americans reflected the trend toward economic inequality since the 1970s. Allowing for inflation, the average weekly earnings of American workers in 2000 were less than in 1970. The decline of manufacturing meant the loss of relatively high-paying jobs. Employers were determined to hold down the growth of wages and salaries. Workers, facing threats from downsizing and outsourcing, were reluctant to demand big wage increases, as were labor unions, which continued to have difficulty organizing workers.

To stay even, Americans borrowed and worked more than before. Many families now had both parents in the paid workforce. In 1960, only a fifth of women with children under six held paid jobs; in 1995, two-thirds worked for pay. Partly because they now held two and even three jobs, many people put in much more time at work. In 1960, Americans worked less—1,795 hours a year—than their counterparts in Britain, France, Germany, and Japan. By 1997–1998, they worked more—1,966 hours a year.

Meanwhile, the wealthy fared exceptionally well. In 2000, the richest 400 Americans had an average annual income of $174 million, almost quadruple their earnings only eight

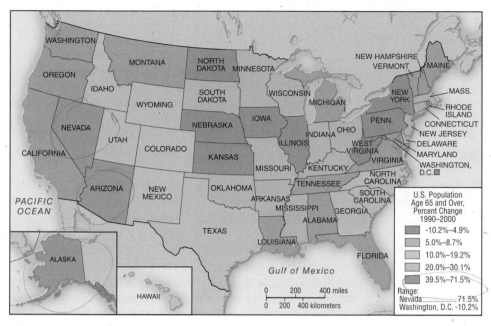

Map 31–2   Aging in America The increase in the percentage of the US population age 65 and over from 1980 to 2000 helped fuel worries about health care and social security. *Data Source: US Census Bureau, Population Estimates, July 1, 2000 to July 1, 2006. Data Source: He, Wan, Manisha Sengupta, Victoria A. Velkoff, and Kimberly A. DeBarros, US Census Bureau, Current Population Reports, P23-209, 65+ in the United States: 2005, US Government Printing Office, Washington, DC, 2005.*

years earlier. That year, the richest 1 percent of American households owned 40 percent of the nation's wealth, about as much as in the 1920s.

Several factors spurred the rebirth of great fortunes. The stock market boom of the 1990s, fed by the information revolution, rewarded Bill Gates and other wealthy men and women with vast profits. The tax cuts of the Reagan Revolution allowed the rich to keep more of their gains. And a "winner-take-all" culture validated wide differences in income that had seemed unacceptable for decades.

By 2000, the United States, the richest country in the world, was also the country with the largest gap between rich and poor. Many observers wondered whether strong social class differences, which had decreased in the mid-twentieth century, would once again define the nation and limit democracy.

The Power of Conservatism

After the Reagan Revolution of the 1980s, American politics seemed set on a conservative path. In 1988, Reagan's vice president, George H. W. Bush of Texas, easily defeated the colorless liberal Democratic nominee, Governor Michael Dukakis of Massachusetts, to become the nation's 41st president. But hopes of continuing the Reagan Revolution faded as voters left the Democrats in control of the House and Senate. Squabbling with Congress, Bush vetoed 40 bills and even briefly closed down the government in a budget dispute. Yet Bush also alienated conservatives. He supported new environmental controls and federal funding for education. He broke his campaign pledge not to raise taxes.

The Democratic Ticket, 1992 Presidential nominee Bill Clinton (right) would be elected president in 1992 and 1996; Al Gore (left) would win the vice presidency twice before losing the presidential election of 2000.

Running a tired campaign for reelection in 1992, Bush faced a surprisingly strong third-party challenge from Texas businessman H. Ross Perot. The pugnacious, plainspoken billionaire played to Americans' unhappiness with the political system by promising to end gridlock, balance the budget, and reform campaign finances. But it was Governor Bill Clinton of Arkansas, a moderate "New Democrat," who seemed the best chance for change. Bush's broken tax promise and a weak economy doomed his campaign. Winning with only 43 percent of the popular vote, Clinton had a chance to partner with the Democratic-controlled Congress to move toward liberalism. But when the president proposed a liberal solution to the nation's health care crisis in 1993, Congress rejected the plan as too expensive and intrusive. By 1994, only 14 percent of Americans believed they could trust the federal government. That November, the Republicans won control of Congress for the first time in 40 years.

Fighting for his political future, Clinton moved right. "The era of big government is over," he declared. Through budget cuts and tax increases, he managed to end the budget deficit. In 1996, he signed a welfare bill that significantly reduced federal support for the poor, especially children. The bill limited welfare recipients to five years of assistance over their lifetimes and required heads of households on welfare to find work within two years. Many Democrats and liberals angrily claimed that the president had betrayed the poor.

To keep the economy booming, Clinton blended liberal and conservative financial policies. In 1995, liberals were pleased by the revised Credit Reinvestment Act, which encouraged banks to offer "subprime" mortgages—home loans to low-income Americans who did not traditionally qualify for such financing. Clinton also endorsed the conservative goal of easing federal regulation of the financial industry. In 1999, he signed the Financial Services Modernization Act (the Gramm-Leach-Bliley Act), which removed longstanding restrictions and permitted commercial banks, investment banks, and insurance companies to compete for one another's business. In the short run, subprime mortgages and deregulation helped sustain the economic boom and President Clinton. But in little more than a decade, these actions would become much more controversial.

Thanks to his conservative tilt and the continuing boom, Clinton easily beat the Republican presidential nominee, Senator Bob Dole of Kansas, in 1996. But Clinton's second term nearly collapsed in scandal over his real estate dealings and adulterous affairs. In 1998, the House of Representatives voted two articles of impeachment charging the president with perjury and obstruction of justice. Only the second president to go on trial in the Senate, Clinton remained popular. Most Americans seemed willing to separate his private and public lives and wanted to keep him in office. Reflecting popular opinion, the Senate voted to acquit Clinton on both articles of impeachment.

Although Clinton charted a moderate course between liberalism and conservatism, his scandal-ridden presidency did not guarantee Democratic success. In one of the closest elections in history, his vice president, Al Gore of Tennessee, lost to Governor George W. Bush of Texas, the son of the first President Bush, in 2000. Although Gore won the popular ballot by 550,000 votes, Bush appeared to capture a narrow majority of the Electoral College. It took the intervention of the Supreme Court to halt a controversial recount of Florida's vote and thereby make him the 43rd president.

Influenced by Reagan's success, the younger Bush was more conservative than his father. In his first term, "Bush 43" pushed successfully for tax cuts and weakened regulation of the financial industry. But Bush also accepted a classic liberal initiative, an expensive drug benefit program for retired Americans.

In 2004, Bush faced another liberal Democrat, Senator John Kerry of Massachusetts, who tried to capitalize on worries over outsourcing and economic change. Yet Bush prevailed with 50.7 percent of the popular vote and a solid electoral majority. Buoyed by his victory, the president promised new conservative initiatives, including a reform of the social security system. His plans went nowhere, particularly after the Democrats won control of both houses of Congress in 2006. Thanks to Bush's tax cuts, drug plan, and military expenditures, the federal government ran a budget deficit again—another disappointment to conservatives, who yearned for leaner government.

Contesting Globalization

Republican and Democratic leaders generally agreed with big business that globalization represented a triumph for American institutions and values, including capitalism, free trade, and democracy. Despite tough international economic competition, American leaders thought the nation was still better off than in a divided world without free trade.

In contrast, many middle- and working-class Americans questioned whether globalization made their lives better. The presence of several million illegal immigrants from Mexico angered many American citizens, particularly in Texas and California. Their argument was familiar: illegal aliens drove down wages and took jobs from native-born Americans who paid higher taxes to provide services and benefits to tax-evading immigrants. Supposedly, Spanish would rival English, and whites would lose political power and cultural influence. In 1994, California voters passed Proposition 187, a referendum denying illegal aliens access to public education and other benefits. Two years later, Congress increased efforts to stop the flow of illegal immigrants.

The anti-immigrant movement would continue. But business generally welcomed immigration because it provided workers. Calculating the rapid growth of the Hispanic population, political leaders did not wish to antagonize an increasingly powerful group of voters. Many native-born Americans, themselves descendants of immigrants, believed immigration would invigorate the economy and the culture.

International trade also provoked a battle. The US government, faced with the rapid-fire appearance of regional economic alliances, moved to create its own economic bloc. In

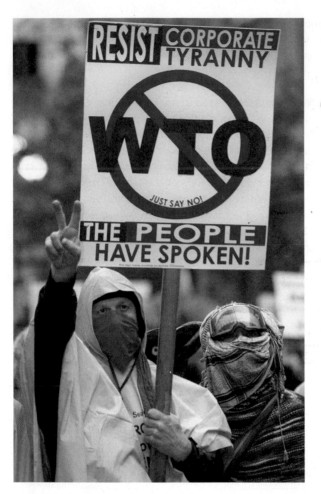

1992, the United States joined with Canada and Mexico in the North American Free Trade Agreement (NAFTA), which established the world's largest and richest low-tariff trading zone. Fearing more lost jobs, organized labor opposed the agreement. So did many environmentalists, who believed corporations would get around US environmental laws by moving operations to Mexico. But the leadership of both major parties favored the agreement, and in 1993, the Senate ratified NAFTA.

Opposition to globalization flared again at a meeting of the WTO in Seattle, Washington, in 1999. Labor unions, environmentalists, consumer activists, women's groups, and other organizations staged parades, meetings, and street theater. Demonstrators charged that the WTO favored corporations and developed nations, damaged the environment, allowed AIDS to spread, and destroyed indigenous cultures. Fears of protest and terrorism led to cancelation of the WTO meetings scheduled for 2001.

Globalization was hard to contest. It would take more than isolated protests to halt the movement of people, ideas, technologies, goods, and capital in the twenty-first century.

A Changing People

Globalization was one of several forces reshaping American society and culture at the turn of the twenty-first century. As Hispanics became the largest minority group, the time neared when people of color would become the majority of the population. As the experience of African Americans underscored, race and rights remained divisive issues. Concern about rights also sparked "culture wars" over family and sexual values and the status of women and homosexuals. In general, these struggles moved American society in a liberal direction: the changing population became more tolerant of diversity and more willing to extend rights to disadvantaged groups.

A Diverse Society of Color

The racial and ethnic composition of the United States changed rapidly at the turn of the twenty-first century (see Map 31–3). In 2001, Americans of Hispanic origin outnumbered African Americans and became the largest minority group. Thanks to a strong job market, the Hispanic population had spread well beyond traditional concentrations in south Florida and the states from Texas to California. Mexican immigrants moved to small midwestern towns and cities where semiskilled and unskilled jobs paid 10 and 15 times more than jobs in Mexico. By 2004, nonwhites made up one-quarter of the population. Americans of Hispanic or Latino origin, white and nonwhite, numbered about 40 million—almost 14 percent of the population. Expecting the number of Hispanics and Asians to triple in the next 50 years, the Census Bureau predicted that the United States would become a diverse society of color, with a nonwhite majority.

As the population changed, the concept of race became more complicated. To many Americans, race was largely a divide between black and white. But the growth of the Hispanic population confounded this simple division.

Moreover, many Americans, especially younger ones, felt that mixed racial background was a basic and distinctive part of their identity. In 2000, the Census Bureau let people choose more than one race to describe themselves. Hispanics, epitomizing the

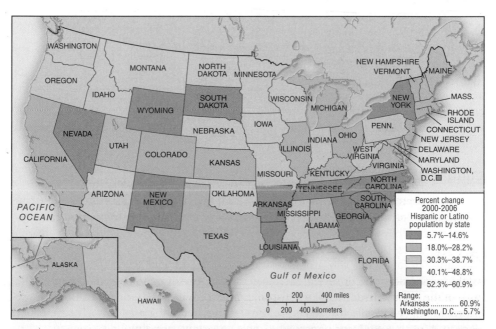

Map 31–3 The Growing Population of Americans of Hispanic or Latino Origin: Percent Change, 2000–2006 The Hispanic and Latino population increased dramatically across the country in the early 21st century. *Data Source: US Census Bureau, Population Estimates, July 1, 2000 to July 1, 2006.*

complications of race, were allowed to identify themselves both as Hispanic and as members of any race. Although officially labeled Hispanic, many Americans increasingly considered themselves Latinos or Latinas.

African Americans in the Post–Civil Rights Era

As Americans pondered the future, the African American experience reminded them that issues of race and rights remained volatile and unresolved. Half a century after *Brown v. Board of Education*, African Americans had made notable gains. In 1957, only 18 percent of black adults had graduated from high school. By 2010, 84 percent had, just under the 87 percent national rate.

African Americans had also made notable economic and political gains. The black middle class continued to grow. But African Americans were consistently more likely to be unemployed than were whites. By 1992 there were more than 10,000 black officeholders nationwide. In 2001, Colin Powell became the first African American secretary of state, and Condoleezza Rice became the first African American (and female) national security advisor. Four years later, Rice became secretary of state.

These and other firsts did not mean the end of racial injustice and conflict. In 1991, white police in Los Angeles stopped a black motorist, Rodney King, for drunk driving and then savagely beat him. Despite a videotape of the beating, an all-white jury acquitted four of the policemen of all charges. The verdict set off a riot in the predominantly African American community of South Central Los Angeles, including the Watts section that had been the center of rioting in 1965. Three days of violence left 51 people dead, 1,800 injured, and nearly 3,700 buildings burned. In the aftermath, Americans debated whether the legal system offered justice to African Americans, while liberals and conservatives blamed each other for the poverty and despair of many black communities. Eventually a federal court convicted two of the police officers for depriving King of his civil rights and another court awarded him $3.8 million in damages.

Despite the riots, governments took few new steps to deal with racial inequality. In an age of pessimism about government, few Americans believed that any activist programs could secure equal conditions for African Americans. Nevertheless, Americans did not want to undo the achievements of the past. Despite conservative opposition, affirmative action and other civil rights programs remained largely in place.

Culture Wars

Concerns about rights also drove a cluster of controversies, known as "culture wars," centering on the family, marriage, gender, and sexuality. By 2010, the transformation of the American family was unmistakable. In the 1950s, two out of three families had a parent staying at home full-time; in 2000, with so many mothers in the workforce, less than one family in four had a stay-at-home parent. The "traditional" nuclear family of father, mother, and children no longer predominated in American households. Married couples with children made up fewer than half of all households by 2010 (see Table 31–1). Households of only one person rose to over a third of total households by 2011. That year, over 17 percent of all households contained a single parent, usually a mother.

A number of factors led to these trends. Americans were marrying later, having fewer children, and having them later in life. The divorce rate doubled from 1960 to 1990. In the

Table 31-1 The Changing American Household, 1960–2011*

Year	Households	Families	Married-Couple Families % of Total Households	Single-Parent Families % of Total Households	One-Person Households % of Total Households
1960	52,799	44,905	74.3%	10.7%	15.0%
1970	63,401	51,456	70.5%	10.6%	18.8%
1980**	80,776	59,550	60.8%	12.9%	26.3%
1990	93,347	66,090	56.0%	14.8%	29.2%
2000	104,705	72,025	52.8%	16.0%	31.2%
2010	117,538	78,833	49.7%	17.4%	32.9%
2011	118,682	78,613	48.9%	17.3%	33.8%

Source: U.S. Census Bureau, Current Population Survey, March and Annual Social and Economic Supplements, 2011 and earlier.
http://www.census.gov/population/socdemo/hh-fam/hh1.xls
*Numbers given in thousands.
**Revised using population controls based on the 1980 census.

1990s about half of all marriages were ending in divorce. As women's wages rose, more women could afford to live alone or to head families by themselves.

Many conservatives and Republicans blamed these developments on an alleged moral decline. In their view, the counterculture of the 1960s, liberals, the media, feminists, and gays had undermined "family values." "It is a cultural war, as critical to the kind of nation we will one day be as was the cold war itself," thundered Patrick Buchanan in 1992.

To defend the family, some conservatives argued that single mothers should receive fewer welfare benefits and that divorce should be made more difficult. In response, liberals claimed that the family was not dying but simply adapting to change, as it always had. The different forms of the family, like social diversity in general, could be viewed as a good thing.

Conservatives found the battle for "family values" hard to win. The underlying factors of family life were almost impossible to influence.

Women in the Postfeminist Era

Women were also at the center of the culture wars because their position in society had changed dramatically since the 1960s. The percentage of adult women in the workforce rose, as did the percentage of women in high-paying white-collar jobs. Women were more visible in politics. After the 1992 elections, a record 53 women held seats in Congress. In 1993, Janet Reno became the first female attorney general, and Madeleine Albright became the first female secretary of state.

Yet there was a sense of stagnation in the new century. In 2009, women earned on average 77 percent as much as men—little better than 15 years before. Women were still more likely than men to live in poverty. Bill Clinton's adulterous affairs dramatized women's insistence that men "just don't get it" about relationships between the sexes. Nearly half of women believed the women's movement had made their lives better, but the movement was now less visible and less vocal. The 2000s were both the "post–civil rights era" and the "postfeminist era."

Still, conservatives could not turn back the clock. Forced to raise troops without a draft, the military, one of the last and most intensely masculine preserves, needed female volunteers. In 1994, the Department of Defense rescinded the "Risk Rule" that kept women out of units in which they could be harmed or captured.

Conservatives also tried to limit women's access to abortion. At the grassroots level, the Right to Life movement picketed abortion clinics and tried to discourage pregnant women from having abortions. Some radicals resorted to violence, including the murder of clinic workers. Meanwhile, both presidents Bush opposed abortion and named anti-abortion judges to the federal courts.

In spite of the protests and political maneuvers, abortion continued. In *Planned Parenthood v. Casey* in 1992, the Supreme Court narrowly voted to uphold much of a Pennsylvania law limiting access to abortions while also declaring that a woman's right to choose an abortion was "a component of liberty we cannot renounce." President Clinton chose proabortion justices and vetoed antiabortion legislation.

Winning Gay and Lesbian Rights

Homosexuality was one more front in the culture wars. Although most Americans believed businesses should not discriminate on the basis of sexual preference, a majority in the 1990s believed that homosexuality was morally wrong. Every year, there were hundreds of documented instances of violence against gays and lesbians.

As homosexuals pressed for equal rights, evangelical Christians and conservatives fought back. In 1992 Colorado voters passed a referendum forbidding communities to pass laws protecting gay rights, but the state supreme court declared it unconstitutional. In 1996, Congress passed the Defense of Marriage Act, which denied federal benefits to same-sex couples and allowed states to refuse to recognize same-sex marriages from other states.

The military was another battle zone. Officially barred from serving, homosexuals had long concealed their sexual orientation in order to remain in the military. Then, in 1992, a federal court ordered the navy to reinstate an openly gay petty officer who had been discharged. The next year, President Clinton instituted a "don't ask, don't tell" policy. The military would no longer ask recruits whether they were gay, and gays and lesbians would continue to conceal their sexual orientation.

These developments reflected a gradual turning of the tide. As AIDS spread more slowly among the gay population and heterosexuals contracted the disease, Americans were less likely to consider it "gay cancer" or God's punishment. Meanwhile, gays became a more accepted presence in society. Television shows positively depicted homosexuality. Openly gay men and women served in Congress. Many businesses, including Disneyland, welcomed gay customers. Leading corporations, including Ford and General Motors, began providing benefits to the partners of gay employees. In the process, Americans developed a more nuanced understanding of nonheterosexual identities, including bisexual and transgendered as well as lesbian and gay. By the 2000s, the increasing use of the inclusive term "LGBT" reflected this new awareness.

Americans, especially younger ones, increasingly accepted the legitimacy of nonheterosexual relationships. In *Lawrence v. Texas* in 2003, the US Supreme Court struck down state antisodomy laws and effectively legalized gay sexual behavior. After *Lawrence*,

The Spread of Same-Sex Marriage In June 2008, a ruling by the California State Supreme Court allowed same-sex couples, including this one, to marry.

there was new support for legalizing same-sex marriage. In 2004, the mayor of San Francisco, flouting state law, issued marriage licenses to same-sex couples. Liberal Massachusetts became the first state to legalize same-sex marriages, and couples flocked there to be married. Despite the support of conservatives and George W. Bush, a constitutional amendment banning gay marriage failed to pass that year. In 2008, a majority of California voters passed a referendum imposing a ban on gay marriage, but courts soon blocked the measure.

The battles over family values did little to alter the direction of social change in the United States. Despite the culture wars, Americans seemed willing to balance conservative economic policy with more liberal social values.

America in the Post–Cold War World

With the end of the cold war, America's role in the world, so clear for nearly half a century, suddenly became unclear. In 1991, the American-led victory in the Persian Gulf War briefly suggested that the United States might serve as an international police officer in a "New World Order." But Americans remained reluctant about further intervention abroad. Then the attacks of September 11, 2001, forced the United States into the lengthy global war on terror.

The New World Order

As the cold war ended, many Americans hoped the United States would play a less active role in the world. Still remembering the Vietnam War, they were reluctant to endorse armed intervention abroad. Liberals hoped, too, that the end of the cold war would bring a "peace dividend"—savings on foreign aid and military expenditures to be spent on domestic needs. Some Republicans also wanted a less internationalist foreign policy. Echoing conservatives of the 1940s and 1950s, they insisted that the United States should no longer provide financial aid and military protection to other countries.

In contrast, internationalists in both the Democratic and Republican Parties believed the United States could protect itself and advance its interests only by remaining active in world affairs. The most powerful internationalist was President George H. W. Bush. Believing that American isolationism had encouraged fascist aggression and world war, he argued that the United States had to maintain its overseas commitments. With the help of other powerful countries, America should use foreign aid, military strength, NATO, and the United Nations to maintain a stable international system, a profitable "New World Order," of democracy, capitalism, free trade, prosperity, and the rule of law.

Bush's "New World Order," like the cold war, would serve American interests, but it required costs the nation might not want to pay.

The Persian Gulf War

The test of the New World Order came quickly. On August 2, 1990, Iraq, led by President Saddam Hussein, overran Kuwait, its oil-rich but defenseless neighbor to the south. Entrenched in Kuwait, Iraq threatened its much larger western neighbor, oil-producing Saudi Arabia. Hussein's actions clearly jeopardized America's oil supply and its Saudi Arabian ally. The Kuwaiti invasion also challenged Bush's calls for a stable global system.

Comparing Hussein to Adolf Hitler, Bush created an international coalition opposing Iraq. By the end of 1990, over half a million US troops had joined with forces from 36 nations in Operation Desert Shield to protect Saudi Arabia (see Map 31–4). Meanwhile, Bush persuaded the United Nations to authorize military action if the Iraqis did not withdraw by January 15, 1991. He also obtained congressional approval for the use of force.

When Hussein refused to pull back by the deadline, Operation Desert Shield became Operation Desert Storm. Covered live by CNN, coalition missiles and planes struck Iraq on the night of January 17. In response, Hussein launched ineffective Scud missiles against America's ally, Israel. Ground forces led by US general Norman Schwarzkopf swept into Kuwait, devastated the Iraqi army, and pushed into Iraq in just 100 hours. Fearing accusations of cruelty, Bush halted the invasion before it reached the Iraqi capital of Baghdad and toppled Hussein.

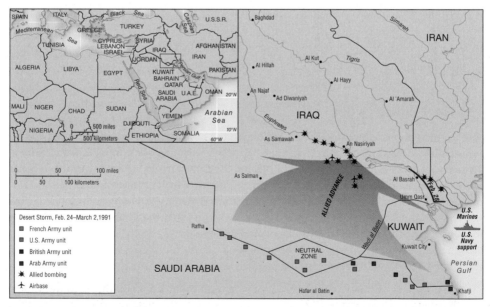

Map 31–4 The Persian Gulf War Operation Desert Storm, the allied attack on the forces of Iraq, tested President George H. W. Bush's vision of a "New World Order" in the oil-rich heart of the Middle East. *Mark C. Carnes et al.,* Mapping America's Past *(New York: Henry Holt, 1996), p. 267;* Hammond Atlas of the Twentieth Century *(New York: Times Books, 1996), p. 166.*

The Persian Gulf War seemed a great victory for the United States and the New World Order. American technology appeared to work perfectly. Coalition forces suffered only about 220 battle deaths while killing thousands of Iraqis. American leadership and power had halted aggression and restored freedom abroad.

Americans' euphoria did not last. Studies showed that US weapons had not worked quite so well. As many as a quarter of Gulf War veterans suffered major health problems caused by exposure to chemical pesticides and, ironically, pills intended to protect them from Iraqi chemical weapons. Despite his defeat, Hussein held on to power and ruthlessly repressed the Shiite and Kurdish populations. He would remain a threat to his neighbors and to American interests. The goals of the New World Order had not been fully achieved after all.

Retreating from the New World Order

In the years after the Persian Gulf War, the United States retreated from Bush's vision. Unwilling to maintain cold war spending levels, the nation cut troops, closed bases, and canceled weapons, including Reagan's Strategic Defense Initiative. The Central Intelligence Agency and other intelligence operations struggled with tight budgets, low morale, and public criticism. The foreign aid budget also stagnated.

As US power diminished, the Vietnam syndrome returned: Americans were reluctant to intervene overseas with no critical military or economic interest at stake. Both Bush and Clinton provided US troops to a United Nations peacekeeping mission in the famine-plagued, war-ravaged African nation of Somalia. But when a local warlord's forces massacred 32 US troops, a chastened Clinton promised that US troops would only join peacekeeping operations that benefited US interests and preserved international security.

The United States was also reluctant to intervene in the violence following collapse of Communist rule in Yugoslavia. As this Balkan country broke apart in the early 1990s, three ethnic groups—Serbs, Croats, and Muslim Slavs—fought a bitter civil war in the newly independent province of Bosnia-Herzegovina. The remnants of the old Yugoslavia, under the harsh leadership of Slobodan Milosevic, helped Serbs carry out "ethnic cleansing," the forcible expulsion of Muslims and Croats from their homes. Faced with the worst mass brutality in Europe since World War II, Bush and Clinton were unwilling to risk American lives in a ground war. As the slaughter continued, Clinton finally unleashed US planes and missiles, operating with NATO, in 1994. When he committed 20,000 troops to help keep the peace, most Americans opposed the move. In 1999, Clinton faced the same dilemma again, when the Milosevic regime attacked ethnic Albanians in the region of Kosovo. Avoiding a ground war, his administration joined a devastating 78-day NATO air offensive that ended the fighting without any US casualties. Despite this success, there was no longer any talk about a US-led New World Order.

Al Qaeda and 9/11

As Americans shied away from international commitment, a mortal threat to the United States emerged. In February 1993 an explosive-laden truck blew up in an underground garage beneath New York City's World Trade Center. Six people were killed and more than a thousand injured in the first major international terrorist incident inside the United States. Investigators traced the attack to followers of a radical Islamist spiritual leader from

Egypt, Sheikh Omar Abdel-Rahman, who lived in New Jersey. Rahman and over a dozen associates were convicted for the bombing and other plots.

Despite the attack, most Americans ignored terrorism. US authorities ignored the plotters' connections to a transnational terrorist organization, Al Qaeda, led and financed by a wealthy Saudi Arabian exile, Osama bin Laden. A veteran of the resistance to the Soviet invasion of Afghanistan, bin Laden had made Al Qaeda—Arabic for "base" or "foundation"—into an anti-Western movement dedicated to restoring the supposedly lost glory of Islam. He particularly hated the United States for its support of Israel and its military presence in the Middle East. In 1995 and 1996, the organization was involved in deadly terrorist attacks on US soldiers in Saudi Arabia. In 1996, bin Laden declared *jihad*—holy war—on the United States.

Although Clinton called terrorism "the enemy of our generation," Americans still largely ignored it. In 1998, truck bombs at US embassies in Kenya and Tanzania killed at least 224, including 12 Americans, and wounded 5,000. Blaming Al Qaeda, the Clinton administration launched missile attacks on terrorist facilities in Sudan and Afghanistan and tried unsuccessfully to kill bin Laden. In 2000, Al Qaeda members slammed an explosive-laden motorboat into the side of the US destroyer *Cole*. Although 17 American sailors died, Clinton did not retaliate.

Despite warnings, Clinton's successor, George W. Bush, paid little attention to Al Qaeda. Then, on the morning of September 11, 2001, the most ambitious Al Qaeda plot took place in a clear blue morning sky. Nineteen Middle Eastern members of bin Laden's organization walked through security at East Coast airports and boarded four passenger jets. In flight, the terrorists, brandishing box cutters and Mace or pepper spray, overwhelmed flight attendants and passengers, killed or wounded the pilots, took the controls, and redirected the flights. At 8:46 a.m., American 11 sped into the North Tower of the World Trade Center; 17 minutes later, United 175 hit the Trade Center's South Tower. At 9:37, American 77 struck the west wall of the Pentagon, outside Washington, DC. Aboard

Map 31–5   The Global Reach of Al Qaeda *Data Source: National Consortium for the Study of Terrorism and Responses to Terrorism (START), 2011. Global Terrorism Database [Data file]. Retrieved from http:// www.start.umd.edu/gtd.*

United 93, apparently headed toward Washington, there were sounds of struggle, a voice shouted, "Allah is the Greatest," and the jet crashed into an empty field in Shanksville, Pennsylvania, at 10:03. By then, the North Tower of the World Trade Center had collapsed in a cloud of smoke and debris. The South Tower followed at 10:28.

The tragedy, which became known as "9/11," killed the 19 hijackers, 40 people in the crash at Shanksville, 184 at the Pentagon, and 2,751 at the World Trade Center. More Americans died on 9/11 than had died in the Japanese attack at Pearl Harbor on December 7, 1941. Only the Civil War battles of Antietam and Cold Harbor had been deadlier days. The United States had suddenly discovered its place in the post–cold war world.

The Global War on Terror

In the days after 9/11, stunned Americans felt the attacks had "changed everything." Much stayed the same, but the catastrophe did reshape American foreign and security policy. Vowing privately on 9/11 "to kick some ass," President Bush declared publicly that evening, "We will make no distinction between the terrorists who committed these acts and those who harbor them." When Afghanistan's Taliban refused to turn over bin Laden, the United States and other NATO countries responded in October by launching air strikes against Al Qaeda and Taliban targets and sending troops to hunt down bin Laden, destroy his camps, and drive out the Taliban. What the Bush administration called the "Global War on Terror" had begun.

Afghanistan, weak and impoverished, fell quickly, but bin Laden and many Al Qaeda and Taliban fighters escaped in the remote, mountainous terrain to continue their struggle. US and NATO forces remained to protect the new government and find bin Laden.

Meanwhile, the Bush administration reorganized the federal government to combat terror. Within a month of 9/11, Bush chose the first Director of Homeland Security to protect US borders and infrastructure and to respond in the event of a terrorist strike. In 2002, Congress elevated the position to cabinet rank in a new Department of Homeland Security. Two years later, Congress answered harsh criticism of the CIA and FBI for failing to detect the 9/11 plot by transferring oversight of all US intelligence agencies from the head of the CIA to a new Director of National Intelligence.

More controversially, the Bush administration worked what Vice President Dick Cheney called "the dark side"—practices traditionally condemned by American law and culture. The government maintained a detention center at Guantánamo Bay, Cuba, where captured "enemy combatants" were denied trials and the protections of the Geneva Convention on prisoners of war and were, in some cases, tortured. In 2006 and 2008, the US Supreme Court asserted the rights of the Guantánamo detainees and reminded Bush that "a state of war is not a blank check for the president."

Bush also wanted the government to be able to gather more information about its own citizens. In October 2001, Congress hastily passed the USA Patriot Act, which made it easier for the federal government to spy on Americans. It also allowed the attorney general to imprison indefinitely, without trial, noncitizens considered threats to national security.

Opponents condemned the Patriot Act as an unlawful and unequaled deprivation of civil liberties. In 2004, a federal judge declared part of the measure an unconstitutional infringement on First Amendment rights. But the Bush administration secured the renewal and expansion of the act.

Bush also rethought the use of American military power. In the past, presidents had rejected preemptive peacetime attacks on other nations. But Bush believed that

AMERICAN LANDSCAPE

>> Gitmo, "The Least Worst Place"

From the camera eye of a satellite miles above, Guantánamo Bay stood out from the rest of eastern Cuba. The inlet was a horseshoe of brown and gray amid the lush green of the island and the bright blue of the Atlantic. To the administration of George W. Bush, Guantánamo Bay was a gray area, too: one of the few places on earth that was American and yet not American, a drab anomaly perfect for one of the most controversial phases of the war on terror.

Guantánamo Bay, 520 miles from Miami, Florida, had been an anomaly for more than a century. After the Spanish-American War of 1898, the US government had taken the spot for a well-protected naval base. The Cuban-American Treaty of 1903 effectively gave America perpetual control over the base. For less than $4,000 a year, the United States could keep the facility until both Washington and Cuba agreed to end the arrangement.

Even when Fidel Castro came to power in 1959, the US base remained. Castro objected to the base but did not try to drive out the United States. So Guantánamo Bay, or "Gitmo," as Americans called it, remained the oldest US overseas naval base and the only one in a Communist country.

Gitmo became less and less valuable over the years. As the cold war ended and the United States closed down military bases, there was no real need for a naval installation so close to the US mainland. Then the war on terror began. The Bush administration needed to put captured Taliban fighters and other "enemy combatants" somewhere safe. It was too risky to leave detainees in unstable Afghanistan or Iraq, but it was also too risky to bring them to the United States, where courts, Congress, and public opinion could interfere in their imprisonment. So the Bush administration looked, in the words of Secretary of Defense Donald Rumsfeld, for "the least worst place" to hold those captured in the war on terror.

They found it at Guantánamo Bay. The US military controlled the base, but US civil law did not apply. Gitmo, with its gray, pebbly beaches, was the perfect gray area for an administration determined to find a way around the law to prosecute the war on terror. Before 2001 was over, detainees began to arrive from Afghanistan. By the end of 2008, some 775 people had been incarcerated at Gitmo. To accommodate them, the United States built no fewer than seven separate prison facilities; one of them, known only as "Camp 7," remained secret. Thousands of Americans streamed in to run Gitmo.

For a time, the base provided the Bush administration with the freedom it wanted and needed. CIA, FBI, and military interrogators, apparently copying Chinese Communist techniques from the 1950s, tortured some prisoners. According to detainees, their captors used sleep deprivation and beatings; they also mocked detainees' religious practices by defacing the Qur'an or flushing it down the toilet. Lacking the rights of captured military prisoners under the Geneva Convention, the detainees were deprived of the right to trial—a feature of justice in the United States. These conditions took a heavy toll on prisoners; an unknown number committed suicide.

As details of life at Gitmo leaked out, critics of the Bush administration argued that the laws of the United States should apply to prisoners at the base; they deserved the protections of the Geneva Convention and the right to trial. They saw Gitmo as proof that the war on terror, like other wars, had eroded due process, human rights, and other features of democracy, all in the name of battling for democracy.

Even though the US Supreme Court seemed to agree, in its rulings of 2006 and 2008, that Gitmo was an assault on democratic values, the facility remained open—a swath of gray amid all the green and blue.

terrorism, "a threat without precedent," might require the nation to strike even before a threat emerged. Bush further broke with cold war presidents, including his father, by calling for the United States to act alone when necessary rather than through alliances and the United Nations.

The Bush Doctrine of preemption and unilateral action risked isolating the United States and making it seem selfish, dangerous, and illegitimate. Yet Bush, confident of American power and virtue, was willing to go it alone.

The Iraq War

It was not enough to go after terrorist organizations, Bush declared in January 2002. The United States must also "prevent regimes that sponsor terror from threatening America or our friends and allies with weapons of mass destruction." He identified Iran, Iraq, and North Korea as an "axis of evil," potentially able to arm terrorists with nuclear, chemical, or biological weapons to threaten the United States directly.

Iraq was the focus of Bush's attention. In his view, Saddam Hussein had plotted the assassination of the president's father, forced United Nations weapons inspectors to leave, resumed attempts to gain weapons of mass destruction (WMD), and supported Al Qaeda. Bush was also influenced by advisors including Vice President Cheney, Secretary of Defense Donald Rumsfeld, and Undersecretary of Defense Paul Wolfowitz, who advocated neoconservatism, the idea that the United States should aggressively promote democracy abroad in order to make a better and more secure world. Replacing Hussein with a democratic regime would, these neoconservatives insisted, encourage the spread of democracy in the Middle East and make US ally Israel safer.

As Bush moved to confront Iraq, nearly all of America's European allies, as well as Russia, China, and Middle Eastern countries, opposed a unilateral US war. Bush did assemble a "coalition of the willing," but only Great Britain, Australia, and Poland joined the United States in committing troops.

On the night of March 19, 2003, Operation Iraqi Freedom began with a hail of Tomahawk cruise missiles aimed at Baghdad in an unsuccessful attempt to kill Hussein. On March 21, some 1,300 bombs and missiles rained down on Baghdad in a display of "shock and awe" meant to demoralize Iraqi leadership. Sweeping into Iraq, US troops occupied Baghdad and British forces seized a key port to the south. American technology, particularly missiles and smart bombs, worked well. Offering little resistance, much of the Iraqi

The Fall of Saddam Hussein As the coalition invasion overthrew the Iraqi regime, jubilant Iraqis pulled down the statues of Saddam Hussein, like this one, in the spring of 2003.

army disappeared into the civilian population. Hussein disappeared, too. By mid-April, his statues were toppling.

Swift and short, like the Gulf War 12 years before, the war with Iraq seemed to be everything that the Bush administration had hoped. Only 138 US soldiers had died. Standing before a huge banner declaring "Mission Accomplished" aboard an aircraft carrier on May 1, the president jubilantly announced, "Major combat operations in Iraq have ended." The United States seemed well on the way to winning the war on terror and reshaping the Middle East.

America in Crisis

It was not that easy. The global war on terror dragged on without victory in either Iraq or Afghanistan. In 2008, financial catastrophe touched off a harsh recession and set the stage for a precedent-setting presidential election. In the next years, the United States avoided a depression and finally drew the two wars toward a conclusion. Even so, the nation faced a crisis rooted in long-term economic problems and political discontent.

Iraq and Afghanistan in Turmoil

The jubilation of "Mission Accomplished" soon gave way to sober realities in Iraq during 2003. WMD, a chief justification of the war, were never found. Unable to prove Hussein's ties to Al Qaeda, the Bush administration faced charges of fighting a needless war in Iraq while bin Laden went free in Afghanistan. Meanwhile, the United States struggled to restart the Iraqi economy, train new police and military, and create a popular, democratic regime.

Soon, a violent insurgency, perhaps orchestrated by Hussein, tried to destabilize Iraq and drive out the United States. Although US forces captured Hussein in December 2003, the conflict went badly. Hussein's brutal execution and revelations of the humiliation and torture of Iraqis at a prison in Abu Ghraib humiliated the United States. "Al Qaeda in Iraq," a new terrorist group to loyal to bin Laden, joined the fight. Although the Bush administration handed over sovereignty to an American-chosen Iraqi government in 2004, over 100,000 US troops had to remain to keep the peace. By the end of 2006, 3,000 had died amid the turmoil.

Facing failure, Bush responded with a controversial "surge," a temporary troop increase that succeeded, along with changes in Iraqi politics, in decreasing the violence by mid-2008. But American public opinion had largely turned against the continuing war.

Meanwhile, the Afghanistan conflict had worsened. As the United States focused on Iraq, the Taliban, aided by foreign fighters, had gradually regained strength and the pro–United States government had lost power. Osama bin Laden remained at large. By 2008, over 600 US soldiers and uncounted Afghans had died in seven years of fighting.

The wars in Afghanistan and Iraq cost the United States popularity and influence around the globe. Sympathetic to Americans after 9/11, many people no longer supported US military action in the Middle East. Critics argued that war, torture, and civilian casualties helped rather than hurt the terrorist cause. Moreover, the United States no longer seemed like an unstoppable military and economic superpower able to reshape the world in its image.

The Economy in Jeopardy

The economic boom of the 1990s and 2000s looked a lot like the boom of the 1920s. In both periods, optimistic American consumers, buoyed by good times, borrowed money to buy houses, cars, and stocks. All that buying spurred the economy and drove the stock market to record heights. But eventually all that borrowing reached its limits: unable to meet their debts, many Americans could not borrow any more. In both periods, business leaders and government officials paid too little attention to dangerous financial practices until it was too late.

By the early 2000s, the housing industry was developing a classic "bubble," an unrealistic inflation of prices. As Americans—some of them aided by subprime mortgages—bought houses in record numbers, homes seemed like risk-free investments whose value would only increase. Some people bought houses they could not afford, and many used houses as collateral for loans. Banks made loans they should not have made. Moreover, financial institutions obscured the reality of bad mortgage loans by folding them into complex, risky new financial instruments, known as Collateralized Debt Obligations (CDOs), that sold around the world. As a result, firms that bought CDOs were vulnerable to trouble in housing but did not understand the danger.

In 2005, US house prices stagnated and began to fall. As the housing bubble burst, many homeowners discovered they were not as wealthy as they had thought. Some, particularly those with subprime loans, had trouble making their payments; foreclosures—banks' repossession of homes for unpaid mortgages—increased. In consequence, the home-construction industry suffered, and it became harder for consumers to get credit.

The most dramatic consequences befell financial institutions. In the spring of 2008, the investment bank Bear Stearns, involved in subprime mortgage loans and other risky practices, avoided bankruptcy only with federal help and then a takeover by banking giant JPMorgan Chase. In the summer, the nation's largest mortgage lender, IndyMac Bank, failed; the federal government had to guarantee depositors' money. Then, Washington took over two key private corporations that bought and sold mortgages—the Federal National Mortgage Association, known as "Fannie Mae," and the Federal Home Loan Mortgage Corporation, known as "Freddie Mac."

At the same time, developments linked to globalization also threatened the United States and other nations. Globalized free trade suffered when the World Trade Organization's round of trade talks in Doha, Qatar, ended in failure. Oil prices, driven by demand from the growing economies of China and India, hit record levels. High oil prices drove up the prices of other goods, including food. They particularly hurt the American auto industry, whose gas-guzzling SUVs became hard to sell. Felt worldwide, these events especially hit the United States as the global value of the dollar declined and American consumers, particularly those with big credit card balances, lost confidence. As the Dow Jones industrial average fell from a record high over 14,000 in October 2007 to the 11,000s in early September 2008, many Americans were less wealthy.

Despite the signs, most people were unprepared when disaster struck that month. Within days, the US financial industry nearly collapsed: Lehman Brothers, another investment firm caught up in the subprime debacle, became the most valuable American corporation ever to fail; the Bank of America bought Merrill Lynch, still another near-bankrupt victim of dubious mortgage and other financial practices; and AIG, an insurance giant heavily involved in CDOs, had to be bought by the Federal Reserve.

Meanwhile, US and foreign stock markets buckled. The Dow Jones lost more than 4 percent of its value on September 15, and another 4 percent two days later. As governments and financial institutions around the world scrambled to save banks, keep the financial system operating, and prop up stock markets, Americans feared a repeat of the great crash of 1929. At the end of the month, a panicked Congress approved the Emergency Economic Stabilization Act of 2008, a $700 billion financial package, which created the Troubled Asset Relief Program (TARP) to bail out the US financial industry, ensure the availability of credit to borrowers, and save the nation from depression.

The Presidential Election of 2008

Against this frightening backdrop, Americans chose their 44th president. First-term senator Barack Obama of Illinois, the son of a black Kenyan father and a white American mother, won the Democratic nomination on a platform of an end to the Iraq War and "change" for America. A symbol of the diverse, globalized nation, Obama became the first African American major-party presidential nominee. His Republican opponent, Senator John McCain of Arizona, reinforced a reputation as an independent "maverick" by choosing the second female major-party candidate for the vice presidency, Governor Sarah Palin of Alaska. But the 72-year-old McCain, a generation older than Obama, seemed more like a defender of the status quo, including Bush's policies.

The intensifying economic crisis mortally wounded the Republican cause. Saddled with the unpopular wars and weak economy of the Bush administration, McCain seemed old and uncertain. On November 4, voters did what had seemed unthinkable

"Change We Can Believe In" Democratic nominee Barack Obama campaigns for the presidency in 2008.

even after the civil rights movement of the 1960s: they made an African American the president of the United States. Obama won a clear victory, with 52.8 percent of the popular vote, the highest in 20 years, and 365 electoral votes. The Democrat seemed to have his mandate for "change."

The Obama Administration

He would need it. Even before the celebration of Obama's history-making victory ended, the economic crisis deepened. In mid-November, the stock market lurched below 8,000. As Chrysler, Ford, and GM headed toward bankruptcy, President Bush provided 13 billion dollars in TARP funds to the troubled automakers. Consumer spending fell and unemployment rose.

Taking office amid hardship and war in January 2009, Obama optimistically promised a new politics. "We have chosen hope over fear, unity of purpose over conflict and discord," he declared. "We come to proclaim an end to the petty grievances and false promises, the recriminations and worn-out dogmas that for far too long have strangled our politics."

To restore prosperity, Obama pushed successfully for major economic legislation. The American Recovery and Reinvestment Act of 2009, known as the stimulus package, included tax incentives and money for housing, health care, educational programs, food stamps, retirees, scientific research, highways, and other infrastructure. Costing three-quarters of a trillion dollars, the measure was the sort of deficit spending that liberals had long advocated to end recession or depression. Some liberals, however, believed the stimulus spent too little, while conservatives charged that the act spent far too much and irresponsibly increased federal power and the national debt.

To save Chrysler and General Motors in 2009, the US government stepped in to support swift bankruptcies for the two manufacturers, which quickly reemerged as new, restructured companies with less debt and new ownership. To Republicans' dismay, the United States Treasury temporarily became the majority owner of General Motors. Despite the controversy over this supposed "socialism," the bailout worked: the American automakers survived and the federal government sold off its majority ownership of GM.

Rather than punish the financial leaders for their role in the economic crisis, Obama focused on protecting consumers and regulating banks and insurance companies. In 2009, Congress passed new rules for credit card companies. The next year, the president signed the Wall Street Reform and Consumer Protection Act, known as Dodd-Frank, perhaps the most significant overhaul of federal financial regulation since the 1930s. But it was unclear whether the law would prevent a future banking crisis.

As the stock market climbed up again and the danger of depression receded, Obama concentrated on winning a longtime liberal goal, national health care. After a lengthy congressional battle, the president signed the Patient Protection and Affordable Health Care Act of 2010 and the Health Care and Educational Reconciliation Act of 2010. The two measures helped uninsured and self-employed Americans buy health insurance, made more poor people eligible for Medicaid, increased the number of years children could be covered under their parents' health insurance, prevented insurance companies from denying coverage on the basis of preexisting conditions, and encouraged large employers to provide health care plans. Through Medicare taxes and benefit cuts, the measures would reduce the federal budget deficit. Finally, a controversial "individual mandate" required all adults to obtain health care beginning in 2014 or pay a penalty. In all, Obama had achieved what previous Democratic presidents had not. But his landmark reform was poorly understood by the public and passionately attacked by conservatives as more government "socialism."

In the midst of economic crisis, Americans worried less about some of the social issues that divided them. Immigration remained a major concern for some people, particularly along the border with Mexico, but hard times lowered the number of illegal immigrants. As public opinion increasingly favored GLBT rights, the Obama administration stopped enforcing the Defense of Marriage Act, Obama and Congress ended "don't ask, don't tell," and more states recognized same-sex marriage.

Obama coupled his activist domestic agenda with an aggressive foreign policy. To the disappointment of supporters, the president did not close the detention center at Guantánamo Bay, as he had promised. But Obama did redeem his promise to bring the Iraq War to a close. In October 2011, he declared that American troops would leave the country by the end of the year. Whether the United States had achieved its goals of a stable Iraq was unclear.

Believing the fate of Afghanistan crucial to the fight against terrorism, the president ordered 30,000 more troops into the nation in 2009. Although US military leaders changed tactics, American troops faced the same difficult battle that Lieutenant Craig Mullaney had fought to defeat the Taliban and Al Qaeda and win over the Afghan people.

Meanwhile, Obama aggressively used other means to go after terrorists and their supporters. To the surprise of many, he greatly increased the use of unmanned, rocket-firing CIA drones to hunt down and kill suspected terrorists, even inside Pakistan. The president also used the CIA and Special Forces to go after terrorist leaders. On May 1, 2011, nearly a decade after 9/11, a daring helicopter raid by US Special Forces inside Pakistan succeeded in killing Osama bin Laden. His presence in Pakistan raised troubling questions about that country's relationship with the United States, but Americans finally could celebrate a key turning point in the war on terror.

As the United States struggled with the heavy human and financial costs of war, Obama intervened less dramatically in other places around the world. In the Middle East and Africa in 2011, the "Arab Spring" saw popular uprisings against repressive leaders in nations including Tunisia, Egypt, and Libya. In the face of criticism for doing either too

>> Time Line

▼1988
George H. W. Bush elected president

▼1989
Collapse of Communist regimes in Eastern Europe
Invasion of Panama

▼1990
Partial shutdown of federal government

▼1991
Persian Gulf War
Collapse of the Soviet Union
Dow Jones Industrial Average over 3,000 for first time

▼1992
Los Angeles riot after first Rodney King verdict
US troops sent to Somalia
Bill Clinton elected president

▼1993
Terrorist truck bombing of World Trade Center, New York City
Ratification of North American Free Trade Agreement (NAFTA)

▼1994
End of "Risk Rule" for women soldiers

little or too much, the president partnered with NATO and carefully used airpower, without an American military casualty, to help overthrow Libya's Muammar Qaddafi, who had supported terrorism against the United States.

Continuing Crisis

Obama's foreign policy successes earned him little credit because the economy did not recover as strongly as he and his advisers had expected. The economic crisis, more severe than economists had first recognized, continued to strain American society. Although the economy grew, unemployment peaked at 10 percent in 2009 and remained at 9 percent.

Against this backdrop of hardship and frustration, the president's optimistic call for a new politics went unheeded. Obama found himself whipsawed in an often nasty debate. On one hand, he disappointed many of his supporters, who had expected more aggressive leadership, a better economy, and more "change" generally. More liberal Democrats and independents, who increasingly called themselves "progressives," felt that Obama should have punished Wall Street and expanded federal regulation and spending still further. On the other hand, conservatives were horrified by what Obama

had accomplished. In 2009, the Tea Party movement, evoking the spirit of the Boston Tea Party of 1773, before the American Revolution, voiced

"Impeach the Beltway Pirates" Members of the conservative Tea Party movement protest the power of federal officials in Washington, DC (which is encircled by the US Highway 495, also known as the Capital Beltway).

continued

conservative anger at federal activism. Composed mostly of white, older Americans, the movement served primarily as a pressure group within the Republican Party pushing more conservative candidates and policies.

While most Americans endorsed neither the Tea Party nor the progressives, there was considerable disappointment with Obama's presidency. In the 2010 elections, Republicans recaptured the House of Representatives. Once again the United States had divided partisan control of the federal government, and once again, as in the 1990s, the result was legislative gridlock. As unemployment stayed high, Obama pushed fruitlessly for legislation to stimulate the economy and lower the deficit. Influenced by the Tea Party, Republican leaders wanted to lower taxes and spending. Democrats generally refused to cut Medicare and other social programs. In the summer of 2011, the president and the parties finally made a modest bargain to cut the deficit, but not before the United States, for the first time in its history, nearly failed to meet its financial obligations. Many Americans criticized Obama as a weak leader who did not care enough about the nation's financial plight. But they condemned Congress and Republicans even more.

Meanwhile, evidence of America's economic travail continued to mount. While the People's Republic of China developed into a world economic power with breathtaking speed, the United States fell deeper into debt to its rival. By 2010, 15 percent of Americans lived in poverty, the highest level in nearly three decades. Suburbs, long the focus of the American dream, saw poverty reach record levels. Inequality had increased dramatically, too. Households headed by people 65 and older were now 47 times as wealthy as households headed by people 35 and under. While the elderly benefited from Social Security and Medicare, young people suffered from unemployment and the cost of education. In addition, the top one percent of Americans controlled ever more income and wealth.

Such statistics helped drive another protest, the "Occupy" movement, which demonstrated in places around the world, including Wall Street, on behalf of the "99 Percent" against the "One Percent." While the Tea Party blamed the federal government for the nation's woes, Occupy blamed financial elites. More fundamentally, inequality was also the result of the long-term impact of globalization and deindustrialization. No one had a clear way to deal with these complex developments.

>> Time Line *continued*

▼2002
Creation of Department of Homeland Security

▼2003
US Supreme Court gay rights ruling, *Lawrence v. Texas*
"Operation Iraqi Freedom," Coalition invasion of Iraq

▼2004
George W. Bush reelected

▼2007
US military "surge" in Iraq

▼2008
Collapse of Doha world trade talks
US financial crisis
Barack Obama elected president

▼2009
American Recovery and Reinvestment Act (the stimulus package)

Tea Party founded

▼2010
Patient Protection and Affordable Health Care Act
Health Care and Educational Reconciliation Act

▼2011
Death of Osama bin Laden
End of Iraq War

Conclusion

In the generation from the end of the cold war to the collapse of the economic boom, the United States completed its transformation into a globalized, information-based, diverse nation. Americans accepted social and cultural diversity with less upheaval than might have been expected. But the end of the cold war had not brought the peace many people anticipated: the United States, confronting terrorism, seemed perpetually at war. The promise of the information economy had not yet matched the tests of globalization and deindustrialization. Confronting social change, war, and economic hardship, the democratic political system struggled to serve the country effectively. One hundred and fifty years after Abraham Lincoln spoke on the battlefield at Gettysburg, Americans still faced the challenge of creating a government and a nation "of the people."

Who, What

George H. W. Bush ("Bush 41") 953

George W. Bush ("Bush 43") 955

Bill Clinton 954

Saddam Hussein 962

Osama bin Laden 964

Ted Turner 947

"Family values" 959

Bush Doctrine 967

Globalization 946

Information economy 950

Neoconservatism 967

New World Order 961

NGOs 947

Subprime mortgages 954

World Trade Organization 948

Review Questions

1. What innovations spurred globalization after the cold war?

2. What were the main features of the information economy?

3. Why were Americans so often frustrated by the political system after the cold war?

Critical-Thinking Questions

1. What set apart the globalization of the 1990s and 2000s from earlier linkages between the United States and the rest of the world?

2. How did the foreign and security policies of the two presidents Bush differ? Which was more successful?

3. Did the global war on terror change American life in a fundamental way?

For further review materials and resource information,
please visit www.oup.com/us/ofthepeople

1) Globalization and the emerging postindustrial information economy brought new challenges and opportunities.

2) While politics tended toward conservatism on economic issues, social attitudes generally became liberal as the United States became more diverse.

3) Globalization was one factor encouraging US involvement abroad despite the end of the cold war.

4) The continuing war on terror and the weakness of the globalized information economy created a national crisis during the presidencies of George W. Bush and Barack Obama.

The Age of Globalization

The Politics of a New Economy

A Changing People

America in the Post–Cold War World

America in Crisis

The Cold War and Globalization In various ways, the cold war spurred globalization even as it inhibited relations between the US and Soviet blocs.

New Communications Technologies New communication technologies, speeding the flow of news, ideas, and money, were critical to globalization.

Multinationals and NGOs The rapid spread of multinational corporations and nongovernmental organizations further bound the world together.

Expanding Trade Trade agreements and regional economic alliances played a key role in globalization by removing barriers to the movement of goods and services across national borders.

Moving People Regional economic agreements and the end of the cold war facilitated the global movement of people, including an increase in US immigration.

The Information Economy Technological advances helped complete the transition from an industrial-centered economy to an information-centered economy.

A Second Economic Revolution? The information economy did not seem to bring a dramatic long-term improvement in Americans' standard of living.

Boom and Insecurity Despite sustained economic growth in the 1990s, the new economy produced worries about downsizing, outsourcing, health care, and retirement for many Americans.

The Return of Inequality The new economy intensified the trend toward economic inequality.

The Power of Conservatism National politics and economic policy remained fairly conservative.

Contesting Globalization While presidents and elites celebrated globalization, many Americans questioned its impact on their lives.

A Diverse Society of Color The rapid growth of the Hispanic and Latino population brought the US closer to becoming a majority nonwhite society.

African Americans in the Post-Civil Rights Era Despite noticeable political and economic gains, African Americans still faced racial injustice.

Culture Wars Conservatives tried with little success to undo changes to the "traditional" family.

Women in the Postfeminist Era Although women's gains slowed somewhat, conservatives did not manage to undo the long-term changes in the status of women since the 1960s.

Winning Gay and Lesbian Rights Lesbian, gay, bisexual, and transgendered Americans made substantial gains in their battle for equal rights.

The New World Order President George H. W. Bush proposed continuing activist American leadership in the world.

The Persian Gulf War Victory in Iraq seemed to validate Bush's New World Order in the early 1990s.

Retreating from the New World Order Americans were unwilling to risk significant casualties in order to intervene around the world in the mid-1990s.

Al Qaeda and 9/11 The growing threat of terrorism culminated in Al Qaeda's 9/11 attacks.

The Global War on Terror The "war on terror" brought war in Afghanistan and major social changes in the United States.

The Iraq War As part of the war on terror, the administration of George W. Bush went to war in Iraq to overthrow Saddam Hussein in 2003.

Iraq and Afghanistan in Turmoil America's wars in Iraq and Afghanistan proved difficult to win.

The Economy in Jeopardy In 2008, a housing bubble brought the financial system near to collapse and plunged the economy into a deep recession.

The Presidential Election of 2008 Barack Obama became the first African American president.

The Obama Administration Obama coupled an activist domestic agenda to combat the recession with an aggressive foreign policy to defeat terrorism and end the war in Iraq.

Continuing Crisis Despite foreign policy successes, the continuing economic crisis spurred popular discontent and threatened Obama's presidency.

Appendix A

Historical Documents

The Declaration of Independence

When in the course of human events, it becomes necessary for one people to dissolve the political bands which have connected them with another, and to assume, among the powers of the earth, the separate and equal station to which the Laws of Nature and of Nature's God entitle them, a decent respect to the opinions of mankind requires that they should declare the causes which impel them to the separation.

We hold these truths to be self-evident, that all men are created equal, that they are endowed by their Creator with certain unalienable Rights, that among these are life, liberty and the pursuit of happiness. That to secure these rights, governments are instituted among men, deriving their just powers from the consent of the governed; that whenever any form of government becomes destructive of these ends, it is the right of the people to alter or to abolish it, and to institute new Government, laying its foundation on such principles and organizing its powers in such form, as to them shall seem most likely to effect their safety and happiness. Prudence, indeed, will dictate that Governments long established should not be changed for light and transient causes; and, accordingly, all experience hath shown, that mankind are more disposed to suffer, while evils are sufferable, than to right themselves by abolishing the forms to which they are accustomed. But when a long train of abuses and usurpations, pursuing invariably the same object evinces a design to reduce them under absolute despotism, it is their right, it is their duty, to throw off such government, and to provide new guards for their future security. Such has been the patient sufferance of these colonies; and such is now the necessity which constrains them to alter their former systems of government. The history of the present King of Great Britain is a history of repeated injuries and usurpations, all having in direct object the establishment of an absolute tyranny over these States. To prove this, let facts be submitted to a candid world:

He has refused his assent to laws, the most wholesome and necessary for the public good.

He has forbidden his governors to pass laws of immediate and pressing importance, unless suspended in their operation till his assent should be obtained; and, when so suspended, he has utterly neglected to attend to them.

He has refused to pass other laws for the accommodation of large districts of people, unless those people would relinquish the right of representation in the legislature, a right inestimable to them and formidable to tyrants only.

He has called together legislative bodies at places unusual, uncomfortable, and distant from the depository of their public records, for the sole purpose of fatiguing them into compliance with his measures.

He has dissolved representative houses repeatedly, for opposing with manly firmness his invasions on the rights of the people.

He has refused for a long time, after such dissolutions, to cause others to be elected; whereby the legislative powers, incapable of annihilation, have returned to the People at large for their exercise; the State remaining in the mean time exposed to all the dangers of invasion from without, and convulsions within.

He has endeavored to prevent the population of these States; for that purpose obstructing the laws for naturalization of foreigners; refusing to pass others to encourage their migrations hither, and raising the conditions of new appropriations of lands.

He has obstructed the administration of justice, by refusing his assent to laws for establishing judiciary powers.

He has made judges dependent on his will alone, for the tenure of their offices, and the amount and payment of their salaries.

He has erected a multitude of new offices, and sent hither swarms of officers to harass our people, and eat out their substance.

He has kept among us, in times of peace, standing armies without the consent of our legislatures.

He has affected to render the Military independent of, and superior to, the civil power.

He has combined with others to subject us to a jurisdiction foreign to our constitution and unacknowledged by our laws; giving his assent to their acts of pretended legislation:

For quartering large bodies of armed troops among us;

For protecting them, by a mock trial, from punishment for any murders which they should commit on the inhabitants of these States;

For cutting off our trade with all parts of the world;

For imposing taxes on us without our Consent;

For depriving us, in many cases, of the benefits of Trial by Jury;

For transporting us beyond Seas to be tried for pretended offences;

For abolishing the free System of English Laws in a neighbouring Province, establishing therein an Arbitrary government, and enlarging its Boundaries so as to render it at once an example and fit instrument for introducing the same absolute rule into these colonies;

For taking away our charters, abolishing our most valuable laws, and altering fundamentally the forms of our governments;

For suspending our own legislatures, and declaring themselves invested with power to legislate for us in all cases whatsoever.

He has abdicated government here, by declaring us out of his protection and waging war against us.

He has plundered our seas, ravaged our coasts, burnt our towns, and destroyed the lives of our people.

He is at this time transporting large armies of foreign mercenaries to complete the works of death, desolation and tyranny, already begun with circumstances of cruelty and perfidy scarcely paralleled in the most barbarous ages, and totally unworthy the head of a civilized nation.

He has constrained our fellow citizens taken captive on the high seas to bear arms against their country, to become the executioners of their friends and brethren, or to fall themselves by their hands.

He has excited domestic insurrections amongst us, and has endeavored to bring on the inhabitants of our frontiers, the merciless Indian savages, whose known rule of warfare, is an undistinguished destruction of all ages, sexes and conditions.

In every stage of these oppressions we have petitioned for redress in the most humble terms; our repeated petitions have been answered only by repeated injury. A prince whose character is thus marked by every act which may define a tyrant, is unfit to be the ruler of a free people.

Nor have we been wanting in attentions to our British brethren. We have warned them from time to time of attempts by their legislature to extend an unwarrantable jurisdiction over us. We have reminded them of the circumstances of our emigration and settlement here. We have appealed to their native justice and magnanimity, and we have conjured them by the ties of our common kindred to disavow these usurpations, which, would inevitably interrupt our connections and correspondence. They, too, have been deaf to the voice of justice and of consanguinity. We must, therefore, acquiesce in the necessity, which denounces our separation, and hold them, as we hold the rest of mankind, enemies in war, in peace friends.

We, therefore, the representatives of the United States of America, in general Congress, assembled, appealing to the Supreme Judge of the world for the rectitude of our intentions, do, in the name, and by the authority of the good people of these colonies, solemnly publish and declare, that these united colonies are, and of right ought to be free and independent states; that they are absolved from all allegiance to the British Crown, and that all political connection between them and the state of Great Britain, is and ought to be totally dissolved; and that, as free and independent states, they have full power to levy war, conclude peace, contract alliances, establish commerce, and to do all other acts and things which independent states may of right do. And for the support of this declaration, with a firm reliance on the protection of Divine Providence, we mutually pledge to each other our lives, our fortunes and our sacred honor.

The Constitution of the United States of America

We the People of the United States, in Order to form a more perfect Union, establish Justice, insure domestic Tranquility, provide for the common defence, promote the general Welfare, and secure the Blessings of Liberty to ourselves and our Posterity, do ordain and establish this Constitution for the United States of America.

Article I
Section 1

All legislative Powers herein granted shall be vested in a Congress of the United States, which shall consist of a Senate and House of Representatives.

Section 2

The House of Representatives shall be composed of Members chosen every second Year by the People of the several States, and the Electors in each State shall have the Qualifications requisite for Electors of the most numerous Branch of the State Legislature.

No Person shall be a Representative who shall not have attained to the Age of twenty five Years, and been seven Years a Citizen of the United States, and who shall not, when elected, be an Inhabitant of that State in which he shall be chosen.

Representatives and direct Taxes shall be apportioned among the several States which may be included within this Union, according to their respective Numbers, which shall be determined by adding to the whole Number of free Persons, including those bound to

Service for a Term of Years, and excluding Indians not taxed, three fifths of all other Persons. The actual Enumeration shall be made within three Years after the first Meeting of the Congress of the United States, and within every subsequent Term of ten Years, in such Manner as they shall by Law direct. The Number of Representatives shall not exceed one for every thirty Thousand, but each State shall have at Least one Representative; and until such enumeration shall be made, the State of New Hampshire shall be entitled to choose three, Massachusetts eight, Rhode-Island and Providence Plantations one, Connecticut five, New York six, New Jersey four, Pennsylvania eight, Delaware one, Maryland six, Virginia ten, North Carolina five, South Carolina five, and Georgia three.

When vacancies happen in the Representation from any State, the Executive Authority thereof shall issue Writs of Election to fill such Vacancies.

The House of Representatives shall choose their Speaker and other Officers; and shall have the sole Power of Impeachment.

Section 3

The Senate of the United States shall be composed of two Senators from each State, chosen by the Legislature thereof for six Years; and each Senator shall have one Vote.

Immediately after they shall be assembled in Consequence of the first Election, they shall be divided as equally as may be into three Classes. The Seats of the Senators of the first Class shall be vacated at the Expiration of the second Year, of the second Class at the Expiration of the fourth Year, and of the third Class at the Expiration of the sixth Year, so that one third may be chosen every second Year; and if Vacancies happen by Resignation, or otherwise, during the Recess of the Legislature of any State, the Executive thereof may make temporary Appointments until the next Meeting of the Legislature, which shall then fill such Vacancies.

No Person shall be a Senator who shall not have attained to the Age of thirty Years, and been nine Years a Citizen of the United States, and who shall not, when elected, be an Inhabitant of that State for which he shall be chosen.

The Vice President of the United States shall be President of the Senate, but shall have no Vote, unless they be equally divided.

The Senate shall choose their other Officers, and also a President pro tempore, in the Absence of the Vice President, or when he shall exercise the Office of President of the United States.

The Senate shall have the sole Power to try all Impeachments. When sitting for that Purpose, they shall be on Oath or Affirmation. When the President of the United States is tried, the Chief Justice shall preside: And no Person shall be convicted without the Concurrence of two thirds of the Members present.

Judgment in Cases of Impeachment shall not extend further than to removal from Office, and disqualification to hold and enjoy any Office of honor, Trust or Profit under the United States: but the Party convicted shall nevertheless be liable and subject to Indictment, Trial, Judgment and Punishment, according to Law.

Section 4

The Times, Places and Manner of holding Elections for Senators and Representatives, shall be prescribed in each State by the Legislature thereof; but the Congress may at any time by Law make or alter such Regulations, except as to the Places of chusing Senators.

The Congress shall assemble at least once in every Year, and such Meeting shall be on the first Monday in December, unless they shall by Law appoint a different Day.

Section 5

Each House shall be the Judge of the Elections, Returns and Qualifications of its own Members, and a Majority of each shall constitute a Quorum to do Business; but a smaller Number may adjourn from day to day, and may be authorized to compel the Attendance of absent Members, in such Manner, and under such Penalties as each House may provide.

Each House may determine the Rules of its Proceedings, punish its Members for disorderly Behaviour, and, with the Concurrence of two thirds, expel a Member.

Each House shall keep a Journal of its Proceedings, and from time to time publish the same, excepting such Parts as may in their Judgment require Secrecy; and the Yeas and Nays of the Members of either House on any question shall, at the Desire of one fifth of those Present, be entered on the Journal.

Neither House, during the Session of Congress, shall, without the Consent of the other, adjourn for more than three days, nor to any other Place than that in which the two Houses shall be sitting.

Section 6

The Senators and Representatives shall receive a Compensation for their Services, to be ascertained by Law, and paid out of the Treasury of the United States. They shall in all Cases, except Treason, Felony and Breach of the Peace, be privileged from Arrest during their Attendance at the Session of their respective Houses, and in going to and returning from the same; and for any Speech or Debate in either House, they shall not be questioned in any other Place.

No Senator or Representative shall, during the Time for which he was elected, be appointed to any civil Office under the Authority of the United States, which shall have been created, or the Emoluments whereof shall have been increased during such time; and no Person holding any Office under the United States, shall be a Member of either House during his Continuance in Office.

Section 7

All Bills for raising Revenue shall originate in the House of Representatives; but the Senate may propose or concur with Amendments as on other Bills.

Every Bill which shall have passed the House of Representatives and the Senate, shall, before it become a Law, be presented to the President of the United States: If he approve he shall sign it, but if not he shall return it, with his Objections to that House in which it shall have originated, who shall enter the Objections at large on their Journal, and proceed to reconsider it. If after such Reconsideration two thirds of that House shall agree to pass the Bill, it shall be sent, together with the Objections, to the other House, by which it shall likewise be reconsidered, and if approved by two thirds of that House, it shall become a Law. But in all such Cases the Votes of both Houses shall be determined by yeas and Nays, and the Names of the Persons voting for and against the Bill shall be entered on the Journal of each House respectively. If any Bill shall not be returned by the President within ten Days (Sundays excepted) after it shall have been presented to him, the Same shall be a Law, in like Manner as if he had signed it, unless the Congress by their Adjournment prevent its Return, in which Case it shall not be a Law.

Every Order, Resolution, or Vote to which the Concurrence of the Senate and House of Representatives may be necessary (except on a question of Adjournment) shall be presented to the President of the United States; and before the Same shall take Effect, shall be approved by him, or being disapproved by him, shall be repassed by two thirds of the Senate and House of Representatives, according to the Rules and Limitations prescribed in the Case of a Bill.

Section 8

The Congress shall have Power

To lay and collect Taxes, Duties, Imposts and Excises, to pay the Debts and provide for the common Defence and general Welfare of the United States; but all Duties, Imposts and Excises shall be uniform throughout the United States;

To borrow Money on the credit of the United States;

To regulate Commerce with foreign Nations, and among the several States, and with the Indian Tribes;

To establish an uniform Rule of Naturalization, and uniform Laws on the subject of Bankruptcies throughout the United States;

To coin Money, regulate the Value thereof, and of foreign Coin, and fix the Standard of Weights and Measures;

To provide for the Punishment of counterfeiting the Securities and current Coin of the United States;

To establish Post Offices and post Roads;

To promote the Progress of Science and useful Arts, by securing for limited Times to Authors and Inventors the exclusive Right to their respective Writings and Discoveries;

To constitute Tribunals inferior to the supreme Court;

To define and punish Piracies and Felonies committed on the high Seas, and Offences against the Law of Nations;

To declare War, grant Letters of Marque and Reprisal, and make Rules concerning Captures on Land and Water;

To raise and support Armies, but no Appropriation of Money to that Use shall be for a longer Term than two Years;

To provide and maintain a Navy;

To make Rules for the Government and Regulation of the land and naval Forces;

To provide for calling forth the Militia to execute the Laws of the Union, suppress Insurrections and repel Invasions;

To provide for organizing, arming, and disciplining the Militia, and for governing such Part of them as may be employed in the Service of the United States, reserving to the States respectively, the Appointment of the Officers, and the Authority of training the Militia according to the discipline prescribed by Congress;

To exercise exclusive Legislation in all Cases whatsoever, over such District (not exceeding ten Miles square) as may, by Cession of particular States, and the Acceptance of

Congress, become the Seat of the Government of the United States, and to exercise like Authority over all Places purchased by the Consent of the Legislature of the State in which the Same shall be, for the Erection of Forts, Magazines, Arsenals, dock-Yards, and other needful Buildings;—And

To make all Laws which shall be necessary and proper for carrying into Execution the foregoing Powers, and all other Powers vested by this Constitution in the Government of the United States, or in any Department or Officer thereof.

Section 9

The Migration or Importation of such Persons as any of the States now existing shall think proper to admit, shall not be prohibited by the Congress prior to the Year one thousand eight hundred and eight, but a Tax or duty may be imposed on such Importation, not exceeding ten dollars for each Person.

The Privilege of the Writ of Habeas Corpus shall not be suspended, unless when in Cases of Rebellion or Invasion the public Safety may require it.

No Bill of Attainder or ex post facto Law shall be passed.

No Capitation, or other direct, Tax shall be laid, unless in Proportion to the Census or enumeration herein before directed to be taken.

No Tax or Duty shall be laid on Articles exported from any State.

No Preference shall be given by any Regulation of Commerce or Revenue to the Ports of one State over those of another; nor shall Vessels bound to, or from, one State, be obliged to enter, clear, or pay Duties in another.

No Money shall be drawn from the Treasury, but in Consequence of Appropriations made by Law; and a regular Statement and Account of the Receipts and Expenditures of all public Money shall be published from time to time.

No Title of Nobility shall be granted by the United States: And no Person holding any Office of Profit or Trust under them, shall, without the Consent of the Congress, accept of any present, Emolument, Office, or Title, of any kind whatever, from any King, Prince, or foreign State.

Section 10

No State shall enter into any Treaty, Alliance, or Confederation; grant Letters of Marque and Reprisal; coin Money; emit Bills of Credit; make any Thing but gold and silver Coin a Tender in Payment of Debts; pass any Bill of Attainder, ex post facto Law, or Law impairing the Obligation of Contracts, or grant any Title of Nobility.

No State shall, without the Consent of the Congress, lay any Imposts or Duties on Imports or Exports, except what may be absolutely necessary for executing it's inspection Laws: and the net Produce of all Duties and Imposts, laid by any State on Imports or Exports, shall be for the Use of the Treasury of the United States; and all such Laws shall be subject to the Revision and Control of the Congress.

No State shall, without the Consent of Congress, lay any Duty of Tonnage, keep Troops, or Ships of War in time of Peace, enter into any Agreement or Compact with another State, or with a foreign Power, or engage in War, unless actually invaded, or in such imminent Danger as will not admit of delay.

Article II
Section 1

The executive Power shall be vested in a President of the United States of America. He shall hold his Office during the Term of four Years, and, together with the Vice President, chosen for the same Term, be elected, as follows:

Each State shall appoint, in such Manner as the Legislature thereof may direct, a Number of Electors, equal to the whole Number of Senators and Representatives to which the State may be entitled in the Congress: but no Senator or Representative, or Person holding an Office of Trust or Profit under the United States, shall be appointed an Elector.

The Electors shall meet in their respective States, and vote by Ballot for two Persons, of whom one at least shall not be an Inhabitant of the same State with themselves. And they shall make a List of all the Persons voted for, and of the Number of Votes for each; which List they shall sign and certify, and transmit sealed to the Seat of the Government of the United States, directed to the President of the Senate. The President of the Senate shall, in the Presence of the Senate and House of Representatives, open all the Certificates, and the Votes shall then be counted. The Person having the greatest Number of Votes shall be the President, if such Number be a Majority of the whole Number of Electors appointed; and if there be more than one who have such Majority, and have an equal Number of Votes, then the House of Representatives shall immediately choose by Ballot one of them for President; and if no Person have a Majority, then from the five highest on the List the said House shall in like Manner choose the President. But in choosing the President, the Votes shall be taken by States, the Representation from each State having one Vote; A quorum for this purpose shall consist of a Member or Members from two thirds of the States, and a Majority of all the States shall be necessary to a Choice. In every Case, after the Choice of the President, the Person having the greatest Number of Votes of the Electors shall be the Vice President. But if there should remain two or more who have equal Votes, the Senate shall choose from them by Ballot the Vice President.

The Congress may determine the Time of choosing the Electors, and the Day on which they shall give their Votes; which Day shall be the same throughout the United States.

No Person except a natural born Citizen, or a Citizen of the United States, at the time of the Adoption of this Constitution, shall be eligible to the Office of President; neither shall any Person be eligible to that Office who shall not have attained to the Age of thirty five Years, and been fourteen Years a Resident within the United States.

In Case of the Removal of the President from Office, or of his Death, Resignation, or Inability to discharge the Powers and Duties of the said Office, the Same shall devolve on the Vice President, and the Congress may by Law provide for the Case of Removal, Death, Resignation or Inability, both of the President and Vice President, declaring what Officer shall then act as President, and such Officer shall act accordingly, until the Disability be removed, or a President shall be elected.

The President shall, at stated Times, receive for his Services, a Compensation, which shall neither be increased nor diminished during the Period for which he shall have been elected, and he shall not receive within that Period any other Emolument from the United States, or any of them.

Before he enter on the Execution of his Office, he shall take the following Oath or Affirmation:—"I do solemnly swear (or affirm) that I will faithfully execute the Office of President of the United States, and will to the best of my Ability, preserve, protect and defend the Constitution of the United States."

Section 2

The President shall be Commander in Chief of the Army and Navy of the United States, and of the Militia of the several States, when called into the actual Service of the United States; he may require the Opinion, in writing, of the principal Officer in each of the executive Departments, upon any Subject relating to the Duties of their respective Offices, and he shall have Power to grant Reprieves and Pardons for Offences against the United States, except in Cases of Impeachment.

He shall have Power, by and with the Advice and Consent of the Senate, to make Treaties, provided two thirds of the Senators present concur; and he shall nominate, and by and with the Advice and Consent of the Senate, shall appoint Ambassadors, other public Ministers and Consuls, Judges of the supreme Court, and all other Officers of the United States, whose Appointments are not herein otherwise provided for, and which shall be established by Law: but the Congress may by Law vest the Appointment of such inferior Officers, as they think proper, in the President alone, in the Courts of Law, or in the Heads of Departments.

The President shall have Power to fill up all Vacancies that may happen during the Recess of the Senate, by granting Commissions which shall expire at the End of their next Session.

Section 3

He shall from time to time give to the Congress Information of the State of the Union, and recommend to their Consideration such Measures as he shall judge necessary and expedient; he may, on extraordinary Occasions, convene both Houses, or either of them, and in Case of Disagreement between them, with Respect to the Time of Adjournment, he may adjourn them to such Time as he shall think proper; he shall receive Ambassadors and other public Ministers; he shall take Care that the Laws be faithfully executed, and shall Commission all the Officers of the United States.

Section 4

The President, Vice President and all civil Officers of the United States, shall be removed from Office on Impeachment for, and Conviction of, Treason, Bribery, or other high Crimes and Misdemeanors.

Article III
Section 1

The judicial Power of the United States shall be vested in one supreme Court, and in such inferior Courts as the Congress may from time to time ordain and establish. The Judges, both of the supreme and inferior Courts, shall hold their Offices during good Behaviour, and shall, at stated Times, receive for their Services a Compensation, which shall not be diminished during their Continuance in Office.

Section 2

The judicial Power shall extend to all Cases, in Law and Equity, arising under this Constitution, the Laws of the United States, and Treaties made, or which shall be made, under their Authority;—to all Cases affecting Ambassadors, other public Ministers and Consuls;—to all Cases of admiralty and maritime Jurisdiction;—to Controversies to which the United States shall be a Party;—to Controversies between two or more States;—between a State and Citizens of another State;—between Citizens of different States;—between Citizens of the same State claiming Lands under Grants of different States, and between a State, or the Citizens thereof, and foreign States, Citizens or Subjects.

In all Cases affecting Ambassadors, other public Ministers and Consuls, and those in which a State shall be Party, the supreme Court shall have original Jurisdiction. In all the other Cases before mentioned, the supreme Court shall have appellate Jurisdiction, both as to Law and Fact, with such Exceptions, and under such Regulations as the Congress shall make.

The Trial of all Crimes, except in Cases of Impeachment, shall be by Jury; and such Trial shall be held in the State where the said Crimes shall have been committed; but when not committed within any State, the Trial shall be at such Place or Places as the Congress may by Law have directed.

Section 3

Treason against the United States, shall consist only in levying War against them, or in adhering to their Enemies, giving them Aid and Comfort. No Person shall be convicted of Treason unless on the Testimony of two Witnesses to the same overt Act, or on Confession in open Court.

The Congress shall have Power to declare the Punishment of Treason, but no Attainder of Treason shall work Corruption of Blood, or Forfeiture except during the Life of the Person attainted.

Article IV
Section 1

Full Faith and Credit shall be given in each State to the public Acts, Records, and judicial Proceedings of every other State. And the Congress may by general Laws prescribe the Manner in which such Acts, Records and Proceedings shall be proved, and the Effect thereof.

Section 2

The Citizens of each State shall be entitled to all Privileges and Immunities of Citizens in the several States.

A Person charged in any State with Treason, Felony, or other Crime, who shall flee from Justice, and be found in another State, shall on Demand of the executive Authority of the State from which he fled, be delivered up, to be removed to the State having Jurisdiction of the Crime.

No Person held to Service or Labour in one State, under the Laws thereof, escaping into another, shall, in Consequence of any Law or Regulation therein, be discharged from such Service or Labour, but shall be delivered up on Claim of the Party to whom such Service or Labour may be due.

Section 3

New States may be admitted by the Congress into this Union; but no new State shall be formed or erected within the Jurisdiction of any other State; nor any State be formed by the Junction of two or more States, or Parts of States, without the Consent of the Legislatures of the States concerned as well as of the Congress.

The Congress shall have Power to dispose of and make all needful Rules and Regulations respecting the Territory or other Property belonging to the United States; and nothing in this Constitution shall be so construed as to Prejudice any Claims of the United States, or of any particular State.

Section 4

The United States shall guarantee to every State in this Union a Republican Form of Government, and shall protect each of them against Invasion; and on Application of the Legislature, or of the Executive (when the Legislature cannot be convened), against domestic Violence.

Article V

The Congress, whenever two thirds of both Houses shall deem it necessary, shall propose Amendments to this Constitution, or, on the Application of the Legislatures of two thirds of the several States, shall call a Convention for proposing Amendments, which, in either Case, shall be valid to all Intents and Purposes, as Part of this Constitution, when ratified by the Legislatures of three fourths of the several States, or by Conventions in three fourths thereof, as the one or the other Mode of Ratification may be proposed by the Congress; Provided that no Amendment which may be made prior to the Year One thousand eight hundred and eight shall in any Manner affect the first and fourth Clauses in the Ninth Section of the first Article; and that no State, without its Consent, shall be deprived of its equal Suffrage in the Senate.

Article VI

All Debts contracted and Engagements entered into, before the Adoption of this Constitution, shall be as valid against the United States under this Constitution, as under the Confederation.

This Constitution, and the Laws of the United States which shall be made in Pursuance thereof; and all Treaties made, or which shall be made, under the Authority of the United States, shall be the supreme Law of the Land; and the Judges in every State shall be bound thereby, any Thing in the Constitution or Laws of any State to the Contrary notwithstanding.

The Senators and Representatives before mentioned, and the Members of the several State Legislatures, and all executive and judicial Officers, both of the United States and of the several States, shall be bound by Oath or Affirmation, to support this Constitution; but no religious Test shall ever be required as a Qualification to any Office or public Trust under the United States.

Article VII

The Ratification of the Conventions of nine States, shall be sufficient for the Establishment of this Constitution between the States so ratifying the Same.

The Word, "the," being interlined between the seventh and eighth Lines of the first Page, the Word "Thirty" being partly written on an Erazure in the fifteenth Line of the first Page, The Words "is tried" being interlined between the thirty second and thirty third Lines of the first Page and the Word "the" being interlined between the forty third and forty fourth Lines of the second Page.

Attest William Jackson Secretary

Done in Convention by the Unanimous Consent of the States present the Seventeenth Day of September in the Year of our Lord one thousand seven hundred and Eighty seven and of the Independence of the United States of America the Twelfth In witness whereof We have hereunto subscribed our Names,

G°. Washington
Presidt and deputy from Virginia

Delaware
Geo: Read
Gunning Bedford jun
John Dickinson
Richard Bassett
Jaco: Broom

Maryland
James McHenry
Dan of St Thos. Jenifer
Danl. Carroll

Virginia
John Blair
James Madison Jr.

North Carolina
Wm. Blount
Richd. Dobbs Spaight
Hu Williamson

South Carolina
J. Rutledge
Charles Cotesworth Pinckney
Charles Pinckney
Pierce Butler

Georgia
William Few
Abr Baldwin

New Hampshire
John Langdon
Nicholas Gilman

Massachusetts
Nathaniel Gorham
Rufus King

Connecticut
Wm. Saml. Johnson
Roger Sherman

New York
Alexander Hamilton

New Jersey
Wil: Livingston
David Brearley
Wm. Paterson
Jona: Dayton

Pennsylvania
B Franklin
Thomas Mifflin
Robt. Morris
Geo. Clymer
Thos. FitzSimons
Jared Ingersoll
James Wilson
Gouv Morris

Articles

In addition to, and Amendment of the Constitution of the United States of America, proposed by Congress, and ratified by the Legislatures of the several States, pursuant to the fifth Article of the original Constitution.

(The first ten amendments to the U.S. Constitution were ratified December 15, 1791, and form what is known as the "Bill of Rights.")

AMENDMENT I

Congress shall make no law respecting an establishment of religion, or prohibiting the free exercise thereof; or abridging the freedom of speech, or of the press; or the right of the people peaceably to assemble, and to petition the Government for a redress of grievances.

AMENDMENT II

A well regulated Militia, being necessary to the security of a free State, the right of the people to keep and bear Arms, shall not be infringed.

AMENDMENT III

No Soldier shall, in time of peace be quartered in any house, without the consent of the Owner, nor in time of war, but in a manner to be prescribed by law.

AMENDMENT IV

The right of the people to be secure in their persons, houses, papers, and effects, against unreasonable searches and seizures, shall not be violated, and no Warrants shall issue, but upon probable cause, supported by Oath or affirmation, and particularly describing the place to be searched, and the persons or things to be seized.

AMENDMENT V

No person shall be held to answer for a capital, or otherwise infamous crime, unless on a presentment or indictment of a Grand Jury, except in cases arising in the land or naval forces, or in the Militia, when in actual service in time of War or public danger; nor shall any person be subject for the same offence to be twice put in jeopardy of life or limb; nor shall be compelled in any criminal case to be a witness against himself, nor be deprived of life, liberty, or property, without due process of law; nor shall private property be taken for public use, without just compensation.

AMENDMENT VI

In all criminal prosecutions, the accused shall enjoy the right to a speedy and public trial, by an impartial jury of the State and district wherein the crime shall have been committed, which district shall have been previously ascertained by law, and to be informed of the nature and cause of the accusation; to be confronted with the witnesses against him; to have compulsory process for obtaining witnesses in his favor, and to have the Assistance of Counsel for his defence.

AMENDMENT VII

In Suits at common law, where the value in controversy shall exceed twenty dollars, the right of trial by jury shall be preserved, and no fact tried by a jury, shall be otherwise re-examined in any Court of the United States, than according to the rules of the common law.

AMENDMENT VIII

Excessive bail shall not be required, nor excessive fines imposed, nor cruel and unusual punishments inflicted.

AMENDMENT IX

The enumeration in the Constitution, of certain rights, shall not be construed to deny or disparage others retained by the people.

AMENDMENT X

The powers not delegated to the United States by the Constitution, nor prohibited by it to the States, are reserved to the States respectively, or to the people.

AMENDMENT XI

Passed by Congress March 4, 1794. Ratified February 7, 1795.

Note: Article III, Section 2, of the Constitution was modified by Amendment XI.

The Judicial power of the United States shall not be construed to extend to any suit in law or equity, commenced or prosecuted against one of the United States by Citizens of another State, or by Citizens or Subjects of any Foreign State.

AMENDMENT XII

Passed by Congress December 9, 1803. Ratified June 15, 1804.

Note: A portion of Article II, Section 1, of the Constitution was superseded by the Twelfth Amendment.

The Electors shall meet in their respective states and vote by ballot for President and Vice-President, one of whom, at least, shall not be an inhabitant of the same state with themselves; they shall name in their ballots the person voted for as President, and in distinct ballots the person voted for as Vice-President, and they shall make distinct lists of all persons voted for as President, and of all persons voted for as Vice-President, and of the number of votes for each, which lists they shall sign and certify, and transmit sealed to the seat of the government of the United States, directed to the President of the Senate;—the President of the Senate shall, in the presence of the Senate and House of Representatives, open all the certificates and the votes shall then be counted;—The person having the greatest number of votes for President, shall be the President, if such number be a majority of the whole number of Electors appointed; and if no person have such majority, then from the persons having the highest numbers not exceeding three on the list of those voted for as President, the House of Representatives shall choose immediately, by ballot, the President. But in choosing the President, the votes shall be taken by states, the representation from each state having one vote; a quorum for this purpose shall consist of a member or members from two-thirds of the states, and a majority of all the states shall be necessary to a choice. [And if the House of Representatives shall not choose a President whenever the right of choice shall devolve upon them, before the fourth day of March next following, then the Vice-President shall act as President, as in case of the death or other constitutional disability of the President.—]* The person having the greatest number of votes as Vice-President, shall be the Vice-President, if such number be a majority of the whole number of Electors appointed, and if no person have a majority, then from the two highest numbers on the list, the Senate shall choose the Vice-President; a quorum for the purpose shall consist of two-thirds of the whole number of Senators, and a majority of the whole number shall be necessary to a choice. But no person constitutionally ineligible to the office of President shall be eligible to that of Vice-President of the United States.

*Superseded by Section 3 of the Twentieth Amendment.

AMENDMENT XIII

Passed by Congress January 31, 1865. Ratified December 6, 1865.

Note: A portion of Article IV, Section 2, of the Constitution was superseded by the Thirteenth Amendment.

Section 1

Neither slavery nor involuntary servitude, except as a punishment for crime whereof the party shall have been duly convicted, shall exist within the United States, or any place subject to their jurisdiction.

Section 2

Congress shall have power to enforce this article by appropriate legislation.

AMENDMENT XIV

Passed by Congress June 13, 1866. Ratified July 9, 1868.

Note: Article I, Section 2, of the Constitution was modified by Section 2 of the Fourteenth Amendment.

Section 1

All persons born or naturalized in the United States, and subject to the jurisdiction thereof, are citizens of the United States and of the State wherein they reside. No State shall make or enforce any law which shall abridge the privileges or immunities of citizens of the United States; nor shall any State deprive any person of life, liberty, or property, without due process of law; nor deny to any person within its jurisdiction the equal protection of the laws.

Section 2

Representatives shall be apportioned among the several States according to their respective numbers, counting the whole number of persons in each State, excluding Indians not taxed. But when the right to vote at any election for the choice of electors for President and Vice-President of the United States, Representatives in Congress, the Executive and Judicial officers of a State, or the members of the Legislature thereof, is denied to any of the male inhabitants of such State, being twenty-one years of age,* and citizens of the United States, or in any way abridged, except for participation in rebellion, or other crime, the basis of representation therein shall be reduced in the proportion which the number of such male citizens shall bear to the whole number of male citizens twenty-one years of age in such State.

Section 3

No person shall be a Senator or Representative in Congress, or elector of President and Vice-President, or hold any office, civil or military, under the United States, or under any State, who, having previously taken an oath, as a member of Congress, or as an officer of the United States, or as a member of any State legislature, or as an executive or judicial officer of any State, to support the Constitution of the United States, shall have engaged in insurrection or rebellion against the same, or given aid or comfort to the enemies thereof. But Congress may by a vote of two-thirds of each House, remove such disability.

Section 4

The validity of the public debt of the United States, authorized by law, including debts incurred for payment of pensions and bounties for services in suppressing insurrection or rebellion, shall not be questioned. But neither the United States nor any State shall assume or pay any debt or obligation incurred in aid of insurrection or rebellion against the United States, or any claim for the loss or emancipation of any slave; but all such debts, obligations and claims shall be held illegal and void.

Section 5

The Congress shall have the power to enforce, by appropriate legislation, the provisions of this article.

*Changed by Section 1 of the Twenty-sixth Amendment.

AMENDMENT XV

Passed by Congress February 26, 1869. Ratified February 3, 1870.

Section 1

The right of citizens of the United States to vote shall not be denied or abridged by the United States or by any State on account of race, color, or previous condition of servitude.

Section 2

The Congress shall have the power to enforce this article by appropriate legislation.

AMENDMENT XVI

Passed by Congress July 2, 1909. Ratified February 3, 1913.

Note: Article I, Section 9, of the Constitution was modified by Amendment XVI.

The Congress shall have power to lay and collect taxes on incomes, from whatever source derived, without apportionment among the several States, and without regard to any census or enumeration.

AMENDMENT XVII

Passed by Congress May 13, 1912. Ratified April 8, 1913.

Note: Article I, Section 3, of the Constitution was modified by the Seventeenth Amendment.

The Senate of the United States shall be composed of two Senators from each State, elected by the people thereof, for six years; and each Senator shall have one vote. The electors in each State shall have the qualifications requisite for electors of the most numerous branch of the State legislatures.

When vacancies happen in the representation of any State in the Senate, the executive authority of such State shall issue writs of election to fill such vacancies: Provided, That the legislature of any State may empower the executive thereof to make temporary appointments until the people fill the vacancies by election as the legislature may direct.

This amendment shall not be so construed as to affect the election or term of any Senator chosen before it becomes valid as part of the Constitution.

AMENDMENT XVIII

Passed by Congress December 18, 1917. Ratified January 16, 1919. Repealed by Amendment XXI.

Section 1

After one year from the ratification of this article the manufacture, sale, or transportation of intoxicating liquors within, the importation thereof into, or the exportation thereof from the United States and all territory subject to the jurisdiction thereof for beverage purposes is hereby prohibited.

Section 2

The Congress and the several States shall have concurrent power to enforce this article by appropriate legislation.

Section 3

This article shall be inoperative unless it shall have been ratified as an amendment to the Constitution by the legislatures of the several States, as provided in the Constitution, within seven years from the date of the submission hereof to the States by the Congress.

AMENDMENT XIX

Passed by Congress June 4, 1919. Ratified August 18, 1920.

The right of citizens of the United States to vote shall not be denied or abridged by the United States or by any State on account of sex.
　　Congress shall have power to enforce this article by appropriate legislation.

AMENDMENT XX

Passed by Congress March 2, 1932. Ratified January 23, 1933.

Note: Article I, Section 4, of the Constitution was modified by Section 2 of this amendment. In addition, a portion of the Twelfth Amendment was superseded by Section 3.

Section 1

The terms of the President and the Vice President shall end at noon on the 20th day of January, and the terms of Senators and Representatives at noon on the 3d day of January, of the years in which such terms would have ended if this article had not been ratified; and the terms of their successors shall then begin.

Section 2

The Congress shall assemble at least once in every year, and such meeting shall begin at noon on the 3d day of January, unless they shall by law appoint a different day.

Section 3

If, at the time fixed for the beginning of the term of the President, the President elect shall have died, the Vice President elect shall become President. If a President shall not have been chosen before the time fixed for the beginning of his term, or if the President elect shall have failed to qualify, then the Vice President elect shall act as President until a President shall have qualified; and the Congress may by law provide for the case wherein neither a President elect nor a Vice President shall have qualified, declaring who shall then act as President, or the manner in which one who is to act shall be selected, and such person shall act accordingly until a President or Vice President shall have qualified.

Section 4

The Congress may by law provide for the case of the death of any of the persons from whom the House of Representatives may choose a President whenever the right of choice shall have devolved upon them, and for the case of the death of any of the persons from whom the Senate may choose a Vice President whenever the right of choice shall have devolved upon them.

Section 5

Sections 1 and 2 shall take effect on the 15th day of October following the ratification of this article.

Section 6

This article shall be inoperative unless it shall have been ratified as an amendment to the Constitution by the legislatures of three-fourths of the several States within seven years from the date of its submission.

AMENDMENT XXI

Passed by Congress February 20, 1933. Ratified December 5, 1933.

Section 1

The eighteenth article of amendment to the Constitution of the United States is hereby repealed.

Section 2

The transportation or importation into any State, Territory, or Possession of the United States for delivery or use therein of intoxicating liquors, in violation of the laws thereof, is hereby prohibited.

Section 3

This article shall be inoperative unless it shall have been ratified as an amendment to the Constitution by conventions in the several States, as provided in the Constitution, within seven years from the date of the submission hereof to the States by the Congress.

AMENDMENT XXII

Passed by Congress March 21, 1947. Ratified February 27, 1951.

Section 1

No person shall be elected to the office of the President more than twice, and no person who has held the office of President, or acted as President, for more than two years of a term to which some other person was elected President shall be elected to the office of President more than once. But this Article shall not apply to any person holding the office of President when this Article was proposed by Congress, and shall not prevent any person who may be holding the office of President, or acting as President, during the term within which this Article becomes operative from holding the office of President or acting as President during the remainder of such term.

Section 2

This article shall be inoperative unless it shall have been ratified as an amendment to the Constitution by the legislatures of three-fourths of the several States within seven years from the date of its submission to the States by the Congress.

AMENDMENT XXIII

Passed by Congress June 16, 1960. Ratified March 29, 1961.

Section 1

The District constituting the seat of Government of the United States shall appoint in such manner as Congress may direct:

A number of electors of President and Vice President equal to the whole number of Senators and Representatives in Congress to which the District would be entitled if it were a State, but in no event more than the least populous State; they shall be in addition to those appointed by the States, but they shall be considered, for the purposes of the election of President and Vice President, to be electors appointed by a State; and they shall meet in the District and perform such duties as provided by the twelfth article of amendment.

Section 2

The Congress shall have power to enforce this article by appropriate legislation.

AMENDMENT XXIV

Passed by Congress August 27, 1962. Ratified January 23, 1964.

Section 1

The right of citizens of the United States to vote in any primary or other election for President or Vice President, for electors for President or Vice President, or for Senator or Representative in Congress, shall not be denied or abridged by the United States or any State by reason of failure to pay poll tax or other tax.

Section 2

The Congress shall have power to enforce this article by appropriate legislation.

AMENDMENT XXV

Passed by Congress July 6, 1965. Ratified February 10, 1967.

Note: Article II, Section 1, of the Constitution was affected by the Twenty-fifth Amendment.

Section 1

In case of the removal of the President from office or of his death or resignation, the Vice President shall become President.

Section 2

Whenever there is a vacancy in the office of the Vice President, the President shall nominate a Vice President who shall take office upon confirmation by a majority vote of both Houses of Congress.

Section 3

Whenever the President transmits to the President pro tempore of the Senate and the Speaker of the House of Representatives his written declaration that he is unable to discharge the powers and duties of his office, and until he transmits to them a written declaration to the contrary, such powers and duties shall be discharged by the Vice President as Acting President.

Section 4

Whenever the Vice President and a majority of either the principal officers of the executive departments or of such other body as Congress may by law provide, transmit to the President pro tempore of the Senate and the Speaker of the House of Representatives their written declaration that the President is unable to discharge the powers and duties of his office, the Vice President shall immediately assume the powers and duties of the office as Acting President.

Thereafter, when the President transmits to the President pro tempore of the Senate and the Speaker of the House of Representatives his written declaration that no inability exists, he shall resume the powers and duties of his office unless the Vice President and a majority of either the principal officers of the executive department or of such other body as Congress may by law provide, transmit within four days to the President pro tempore of the Senate and the Speaker of the House of Representatives their written declaration that the President is unable to discharge the powers and duties of his office. Thereupon Congress shall decide the issue, assembling within forty-eight hours for that purpose if not in session. If the Congress, within twenty-one days after receipt of the latter written declaration, or, if Congress is not in session, within twenty-one days after Congress is required to assemble, determines by two-thirds vote of both Houses that the President is unable to discharge the powers and duties of his office, the Vice President shall continue to discharge the same as Acting President; otherwise, the President shall resume the powers and duties of his office.

AMENDMENT XXVI

Passed by Congress March 23, 1971. Ratified July 1, 1971.

Note: Amendment XIV, Section 2, of the Constitution was modified by Section 1 of the Twenty-sixth Amendment.

Section 1

The right of citizens of the United States, who are eighteen years of age or older, to vote shall not be denied or abridged by the United States or by any State on account of age.

Section 2

The Congress shall have power to enforce this article by appropriate legislation.

AMENDMENT XXVII

Originally proposed Sept. 25, 1789. Ratified May 7, 1992.

No law, varying the compensation for the services of the Senators and Representatives, shall take effect, until an election of representatives shall have intervened.

Lincoln's Gettysburg Address

Four score and seven years ago our fathers brought forth on this continent, a new nation, conceived in Liberty, and dedicated to the proposition that all men are created equal.

Now we are engaged in a great civil war, testing whether that nation, or any nation so conceived and so dedicated, can long endure. We are met on a great battle-field of that war. We have come to dedicate a portion of that field, as a final resting place for those who here gave their lives that that nation might live. It is altogether fitting and proper that we should do this.

But, in a larger sense, we can not dedicate—we can not consecrate—we can not hallow—this ground. The brave men, living and dead, who struggled here, have consecrated it, far above our poor power to add or detract. The world will little note, nor long remember what we say here, but it can never forget what they did here. It is for us the living, rather, to be dedicated here to the unfinished work which they who fought here have thus far so nobly advanced. It is rather for us to be here dedicated to the great task remaining before us—that from these honored dead we take increased devotion to that cause for which they gave the last full measure of devotion—that we here highly resolve that these dead shall not have died in vain—that this nation, under God, shall have a new birth of freedom—and that government of the people, by the people, for the people, shall not perish from the earth.

Appendix B

Historical Facts and Data
U.S. Presidents and Vice Presidents

Table App B-1 Presidents and Vice Presidents

	President	Vice President	Political Party	Term
1	George Washington	John Adams	No Party Designation	1789–1797
2	John Adams	Thomas Jefferson	Federalist	1797–1801
3	Thomas Jefferson	Aaron Burr George Clinton	Democratic Republican	1801–1809
4	James Madison	George Clinton Elbridge Gerry	Democratic Republican	1809–1817
5	James Monroe	Daniel D. Tompkins	Democratic Republican	1817–1825
6	John Quincy Adams	John C. Calhoun	Democratic Republican	1825–1829
7	Andrew Jackson	John C. Calhoun Martin Van Buren	Democratic	1829–1837
8	Martin Van Buren	Richard M. Johnson	Democratic	1837–1841
9	William Henry Harrison	John Tyler	Whig	1841
10	John Tyler	None	Whig	1841–1845
11	James Knox Polk	George M. Dallas	Democratic	1845–1849
12	Zachary Taylor	Millard Fillmore	Whig	1849–1850
13	Millard Fillmore	None	Whig	1850–1853
14	Franklin Pierce	William R. King	Democratic	1853–1857
15	James Buchanan	John C. Breckinridge	Democratic	1857–1861
16	Abraham Lincoln	Hannibal Hamlin Andrew Johnson	Union	1861–1865
17	Andrew Johnson	None	Union	1865–1869
18	Ulysses Simpson Grant	Schuyler Colfax Henry Wilson	Republican	1869–1877
19	Rutherford Birchard Hayes	William A. Wheeler	Republican	1877–1881
20	James Abram Garfield	Chester Alan Arthur	Republican	1881
21	Chester Alan Arthur	None	Republican	1881–1885
22	Stephen Grover Cleveland	Thomas Hendricks	Democratic	1885–1889
23	Benjamin Harrison	Levi P. Morton	Republican	1889–1893

continued

Table App B-1 *continued*

	President	Vice President	Political Party	Term
24	Stephen Grover Cleveland	Adlai E. Stevenson	Democratic	1893–1897
25	William McKinley	Garret A. Hobart Theodore Roosevelt	Republican	1897–1901
26	Theodore Roosevelt	Charles W. Fairbanks	Republican	1901–1909
27	William Howard Taft	James S. Sherman	Republican	1909–1913
28	Woodrow Wilson	Thomas R. Marshall	Democratic	1913–1921
29	Warren Gamaliel Harding	Calvin Coolidge	Republican	1921–1923
30	Calvin Coolidge	Charles G. Dawes	Republican	1923–1929
31	Herbert Clark Hoover	Charles Curtis	Republican	1929–1933
32	Franklin Delano Roosevelt	John Nance Garner Henry A. Wallace Harry S. Truman	Democratic	1933–1945
33	Harry S. Truman	Alben W. Barkley	Democratic	1945–1953
34	Dwight David Eisenhower	Richard Milhous Nixon	Republican	1953–1961
35	John Fitzgerald Kennedy	Lyndon Baines Johnson	Democratic	1961–1963
36	Lyndon Baines Johnson	Hubert Horatio Humphrey	Democratic	1963–1969
37	Richard Milhous Nixon	Spiro T. Agnew Gerald Rudolph Ford	Republican	1969–1974
38	Gerald Rudolph Ford	Nelson Rockefeller	Republican	1974–1977
39	James Earl Carter Jr.	Walter Mondale	Democratic	1977–1981
40	Ronald Wilson Reagan	George Herbert Walker Bush	Republican	1981–1989
41	George Herbert Walker Bush	J. Danforth Quayle	Republican	1989–1993
42	William Jefferson Clinton	Albert Gore Jr.	Democratic	1993–2001
43	George Walker Bush	Richard Cheney	Republican	2001–2009
44	Barack Hussein Obama	Joseph Biden	Democratic	2009–

Admission of States into the Union

Table App B-2 Admission of States into the Union

	State	Date of Admission		State	Date of Admission
1	Delaware	December 7, 1787	26	Michigan	January 26, 1837
2	Pennsylvania	December 12, 1787	27	Florida	March 3, 1845
3	New Jersey	December 18, 1787	28	Texas	December 29, 1845
4	Georgia	January 2, 1788	29	Iowa	December 28, 1846
5	Connecticut	January 9, 1788	30	Wisconsin	May 29, 1848
6	Massachusetts	February 6, 1788	31	California	September 9, 1850
7	Maryland	April 28, 1788	32	Minnesota	May 11, 1858
8	South Carolina	May 23, 1788	33	Oregon	February 14, 1859
9	New Hampshire	June 21, 1788	34	Kansas	January 29, 1861
10	Virginia	June 25, 1788	35	West Virginia	June 20, 1863
11	New York	July 26, 1788	36	Nevada	October 31, 1864
12	North Carolina	November 21, 1789	37	Nebraska	March 1, 1867
13	Rhode Island	May 29, 1790	38	Colorado	August 1, 1876
14	Vermont	March 4, 1791	39	North Dakota	November 2, 1889
15	Kentucky	June 1, 1792	40	South Dakota	November 2, 1889
16	Tennessee	June 1, 1796	41	Montana	November 8, 1889
17	Ohio	March 1, 1803	42	Washington	November 11, 1889
18	Louisiana	April 30, 1812	43	Idaho	July 3, 1890
19	Indiana	December 11, 1816	44	Wyoming	July 10, 1890
20	Mississippi	December 10, 1817	45	Utah	January 4, 1896
21	Illinois	December 3, 1818	46	Oklahoma	November 16, 1907
22	Alabama	December 14, 1819	47	New Mexico	January 6, 1912
23	Maine	March 15, 1820	48	Arizona	February 14, 1912
24	Missouri	August 10, 1821	49	Alaska	January 3, 1959
25	Arkansas	June 15, 1836	50	Hawaii	August 21, 1959

Glossary

Antinomianism   The belief that moral law was not binding on true Christians. The opposite of Arminianism, antinomianism held that good works would not count in the afterlife. Justification, or entrance to heaven, was by faith alone. *See* Calvinism.

Arminianism   Religious doctrine developed by the Dutch theologian Jacobus Arminius that argued that men and women had free will and suggested that hence they would earn their way into heaven by good works.

Armistice   A cessation of hostilities by agreement among the opposing sides; a cease-fire.

Associationalism   President Herbert Hoover's preferred method of responding to the Depression. Rather than have the government directly involve itself in the economy, Hoover hoped to use the government to encourage associations of businessmen to cooperate voluntarily to meet the crisis.

Autarky   At the height of the world depression, industrial powers sought to isolate their economies within self-contained spheres, generally governed by national (or imperial) economic planning. Japan's Co-Prosperity Sphere, the Soviet Union, and the British Empire each comprised a more or less closed economic unit.

Benevolent Empire   The loosely affiliated network of charitable reform associations that emerged (especially in urban areas) in response to the widespread revivalism of the early nineteenth century.

Berdache   In Indian societies, a man who dressed and adopted the mannerisms of women and had sex only with other men. In Native American culture, the berdache, half man and half woman, symbolized cosmic harmony.

Blockade   A military tactic used in both land and naval warfare by which a location is sealed off to prevent goods or people from entering or leaving.

Budget deficit   The failure of tax revenues to pay for annual federal spending on military, welfare, and other programs. The resulting budget deficits forced Washington to borrow money to cover its costs. The growing budget deficits were controversial, in part because the government's borrowing increased both its long-term debt and the amount of money it had to spend each year to pay for the interest on loans.

Busing   The controversial court-ordered practice of sending children by bus to public schools outside their neighborhoods in order to promote racial integration in the schools.

Calvinism   Religious doctrine developed by the theologian John Calvin that argued that God alone determines who will receive salvation and, hence, men and women cannot earn their own salvation or even be certain about their final destinies.

Carpetbagger   A derogatory term referring to northern whites who moved to the South after the Civil War. Stereotyped as corrupt and unprincipled, "carpetbaggers" were in fact a diverse group motivated by a variety of interests and beliefs.

Charter colony   Settlement established by a trading company or other group of private entrepreneurs who received from the king a grant of land and the right to govern it.

The charter colonies included Virginia, Plymouth, Massachusetts Bay, Rhode Island, and Connecticut.

City busting   As late as the 1930s, President Roosevelt and most Americans regarded attacking civilians from the air as an atrocity, but during World War II cities became a primary target for U.S. warplanes. The inaccuracy of bombing, combined with racism and the belief that Japanese and German actions justified retaliation, led American air commanders to follow a policy of systematically destroying urban areas, particularly in Japan.

Communist   Member of the Communist Party or follower of the doctrines of Karl Marx. The term (or accusation) was applied more broadly in the twentieth century to brand labor unionists, progressives, civil rights workers, and other reformers as agents of a foreign ideology.

Communitarians   Individuals who supported and/or took up residence in separate communities created to embody improved plans of social, religious, and/or economic life.

Commutation   The controversial policy of allowing potential draftees to pay for a replacement to serve in the army. The policy was adopted by both the Union and Confederate governments during the Civil War, and in both cases opposition to commutation was so intense that the policy was abandoned.

Consent   One of the key principles of liberalism, which held that people could not be subject to laws to which they had not given their consent. This principle is reflected in both the Declaration of Independence and the preamble to the Constitution, which begins with the famous words "We the people of the United States, in order to form a more perfect union."

Conspiracy theory   A belief that history is shaped intentionally by unseen powers. Conspiracy theory lay behind the McCarthy anti-Communism hearings, which assumed that American society and government had been infiltrated by countless Communist spies.

Constitutionalism   A loose body of thought that developed in Britain and the colonies and was used by the colonists to justify the Revolution by claiming that it was in accord with the principles of the British Constitution. Constitutionalism had two main elements. One was the rule of law, and the other the principle of consent, that one cannot be subject to laws or taxation except by duly elected representatives. Both were rights that had been won through struggle with the monarch. Constitutionalism also refers to the tendency in American politics, particularly in the early nineteenth century, to transpose all political questions into constitutional ones.

Consumer revolution   A slow and steady increase over the course of the eighteenth century in the demand for, and purchase of, consumer goods. The consumer revolution of the eighteenth century was closely related to the Industrial Revolution.

Consumerism   An ideology that defined the purchase of goods and services as both an expression of individual identity and essential to the national economy. Increasingly powerful by the 1920s and dominant by the 1950s, consumerism urged people to find happiness in the pursuit of leisure and pleasure more than in the work ethic.

Containment   The basic U.S. strategy for fighting the cold war. As used by diplomat George Kennan in a 1947 magazine essay, "containment" referred to the combination of diplomatic, economic, and military programs necessary to hold back Soviet expansionism after World War II.

Contraband of war   In its general sense, contraband of war was property seized from an enemy. But early in the Civil War the term was applied to slaves running to Union lines as a way of preventing owners from reclaiming them. The policy effectively nullified the fugitive slave clause of the U.S. Constitution. It was a first critical step in a process that would lead to a federal emancipation policy the following year.

Cooperationists   Those southerners who opposed immediate secession after the election of Abraham Lincoln in 1860. Cooperationists argued instead that secessionists should wait to see if the new president was willing to "cooperate" with the South's demands.

Copperhead   A northerner who sympathized with the South during the Civil War.

Crop lien   The first right to the proceeds of a harvested crop, given by farmers to their creditors. At the beginning of the growing season, farmers paid on credit for seeds, supplies, and food to get them through the year. They repaid these debts when the crop was sold.

Deindustrialization   The reverse of industrialization, as factory shutdowns decreased the size of the manufacturing sector. Plant closings began to plague the American economy in the 1970s, prompting fears that the nation would lose its industrial base.

Democratic Republicans   One of the two parties to make up the first American party system. Following the fiscal and political views of Jefferson and Madison, Democratic Republicans generally advocated a weak federal government and opposed federal intervention in the economy of the nation.

Détente   This French term for the relaxation of tensions was used to describe the central foreign policy innovation of the Nixon administration—a new, less confrontational relationship with Communism. In addition to opening a dialogue with the People's Republic of China, Nixon sought a more stable, less confrontational relationship with the Soviet Union.

Diffusion   The controversial theory that the problem of slavery would be resolved if the slave economy was allowed to expand, or "diffuse," into the western territories. Southerners developed this theory as early as the 1800s in response to northerners who hoped to restrict slavery's expansion.

Disfranchisement   The act of depriving a person or group of voting rights. In the nineteenth century the right to vote was popularly known as the franchise. The Fourteenth Amendment of the Constitution affirmed the right of adult male citizens to vote, but state-imposed restrictions and taxes deprived large numbers of Americans— particularly African Americans—of the vote from the 1890s until the passage of the Voting Rights Act of 1964.

Domestic patriarchy   The practice of defining the family by the husband and father, and wives and children as his domestic dependents. Upon marriage a wife's property became her husband's, and children owed obedience and labor to the family until they reached adulthood. In combination with an exclusive male suffrage, domestic patriarchy described the political as well as the social system that prevailed among free Americans until the twentieth century.

Downsizing   American corporations' layoffs of both blue- and white-collar workers in an attempt to become more efficient and competitive. Downsizing was one of the factors that made Americans uneasy about the economy in the 1990s, despite the impressive surge in the stock market.

Dust Bowl   Across much of the Great Plains, decades of wasteful farming practices combined with several years of drought in the early 1930s to produce a series of massive dust storms that blew the topsoil across hundreds of miles. The area in Texas and Oklahoma affected by these storms became known as the Dust Bowl.

E-commerce   Short for "electronic commerce," this was the term for the Internet-based buying and selling that was one of the key hopes for the computer-driven postindustrial economy. The promise of e-commerce was still unfulfilled by the start of the twenty-first century.

Encomienda   A system of labor developed by the Spanish in the New World in which Spanish settlers (encomenderos) compelled groups of Native Americans to work for them. The encomendero owned neither the land nor the Indians who worked for him, but had the unlimited right to compel a particular group of Indians to work for him. This system was unique to the New World; nothing precisely like it had existed in Europe or elsewhere.

"Establishment"   The elite of mainly Ivy League–educated, Anglo-Saxon, Protestant, male, liberal northeasterners that supposedly dominated Wall Street and Washington after World War II. The Establishment's support for corporations, activist government, and containment engendered hostility from opposite poles of the political spectrum—from conservatives and Republicans like Richard Nixon at one end and from the New Left and the Movement at the other. Although many of the post–World War II leaders of the United States did tend to share common origins and ideologies, this elite was never as powerful, self-conscious, or unified as its opponents believed.

Eugenics   The practice of attempting to solve social problems through the control of human reproduction. Drawing on the authority of evolutionary biology, eugenists enjoyed considerable influence in the United States, especially on issues of corrections and public health, from the turn of the century through World War II. Applications of this pseudoscience included the identification of "born" criminals by physical characteristics and "better baby" contests at county fairs.

Farmers' Alliance   A group organized in the late nineteenth century to help farmers pool their knowledge and resources. By 1890 it had entered politics, endorsing candidates and building the political connections in the South and West that would lead to the Populist Party.

Federalists   One of the two political parties to make up the first American party system. Following the fiscal and political policies proposed by Alexander Hamilton, Federalists generally advocated the importance of a strong federal government, including federal intervention in the economy of the new nation.

Feminism   An ideology insisting on the fundamental equality of women and men. The feminists of the 1960s differed over how to achieve that equality: while liberal feminists mostly demanded equal rights for women in the workplace and in politics, radical feminists more thoroughly condemned the capitalist system and male oppression and demanded equality in both private and public life.

Feudalism   A social and political system that developed in Europe in the Middle Ages under which powerful lords offered less powerful noblemen protection in return for their loyalty. Feudalism also included the economic system of manorialism, under which dependent serfs worked on the manors controlled by those lords.

Fire-eaters   Militant southerners who pushed for secession in the 1850s.

Flexible response   The defense doctrine of the Kennedy and Johnson administrations. Abandoning the Eisenhower administration's heavy emphasis on nuclear weapons, flexible response stressed the buildup of the nation's conventional and special forces so that the president had a range of military options in response to Communist aggression.

Front   Early twentieth-century mechanized wars were fought along a battle line or "front" separating opposing sides. By World War II, tactical innovations—blitzkrieg, parachute troops, gliders, and amphibious landings—complicated warfare by breaking through, disrupting, or bypassing the front. The front thus became a more fluid boundary than the fortified trench lines of World War I. The term also acquired a political meaning, particularly for labor and the left. A coalition of parties supporting (or opposing) an agreed-upon line could be called a "popular front."

Galveston Plan   A system of municipal government by appointed commissioners, each with responsibility for a utility or service. After a hurricane devastated Galveston, Texas in 1900, unelected commissioners temporarily took charge to oversee relief and rebuilding efforts.

Gentility   A term without precise meaning that represented all that was polite, civilized, refined, and fashionable. It was everything that vulgarity was not. Because the term had no precise meaning, it was always subject to negotiation, striving, and anxiety as Americans, beginning in the eighteenth century, tried to show others that they were genteel through their manners, their appearance, and their styles of life.

Glass ceiling   The invisible barrier of discrimination that prevented female white-collar workers from rising to top executive positions in corporations.

Globalization   This term first came into use during the 1980s to describe the web of technological, economic, military, political, and cultural developments binding people and nations ever more tightly together. America had been defined by its relationship to the world for centuries, but the coining of the term *globalization* reflected the emergence of closer international ties.

Great Society   President Lyndon Johnson's ambitious legislative program embodying the vision of the activist new liberalism of the 1960s. Enacted from 1965 to 1968, the Great Society sought to wipe out poverty, end segregation, and enhance the quality of life for all Americans.

Greenbackers   Those who advocated currency inflation by keeping the type of money printed during the Civil War, known as "greenbacks," in circulation.

Gridlock   The political traffic jam that tied up the federal government in the late 1980s and the 1990s. Gridlock developed from the inability of either major party to control both the presidency and Congress for any extended period of time. More fundamentally, gridlock reflected the inability of any party or president to win a popular mandate for a bold legislative program.

Horizontal integration   More commonly known as "monopoly." An industry was "horizontally integrated" when a single company took control of virtually the entire market for a specific product. John D. Rockefeller's Standard Oil came close to doing this.

Humanism   A Renaissance intellectual movement that focused on the intellectual and artistic achievements of humankind. Under the patronage of Queen Isabel, Spain became a center of European humanism.

Immediatism   The variant antislavery sentiment that demanded immediate (as opposed to gradual) personal and federal action against the institution of slavery. This approach was most closely associated with William Lloyd Garrison and is dated from the publication of Garrison's newspaper, *The Liberator*, in January 1831.

Imperialism   A process of extending dominion over territories beyond the national boundaries of a state. In the eighteenth century, Britain extended imperial control over North America through settlement, but in the 1890s, imperial influence was generally exercised through indirect rule. Subject peoples generally retained some local autonomy while the imperial power controlled commerce and defense. Few Americans went to the Philippines as settlers, but many passed through as tourists, missionaries, traders, and soldiers.

Individualism   The social and political philosophy celebrating the central importance of the individual human being in society. Insisting on the rights of the individual in relationship to the group, individualism was one of the intellectual bases of capitalism and democracy. The resurgent individualism of the 1920s, with its emphasis on each American's freedom and fulfillment, was a critical element of the decade's emergent consumerism and Republican dominance.

Industrious revolution   Beginning in the late seventeenth century in western Europe and extending to the North American colonies in the eighteenth century, a fundamental change in the way people worked, as they worked harder and organized their households to produce goods that could be sold, so they could have money to pay for the new consumer goods they wanted.

Information economy   The post-industrial economy, gradually emerging in the mid- and late-twentieth century, in which sophisticated communications, computing, biomedical technology, and services took the place of manufacturing.

Initiative, recall, and referendum   First proposed by the People's Party's Omaha Platform (1892), along with the direct election of senators and the secret ballot, as measures to subject corporate capitalism to democratic controls. Progressives, chiefly in western and midwestern states, favored them as a check on the power of state officials. The initiative allows legislation to be proposed by petition. The recall allows voters to remove public officials, and the referendum places new laws or constitutional amendments on the ballot for the direct approval of the voters.

Interest group   An association whose members organize to exert political pressure on officials or the public. Unlike political parties, whose platforms and slates cover nearly every issue and office, an interest group focuses on a narrower list of concerns reflecting the shared outlook of its members. With the decline of popular politics around the turn of the twentieth century, business, religious, agricultural, women's, professional, neighborhood, and reform associations created a new form of political participation.

Isolationist   Between World War I and World War II, the United States refused to join the League of Nations, scaled back its military commitments abroad, and sought to maintain its independence of action in foreign affairs. These policies were called isolationist, although some historians prefer the term "independent internationalist," in recognition of the United States' continuing global influence. In the late 1930s, isolationists favored policies aimed at distancing the United States from European affairs and building a national defense based on air power and hemispheric security.

Jim Crow laws   Statutes discriminating against nonwhite Americans, particularly in the South. The term specifically refers to regulations excluding blacks from public facilities or compelling them to use ones separate from those allotted to whites.

Joint-stock company   A form of business organization that was a forerunner to the modern corporation. The joint-stock company was used to raise both capital and labor for New World ventures. Shareholders contributed either capital or their labor for a period of years.

Judicial nationalism   The use of the judiciary to assert the primacy of the national government over state and local government and the legal principle of contract over principles of local custom.

Keynesian economics   The theory, named after the English economist John Maynard Keynes, that advocated the use of "countercyclical" fiscal policy. This meant that during good times the government should pay down the debt, so that during bad times, it could afford to stimulate the economy with deficit spending.

Knights of Labor   The first national federation of trade unions, led by Terence V. Powderly. The Knights grew to its fullest size in the mid-1880s before a steep decline. The federation was based on the premise of a common interest of all producers (for example, farmers and industrial workers), and it supported reform as well as united action by workers.

Liberalism   A body of political thought that traces its origins to John Locke and whose chief principles are consent, freedom of conscience, and property. Liberalism held that people could not be governed except by their own consent and that the purpose of government was to protect people as well as their property.

Linked economic development   A form of economic development that ties together a variety of enterprises so that development in one stimulates development in others, for example, those that provide raw materials, parts, or transportation.

Longhorn cattle   Rangy, tough, resourceful cattle found on the southern Great Plains. They were ideal for long cattle drives like those along the Abilene Trail.

Lyceum movement   A voluntary adult-education movement that swept New England and the Mid-Atlantic states in the early and mid- nineteenth century, credited in large part to the efforts of Josiah Holbrook. Lyceum organizations hosted educational lectures in towns and cities. Lecturers included such prominent speakers as Ralph Waldo Emerson, Mark Twain, and Abraham Lincoln.

Manifest destiny   A term first coined in 1845 by journalist John O'Sullivan to express the belief, widespread among antebellum Americans, that the United States was destined to expand across the North American continent to the Pacific and had an irrefutable right to the lands absorbed in this expansion. This belief was frequently justified on the grounds of claims to political and racial superiority.

Market revolution   The term used to designate the period of the early nineteenth century, roughly 1815–1830, during which internal dependence on cash markets and wages became widespread.

Mass production   A system of efficient, high-volume manufacturing based on division of labor into repetitive tasks, simplification, and standardization of parts, increasing use of specialized machinery, and careful supervision. Emerging since the nineteenth century, mass production reached a critical stage of development with Henry Ford's introduction of the moving assembly line at his Highland Park automobile factory. Mass production drove the prosperity of the 1920s and helped make consumerism possible.

Massive resistance   The rallying cry of southern segregationists who pledged to oppose the integration of the schools ordered by the Supreme Court in *Brown v. Board of*

Education in 1954. The tactics of massive resistance included legislation, demonstrations, and violence.

Massive retaliation   The defense doctrine of the Eisenhower administration which promised "instant, massive retaliation" with nuclear weapons in response to Soviet aggression.

McCarthyism   The hunt for Communist subversion in the United States in the first years of the cold war. Democrats, in particular, used the term, a reference to the sometimes disreputable tactics of Republican Senator Joseph R. McCarthy of Wisconsin, in order to question the legitimacy of the conservative anti-Communist crusade.

Mercantilism   An economic theory developed in early-modern Europe to explain and guide the growth of European nation-states. Its goal was to strengthen the state by making the economy serve its interests. According to the theory of mercantilism, the world's wealth, measured in gold and silver, was fixed; that is, it could never be increased. As a result, each nation's chief economic objective must be to secure as much of the world's wealth as possible. One nation's gain was necessarily another's loss. Colonies played an important part in the theory of mercantilism. Their role was to serve as sources of raw materials and as markets for manufactured goods for the mother country alone.

Middle ground   The region between European and Indian settlements in North America that was neither fully European nor fully Indian, but rather a new world created out of two different traditions. The middle ground came into being every time Europeans and Indians met, needed each other, and could not (or would not) achieve what they wanted through use of force.

Millennialism   A strain of Protestant belief that holds that history will end with the thousand-year reign of Christ (the millennium). Some Americans saw the Great Awakening, the French and Indian War, and the Revolution as signs that the millennium was about to begin in America, and this belief infused Revolutionary thought with an element of optimism. Millennialism was also one aspect of a broad drive for social perfection in nineteenth-century America.

Minstrel show   Form of popular entertainment in the nineteenth century, with black performers or white ones pretending to be black. Minstrel shows included music, comedy acts, and drama.

Modern Republicanism   President Dwight Eisenhower's middle-of-the-road legislative program of the 1950s. Reflecting traditional Republican faith in limited government and balanced budgets, Modern Republicanism still left alone such liberal programs as Social Security and farm subsidies.

Modernization   The process by which developing countries in the third world were to become more like the United States—i.e., capitalist, independent, and anti-Communist. Confidence about the prospects for modernization was one of the cornerstones of liberal foreign policy in the 1960s.

Moral suasion   The strategy of using persuasion (as opposed to legal coercion) to convince individuals to alter their behavior. In the antebellum years, moral suasion generally implied an appeal to religious values.

Mugwump   Name applied to liberal reformers in the late nineteenth century. Unattached to either major party, Mugwumps would endorse any candidate supportive of civil service reform, a secret ballot, and honest government.

Mutual aid societies   Organizations through which people of relatively meager means pooled their resources for emergencies. Usually, individuals paid small amounts in dues and were able to borrow large amounts in times of need. In the early nineteenth century, mutual aid societies were especially common among workers in free African American communities.

National Republicans   Over the first 20 years of the nineteenth century, the Republican Party gradually abandoned its Jeffersonian animosity toward an activist federal government and industrial development and became a strong proponent of both of these positions. Embodied in the American system, these new views were fully captured in the party's designation of itself as National Republicans by 1824.

Nativism   A bias against anyone not born in the United States and in favor of native-born Americans. This attitude assumes the superior culture and political virtue of white Americans of Anglo-Saxon descent, or of individuals assumed to have that lineage. During the period 1820–1850, Irish immigrants became the particular targets of nativist attitudes.

Neoconservatism   Form of conservative ideology that advocated the aggressive promotion of democracy abroad by the United States in order to make a better and more secure world. Emerging in the 1970s and 1980s, neoconservative ideas influenced the foreign policy of President George W. Bush.

New conservatism   The resurgent conservative ideology of the 1950s and 1960s reiterated the old conservatism's faith in individual freedom and liberal government and added an aggressive, anti-Communist defense policy.

New Federalism   Conservative policy of President Richard Nixon intended to limit the federal government by returning revenue and control to state and local government.

New Left   The radical student movement that emerged in opposition to the new liberalism in the 1960s. The New Left condemned the cold war and corporate power and called for the creation of a true "participatory democracy" in the United States. Placing its faith in the radical potential of young, middle-class students, the New Left differed from the "old left" of the late nineteenth and early twentieth centuries, which believed workers would lead the way to socialism.

New Right   The conservative movement that swept Ronald Reagan into power in 1980 and sustained his presidency. The New Right was much like the new conservatism of the 1950s and 1960s, but with greater emphasis on social issues such as abortion.

Nickelodeon   The first venue for motion pictures, a machine that showed a movie (lasting several minutes) for a nickel. Galleries with dozens of such machines, and the first movie theaters, came to be called "nickelodeons" as a result.

Omaha Platform   The Populist Party's program endorsed at the party's national convention in Omaha in 1892. Among its planks were government ownership of railroads and telegraph lines, the direct election of senators, a subtreasury system, and an expansion of the money supply.

Patriotism   Love of country. Ways of declaring and displaying national devotion underwent a change from the nineteenth to the twentieth centuries. Whereas politicians were once unblushingly called patriotic, after World War I the title was appropriated to describe the sacrifices of war veterans. Patriotic spectacle in the form of public oration and electoral rallies gave way to military-style commemorations of Armistice Day and the nation's martial heritage.

Patronage   *See* spoils system.

Political economy   Traditionally, the study of the connections between economics and politics. In this text, political economy refers to the relationships between the economy, politics, and the daily lives of ordinary people. Use of the term underscores the importance of the economy in shaping American life and the importance of politics in shaping the economy. However, the economy and politics did not simply shape, but were in turn shaped by, the lives and cultural values of ordinary men and women.

Political machine   An organization controlling a party, usually dominated by a "boss" and held together by loyalty and the distribution of rewards to those who had done the organization service.

Political virtue   In the political thought of the early republic, the personal qualities required in citizens if the republic was to survive.

Popular sovereignty   A solution to the slavery controversy espoused by leading northern Democrats in the 1850s. It held that the inhabitants of western territories should be free to decide for themselves whether or not they wanted to have slavery. In principle, popular sovereignty would prevent Congress from either enforcing or restricting slavery's expansion into the western territories.

Populism   The ideology of the People's (Populist) party in the 1890s, opposing the eastern economic elites and favoring government action to help producers in general and farmers in particular.

Postindustrial economy   The service- and computer-based economy that was succeeding the industrial economy, which had been dominated by manufacturing, at the end of the twentieth century.

Principle of judicial review   The principle of law that recognizes in the judiciary the power to review and rule on the constitutionality of laws. First established in *Marbury v. Madison* (1803) under Chief Justice John Marshall.

Producers ideology   The belief that all those who lived by producing goods shared a common political identity in opposition to those who lived off financial speculation, rent, or interest.

Proprietary colony   Colony established by a royal grant to an individual or family. The proprietary colonies included Maryland, New York, New Jersey, Pennsylvania, and the Carolinas.

Public opinion   Not quite democracy or consent, public opinion was a way of understanding the influence of the citizenry on political calculations. It emerged in the eighteenth century, when it was defined as a crucial source of a government's legitimacy. It was associated with the emergence of a press and a literate public free to discuss, and to question, government policy. In the twentieth century, Freudian psychology and the new mass media encouraged a view of the public as both fickle and powerful. Whereas the popular will (a nineteenth century concept) was steady and rooted in national traditions, public opinion was variable and based on attitudes that could be aroused or manipulated by advertising.

Realism   A major artistic movement of the late nineteenth century that embraced writers, painters, critics, and photographers. Realists strove to avoid sentimentality and to depict life "realistically."

Reconquista   Literally "reconquest." Between the eleventh and the fifteenth centuries, Christian nobles in Spain and Portugal fought to eject Muslim conquerors who had come from North Africa in the seventh and eighth centuries. In 1492, Ferdinand and Isabel defeated the last remaining Muslim ruler.

Reconversion   The economic and social transition from the war effort to peacetime. Americans feared that reconversion might bring a return to the depression conditions of the 1930s.

Re-export trade   Marine trade between two foreign ports, with an intermediate stop in a port of the ship's home nation. United States shippers commonly engaged in the re-export trade during the European wars of the late eighteenth and early nineteenth centuries, when England and France tried to prevent each other from shipping or receiving goods. United States shippers claimed that the intermediate stop in the United States made their cargoes neutral.

Republicanism   A set of doctrines rooted in classical antiquity that held that power is always grasping and dangerous and presents a threat to liberty. Republicanism supplied constitutionalism with a motive by explaining how a balanced constitution could be transformed into a tyranny as grasping men used their power to encroach on the liberty of citizens. In addition, republicanism held that people achieved fulfillment only through participation in public life, as citizens in a republic. Republicanism required the individual to display virtue by sacrificing his (or her) private interest for the good of the republic.

Requerimiento (the Requirement)   A document issued by the Spanish Crown in 1513 in order to clarify the legal bases for the enslavement of hostile Indians. Each conquistador was required to read a copy of the Requerimiento to each group of Indians he encountered. The Requerimiento promised friendship to all Indians who accepted Christianity, but threatened war and enslavement for all those who resisted.

Safety-valve theory   An argument commonly made in the nineteenth century that the abundance of western land spared the United States from the social upheavals common to capitalist societies in Europe. In theory, as long as eastern workers had the option of migrating west and becoming independent farmers, they could not be subject to European levels of exploitation. Thus the West was said to provide a "safety-valve" against the pressures caused by capitalist development.

Scab   Slang term for a worker employed during a strike; a strikebreaker.

Scalawag   A derogatory term referring to southern whites who sympathized with the Republicans during Reconstruction.

Second-wave feminism   The reborn women's movement of the 1960s and 1970s that reinterpreted the first wave of nineteenth- and early twentieth-century feminists' insistence on civil rights and called for full economic, reproductive, and political equality.

Separation of powers   One of the chief innovations of the Constitution and a distinguishing mark of the American form of democracy, in which the executive, legislative, and judicial branches of government are separated so that they can check and balance each other.

Sharecropping   The practice of a tenant farming the landlord's ground for a share of the crop, sold when the harvest came in. This became a common form of employment for former slaves in the post-Civil War South.

Slave power   In the 1850s northern Republicans explained the continued economic and political strength of slavery by claiming that a "slave power" had taken control of the federal government and used its authority to keep slavery alive artificially.

Slave society   A society in which slavery is central to the economy and political structure, in contrast to a society with slaves, in which the presence of slaves does not alter the fundamental structures of the society.

Slavery   A system of extreme social inequality distinguished by the definition of a human being as property, or chattel, and thus, in principle, totally subordinated to the slave owner.

Social Darwinism   Darwin's theory of natural selection transferred from biological evolution to human history. Social Darwinists argued that some individuals and groups, particularly racial groups, were better able to survive in the "race of life."

Spoils system   The practice of politicians rewarding their friends with offices and contracts.

Stagflation   The unusual combination of stagnant growth and high inflation that plagued the American economy in the 1970s.

Strict constructionism   The view that the Constitution has a fixed, explicit meaning which can be altered only through formal amendment. Loose constructionism is the view that the Constitution is a broad framework within which various interpretations and applications are possible without formal amendment.

Subtreasury   A government-run bank in which farmers could get low-interest loans using their crops as collateral. The creation of subtreasuries formed a key plank in the Populist platform.

Suburbanization   The spread of suburban housing developments and, more broadly, of the suburban ideal.

Supply-side economics   The controversial theory, associated with economist Arthur Laffer, that drove "Reaganomics," the conservative economic policy of the Reagan administration. In contrast to liberal economic theory, supply-side economics emphasized that producers—the "supply side" of the economic equation—drove economic growth, rather than consumers—the "demand side." To encourage producers to invest more in new production, Laffer and other supply-siders called for massive tax cuts.

Tammany Hall   A fraternal organization in New York City that developed into a Democratic political machine, electing officials, mobilizing voters, and allotting contracts. Its enemies saw it as a symbol of corrupt, selfish, and incompetent government.

Tariff   A tax on goods moving across an international boundary. Because the Constitution allows tariffs only on imports, as a political issue the tariff question has chiefly concerned the protection of domestic manufacturing from foreign competition. Industries producing mainly for American consumers have preferred a higher tariff, while farmers and industries aimed at global markets have typically favored reduced tariffs. Prior to the Civil War, the tariff was a symbol of diverging political economies in North and South. The North advocated high tariffs to protect growing domestic manufacturing ("protective tariffs"), and the South opposed high tariffs on the grounds that they increased the cost of imported manufactured goods.

Taylorism   A method for maximizing industrial efficiency by systematically reducing the time and motion involved in each step of the production process. The "scientific" system was designed by Frederick Taylor and explained in his book *The Principles of Scientific Management* (1911).

Temperance   Moderation, or the use of something with restraint. In the Gilded Age, the temperance movement opposed the use of alcohol.

Trusts   Corporate arrangements to unify action in production and distribution among different firms. Shareholders handed over control of their stock to a board that held the shares in trust and operated the combined concerns.

Universalism   Enlightenment belief that all people are by their nature essentially the same.

Vaudeville   A type of variety show popular in the late 1800s and early 1900s. Vaudeville was family friendly and included songs, band performances, skits, comedy routines, and circus acts.

Vertical integration   The practice of taking control of every aspect of the production, distribution, and sale of a commodity. For example, Andrew Carnegie vertically integrated his steel operations by purchasing the mines that produced the ore, the railroads that carried the ore to the steel mills, the mills themselves, and the distribution system that carried the finished steel to consumers.

Virtual representation   British doctrine that said that all Britons, even those who did not vote, were represented by Parliament, if not "actually," by representatives they had chosen, then "virtually," because each member of parliament was supposed to act on behalf of the entire realm, not only his constituents or even those who had voted for him.

Voluntarism   A style of political activism that took place largely outside of electoral politics. Voluntarism emerged in the nineteenth century, particularly among those Americans who were not allowed to vote. Thus women formed voluntary associations that pressed for social and political reforms, even though women were excluded from electoral politics.

Waltham system   Named after the system used in early textile mills in Waltham, Massachusetts, the term refers to the practice of bringing all elements of production together in a single factory setting with the application of non-human-powered machinery.

Wampum   Shell beads used by Indians of the Eastern Woodlands to make jewelry and to memorialize political agreements; later used as currency in the trade networks established between Europeans and Indians.

Watergate   The name of the Washington, DC, office and condominium complex where five men with ties to the presidential campaign of Richard Nixon were caught breaking into the headquarters of the Democratic National Committee in June 1972. "Watergate" became the catchall term for the wide range of illegal practices of Nixon and his followers that were uncovered in the aftermath of the break-in.

Whig Party   The political party founded by Henry Clay in the mid-1830s. The name derived from the seventeenth- and eighteenth-century British antimonarchical position and was intended to suggest that the Jacksonian Democrats (and Jackson in particular) sought despotic powers. In many ways the heirs of National Republicans, the Whigs supported economic expansion, but they also believed in a strong federal government to control the dynamism of the market. The Whig Party attracted many moral reformers.

Whitewater   With its echo of Richard Nixon's "Watergate" scandals in the 1970s, "Whitewater" became the catchall term for the scandals that plagued Bill Clinton's presidency in the 1990s. The term came from the name of a real estate development company in Arkansas. Clinton and his wife Hillary supposedly had corrupt dealings with the Whitewater Development Corporation in the 1970s and 1980s that they purportedly attempted to cover up in the 1990s.

Women's rights movement   The antebellum organizing efforts of women on their own behalf, in the attempt to secure a broad range of social, civic, and political rights. This movement is generally dated from the convention of Seneca Falls in 1848. Only after the Civil War would women's rights activism begin to confine its efforts to suffrage.

Photo Credits

Chapter 1: Lloyd Townsend Mural, Cahokia Mounds State Historic Site. Photo by Art Grossman, 2, 7; Gianni Dagli Orti/National History Museum, Mexico City/The Art Archive, 3; © Trustees of the British Museum, 13; The Granger Collection, 22; Benson Latin American Collection, University of Texas, Austin, 27.

Chapter 2: Private Collection/Bridgeman Art Library, 32; Collection of the New-York Historical Society/Bridgeman Art Library, 46; Service Historique de la Marine, Vincennes, France/Giraudon/Bridgeman Art Library, 53; Service Historique de la Marine, Vincennes, France/Giraudon/Bridgeman Art Library, 54; The Art Archive/British Museum, 56.

Chapter 3: Preservation Virginia, 60, 64; Private Collection/Peter Newark American Pictures/Bridgeman Art Library, 61; Marilyn Angel Wynn/Nativestock.com, 67 (left); Ira Block/National Geographic Stock/Getty Images, 67 (right); Pilgrim Hall Museum, Plymouth, MA, 78.

Chapter 4: Giraudon/Bridgeman Art Library, 90, 121; illustration by Walter Rane, 91; North Carolina State Archives, Division of Archives and History, 98; Plymouth County Commissioners, Plymouth Court House, Plymouth, Mass./Dublin Seminar for New England Folklife, Concord, MA, 106; Courtesy of The Newberry Library, Chicago. Ayer Ms map 30, Sheet 77, 116; Kevin Fleming/Corbis, 18.

Chapter 5: The Granger Collection, 126, 134; Private Collection/Bridgeman Art Library, 127; Print Collection, Miriam and Ira D. Wallach Division of Art, Prints and Photographs, New York Public Library, 140; Gibbes Museum, Gift of Mr. Joseph E. Jenkins © Image Gibbes Museum of Art/Carolina Art Association, 1968.005.0001, 142.

Chapter 6: The Granger Collection, 160, 167; *A Narrative of the Captivity of Mrs. Johnson* (Bowie, Md.: Heritage Books, Inc., 1990), p. v, 161; Library and Archives Canada, 169; The Granger Collection, 179.

Chapter 7: Library of Congress, Prints and Photographs Division, Washington, D. C., 192, 198; The Granger Collection, 193; The Granger Collection, 197; Reunion des Musées Nationaux/Art Resource, NY, 207.

Chapter 8: National Park Service/Archil Pichkhadze, 229; Courtesy Winterthur Museum, Garden and Library. 1961.1427, 228, 235; Courtesy Winterthur Museum, Garden and Library. 1953.0178.002, 238.

Chapter 9: Collection of the New-York Historical Society/Bridgeman Art Library, 262, 272; Mabel Brady Garvan Collection, 1936.302, Yale University Art Gallery/Art Resource, NY, 263; American Antiquarian Society, 269; National Portrait Gallery, Smithsonian Institution/Art Resource, NY, 285.

Chapter 10: Gilcrease Museum, Tulsa OK, 296, 319; Bentley Historical Library, University of Michigan, 297; The Granger Collection, 299; The Granger Collection, 307; Library of Congress, Prints and Photographs Division, Washington, D. C., 315.

Chapter 11: Geoffrey Clements/Corbis, 326, 335; The Granger Collection, 327; The Granger Collection, 329; The Granger Collection, 341; The Granger Collection, 347.

Chapter 12: The Granger Collection, 352, 362. New Haven Colony Historical Society, 353. Collection of the New-York Historical Society, acc. 1953.251, 360.

Chapter 13: Thomas Cole, *The Hunter's Return* 1845, Oil on canvas, 40 1/8 × 60 1/2 inches. The Amon Carter Museum Fort Worth, Texas, 1983.156. Purchased by the Friends of Art, Fort Worth Art Association, 1925; acquired by the Amon Carter Museum, 1990, from the Modern Art Museum of Fort Worth through grants and donations from the Amon G. Carter Foundation, the Sid W. Richardson Foundation, the Anne Burnett and Charles Tandy Foundation, Capital Cities/ABC Foundation, Fort Worth Star-Telegram, The R. D. and Joan Dale Hubbard Foundation and the people of Fort Worth, 380, 387; Smithsonian American Art Museum, Washington, DC/Art Resource NY, 396; Library of Congress, Prints and Photographs Division, Washington, D. C., 384; Hulton Archive/Getty Images, 404.

Chapter 14: The Granger Collection, 410, 433. Image copyright © The Metropolitan Museum of Art/Art Resource, NY, 411; Collection of the New-York Historical Society/The Bridgeman Art Library, neg#189006, 413; Bettmann/Corbis, 419; The Granger Collection, 420.

Index

Italicized page numbers indicate a figure or photo. Page numbers followed by t indicate a table. Page numbers followed by m indicate a map.

CANADA

Lake Superior

INNESOTA

St. Paul
Minneapolis

WISCONSIN
Green Bay

Madison

MICHIGAN

Lake Michigan

Lake Huron

NEW HAMPSHIRE

VERMONT

MAINE
Bangor

Augusta

Montpelier

Concord

Lansing

Flint

Detroit

Lake Erie

Lake Ontario

Albany

Buffalo

NEW YORK

Boston MASSACHUSETTS

Providence

Hartford RHODE ISLAND

CONNECTICUT

IOWA

Cedar
Rapids

Des Moines

Chicago

Fort
Wayne

Toledo

Cleveland

New York

Peoria

INDIANA

OHIO

Columbus

PENNSYLVANIA

Harrisburg

Pittsburgh

Trenton

Philadelphia

NEW JERSEY

ILLINOIS

Springfield

Indianapolis

Cincinnati

WEST
VIRGINIA

Baltimore

Annapolis

Washington, D.C.

Dover DELAWARE

MARYLAND

Kansas
City

Jefferson
City

St. Louis

Louisville

Frankfort

Charleston

Richmond

VIRGINIA

MISSOURI

Springfield

KENTUCKY

Nashville

Knoxville

Raleigh

NORTH
CAROLINA

Charlotte

ulsa

Fort Smith

Little Rock

Memphis

TENNESSEE

Wilmington

ARKANSAS

Tupelo

Columbia

SOUTH
CAROLINA

El Dorado

Shreveport

Jackson

Birmingham

Atlanta

Augusta

Charleston

MISSISSIPPI

ALABAMA

GEORGIA

Savannah

ATLANTIC
OCEAN

LOUISIANA

Baton
Rouge

Biloxi

Mobile

Pensacola

Montgomery

Valdosta

Tallahassee

Jacksonville

New
Orleans

sti

Gulf of Mexico

Orlando

Tampa

FLORIDA

BAHAMAS

Miami

0   20   40 miles

0   20   40 kilometers

PUERTO RICO

San Juan

Bayamón   Carolina

Ponce

CUBA